The Way of the West

VOLUME 3

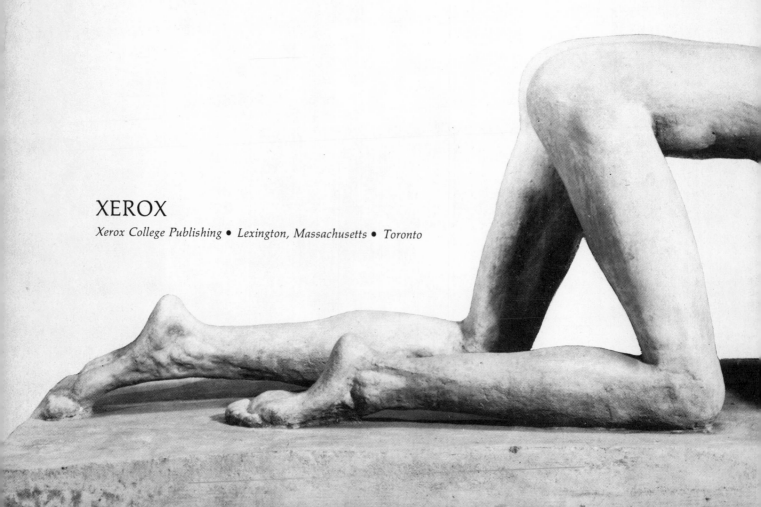

XEROX

Xerox College Publishing • *Lexington, Massachusetts* • *Toronto*

THE ERA OF WORLD DOMINION, 1760–PRESENT

Arthur J. Slavin

University of California, Irvine

Cover photograph by Arthur J. Slavin
Half-title page photograph courtesy Kunsthaus Zurich
Title page photograph courtesy Wilhelm Lehmbruck Museum
Index page photograph courtesy Museum of Fine Arts, Boston

Editor, Diane Shluger
Design, Mark T. Fowler and Martha Johnson
Picture Research, Dianne C. Smith
Copy Editor, Constance Baher
Cover Design, Edgar H. Allard
Maps, Richard D. Pusey

ISBN: 0-536-00889-2

Library of Congress Catalog Card Number: 72–91059

Printed in the United States of America.

PREFACE

The title of this book suggests that we have put before students a complete history of our civilization. It also suggests a clear sense of the "way" of Western civilization, or the paths by which we have reached the place in history in which we find ourselves. We want to make clear in this Preface in what sense both statements about our book are true. And, in order to do so, some words directed more to the student than to the instructor are necessary.

No satisfactory history of a single event, much less anything as complex as the series of events in time we label a civilization, can be written without a solid grasp and sure placement of facts. Nor can such a satisfactory history be written merely within the frame of an authoritative recital of agreed-upon facts. The question of a securely placed and adequate stock of reliable data does not present many hard problems even to students new to historical study. They know it is essential to put George Washington in the *presidency* at the *start* of our national history, not during the Civil War between 1861 and 1865, if any sense at all is to be made of the American past.

Questions do arise, however, when we confront the problem of the frame within which agreed-upon facts are displayed. One is certainly this: Do all historians writing histories of the same subject display the same recognized facts? A second derives from the *negative* answer we must give to the first question: Why do historians choose to emphasize different facts in writing the history of the same events and series of events? Before commenting on this, we may consider why the original question is given a negative answer.

The largest "fact" of all about the past is that it is really many pasts! Just as travelers to the Congress on Capitol Hill may all look at the same building without seeing exactly the same things, so historians and students viewing a particular past may not select the same vantage points or even the same points of focus within the past on which to concentrate their observations. Several travelers seeing the same thing will emphasize different facts in trying to convey what they have seen in Washington. Moreover, they will usually put whatever facts they mention—even common facts of their own observation—in quite different settings. One may speak of the rotunda by emphasizing the technological achievement in putting in place that huge dome. Another may stress the pink shades the dome absorbed from a setting sun. Still another may remark on the pleasing combination of arcs and straight lines which together improve the appeal of what might otherwise have been a very severe building.

Hence, even when facts themselves are not in

dispute, historical accounts employing them have decidedly different impacts One reason for this is that we select different sets of facts in seeking to convey what a particular past was like. Choice is necessary for every student of history, if for no other reason than that the range of facts is too vast to allow a complete display of all of them of proven relevance to the history of any topic. It is not, however, only their very bulk which makes choice necessary and therefore gives to every history its character of wholeness within the limits of selection.

Historians who admit the necessity of choice also make different selections. And this fact is of the greatest relevance to any book we call a complete history of Western civilization. Historical completeness lies in the unity of concepts employed in selecting the facts and the frame in which evidence is put. It is *unity of vision* in the historian that enables his or her work to convey to students a sense of the meaningfulness of past events and hence of the wholeness of the past.

Some historians elect to unify their work through the simplest device of all: the straight chronological account of whatever subject they have in hand. With a subject as large as a civilization, this choice often means writing separate accounts of the major constituent parts, which are more often than not seen as countries or nations. These accounts are then connected from time to time, by efforts to compare and contrast the truly separate "histories" presented. One example of this practice would be to write the history of the Renaissance in each European country, say between 1350 and 1600, and then to draw from these histories a set of shared experiences which justifies speaking of a Renaissance at all. Other accounts may elect certain topics or themes for focus. Studied chronologically, these then became the core of Western history.

In the writing of texts for students the most frequent choices have been two: the history of politics, war, and diplomacy, viewed from the top level of a society of politically articulate groups of people—the elite in most cases; or the history of ideas and high culture centered around the few creators of "culture" rather than the consumers. The "way of the West" will seem quite different from these frameworks.

Our own concern has been to write neither a "political" nor an "intellectual" history of Western civilization, neither a topical nor a national history. We do not think any partial view or any view from the top makes the best sense out of our past for modern students. Nor do we suppose the best alternative to such history is the sort of "popular social history" which focuses almost as exclusively on "pots and pans," or the mere round of daily work of ordinary people. Such "little" history is different from "big" history. Is it better?

We think not. Our own choice has been to make the relationship between human material and mental culture the main focus. Our intention is to provide students with a unified view of Western life within the circumstances of certain *relationships* between economic resources and systems of politics and ideas. We are less concerned to store up facts for posterity than to convey a dynamic sense of how and why the shape of Western society changed. The nature of our concern is, therefore, central to the shape and character of our history.

We have chosen to display facts in a setting which is deeper than the top crust of politicians and princes in realms of ideas. Moreover, we have consistently chosen not only to show facts but to try to display them in a framework of explanation. It is one thing to say authoritatively, that Louis XIV's drive for absolute power was inhibited by the failures of French agriculture. It is an altogether different matter to explain to students how and why and in what ways agriculture in France "failed."

We have tried consistently to explain, to take students into partnership in the historical inquiry we call *The Way of the West.* This has required of us the establishment of a thick, rich texture of evidence and argument. And it has made it seem wise to employ techniques of presentation more complicated than simple chronological narrative. Often our approach has been to compare and contrast certain social, political, intellectual, and economic events over broad reaches of space and time. For example, to use the case of Louis XIV again, we have treated his wars as a *social* "event" for the whole of Europe in order to provide an understanding of how political decisions made by leaders have affected the mass of followers. This means a diminished commitment to narrations of campaigns and the treaties which ended the wars. It also means an increased effort to explain how the demands of war on a large scale impinged on aristocrats and peasants, officials responsible for gathering new taxes and artisans who resented paying them.

Our work is thus frankly comparative, social, and explanatory in character, rather than basically national, political, and authoritative. We are more concerned with the student's comprehension of the relationship between population, land resources, and standards of living than with the history of either diplomacy or secular dramatic literature. Yet, we have tried to integrate even the most subtle diplomacy and the most esoteric fine art into our broad concern for the shape of society and the relation between the groups which at any one time made it an exciting adventure in the history of human communities.

Writing history is a social act. So, too, is studying it. It is our hope that we will engage students and their instructors in lively discussion about the shape of our past, if for no other reason than the shape of our future depends so much on our historical consciousness and conscience.

Because writing history is a social act, the help of students and colleagues who have made possible this book and who have improved the text of it must be acknowledged. My first debt is to the many students, UCLA undergraduates especially, who have talked with me about their perceptions of the text. I want also to make special mention of colleagues who have read parts of this book in manuscript, thereby rescuing me from error and the text from obscurity at many points: Professors Peter H. Amann, Robert M. Berdahl, David Bien, James D. Hardy, Jr., Boyd H. Hill, Jr., Robert B. Holtman, and Jere C. King. Lastly, I must thank especially Diane Shluger, the editor, who was instrumental in developing every phase of this book, and also William Frohlich of Xerox College Publishing, whose friendship and devotion to this book extend well beyond its pages.

TO THE INSTRUCTOR

The organization of this book should permit its use in a variety of Western civilization courses with widely spread chronological breaking points. The first volume has special advantages for professors wishing to stress the ancient and medieval roots of modern civilization in the West. The treatments of evolution, prehistory, and the Mediterranean world through the medieval period (to 1300) are broader and deeper in this book than in others. A special feature is the attention given to how non-Western peoples impinged on the West, were absorbed in its civilization, or were rejected as alien. Moreover, the focus in Book Five of Volume I—on the profound shifts in material and mental culture in the "higher" Middle Ages—should fit well into a quarter-system program in which the second quarter of instruction is devoted to the transition to "early modern" history.

The Way of the West incorporates into Volume II a feature with decided advantages for understanding social change in one civilization. The first three Books form a cycle of overlapping studies of economic, political, and intellectual development and change in the period from about 1300 to 1650. Book Four (covering the period from 1650 to 1760) sets in place, by description and analysis, the character of the Old Regime, focusing on government in relation to society, the shaping of maritime economies, absolutism, and scientific and philosophical ideas in the context of social welfare. The first three Books will convey to students a connected sense of what the transformation from a traditional agrarian civilization to a commercial civilization involved, and what ideas and institutions set off the great maritime powers from the other European states in the eighteenth century.

Instructors will, we believe, find in this comparative approach, with its extended descriptions and explanations, a welcome integrating technique for material too often merely strung together in a series of little national and topical histories.

The organization of the second volume also facilitates the study of the revolutionary movements after 1760 which shaped the modern world—democracy in politics and machine industry in economy. By directing attention toward the transition from traditional society to commercial societies in a world setting, the second volume establishes a basis for examining yet another major transformation. The third volume has its essential focus in two additional related themes: the genesis in the West of liberal industrial societies in competition on a world stage and how and why the relations between competing modes of society in the West assumed the character they did in the age of imperialism and in the twentieth century. This orientation of the material helps the student grasp the problem of relating Western values and institutions to the emerging states of the westernized but non-Western world of our own time.

We have explored revolution in politics (1760–1815) and ideas in the first Book of the third volume. The development of industrial societies on a mass political basis is the central theme of the next group of chapters; and it is on this double base that we have set the imperialism and war, as well as the ideological struggles, of the period from about 1870 to 1920. The last Book deals primarily with the shape of modern society. The focus is on the relationship between liberal values and ideas, whether expressed in politics, literature, motion pictures, or the fine arts. Just as a special feature of Book One is the effort to relate revolutionary slogans to political realities, so the essential theme of the last Book of *The Way of the West* is a question: Have technology and the concentration of power in superstates and super-corporations altered fundamentally the nature of our civilization *within* the modern era of our history?

This history embraces extended analysis and explanation in comparative settings. It is, however, governed by a firm sense of chronological continuity.

For instructors in colleges and universities on two-term systems, volumes I and II may easily be used for courses with traditional breaks during the period 1650 to 1760. Similarly, for courses in which the break is earlier, say with the Renaissance-Reformation, volumes II and III ought to function smoothly in providing students with a sound core of study.

CONTENTS

MAPS

BOOK ONE

The Old Order Changeth, 1760–1815

The years 1760–1815 produced important revolutionary movements on three continents. In dozens of countries the Old Regime either was destroyed or was transformed in important respects by the agitation for change backed by the threat of revolution.

The early chapters of this Book deal with the conditions of material life in relation to ideas on the one hand and concrete proposals for change on the other, as well as with the course of events within certain states. France and England are treated at length because our earlier narrative and analysis established their significance as representatives of two different kinds of government and two different types of society. Our approach has been to treat in detail the patterns of ideas and politics in each system and to show how the liberal English came to be the chief enemy of the "liberal" revolution in France.

In order to do so, we have devoted the second part of this Book almost entirely to a study of the French Revolution, at home and abroad during the era of the Revolutionary and Napoleonic wars. We have given special emphasis in this study to three elements: the actual course of the Revolution, because the character of the regimes in succession cannot be understood without an adequate narrative; the turn toward expansion of the Revolution, and the nature of the threat posed to the Old Regime outside of France; and the question of ideology.

What exactly were the revolutionaries in France seeking? To what extent was Napoleon a continuator of the Revolution? How did French ideas penetrate Europe east of the Rhine? And why were they received so eagerly by some?

The exploration of political systems in the context of radical ideas, especially the idea of democracy and that of a government responsible to its people, is thus the core of this introduction to the modern West.

Prologue

THE ISLE OF CYTHERA

HIGH SOCIETY AND *FÊTES GALANTES*

In 1698 the minor French poet and dramatist Florent Carton Dancourt provided a musical interlude in his play *The Three Cousins* (*Les Trois Cousines*).[2] One song among others was the "Isle of Cythera," about a land of legend famed for gentle love, peace, and bliss. Nearly twenty years later, the greatest French painter of the age, Jean Antoine Watteau (1684–1721), made the mythical island of love the setting for a painting which more than any other work of art captures the essential frivolity of aristocratic life in Louis XIV's age and that of his successors.

Watteau's *Return from the Island of Cythera* (1717)[3] deserves attention on several counts. The painting was presented by Watteau to the French Royal Academy as his diploma work, five years after his election. Works marking the "reception" of a man into the Academy confirmed the "election." They were graded by subject; and, unless one was willing to be accorded a low status in the Academy, custom demanded a serious theme, usually taken from history, mythology, or religion. Watteau's work contained no person identifiable in ancient myth, history, or religion. Indeed, there are no faces clearly revealed. Cupids hover over the couples; and small groups, who either suggest a movement toward a waiting boat or appear engrossed in some attitude of courtship and love, occupy the canvas. The focus is less on any historical reality than on the expressive encounters among men and women interested in little beyond their private emotions. The popularity at the French court of the Cythera theme in literature, ceremony, and painting was Watteau's warrant for what would otherwise have been a daring and "unacademic" submission by any artist.

If the *Return* did not belong to any "serious" genre of painting, it did belong to an aristocratic mode of culture called *fêtes galantes,* or noble dances and games of love. The title Watteau actually had as court painter was "painter of *fêtes galantes*." He thus brought to its climax a mood first expressed by Louis XIV at Versailles. The young king longed for revels

1. My translation from the French text in A. C. Sewter, *Baroque and Rococo Art* (London: Thames & Hudson, 1972), p. 163.
2. The play was first performed in Paris in 1700.
3. He painted a second version of *Return from the Island of Cythera* before his death; it is in Berlin's Dahlem Museum.

in places where cares of state could not reach. In 1664 he had created a pageant, or masque,[4] entitled "Pleasures of an Enchanted Island"; and at regular intervals after 1664 similar programs expressed the king's need to escape the harsh and ugly reality of politics and war. Versailles became the showplace of Europe, the theater of pastorales, festivals, peaceful love affairs (*amour paisible*), and numerous mock pilgrimages in classical parklike settings of palaces, gardens, and wooded retreats.

The *fêtes galantes* were not new in Louis XIV's time, either in painting or in the splendidly acted out escape fantasies. Italian Renaissance princes had participated in such masquerades. In the sixteenth century in England Henry VIII's court had raised the office of Master of the Revels to a new dignity. And in the England of the Stuarts the greatest artists, architects, poets, and musicians had collaborated on grand masques. Inigo Jones (1573–1652) had built a Banqueting House at Whitehall in London[5] and worked with Ben Jonson (1572–1637)[6] in producing pageants for the English court.

Under Charles II (1660–1685), the French ceremonies and festivities of Versailles influenced English taste. Henry Purcell (1659–1695), the best English composer of the century, wrote many "semioperas," or combined plays, operas, ballets, and masques. These were sometimes on wholly English themes (*King Arthur*), but often the French-inspired craze for Indian, Persian, and Chinese stories was influential. In settings built by Sir Christopher Wren and decorated by Peter Lely, works like Purcell's *The Indian Queen* provoked admiration.

4. A form of private entertainment featuring elaborate costumes, scenery, dancing, and music.
5. 1619–1622.
6. The great dramatist and poet, whose *Volpone* and *The Alchemist* are often performed today.

Antoine Watteau's Return from the Island of Cythera *depicts the wistful departure of young couples from the island of love. The garlanded bust of Venus at right presides over the scene, which is composed in Watteau's highly personal, unacademic style. The figures are strewn in a graceful curve, while the beautiful, misty landscape increases the sense of fantasy. These elegant lovers are refined, ephemeral, and more characteristically French than their predecessors in Rubens's* Garden of Love. *Watteau lived a short, unhappy existence and his melancholy vision of love's beautiful fleeting moments is in a larger sense a comment on the brevity of life itself. Louvre.*

The painters looked back to a tradition begun by Giorgione (1478–1510).[7] His *Fête champêtre* had put two nude women in a frankly erotic situation, deep in a wooded area where the landscape has a feeling of mystery.[8] Three generations of painters from the Flemish family of Pourbus continued this tradition, especially Pieter Pourbus (1510–1584) in his *Love Feast,* and Frans the Younger, who in 1609 came to Paris under Marie de' Medici's patronage. Perhaps the greatest inspiration for Watteau, however, was in Peter Paul Rubens' *Garden of Love,* a frankly erotic painting done for the Spanish court between 1632 and 1634, and the large cycle of paintings done for Marie de' Medici, glorifying the queen, in Paris between 1622 and 1625.

Watteau, from the town of Valenciennes, was himself of Flemish origins, like Rubens, and he had studied Rubens's Paris cycle as a student of Claude Audran III (1658–1734), curator of the Luxembourg Palace.[9] Audran was the son of the decorator who was, with Charles Le Brun,[10] responsible for the apartments of Louis XIV at Versailles. Watteau was thus thoroughly schooled in the traditions of secular painting and court life which lay at the heart of the style often called rococo.

7. The Venetian painter Giorgio Barbarelli.
8. Many critics attribute this picture to Titian; but it seems likely that Titian merely changed a Giorgione setting.
9. Where Rubens's Paris works were kept before removal to the Louvre.
10. A French painter; his dates are 1619–1690.

The Garden of Love *is a testimony of Rubens's love for his wife Hélène Fourment, who is shown seated on the ground at left-center. The elegant voluptuousness of the scene, where cupids whisper words of advice and encouragement in lovers' ears, is derived from Venetian masters such as Giorgione and Titian whom Rubens admired. The baroque composition is characterized by the diagonal groupings of figures, loose exuberant brushstrokes, brilliant colors, and a flickering light. Roman baroque architecture and the idyllic landscape setting forcefully recall Rubens's debt to Italian classical traditions.* The Garden of Love *achieved widespread fame through prints and replicas, thus influencing similar scenes in the eighteenth century. Prado, Madrid.*

THE FRENCH CENTURY AND THE FRENCH STYLE

This style probably owes its name to the French word *rocaille,* which refers to the generous use of rock, shell, plant, and scroll motifs in decorative arts. It was above all else a style of ornament. Rococo aimed to please, not to evoke either the profound sense of religious emotion we often associate with the baroque, or the equally profound sense of harmony and order we associate with French classicism. The focus on pleasure is clear in Watteau's *Return* as well as in his other famous *fête* paintings: *Fête en parc, The Elysian Fields, Fête Vénitienne, Jupiter,* and *Antiope.*

The emphasis is always on gracefulness, intricate decorations, the suggestion of erotic sensuality carried by the contrast between the naked statues and clothed lovers, and romantic delicacy. Watteau's imaginative world, like that of his pupils and imitators, was thus one of the bridges between the time of Louis XIV and the century of Enlightenment and Revolution.

In lesser artists, Watteau's acute psychological insight into the melancholy of love was lacking. In François Boucher (1703–1770), who received the patronage of Madame de Pompadour,[11] the voluptuous pleasures triumphed completely. His *Cupid Captive* (1754) dwells only on eroticism, while the court portrait painter Jean Marc Nattier (1685–1766) took up Watteau's theme of seductive ladies in a series of works devoid of intellectual depth. The work of the last great rococo master, Jean Honoré Fragonard (1732–1806), was until the Revolution wholly involved with the parasitic milieu of idle patrons, whose amorous dalliances he portrayed in *Love Letters* (1773). Even landscapes became excessively artificial and devoid of feeling in Fragonard's paintings, just before the Revolution destroyed the market for his talent by destroying the social class in which he found patronage.

The decorative and painting interests of rococo were elegant, if frivolous. Yet it was not only in silks for costumes, porcelain vases, mirror frames of gold scrolls, finely carved furniture, and tableware that Louis XIV's Versailles patterns impressed themselves on European taste. Side by side with the work of Le Brun and the other decorators of Versailles, a literary movement arose to sharpen the aristocratic milieu which also flourished in painting and architecture.

Voltaire, writing in the 1750s, had praised the age of Louis XIV as a "grand century," one in which great politics flowed together with splendid achievements in civilization. Much of what the *philosophe* praised, remarking that French civilization was "classical" in the same sense as Greece had been under Pericles or Rome under Augustus—a model for contemporaries and later imitators—did belong to Louis's age.

Yet the roots of this French "classical" culture and its elements of style were often foreign. In literature Spanish influences from Seville had penetrated France along with cargoes entering Rouen and La Rochelle. The works of the three main writers of Spain's "golden age,"[12] Calderón, Cervantes, and Lope de Vega, were familiar to the French dramatist Pierre Corneille (1606–1684). Indeed, in 1636 Corneille put on the tragicomedy *The Cid,* a play based on the heroic deeds of the Cid, Rodrigo, a Spanish knight admired for prowess, honor, and courtesy. The noble hero in other guises was, of course, already familiar on the stage in England, especially through the plays of Marlowe and Shakespeare. But in France this drama of human passions had not yet given rise to a theater glorifying aristocratic ideals of grandeur, war, great sword fights, and even greed.

When the aristocratic court of Versailles did support such a theater, it was only after the people of Paris had first created a demand for it. Corneille, Racine (1639–1699), and Molière (1622–1673), France's greatest dramatists, were all successful before Louis XIV brought them from Paris to Versailles in the decade 1664–1674. The society of the French capital had already been won over to the theater of Corneille and Racine and its celebration of heroic passions. Molière, however, focused on human folly. He gave aristocratic pretensions a bad press in *Don Juan* and *Tartuffe,* while in *The Misanthrope* and *Would-Be Gentleman* (*Le Bourgeois Gentilhomme*) he had ridiculed both the courtiers who lived only for the ceremonies of the King's *levée*[13] and the bourgeoisie who wished to cease honest work, acquire a title, and become members of the courtier class.

Art and architecture exhibited the rigorous form and sense of harmony we find in Racine's *Phaedra* in 1677, a tragedy on Greek models written under Louis XIV's patronage. If Racine's inspiration came from ancient

11. Louis XV's mistress.
12. It ran from perhaps 1550 to 1650 in Spanish literature.
13. His rising from bed in the morning; similarly there were evening rites when the King retired, the *grand* or *petit coucher.*

Greece, however, the supreme influence in the visual arts came from Italy.
French baroque painting had some roots in Florence, where Jacques Callot
(1592–1635)[14] had studied the "classical" style of Raphael, and in the
"Italian" style of Rubens. Some painters developed a lyric, sensuous,
Rubenesque, and full-blown emotional style. But others, especially Philippe
de Champaigne (1602–1674), endorsed a restrained and naturalistic mode of
painting. Nicolas Poussin (1594–1665) was the most important exponent of
French baroque "classicism." He was influenced by Raphael and also by his
own studies of Roman sculpture and poetry. Poussin's work in its mature
form[15] sacrificed sensualism to a more formal and rational control of both
subject and technique. In landscape painting Claude Lorrain (1600–1682)
placed a similar emphasis on calm and control, gracefulness, and an almost
geometric precision in composition. Lorrain proclaimed the artistic duty to
improve nature by appropriating poetic visions of order, especially Virgil's
pastoral sense of harmony.

When we consider architecture, the classicism of French baroque also
appears dominant. Early in the seventeenth century, buildings stressing
great power and nervous movement were built in France, especially by
Jacques Lemercier (ca. 1585–1654). A good example is his Church of the

14. His last year of work at Florence was 1621; returning to France, he published the *Miseries
of War* (1633), a series of engravings based on the Thirty Years' War.
15. In such paintings as *The Triumph of David, The Inspiration of the Poet,* and *Shepherds of
Arcadia.*

Sorbonne in Paris. But his successors quickly imposed severe restraints on the Roman baroque influence. By 1665, the victory of a distinctly "classical" variety of French building was evident. Louis XIV in that year refused certain designs of Bernini, who had come to France at royal invitation to rebuild part of the Louvre. A French architect, Claude Perrault, got the commission, and Bernini's vast plans, including a square on the model of the piazza in front of Saint Peter's in Rome, gave way to a design with no detached columns or undulating facades. The east wing of the Louvre rose to a flat roof, and the facade was severe, regular, and elegant.

Severity, regularity, and elegance became the architectural rule of thumb in the central decades of Louis XIV's reign. Secular buildings and churches exhibited classicism: Le Vau's[16] great châteaux; Jules Mansart's[17] Grand Trianon at Versailles and his Dôme des Invalides in Paris; Mansart's Royal Chapel at Versailles.

The central monument of the French style was, however, Versailles itself. Begun by Louis XIII under the direction of Lemercier, it was enlarged and completed by Louis XIV. Charles Le Brun employed Mansart, André Le Nôtre, Le Vau, and nearly every other architect of prominence to build the retreat from Paris to which Louis XIV officially moved the court in 1682.

16. Louis Le Vau (1612–1670).
17. 1646–1708.

Landscapes by Nicolas Poussin and Claude Lorrain, two French artists who lived and worked in Rome, are artistic equivalents of the rational clarity associated with the philosophy of Descartes. Parnassus *shows how these artists submitted nature to the rules of the intellect: the large mass at the right comprising the temple and figures is asymmetrically balanced by the small tree which closes the composition at the left. Between these two features there is a carefully delineated succession of planes leading the viewer's eye into a third dimension. The classical subject reveals Lorrain's love of Arcadian poetry. Appolo is surrounded by the Muses in the sacred grove on Mount Helicon. Beneath them is the placid Hippocrene spring, a source of inspiration for poets. Courtesy, Museum of Fine Arts, Boston.*

And it was at Versailles that the entire style of high culture coalesced. The music of Jean Baptiste Lully (1632–1687),[18] Denis Gaultier (1600–1672), and Louis Couperin (1626–1661) gave work to court orchestras also employed in the production of Italian operas and the musical interludes in plays by Racine and Molière. Louis XIV brought to Versailles whatever had succeeded in Paris. And this was usually an art of restrained feelings, of passions mastered. It was an art and environment suitable to an age in which Louis XIV bled France to the point of exhaustion in war and also reduced the nobility to attendants on their prince's *petit coucher.*

The elaboration of the Versailles court culture was not a French monopoly, however. Ambassadors and other visitors took home with them tales of French ceremonies, plays, operas, decorations, gardens, buildings, and music. Everywhere, as Voltaire noted in his *Age of Louis XIV (Siècle de Louis XIV,* 1751), kings and courtiers imitated Versailles. Charles II of England would have no music master but a French one; Italian literary men gathered in Tuscan academies to hear translations of Molière; Danish and Swedish kings built palaces on the French model; German rulers, especially in Prussia, founded "royal" academies for the arts and sciences,[19] long before Frederick II brought to Potsdam a palace complex based on that of "the King of Versailles."

Even the Versailles habit of taking coffee or tea in special houses or *salons* where news and literary gossip circulated was imitated, first in the French provincial towns and then in every place in contact with Versailles and Paris and enjoying pretensions to French grandeur.

COURTS AND CULTURE IN THE EIGHTEENTH CENTURY

The festivities of royal courts in France were not interrupted by Louis XIV's death in 1715. Indeed, September 1715 ushered in an age of aristocratic *fêtes,* which reached from the Versailles fireworks displays put on immediately after Louis XIV's death to the performances of *Le nozze di Figaro*[20] enjoyed by Louis XVI's queen, Marie Antoinette, on the eve of the French Revolution.

French society at the level of the court and the lesser aristocracy seemingly safe in their country chateaux was a society living for witty saying, gorgeous displays, comedies of manners, and the acting out of the scenes in Watteau's paintings. The tone was set at once during the Regency (1715–1723). Watteau ruled canvas realms. Lully's sweet tunes gave way to those by Rameau (1683–1764) and François Couperin (1668–1733), who delighted audiences with masterpieces of worldly music, often on exotic themes set in the Indies or other dreamlands. On the edges of the court and in countless towns, worldliness and sensualism overwhelmed the taste of magistrates, traders, and aristocrats. Women rose to the social eminence of the presidency of fashionable salons where *bons mots*—witticisms— achieved a place once held by serious thoughts. The grand style of Versailles was reproduced in miniature in such salons, just as the Petit Trianon provided Marie Antoinette a more intimate setting in which she and her court followers played at being shepherds in an endless bucolic idyll.

Even on a smaller scale, as French society retreated from the grandeur of Louis XIV, the emphasis was on elegance and detachment from the

18. The Superintendent of Music, primarily a composer of ballets and operas.
19. With constitutions modeled on those of the French academies.
20. An opera in four acts by Mozart based on the play *The Marriage of Figaro (La Folle Journée ou Le Mariage de Figaro)* by Beaumarchais.

ordinary circumstances of life. Foreigners eagerly fell to imitating Regency furniture and the modes preferred by Louis XV—small, fine in detail, and focused on a delicacy which was in rococo decorative arts the counterpart to Watteau's technique in depicting fine women. In the salons people spoke knowingly of Rameau concert pieces and his opera-ballets on classical themes or those on love *fêtes*.[21]

Indeed, it was the work of the age of Rameau and Watteau which represented French civilization abroad in the eighteenth century. A copy of the Cythera painting reached Berlin in 1720. Paintings by Boucher and Lancret[22] were in demand at every court. The French language became the necessary accomplishment for would-be courtiers at Potsdam and in Moscow or Saint Petersburg, where Frederick II and Catherine the Great were devotees of all things French. No English gentleman could be said to be well educated without a stay in Paris on the Grand Tour. In the late 1750s the great Scottish philosopher and man of letters David Hume (1711–1776) found it an advantage to have visited the Paris salon of Baron d'Holbach, where he cemented his reputation with the recommendation of the *philosophe*.

Frenchmen at the time might be wildly enthusiastic about everything foreign. Voltaire heaped praise on English institutions in his *Letters concerning the English Nation* (1732),[23] especially on the writ of habeas corpus.[24] Paris musicians correctly saw in the German Bach (1685–1750) and the Italian Vivaldi (1675?–1741) masters of secular and church music greater than anything produced in France; the Parisians acknowledged the foreigners' supremacy in works for the organ, for violin, in the forms of oratorio, cantata, concerto, and symphony. French writers such as Montesquieu reached sympathetic responses with works like *Persian Letters* (*Lettres persanes*), which put a premium on the achievements of non-European peoples. The vogue for Chinese objects and civilization was so great that *chinoiserie*[25] threatened to eclipse the native styles.

Yet Mozart (1756–1791) sought the applause of Paris eagerly and dedicated works[26] to the city he so enjoyed. The genius Haydn (1732–1809) went to Paris to compose six of his greatest works in 1786.[27] *La Logue olympique* in Paris was considered to be the most important concert hall in Europe. And the most gifted young writer in Europe, the German Goethe (1749–1832), after an early visit to France, seriously considered writing in French rather than in the German spoken at the sophisticated court of Weimar.

No better clue to the French dominance of high culture exists. Even in the smallest German states "civilization" often meant a French culture. To be a nobleman in Saxony, Austria, Weimar, or Prussia about 1760 meant to have an education in the French language, a French dancing master, a taste for French painting, and a wish to build in the French style.

Frederick II's own Academy of Sciences was from 1741 to the 1770s so dominated by Frenchmen that German philosophical and literary figures exercised very little influence in it. Educated Germans preferred to read French books or translations of Racine, Molière, Corneille, and also

21. His *Castor and Pollux* for example, or *Surprises of Love*.
22. A French painter (1690–1743) noted for his gay court and garden scenes.
23. This work appeared in 1733 in French as *Lettres philosophiques*.
24. The legal device which safeguarded against arbitrary imprisonment.
25. An elaborate style of ornamentation characterized by intricate patterns reflecting Chinese influence.
26. The *Paris Symphony,* for example (1778).
27. The *Paris Symphonies,* numbered 82 to 87 in the standard sequence of his works.

English writers.[28] When Goethe wished to praise Leipzig for the richness of its intellectual life, the best tribute he could find was, "It is a little Paris." Frederick the Great said in 1780 that German literature was not fit to set beside the "Augustan" achievements of Frenchmen between 1660 and the 1760s. Goethe he labeled a bizarre imitator of Shakespeare's aberrations. The royal pundit did not even mention a writer as famous as G. E. Lessing (1729–1781), who revived moral philosophy and laid the foundations for modern German drama in his criticism and plays, especially *Minna von Barnhelm* and *Nathan the Wise* (*Nathan der Weise*). Germany, according to the King's essay *On German Literature*, had neither good taste nor a language suitable for literature.

Some Germans remained partly outside the attractive pull of French ways, especially the philosopher Immanuel Kant (1724–1804), whose debt to Locke and Hume was profound. Yet even Kant was under Descartes's influence, at least to the extent that he undertook a refutation of the French trust in reason over reality.

Frederick the Great was more representative, however, and he found support for his opinions among other princes in Germany and northern Europe. In France itself, despite the great influence exercised by rococo ideas and styles, the arts often had an existence entirely independent of the "fashion." The French seascape artist Claude Joseph Vernet (1714–1789) led a reaction against "bedroom rococo." He liked the more austere paintings of the English school of Richard Wilson (1714–1782)[29] and also those of the Italian Salvator Rosa (1615–1673), a satirist and painter of picturesque landscapes. Louis XV gave support to this reaction by commissioning Vernet to do a series of paintings of the major French ports. Hubert Robert (1733–1808) also fell under the Italian influence, especially that of the printmakers Giovanni Paolo Panini (1692–1765) and Giovanni Battista Piranesi (1720–1778).

Panini and Piranesi were primarily painters and engravers of what the Italians called town scenes or *vedute*. Panini had also pioneered views of archaeological ruins, which became a French rage through his classes at the French Academy in Rome. It was Piranesi who exercised the greater influence, however, on a European scale. His series of 137 etchings, *Scenes of Rome* (*Le Vedute di Roma*, 1745), quickly found English admirers and French imitators.

Italian ideas moved easily into Spain via the Bourbon courts of Naples and Sicily, into Austria by way of the close connections between the Piedmont house of Savoy and the Habsburg court, and into Austria through the house of Lorraine, which succeeded the Medici in Florence and was tied dynastically to France. The Austro-French wars in Italy also formed a natural conduit for the circulation of Italian civilization. High culture in Italy

28. Most notably Defoe, whose *Robinson Crusoe* (1719) produced the genre of *Robinsonaden* for a half century; but also Richardson, Fielding, Goldsmith, and Sterne.
29. Who was Welsh by birth and neoclassical in style.

The decorative arts of furniture, porcelain, metalwork, and delicate wood carving attained perfection in eighteenth-century France. The rococo style of decoration created its effect by a sense of total unity, with every object in a room carefully conceived to enhance the overall plan. These carved and gilded wooden wall panels are typical of a late phase of rococo art already permeated by some neoclassic motifs such as the Grecian drapery on the figures. The panels would have been coordinated with a specially made set of furniture and fashionable decorative paintings above the doors. Courtesy, Museum of Fine Arts, Boston.

was concentrated in five cities: Genoa, Naples, Rome, Venice, and Turin. Europeans from north of the Alps generally included one or more of the cities in their educational "tours." There was thus an ample variety of ways in which Italian alternatives to French rococo might enter the mainstream of court culture.

That movement was easy we may see in the work of the second-rate painter Sebastiano Ricci (1659–1734). This Venetian executed works in the Schönbrunn Palace in Vienna, Burlington House in London, and at the French court. The best painter of the next generation followed an even more elaborate route of aristocratic patronage. For Giovanni Battista Tiepolo (1696–1770) scattered his saints, historical paintings, and mythological scenes from his native Venice to Madrid and the Kaisersaal in Würzburg. Lesser artists who embodied Tiepolo's light, brilliant, and artificial images were in demand everywhere: in England Sebastiano and Marco Ricci; Jacopo Amigoni in Germany and Spain; Antonio Pellegrini in France and Germany; Francesco Fontebasso in Russia.

The English bought the Venetian scenes of Antonio Canale (1697–1768), called Canaletto, with devotion, perhaps because the English were prosaic and absorbed with the accurate observation of bourgeois life. But that explanation will not help us to understand why Frederick Augustus II of Saxony and Russian czars bid for Canaletto's pictures, or why a pupil, Bernardo Bellotto (ca. 1724–1780), should have been in turn court painter in Saxony, Poland, and Vienna.

In England as well as in certain other states there seemed to be a certain immunity to what was sometimes called the decadence of French rococo. In Italy, of course, there was native pride in the painting, music, and architecture that made Naples, Venice, and Turin great centers of culture. Elsewhere, however, resistance to the French, when it developed, had other bases. Peter III of Russia admired Frederick the Great and hated the Bourbons. Joseph II of Austria actually forbade the imitation of French manners and styles. The English responded to the severely restrained and "classical" elements in French civilization, while eschewing excessive decorative brilliance. The earl of Shaftesbury had remarked that good art

Artists who were adept at painting cityscapes and public spectacles were much in demand by eighteenth-century patrons. One of the most successful was Antonio Canale, known as Canaletto, whose paintings of Venice were avidly collected by English tourists. Acquiring appropriate art for one's country house was an important aspect of the noble Englishman's "grand tour" of the Continent, and a work by Canaletto or his chief rival Francesco Guardi was a required souvenir of Venice. Even in Canaletto's time Venice was decayed and politically impotent, living off tourists who came to enjoy the unique setting and matchless architecture such as the Church of Santa Maria della Salute *shown here. Staatliche Museen, Berlin.*

was simple, clear, unaffected, and devoid of anything either too gaudy or too luscious.

English patrons and consumers seemed to embody the earl's norms in their taste. In music they preferred the chaste and solemn works of Handel (1685–1759), whose roots were in serious Italian opera. In portrait painting the standard was set by Sir Godfrey Kneller, a German trained in Amsterdam. Kneller (1646–1723) valued somber, direct representation, and his head of Newton showed the next generation how to paint people expressively but with restraint. This mode William Hogarth (1697–1764) took up in such works as "The Artist's Servants," and he exercised great influence on subsequent portrait painting.

But for a time rococo enthusiasm for decoration, lightness, even sensualism, did seem to triumph over severity. The portraits of Allan Ramsay (1713–1784) were "French" in feeling. The silver of Paul de Lamerie, the elaborate pleasure gardens at Vauxhall, Chippendale furniture, and Bow porcelains formed the backdrop for the early rococo paintings of Thomas Gainsborough (1727–1788)—his figure of Mary, Countess Howe, for example. Yet Gainsborough's later work stresses a real communion with nature (*Haymaker and Sleeping Girl, Peasant Girl Gathering Sticks*) which has more in common with Hogarth than with either Fragonard or the classical portraits and mythological scenes of Sir Joshua Reynolds (1723–1792).[30]

CULTURE AND THE COMMON MAN

Art, whether we mean music, literature, painting, or architecture and sculpture, was never entirely confined to courts, salons, and ecclesiastical buildings. In palaces and churches, however, the arts merged in gorgeous displays only princes and prelates could afford. This was especially true in rococo architecture, which was above all else a decorative medium rather than a new elaboration of fundamental principles.

The masters of rococo building did not do what Brunelleschi, Palladio, and Bernini had done: elaborate a new language of forms to make sense of novel ideas. They were content for the most part to decorate expensively: witness the stupendous royal hunting lodge done at Turin by Filippo Juvara (1678–1736) for the duke of Savoy, or Gabriel Germain's[31] Hôtel de Soubise in Paris, or Johan von Hildebrandt's[32] Upper Belvedere Palace (Vienna), or Francois Curvillié's[33] "Hall of Mirrors" in the Amalienborg Castle in Copenhagen. The basic structural ideas are baroque and can be traced to Roman baroque or classical sources. The fantastic facades and molded walls derive from the decorative styles of Italian baroque or the luxurance of Le Brun at Versailles. French decorative influence might be successfully

---

30. Even Reynolds escaped his own neoclassical dogmas, in a rococo direction in *Mrs. Lloyd* where the subject is shown writing her lover's name on a tree, and in straightforward portraits such as *Mrs. Robinson* and *Lady Price.*
31. 1667–1754.
32. 1668–1745.
33. 1695–1768.

Although he began as a landscape artist, Thomas Gainsborough is primarily remembered as a popular portraitist of British society. The Honorable Frances Duncombe *is a casually elegant work in which the patron is shown strolling in the outdoors, one of the artist's favorite devices for indicating a sensitive rapport with nature. Rather than being rigidly posed, the lady seems to be caught unaware of the viewer, and she casts a charming gaze to the side. Gainsborough took the magnificent court portraiture of the seventeenth-century artist Van Dyck as his ideal, but he avoided all stiffness and formality while emulating Van Dyck's brushwork and strong interest in the handling of drapery. Copyright The Frick Collection, New York.*

avoided here or there, at Dresden, for example, where fantastic elements of medieval decoration were more important. But Frederick II sent his chief builders to Paris to study for the programs executed at Charlottenburg and Sans Souci.[34] And the Russian Empress Elizabeth employed an Italian architect, Bartolomeo Rastrelli, a son of Peter the Great's favorite sculptor. She sent him to Paris, however, to study under French masters, before entrusting to him the building of the Winter Palace at Saint Petersburg (1749–1756).

Far from the luxury and fantasy of the Petit Trianon, we may wonder what ordinary men and women thought of the culture of the courts. And we may also ask what the creators of high culture thought of them.

Certainly most music had no time for common people in its round of concerts and operas based on court orchestras, ecclesiastical patronage, themes from aristocratic life, and tours of Europe's great halls and palaces. Inasmuch as the musical culture of the age for common people reached beyond popular ballads and ditties, it was through compositions written for church settings, the only really "public" concerts. A few painters, however, had departed from the norms of aristocratic elegance and frivolity. The portraitists Jean Baptiste Perronneau (1715–1783) and Quentin de la Tour (1704–1788) stressed simplicity in subjects devoid of aristocratic connections. Jean Baptiste Chardin (1699–1779) took up the line of Dutch painting concerned with domestic life, and he made the bourgeoisie the subject of very direct, unaffected observation. Jean Baptiste Greuze (1725–1805) not only expressed the order of bourgeois life. His *The Village Bride* (1761) showed sympathetically a betrothal celebrated in the house of a prosperous peasant.

Greuze clearly had a social conscience which was too active to be content with the subjects of Fragonard. Yet he idealized peasant life. His works did not help those who viewed them to see realistically levels of society below that of the salon.

In England, Hogarth had done just that. From the 1720s until his death, he published engravings based on his own painted observations of life and on literary reflections of reality. His *A Harlot's Progress* (1732) took up the theme already familiar in Daniel Defoe's *Moll Flanders.* The sympathetic representation of the "fallen woman" obviously pointed a finger at the society in which men of little virtue sneered at women of easy virtue. *A Rake's Progress* (1735), *Marriage à la Mode* (1745), *Industry and Idleness* (1747), and *The Four Stages of Cruelty* (1751) appeared before admiring audiences.

Hogarth was unique among painters and had few equals even among literary artists when it came to exposing degenerate aristocrats, greedy city merchants, quack doctors, rapacious lawyers, corrupt "statesmen," fancy teachers of French dances, or the other legions of elegant but vicious people whose victims he also showed in his great drawings of the gin-soaked, hopeless urban masses of London. If he was rococo in his fine technique, still the depth of his social conscience, his realism, and his critical interests set him apart. So, too, did his economy as an artist. Long before the Revolution in France destroyed the patterns of patronage Fragonard needed, the Englishman had freed himself from both patrons and art dealers. He published his own engravings, which were protected by the Copyright Act of 1735, for which he was a chief lobbyist. He could thus afford to cater to bourgeois tastes, even at the level of literate artisans.

In the market for art, as in so many other things, English society was

The Scullery Maid is typical of J. B. Chardin's solemn scenes of the simple activities of a bourgeois household. These genre paintings, which continued Dutch seventeenth-century traditions, are intimate in scale and composition. Although genre painting as a category was considered inferior to scenes painted from mythology and history, Chardin's work was highly prized and found its place on the walls of the greatest salons in Paris. This was due to the artist's brilliant handling of paint and mastery of his craft. Even Diderot, who considered social consciousness and a sense of drama to be the paramount attributes in a work of art, could not resist the sheer beauty of Chardin's painting. University of Glasgow, Hunterian Collection.

34. Frederick II's magnificent palace, built between 1745 and 1747 at Potsdam, Germany.

William Hogarth revitalized the English school of painting with his moral subjects which he compared to "representations on the stage." His most successful works were series of paintings—engraved in sets for popular sale—which were visual morality plays. The Orgy *(scene 3 from* The Rake's Progress *ca. 1734) tells the tale of a young profligate enjoying women and wine. In subsequent scenes the Rake loses his fortune and ends his days as a poverty-stricken madman. Hogarth was inspired by Dutch seventeenth-century art, particularly the low-life paintings of Jan Steen. Like the Dutch masters, he filled his scenes with a copious amount of allegorical detail which delighted and intrigued his audience. Courtesy, Trustees of Sir John Soane's Museum.*

already at odds with the court-based aristocracies of most of the Continent. Hogarth's affinities as a social critic were not with the plastic artists and painters of rococo Europe, but rather with the small band of thinkers we style the *philosophes,* who made the Enlightenment a synonym for revolutionary ideas.

BIBLIOGRAPHY

BUKOFZER, M. *Music in the Baroque Era.* New York: John Wiley & Sons, 1947. A standard work on the age of Bach.

FOSCA, FRANÇOIS. *The Eighteenth Century.** Geneva: Skira, 1953. A beautifully illustrated survey of painting.

SEWTER, A. C. *Baroque and Rococo Art.** London: Thames & Hudson, 1972. A sound analysis of painting, architecture, and sculpture.

TURNER, W. J. *Mozart: The Man and his Work.** New York: Barnes & Noble, 1966. Very good on the problems of patronage in aristocratic circles.

Asterisk indicates a paperbound edition.

ENLIGHTENMENT AND OPPRESSION

There is a mighty light which spreads itself over the world, especially in those two free nations of England and Holland, on whom the affairs of all Europe now turn.

<small>ANTHONY ASHLEY COOPER</small>, Letter to Le Clerc (March 6, 1706)[1]

If someone asks, are we living in an enlightened age today? the answer would be No. But we are living in an Age of Enlightenment.

<small>IMMANUEL KANT</small>, *What Is Enlightenment?* (1784)[2]

ENLIGHTENMENT AND THE ENLIGHTENMENT

In the three generations separating Lord Shaftesbury's assertion from Kant's answer to the question, What is Enlightenment, Europe witnessed the rise of the *philosophes,* "the party of humanity."[3] Lord Shaftesbury was not one of the persons ordinarily comprehended in the term *philosophes.* Kant was in many ways more closely tied to the development of nineteenth-century thought than to the French-based movement on which the Enlightenment centered. Yet Shaftesbury was hailed by the French thinkers as a father of enlightened ideas. And Kant was the greatest of the German thinkers to undertake an answer to the question posed in 1784 by the *Berlin Monthly.*[4]

Our task here is to set in context the *philosophes,* especially the movement which included the greatest names in French letters in the eighteenth century—Montesquieu, Voltaire, Diderot, and Rousseau. To do so we must establish the character of the Enlightenment and what we mean by enlightenment. This will require investigating thinkers other than French ones:[5] among others, Kant in Germany, Hume in Scotland, Count Verri in Italy, Ben Franklin in America. It will also be necessary to focus attention on what attitudes and habits of thought linked Frenchmen and foreigners.

1. Cooper was the famous earl of Shaftesbury and was here addressing the French thinker Jean Le Clerc. From Benjamin Rand, *Life, Unpublished Letters, and Philosophical Regimen* (London: Longmans, 1900), p. 353.
2. From Kant's *Beantwortung der Frage: Was ist Aufklärung,* quoted in Peter Gay, *The Enlightenment: An Interpretation; The Rise of Modern Paganism* (New York: Alfred A. Knopf, 1967), p. 20.
3. The phrase is from Peter Gay's title: *The Party of Humanity: Essays in the French Enlightenment* (New York: Alfred A. Knopf, 1964).
4. "Was ist Aufklärung?" or "What is Enlightenment?"
5. In this chapter and the following one.

Madame de Pompadour adroitly used her position as official mistress to Louis XV to become one of the most powerful individuals in France. Although her political influence was formidable, she is best remembered as a patron of the arts. In this portrait by François Boucher she is surrounded by the elegant rococo furniture and decorative arts she loved. The piano and objects of learning in the lower right corner refer to her accomplishments as a musician, artist, and thinker. Like any amateur of her time, she took these avocations very seriously. She had much contact with the philosophes and supplied both encouragement and protection to the editors of the Encyclopédie. *Louvre.*

No mere descriptive catalogue of philosophical thinkers and their ideas will suffice, however. We want to know something about the institutions of enlightenment also, something about the role of the salon, publications like the *Encyclopédie*, and the academic societies (academies) in which the *philosophes* were read, imitated, and often made the basis for practical reform activities. We need to know more than the ideas of a few famous publicists if we hope to understand at all the relationship between the ideas of the "party of humanity" and the active agitation for reform and social change in France and Europe in the last decades of the Old Regime.

Our practical concern has its foundation in the fact of the practical concerns of the *philosophes* themselves. Denis Diderot (1713–1784) set the tone when he criticized any philosophical work that was silent on government or the role of the church and religion in contemporary life. He said that a writer who ignored such practical questions had nothing to say! Hence it appears less important to trace the ideas of the *philosophes* back to their origins than it is to study the function of both the *philosophes* and their ideas in the real world of the eighteenth century.[6] Political and social ferment were the natural environment in which the *philosophes* grew to

6. See especially the next chapter for the academies and social change, for example.

maturity. And the motto Kant proclaimed, *sapere aude* ("dare to know"), had in it the implication that to know the truth was to be set free.[7]

Before Kant used the motto in 1784, it had been adopted by the so-called enlightened despots in Poland and Austria and had heralded a German translation of Lord Shaftesbury's works. For Kant and the *philosophes* on the eve of the French Revolution the slogan *sapere aude* clearly had a polemical sense. To know was to challenge obscurantism and to lay bare the nakedness of any authority unable to produce an improvement in human welfare.

To say this is not to say that the Enlightenment belongs more to the social history of reform and revolution than to the history of ideas. It is to say that an approach to the character of enlightened thought which does not look at society as well as ideas—at groups as well as individuals, at the shape of opinion as well as the philosophic analysis of elements of thought—will fail to grasp the significance of the Enlightenment.

The truth of this assertion will appear especially clear to every student who asks why reform failed in France while succeeding in Tuscany. In each place small elites embraced certain changes as desirable. Writers, engineers, professors, doctors, bureaucrats, and articulate citizens came together in Paris and in Florence eager to create effective instruments of concrete action. In each place men with zeal for reform wished *to know* in order to change the world by political means. Why one group failed and another succeeded we may know only by looking at the *philosophes* in their habitats.

THE *PHILOSOPHES*

Many different men and strands of thought made up the whole cloth of the Enlightenment. The *philosophes* were scattered from the east coast cities and plantations of North America to the capitals of Europe. Some were chiefly general critics of culture. Others were skeptics at war with established religion. Many openly advocated political reform. A few were serious, systematic philosophers.

What linked Franklin and Jefferson in Philadelphia and Virginia to Voltaire and Diderot in Paris, Hume in Edinburgh, and Kant in Königsberg was not therefore an identity of ideas in particular. The *philosophes* also lacked any formal organization across national lines. They were in fact cosmopolitan in nature and somewhat suspicious of any loyalty less broad than that to humanity. They were, however, all "secular" thinkers, committed to welfare in this world. And they were all apostles of freedom.

Voltaire (1694–1778), Kant (1724–1804), and Franklin (1706–1790) were dedicated to freedom in every form. Franklin fought for freedom of the press. So did Kant and Voltaire. Kant made the freedom of each man to develop his moral sense the keystone of his philosophy. Voltaire wrote again and again of the freedom to hold whatever ideas were consistent with a man's aesthetic and intellectual judgments. Franklin became a revolutionary spokesman for the concrete forms of freedom of thought which drew their nourishment from a politically free constitutional agreement.

The *philosophes* were also united in their diversity by their devotion to moral freedom, which Kant expressed as the right of a moral man to be an end in himself, not merely a means to ends pursued by other men.

The *philosophes* remained divided on concrete issues. Where the Ameri-

---

7. The motto was itself classical and occurs in the Latin poet Horace. As early as 1736, it was found in an emblem used on a medal struck in Berlin by reform-minded servants of King Frederick William I.

can political situation encouraged activism in the decades before the Revolution of 1776, the German partisans of reform faced stern repressive measures in the 1770s. The English counterparts of the Paris-based thinkers were not confronted by a regime mired in failure and were not at odds with the "liberal" institutions at home. They had in any event had their revolutions in 1649 and 1689. Nor were all the Italians driven to revolutionary action rather than peaceful agitation. In Tuscany and in Lombardy the authorities actually seemed bent on using the state to put in force an enlightened policy.

The *philosophes* were thus arranged along a political spectrum which reached from the benign regimes in Florence and London to the Prussian one which made politics taboo for professors and the French atmosphere in which radical thinkers faced either jail or exile as rewards for freethinking.

The often temperamental leaders of enlightened thinking also were out of step with each other on stylistic and personal issues. Voltaire and Diderot labeled the ideas of Jean Jacques Rousseau (1712–1778) "primitive."[8] David Hume (1711–1776) mistook the breezy wit of Voltaire for social irresponsibility. Diderot never forgave writers who deserted his project of the *Encyclopédie*. Rousseau criticized Voltaire bitterly in print, and Diderot avoided meeting Voltaire, the most famous of the pundits of the age, until 1778, the year of Voltaire's death. Even David Hume finally fell out with the nearly paranoid, suspicious, and often petty Rousseau.

Yet the basic loyalties often proved stronger than the conflicts. In France official persecution drew *philosophes* together; when court journalists denounced Diderot; or in 1758, when Claude Helvétius's work *Essays on the*

In this mid-century engraving, leading philosophes *are engaged in conversation over the dinner table. Held in awe by his contemporaries, Voltaire appropriately seems to be the center of attention as he makes an animated gesture. Diderot, the editor of the* Encyclopédie, *sits at his right, while other contributors to that great enterprise round out the company. The writings of these liberal thinkers helped pave the way for the democratic revolutions and increasing emphasis on individual liberty characteristic of the late eighteenth century. Bibliothèque Nationale.*

8. See later in this chapter for a sketch of his main ideas.

Mind (*De l'esprit*) was condemned; or in 1759, when Diderot's *Encyclopédie* was prohibited. The *philosophes* defended one another[9] for a variety of reasons, of course. But it was common knowledge in the 1750s that they shared certain attitudes about authority in church and state. The common experience of persecution insured that, as it tended to make more cohesive their attack on absolutism and established religion. So, too, did their common resort to classical literature and the scientific traditions of the seventeenth century.

The *philosophes* also shared a dedication to the international circulation of ideas. Montesquieu's elegant *Persian Letters* were read by Gaetano Filangieri in Naples, and the Italian acknowledged that his own *Science of Legislation* (*La Scienza della legislazione*) was inspired by the graceful French work. Hume paid a similar compliment when the matter of his historical writings was at issue.[10] The economist Adam Smith learned from Turgot and Quesnay[11] during his Paris visit from 1764 to 1766. Kant freely acknowledged that Locke's and Hume's critique of rationalism first woke him from "dogmatic slumber," and paid tribute to Rousseau's respect for the common man. The German writer Lessing criticized the classical theater of France, especially Racine and Corneille; but he did so after the fashion set by Diderot. Thomas Jefferson turned to Montesquieu and Locke for his fundamental stock of political ideas, just as Ben Franklin looked to Locke, Newton, and Voltaire for certain elements of his social, scientific, and political ideas.

This constant admission abroad of the impact of Newton, Locke, and certain French popularizers of English scientific and political thought points to another important aspect of the Enlightenment. The most fundamental contributors to enlightened thought were seventeenth-century Englishmen. The German contributor to Diderot's *Encyclopédie*, Baron Grimm (1723–1807), explained the rise of French "popular" philosophy by pointing out how Montesquieu and Voltaire had taken over English ideas. In Italy, English science, the English constitution, and the philosophy of Shaftesbury, Locke, and Hume were hailed as the essential elements of *illuminismo* (enlightenment).

Even in France, which we sometimes identify as the home ground of enlightenment because the word *philosophe* is French, the debt to England was frankly recognized. Voltaire himself came back from London in 1728 to proclaim his addiction to Shaftesbury's deism and Newtonian science. From Lord Shaftesbury he learned to think of a world governed by the reason of a God stripped of the character given him by orthodox religion— that of a meddling, vindictive, and petty tyrant. And from Newton he took over both the mechanical view of natural order and sense of reason in nature. Voltaire readily confessed to "Anglomania" in 1764.

It was thus the case that the cosmopolitan French literature of enlightenment was the result of mixing British empiricism with French rationalism and clarity of expression. If it was as men of letters writing brilliant and witty books and essays that Frenchmen astutely propagandized other Europeans, it was largely the English example and tradition which lay at the heart of the matter. Moreover, it was as city dwellers that the articulate citizens of the world-state of enlightenment made their mark. The high

Among the great salons of mid–eighteenth-century Paris, none was more brilliant than that of Madame Geoffrin. Her regular dinners provided an agreeable atmosphere for the free exchange of ideas among the great minds of the Enlightenment. In this work by the genre painter Lemoinnier, the actor Le Kain reads to an assortment of philosophes, amateurs, and artists including Diderot, Rousseau, and, seated toward the right, Madame Geoffrin. With a good deal of artistic license, Lemoinnier shows a number of bitter enemies seated together in harmony. In fact, Madame Geoffrin was a perfect hostess and scrupulously avoided mixing antagonistic factions. Lauros-Giraudon.

---

9. Except Rousseau after 1762; all joined in persecuting the Genevan radical.

10. Hume's *History of England* was one of the greatest works of Enlightenment historiography; it remained a "best seller" from the 1760s to the 1820s.

11. Anne Robert Jacques Turgot (1727–1781) and François Quesnay (1694–1774), both noted French economists.

This amusingly satirical engraving conveys the unrefined atmosphere of an eighteenth-century London coffeehouse. Such establishments played an important role as meeting places for artists, writers, scientists, and politicians who sought the stimulation of intellectual conversation in an easy ambience. An aura of political agitation and intellectual radicalism came to be associated with these places. By courtesy of the Trustees of the British Museum.

culture we described in the Prologue was court based. The culture of the *philosophes* broke out of that orbit.

It is true that Montesquieu, Grimm, and Holbach were barons, that Jefferson was a landed aristocrat, and that Jean Le Rond d'Alembert (1717–1783) was bound to the Old Regime by birth and the five pensions he had from kings, their academies, and his own family.[12] Yet he drew sustenance from Paris, not from Versailles. Like other *philosophes,* he was tied to the city press, to bourgeois coffeehouses, urban salons like that of Baron d'Holbach or Sophie Volland,[13] and the excitement of the capital. Like the gentlemen on the Grand Tour, the internationally migrant *philosophes* moved from London to Paris to Milan to Rome to Geneva. David Hume was drawn to Paris because it was *the* city, and only a city supplied the man of letters with his natural audience. When we think of Franklin, we put him in Boston and Philadelphia. When we think of Voltaire, Diderot, and d'Alembert we put them in Paris as automatically as we put Kant in Königsberg and Rousseau in Geneva.

The city salon was cosmopolitan in Paris in the same sense that the literary clubs and coffeehouses were in London and Edinburgh. Voltaire avoided Paris from 1750 to 1778, but he made his exile at Ferney bearable by bringing to his country house the society of Paris, not by imitating the society of Versailles. Indeed, in describing the *philosophes*, we speak

12. D'Alembert gave away most of his earnings, but he retained pensions from Frederick the Great, Louis XVI, the French Academy, the Academy of Science, and his father.
13. Diderot's mistress.

readily of their *urbane* wit and their general *urbanity*. Kant, in speaking of the tone of European ideas in his own life, said that there was a revolt against superstition, authority, and absolutism in every civilized country, especially among the *civilized* classes. The German philosopher's use of the word *civilized* is revealing. For the precise meaning of the word cannot be separated from its Latin root, *civilis,* pertaining to life in the city of classical times.

The Enlightenment was for Kant the "revolt" itself. The leaders he called *Aufklärer,* or bearers of enlightenment. In Italian and French, terms such as *illuminismo* and *lumières* suggested both the process of being enlightened which Kant discussed and also the carrying of that light of philosophy to the rest of the Western world. By "revolt" *philosophes* in Kant's time did not mean political revolution or the violent overthrow of governments. Change was meant, however, and it was often recognized that the changes thought necessary would be resisted by the guardians of the old order. There were radical ideas afoot in psychology, politics, economics, theology, science, education, and even in those areas of thought concerning the nature and purpose of society as a whole. The partisans of these ideas were belligerent toward the "enemies of philosophy,"[14] no matter how divided they might be among themselves.

VOLTAIRE AND MONTESQUIEU: THE FIRST GENERATION

To appreciate more fully the nature of the revolt made against tradition by the *lumières* we must distinguish the main phases of the Enlightenment. The movement as a whole extended in time from the late 1680s to the late 1780s. It embraced the publication of Newton's *Principia* (Mathematical principles of natural philosophy) and the "Glorious Revolution"[15] at one end and the Declaration of Independence and the Declaration of the Rights of Man at the other. It was alive in 1689, when Montesquieu was born and William III sat on an English throne. And it was dying in 1789, when Baron d'Holbach died and the Revolution in France began. It was punctuated by Hume's death in 1776, a year in which Adam Smith published his *Wealth of Nations* and Thomas Jefferson put the final touches to America's revolutionary manifesto. It had a great monument in the 1750s in the *Encyclopédie* and another in Voltaire's work on Louis XIV.

The Enlightenment was thus the work of several generations of men. Early in the eighteenth century it was shaped by Montesquieu and Voltaire, whose respective birthdates were 1689 and 1694. By the 1740s, however, despite Voltaire's continuing influence, men born in the eighteenth century came to dominate: Franklin (1706), Hume (1711), Rousseau (1712), Diderot (1713). Only Franklin lived through both the American Revolution and the beginning of the one in France. And in the 1770s and 1780s he was already a senior statesman and a venerated literary and scientific man. The ongoing leadership then rested with the third generation of *philosophes,* men like Kant, Deleyre, Beccaria, and Jefferson, all born when Voltaire was already in middle age[16] and for the most part still alive when Napoleon had substituted his own brand of enlightened despotism for the dream of republican liberty.[17]

---

14. Diderot used the phrase repeatedly in letters and published articles.
15. This refers to the events of 1688–1689 in England, the result of which were the abdication of James II and the accession of William and Mary.
16. 1724, 1730[?], 1738, and 1743, respectively.
17. Jefferson died in 1826, Kant in 1804, Deleyre in 1797, and Beccaria in 1794, when the reaction to radical republicanism took power in France.

What was characteristic in the successive generations we may illustrate by focusing in turn on Montesquieu and Voltaire, Diderot and Rousseau, Kant and Deleyre.[18]

"Voltaire" was the pen name of a wealthy bourgeois writer, François Marie Arouet. As a young man, he exhibited brilliance of style, but his epigrams, plays, and epic poetry were not the stuff of greatness. Indeed, his satiric wit and withering ridicule got him into trouble during the Regency. He was twice jailed, once for alleged insults to the regent, the duke of Orléans, and a second time because of a scrape with a powerful nobleman, the Chevalier de Rohan. A powerful friend[19] helped him to regain both freedom and some favor, however, and by 1730 Voltaire was the holder of a pair of court offices: he was court historiographer and gentleman of the King's Chamber.

By 1730 Voltaire's future career had also been influenced in another direction. His trip to England had converted him to Newtonian science, constitutional liberty, and freethinking, views expressed in his *Letters concerning the English Nation* (1732) and *Elements of the Philosophy of Newton* (*Éléments de la philosophie de Newton*, 1738). Both books were elegant popular accounts of what Voltaire found admirable in England: religious liberty and political freedom. The Frenchman especially valued Locke's psychology of experience, Lord Bacon's empiricism, and Newton's sense of the regularity of the cosmos.

Yet Voltaire was no antiroyalist, however much he opposed religious beliefs based on dogma. He was the friend of Frederick the Great, Louis XV's servant, and the eulogizer of Louis XIV. By 1740 in fact his main political opinions were linked to his pleas for religious toleration. He publicized the infamous prosecutions of victims of religious bigotry: Jean Calas, a Protestant accused wrongfully of murdering his son to keep the youth from converting to Catholicism; and Jean François La Barre, a boy charged with acts of desecrating crosses.

From his English experiences and the public defenses he made in France after 1759, Voltaire shaped an overall critique of religion in general and of the Catholic Church in particular. The religion proper to rational men was not that "revealed" in scriptures, but only the "natural" morality and veneration inspired by the application of reason to the laws of nature. The Deity (God) was a general force of order in the world, and this order was incompatible with traditional beliefs, which Voltaire called superstitions. Supernaturalism in belief made men perpetual adolescents, always waiting for the pleasures or pains given them by an all-powerful and capricious God.

The deism Voltaire expounded was set in the context of a thoroughly secular notion of history and culture. In the *Essay on the Manners and Spirit of Nations* (*Essai sur les moeurs et l'esprit des nations*, 1756), which is a universal history, Voltaire broke with the Christian tradition of writing

18. In the remainder of this chapter we will be concerned chiefly with the first two generations of *philosophes*. See Chapter 2 for the men of the "Age of Revolutions," from 1776 to 1789.
19. Louis XV's bourgeois mistress, Madame de Pompadour.

Like his contemporary David, the sculptor Jean Antoine Houdon used a classical idiom to immortalize the great figures of his age. Archaeological discoveries in Italy provided the eighteenth century with impressive evidence of the superiority of ancient sculpture, and Houdon has endowed Voltaire with the flowing robes and authoritative posture of a classical sage. The startlingly emaciated face, which seems to pierce the viewer with a kindly tolerant yet cynical gaze, may have been inspired by the Roman portrait busts which Houdon knew. Giraudon.

about the events in Palestine which led to the birth of Jesus, Christ's mission and sacrifice, and the spread of the Church in the Roman world. Voltaire began instead with China, ignoring Creation altogether, and went forward by describing and comparing various early civilizations. Thus the Christian religion and Western ideas and institutions were presented as one set of social experiences and opinions. They were stripped of their sanction in Scripture.

Voltaire's liberalism in religion made him an outspoken critic of Rome. He advocated the eradication of established churches, because of their intolerance and bigotry. *Écrasez l'infâme*—"Crush the infamous thing"— became his battle cry against the clergy. His anticlericalism did not make Voltaire universally tolerant, however. In an article for his *Philosophical Dictionary,* he gave vent to anti-Semitic passions. While urging Christians not to burn Jews, Voltaire described them as ignorant, barbaric, avaricious, and invincibly superstitious and cruel. Voltaire's intolerance for some thus grew directly out of his doctrine of tolerance. The sects were equal in their devotion to "truths" not subject to proof. A reasonable life demanded the abolition of all religious groups willing to use verbal or physical violence to enforce obedience to unproved dogmas. The best way to rid the world of the enemies of reason, however, was not persecution; violence begat violence.

Voltaire was thus selective in his hostility and his favor: he loathed the Jews, Rome, the Jesuits, officious bishops; he praised a God who created the world on sound mechanical principles, and he thought religion a necessary social sentiment. Without it order and the security of property would be impossible! Politically, the same Voltairian distrust of truly radical measures surfaced. The sage of Ferney was no democrat. Like Frederick the Great, he thought the masses incapable of managing their own affairs. Only a powerful but enlightened government could subordinate the clergy, advance freedom of thought, and insure material progress. Voltaire's politics were thus the politics of enlightened despotism: he advocated a strong state ruled by kings and *philosophes.*

Charles de Secondat, Baron de la Brède et de Montesquieu, made a more fundamental contribution to enlightened politics than did Voltaire. Like him, Montesquieu was tied to the Old Regime by interest. A *seigneur* (manorial lord) from southern France, he inherited a seat in the *parlement de Bordeaux* from an uncle. He was active during the Regency in the aristocratic reaction to absolutism. And he was sympathetic to the elitist ideas we have already seen at work in Voltaire. His friends among the *philosophes* sought to convince Montesquieu not to publish his great work *The Spirit of the Laws* (*De l'esprit des lois,* 1748), on the ground that the book was too conservative.

Yet it is because of *The Spirit of the Laws* even more than the *Persian Letters*[20] that we place Montesquieu in the first rank of *philosophes.* The *Persian Letters* was a radical book, in fact one of the two most radical works issued before 1740, the other being Voltaire's *Letters concerning the English Nation.* In his *Persian Letters,* Montesquieu made a devastating rationalist critique of Europocentric ideas of culture, in exactly the same vein as Diderot's later *Voyage de Bougainville.* But *The Spirit of the Laws* is a systematic critique of politics. Moreover, it is one of the main links in the

Montesquieu's peculiar looks are exaggerated in this caricature by Pier Leone Ghezzi. But a protruding nose, short stature, and habitual absent-mindedness were minor imperfections compared to the philosopher's penetrating insight into human nature and society. Heavily influenced by English writers and institutions, he helped introduce the rationalistic ideas of Locke to France and argued against the absolute power of the French monarchy. Along with Voltaire, Montesquieu was an influential figure in the early years of the French Enlightenment. The Bettmann Archive.

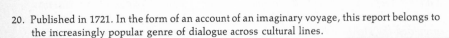

20. Published in 1721. In the form of an account of an imaginary voyage, this report belongs to the increasingly popular genre of dialogue across cultural lines.

chain of transmission by which Locke's *A Treatise of Civil Government* reached a wide European and American readership.

Montesquieu, like Edmund Burke (1729–1797) in England and Giovanni Battista Vico (1668–1744) in Italy, held a *social* doctrine of mankind. Human beliefs and ideas were a natural growth conditioned by environment and the groups within which people grew to maturity. Nothing in man's "nature" was predetermined by God or any supernatural forces. Some forces of nature were beyond human control—climate for example. But men were shaped by things they also shaped: economies, governments, religion, and the laws which set limits to action. Laws were for Montesquieu not arbitrary, but the necessary result of the disposition of natural forces and human institutions.

Montesquieu shared with Voltaire a pluralist theory of society. There was no single pattern of social rights and obligations ordained for mankind. The patterns in existence within the whole human community differed because in each country methods of education differed, churches differed, climates differed, the structure of families differed. Efforts to impose a "system" of government foreign to the natural disposition of things were therefore both tyrannical and contrary to nature. Pluralism was incompatible with any doctrine of absolutism within a state, because the rights and obligations of the various groups derived from no individual, not even the king, but rather from the "corporations" to which men belonged by birth and free association.

In France Montesquieu applied his ideas to argue against despotism, which was the term he used for royal absolutism. Power in France, he said, was actually divided naturally between the crown and other bodies and social groups: towns, the nobility, the clergy, *parlements.* Each was essential to check the other. The monarchical "principle" embodied in the king and his council was balanced by the aristocratic and democratic forces of the nobility, the parliaments, and the Church, as well as by the bourgeoisie in the chartered towns. In England, which Montesquieu admired and misinterpreted,[21] he saw the three principles embodied in the king, the Lords, and the Commons. And he also imagined that English liberty was safeguarded by a mechanical separation of executive, legislative, and judicial powers.

Montesquieu balanced his English examples with citations from the classics, but it was the spectacle of English liberty and the theory he extracted from Locke's *Treatise* which supplied him with his basic arguments. England is the model government of Europe, he said. Citizens are secure in their lives, liberty, and property. The king makes no law by himself and is bound to obey whatever laws are made by the whole political community, the supreme legislature. The independence of the courts is insured by the tenure enjoyed by judges. No royal army forces submission on an unwilling people. And the church and aristocracy are strong enough supports for the monarchy to keep out mere mob rule, or the triumph of a democratic republic over the balancing principles of kingship and nobility.

Naturally, the consequences one might see in such ideas varied according to how one viewed one's own situation. A person reading Montesquieu and very dissatisfied with affairs at home might use the ideas of separation of powers and balance of forces to argue that centralized and despotic monarchy was unnatural and hence fair game for reform, even for change through revolution. Montesquieu himself was no revolutionary, but he did

21. The English government had neither a formal nor a functional balance of powers: Parliament was a legislature and a court; the king was part of it, etc.

say that in France the monarchy was ripe for reform. The advance of "despotism" had weakened monarchy:

Monarchies become corrupt when the prerogatives of corporations and the privileges of towns are gradually taken away. . . . Monarchy itself perishes when the ruler . . . summons the state to his capital, the capital to his court, and the court to his person.[22]

Montesquieu clarified this implied criticism of Louis XIV's absolutism and the royal power to do wrong with impunity. He contrasted the French king's arbitrary powers of arrest by *lettres de cachet* with the English writ of *habeas corpus*, which limited and controlled the king by law. Of course Montesquieu's call for a resurgence of aristocratic and high bourgeois corporate influence can be said to be part of a selfish aristocratic reaction. But *The Spirit of the Laws* reached a much wider audience than that concerned with weakening the Versailles regime by restoring the provincial elites. The appeal of the *philosophe* was to "natural" arrangements against the usurpation of power by unnatural kings. And that appeal might be construed to be valid everywhere.

THE SECOND GENERATION: DIDEROT AND ROUSSEAU

Montesquieu's great book about society and government illuminated the conditions of the then modern monarchies and their discords. *The Spirit of the Laws* also devoted much space to republics, commenting on their size, federal systems (Holland, Switzerland), their spirit of moderation and peace, and the danger to free institutions arising from the ambitions of aristocrats who are courtiers rather than true citizens. Such courtiers, he said, suffer from an aversion to truth, the disease of flattery, and prefer inflated honor to virtue. In a sound republic, virtue formed the principle of government. The republics of Europe in 1748, however, were not republics of virtue. In Holland and Venice, debauched aristocracies no longer held to the ideal of virtue and did not inform politics with the spirit of true law. They preferred private morality to the public good.

England had passed through a similar experience in the 1640s and 1650s, when men without virtue made a republican revolution and could not maintain it. After the collapse of the Commonwealth in 1660, the republican ideals of virtue achieved by a citizen body participating in government were kept alive in England. Republican thought had been transmitted from the Commonwealth spokesmen[23] by way of Locke and his patron, Lord Shaftesbury.[24]

In France, the ideas of the third earl of Shaftesbury and his contemporaries[25] were never ignored. During the revolutionary epoch, even the obscure writings of Walter Moyle (1672–1721) on republican Rome were reprinted and translated.[26] Few of the English writers were democrats, but nearly all agreed that even a corrupted republic (i.e., a democracy) was preferable to any tyranny, in much the same sense that Shaftesbury, who was a deist, thought even atheism better than superstition.

22. Quoted in Norman Hampson, *The First European Revolution, 1776–1815* (New York: Harcourt, Brace & World, 1970), p. 13.
23. John Milton and James Harrington among others.
24. The first earl of Shaftesbury. Locke also supervised the education of Lord Shaftesbury's grandson, the third earl of Shaftesbury, the English philosopher.
25. Robert Molesworth, Anthony Collins, John Toland, and other writers on science, deism, and republicanism.
26. In 1801, as *Essai sur le gouvernement de Rome;* the book appeared first in English (*Essay on Roman Government*) in 1696.

These were ideas any *philosophe* might embrace in searching for the path toward a society at once free and powerful. This was especially true of Denis Diderot, in whose work the struggle for enlightenment and free thought made clear the connection between politics and ideas.

In 1745 Diderot published his *Principles of Moral Philosophy, or The Essay of Lord Shaftesbury on Merit and Virtue.*[27] A year later he had printed his *Philosophical Thoughts (Pensées philosophiques),* a book in which he glossed Shaftesbury's doctrines, as an appeal for liberation against the forces of oppression. Diderot took from his English hero the following argument. Religious enthusiasms derived from revelation were antisocial. By setting belief against belief, churches set man against man. They thus inhibited the basic human ethical drive to live happily in a world society. On a secular plane, patriotism played the same role. By promoting war, patriotism destroyed cosmopolitan ideas. The drive for absolute power within a state had cast states into competition. The net result was to destroy freedom. Hence all forms of absolute power and belief were inimical to free thought and free institutions. Or, as Shaftesbury himself had said, "Absolute power annuls the publick. . . . [28] by destroying the social sentiment of confederacy, the league for the common good, or true patriotism.

The maturing of Diderot's own thought took more than twenty years; it was not complete until 1772, when the last of the twenty-eight volumes of the *Encyclopédie* appeared. But already in 1751 Diderot had contributed the article in Volume One on *autorité politique* (political authority), which was the political manifesto of the second-generation *philosophes.*

In that early article Diderot wrote for an audience wider than that of the salons. He appealed to the *parlementaires*[29] and the bourgeoisie of the towns and suburbs, to the reading public wherever it was, including the village *curé* (parish priest), the rural court clerk, even the literate peasant and house servant who went to town once a week or once a month to sell produce or buy the supplies to satisfy their own or their masters' needs. Like Voltaire, Diderot addressed himself to that new thing—public opinion.

His appeal was against the monarchy shrouded in the myths of absolutism. While Diderot did not embrace republicanism and shared the basic *philosophe* ambivalence toward directly revolutionary ideas, he did strike strongly:

The crown, government, and public authority are goods of which the whole body of the nation is proprietor. Princes are merely users of the fruits of these goods and their ministers the trustees. The whole nation possesses a right to maintain the contract made in its behalf, and there is no power able to change the agreement. . . .[30]

The *Encyclopédie* edited by Diderot and the scientist d'Alembert was much more than a manifesto of the new political ideas. The title page of the first volume bore the legend *Encyclopédie, ou Dictionnaire raisonné des sciences, des arts et des métiers.*[31] It was a handbook of scientific, technical, and historical knowledge. *Raisonné* in the title made explicit the critical function and the rational, skeptical stance taken by the famous contributors. As volume followed volume, the reading public found Voltaire, Diderot, d'Alembert, Rousseau, Quesnay, Turgot, Buffon, and many other

27. *Principes de la philosophie morale ou Essai de M.S. sur le mérite et la vertu.*
28. *Characteristicks of Men, Manners, Opinions, Times* (London: n.p., 1711), 3:131.
29. The lawyers of the *parlements.*
30. My translation from the French in *Encyclopédie* (Paris, 1751), 1:899.
31. *Encyclopedia, or a Critical Dictionary of the Sciences, Arts and Crafts.*

philosophes evading the loose network of censorship. Forbidden to directly criticize the government or the Church, the "encyclopedists" spoke in parables, described the good customs of the Chinese, the American Indians, the Persians, and the English. The criticism of French society and institutions was obvious.

The whole reading public knew that Diderot and his friends wanted to demonstrate how human knowledge could be made to advance the general interest of humanity. This they hoped to do not by creating a new system. They distrusted systems and dogmas. Instead, they had faith in the idea that each science, art, and craft, if honestly expounded, would reveal the beneficial connections between diverse sorts of knowledge. Above all else, Diderot and d'Alembert infused their pages with a belief in progress through applied science. The *Encyclopédie* was an eighteenth-century *summa,* ranging from Buffon's denial of Creation according to Genesis[32] to articles in which the despotism of France is the target. The encyclopedists were apologists of human progress, and the scientific and technological leaning of the work set the seal to the triumph of the Newtonian spirit which Voltaire had popularized in the 1730s.

One interest of Diderot, in the origins of social life and its consequences, had a profound impact on the irascible Swiss exile from Geneva, Rousseau. Born in Geneva in 1712, Jean Jacques was a Protestant of lower-class origins. As a child he was neglected.[33] At the age of sixteen he was a runaway. In the 1730s and 1740s he lived at odd jobs, fathered five children[34] by an illiterate girl, and became an unhappy, sexually frustrated, poor, and lonely man.

Diderot had befriended the little Genevan in 1749. Rousseau, inspired by his new place in French literary society, competed for a prize in the Dijon Academy's contest on the question of the relationship between civilization and human nature. His 1750 essay, *Discourse on the Arts and Sciences (Discours sur les arts et les sciences),* won the prize, despite the unflattering paradox Rousseau maintained: that civilization and artistic progress corrupt mankind. Men in the state of nature are good; society corrupts them. Every refinement is a distortion of what is natural and good. Four years later Rousseau again competed for the Dijon prize, this time on the subject of the origins of inequality among men. The 1754 essay, *Discourse on the Origin of Inequality among Men (Discours sur l'origine de l'inégalité des hommes),* expounded the same theme. Man, the "noble savage," is degraded by civilization. In nature equal and just, men in society are predators. The inequality we see in the distribution of liberty, property, and fundamental happiness, Rousseau said, was an evil produced by such "civilized" institutions as property and monarchy.

These ideas shocked Diderot and Voltaire, but no more than Jean Jacques's resolve to retire from the civilization of Paris to a life of rural solitude. Diderot publicly criticized Rousseau, urging him to recognize that man is good only in society. Voltaire complained that Rousseau degraded the civilized ideals the *philosophes* championed. Most of the *philosophes* treated Rousseau's rejection of society as a return to a monastic ideal and thus a blow at the social drive toward progress to which they were dedicated. After 1755, Rousseau was persecuted by the French *lumières,* as the Genevan's ideas took new, radical, turns in his great works on education and society, *Émile, Social Contract (Contrat social), La Nouvelle*

32. A denial he had published in 1749 as a book, *Theory of the Earth (Théorie de la terre).*
33. He was illegitimate.
34. All deposited in an orphanage.

Héloïse, and *Considerations on the Government of Poland (Considérations sur le gouvernement de la Pologne).*

In the novels *La Nouvelle Héloïse* (1761) and *Émile* (1762) Rousseau developed some of his basic ideas about child rearing, education, and human nature. In them he took up the cause of honest emotion at the expense of reason, advocating spontaneity, gentleness, reverence toward nature, tenderness. He wrote beautifully about common men and women and common things, from the breast-feeding of babies by their own mothers to the abolition of corporal punishment in schools. His appeal to compassion and pity attracted a wide audience, and his sentimentalism was viewed by Diderot as the elevation of feeling over reason. He was not entirely mistaken, for Rousseau was at war with the artificiality of aristocratic society, privilege, and every social institution inimical to his own sense of humanitarian order.

The great weapon in Rousseau's personal war was the 1762 *Social Contract.* In this book Jean Jacques put in order certain themes already evident in the works of 1750–1754 and the novels. In the 1754 *Discourse,* Rousseau had said he was looking for a place to live in which civil society and government were identical, a place in which the governed and the governors were the same, in which the people were sovereign, the law ruled, and men sought virtue. He said also that Geneva was such a place.

Critics said what he saw was not Geneva, but a utopia. Rousseau replied that only visionaries could alter reality, and that the French *philosophes* were wrong to think they could reform a corrupt society. No free and fair state could be dug out of the fossilized absolutism of the Old Regime, Rousseau believed, any more than conscience could prosper in a godless world. This sentence in *La Nouvelle Héloïse* convinced Diderot that the Swiss was a religious reactionary, just as Madame de Wolmar's thought[35] that simple men and women need not climb the social ladder convinced other *philosophes* that Rousseau was at bottom paternalistic and authoritarian.

Rousseau's critics were both right and wrong. The *Social Contract* is at once a democratic and an authoritarian book, libertarian and paternalistic. Its general argument is simple. Rousseau began again with the argument of 1750, that the evils of society produced badness in men. Now, however, instead of advocating a return to nature, Rousseau argued that only a better society could produce better men. This better society was itself the product of a contract. Unlike Locke, whose theory invoked a *political* contract between a people and a ruler, Rousseau wrote of a contract that was *social.* The people themselves agreed among themselves to form a society. The society or community was no extrinsic *political* thing, but the agreement of the people. The content of this contract was a mutual surrender of natural liberty and individual will to the association of all the people, not to an

35. She was the novel's heroine.

A friend of the philosophes *and one of the first to stress the social utility of the arts, the dedicated amateur C. N. Cochin was invited to provide the frontispiece for the* Encyclopédie. *His curious allegory uses the format of a baroque religious scene to reveal the rational aims of the new publication. Light radiates from Truth in the center, while Reason and Philosophy pull away her veil. The various arts are seated at the left beneath Imagination who prepares to crown Truth. The sciences are shown at the right, while Theology basks in Truth's light at her feet. The Bettmann Archive.*

external ruler. The "general will" was the expression of this popular association. This was not a mere consensus, the result of a majority vote. It was instead the absolute, sacred, and inviolable will of the society. The general will was objectively whatever advanced the common interest of the community, which knew its interest by a sort of reasonableness which received no satisfactory explanation in the pages devoted to it. The general will was in fact the sovereign power and resided in the people. Rousseau had little to say about the practical arrangements of government, to which he devoted space in *Considerations on the Government of Poland*.[36]

What concerned Rousseau was a state of mind. Against the cosmopolitanism of Paris, Rousseau revived patriotism. He praised Sparta because it had trained soldiers to be suspicious of foreigners. Madame de Wolmar always knew the objective interests of the peasants on her estates. And for many of Rousseau's critics this "sense" was a taste of the authoritarian states which might result from Rousseau's doctrine of general will. But neither the praise of Sparta nor Madame de Wolmar's paternalism gets to the core of Rousseau.

His basic concern was with the *experience of belonging,* and belonging as the condition of equals. A community of equals was the indispensable requirement for social harmony; inequality produced egoistic and antisocial intentions.

Himself an outsider, bitter, maladjusted, and physically unattractive, Rousseau longed to belong. His idealization of Geneva was an act of homage to the city he adopted. He recognized the popular need for membership, and the sense of community he wrote about praised a fellowship that was emotional. The general will was at the psychological level the only basis for real citizenship. Rousseau was saying that participation alone made effective and responsible citizenship. Moral solidarity was the result of the sense of personal freedom to be involved. And this freedom was more basic to a healthy politics than how votes were decided. Men knew by instinct when the "sovereign power" advanced their true interests. When it seemed not to do so, it was a perversion and subject to revolutionary correction. The general will was common well-being in action.

Rousseau thus took the Enlightenment in a new direction. Freedom was not a matter of logic. It was a matter of instinct, of conscience, of emotion, of identification by shared experience. Thus Rousseau was a democrat, not an aristocratic rationalist playing at reform but bound to the established order. Against Montesquieu, who taught that rights were corporate, Rousseau said they were *personal*: what a man feels to be right is right. Rousseau opposed Voltaire's view that virtue was not for simple souls. Even uneducated men could hear the voice of conscience, Rousseau said in 1750.

It was thus not true to say Rousseau opposed progress and cared nothing for man's material well-being. He believed that moral qualities were the key even to economics, however, and that no good distribution of wealth could be made by the abstract manipulation of property. Rather, like Marx a hundred years later, he taught that social depravity resulted from the arrangement of property. It was no good to talk of agricultural improvement and free trade when peasants were robbed of their produce. Private property lay at the bottom of inequality among men and political oppression. The love of profit itself led men to perdition. Economics made men insensitive to suffering and diminished respect for the morally infallible general will.

36. A sketch for a constitution along Genevan lines, written during the wars to partition the Polish state.

Upon hearing of Rousseau's death, the sculptor Jean Antoine Houdon hastened to Rousseau's home and took a cast of the dead man's face; from this he developed the portrait bust shown here. In his portrait busts Houdon displayed a keen sense of characterization and great artistic powers of selection and organization. He created some 200 busts, the later ones anticipating classicism. Musée de Versailles.

Kant understood Rousseau very well indeed. Jean Jacques was not obliterating conscience before the abstract notion of the general will. On the contrary, he was saying that society must identify its interests as a whole. These interests must then take precedence over the particular wants of men whose private desires are often antisocial in character. Rousseau may have been foolish to believe that citizens would not combine to tyrannize over other citizens, or to suppose that a democratic elitism or absolutism might now arise in place of a royal one. But he was no partisan of absolutism, as Kant wrote:

I once thought that it was only knowledge that constituted the dignity of man and I despised the ignorant masses. But Rousseau set me on the right road. I have learned to honor man for himself. . . . [37]

THE THIRD GENERATION

On what road did Rousseau set Kant and other *philosophes* of the third generation? There is no one answer, but a variety of answers. For Rousseau, revolution would not have seemed necessary in Geneva. But what about Rousseau had he been not a Swiss citizen but a French subject? For Franklin in America, as we shall see, the consideration of the common good led to the signing of a revolutionary manifesto—the Declaration of Independence. Most of the French *philosophes* had a sense of mission. But that mission did not include making a revolution by violent means to topple the Bourbon monarchy. Their focus had shifted from deism to politics in the second generation. Yet Voltaire in 1759 published his *Candide*.[38] Apart from its complaint against priests and its trenchant defense of reason against faith, neither *Candide* nor most other works of the Paris-based writers on enlightenment embraced revolutionary politics.

The plain fact was that the *philosophes* were materialists and reformers more than half at home in the Old Regime. Voltaire retained his royal offices until his death. Like Montesquieu and Diderot, and unlike the outcast Rousseau, the sage of Ferney was a defender of the civilization of the Old Regime, however much he disguised his debts to Christian ideas and muted the tone of his respect for monarchy. Rousseau's direct attacks on hierarchy in *Émile* and the *Social Contract* frightened men who enjoyed their powerful connections. Buffon was curator of the Jardin du Roi (the Royal Garden). We have enumerated d'Alembert's pensions. Voltaire went so far as to defend Louis XV's "reforms" against the *parlementaires*—and rightly so. The King had decided to tax the clergy, and the clergy's allies were determined to nip that invasion of privilege in the bud.

This was not the stuff of revolution, however. Indeed, Voltaire, so long-lived that he died after many of the younger *philosophes* of the second generation, best represents the ambiguity of the first two phases of the Enlightenment. He called for the dissolution of the Jesuits. He wrote a *Philosophical Dictionary* full of rationalist attacks on authority—and utterly hostile to democracy. He defended Rousseau against censorship, but saw in Jean Jacques a fundamental menace to the civilized life of salons and courts in which the *philosophes* moved.

Yet not all the younger encyclopedists reacted to either Rousseau or his "attacks" on civilization in the same way. In 1752 a young man from the Garonne region, near Montesquieu's estates, arrived in Paris with an

---

37. Quoted in Hampson, *The First European Revolution*, p. 39.
38. Samuel Johnson's *Rasselas* appeared in the same year.

introduction from the aged master of Bordeaux. Alexander Deleyre was twenty years old. He met Rousseau and through him Diderot, before the break brought about by Jean Jacques's 1754 *Discourse.* Deleyre contributed two articles to the *Encyclopédie,* in which he wrote of the division of labor and against institutional religion.[39] In 1755 he published a book on Bacon's philosophy of progress.

The conflict between Diderot and Rousseau shocked Deleyre greatly, since it posed the question of the relationship of progress and revolt, peaceful persuasion and open violence. By 1758 he had decided for Rousseau, writing to tell Jean Jacques that here was a kindred spirit, another revolutionary against the world. He confessed also his disappointment in the *philosophes,* who had abandoned the ideal of a society of *free and equal men.*[40]

Deleyre left Paris in 1758 and began a period of search. What he was looking for is hard to define, but he wrote enthusiastically about popular rebellions in Italy, especially that led by Pasquale Paoli in Corsica and at Genoa.[41]

In the seven years from 1751 to 1758, Deleyre had come a long way along the road to revolution. In 1752 he had accepted the accommodations with absolutism made by the *philosophes.* In 1756 he criticized Diderot's article on political authority for its compromises. In 1758, exiled from Paris and no longer welcome as a contributor to the *Encyclopédie,* the third-generation *Aufklärer* Alexander Deleyre wrote for the *Encyclopedic Journal (Journal encyclopédique)* a piece entitled "Thoughts of a Republican" (*Pensées d'un républicain*). Deleyre's "Thoughts" brought together a sense of moral outrage and a charge against the Old Regime. Palaces and objects of art were purchased with the unhappy lives of a hundred thousand unfortunate people. Poverty was the other side of the coin of luxury. Injustice and liberty were incompatible. Everywhere, the rich crushed the poor!

There was in Europe a "civil slavery" as odious as the black slavery in America which Montesquieu had restored to the list of grievances against Christian culture. Kings made wars; their subjects died in them. Yet most of the *philosophes* drew back from the question of holding monarchs to account. Deleyre did not. In the "Thoughts" he pictured a day in which the people would bring to trial their kings. More than thirty years later, in 1793, Deleyre was a member of the revolutionary assembly called the Convention. He was one of the men who condemned Louis XVI to death by ballot; and, far from shrinking from the act, he wrote an *Opinion* justifying it.[42] When he died in 1797, his eulogist, writing in the revolutionary journal *Philosophic Decade (Décade philosophique),* observed rightly that Deleyre was "*républicain par sentiment et par principes*"—republican in word and deed.

Deleyre was not akin to those revolutionaries in America whom Samuel Johnson had in mind when he noted the paradox of American politics. Thomas Jefferson doubtless was. For Johnson must have thought of the *philosophe* drafter of the Declaration of Independence when he asked rhetorically: "How is it that we hear the loudest *yelps* for liberty among the

39. Under the titles "Pin" (*Epingle*) and "Fanaticism" (*Fanatisme*).
40. See Deleyre's letter of October 28, 1758, in Jean Jacques Rousseau, *Correspondence complète,* ed. R. A. Leigh (Geneva: Droz, 1967), 5:195, no. 720.
41. Insurrections in the Corsican and Genoese territory were of long duration, dating from at least 1734. Paoli figured in the 1746 risings, and in the 1760s he was still active.
42. On the Convention, see Chapter 3. Deleyre's work was printed by the Convention: *Opinion d'Alexandre Deleyre . . . sur la question du jugement de Louis XVI.*

drivers of negroes?"[43] How indeed? How could any *philosophe,* mindful of the necessity to treat every man as an end in himself, never as a means,[44] countenance either the "civil slavery" Deleyre protested or the body slavery of the blacks?

BIBLIOGRAPHY

BECKER, CARL. *The Heavenly City of the Eighteenth Century Philosophers.** New Haven: Yale University Press, 1932). Witty and critical view of the major thinkers as latter-day "Scholastics" bemused by reason.

BRINTON, CRANE, ed. *The Portable Age of Reason Reader.** New York: The Viking Press, 1956. A very useful anthology.

CASSIRER, ERNST. *The Philosophy of the Enlightenment.** Boston: Beacon Press, 1955. Serious analytic work by the greatest interpreter of our age.

COBBAN, ALFRED. *In Search of Humanity.** London: Jonathan Cape, 1960. Essentially a sympathetic evaluation of the impact of moral doctrine on politics.

CROCKER, LESTER. *An Age of Crisis.* Baltimore: The Johns Hopkins Press, 1959. A very keen analysis by one of the best critics of Diderot, Rousseau, and French thought in general.

GAY, PETER. *Voltaire's Politics.** Princeton: Princeton University Press, 1959. A lucid analysis, friendly to its subject.

HALÉVY, ELIE. *The Growth of Philosophic Radicalism.** Boston: Beacon Press, 1955. Classic work, especially good on utilitarian ideas in England.

MANUEL, FRANK. *The Age of Reasons.** Ithaca: Cornell University Press, 1951. A judicious, brief, but stimulating survey.

PALMER, R. R. *Catholics and Unbelievers in Eighteenth Century France.** New York: Cooper Square Publishers, 1961. Good on popular attitudes toward God and religion in general.

Asterisk indicates a paperbound edition.

43. Quoted without attribution of source, in David Brian Davis, *The Problem of Slavery in Western Culture* (Ithaca: Cornell University Press, 1966), p. 3.
44. This version of the Golden Rule Kant transformed philosophically into his famous "categorical imperative": the moral law must be that people accept freely the duty expressed in maxims, which contain the practical principles of general legislation. Men must never act in such a way that they could not will their actions should become universal law.

2

REFORM AND REACTION: THE GATHERING STORM

The use of force alone is but temporary. It may subdue for a moment; but it does not remove the necessity of subduing again; and a nation is not governed, which is perpetually to be conquered.
EDMUND BURKE, *Conciliation with America* (1775)[1]

THE WEED THAT GROWS ON EVERY SOIL

In his celebrated speech defending the American colonists' right to resist a government they found oppressive, Burke returned again and again to a theme he had taken up a year earlier. Speaking on the question of whether certain Americans ought to pay taxes imposed by the British ministry of Lord North,[2] Burke had said a startling thing: The payment of twenty shillings would not ruin a Virginia planter, but on the principle it was required, payment would make of him a slave.[3]

Slavery was a thing much on people's minds during the Enlightenment. Samuel Johnson accused Americans of hypocrisy because of it. Deleyre thought monarchy on French lines imposed a "civil slavery" on people. Burke warned Englishmen that slavery was a weed easy to grow on any soil, but liberty was a delicate bloom needing careful nurture. The Scottish poet Robert Burns (1759–1796) evoked the memory of freedom in his countrymen when he said Edward I's campaigns in Scotland in the thirteenth century had given Scots "chains and slaverie!"[4] The British poet James Thomson (1700–1748), proud of England's fight against French hegemony in Europe, shaped a familiar refrain:

> Rule, Britannia, rule the waves;
> Britons never will be slaves.[5]

Oliver Goldsmith (1728–1774), another poet, confessed to hating the French because "they are all slaves."[6] Statesmen of the first rank joined writers in denouncing the voluntary slavery some submitted to in society. William Pitt the Elder, Lord Chatham (1708–1778), defended the American rebels:

I rejoice that America has resisted. Three millions . . . so dead to all feelings of liberty, as voluntarily to submit to be slaves, would have been fit instruments to make slaves of the rest.[7]

1. Burke delivered this speech before Parliament on March 22, 1775.
2. Frederick North, the second earl of Guilford (1732–1792).
3. From Burke's *Speech on American Taxation*.
4. In *Scots, Wha Hae.*
5. *Alfred: A Masque* (1740), act 2, sc. 3. Thomson wrote this jointly with his friend David Mallet.
6. "Distresses of a Common Soldier," *Essays.*
7. From a speech in the House of Commons, January 14, 1766.

Seventeen years later, when the American Revolution was over, his son,[8] the future prime minister, again speaking in the Commons against Britain's policy and that of despots everywhere, made this comment on politics: "Necessity is the plea for every infringement of human freedom. It is the argument of tyrants; it is the creed of slaves."[9]

Politicians and authors everywhere in the European republic of letters easily conjured up images of civil slavery for the simplest of reasons. Within Europe, serfdom was still a familiar fact, even in the third generation of the Enlightenment. And wherever Europeans had established empires, real body slavery had been sure to follow, as a result of the sale of Africans either captured directly or purchased from traders who did the hunting. It was difficult for liberal Europeans and Americans in the colonies of Portuguese, Spanish, French, Dutch, and English governance to escape the question, Can we be free until we emancipate our slaves?

The tension arose naturally out of the fact that *philosophes* and enlightened statesmen saw in America a vision of liberation from the European

French slave ships such as this one, along with ships of the British, the Dutch, the Spanish, and the Portuguese, brought blacks from Africa for sale in the southern American colonies, the West Indies, and Brazil. To save space, the human cargo (as many as 500 blacks) was laid down side by side, pairs of black males often manacled to the deck. The space between decks, at most perhaps five feet, was often subdivided by additional "shelves" of slaves. At the height of the slave trade, these ships transported an estimated total of 70,000 slaves a year. Musée des Arts Décoratifs, Nantes; Studio Madec.

8. William Pitt the Younger (1759–1806).
9. From a speech given November 18, 1783.

chains of hierarchy. Yet America had been since its settling a land of masters and slaves. Utopian writers had followed Thomas More's 1516 example,[10] by putting their more perfect societies in the Western Hemisphere. Yet even in More's time the romantic view of American freedom had been jolted by Spanish priests who exposed the enslavement of the Indians. The early colonists had found in various forms of slave labor a solution to the problems of production at a profit.

Hence material progress, even luxury and a measure of political liberty at home, was purchased by the blood and sweat of stolen blacks and those "legally" bought in the world's markets. From the Rio de la Plata in the Argentine to the Saint Lawrence River, slavery was a basic institution of the Western world. By the 1760s Europeans participated widely in "tea and coffee" slavery, as addicted to America's products or those of the Oriental plantations as were the slaves bound to their work by slave codes and laws. The more northern American colonies supplied goods to the plantations in the South in exchange for the staple crops of sugar, rice, tobacco, cotton, and dyestuffs.

The same varieties of staples crossed the Atlantic in exchange for iron, textiles, weapons, and refined products (rum for example) made from the American staples. Such goods were also basic to the slave trade itself, and Africa was a vast market in the triangular trade that linked America to Europe and to Africa. Profits arose out of the sale of goods in Africa in exchange for slaves, and the sale of slaves in America in exchange for staples. The staples, in turn, were exchanged in Europe for the goods that would buy more slaves in Africa. The slave trade helped to build capital and to spur investment, banking, shipbuilding, canal construction, and even the growth of huge French and English urban centers.[11]

It was hard to escape the conclusion that black slavery was a major force shaping European society and institutions in the Age of Enlightenment. It was even harder for the *philosophes* and their political allies to escape another conclusion, that where some were slaves, none were free.

The standard works of legal and moral philosophy in the eighteenth century treated the matter at length. In France, Montesquieu sharpened the discussion in his *Spirit of the Laws,* and Abbé Raynal set forth the influence of slavery on Europe in 1770.[12] In Britain, the jurist William Blackstone and the writer on ethics William Robertson took up the question long before there was an effective abolition movement. In America, Jefferson became an early critic of the institution of slavery, despite his own holdings in Virginia.

10. His *Utopia* was published in that year.
11. Bordeaux and Liverpool, among others.
12. Guillaume Thomas François Raynal, a *philosophe,* in his book *A History of the Two Indies* (*Histoire philosophique et politique des établissements et du commerce des Européens dans les deux Indes*).

Native Indians were the first slaves in the West Indies, but, unable to withstand the rigors of forced labor, they were soon replaced by blacks. In the latter part of the eighteenth century, 12½ percent of the blacks shipped to the West Indies on English slavers died en route; the rest were lucky if they survived ten years of labor on the sugar plantations. British agitation in such antislavery tracts as this one, published in 1793, called attention to the barbarities of West Indian slavery and finally resulted in the outlawing of the British slave trade in 1807 and the abolition of British slavery in 1833. Rare Book Division, The New York Public Library, Astor, Lenox and Tilden Foundations.

FIG. I.

Reprefents the manner of Yoking the Slaves by the Mundingoes, or African Slave Merchants, who ufually march annually in eight or ten parties, from the River Gambia to Bambarra; each party having from one hundred to one hundred and fifty Slaves.

FIG. III.

Where the roads lay through woods, the captive inhabitants are made to travel feveral hundred miles with a log hung as here defcribed.

FIG. V.

The Hufband and Wife, after being fold to different purchafers, violently feparated—probably never to fee each other more!

FIG. VII.

A front and profile view of an African's head with the mouth piece and necklace, the hooks round which, are placed as a preventative to an efcape when purfued in the woods, or, to procuring of reft by laying the head down.

N.B. At A is a piece of flat iron which goes into the mouth—and fo effectually keeps down the tongue, that nothing can be fwallowed, not even the faliva, a paffage for which is made through holes in the mouth plate.

FIG. IX.

An enlarged view of the mouth piece—which when long worn—becomes fo heated as frequently to bring off the fkin along with it.

N.B. A late refpectable tradefman in London, had an order for a great number of thefe and other fuch like inftruments—but after they were made, finding the ufes they were intended for, he declined fending them.

FIG. XI.

The manner in which fome Slaves are placed to be flogged.

FIG. II.

These Log-Yokes are made of the roots of trees—and so heavy as to make it extremely difficult for the person who wears it to walk, much more to escape or run away.

FIG. IV.

A view of the leg bolts or shackles, as put upon the legs of the Slaves on ship board, in the middle passage.

FIG. VI.

When Slaves are purchased by the dealers they are generally marked on the breast with a red hot iron.

FIG. VIII.

A representation of a Slave at work as cruelly accoutered—with a head frame and mouth piece to prevent his eating—with boots and spurs (as they are called) round his legs, and an half hundred weight chained to his body to prevent his absconding.

FIG. X.

An enlarged view of the Boots and Spurs, as seen used on some plantations in Antigua.

FIG. XII.

Another method of fixing the poor victims on a ladder to be flogged, which is also occasionally laid flat on the ground for severer punishments.

Some, like Raynal, approached the fact of slavery from a moral point of view rooted in natural law, holding slavery to be unnatural and hence wrong. Raynal controverted Montesquieu's doctrine that at least in Europe slavery had been abolished by raising the question of the serf codes east of the Elbe River. Raynal believed that the lust for power and profit had degraded whole peoples. The habit of lording over blacks in America had its counterpart in Europe in the cruelty and arbitrariness with which even the free peasant was treated at home. Progress and the redemption of society from despotism, Raynal said, were impossible for as long as the habit of mastership abroad accustomed people at home to the worst vice of all— treating another human being as a living tool. If it were claimed that without slave labor and serfdom the profits of the world could not be, Raynal answered: then let the lands lie fallow and the mines go unworked!

America, Raynal believed, would shake off slavery and lead the rest of the world to true liberty. Reason and the laws of nature would triumph there, he wrote in 1781,[13] throwing off the shackles of the European social order. Then, when the revolution for liberty was won, and black revolutionaries had won the freedom for themselves which Jefferson claimed for the British colonists against King George III, a new order in America would free Europe from slavery, by destroying the commerce in people which degraded master and slave alike.

ENGLAND: THE CRITICAL YEARS

That a French *philosophe* could place in America's struggle for independence from Britain the hope for a new ethic of humanitarianism and a new politics of freedom is interesting, if for no other reason than the contrast such hope offers to Samuel Johnson's native English skepticism about the American revolutionaries. What reason was there to cherish the belief that a rebellion against the most liberal government in the West would advance the ideal of freedom? The Americans kept slaves while rebelling against their own political enslavement. Liberal Europeans took positions similarly ambiguous.

Even some of the severest English critics of the barbarities of American slavery maintained that slavery in theory was not evil. Daniel Defoe, for example, had as early as 1702[14] recognized the despair of black men, whose release was more likely to come from famine, plague, disease, and death than from Christian charity. And in the year 1774, when Thomas Day dedicated his antislavery tract, the *Dying Negro,* to Rousseau,[15] the "liberal" British economists were arguing that dealing with slave traders and owners was just, so long as they paid their bills!

Despite such facts, the *philosophes* who admired *habeas corpus* and the British system of constitutional monarchy, however erroneously Montesquieu had interpreted it, were not wholly misguided in looking to England's American cousins and their revolution. England in the 1760s and 1770s was a society acutely racked by protest and demands for liberty. The distant American "Englishmen" were blessed by geography. Since they were so far from home, it was more difficult for the partisans of the old hierarchy and subordination to subdue malcontents or impose on Americans a form of conquest.

13. In a second edition of his *History,* published during the Revolutionary War.
14. In his *Reformation of Manners, A Satyr* (London, 1702), pp. 17–18.
15. Day (1748–1789) was a lawyer, a writer, and an active reformer interested in applying some of Rousseau's ideas to the reform of the poor.

Even at home the government of George III had suffered setbacks in its struggle to contain aspirations for a politics of participation and wider liberty.

Britain had emerged from the Seven Years' War victorious in Europe, America, and India. The cost had been great, however. George II (1727–1760) had supported the European adventures at least in part because he was a Hanoverian tied to his family's German interests. But doing so had brought a halt to a promising series of acts of domestic reform. From 1746 to 1756, under the leadership of Henry Pelham, the duke of Newcastle's brother, debt consolidation was so successful that by 1751 the government had no bonds outstanding at more than 3 percent interest. Europe's first professional urban police had been established in London. Calendar reform had brought to England the calculations of the date used in Europe since 1582.[16] There had been legislation allowing Jews and Christian Nonconformists a larger share in civil life.

The outbreak of war brought to power Pitt the Elder, who managed the "German business" effectively, while focusing his energy on defeating the French in America and Asia. He was aided in this by the spirit of partnership with the colonials he favored. For example, to Colonel George Washington of the Virginia militia he gave powers equal to those of royal commanders. He also convinced the Americans that his war to expand the British Empire represented a vast expenditure of treasure to protect the interests of colonial planters and merchants from the Bahamas through Georgia and clear up to the Canadian border. The colonies saw in this some truth, since the security of their internal trade was as much at stake as was the exchange between Britain and her dependencies. If 90 percent of all New Yorkers wore clothes made in England, the total volume of New York's trade with the Bahamas was larger than that with the mother country.

By 1760, when Pitt's forces had effectively defeated the French in America, the £2,000,000 annual trade with the thirteen seaboard colonies made the expense seem worth the sacrifices. The Prime Minister was not slow to tell the Americans that over one-third of the war expenditures of nearly £4,000,000 were for American defense.

The death of George II in 1760 brought to an end Pitt's control of the government and also rapport between London and America. George III cared not at all for the Hanoverians' German interests. He wished a quick end to the war. He claimed to want a return to domestic reform, but Pitt accused his king of perfidy in deserting England's European allies. He also ridiculed the idea that the King's new chief minister, Lord Bute, had the confidence of Parliament. He proved a good prophet. Bute[17] resigned in 1763, having thoroughly alienated the London masses by the imposition of a tax on cider.

This measure was one of the many passed in the 1760s and 1770s to reduce the war debt and fund the administration of a vastly enlarged empire. The debt had swelled from about £80,000,000 in 1750 to £115,000,-000 in 1763. Postwar unemployment, the misery of veterans concentrated in London slums, and some harvest failures combined to breed urban unrest. And Bute's successor, George Grenville (1712–1770), did not help relieve tensions. In an effort to reduce the cost of government, he trimmed the imperial defenses. This alarmed the colonials, who wished to know what

George Grenville, depicted here in a mock burial ceremony for the Stamp Act of 1765, had not anticipated the antagonism that this revenue measure would arouse in the colonies. Benjamin Franklin, in London at the time, had urged Americans to accept the tax and had even sought a position for one of his friends as stamp distributor in Philadelphia. The colonies, however, met the Stamp Act with immediate opposition; Grenville was dismissed from office later in 1765, and in 1766 the Stamp Act was repealed. The John Carter Brown Library, Brown University.

16. Until 1752 England used the Julian calendar and was eleven days behind the countries on the Gregorian one.
17. A Scot, John Stuart (1713–1792).

had become of the promises made by Pitt—to spare no expense in their defense. The cuts in defense costs were popular at home, however, even if the new taxes on a wide variety of imports were not.

Groaning under the new taxes, ordinary Englishmen asked why the Americans paid no share of the cost of their own defense. Grenville responded to domestic pressures with two acts to pass the costs at least in part to America: the Sugar Act (1764) and the Stamp Act (1765). Both had precedents,[18] but none of the earlier taxes had been collected in the colonies. Popular with the country gentry who were Grenville's chief supporters, since they promised to ease the burden of taxes on land, these two new acts were unpopular with the commercial classes, especially in London and the western English ports. In America, Grenville's program provoked resistance.[19]

The issue of taxes levied by Parliament in the colonies ran parallel to a challenge given to legislative authority at home. The British legislature made no pretense at representing the people in a direct way. Instead, it embodied a doctrine of virtual representation rather than actual representation. The colonists were dissatisfied over this doctrine, which denied them the right to play a direct role in making the laws binding on them. It was not enough to send agents to plead their cause with sympathetic members of the Parliament. This feeling was widely shared among the unfranchised London masses, who found themselves taxed without representation also. Events were to reveal the close link between colonial unrest and domestic demands for reform.

18. The Molasses Act of 1733 and the old laws requiring tax stamps for legal papers.
19. See later in this chapter.

On another front, the government was under severe attack. One of Pitt's followers, John Wilkes, had attacked Bute over the concessions to France in the Treaty of Paris of 1763. It mattered little that Wilkes (1727–1797), a good cavalry officer, and member of Parliament since 1757, was also a lecher who abandoned his wife and children and joined the orgies and peculiar devotions of London's rakish Hellfire Club. He was a political journalist of genius. Since 1762 he had put out a journal, the *North Briton,* which in its number 45, of April 23, 1763, directly attacked the King.

Wilkes in fact accused George III of aspiring to absolutism. Readers on that Saturday were astounded to see Wilkes go from his characterization of Bute as an "insolent, incapable, despotic minister" to this attack on Grenville's policy and the King's intentions:

A nation as sensible as the English will see that a spirit of concord when they are oppressed[20] . . . means a tame submission to injury, and that a spirit of liberty ought then to arise, and I am sure ever will, in proportion to the weight of grievance they feel. Every legal attempt of a contrary tendency to the spirit of [submissive] concord will be deemed a justified resistance . . . [to] the slavish doctrines of the absolute, independent, unlimited power of the crown. . . . The people too have their prerogative, and I hope the fine words of Dryden[21] will be engraven on our hearts: Freedom is the English Subject's Prerogative.[22]

The result of Wilkes's setting up as a tribune of the people was a general warrant for a series of arrests, forty-nine publishers and printers in all being imprisoned for seditious libel on no greater authority than the signature of the secretary of state. Wilkes called this procedure by *lettre de cachet* an evidence that his charges against the government were valid. General warrants specified the alleged crime, but left blank the place for the names of the accused persons. As such, Wilkes said, the warrants were oppressive and a threat to every man's liberty. Huge London crowds demonstrated for "Wilkes and liberty," harangued by Pitt's "imperialist" agitators. Wilkes won release on grounds of his immunity from arrest as a member of Parliament.

"That devil Wilkes," as George III called him, was not content thus to resolve the issue of censorship and general warrants. He instituted suits for damages, which were finally decided in his favor in 1769. Meanwhile, in 1763–1764 the new popular hero reprinted the *North Briton's* number 45, publishing as well a pornographic *Essay on Women* and an obscene paraphrase of the religious hymn *Veni Creator.* This turn toward an attack on social convention shocked his aristocratic friends, and Wilkes fled to Paris to escape prosecution on new charges of sedition, libel, and obscene publications.

During his Paris exile, one thing of great importance for the history of English radicalism happened. In 1766 the courts and Parliament declared general warrants unconstitutional. Wilkes returned to agitation in England in 1768, having been assured that earlier prosecutions would be dropped.[23] Devoid of high-ranking supporters, he now appealed directly to the London masses. Defeated in a bid for a London seat in the Commons, he ran in 1769

---

20. By taxes and a false peace.
21. The poet John Dryden (1631–1700).
22. All quotes from the *North Briton,* no. 45, are from the reprint in Robert and Elborg Foster, eds., *European Society in the Eighteenth Century* (New York: Harper & Row, Publishers, Torchbooks, 1969), pp. 390–394.
23. He was actually imprisoned on new libel charges, before being released in a reaction to a period of intense pro-Wilkes riots.

for Middlesex County. Wherever he campaigned there were riots. When soldiers killed a supporter with rifle fire, the boy's body was taken through the streets of London to arouse opposition to the government. Soldiers shot down more people. There were "risings" of sailors, sawyers, coal heavers, and yardmen sabotaged naval vessels. The Commons saw in Wilkes a challenge to the established order. They refused to accept his election and disbarred him from membership. His supporters returned him over his opponent in three new elections, but Parliament actually seated the *defeated* candidate.

Wilkes's career after 1769 became even more spectacular and notorious. Unable to seat their man in the Commons, the Middlesex men elected him sheriff of the county. Londoners made him sheriff of the City. In 1774 he was again elected member of Parliament for Middlesex. This time he was seated, without opposition, doubtless because the House would not again risk the wrath of the Londoners, who in that same year had also elected Wilkes their lord mayor, thus giving him the highest office in Europe's richest, largest capital.

More important than the further details of Wilkes's career[24]—he relapsed into respectability in his declining years—was his impact on the politics of Britain. Wilkes's various struggles not only took general warrants out of the realm of law. The matter of prior censorship arose in the trial on the charges associated with the *North Briton's* number 45. Lord Chief Justice Mansfield[25] of the Court of Common Pleas defined freedom of the press to include freedom from prior restraint, while acknowledging that the exercise of that freedom might produce a libel action, even if a writer and publisher told the truth. This restraining definition set the limit of a free press in the Anglo-American tradition, by protecting the right to publish while providing aggrieved parties remedies at law.

Mansfield also warned the government that seizure of a newspaper on grounds of "public necessity" was illegal. Public policy, he said, in a free country was no argument at law. This dictum was especially important to Wilkes, because one thing he did was to make public certain debates on policy in Parliament on the ground that secrecy inhibited responsible opinion among the electorate.

The issue of opinion and the vote lay at the heart of Wilkes's popular politics. The old slogan, "Wilkes and liberty," became the rallying cry of an association formed in 1769, the Society of the Supporters of the Bill of Rights. The Society and Wilkes said the refusal to seat the Middlesex member (Wilkes) had exposed the House of Commons as an "unrepresentative" body. Against that "club of oligarchs," as Wilkes contemp-

24. He was City chamberlain in 1779, an office he held until his death. He led the London radicals who opposed the government's policy toward America. Samuel Johnson called this treason.
25. William Murray, first earl of Mansfield, 1705–1793. He was Lord Chief Justice from 1756 until 1788.

John Wilkes, agitator for parliamentary reform and friend of the American colonies, led a stormy life in his ceaseless campaigns for individual liberty. Arrested and imprisoned in 1763, twice expelled from the House of Commons, convicted of seditious libel, arrested as an outlaw (serving 22 months in prison), refused a seat in Parliament four times, he nonetheless rose to the lord mayorship of London and again entered Parliament in 1774. With a private life characterized as lecherous and a satiric pen that helped drive a prime minister from office, Wilkes was far from universally popular. He antagonized, among others, the artist William Hogarth, who retaliated with this caricature. By courtesy of the Trustees of the British Museum.

tuously called the Commons, the only appeal was to the franchised people. The Society's program advocated the rights of electors, the dissolution of false parliaments, the dismissal of George III's ministers, and a radical extension of the franchise to those the oligarchs called "the Mob." Wilkes raised the banner of mass politics, of democracy through universal manhood suffrage, and of the incorporation of the unpropertied classes into a wider political nation. The first political pressure group sponsored a second in 1770, the Society for Constitutional Information. And this group agitated among the urban working classes, especially on the franchise question and the need to purge members of Parliament who sat from "rotten boroughs" and family seats, where half a dozen electors returned a member whose vote counted for as much as the vote of a member representing the Bristol electorate of 6,000 or London's 12,000 enfranchised men.

Vote buying and the waste of tax revenue were issues with popular appeal far from London. In 1780 a farming gentleman from Yorkshire founded the Yorkshire Association. Christopher Wyvill (1740–1822) attacked the corruption of the courts and government by aristocratic cliques. He wanted to exclude "placemen" (crown officials and patronage recipients) from Parliament. His Association had by 1785 a program of franchise extension and cooperated with the southern urban societies. Wyvill also advocated a major reform of national politics by convoking a "constituent assembly" empowered to force parliamentary reforms.

A vigorous literature supported the street riots and organized pressure groups. While the London *Annual Register* in 1775 complained that outrages once reported from afar—in Poland or on the Danube—now reigned in London's streets, favorable doctrines spread. Catherine Macaulay (1731–1791), an ardent friend of the American Revolution, urged radical action in her *History of England from the Accession of James I*.[26] John Cartwright (1740–1824) mixed antislavery sentiments with political reform in a pamphlet of 1776 entitled *Take Your Choice.* His arguments carried on the tradition of the anonymous publicist called Junius who had published a stream of letters[27] attacking the King's government, filled with echoes of the Glorious Revolution. John Horne Tooke (1736–1812), a parson and friend of Wilkes and Voltaire, was repeatedly fined and imprisoned for publishing resolutions subscribing funds to aid the American rebels.

Another minister of God, Joseph Priestley (1733–1804),[28] advocated in politics the rule that government was legitimate only when it secured the greatest happiness for the greatest number. His debt to Rousseau was deep in his fiery *First Principles of Government.* Yet another preacher, Dr. Richard Price (1723–1791), who was a close friend of Ben Franklin, accused George III of betraying the Englishmen at home by the war he made on their American friends and relatives. His *Observations on Civil Liberty* (1776)[29] caused a sensation by asking whether God was more likely to favor the whoremongers and dicers of George III's court or those fasting and praying fighters for liberty at Lexington and Concord.

Burke's *Thoughts on the Causes of the Present Discontents* had tried to steer the demand for reform into the still waters of moderation in 1770. But in 1775 even that inherently conservative voice asked whether George III supposed he could govern men impatient of servitude on any principle but that of freedom.

26. Eight volumes appeared between 1763 and 1783.
27. Between 1769 and 1772.
28. He was also a famous chemist and was credited with discovering oxygen.
29. The full title of this pamphlet is *Observations on the Nature of Civil Liberty, the Principles of Government, and the Justice and Policy of War with America.*

The emblem of the snake, whose separate parts represent the thirteen colonies, and the motto beneath dramatized the need for colonial unity. Of the 13 colonies, 7 were governed as crown colonies, 3 others as proprietary colonies, and the remaining 3 as corporate colonies. These differing forms of government, plus differing economies, religions, and populations, threatened to defeat beforehand any attempts by the colonies at concerted opposition to Britain. As John Adams put it, the problem of the American Revolution was to make thirteen clocks strike as one. The Historical Society of Pennsylvania.

AMERICA: REBELLION AND REVOLUTION

As Wilkes and his supporters unfurled the banner of protest and reform at home, opinion in the colonies turned toward disenchantment. Grenville, who was much misliked by his sovereign, was hated by the Americans. The combination of new taxes and reduced defenses promised less security at a greater cost. Grenville had also tightened the collection of customs duties in the American ports. The net effect of English import duties and safeguards against smuggling was to impede both free trade and illegal trade.

Events moved rapidly in 1765, after the imposition of the Stamp Act. George III accepted Grenville's resignation and gave power to Lord Rockingham,[30] the third prime minister in three years. Despite his intention to mollify the colonists, Rockingham discovered how easily bad goes to worse.

The colonies were traditionally aloof from one another. Arrangements in Connecticut and Rhode Island had little in common with those in the Carolinas, or those in Virginia with the structure of society and politics in New York. Not only was there no central direction of colonial affairs from London. The settlements were internally divided. The Carolinas and Georgia were effectively royal colonies controlled by nominated governors. Virginia was an aristocratic republic under planter control. New York was a commercial and landed oligarchy. Connecticut, like Rhode Island, was virtually a self-ruling state. In some colonies slave labor dominated, while even in the northern "free" colonies perhaps 10 percent of the population was slave. Maryland was a refuge for Catholics. Virginia was Church of England territory. Most of New England showed various shades of Puritanism and rugged Nonconformity.

These divergent little colonies had been unable to cooperate even in their own defense from 1756 to 1763. The Albany Plan of Union drafted by Ben Franklin was rejected by the colonial legislatures. While British troops defended against the French, Americans traded with the enemy. Only three of the thirteen colonies raised decent armies. This performance did not

30. Charles Watson-Wentworth, marquess of Rockingham, a liberal-minded politician (1730–1782).

surprise Britain, which had come to view the colonials as lawless. The Americans had for decades evaded customs, traded illegally with the French, and refused taxes not approved by local legislatures.

What did startle George III and his ministers was the reaction to the Sugar Act and the Stamp Act. Resistance, even scattered violence against collectors, was anticipated. But the demand the Americans pay for stamps on all forms of paper—legal, commercial, even newspapers—loosed more than resistance. Led by the classes normally most lawful—the editors, lawyers, and big merchants—the colonists organized a "congress." Delegates from nine colonies met in the New York Stamp Act Congress, where they told Rockingham by proclamation that no ministry in Britain had the right to tax the Americans. This position was supported by Pitt in Parliament, and Rockingham withdrew the Stamp Act. Even the repeal and consequent lowering of the sugar duty did not ease the pressure of American riots and boycotts, however. The British government had tried to save face with a Declaratory Act, in which the larger issue was squarely joined.

The Declaratory Act stated that the American "plantations" were by right subordinate to the crown and Parliament of Great Britain. Ministers might come and go in London in rapid succession over the next five years.[31] The issue would not lie down. Pitt's regime, which the colonists looked to for relief, was in fact presided over less by the aged and nearly senile statesman than by Charles Townshend.[32] In 1766 "Champagne Charley" pledged to find a "revenue for America." As chancellor of the exchequer he established customs officers in America and levied port taxes. When the New York legislature resisted the dual imposition (customs and excise), Townshend actually suspended the legislative functions of that assembly in 1767. The ministry of the duke of Grafton[33] continued in effect also Townshend's program of duties on paper, paint, lead, glass, and tea. When new resistance to these imposts on imports into the colonies grew, repeal was again carried. But another "saving" gesture was made; the duty on tea was kept, as a proof of the doctrine of the Declaratory Act.

We need give only a rapid summary of the more familiar events from 1770 to 1776. Lord North's government was bent on reform in America, India, and at home, but was unsuccessful. Direct rule in India was attempted under the Regulating Act of 1774, and India submissively went along with this act. But America responded differently to North's efforts to consolidate relations with the empire. From 1768 to 1773 militancy had increased in the major ports, especially Boston. A "massacre" there in 1770 of five colonists by royal musketeers set the pace for increased violence. In 1772 colonists burned a customs ship. North's inquiry boards found some sympathetic responses, in New York for example, as an end to rioting seemed desirable. But in 1773 the financial collapse of the East India Company renewed the pressure on the western part of the empire.

North tried to compensate and revive the East India Company through its tea trade. The Tea Act of 1773 allowed the Company to ship tea directly to America.[34] The remitted duty of 5 percent would help the Company to solvency, because it could now sell tea more cheaply in America than could the Dutch. The act gave the Company a monopoly of sale, however, and

Four thousand British troops arrived in Boston in 1768 to protect royal officials and enforce the British acts of trade. Resented by the radical politicians, the British troops were constantly harassed by the townspeople. When, on March 5, 1770, a British customs house sentry became the target of icy snowballs thrown by local men and boys, other British soldiers came to his aid, and a full-scale riot erupted in front of the State House, shown here (center). The troops fired, and five men were killed in what the patriots labeled the Boston Massacre. A murder trial was held (with John Adams and Josiah Quincy as defense lawyers), but the British sentry was acquitted. Library of Congress.

31. Pitt (1766–1768), Grafton (1768–1770), and Lord North, who began a twelve-year regime in 1770.
32. 1725–1767, a successful ministerial politician first elected to Parliament in 1747.
33. Augustus Henry Fitzroy (1735–1811), also a minister under Rockingham and Pitt and again under Lord North.
34. Rather than through London customs first, where it was taxed and then sold at auction to merchants who resold it.

this had the effect of putting out of business the American merchants who in the past had bought tea in London for sale in the colonies.

Led by New England merchants such as Sam Adams and John Hancock, a systematic boycott of Company tea followed. The Americans, Adams said, would not sell their liberty for cheap tea! To give support to the point, on December 16, 1773, a band of boycotters dumped 298 casks of tea into the Boston harbor. London responded with severity. Lord North proclaimed the closure of Boston harbor, thus threatening economic ruin to the most English of American cities. The Massachusetts legislature was suspended. Local elections and town meetings were banned.

An apparently unrelated act in 1774 also underlined the meaning of the theory of sovereignty stated in the 1766 Declaratory Act. The Quebec Act integrated the conquered Canadian provinces into the empire by preserving French civil law and Catholic religious freedom. It also gave Quebec the land north of the Ohio River,[35] which western-oriented colonists had hoped

35. Later the states of Ohio, Wisconsin, Michigan, Illinois, and Indiana.

Britain's General Gage sent troops, under Lieutenant Colonel Francis Smith and Major John Pitcairn (shown in the foreground of this engraving by a Connecticut militiaman), to destroy colonial powder stores at Concord. After an opening skirmish on April 19, 1775, in Lexington, where eight minutemen fell, the British marched on into Concord, as shown here. The patriots repulsed the well-regimented British at Concord's North Bridge, forcing them to make a bloody retreat back toward Boston. The American Revolution had begun. Prints Division, The New York Public Library, Astor, Lenox and Tilden Foundations.

to make their own. The act also made no provision for representative institutions. To the Americans, already engulfed in what they thought was an assault on their liberty, the Quebec Act seemed a confirmation of their worst fears. They regarded it as pro-French, pro-Catholic, and one of the "Intolerable Acts" by which Parliament meant to show America where sovereign power resided.

The American answer to London's efforts at putting the whole empire in order was revolution. In 1774 a new "congress" met in Philadelphia. This Continental Congress not only made the boycott of British goods total; it provided vigilante groups to enforce its decrees on those loyal to king and Parliament. In April of 1775 fighting began, when troops under royal orders tried to seize contraband weapons at Concord, Massachusetts. The skirmish at Concord and Lexington prompted a Second Continental Congress, which outlined a truly revolutionary policy. An army of "America" would be raised; expeditions to Quebec were to persuade the French into the "union." Diplomats were sent to France, to persuade England's chief rival that there would be advantages to the Bourbons in helping break apart the British Empire.

The Americans were terribly divided among themselves, and there were probably as many loyalists as there were secessionists, as well as a large majority of neutrals. But the vanguard of activists on each side reduced the possibility of neutrality in armed engagements. The radical pamphleteer Thomas Paine (1737–1809), who had come to America in 1774, said in *Common Sense* (January 1776) that only revolution would guarantee the English in America their liberty. Six months later, Jefferson's draft of the Declaration of Independence gained the assent of Congress for the propositions of Paine's incendiary book. Britain had tried to rule not by reason but by force. In the future it must be America for itself. Once the facts of tyranny were submitted to a candid world, the cause of independence would be upheld.

The War of American Independence was more than a revolutionary struggle, however.[36] France gave aid to the rebels. The Dutch, Prussians, Swedes, Portuguese, Danes, and Turks so resented the British efforts to blockade America that they became armed neutrals. A new war for empire was thus attached to the American struggle. And the French army and navy forces proved essential to the American victory, as the colonists were disunited internally and hard up for troops and cash.

The events ended by the concession of independence at Paris in 1783 were significant in yet another sense, one having nothing to do with the

36. A narrative of its course is inappropriate here. Our subject is only the growth of revolutionary tensions in the West ca. 1770–1790.

When the American Revolution began, Britain was the richest nation and the most powerful military force in the world; the colonies, in their thirteen individual militias and the infant Continental Army, had untrained, undisciplined soldiers, many of them independent-minded farmers and artisans. The colonial soldiers, two of whom are depicted on this Pennsylvania German earthenware plate (ca. 1800), were often ill fed, ill clothed, and ill equipped: in the summer of 1775 the Continentals had 9 cartridges per man against the British regulars' 60 apiece. At the end of the war, there were approximately 30,000 British troops in America; at the most the Continental Army had mustered 18,000. Philadelphia Museum of Art.

new phase of the Anglo-French struggle. From 1783 to 1789 the new nation on the Atlantic's western edge struggled to express its destiny in a stable political form. The *philosophes* and every liberal statesman in Europe watched closely the outcome of the struggle in the distant crucible of human rights. The 1776 Declaration had taken its stand for more than secession. It had claimed more than a popular right to resist tyranny. It had taken over the Enlightenment doctrines of natural law, the equality of men, their endowment by the Creator with unalienable rights of "Life, Liberty and the pursuit of Happiness."

What this meant in practice was soon evident, not only in the Constitution submitted for ratification in 1787, but in the real politics and social systems of the Union. After the revenge had been visited on those loyal to Britain,[37] the decision had still to be made as to what "home rule" should mean. Often violence determined who should rule at home as the new political system took shape. Religious toleration was without limitation. The propertied classes were often forced to extend the franchise to common artisans and poor farmers. The principle was adopted that representatives in the various legislatures, state and federal, should represent equal numbers of citizens, although slaves were not to be counted equally with free men.[38] A start was made toward Abbé Raynal's prediction: all states north of Maryland acted to end slavery.

Everywhere, old institutions modeled on European hierarchy gave way to a more open vision of society. Established churches were weakened. Tithes were no longer legally enforceable. Feudal tenures of land were outlawed, along with manorial dues and the systems of land law (primogeniture and entail) which facilitated large, inherited estates.

If much wealth changed hands and power was more widely distributed, the new Union was no perfect democracy, however. Kings, nobles, bishops, and courts were gone. There were still aristocratic and oligarchic politicians who controlled power in New York and Virginia. Slavery still existed. Religion was still important in determining who governed in New England. Property qualifications for the franchise remained in effect in most states. Policy toward the Indians was genocidal.

Yet constitutional guarantees of liberty existed. A "Bill of Rights" was added to the Constitution. There was a separation of legislative, judicial, and executive powers, as well as a supreme court to check the executive and legislative branches. Government was told quite frankly what it could not do. The citizens of the separate states were able to protect themselves against the federal system, while moving freely from state to state with equal rights in all. The whole "people" constituted one nation, in which what the *philosophes* had said was natural for mankind seemed to be being put to a test.

To the Europeans, the lesson was brought home by politicians and pamphleteers in the 1780s, as well as by adventurers who had gone to

37. The Tories and imperial loyalists.
38. By the three-fifths rule of apportionment. See the Constitution.

The American Revolution was more than a year old when the Declaration of Independence was adopted. Though independence had been urged by some, others feared that such a bold step would frighten off many from the patriot cause. When the final draft of the Declaration was adopted by the Second Continental Congress on July 4, 1776, the colonists cheered, firing salutes despite the shortage of gunpowder, burning the King's Arms, and, as shown in this scene, raising a liberty pole in defiance of tyranny and in celebration of freedom. Courtesy of Kennedy Galleries, Inc.

America to help in the struggle for liberty: Tom Paine from Britain, General Lafayette from France, and the Polish "nationalist" Kosciusko. The new system was also brought into focus by Europeans who went to visit after the war had been won: the Frenchmen who made their own revolution a European concern and German soldiers like Gneisenau (1760–1831), the Prussian reformer. The word was also taken to Europe by the Americans Franklin and Jefferson, who were greeted as heroes by liberals in Paris and the other centers of monarchy.

REVOLUTIONARY ENTHUSIASM IN EUROPE

Partisans of political and social change in Europe drew hope from the American experiment, which seemed to many to prove the nonutopian character of enlightened ideas. An alternative to royal despotism, even enlightened despotism, *existed* in reality as well as in speech and writing.

The point was not missed in Britain itself. Adam Smith and Jeremy Bentham, in their 1776 books (*The Wealth of Nations* and *The Fragment on Government*), maintained that secure freedom and human happiness were the sole objects of government. Charles James Fox (1749–1806) carved out a political career by advocating reforms along radical lines. He went about London in clothes modeled on the uniform of General Washington's soldiers. As a leading minister in the 1780s, in addition to pressing for educational as well as parliamentary reforms, he advocated repeal of religious tests for public office. He had drawn liberal conclusions, he said, from the revolution in America and the anti-Catholic riots of 1780 in London. He might just as well have cited the audacious resolution introduced in the Commons in 1780 by John Dunning: that the influence of the crown had increased, and ought to be diminished.[39]

Elsewhere in Europe people spoke of a revolutionary crisis. They did so not because the ideas of the *philosophes* spurred people to revolution, but because the social, economic, and political systems of the Old World were not responsive to the pressure for reform.

Regarded as a system of international competitors, the monarchies looked to the past. The Holy Roman Empire of the Habsburgs was weak. Germany was an aggregation of great states with antagonistic interests—Prussia, Austria, Bavaria, and Saxony—plus some 300 or more "imperial" states owing allegiance to the emperor. Habsburg politics were based on protecting the tiny states from the largest ones, while the bigger secondary states sought the status of kingdoms on the Prussian model. This gave Prussia scope to pose as the anti-Habsburg power in Germany and to speak for modernity against anachronism. Blocked in Germany, the Habsburgs sought compensation in Italy[40] and the Balkans.

In the north, Sweden had lapsed finally from great-power status. Denmark, which controlled Norway and also a large navy in the Baltic, was considered a valuable potential ally by all the Western powers. But Sweden was left to be defended by Finland against the expansionist ambitions of Russia.

Indeed, Russia was by the 1780s clearly the dominant Eastern power. Russia had profited from a partition of Poland in 1772. Catherine the Great also sought to expand southward and eastward, in the Ottoman-controlled Balkans. Russian agents sought to stir the Greek and Slav Christians to revolt against the Turks. Poland, under the able but powerless elective kingship of Stanislaus Poniatowski (1764–1795), having lost territory in

---

39. Dunning (1731–1783) later became Baron Ashburton. He carried his resolution!
40. See the last section of this chapter for the Italian situation.

1772 to Austria and Prussia as well as Russia, tottered toward dismemberment in 1793, during the wars of the French Revolution.[41]

Economically, the European states were tension-racked. The unrest in England we have already attributed in part to severe economic dislocations. It was also the case that the onset of industrialization[42] reached Britain before continental Europe, causing massive transfers of population to the northern mining and textile towns. No matter how hopeful for the future increased production and urbanization might be, in the 1780s the visible result was often slum crowding and despair.

The Continent lagged Britain in economic development. Only northern France and the southern Netherlands showed much evidence of economic growth. German industry was backward, and in the East only the Russian iron mines in the Urals were vital. But even those were worked in part by serfs. Economically, there was little to promote the hope that relief from hardship and material deprivations would soon produce a better life for the masses of Europeans.

The combined effect of what seemed an almost static economic life and a hopelessly anachronistic high politics was to sharpen the awareness of social distinctions.

Setting aside Britain, where society was less rigid and stratified than elsewhere, and France, whose revolutionary tension will be fully described in the next chapter, we can well say that the European social order was rigorously hierarchic. In Germany blood counted for more than landed

41. The situation in prerevolutionary France forms the subject of the early sections of the next chapter.
42. See Chapter 8 for a full treatment.

Poland and the Great Powers, 1772–1795

Areas of Poland Annexed in First Partition, 1772
Areas of Poland Annexed in Second Partition, 1793
Areas of Poland Annexed in Third Partition, 1795

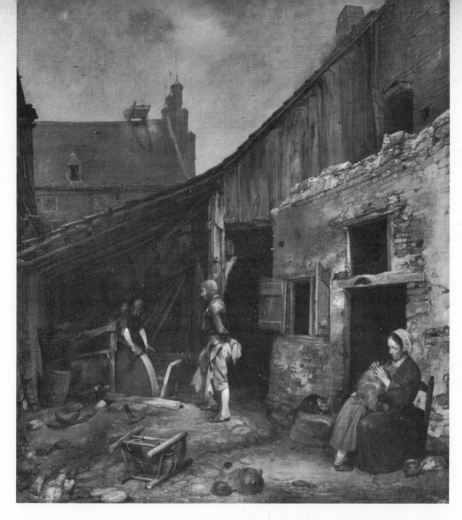

During the latter half of the seventeenth century the poor could expect little but hardship, undernourishment, and toil. In his rendering of a wheelwright and his family Gerard ter Borch of Deventer has realistically portrayed the squalor and despair that were the lot of the peasant population. Staatliche Museen, Berlin.

wealth, which in most places counted most. Prussian laws did not allow common people to buy the estates of hard-up nobles and forbade aristocrats to marry commoners. The Venetian aristocracy suffered under the same prohibition, on the pain of forfeiting patrician status. Nobles and gentlemen nearly everywhere else were separated from the ordinary free folk—to say nothing of the serfs in Eastern lands—by codes of law and codes of honor. These were especially sharp in southern Italy and Spain.

Everywhere the social standard was set by the aristocracies. The most successful merchants and bankers, even in France and Britain, adopted "noble" life-styles. This often had a stifling impact on economic development on the Continent, where capital growth was inhibited by the willingness of investors to forgo higher profits in order to get the respectably low ones from land, office, and *rentes* (state bonds). On a lower social level, the push of small merchants was to become like the greater bourgeoisie of the major ports and banking centers. And craftsmen often sought to evade guild law and make it into the various grades of small businessmen. Among laborers wages were kept down by traditional laws restraining them. Thus the social goals of even upwardly mobile people were conservative, while their mobility itself was a destabilizing force.

European society was thus shot through with contradictions between restless and mobile people and those structures of law and custom which blocked them from the top politically, economically, and socially. The vast peasant masses were locked into static situations. Towns grew rapidly in population because of natural increase and migration from rural to urban areas, especially after 1750. But food distribution was inefficient, and urban bread riots were a powerful challenge to law and order in Cracow, Paris,

Florence, and even London. The towns were also troubled by the presence of outsiders, especially the Jews in eastern and central Europe, gathered in ghettos and largely indifferent to the fate of governments indifferent toward them.

Society was static, unyielding, exploitative. If there was a revolution of rising expectations wherever enlightened ideas reached, it seemed to be thwarted by powerful currents of aristocratic reaction. Autocrats played at enlightened despotism, but we have seen how little things changed, even in Austria.

In the 1780s especially, it seemed that the partisans of reaction were ascendant. There were revolutionary agitations across Europe in that decade, swinging from west to east in a wide arc. Britain and Ireland seemed on the verge of open revolution during the Gordon Riots in 1780. In 1782 it was in Geneva that unrest was most violent. France, Zurich, and Bern intervened on the side of the oligarchs. The Netherlands from 1783 to 1787 was torn by riots and the formation of popular political associations. In the Dutch struggles Prussia intervened on the side of the oligarchs and the "monarchists" favorable to the house of Orange. By 1788 revolutionary agitation for political participation and social change was carried by liberal bourgeoisie into the Austrian Netherlands, Sweden, and Poland.

Intervention in Poland took the form of the crushing partition of 1793, worked out by Prussia and Russia, against the "patriot" revolution in behalf of a liberal, enlightened policy pursued by Poniatowski.

Thus, wherever native groups sought real change, foreign intervention was in the interest of the Old Regime. The American case seemed an exception, but it can be argued that France sought to redress her defeats there; and no result could have been more reactionary, had France really emerged in 1783 as stronger than Britain. Only in Austria and Sweden did energetic monarchs—Joseph II and Gustavus III—react to the internal agitation by imposing from the top a truly enlightened, more liberal, system of government. It is also true that radical politics in the small, weak states—Geneva, the Netherlands, and Poland—were no match for the conservative interests of the surrounding giants: France, Prussia, and Russia.

THE EXAMPLE OF ITALY

If we look for a place where the combined weight of liberal ideas and resentment over restrictive social, economic, and political systems triumphed, Italy provides a case as vital as the victory of the Americans over Britain. In Tuscany's cities the intervention of a foreign dynasty was critical for the success of the liberals. Elsewhere, intervention was conservative, for the patriciates of Geneva and Holland, and against Polish national patriotism. There was no parallel to the situation in the Austrian Netherlands, where Joseph II, so liberal at home, abrogated the 1355 "constitution" of self-government.[43] Nor was there any place "popular" revolution along the lines of that led by Wilkes or Wyvill.

Politically, the Tuscan countryside experienced three changes in regime between 1670 and 1790. The last two Medici dukes[44] ruled from 1670 to 1737. They had all effective power in the prince's hands, while allowing the free play of powerless and overlapping civil and ecclesiastical magistracies

43. Thus bringing to prominence Jean François Vonck (1743–1792), who led the "patriots" to expel the Austrians and form an Act of Union based on the American Articles of Confederation. His group called themselves the Democrats.
44. Cosimo III (1670–1723) and Gian Gastone (1723–1737).

in the dependent city-states. From 1737 to 1765 a regency[45] existed throughout the duchy of Tuscany, exercising power for an absentee lord.

This was Francis Stephen,[46] duke of Lorraine by birth, and the husband of Maria Theresa, the Habsburg heiress. He had exchanged Lorraine for Tuscany in furtherance of Habsburg policy in Italy. But Maria Theresa's inheritance of the Holy Roman Empire preoccupied her husband in the tasks of Vienna, where he was actually named emperor.[47] In 1737 the new grand duke's agents were chiefly French officials from Lorraine. Accustomed to the efficient ducal government at home, they told Francis Stephen that Tuscany was a "chaos impossible to disentangle," whether one regarded political or economic affairs, lay or clerical life.

When Francis Stephen died in 1765, his regency in Tuscany gave way to the direct rule of his Austrian son, Peter Leopold,[48] the brother of Joseph II and his successor as emperor in 1790. Under Peter Leopold especially, but during the "Austrian" ducal era as a whole, in little more than fifty years, Tuscany experienced a revolution.

When Leopold II left Tuscany in 1790 to take up the duties of Holy Roman emperor, a state once the most backward in Europe was thoroughly reformed. Gone were the civil jurisdiction of the clergy, commercial restrictions, restraints on manufacturing, aristocratic power based on inalienable landholding, and the conflicting hierarchies of administration. In their place stood a rationalized system of courts of law, uniform municipal councils, "royal" ministries with fully subordinated bureaucracies, and a whole corpus of economic measures establishing a freedom of production and distribution thought ideal by England's liberal economists. A unified state had been created, and it was given a draft constitution dedicated to the welfare of its subjects.[49]

Most of the most important changes were made in the 1780s, exactly when reaction was triumphant in much of Europe. Where had the impetus come from? Some said from the French officials, who brought in their baggage Montesquieu, Locke, and the Physiocrats. Others credited the Viennese influence, noting how similar Peter's policies were to Joseph II's. A few stressed the maturing of native Italian reform ideas and the objective need for economic modernization. What cannot be doubted is that Italians increasingly quoted foreign writers, and that *illuminismo* slowly spread out from the ancient academies to reach literate citizens throughout Tuscany. By the 1780s, too, the need for change was clear to all and eagerly endorsed by the foreign prince whose popular support was more general than that ever given the native Medici.

The origins of the reforms can be seen in the transformation of the Tuscan academies. These academies dated back to the fifteenth and sixteenth centuries and in their organization reproduced the offices of the free communes in which they had their origins.[50] By 1540, however, when the first Medici grand duke ruled the once free cities, the semipolitical functions of the academies had been suppressed. They were still societies with written constitutions, elected officers, and regular meetings. But where once the humanists had debated public policy in such famous academic

---

45. This was a body of regents appointed to rule in Francis's place.
46. Francesco Stefano to the Italians.
47. Maria Theresa was queen of Bohemia and Hungary and archduchess of Austria. Francis was coregent in Austria as well. Francis gained Tuscany because of the extinction of the Medici; he was a close relative.
48. Pietro Leopoldo (1747–1792), grand duke of Tuscany, and Emperor Leopold II (1790–1792).
49. Written in part by Peter Leopold, this was published early in the new century.
50. They were governed by consuls, councillors, secretaries, censors.

societies as the Accademia Fiorentina's parent group,[51] by the mid–sixteenth century a new routine had come to prevail.

The disastrous political events between 1494 and 1540 had destroyed republican liberty. The interests of the intellectual classes were no longer civic in the sense of general politics. The academics were in fact actually forbidden to discuss politics or religion by Cosimo I in 1542. Proclaiming that the social and political order were the sole business of the prince, the Medici imposed prior restraint on both speech and writing. Even questions of literature and language touching Tuscan public life were prohibited. What distinguished the academies in the late 1500s and in the seventeenth century was scientific investigations. Cosimo III finally prohibited work in medicine and botany—Galileo's ideas had long ago been stilled—on the grounds these studies undermined faith.

Thus it was that early in the 1700s the dozens of academies and their hundreds of members throughout Tuscany were engaged in sterile activities. In theology the academies could not discuss the Reformation. In science Copernicus and Galileo were forbidden. In place of politics and popular literature there was endless recitation of chiefly bad original verse, worse plays, and scholarly dissertations on classical poets or the vocabulary of the Tuscan language, or the work of Dante and Petrarch. The world of learning had nothing to say either about the price of bread or the cure of souls. Yet the academies enrolled all of the top professionals (doctors, lawyers, notaries), the printers and booksellers, the leading ecclesiastics, most educators, and the leading landowners active in the patronage of urban cultural life.

It was only in the 1730s that "philosophy" once again entered the discussions of the academies. Francis Stephen's regents permitted the reintroduction of political discussion, treatises on economics, the sciences, and questions of patriotism. Francis and Peter Leopold allowed their ministers to accept honorary and active membership in the leading academies[52] whose interests were often specialized in such matters as physics, botany, agriculture, and trade. But during the regency, in fact as late as 1767, it was still the case that voluntary associations could take no political initiatives. Hence no "legislative" suggestions made by academics were fruitful until some time into Peter Leopold's regime. As grand duke he was so favorable to change that he sponsored prizes on important reform issues among the chief academies.

There was thus reborn the original premise of the most ancient learned societies: that philosophy had a role to play within the body politic. The academies were no longer little body politics forbidden to relate the republic of ideas to the state of landlords, peasants, merchants, police work, taxes, law codes, or the *corpo politico* (body politic) of Tuscany. Partisans of *illuminismo* in Tuscany now had the influence which *philosophes* elsewhere struggled to wield against hostile authorities.

Citizens no longer viewed the academies as a polite escape from the repressive politics of the real world. Indeed, a new Accademia degli Arcadi had in its constitution the principle that the role of the academies was to suggest changes in the society as a whole, beginning with the idea of a written constitution—and this years before Peter Leopold actually began to draft one for Tuscany. Regency officials had actually drawn practical ideas

51. The Accademia Fiorentina was actually incorporated in 1540, but was based on an older society. The most famous society was the Accademia della Crusca (1582), in which Galileo and Michelangelo had been members.
52. Fiorentina, Umidi, Crusca, Fisiocritici, Botanica, Georgofili.

from academic specialists since 1753, when the Georgofili were asked to comment on reform legislation "without fear of offending the Sovereign."[53]

What the *philosophes* everywhere had asked was such power, not to run the state, but to criticize, to suggest, to help remake the world by communicating to the politicians the needs and aspirations of subjects. The Enlightenment had broadened the scope of useful knowledge, chiefly by redefining science in such a way as to apply its concepts to political, social, and economic questions. In Italy endeavors focusing on even the more limited sense of practical importance, as seen in the fields of physics and medicine, had labored under harsh censorship for generations. Now, in Tuscany and also in Lombardy, not only was learning being reincorporated into the political order; it was freed from the censorship against which Diderot and the encyclopedists in France still struggled. Peter Leopold had endorsed the basic truth of the Enlightenment: that the spirit of discovery was dedicated to utility in the real world.

The Prince's acceptance of the idea that the obligation of learning was to the improvement of society made fruitful years spent in building laboratories, libraries, and museums of natural history. It also turned to social causes the academic printing houses. Under Peter Leopold especially, both civil and ecclesiastical censors were nominated from men in harmony with the ducal enthusiasm for change. Hence the diffusion of useful knowledge received impetus from the existing *Acts* and *Transactions* which suddenly were permitted to publish relevant materials.

Some of these practical achievements may be cited as a way of giving concreteness to the general list of reforms whose sum we called a revolution in Tuscan life.

The Georgofili published agricultural books and even peasant calendars to aid the uneducated in better farming methods. They also opened their library and museum to the general public and inspired teachers to insert agricultural textbooks into the general course of studies for children of farm families. In the 1780s many academics took a step beyond local patriotism by spreading the idea that an "Italian" language was now even more important than a purified Tuscan dialect. This insistence on awareness of the larger world extended beyond the Alps as well. Tuscan presses were allowed to translate the *Encyclopédie*, and the grand duke allowed a bookstore to be set up expressly for the sale of "European" works of enlightenment.

On the side of science, from 1737 lectures on Galileo were again allowed. The Fisiocritici advocated Newton's doctrines publicly from the 1740s. This new freedom had the result intended. There was a rapid spread of the idea that experiment and experience and the collection of data would reveal the natural laws which, once known, would produce not only new truths but beneficial applications. Tuscan botanists, for example, quickly made important discoveries about herbs and fungi, including the fact that fungi were plants which reproduced by scattering spores. This enabled them to prove that grain rust, the chief blight on Tuscan harvests, was caused not by humidity or the drying of sap in leaves, but by infection caused by microscopic spores. This discovery by Everardo Micheli set in motion the solution to one problem of crop failure and thus brought about the relief of famine and the lowering of the cost of bread. Other botanical studies

53. The phrase is from a letter of 1767, actually, written by the regent to the Georgofili; quoted in Eric W. Cochrane, *Tradition and Enlightenment in the Tuscan Academies* (Chicago: University of Chicago Press, 1961), p. 54.

produced important medical results, as "gardens" attached to hospitals became medical laboratories.

Another important Tuscan contribution to the relief of human suffering lay in the medical field. Mercury was used in the treatment of syphilis, and the healing power of certain vaporous springs passed from the realm of miracles into that of preventive medicine. Another fruit of free inquiry was the development in 1754 at Florence and Siena of inoculations against smallpox, a breakthrough first described in the *Acts (Atti)* of the Fisiocritici. The grand duke himself submitted to immunization, and the example he gave defeated opposition. On a more esoteric level, from the 1740s the collection of fossils in Tuscany set in motion the idea that Tuscany had once had an arctic climate and also a tropical one. Freethinkers challenged the biblical account of Creation on such grounds.

Of greater practical importance were three other developments. The Georgofili studied grain distribution in Tuscany. They were able to show that periodic shortages were not only the result of natural causes. A few merchants had sold grain abroad in scarce years. Prices soared; famine followed, and workers were thrown back on charity for their survival. Increasing the area under cultivation provided some help after agitation by the academics in 1765. So, too, did the introduction of new grains (barley and oats) to diversify the two-crop agriculture in wheat and grapes. And the cultivation of wasteland drained by artificial methods, or made usable by controlling mosquitoes responsible for malaria, also aided toward the end of a good food supply.

But scientific agriculture was not enough. The Georgofili and Fisiocritici argued that legislation to regulate the grain trade was perverse. It allowed exports, even in times of dearth, and prohibited competitive imports. Political power had to reverse this economically catastrophic policy. It was said that the poverty of the land lay less in the perversity of nature than in that of men! Scientists and literary men agitated for new tax structures and free trade, which they said were the proper concerns of all citizens. From 1767 on the minister Orsini Rosemberg began to repeal old laws and to codify new ones on the principle that such statutes should be useful to trade, industry, and agriculture. By 1775, the "political and human" causes of hunger were under strong attack. The Physiocrats were quoted in Florence in the course of agitation to improve distribution by building new roads, giving land to landless peasants, allowing the free import of commodities, and creating fiscal policies to foster economic growth.

Peter Leopold took up the cause of peasant proprietorship and free trade. He sponsored law reform and tax reform. He abolished restrictive toll systems. And he endorsed these Enlightenment ideas: that reason and utility were one, that social interests were determinable by study, that all economic activity must reconcile private profit to the public good, and that the state was an association of free men acting in harmony for their mutual benefit.

By 1790 much of the legislation Peter Leopold sponsored had put Tuscany on the level of the most progressive states in Europe. Unlike the *philosophes* in France, who were struggling to impose their vision of order in society on an unprepared country and an unwilling government, the Tuscan *illuministi* worked with the government to remake society, to banish unemployment, ecclesiastical oppression, parasitic absentee landlords, conflicting jurisdictions, and to instill in men a civic spirit based on perceptions of common aspirations.

A society once mired in the most abysmal backwardness had been revolutionized. Or at least a start had been made in a new direction. In 1790 there were serious riots in Tuscany. These were partly due to the fact that there were new grain shortages. But rioting had occurred in 1787 and 1788 as well. And those tumults seemed to be a result of ecclesiastical opposition to reform, which had forced Peter Leopold to retreat. *Illuminismo* had gone too far too fast in Tuscany, both in practice as well as in theory. Perhaps the best proof of this was the 1788 popular riots, which were in support of the reformers, or yet again those of 1790. The insurrections of that year in Florence and Leghorn came *after* the departure of the Grand Duke for Vienna. They were made by reactionaries against the new regency. Their hope, in which they succeeded, was to take advantage of the absence of the new emperor to force the withdrawal of twenty years of legislative reform and social revolution. What they did not foresee was that a newly subdued people might prefer the invading army of revolutionary France to a return to the old despotism.

BIBLIOGRAPHY

BAILYN, BERNARD. *The Ideological Origins of the American Revolution.** Cambridge, Mass.: Harvard University Press, 1967. One of the most provocative works on the American pamphleteers in relation to English government of the colonies.

CHRISTIE, I. A. *Wilkes, Wyvill, and Reform.** New York: St. Martin's Press, 1963. This work anchors Wilkes's agitation in the general framework of British reform movements.

DORN, WALTER L. *Competition for Empire.** New York: Harper & Row, Publishers, 1940. A standard survey.

FIELDHOUSE, D. K. *The Colonial Empires.* New York: Delacorte Press, 1967. The early chapters provide a good introduction to prerevolutionary empires.

GERSHOY, LEO. *From Despotism to Revolution, 1763–1789.** New York: Harper & Row, Publishers, 1944. This standard work is still valuable for its discussion of the Continent before the French Revolution.

MILLER, JOHN C. *Origins of the American Revolution.** Stanford: Stanford University Press, 1959. This should be read together with the two books on Wilkes (see entries for Christie and Rudé), for light on the framework of English popular politics.

NAMIER, L. B. *The Structure of Politics and the Accession of George III.** New York: St. Martin's Press, 1957. One of the great analytic studies of British politics, embodying Namier's belief that factions and interests within the aristocracy controlled politics, not "parties" united ideologically.

RUDÉ, GEORGES. *Wilkes and Liberty.** Oxford: Oxford University Press, 1962. Exciting and provocative work by a Marxist-oriented scholar.

THORNTON, A. P. *Doctrines of Imperialism.** New York: John Wiley & Sons, 1965. A good source book of eighteenth-century ideas on empire.

Asterisk indicates a paperbound edition.

*Men are born and live free and equal in rights.
Social distinctions exist, but they have their
foundation solely in the utility of the community.*
Declaration of the Rights of Man (1789)[1]

3

REVOLUTION IN FRANCE: REPUBLIC OF VIRTUE

WHAT WAS THE FRENCH REVOLUTION?

The first sentence quoted above, from the Declaration of 1789, denied the values of the Old Regime. To assert that men were equal in rights was, unlike the assertions of "natural" equality made in the American Declaration of 1776, not to disregard facts of nature. In the debate over the French manifesto on the rights of "Man and Citizen,"[2] it was freely admitted that in nature there were inequalities of every sort. The purpose of Article I, therefore, was neither to ignore nature nor to remake it, but merely to say that in the future men were to have equal rights in law.

This had manifestly not been true in France before 1789. Everyone belonged legally to some social order or "estate," of which three existed: the first estate of clergy; the second of nobility; and the third, which embraced the rest of the population of rich merchants, professionals, workers, and peasants. In a total population of about 24,000,000[3] there were about 100,000 clergy of all types,[4] perhaps 400,000 in the noble order (including women and children), and more than 23,000,000 in the third estate. Membership in each of the three estates conferred different political, social, economic, and juridical rights by law.

The clergy were in decline in 1789, certainly in numbers and perhaps in influence. The Jesuits, for example, had been attacked repeatedly under Louis XV; and in the 1760s France, like Austria, Spain, Portugal, and Naples, expelled them altogether, confiscating their property and schools.[5] Yet the first estate was enormously privileged. The bishops, abbots, religious schools, and *curés* owned about 10 percent of all land. They were entitled to levy a tithe on agriculture by law. Clerical property was not taxable by the state, and this exemption from the

1. My translation of Article I; the text of the Declaration adopted on August 26, 1789, is printed in Philip Joseph Buchez and Pierre Roux, *Histoire parlementaire de la révolution française ou Journal des assemblées nationales depuis 1789 jusqu'en 1815,* 40 vols. (Paris, 1834–1838), 2: 316–318.
2. This phrase comes from the full title, Declaration of the Rights of Man and Citizen.
3. The best modern estimate for the population ca. 1789.
4. Parochial and regular, men and women.
5. The Society of Jesus (the order of the Jesuits) was dissolved entirely by Rome in 1773 and was not reconstituted until 1814.

In this French cartoon of 1789 the structure of society is caricatured by showing the monarchy, clergy, and parlements all astride a blindfolded and shackled third estate. With a whip in his hand, Louis XVI is the "driver" in charge of this faltering structure, and the riders hold papers identifying their special interests and feudal rights. For a number of years the third estate supported the nobility and clergy in their struggle against royal despotism. But by 1788 the third suddenly changed its position, turned on its former allies, and took up the cause of the nation as its own war cry. The Bettmann Archive.

basic land tax (*taille*) was not compensated for by the periodic "gifts" to the treasury. Sons of noblemen occupied every bishopric in France and controlled the greatest part of Church wealth.

This influence of the landed aristocracy in the wealthy Church was merely one aspect of privilege enjoyed by the second estate. The noble order had since 1715, but especially since its resurgence around 1750, gained much political power. The *intendants* were chiefly noblemen, as were most high officials in the army, the Church, and the *parlements* of Paris and the provinces.[6] Nobles were exempt from the taille on principle. And they consistently used their hold on office and judicial institutions to escape the imposition of new taxes.

It was, however, in relations with the third estate that aristocratic legal superiority showed itself most stressfully. The third included wealthy bourgeois merchants and professionals who managed to win privileges of tax exemption by 1789. Yet even the exempt bourgeoisie resented the need to struggle for privileges others had by right. They also regarded the resurgence of aristocratic officeholding as a threat to their own competition for both honors and offices. Thus one element in the coming crisis was the conflict of interest between the more powerful bourgeoisie and the increasingly reactionary aristocracy.

6. This result was achieved by modifications in the law governing office. By the 1780s most posts could be held only by men who could show noble ancestors for four generations consecutively.

Another involved the urban workers, whose tax burden was enhanced by exemptions given to the clergy and aristocracy at a time when the real income of wage earners was shrinking.[7] There was thus a significant tension in towns among proletarians, or the common masses of unpropertied and unprivileged persons.

In the countryside, the impact of aristocratic privilege was even greater. Four-fifths of all the French people lived by agriculture. Yet the peasants owned only 40 percent of the land.[8] There was no legal serfdom and few compulsory labor services. Peasants worked either their own land, or acres rented, or plots exploited on a sharecropping basis. There were, however, an array of restraints on the peasantry arising out of the legal privileges of manorialism, which survived the demise of serfdom. A manor was a legal bundle of rights conferred on the holder, whether he or she was an aristocrat of ancient lineage or a jumped-up clerk, a merchant recently ennobled or even the descendant of prosperous peasants. These rights included hunting and shooting preserves on peasant lands, some token work dues, fees for the use of the manor lord's mills, ovens, and winepresses, collectively called *banalités,* and fines paid to the lord's manorial police and courts. Moreover, although land could be bought, sold, and passed from father to heirs, the right of "eminent domain" gave to the manorial lord small rents and transfer fees symbolic of the older servile dues and aristocratic control over men as well as land.

The social and legal structure of the Old Regime was therefore shot through with survivals of the feudal past. Land, which even for the bourgeois was the most respected form of property, was subjected to tithes, manorial dues, and rights of eminent domain. Like public office and the holding of guild mastership, land was a form of property in which privilege distorted the nature of economic and social relationships. Men and women who performed the basic economic functions of work and production were forced to share the fruits of labor with those who bore no economic relationship to production whatsoever.

And the degree to which this was true, the degree of class antagonism, was one measure of what the Revolution was: a struggle to equalize legal rights by abolishing privilege. The Revolution was also political, economic, and demographic in both its causes and its character, however; and it is therefore necessary to put its coming in a wider context than that of equal rights.

REVOLUTION AND THE OLD REGIME

Class antagonism does not in itself explain the Revolution, of course. Indeed, in recent years it has been demonstrated that the upper bourgeoisie and nobility were closer together in their interests than had once been believed. The upper middle classes preferred the aristocratic, privileged forms of proprietary wealth: land, offices, and *rentes.* These involved low levels of risk and could be made the basis of hereditary family strength. The corporate sense of the family, which was strong at all social levels in France, made merchants regard capitalism and its risks as simply a means to the aristocratic end of establishing a family, achieving hereditary wealth and status, and social climbing.

The relative single-mindedness of rich bourgeoisie and noblemen in socioeconomic values does not take into account other elements of the picture which made revolution possible, however, and cast the third estate as a whole into an antagonistic position relative to the privileged orders.

7. See later in this chapter.
8. The rest was owned by the Church (10 percent), the prosperous bourgeoisie (18 percent), the nobility (22 percent); the crown and common lands made up the other 10 percent.

France in the eighteenth century was probably the richest country in Europe. Its exports to its continental neighbors were greater in value than Britain's. Paris was not only the intellectual focus of Europe. French banking supplied more than half the gold currency then in European circulation. Yet Frenchmen were not the richest Europeans per capita: the Dutch and the English were. The reason for this was not that Versailles bled the nation's wealth for its shows and luxury. Only 5 percent of the annual expenditure of the government went for the court. It was instead the case that war and demographic change contributed more to the economic inequalities of French life and the political failure of French government.

French population had increased from about 13,000,000 in 1500 to 16,-000,000 in 1600. Then, from a figure of perhaps only 15,000,000 after the decline of Louis XIV's reign, it spurted to 24,000,000 in 1789—by far the largest population of any country in Europe.[9] This huge increase was reflected in the fact that urban population grew rapidly *without* any proportional decrease in rural population.[10] Paris had a population of about half a million people. And France had in its teeming population in 1789 one out of every five Europeans!

Despite the vast increases in population, rural France appeared prosperous. People lived longer, for one thing. Life expectancy rose from 23 years to about 30 years in the eighteenth century. This was in part the result of peasant prosperity, but even more basically the statistical effect of the absence of mass famine from 1709 to about 1775.[11] Then, beginning with the accession of Louis XVI, prosperity broke; and the conditions which produced the revolutionary social and political atmosphere set in.

Before 1775, agricultural production had increased, especially after 1730. One reason for this increase was the enclosure of common land for tillage, where once even rich common land had been reserved for village pasture rights. But enclosures, which were often taken at the initiative of *intendants,* destroyed the community rights of peasants. Many peasant grievances filed in 1789[12] concern this threat to rural community solidarity. Yet other peasants agreed to anything which increased production and hence their share in wealth. Thus tension among peasants, and between peasants and enclosing lords, accompanied rising production.

The advent of farming on a larger scale was closely related to improved methods and the use of certain new crops. One such improvement was made under the influence of writers on agrarian improvement at home and abroad. Land once left fallow was brought into production by giving better nutrition to it. This often involved the use of nitrogen-bearing crops— clover, satin, alfalfa, and sainfoin. Also, new and old tillage was put in root crops good for feeding stock—turnips, cabbage, and other fodder plants. Soil enrichment by using the manure of enlarged herds spread grain cultivation on lands once too poor or "heartless" to support grain. And from about 1760 the potato became a popular fodder crop.

Some regions did not participate at all in improvements and were not tied into the expanding urban economies of trade by better roads and canals. These areas remained stubborn pockets of famine. Yet it was not in them that revolutionary agitation among peasants arose most vociferously. Rather, it was in the areas of improvement, where longer life coupled with

9. Some historians cite somewhat higher population figures; those here are based on Georges D. Duby and Robert M. Mandrou, *The Economic and Demographic Revolution* (New York: Random House, 1957), p. 351.

10. It was once thought that towns grew at the direct expense of country districts, as poor peasants left the land.

11. There were famines in 1726–1727, but not great ones.

12. Formal complaints (*cahiers de doléance*) were filed by estate and by class in each electoral district for the Estates General in 1789.

rising wages and stable prices, that discontent was rife after 1775. It was the *brave laboureur,* the able peasant, who was most disturbed by the loss of momentum and prosperity between 1775 and 1789.

So, too, in the towns, where prosperity was closely related to the increased purchasing power of the countryside before 1775, it was the case the revolutionary tensions arose out of newly frustrated rising expectations.

Rural profits entered the towns by increased peasant demands for craft products and even capital goods—tools, for example—useful in agriculture. But there were even more direct links. Since bourgeois landowners as well as lords and clerics who lived in town houses reaped larger tithes, rents, dues, and *banalités* during the surge in production, the money available to the most powerful consuming classes increased. Money, which in the absence of bank notes[13] was nearly the whole medium of exchange, was the basis of urban prosperity. And the monied classes of most towns were growing richer.

It was true that in the Mediterranean towns neither prosperity nor population growth was marked. Indeed in some places, Marseilles for instance,[14] the eighteenth century was one of steady decline, as France was increasingly an Atlantic-oriented country. Most regional centers showed good growth, however; and some, Nantes and Bordeaux, grew remarkably under the impact of rural prosperity and urban demand and investment.

We can see the causes and the results of urban prosperity in a variety of facts. Few of the nobility lived at Versailles. Most preferred town life and amenities to rural isolation; but they lived in local towns or great regional ones like Lyons, Rouen, Dijon, Clermont-Ferrand, and Bordeaux, and especially in Paris. There was a great surge in building after 1715 and an enormous increase in commercial investment as well. Bordeaux and Nantes became important banking centers. French foreign trade grew fourfold between 1716 and 1750, and it grew again in the third quarter of the century. By 1775 it had reached a level five times as great as that of 1715.[15]

The increased consumption of durable goods (fine furniture, homes, carriages, etc.) and fancy decorations for urban *hotels* (houses on a grand scale) gave work to enlarged luxury crafts and trades. But it also unbalanced the relationship between consumption and the investment of profits from land in crafts and commerce directed toward the mass of Frenchmen. Capital produced on the land was not returning to it in large amounts. And thus even urban growth itself reflected one of the sources of class antagonism and embittered opinion. The Physiocrats, not the peasants, were the harshest denouncers of the expropriation of agrarian wealth and its use for city luxury and comfort.

There was yet another aspect of the rise of the building trades and the textile industry.[16] Unlike England, which by the 1760s was revolutionizing industrial production by machinery, France witnessed no early onset of industrialization. The ability to produce articles in heavy demand was limited by handicraft methods. Consequently, the pressure of demand forced prices upward, often beyond the pocketbook of many artisans and most poor workers. The articles in the *Encyclopédie* on the crafts pointed out the need to increase production and lower prices. Little was done, however.

13. See the remarks in Book Four of Volume 2 on French failures to build a strong structure of paper credit, in contrast to the successful efforts of the Dutch and English.
14. Population in 1700 was about 97,000; by 1760 it was not more than 90,000.
15. French foreign trade had grown to an annual value in livres of 1,075 million, up from 215 million in 1715, and 900 million in 1750.
16. The two main "growth" industries in France from 1720 to 1775.

The symmetrical and orderly appearance of present-day Paris results from a series of vast renewal projects begun under the Old Regime, accelerated during the First Empire, and concluded by the great urban planner Baron Haussmann in the 1860s when whole sections of the city were destroyed and reorganized around the famous boulevards. However, as late as the Revolution, much of Paris retained the quaint medieval air captured in this painting. Street life was often disorderly, bawdy, and dangerous, all elements evident here where the happy dancers vie for the viewer's attention with drunks and thieves. Sordid conditions worsened as the urban working class expanded in response to growing industrialization. Lauros-Giraudon.

Consequences abounded. While the upper urban elements of the third estate lived well, the masses in the swollen cities did not. Prices rose about 65 percent for ordinary consumer goods between 1730 and 1775–1789. Urban wages rose only 22 percent in the same period. The living standards of small craftsmen and wage earners plummeted downward. Entrepreneurs complicated the situation by taking advantage of the large labor pool. And when urban workers organized for better wages, capital sought cheap labor by establishing craft production in the smaller towns and villages of every region. The advance in commerce and urban wealth was thus spread narrowly. Coffee and tea remained luxury items of diet at Versailles and in the chief towns, just as sugar sweetened noble and merchant tastes but rarely the palate of workers.

It often seemed to urban workers that the visible prosperity of the country was a reproach to their poverty. While wages lagged behind prices, the fees taken by armies of officials, lawyers, notaries, judges, doctors, and druggists did not. The country was rapidly being unified by better roads, canals, newspapers, and sponsored tourism; but it was not being unified by the distribution of its wealth. And ordinary people often asked whether the government itself was not to blame.

It is hard to say at this distance that it was not. Louis XV may not have said "après nous, le déluge!" (After me, the Flood!).[17] But the cynical comment well characterizes the political failure to ease the tensions of the period of prosperity. Moreover, in the economic crisis of the Old Regime after 1775, Louis XVI acted on that basis, even if unwittingly.

THE COLLAPSE OF THE OLD REGIME

We have until this point avoided the question of enlightened despotism in France. In discussing the other European monarchies, however, we have given great emphasis to the role played by certain monarchs[18] in moving their regimes and peoples toward a concept of government and society more secular, more rational, and more reform oriented than had earlier been the case. To a greater or lesser degree, rulers like Joseph II, Catherine the Great, Frederick the Great, Charles III of Spain, and Peter Leopold in Tuscany had acted as if they accepted some motifs of Enlightenment thought. This seemed to be especially true in the matter of identifying the crown and the subjects' interests within the framework of public welfare ideas.

Yet little was done to meet Rousseau's demand for a practical participation in politics by commoners. Ironically, where the greatest agitation in a democratic direction existed, in the England of Wilkes and in Jefferson's America, it would be wholly wrong to speak of enlightened despots at all. Commoners still gained little in England and America, even though those governments were not despotisms but modified forms, though still controlled largely by aristocrats. And in France, the seat of the Enlightenment, whatever stirrings of enlightened despotism there were failed miserably.

France remained the supreme paradox: perhaps Europe's most important state and the most outwardly unified one, France was also the least reformed. France was the refuge of privileged estates, guilds, towns, and judicial bodies.

Louis XV (1715–1774) had twice tried to implement major reforms. In 1748, chiefly because of the pressure of war expenses, the King had shaken off his dislike of serious work and his distaste for giving offense to the privileged orders. He had named a general finance minister and supported a program to tax *all incomes* arising from landholdings, offices, and *rentes*. This invasion of established privilege provoked a reaction among the first two estates and the *parlements* and privileged bodies of France. The result was a declaration by the *Parlement de Paris* that such taxes were illegal. Louis abandoned the new program.

But the problem of finding an adequate revenue more equally raised from all of the estates would not be dismissed as easily as reform-minded ministers. The system of taxation lay at the root of the government's powerlessness vis-à-vis the resurgent aristocracy of land and privilege. As long as the peasants alone bore the taille, no increase in French prosperity could relieve the poverty of the government. The recognition of this went back to Sully, Richelieu, and Louis XIV's ministers, whose tax experiments had been defeated during the Regency.

17. The remark was attributed to him by many, however.
18. Especially the Austrian ducal rulers of Tuscany.

The practical result of Louis XV's surrender to the nobility was evident in the next two decades. The Seven Years' War and the wars for empire overseas brought new debts as well as defeats. Louis XV again tried to rally his abilities in 1768, and he made the most ambitious effort at centralizing reform of any French king in the eighteenth century. He decided to win control by attacking the obstructive forces directly. Since it was clear that the judicial bodies and assemblies blocked fiscal innovations, the king allowed his new chief minister, the chancellor René Nicolas de Maupeou (1714–1792), to abolish such bodies and reconstitute them.

Maupeou understood that since 1763 the aristocratic resistance to any reduction of tax exemption had hardened. He also knew that the mounting debt was not going to diminish by any means other than an abrogation of privilege. The resistance of the nobles was nothing less than an *aristocratic revolt* in embryo. Maupeou's dissolution of the old parliaments destroyed property in office. The new judges were not hereditary nobles, but bureaucrats, salaried crown officials with no powers to reject decrees or declare policies of taxation illegal. This change cleared the way for two other ones: law codification and a program of tax reform.

For six years Maupeou's efforts aroused cries of pain and charges of absolutism. Voltaire, as we have seen before, knew better. He and other *philosophes* grasped that Louis's chancellor's policies were "enlightened." By destroying privilege, Maupeou might create a free nation.

Louis XV's death brought about the final defeat of reform. The new king, Louis XVI (1774–1792), was twenty years old, irresolute, addicted to Versailles, and fearful of antagonizing the powerful nobles and clergy. He dismissed Maupeou, reinstated the old *parlements,* and thus began his reign by surrendering to the aristocratic revolt against reform. The conflict between privilege and utility had been won by privilege.

That this was so became clear at once. Louis XVI appointed a new controller general of finance in 1774, the aristocrat Anne Robert Turgot, Baron de l'Aulne (1727–1781). Turgot was a *philosophe* and one of the most important political economists of the Physiocrat school. An experienced administrator, he hoped to widen the government's resources by expanding trade, reducing the restrictions imposed on production by obsolete guild rules, abolishing other restrictive monopolies, and relieving the peasants of certain burdens inhibiting agriculture, especially the *corvée,* or compulsory road work levied on them.

Turgot also sought to gain new taxes by widening popular participation in policy making. He planned new provincial assemblies elected by all property owners. The members would sit in consultation as a body, not by estates or orders. This bold scheme on two fronts[19] produced the strongest conservative opposition to date. The guilds, the official nobility, the Church, and the landed classes claimed a judicial right to tax immunity. And the judges in the *parlements* successfully claimed the right to rule on the lawfulness of change. Turgot was forced from office in 1776. And it became clear that by recalling the judicial bodies Maupeou had abolished, Louis XVI had made reform impossible.

Between 1778, when France went to war with Britain again in the American conflict, and 1788, the financial crisis of the Old Regime deepened. The aristocracy, triumphant in their "revolt" against change, continued to consolidate power at the expense of the crown and reform. The new director of finances, the Swiss Jacques Necker (1732–1804), appointed in 1777, advocated Turgot's policies and was dismissed. The privileged

19. Political organization and tax reform.

classes would neither be taxed nor share power. Yet the debt mounted, reaching four billion livres in 1788. Nearly 25 percent of all government income went to the army, but 50 percent went toward the debt. Yet the French debt was not anywhere near as large as the Dutch one or even the English debt.

A new minister, Charles de Calonne (1734–1802), in 1786 and 1787 sought desperately to convince Louis XVI that bankruptcy could be avoided only by stern measures. He advocated a return to representative institutions[20] and the enforcement of a tax on all land, without exemption, in combination with programs to stimulate commerce. He also proposed confiscating some Church wealth. He thus made a revolutionary proposal to defeat the aristocrats' revolution: to tax equally, and to bring peasants and artisans into a political system now imbalanced by the dominance of the clergy and the nobles. To interest the privileged classes in reform, Calonne had Louis XVI convoke an "Assembly of Notables" in 1787. But this group balked, unwilling to go along with reform unless they were given some direct control over government.

Calonne was dismissed. Loménie de Brienne (1727–1794), a careerist in the Church as archbishop of Toulouse, sought to carry the new program. He appealed for approval to the *Parlement de Paris.* The entrenched reactionaries there advised him and the King. They also said only an Estates General could consent to such radical proposals, secure in the belief that such an assembly would be dominated in its proceedings by the first and the second estates.[21] All over the country meanwhile, the aristocratic revolt led to resistance by provincial estates, the army, the *parlements,* and ominous noble "committees of correspondence" and clubs with political axes to grind.

In the French countryside, there was another movement discernible in the years marked by Louis XVI's accession and Calonne's dismissal.

Everywhere, prosperity declined. There was a commercial contraction, small when compared to the seventeenth-century recession and the catastrophe between 1694 and 1709, but perhaps more objectionable. The years of business profits had led to the expectation of more. But these profits were rural in their inspiration. And after 1775 French agriculture was in trouble. The aristocratic revolt and the business slump were running parallel and were partly due to an agrarian crisis.

After 1773 bad weather in a sixteen-year cycle reduced harvests. Large farmers, small farmers, and day laborers felt the shock in reverse order, but by 1789 droughts and famines were affecting even the grandest seigneurs. Landlords with declining rents and other agrarian profits began to increase their pressure on the peasants, by insisting on maintaining and even enlarging the whole bundle of peasant manorial dues and fines. Often insouciant in their patterns of spending, and giving no thought to altering that pattern, the privileged classes sought relief from economic depression in two ways. They revolted against governments anxious to redistribute taxes in order to remain solvent. And they oppressed the less privileged. Thus the coming of the French Revolution may be seen in the double-pronged aristocratic reaction to economic losses, which as a whole well deserves the name some have given it: the feudal reaction.

In the towns, the situation was no better. Peasant hardship decreased demand for ordinary commodities. The slump in incomes derived from agriculture lessened the call for luxury goods. The American war inter-

20. There had been no Estates General since 1614.
21. Voting in an Estates General was always by order rather than by head. Hence conservative majorities in the tiny estates could defeat the wishes of the third.

rupted the supply of Southern cotton; and by 1785 the unemployment and profit losses in the textile towns (Amiens, Rouen, Lyons) were great. The price of wheat was rising because of harvest failures. Workers and vagrants agitated for cheap bread. The classes were at odds with one another. And nearly everybody focused grievances on a government which seemed either unwilling or unable to redress them. France was divided across its breadth and deeply within its communities. For the wealthy the economic crisis meant a struggle to maintain privilege, while cutting back on living standards. But for the poor it meant survival itself, especially in the countryside. For there the aristocracy, armed by its control over policy, was busily revising in their favor the documents (*terriers*)[22] which regulated the dues, *banalités*, fines, hunting grounds, and rights of eminent domain which spoke most eloquently about inequality in the Old Regime.

THE BOURGEOIS REVOLUTION

From the account given here, we ought to conclude that the French Revolution began in 1788, not in 1789. Before the Estates General met, and before the third estate launched a National Assembly and a constitutional reorganization of the kingdom, the clergy and the nobility had triumphed over the crown. In 1788 neither the bourgeoisie nor the peasants had the means to force Louis XVI to convoke an estates general after a vacation of almost 175 years. The privileged groups alone had those means, and they converted the government's financial crisis into a revolution in order to defeat reform.

This revolution began with the King's capitulations in 1787, when he called the Assembly of Notables and subsequently dismissed Calonne. It continued during the provincial resistance campaign (1787) and entered a new phase early in 1788, when the *parlements* forced the withdrawal of reform edicts. It culminated in the decision of Brienne, concurred in by Louis XVI, on July 5, 1788, to call an estates general.[23]

The Revolution was in its first phase thus neither a victory of the peasants over the repressive race for money made by nobles and rich bourgeoisie nor a grab for power by the bourgeoisie at the expense of the privileged orders. Still less was it an overthrow of the Bourbon monarchy by the masses. It was a result of Louis XVI's effort to resist sharing power with the nobles, and the efforts of the nobles to resist sharing their wealth with the King.

Necker was recalled in the summer of 1788, in time to see the *Parlement de Paris* precipitate the second phase of the revolutionary crisis. On the twenty-third of September, the judges ruled that the Estates General should be formed as in 1614, in three separate orders, each equal in the number of deputies and with a single vote. This not only gave the two privileged estates a victory over reform. It meant a common front against the influence of the third—an alliance of 500,000 against more than 23,000,000. The clergy and the nobility struggled against "absolutism," in the name of the nation, but would not be absorbed in the nation.

When the bourgeoisie refused to accept the decision to vote by order, they began the "bourgeois revolution." The bourgeoisie were a purely legal group or class. Unlike the nobility and the clergy, the bourgeoisie were as native to town as to country, as they were mingled with the whole population in their roles as merchants, professionals, teachers, writers, and *rentiers.* Moreover, as a class they detested aristocratic privilege and showed sympathy toward the ideas of the *philosophes,* although their own motives for opposing privilege were less ideological than economic and

22. From *terre* (land); *terriers* were land registers and surveys.
23. Brienne resigned on the twenty-fourth of July; Necker was recalled to office.

social. Cooperating with certain radical nobles who had formed a Committee of Thirty,[24] certain bourgeois leaders began a campaign to revise the form of the Estates General. These maneuvers focused on the question of doubling the third estate, to make it equal in delegates to the combined weight of the first and second.

This would have been a victory of sorts, but would not have touched the question of deciding issues by order. By the time the Estates General opened, on May 4, 1789, therefore, agitation focused on the inadequacy of the concession made in December 1788 to double the representation of the third estate while voting by order. A number of *cahiers*[25] demanded that the *nation* be sovereign, by which they meant the third estate. In so doing, the electorate reflected the thought of Abbé Sieyès (1748–1836) and also certain cartoonists. Pictures circulated showing the third estate as a giant intimidating a frightened clergy and a torpid nobility. Sieyès in his pamphlets[26] had described the privileged classes as a state within the state. He had also said that the third estate, which was now nothing, had to be everything, because it alone had within itself what constituted the nation—"the great French nation"—against the "little nations" of privileged groups who called themselves France.

The nobles had told Louis XVI that a "revolution" loomed in even doubling the third estate. Allowing the December edict to be construed as a

24. Among them the *philosophes* Condorcet and Mirabeau, General Lafayette, and the priests Abbé Louis and the famous Abbé Sieyès.
25. From Angers, Auxerre, Dijon, Dorat, Mâcon, Nîmes, Nivernais, Quimper, Rennes, etc.
26. *What Is the Third Estate? (Qu'est-ce que le tiers état?)* and *On the Royal Veto.*

decision to vote by "head," they now argued, would put the King and the privileged classes at the mercy of commoners. Suffrage for the election of delegates to the third estate was liberal enough to bring in ordinary bourgeoisie, but stringent enough with regard to property qualifications to keep out the peasants—nobody yet feared the peasants. And the bourgeoisie elected in February and March were totally unafraid of the nobility, especially the priests like Sieyès and the lawyers.

Events moved with great rapidity after the fourth of May. Armed with the grievances of their constituents, the leaders of the third estate asserted they had come to Versailles to end absolutism, secure new taxes, guarantee individual liberty and a free press, make certain there would be periodic general estates and provincial ones, and reform the Church. There was as yet no general attack on aristocratic privilege as opposed to tax immunity, much less a demand for democracy. The court refused to sponsor any general reform, however, and the nobles resisted vote by head and all other programs beyond simple tax revisions.

On May 6, the third estate refused to organize as a separate house or take any further steps. Surprisingly, the clergy, who were badly divided by the resentment of the lower clergy against the upper clergy, did the same on the eleventh and joined the third estate in a series of conferences on May 18. Their agreement to recommend organization in one house, with each order to pass on the credentials of its own members, was rejected by the nobles on June 4, 1789. The aristocracy understood what this would mean, since the third estate, which had been doubled, now had much support from disaffected lower clergy.

Sieyès made the refusal of the nobles into a revolutionary cause. On June 10, he called on all delegates to meet with the third estate, saying any who would not were thereby disqualified. This was tantamount to making the third estate into a national legislature without royal consent. A roll call spread over three days (June 12–14) attracted enough priests to compensate for bourgeois defections. And on the sixteenth of June the National Assembly was proclaimed, a decision ratified on the seventeenth by a vote of 491 to 89. On the nineteenth a clerical majority voted to join the third estate.

Necker understood that a revolution had again occurred and that Louis XVI could retain power only by conciliating the third estate, which on the twentieth had taken an oath not to disband and not to resort to violence. The Tennis Court Oath[27] was a prelude to new defiance, for on the twenty-second the rest of the clergy joined the third estate, and even a few nobles did. Louis XVI conceded the vote by head on some matters to the Assembly on the twenty-third, while protesting in behalf of the ancient rights of the crown and the vote by orders on the essentials of the manorial system, the organization of a future Estates General, and honorific privileges. He also addressed the Assembly to propose reforms.

The list of "royal" proposals was itself a symptom of the new revolution's strength. The Estates General was to be given power to raise taxes, equalize levies, allocate funds, secure civil liberty and freedom of "conscience,"[28] oversee provincial estates with vote by head, reform the crown domains, regulate justice, dissolve monopolies, and abolish the *corvée* and vestiges of feudalism. The price, however, was clear: the third estate must preserve an estates general in which privilege was secure. Society was to remain a

During the week preceding the storming of the Bastille political agitation in Paris reached a fever pitch. The dismissal of the popular finance minister Necker and the concentration of largely foreign troops outside the city prompted orators in the gardens of the Palais Royal to call the people to arms, and there was widespread fear that a military coup was about to occur. The duke of Orléans, brother of the king and resident in the Palais Royal, was behind much of the trouble. In this painting the crowd holds aloft wax busts of the heroes, Orléans and Necker. Orléans persisted in trying to further his own position by manipulating democratic sentiment and even voted for the king's death. But the radical momentum eventually engulfed him and he too perished under the blade of the guillotine. Bulloz.

27. So called because the third estate, locked out of its chamber by a royal order that the Assembly be removed from the passions of Paris and reconvene in a "royal" Estates General on June 22, took the oath at a tennis court near the chamber (on June 23).

28. That is, the freedoms of the press, speech, and religious opinion.

A passionate supporter of the Revolution, Jacques Louis David commemorated many of its dramatic moments, such as the Tennis Court Oath. *Events moved so rapidly that the artist never completed the painting. Representatives of the people—the third estate—are shown gathered in a tennis court at Versailles, swearing to remain unified until a constitution could be established. The artist's profound knowledge of classical art was the basis for his contemporary scenes. Many individual poses derive from antique statues and the friezelike composition recalls Roman bas-relief sculpture. Throughout the Revolution and Napoleonic period David's art was a potent weapon of political propaganda. Musée Carnavalet; Bulloz.*

society of legal classes. Louis XVI had chosen the nobles against the commons, directing the second estate to withdraw from further sessions, unless the third submitted. The third refused, and once again Louis XVI caved in. The nobles rejoined the revolutionary National Assembly on June 27, 1789, and the King renounced the use of force against that body.

On the seventh of July, the leaders of the Assembly appointed a Committee of the Constitution. On the ninth a report from this group[29] was adopted, and the Assembly became the Constituent Assembly. On the eleventh Lafayette proposed a committee to draft a Declaration of Rights of Man and Citizen.[30] Unknown to the leadership at first was the fact that Louis XVI had been gathering forces to dissolve the Assembly. But by the eighth of July the threat was clear, scarcely helped by a royal offer to move the Assembly to Soissons, if it feared the troops concentrated in Paris. On the eleventh Necker was dismissed. This alarmed the Parisians who supported the Assembly, and they advocated forming a "civic guard" to defend the Assembly.

29. Headed by Mounier, Target, Gaultier de Biauzat, and other bourgeois partisans of the "juridical" revolution carried on the twenty-seventh.
30. For an analysis of what the debate on the draft Declaration revealed about the political ideas of the Revolution, see Chapter 5.

The intervention of the people characterized the next few months of the unfolding Revolution, which was also marked by an aggressive attack on privilege. Paradoxically, the period of popular agitation from July to October in 1789 did not arise out of any basic class consciousness among workers and peasants. Riots and demonstrations sprang naturally out of the objective conditions prevailing in town and country. Indeed, it is probable that the bourgeois revolutionaries in the Assembly would have been reluctant to use urban wage earners as allies, had the workers been of one political mind. And it is certain that the Assembly had not revolted to satisfy proletarian needs.[31]

The combination of the troops, Necker's dismissal, and the economic crisis put the torch to the powder keg that was Paris. Early in July bread shortages had fired unrest in some worker quarters. By the twelfth popular agitators appeared: Marat (1743–1793), Danton (1759–1794), Desmoulins (1760–1794)—and others perhaps in the pay of Louis Philippe, the duke of Orléans (1747–1793), the King's cousin. On the fourteenth a large mob of artisans and shopkeepers,[32] searching for arms stormed the Bastille, a medieval fortress used also as a jail.

The price of bread in the artisan-dominated quarters of Faubourg Saint Antoine and Quartier Marceau had risen from 2 sous to levels between 4

31. Again, see the discussion of ideology in Chapter 5.
32. With very few wage laborers, some upper bourgeoisie, and a few incendiary leaders.

Under the delusion that the ancient fortress was crammed with political prisoners, Parisian mobs attacked the Bastille on July 14, 1789. Panic spread among the prison guards who fired into the crowd, causing considerable casualties. In this engraving a rebellious detachment of Gardes Françaises join the assault with large cannon. When the prisoners were finally released, it was found that there were only seven, most of whom were guilty of petty crimes. Nonetheless, the fall of the Bastille was a major psychological victory which proved that the King had lost control of Paris. The people demonstrated their victory by demolishing the prison. Bibliothèque Nationale.

and 8 by July 14, at a time when wages for artisans were between 30 and 40 sous a day. In Paris and the provincial towns people believed prices were being artificially raised by hoarding lords and speculators. Some saw Necker's free trade ideas as a free hand for exporters in a time of need. Want, high prices, and fear were all motives for men and women who attacked the Bastille and murdered its governor and six soldiers, while losing ninety-eight men from their own ranks. The mayor of Paris was also slain.

Again, Louis XVI accepted the situation created by others. His army did nothing. He recognized the "National Guard," which in Paris had Lafayette as its commander, as well as the "citizens' committee," the provisional, new municipal government. The Paris popular revolution gave to the movement as a whole its insignia, the tricolor of Bourbon white and the Paris blue-and-red badge.

Meanwhile, in the provinces, both in town and country, the fear of famine and the government's intention to stifle the Assembly was becoming the Great Fear. From July 15, local panics and a widespread peasant fear that the aristocrats would employ foreign mercenaries against them combined with the economic crisis to produce insurrections across the length and breadth of France. We now know that in 1789 millions of people lived in poverty. Begging was endemic.

In the provinces, therefore, Louis XVI's mid-July gestures were meaningless. He might recall Necker, remove the troops, and even appear in public (on July 17) wearing the red, white, and blue cockade. Grain remained scarce. Few peasants believed the local aristocracy would disarm. There were rumors of plans to burn standing crops and of possible British intervention. In Paris the Assembly tried to control popular violence on the twenty-eighth by setting up a revolutionary tribunal to hear denunciations of aristocrats. The house of Madame Roland (1754–1793) became headquarters for a group of radical Assembly members[33] who hinted at a blow at Louis XVI himself, by saying *any* means might be used to defend the Revolution!

Municipal revolutions occurred in many large towns and small regional centers. Rioting and looting were the order of the day, but so too was a revealing demand for control over the price of bread and for the organization of popular governments elected by the urban masses. There was also a widespread organization of urban militias. And, most important of all, town after town submitted voluntarily to the authority of the Assembly, not to that of the King. France was spontaneously reorganizing into a federation of local governments of a revolutionary character.

Even this was not decisive for the fall of privilege, however. It was the intensification of the Great Fear by peasant risings that was. Throughout the countryside peasants now rose to throw off the regime of feudal rights and judges who seemed consistent only in deciding suits against peasant interests, collective rights, and economic independence. Peasant *cahiers* in 1789 criticized the abuses of the agrarian system rather than its principles. Typically, an aggrieved community (in January 1789) wanted the lord to produce authentic documents testifying to the legitimacy of his demands for rents, dues, and fines.

By August, however, a new peasant solidarity had been created by the great events in Paris and the spreading fear of aristocratic counterrevolutionary plots. Hunger had also played a vital role, and even before the fall of the Bastille in 1789 peasants had exercised influence of a violently antiaristocratic sort. Then, from July 17 to 28, peasant revolt spread from Nor-

33. Including the future leaders of the Terror, among them Robespierre, who were members of the "Committee of Inquiry."

mandy to many other regions. Enclosures were pulled down. Money-lenders were attacked. Tithes were refused. Dues of every sort were renounced. The Great Fear grew, as guardsmen at Nantes were mistaken for dragoons. The panic was spread by terrified and excited peasants, until a few provinces alone were not gripped by it.[34] By August 6 the peasants were engaged in a massive defensive action against a "conspiracy" they fully believed was about to strike them.

The situation in the provinces reacted on the forces in Paris. Peasant manifestos demanded that the bourgeoisie in control of the Assembly not ally themselves with privilege, as was often the case in the countryside, where property interests made strange bedfellows. The main focus was the tactic of delay advocated by moderates, who advised delaying any declaration of rights until a constitution had been drafted. The Assembly rejected delay on August 4, when it resolved to begin work with a declaration and to include in it the question of abolishing "feudal" rights. Various preliminary decrees passed[35] between the fifth and the eleventh announced the destruction of the feudal regime.

In order to sugar the pill, it was arranged to propose the abolition of tithes and dues by noble members.[36] The result was the fall of labor services, hunting rights, manorial courts and fines, and Church dues. The question of nationalization of Church lands was raised; titles were taken without compensation. Other motions made on the twenty-second and twenty-third of August raised questions of religious doctrine and worship. Churchmen insisted on maintaining the Catholic Church as a national one. Others argued for freedom of conscience as the only way to complete the work of unifying the nation. On the twenty-sixth a decisive text was passed, giving authority to the radical steps taken since the night of August 4.

The Declaration of Rights of Man and Citizen began the phase of the Revolution dedicated to constitutional monarchy, without ending the period of popular riots and the Great Fear, which merged into the agitations of September and the October Days.

The Declaration clarified the events of July 14–August 4. Seven articles dealt with liberty in general, by which was meant the right to act freely within the necessary restraint of law: no man had a right to harm another. Men were declared free and equal in their right to liberty, property, security, and freedom from oppression; freedom of thought, speech, and religion; freedom from arrest without due process of law; the freedom to hold office, within whatever eligibility requirements the law might establish. The law was to be the same for all citizens, and was to express the general will of the "people" through representatives elected by them. The "nation" was declared sovereign. Every official acted only in its name, as did military forces. Only the nation could raise taxes, and to the nation all servants were accountable. The "state," or the politically constituted people, acted only to realize the common good through the separate branches of its executive, legislature, and judiciary. Article XVII declared property rights sacred and inviolable, *except* where it was for public utility. Then, property might be confiscated and fair compensation paid.

This manifesto to Frenchmen was distributed in tens of thousands of copies in France and also in Europe. The questions it did not answer were those which would have to be answered: What did the words *people, nation,* and *citizen* mean? What would the actual *political constitution* of the now *legally equal* Frenchmen be?

34. Brittany, Lower Languedoc, Lorraine, Alsace, Hainaut.
35. Over aristocratic opposition.
36. The duke of Aiguillon, Lafayette, de Noailles, and others.

One thing decided on August 26 was that France was no longer Louis XVI's to govern. Now it remained to work out a constitution whose specific articles would not contradict the principles of the Declaration, which were in essence not an unlimited charter of democracy but a description of liberties and rights defined by the victorious, self-confident third estate. The bourgeoisie had invoked a doctrine of rights to destroy despotism, but they had not engendered a utopia.

When it became clear that Louis XVI still thought he could reject the Assembly's work and even veto any constitution, the Assembly acted. On September eleventh it proclaimed its independence of royal approval, denied veto powers,[37] and reaffirmed that no bicameral legislature preserving social privilege reflected the will of the people. The King summoned troops on the fourteenth and evaded answering the Assembly, which put the issue of a unitary assembly to him again on the seventeenth. By October 1 the "patriots" or radicals among the constitution-makers decided that an impasse could be avoided only by new popular actions. Either Louis would be coerced, or he might refuse to ratify or publish any constitution. This pressure was increased by the mounting evidence within the Assembly of men determined to stop the Revolution's forward movement.[38]

The "October Days" grew out of this tension over the fate of the Revolution. The Paris municipal government led by the mayor Bailly had little effective control. Some sixty political clubs existed, and through them agitators like Desmoulins reached the masses. Publication was now free of restraint. Both Brissot's journal, *Patriote français,* and Marat's *L'Ami du peuple,* stirred hostility to the Monarchicals and also warned the people of the renewed danger of a military blow at the Revolution. The King's brothers and other nobles had fled to other countries, making plausible the rumor that they were the vanguard of the aristocratic conspiracy. Objectively, social conditions were deteriorating, because the Revolution itself so unsettled trade that money was scarce, prices were more inflated, charity could not feed the poor, peasants avoided taking crops to disordered market towns, and unemployment increased daily.

Courtiers had insulted the cockade on the first of October, and all Paris had the story by the third. Crowds surrounded the Royal Palace on the fourth. On the fifth mobs ("The Women's March") in Paris demonstrated at the City Hall (Hôtel de Ville), after forcing the King and the Assembly to leave Versailles and go to the city. Some of the leaders of a radical club, the Jacobins,[39] including Bertrand Barère (1755–1841) and Robespierre (1758–1794), took a leading part in negotiating terms on which Louis would accept the August decrees and then provision Paris and so satisfy the popular needs.

Louis had been advised to flee for his château at Rambouillet,[40] but went instead to Paris. Once there, he was in effect the prisoner of the mob and at the mercy of the Assembly, which enjoyed popular support. Meeting at the riding academy near the Tuileries from the nineteenth, the Assembly moved to end the "revolution of action" by accepting the flight of the aristocrats[41] and forcing on Louis its constitution.

37. Except a suspensive veto, if Louis accepted all August acts.
38. The so-called monarchicals who favored bicameralism, restricted interpretations of the Declaration, some veto, a halt to nationalization of Church goods and lands. A group of liberal nobles, priests, and some bourgeoisie, they were led by Mirabeau, Lally-Tollendal, and Mounier.
39. So called because they met on the property of a dissolved Jacobin monastery.
40. By his friends, the Queen, the Council of State.
41. The so-called first amputation performed on the social body.

From 1789 (and its October Days) until 1792 the Constituent Assembly and its successor, the Legislative Assembly, carried out the essential task of putting the new regime in order. This involved four main matters: making the Constitution of 1791, fashioning a new administrative system, putting the Church on a new footing, and dealing effectively with the European reaction to the Revolution. These achievements we may quickly sketch, except for the last, which we will examine in detail in another place.[42]

The Constitution put into effect in 1791 was the final work of the Constituent Assembly, which was dissolved by it. This written constitution did not deny the equality of rights in law declared in 1789. It did, however, divide Frenchmen into "active" and "passive" citizens politically. Men who paid taxes equal to three days' wages in their district had the franchise. About one man in three was excluded by this criterion. Domestic servants and women were excluded in principle. With the franchise thus restricted, electors proceeded to provide the new Legislative Assembly with members chosen by an indirect process. Primary assemblies in the districts could name electors who met relatively high property qualifications; and those men in turn selected the "deputies."[43]

Having thus expressed their fear of open democracy, the constitution-makers divided the powers of government unequally. The king was given a veto over legislation that was suspensive, until it was overridden by three successive assemblies. Louis XVI's resistance to reform thus weakened the Constitution, by making its drafters determined on a weak executive power. Nor were the courts given powers similar to those of the old *parlements.* Their business was law enforcement only. This left the state with a strong legislature. For the Legislative Assembly had exclusive control over initiating law, taxes, expenditures, war, and diplomacy.

Within the framework of these separate and unequal branches, the new system of administration fitted uncomfortably. The old conflicting layers of government were stripped away and rationalized. France was made into

During the spring and summer of 1789 bread riots occurred throughout France further aggravating the growing social chaos. On October 5, the women of Paris gathered to demand bread, but, finding no satisfaction, they spontaneously decided to march to Versailles to appeal to the King. After camping on the grounds of the palace, some of the demonstrators invaded the building at dawn the next day, killing several members of the royal bodyguard and nearly penetrating the Queen's apartments before they were stopped. Powerless to protest, the royal family accompanied the mob back to Paris, and, for the first time since Louis XIV had fled the city over a century earlier, a French king was installed in the Tuileries palace. Bibliothèque Nationale.

42. In the context of a connected account of the reaction and the export of the Revolution by French armies; see the next chapter.
43. The proper term applied to Assembly members.

eighty-three departments, or *départements.* Each one had districts (*arron-dissements*); and each district cantons; every canton communes. The *départements* bore no relationship to old provinces rooted in feudal power systems, but derived even their names from natural features. Each had a capital easily reached by citizens at its edge. This decentralization was meant to make government responsive. So, too, was the local system of elected "deliberative" councils, which had executive powers as a local bureaucracy.

This clear effort to dissolve provincial loyalties alienated some, but it was needed to strike again at the tangle of rights and privileges involved in just such loyalties. The problem was to make the new and largely inexperienced local governors responsive, since a strong executive was lacking and the system provided no group to see that enforcement of law and policy existed in the new units. How critical this was became clear in 1792, when the wars of the Revolution broke out and revealed the Assembly's inability both to legislate and to administer.

Since the new order made property the sole basis for distinctions among citizens, it is interesting to see how the Assembly sought to solve the economic crisis to which it owed its own very existence. It did not disown the debts of the Old Regime, perhaps because its members were propertied men and government creditors. When direct taxes on land and other incomes failed to meet the needs for revenue, capital levies were tried on a "patriotic," voluntary basis. Few "patriots" gave enough; the debt mounted, and new measures were needed to finance the new regime. Those measures were found in the solution to another problem, that of the Church.

Before 1789 some three dozen provinces bore names from the feudal past. The Revolution witnessed the division of France into nearly 100 administrative districts based on geographical features.

A second "amputation" was made. The lands of the Church were confiscated, despite the Declaration's guarantees of private property. It was reasoned that the Church was a public corporation performing useful services. Once the state accepted the charges involved in such services, it was for the common good[44] to take back into public hands this private

44. As provided in the Declaration on August 26, 1789.

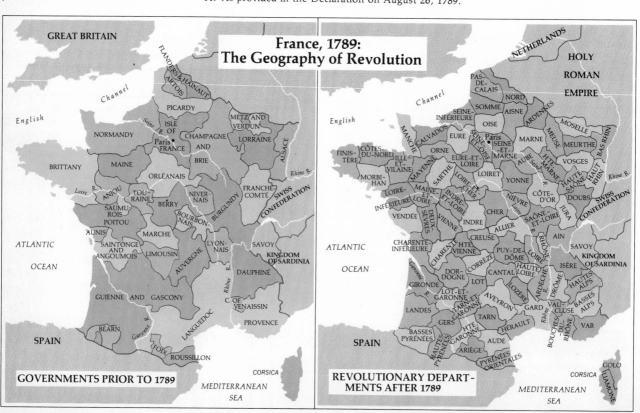

France, 1789:
The Geography of Revolution

GOVERNMENTS PRIOR TO 1789

REVOLUTIONARY DEPART-MENTS AFTER 1789

wealth. And this the Assembly did in November 1789. Then, in order to convert the seized land into usable funds and debt retirement, bonds (*assignats*) bearing interest were assigned to creditors, on the security of the Church lands. Holders had special rights in purchasing such lands; and even those who did not use their rights would be paid off[45] as lands were sold. Paper money thus began to circulate, for the *assignats* were nothing less,[46] and they allowed the government to pay creditors in the coin of inflation.

The Assembly was not content to drop the Church halfway from the lofty perch of privilege, however. Between the thirteenth of February, 1790, and December 26, the Church was refashioned. The clergy were made into salaried state servants by the Civil Constitution of the Clergy. This document also reorganized ecclesiastic government. Old dioceses were abolished and new ones made to coincide with the *départements*. Parish priests were now to be elected by district assemblies, while bishops were named by election by the *département* councils. Monastic houses not suppressed were reformed. And all clergy were required to take an oath to uphold both the constitution of 1791 and the new Civil Constitution of the clergy. Louis XVI accepted this new order, but Pope Pius VI did not. He became in effect the first European sovereign to declare war on the Revolution.

It was the French monarch who made the Constitution a failure, however, and so assured a further movement leftward of the Revolution—which had been his hapless role from the beginning.

Louis was in touch with the *émigrés* who had from early 1789 fled to seek the aid of the Holy Roman emperor, the king of Prussia, and other Europeans, who might help the count of Artois, one of Louis's younger brothers in exile. Louis himself sought the help of Leopold II (1790–1792), the Tuscan reformer. Moreover, neither Mirabeau nor Lafayette, the leading ministers during the constitutional monarchy, succeeded in convincing Louis that he could be a strong king by cooperating with the Assembly.

Louis's disinclination for cooperation gave scope to the radicals of the many political clubs, especially the Jacobins, who were originally the Society of Friends of the Constitution. The Jacobins were the vigilantes of the Revolution and by 1791 had a network of clubs throughout France. Chiefly middle-class men—professionals and businessmen—the Jacobins were disciplined, centralized in their organization, and a clean contrast to the weak executive and floundering administration of the state. Always anti-Bourbon, they pounced on another royal blunder made on June 20, 1791. Louis and his family fled Paris, heading toward the duchy of Luxemburg. There, they were to be joined by Austrian troops sent by Marie Antoinette's brother, Leopold II.

Louis XVI had once again misunderstood the Revolution, which had balanced the abolition of hereditary nobility a year earlier (June 19, 1790) by a law outlawing workers' unions in the month of his flight. Anyway, the plan failed. The royal family was taken at Varennes, on the French side of the border. Louis was seized. The Constitution was promulgated at the end of the summer, already made obsolete by Louis's actions. It had envisioned a weak king as a compliant executive; the Legislative Assembly had on its hands a prisoner whose fate was all but sealed in April 1792, when Leopold II's successor, Francis II, and Frederick William II of Prussia seized certain pretexts to make war on France.[47]

---

45. The *assignats*, or shares in the public debt, would be "retired."
46. A severe inflation already existed and was now pushed on by this "cheap" money.
47. The emperor Leopold had signed the Declaration of Pillnitz on August 27, 1791, in which he said French affairs were the concern of all sovereigns. See Chapter 5.

On the twentieth of April the Jacobin foreign minister Charles François Dumouriez (1739–1823) procured from the Assembly a declaration of war on Austria. The reason was the apparent willingness of the Pillnitz powers to intervene to aid Louis XVI. Prussia joined Austria halfheartedly, however, because its armies were engaged in the East with Russia and a new division of Poland. But the French armies sustained defeats. Morale was on the verge of collapse. The Revolution was in danger.

THE REPUBLIC OF VIRTUE

The reaction to this situation was first dominated by the *Girondins,* or *Girondists,* a group of legislators from the *département* near Bordeaux called the Gironde. Their leader, Brissot de Warville (1754–1793), and others among the Girondins were also Jacobins. The Jacobins were the parent group, but the group split on the issue of royal power, the majority being the more moderate Girondins. The Girondins pushed for war in April because they hoped to bring to power a ministry of their compatriots to run it. They also believed fervently that France could win such a war, and that revolutionary armies could thereby spread the French Revolution in Europe and even overseas, through the European empires. This, in Brissot's eyes, would make *the Revolution* a universal experience and so complete a radical, popular, and ecumenical social change.

Between April and August, 1792, two critical things happened. As the war went badly, the people rallied to the revolutionary cause. But inflation and defeats, as well as deep peasant dissatisfaction with the distribution of land in France and general suffering among workers induced by shortages, alienated the masses from Brissot's leadership. As the summer matured, the potential invaders were near the borders, from where they dictated to the French people the Brunswick Manifesto,[48] threatening to revenge any harm that might be done to the Bourbon royal prisoners.

This suited exactly the needs of a group of Jacobins who had grown more and more radical, to the point of becoming outright opponents of the Girondin faction. These Jacobins were led by Robespierre, Danton, and Marat, who commanded a small and radical group of deputies and also the loyalties of the Paris masses. Against the so-called party of the Plain, chiefly a loosely knit bunch of provincials, the "Mountain," as the Jacobins from Paris's rue Saint-Honoré club were later called, threw the full weight of Paris. The Paris Jacobins in fact exploited the summer discontents to launch a seizure of power and so move the Revolution leftward again.

The left-wing Jacobins had republican feelings at odds with the continuation of the monarchy and the more moderate views of the Girondins. The stirring of the lower classes to action was also a result of the arrival in Paris in the summer of recruits from the countryside, many of them also hostile to Brissot's ministry. One of these groups from Marseilles had brought a marching song—later titled the "Marseillaise"[49]—which expressed the mass enthusiasm for a strike at "tyranny" at home and abroad. Mixing with the Paris mob,[50] shouting their defiance in song, on August 10 the masses rose. They took the Tuileries, after breaking the resistance of the Swiss Guards, and seized Louis XVI and his family.

On that same day the radical Jacobins responded to the pressure they had wanted to see mobilized, while the Girondins drew back. This was decisive

After the flight to Varennes the problem of dealing with the royal family became the basis for bitter arguments in the Constituent Assembly. In August 1792 the constitutional monarchy was overthrown by a popular revolt, and Louis XVI's fate was sealed later in the year with the discovery of his secret correspondence with France's enemies in Austria. Sentenced to death, he was guillotined in the Place de la Révolution in January 1793. His priest, Abbé Edgeworth, prays beside the King's body as the executioner displays his head to the crowd. Louis's death and the subsequent beheadings of the Queen and his sister, Madame Elisabeth, outraged the monarchies of Europe who hastily united to fight the French republicans. Bibliothèque Nationale.

48. July 25, 1792, issued by the Prussian duke of Brunswick, and published in Paris on August 3.
49. This revolutionary anthem soon became what it still is today—the French national anthem.
50. "Mob" here is used to mean the mobilized part of any mass population not organized by political action.

for the future, for the Commune of Paris set up by the mob in forty-eight democratic "sections" abrogated the Constitution of 1791 and dissolved the Legislative Assembly. Proclaiming itself a provisional government, the Commune declared an election for a constitutional convention[51] under universal male suffrage. Before this new body convened on September 20, a wave of violence swept Paris. Danton called for mass arrests and harsh measures against priests and suspected counterrevolutionaries. The mob went beyond the call of duty, however, and instituted in Paris and the provinces a series of "trials" of the "traitors" *within* France. The result was the September Massacres, in which 1,100 were killed.

The situation was one of domestic anarchy mixed with the threat of invasion when the National Convention met to pass decrees against the civil powers of the Church and also to celebrate the first victory of revolutionary arms.[52] The Girondins spoke against mob violence, chiefy because they feared the Paris determination to set up a strong revolutionary government in the wake of Louis XVI's deposition, which had been proclaimed. The Mountain[53] had no such fear, however, and it took the lead in making a formal indictment of "citizen Louis Capet" (Louis XVI) on December 3. On January 16–17, 1793, 387 of the 721 Convention deputies sentenced to death Louis and his family for crimes against France. Not heeding the Brissotins' plea for mercy, the Convention next refused a reprieve and ordered death by guillotine, this time by a vote of 380 to 310!

51. Intentionally recalling the American Constitutional Convention of 1787.
52. The Battle of Valmy, September 20. See the next chapter.
53. So called because these members sat on the high bench of seats on the left side of the hall. Opposite them, on the right side of the hall, sat the Girondins, while on the lower benches on the floor of the hall sat the Plain, or Brissotins and other "moderates."

When Louis was executed on the twenty-first, the Mountain was a step closer to power although the Girondins still held the ministry. The Republic proclaimed in September 1792 was now in being.

The dominant figure in the years 1793 and 1794, the years of the Republic of Virtue, was the provincial lawyer Robespierre. He had been elected to the first revolutionary assembly from Arras[54] as a delegate of the third estate. Quickly, he had established himself as a democrat, in a speech advocating active citizenry for the masses without property, for which he was said to be a vile incendiary. An early opponent of capital punishment, Robespierre had been powerless until 1792, when he opposed the declaration of war. Elected a Convention delegate from Paris, this no longer obscure Jacobin advocated purging the Girondins, and others corrupted not by moderation, but by ordinary sins of bribery and graft. It was now his conviction that the war and the Revolution were sacred and linked together. To survive, the Republic must become pure at home and invincible abroad, which it could do only by purges and the fanatic zeal for "virtue" which Robespierre admired in Rousseau.[55]

Robespierre, whose own purity won for him the title "Incorruptible," thus became the driving force of the Republic of Virtue and also the "Angel of the Terror," the Terror being the program of violent social action and control practiced by the Convention over the two most radical years of the Revolution. This period of two years falls into two clearly different divisions: the period of democratic anarchy between January 21 and early September, 1793; and the period from September 13, 1793, to July 26, 1794, an era of democratic dictatorship which ended in Robespierre's own execution. We must characterize each phase briefly, as well as the succeeding one, which ended in the fall of 1795 (the year III),[56] when Napoleon Bonaparte's actions in Paris helped to bring down the Convention.

During the first nine months of 1793 defeat and anarchy threatened the new Revolution. The economy was falling apart. The radical masses (whose leaders were called *enragés*) distrusted the Jacobins in control of the Convention, because Robespierre and his allies would not be dictated to by the Commune of Paris. The *enragés* wanted controls over food prices and other things affecting the popular standard of living. The Commune's leaders even invaded the Convention in late May, to arrest certain Girondins, including the *philosophe* Condorcet, who escaped.[57] The troubles at home were matched by defeats in the field, especially after the defection in April of the best republican general, Dumouriez. Thus the Mountain had no effective control of France, especially in the provinces, where Girondin fugitives from Paris inspired counterrevolution at Lyons, Bordeaux, and Marseilles, and in the region of the Vendée. Even provincial Jacobin clubs militated against the "bourgeois" parliamentarians in Paris, while the foreign armies seemed about to break France's forces in the field.

Robespierre and his allies responded with what eventually became the full program of the Convention. Haltingly, but with gathering resolve, they shaped an attack on anarchy, domestic counterrevolution, the chaos in the economy, and the foreign enemies of the Revolution.[58]

54. A town in northern France.
55. For whom he had the highest regard as a democratic thinker and a pure example of living.
56. The more radical revolutionary consciousness of 1792 gave birth to a new calendar, in which the year I began on September 22, 1792, with the first full day of business in the Convention.
57. He committed suicide in hiding.
58. On the appointment of Lazare Carnot to "organize victory" in the wars, and for discussion of related questions, see Chapter 4.

Robespierre's personal traits would not have suggested the integral role he was to play in the Reign of Terror. Honest, charitable, and hard working, the young gentleman from the small town of Arras was a highly cultured lawyer noted for his fastidious appearance evident in this portrait. His fanaticism was that of an idealist devoted to Rousseau whose theories on society Robespierre wished to implement by whatever means necessary. As a leader of the Commune he did not invent the machinery of the Terror, but his eloquent oratory helped to make it acceptable. Only a few weeks before his fall, Robespierre enjoyed his greatest moment of triumph when a giant public fête celebrated the new religion of the Supreme Being based on the ideas of Rousseau's Social Contract. Giraudon.

Perhaps the most successful of David's Revolutionary works, the Death of Marat *was hastily painted after the politician's assassination and hung in the Assembly. Marat suffered from a skin disease which forced him to work while sitting in a tub of water, and David has realistically depicted him as he appeared when he was found after the murder. In his hand he holds a letter from the assassin, Charlotte Corday, asking permission for an interview. Despite the acute realism, the starkly simple scene is ennobled by its relation to artistic tradition. Ancient Roman funerary monuments and Italian baroque Christian martyrdom scenes are recalled in a way which underlines the sense of historical importance. Musée de Versailles.*

The instrument of this attack was the Committee of Public Safety,[59] a body of twelve men appointed by the Convention to guide the Revolution. This executive body, which was to be reelected every month, grew out of an earlier Committee of Surveillance, which had sought to control various anarchical tendencies, especially the Commune's Central Revolutionary Committee and the fugitive Girondins. Robespierre entered the Committee on July 27, 1793, and quickly moved it toward a policy of systematic terror

59. Hereafter called the Committee for convenience.

against the "enemies" of the Revolution, where earlier purges had been sporadic and directed chiefly against suspect moderates in and out of the Convention.

Before July, the Committee had instituted some economic controls. It had also shaped a system of trials, under the direction of a Committee of General Security. But the leadership of Danton[60] failed. It had passed in the Convention the "Jacobin" Constitution, which was democratic, while denouncing the Commune and its *enragés* supporters. In July the Jacobin leader Marat was slain in his bath by Charlotte Corday. There was no effective program and no control of the masses.

Robespierre was a systematic man, however, and he realized that to stabilize the Revolution strong law was necessary. The Jacobin Constitution was too diffuse with regard to executive power. Hence it was the Committee's policy after July to centralize control, to institute systematic revolutionary justice, to regulate the economy, and to make the whole nation active in the war. The first major step concerned the war. On August 23 the *levée en masse* was proclaimed, or the recruitment of the masses in a revolutionary army. On the thirteenth of September the Committee effectively seized power,[61] in the wake of Robespierre's election as chairman of the Convention and following an open challenge to the Committee by partisans of the Commune.

The phase of the dictatorship of the Committee thus coincides with a new crisis. The Committee's policy quickly ended speculation about what dictatorship meant. A Law of Suspects was passed to follow up Robespierre's plea, "Let terror reign." Terror was not new, but organized terror was. Criticism of the government was banned. The remaining Girondins were expelled from the Convention. A series of "representatives on mission"[62] was sent into the various regions to implement centralized government by controlling every phase of activity, from army recruitment to food distribution. Armed with the Law of the Maximum, of September 17, which was a comprehensive law of economic regulation, the Committee struck at hoarders, grain speculators, merchants who gave short weight, and every other sort of enemy of cheap bread.

Bogus "foreign plots" were exposed in order to rally the masses to the Committee's slogans of victory, and adequate recompense for the people. A "religion of reason" was proclaimed and inaugurated in November 1793 at Notre Dame Cathedral, in a lurid parody of worship centered on a figure of "philosophy" set up at the main altar. Then, on the fourth of December, 1793, the "Constitution" of the Reign of Terror was passed, which empowered the Committee to publish Bulletins of Laws setting forth the regulations requiring obedience.

The results of the new system of dictatorship were astonishing. The price rise abated at first, before free trade was allowed again. The "nation in arms" won important victories outside of France, spreading republics where it went. The extreme revolutionary anarchists[63] were decimating religionists, especially Christians of very traditional beliefs. "Dechristianization" was unpopular with Robespierre, however, who correctly thought the Hébertists and other extreme revolutionaries were alienating the masses, many of whom were Catholic in sentiment.

60. Along with others later famous as members of the Committee during the Terror: Saint-Just, Couthon, Hérault de Séchelles, Hébert, etc.
61. By gaining a nominating power over its own membership, thus doing away with the monthly elections.
62. Representatives were only sometimes actual members of the Committee.
63. Called Hébertists, after a member of the Paris Commune.

This opposition of Robespierre to the Hébertists figured prominently in the Committee's official terror. By March 1794 the Committee had extended the Terror to both the Hébertists and other "undisciplined" radicals such as the Paris followers of Danton, who were deviating from the Revolution in a conservative direction.[64] Throughout the spring, therefore, the Terror was brought to a new peak. The Commune was attacked. Municipal offices were filled with Robespierre's supporters. New "enemies" were proscribed, adding to the list of victims which included already Marie Antoinette, royalists, Girondins, lukewarm members of the Mountain, and hapless clerks guilty of nothing more serious than denouncing Robespierre's "Festival of the Supreme Being," held in Paris on June 8, 1794.

In all the Terror claimed about 40,000 victims by July 1794, with mass executions in Lyons, the Vendée, and other places considered counter-revolutionary centers. The Terror was blind to age, sex, class, or even past service to the Revolution. While many of the victims were nobles,[65] nearly 15 percent were bourgeoisie. At Nantes 2,000 men, women, and children were killed by being drowned aboard barges. The scientist Lavoisier, a distinguished chemist,[66] was executed because *before* 1789 he had been a tax farmer!

Thus did the Committee make clear the meaning of its policy, which was to concentrate the whole Revolution in its hands and to allow no independent thought or action on its course. The democratic Jacobin Constitution was suspended in the name of order and victory; and this meant in

One of the most effective English caricaturists of contemporary events was Thomas Rowlandson. This watercolor drawing shows French émigrés arriving at Southampton in 1794 after their escape from the Mediterranean port of Toulon. Royalist factions in Toulon revolted in 1793 and turned the city over to the English, but General Bonaparte caused this mass exodus when he succeeded in recapturing it the following year. Thousands of Frenchmen were forced to flee during the Revolution, and they settled mainly in German cities along the Rhine and in England where the Bourbon pretender Louis XVIII resided. Many others, including Talleyrand and the future King Louis Philippe, came to America. Victoria and Albert Museum.

64. Their "deviation" supposedly consisted in financial corruption and, what is probably more true, in opposition to the Committee.
65. Some 6–7 percent.
66. 1743–1794; the "father" of modern chemistry.

practice that the former instruments of popular revolt, which had helped propel the Revolution forward in 1789 and 1791 and 1792, were increasingly the victims of the Terror. The political clubs followed the Commune and the local popular assemblies into disrepute and "illegality."

It is therefore ironic that Robespierre himself became a victim of the Terror on July 28—the tenth day of Thermidor in the new calendar.[67] For the Angel of the Terror was a victim of its success. The Committee had been doubling as a war cabinet through the representatives on mission. By the end of June 1794, the Committee had under its control a successful army of 800,000 men, by far the largest ever raised in Europe. The *levée en masse* produced victories in bunches, as Europe witnessed for the first time war made by a national army of citizens.

The news of victories in the Netherlands in June convinced many Frenchmen that the Revolution was now safe from enemies abroad. Both the Terror and economic controls thus seemed less necessary, especially to the bourgeoisie. The Convention had been alienated by the execution of its leaders, especially Danton. The *enragés* opposed the Committee because of its threatened destruction of the Commune and the clubs. Why, many asked, must the Committee maintain its dictatorship in the eased circumstances? The "narrow way" could no longer be justified by defense.

The Terror itself had long been the chief force of anarchy. Even a majority of the Committee could no longer understand the precise slaughters made by Saint-Just, who had denounced Danton as a traitor—a hero of the Revolution from its start. And the new economic decrees of February and March[68] seemed to embrace sacrifice for its own sake, while giving all legislative power to the Committee. The Ventôse laws had seized the property of "enemies" of the Revolution, supposedly to distribute it to poor peasants, while at the same time courting the merchants with a policy of free trade. Such a policy, doing nothing to relieve the numbing Terror, further alienated the wage earners, who saw bread climb in price again.

Above all raged the question of whether Robespierre was not becoming the dictatorial high priest of terror for its own sake. A group of deputies answered it affirmatively and passed a resolution against Robespierre with the help of the Committee, which he had alienated. On the twenty-sixth of July, Robespierre incautiously predicted that a military dictatorship would follow "attacks" on the Revolution. The Committee participated in a review of this "threat," and on the twenty-seventh (9 Thermidor) a conspiracy to execute Robespierre, Saint-Just, and Couthon was hatched.

The Commune and the Convention were struggling for power now, as the *Thermidorians* put to death the so-called Triumvirate.[69] The extremists and the moderates had combined for a moment to bring to an end the Terror and Robespierre's Republic of Virtue.

In any event, that was the result of what became of what might have seemed just another purge. The moderates quickly suppressed the radicals, completing the destruction of the Commune. Late in the summer the economic decrees of Ventôse were repealed. Terror was dismantled. By November the Paris Jacobin Club was shut down. In December the Law of the Maximum was repealed, along with the Law of Suspects. Early in 1795 Catholic worship was restored. Popular risings in May were suppressed by the National Guard, now under the control of the bourgeois leaders of the

---

67. Where the months were named for seasons or natural aspects—e.g., the heat of summer.
68. Ventôse in the new calendar.
69. So named to arouse memories of Caesar, who rose to his Roman dictatorship with the early aid of Pompey and Crassus.

Thermidorian Reaction. In August the Convention passed the Constitution of the Year III, after suppressing new Paris barricades with army troops from conservative provinces.

The Revolution was over. Or, at the very least, the triumphant, solid bourgeoisie of large merchants, speculators, professionals, and would-be gentlemen had regained control of it, from their places of refuge during the Terror. Convinced that democracy meant Robespierre's Terror, they made the new constitution run in the stiller water of civil liberty on the 1789 model. On October 26, 1795, the Republic came under a government called the Directory, which came into existence just twenty-one days after some insurgents in Paris had been put down by a "whiff of grapeshot" fired by Napoleon Bonaparte.

BIBLIOGRAPHY

BARBER, ELINOR. *The Bourgeoisie in Eighteenth Century France.** Princeton: Princeton University Press, 1955. Important for the influence on government of this class.

FORD, FRANKLIN L. *Robe and Sword.* Cambridge, Mass.: Harvard University Press, 1953. A basic work on the feudal reaction and the relations of the two nobilities to government.

GOODWIN, A., ed. *The European Nobility in the Eighteenth Century.** London: A. & C. Black, 1953. Essays on the various states by specialists; very useful.

LEFEBVRE, GEORGES. *The Coming of the French Revolution.** Princeton: Princeton University Press, 1947. This translation by R. R. Palmer is the classic left analysis by the greatest modern student of the Revolution; it stresses the feudal reaction. This work by LeFebvre should be read in conjunction with his two volumes *The French Revolution* (New York: Columbia University Press, 1961–1964), a fundamental narrative of the events of the 1790s. The classic works of the generation of the First World War are Alphonse Aulard's liberal republican *The French Revolution* and Albert Mathiez's *The French Revolution,* a defense of the radical Jacobins.

PALMER, R. R. *Twelve Who Ruled.** Princeton: Princeton University Press, 1941. Beautifully written account of the domination of the Revolution by the Committee of Public Safety.

RUDÉ, GEORGES. *The Crowd in the French Revolution.** Oxford: Clarendon Press, 1959. Stresses popular participation and class antagonism. This view is severely criticized in Alfred Cobban, *The Social Interpretation of the French Revolution** (Cambridge: Cambridge University Press, 1964).

STEWART, J. H. *A Documentary Survey of the French Revolution.* New York: The Macmillan Company, 1951. One of the best source books.

TILLY, CHARLES. *The Vendée.** Cambridge, Mass.: Harvard University Press, 1964. The best analysis of the counterrevolutionaries, using modern sociological analyses.

TOCQUEVILLE, ALEXIS DE. *The Old Regime and the French Revolution.** New York: Doubleday & Co., Anchor, 1955. This great work focuses on the social breakdown in 1789, from the perspective of a participant in the 1848 revolution.

Asterisk indicates a paperbound edition.

But thy most dreaded instrument,
In working out a pure intent,
Is Man,—arrayed for mutual slaughter,—
Yea, Carnage is thy daughter!
WORDSWORTH, *Ode* (1816)[1]

4

EMPIRE OF IRON: EUROPE AND THE FRENCH REVOLUTION

THE ORIGINS OF THE REVOLUTIONARY WARS

Within a few months of the outbreak of the Revolution in France, there set in across Europe a variety of reactions to it. The impact of the Revolution on artistic and literary expression was profound and deserves detailed examination.[2] Hence it will be our purpose here to explore the effects produced by the new French regime on politics, diplomacy, and the Western system of states.

From the beginning of the National Assembly it was clear the French would not play out a revolutionary drama without anxious attention from Europe's sovereigns and articulate people of every opinion. Even so sympathetic a friend of the American Revolution as Burke distrusted events in France. Now, no speech on "conciliation" came from that corner. Charles James Fox, the radical reformer, proclaimed the fall of the Bastille as the greatest event that had ever happened in the world.[3] Burke, however, rose to the defense of Marie Antoinette and the noble order, calling the one Europe's most "delightful vision" and the other "the Corinthian capital of polished society."[4] What such sentiments portended was clarified when Burke reminded the English that it was prudent to play a little water on one's own house when it was a neighbor's that had caught fire!

It was not in England alone that there arose at once "Jacobins" and "anti-Jacobins," "corresponding" societies for and against the Revolution, and networks of political clubs militating for reforms, constitutional changes, or open intervention against the French despoilers of aristocracy. For the most part, however, pro–French Revolution agitation was strong only in the areas bordering France and in places strongly within the field of the attractive forces of French culture or where social conditions

1. William Wordsworth (1770–1850) first published this ode in 1816; the lines here are from a revised version which appeared in 1845 as pt. 2, stanza 45 of *Poems of the Imagination.*
2. See Chapter 5 for a detailed presentation of the nature of revolutionary thought and the reactions to it.
3. In a letter written on July 30, 1789.
4. In his famous pamphlet *Reflections on the Revolution in France* (1790), from which other remarks attributed to him here also derive.

resembled those dominant within France. These territories consisted chiefly of the Low Countries, the German Rhineland, Savoy, Italy, and Poland. In Britain, the Irish willingly joined English working-class radicals who formed the corresponding societies and distributed Tom Paine's *Rights of Man*. But the Irish did so less out of Jacobin sentiments than because of the natural inclination of the Catholic masses to seize every hope of help in their struggles against Protestant English domination.[5]

Elsewhere in Europe, the seeds of Jacobinism fell on stony soil. Throughout Iberia, Russia, Scandinavia, the Balkans, and the Habsburg dominions, there were few groups of supporters. The same was true in the German heartland of the West, where the relative isolation of weak middle-class sympathizers was underlined by the strong hold of aristocracies on power and the generally fierce conservatism of peasants. Indeed, beyond what we may call the sympathetic bourgeois liberals of the Gallic cultural fringe of Europe, it was only in the United States and in colonial "Latin" America that the French found comfort. The Spanish colonials were preoccupied with their own liberation from Spain, however, and American aid to the French cause was not revolutionary. The United States joined in a war against Britain from 1812 to 1814, but this was inspired by difficulties with Britain.[6]

The material question was not how many intellectuals were for the revolution in France, but what would the other monarchies do? France was

Frightened by the prospect that Jacobin fanaticism might find support in England, Parliament voted to join the war against France in 1793. Here the Tory prime minister, William Pitt, addresses the House of Commons in that year. Opposite him, the Whigs, under the leadership of Charles James Fox, listen attentively. Pitt aggressively waged war for nine years until he resigned in 1802 just as negotiations were leading to the short-lived Peace of Amiens. An aloof and sarcastic individual, Pitt's deepest commitment was not to the interminable war with France but to the consolidation of Britain's colonial interests and the promulgation of a laissez-faire trade and financial system. National Portrait Gallery, London.

5. Many Scots, without the added incentive of religious resistance, were "Jacobin." Scotland was long in the French cultural orbit, however, and also politically tied to the "foreign" Hanoverian dynasty in London by very weak bonds.
6. In any event, it would be perverse to see in Napoleon and President James Monroe ideological allies. The United States used the European wars to expand its power in North America, especially against English and Spanish influence.

fortunate in 1789–1792. Catherine the Great was deeply involved in intrigues concerning new divisions of Poland and also in campaigns against the Turks. The English under William Pitt the Younger, since 1783 the prime minister in a reform-minded government, were so preoccupied by finances, domestic political change, and the problem of governing India that they ignored for a time Burke's warnings. Neither the Iberian nor the Italian states were strong enough or united enough in their reactions to the French situation to lead an effective intervention, which England might have done had it yielded to the demands of Burke.

This meant in practice that the key to the European reaction to France lay in Berlin and Vienna. But Prussia and Habsburg Austria were themselves generally at odds with each other, except in their joint preoccupation to partition Poland in concert with Russia. Frederick the Great had died in 1786, and his Prussian successor, Frederick William II (1786–1797), had cause to worry over the Revolution. He had for a time tried to negotiate with France, hoping to detach the new government from the Habsburg alliance made in 1756. The French refused to be drawn into an alliance, however, and this faced Prussia with a delicate choice. Prussian ambitions in western Germany had led to intervention against revolution in the Dutch Netherlands in 1787. Now, France seemed to be intent on upsetting the newly established order in territories on its borders. The Assembly had seized papal territory at Avignon; and it abrogated the feudal rights of German princes in the disputed lands in Alsace, by extending to them the new laws abolishing feudal and manorial institutions.

The Prussian king saw in this a threat to the role he had played among the lesser German princes, that of winning them away from loyalty to the Holy Roman emperor by posing as protector of "German" rights. Frederick William's fears were thus compounded in 1791 when the Bourbon royal family was taken to prison after the "flight to Varennes." The German princes had already appealed to Emperor Leopold II to protect their rights from French encroachments. He had no stomach for intervention, however. Indeed, he had urged his sister, Louis XVI's queen, to adjust to constitutional politics. By June 1791, however, Leopold II could not so easily ignore the *émigrés* who demanded action. A "brother" who was a king was a prisoner of the Revolution, no longer its royal head on new terms.

The altered situation produced the famous Pillnitz Declaration. In August 1791, Leopold II swore to "restore" France to order, *if* the other European powers joined the crusade against revolution. Leopold meant less than he professed, however. His intention had been to placate the *émigrés,* while avoiding war. It had been his guess that England under Pitt would prevent the condition—*unanimous* agreement of the powers—explicit in the Pillnitz statement.

The Emperor's calculation had not taken into account the political situation within the Revolution. We know how the Girondins reacted and also how the Paris Jacobins stirred outrage against the counterrevolutionary Declaration. The advanced revolutionaries in France not only pushed for a war policy early in 1792. They also established relations with revolutionary groups in the cultural and political areas we described as the "Gallic fringe." The forces of revolution had been crushed in the 1780s by foreign intervention,[7] but they had not been eradicated. These circumstances would have made Leopold's policy difficult to maintain in any event. But he died early in 1792, and Francis II, his successor, was a man fully tuned to the reactionary wishes of the *émigrés* and other aristocrats.

7. As we have already noticed: see Chapter 2.

FRENCH DEMOCRATS *surprizing the Royal Runaways.*

The modern political cartoon developed during the French Revolution when cheap and often vulgar caricatures of the latest events were sold in the streets of London and Paris. French Democrats Surprising the Royal Runaways *is the title of this English cartoon showing the capture of Louis XVI and Marie Antoinette during an attempted flight to freedom. On the night of June 20, 1791, the royal family escaped from Paris and headed toward Metz, where loyalist troops awaited them. Bands of peasants surrounded the party en route at the small town of Varennes, and they were forced to return to Paris as prisoners. Hostile mobs threatened them along the way, and the abortive plot further weakened their lamentable position. By courtesy of the Trustees of the British Museum.*

War fever in France was also made more acute early in 1792 by the miscalculation of Louis XVI's ministers and friends. Mirabeau and Lafayette believed that a war against the German princes would prove Bourbon patriotism. Supported by other moderates, they therefore gave the Girondins and their allies aid in securing the declaration of war on April 20, 1792.

WAR AND POLITICS, 1792–1795

The war declared against Austria in April of 1792 began a period of nearly continuous warfare for twenty-three years. These wars through all their different phases were mainly European. But they spread to the West Indies, South America, the Levant, and India. They were marked by the traditional conflicts for power and empire among Europe's chief states and in that aspect may be regarded as the final phase of the second "Hundred Years' War" between England and France. For they linked the English-Dutch struggles against France late in the Age of Louis XIV to England's leadership of the various alliances against democratic France and Napoleon's Empire.

These wars were also untraditional. They involved an effort to export the revolution from France abroad. Indeed, during their early years, the French wars were at least as much truly revolutionary as they were a continuation of older themes of dominance and exploitation. Even the early campaigns of

Napoleon himself were regarded by contemporaries as struggles for liberation, perhaps in fulfillment of a promise first given to Frenchmen only in 1789, but extended in 1791. On May 15, 1791, an Assembly decree had given civil liberties to "men of color" under French sovereignty. The spread of that sovereignty would therefore involve a fundamental attack on property in slaves as well as other forms of property. And Robespierre's government did not shrink from drawing the necessary conclusion. Slavery was abolished in France and wherever *la grande nation* had expanded.[8]

The "wars of liberation" did finally give way to Napoleon's imperial wars. These continued the revolution in tactics made by the principle of the nation in arms, while substituting dominance and exploitation for liberation. Napoleon even repealed the abolition of slavery, which, along with other acts of enslavement, prompted Beethoven to remove Bonaparte's name from the dedication to his *Eroica Symphony*[9] and led the poet Lord Byron to write, "There sunk the greatest, nor the worst of men."[10] Yet even the Napoleonic phase of the long era of wars helped insure that the Revolution in France would endure, and it is for that reason alone that the wars themselves would command our attention, even if they did not have the largest aspect of a struggle for liberty beyond Europe's Gallic fringe.

During the first phase of the antirevolutionary crusade, the European powers were convinced that they would quickly defeat France. How, they asked, could a kingdom without an officer corps—half of the French officers were noble *émigrés*—fight? How could a nation politically torn between partisans of Louis XVI and adherents of nascent republicanism summon the will to resist?[11]

These questions took on the air of prophecy almost at once, as summer came and turned to fall. The August insurrection in Paris and the September Massacres were productive of new factional fights within France. General Dumouriez's bold strategy of an *offensive* in the Austrian Netherlands backfired on two counts. France's spirited but undisciplined and badly commanded regiments broke in their first engagements; and Britain, until then neutral, now saw in the French thrust in the Low Countries a threat. We have seen already the terror and anarchy defeat produced in Paris in August and early September. This condition was temporarily relieved by the first victory of the revolutionaries, at Valmy, on September 20, the very day on which the National Convention first met.

Austria and Prussia had not committed their full resources to the Netherlands, because of their efforts to partition Poland. Dumouriez had rallied his army and by mid-autumn had seized Antwerp. Pitt found an old enemy poised across the English Channel, already interfering with one focal point of Britain's commercial empire. The Convention proclaimed the Dutch Scheldt River open to ships of every flag, despite a treaty ceding British merchants privileges in return for a guaranteed Dutch control of the river. Already alarmed by this, Pitt's government used the execution of Louis XVI early in 1793 as a pretext to expel the new Republic's diplomats.

8. By a decree made on February 4, 1794.
9. Ludwig van Beethoven (1770–1827). The *Eroica* dedication (the symphony was composed 1803–1804) first read "sinfonia grande: Buonaparte." This was changed to "Sinfonia eroica" to celebrate the memory of a great man, when in 1804 Napoleon took the title "Emperor."
10. *Childe Harold's Pilgrimage,* canto 3, stanza 36.
11. It was in this confident spirit that Prussia and Austria on July 25, 1792, issued the Brunswick Manifesto threatening terrible retribution against Paris if the people of that city harmed their king or queen.

This move seemed to seal the fate of the infant Republic. The Convention reacted belligerently, declaring war on both Britain and Holland. Spain, Sardinia, and Naples immediately joined what was now no longer a German alliance, but had become instead the First Coalition. The Austrians threw fresh troops at Dumouriez in the late winter. Defeats dispirited the French commander, who was under great pressure from the increasingly nervous Paris government. When fresh Coalition forces also defeated the French in the Rhineland, the war seemed nearly over. Dumouriez arranged to betray the Revolution, by ceding the Low Countries to the allies and seizing Paris, restoring monarchy in the bargain.

The effect in Paris was electric, first because the troops refused to join the General's treason, and second because the crisis sharpened the power struggle of the Mountain against the Plain. Bad news blotted out even the loyalty of the recruits, however. The Vendée revolted against government efforts to conscript new troops, with a coalition of staunchly Catholic peasants and reactionary noblemen spreading counterrevolution rapidly to Poitou, Anjou, and Brittany. By May, a Catholic Grand Army of royalists seemed as likely to overturn the Republic as the forces of the Coalition led by Britain and Austria.

This was the combination of circumstances in which the direction of the Republic passed to the Committee of Public Safety, which entrusted military success to the nation in arms, under the ministry of two Jacobin scientists, the minister of the navy Gaspard Monge,[12] and Lazare Carnot, an engineer ever since celebrated as the "organizer of victory."

While the Jacobins in the Committee proscribed the suspected "agents of Pitt," Carnot and Monge organized French science in behalf of the war effort. Carnot himself took personal charge of organizing the broken forces of the Army of the North. The overall command of the eleven republican field armies was revamped by Carnot, who saw that personnel selection was crucial to any new success France might have. With the help of the war minister Bouchotte, Carnot's purge was well under way in September, when, on the sixth, French troops broke the string of allied victories with a stunning triumph of their own at Hondschoote in the Dutch Netherlands.

By November this work of organizing a competent staff was sufficiently done, and Carnot informed the Committee that he must now attend to recruitment and supply. The armies, he correctly said, would fight loyally as presently constituted, taking their orders from the Committee. Even Bouchotte traveled extensively among the troops. Europe was seeing a new kind of army emerge to fight a new kind of war, and the Coalition scarcely seemed to comprehend that the citizen army taking shape would now fight not merely to defend France but to carry the Committee's radical fervor for revolution into the enemy's camps.

While noble generals scoffed that no men of *common birth* could be found able to command armies, the search of the Committee and Carnot proved the Coalition aristocrats wrong. In the next dozen years Europe's armies could not defeat men whose names still fill the histories of great commanders: Jourdan, Hoche, Pichegru, Masséna, Moreau, Lefebvre, and Bonaparte himself.

Jourdan was the designer of a battle plan which produced the victory over the Coalition on October 16 at Wattignies.[13] Although he was soon relieved by Pichegru, a favorite of Robespierre, his initial plan had confirmed the result of Hondschoote. Suddenly the Revolution seemed less likely to be

12. A mathematician and physicist.
13. Where the newly recruited army of *sans-culottes* beat the duke of Coburg.

overthrown from abroad, and the Terror at home was already bringing some hope of reducing the provinces to order. A young Corsican artillery captain, Napoleon Buonaparte[14] (1769–1821), had marked himself for promotion by the role he played in taking back into government hands the royalist naval base at Toulon in December. The recovery of a decent fleet base meant that Britain would not in the future so easily encourage counterrevolutionaries in disaffected provinces, as George III had done in October, by issuing a manifesto to the French people.[15]

New Year's Day in 1794 may thus be taken to mark the end of the beginning for the wars of liberation. The armies had proved their ability to defend France. In 1794–1795, despite the internal convulsions which led to Robespierre's fall, the end of the Terror, and the triumph of the moderates who made the Directory, the same armies overran France's enemies. It is not necessary to narrate in detail the stunning series of victories in two brief years. Yet their general course is inseparable from their effects within France and upon the Coalition, and we must at least sketch those tremendous events.

The revolutionary armies had occupied the Low Countries, the Rhineland, northern Spain, Switzerland, Savoy, and also Liguria. In the Netherlands they were welcomed by the activists, who since 1789 had revived the democratic Vonckist party of Belgium, and also by the northern-based Dutch "patriots" of the ordinary bourgeoisie. These lesser middle-class radicals wished for French help to overthrow the oligarchs. Elsewhere in the Low Countries and in western Germany native Jacobins also openly aided the French. Never strong enough to make their own revolution, they were a genuine revolutionary force.

The early German supporters of France included nearly every leading writer: the philosophers Kant, Herder, Fichte, Schelling, and Hegel; and the literary masters Goethe, Wieland, Klopstock, Schiller, and Hölderlin. Like the Germans, the pro-French elements in northern Italy and Switzerland were too weak to make their own revolution, but not negligible as an aid to the French conquest of their lands. Often a combination of Freemasons and *philosophes*, joined by a small legion of merchants and professionals, these "Jacobins" were therefore not revolutionary shock troops. They were rather suited to another role, unlike the Paris social-revolutionary masses. The true function of the pro-French foreigners was to provide a nucleus about which a series of dependent republics might be created.

In 1795, that development lay in the future, however. The first task of the Directory, as the new government in France was called, was to consolidate the reaction of Thermidor at home. Secondly, it wished to split the now worried Coalition, by detaching from it the geographically nearest, and hence most vulnerable, states. Success in the policy was essential to success in reducing France to a quieter order than the "red terror" of Virtue. This even the Convention had appreciated before its dissolution. Between March and August of 1795 its ministers negotiated peace with Spain and Tuscany. More important still, the Convention appealed to Prussia's anti-Habsburg interests and detached Frederick William II from the alliance now maintained by Austria and Britain.

In August 1795 the Convention had also made the Constitution of the Year III, thus formally constituting a French republic which had in fact existed since the execution of Louis XVI in 1793. The Directory established

14. Hereafter, as before, written either Bonaparte or Napoleon, in the French manner.
15. Smuggled in through Brest and Toulon before they were retaken.

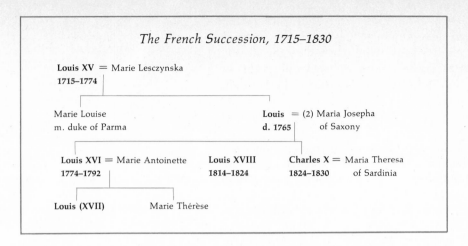

The French Succession, 1715–1830

Louis XV = Marie Lesczynska
1715–1774

Marie Louise
m. duke of Parma

Louis = (2) Maria Josepha
d. 1765 of Saxony

Louis XVI = Marie Antoinette
1774–1792

Louis XVIII
1814–1824

Charles X = Maria Theresa
1824–1830 of Sardinia

Louis (XVII)   Marie Thérèse

under the new instrument of government withstood its first challenge in October, when it broke the resistance of the royalists[16] with the young General Bonaparte's "whiff of grapeshot." The insurrection was essentially aimed at the provision that two-thirds of the new assembly were to be members of the Convention, a step taken to prevent wide gains by monarchists in the elections. As a matter of fact, 506 of the 741 men returned to the new bicameral legislature were former deputies in the Convention (*Conventionnels*) and were thereby dubbed "perpetuals" by their critics.

The new regime enfranchised literate men of property along the lines first set out in 1791. Also taken over was the practice of having the electors choose *département* officials as well as the legislature, which had an upper house, or Council of Ancients (250 members), and an assembly, or Council of Five Hundred. The whole legislature was in turn responsible for selecting a five-man executive board of Directors, from which the regime drew its title of the Directory.

The new regime thus began to rule France on a very narrow basis, by selecting its supporters from among the urban and rural moderates who dominated the post-Robespierre Convention. It sought to safeguard itself against the royalists abroad, who were headed by a man monarchists called Louis XVIII.[17] This man was Louis XVI's brother, the count of Provence, who maintained his claim to the throne from the safety of Verona in Italy, where British funds paid for his grandiose proclamations of a monarchical restoration.

Once again, therefore, a Bourbon's impolitic gestures helped a not too popular government. For few Frenchmen wanted to see a "white" terror by counterrevolutionaries carrying the white Bourbon banners. Most citizens rallied to the Republic, if for no other reason than to protect themselves and their acquisitions of Church lands, whether one considers peasants or the bourgeoisie. Only the more radical left of workers held out for the equality of 1793–1794. And these the Directory was prepared to deal with as harshly as Napoleon had dealt with the October royalists.

It was under these conditions, then, that France faced Britain and Austria in 1795. Britain had determined to fight to the death to preserve its commercial supremacy. And France had insured Austria's bitter opposition

16. On the Paris barricades of 13 Vendémiaire, according to the French revolutionary calendar.
17. The designation Louis XVII royalists reserved for Louis XVI's son, who had died in prison; his reign was supposedly 1793–1795. Louis XVIII actually came to the throne in 1814, but royalists assigned him the dates 1795–1824.

when the Directory extended the Constitution of the Year III to Belgium, thereby making official the will to carve new republics out of the Austrian Netherlands and perhaps other regions soon to be reached by the already broadly deployed armies. As far as Europe was concerned, the events of 1795 had not ended the Revolution, whatever the *enragés* in Paris might think of the Directory.

THE DIRECTORY AND EUROPE

The Convention had stayed in being only by calling in young Bonaparte's provincial troops. And the Directory at once gave evidence of its dependence on its military supporters. This was true not only with regard to the right-wing opposition of the royalists who gathered in the Clichy Club and negotiated with Louis XVI's brother, the pretender count of Provence. It was also true that the Directory needed the army in 1796, when an ambitious young man named "Gracchus" Babeuf,[18] a native of the town of Saint-Quentin, shaped a radical new conspiracy against the victors of Thermidor.

Babeuf (1760–1797) was an unlikely man to lead a communist "Conspiracy of Equals," at least on the surface. He was a member of the despised class of *feudistes,* or provincial lawyers and officials, who sought to compensate for their seigneurial masters' declining rents by squeezing the last obsolete feudal due from the peasantry. Won over to the Revolution, he had rapidly gravitated toward the politics of the wage earners, especially the Paris *sans-culottes,*[19] who derived their name from the fact that they wore trousers rather than the traditional knickers, or *culottes.* Sans-culottism[20] seemed to Babeuf the only alternative to bourgeois radicalism, after the fall of Robespierre and Saint-Just. Socially, Babeuf derived his hatred of the rich from the sans-culottes of the Paris sections. And politically, he drew from Robespierre his doctrine of democratic dictatorship, dressed up in a language also rich with the argot of the clubs and the journalism of Marat and Hébert.

By 1795 Babeuf was perhaps the most determined revolutionary in France, the counterpart of Italians like Filipo Buonarrotti, an organizer of republican resistance to French imperialism.[21] Babeuf and Buonarrotti had together worked out some idea of revolutionary brotherhood based on the dictatorship of the working masses. Babeuf formed a secret brotherhood to work for the seizure of power, which would be followed by a distribution of property to the poor. He did not spell out how the "Equals" would achieve the goals the brotherhood set, including the restoration of the more democratic Constitution of 1793.[22] Betrayed by informers, Babeuf and his followers were executed in 1797.

The episode had serious repercussions in politics, however. For it nearly coincided with the free elections of March 1797, in which a third of the two councils was replaced, including 216 retiring "perpetuals." Of the 150 standing for reelection, only 13 were chosen. Most of the victors were either, at least in a vague sense, royalists or else definite partisans of

18. His name was François Émile, but he took the name Gracchus from the Roman family of radical agrarian reformers.
19. Who were not only laborers, but also paupers, small craftsmen, shopkeepers, even small-scale entrepreneurs.
20. This term refers to the social egalitarian views and politics of the Paris working classes who distrusted the bourgeoisie.
21. The Carbonari were also active when Napoleon was extending his empire, as mentioned in Chapter 5.
22. Which had never been implemented.

constitutional monarchy. Such a restoration was absolutely unacceptable to the strongest force in the Republic, however—the army—nor was it acceptable to its most rapidly rising power, the Corsican general (then not yet thirty years old), Bonaparte.

While the Directory at home had stumbled between the Scylla of the royalists and the Charybdis of Babeuf,[23] the armies had marched straight to a new string of victories abroad. The triumphs were won in Italy at Austria's expense, by forces under the command of Bonaparte. And the policy in Italy became in fact that of the successful general who had in 1795 been made commander of the Army of the Interior.

Napoleon's useful work in buttressing the Directory at home aroused in him a keen sense of the French political situation, but he ached for a role of conquest. So, in 1796, he had secured a field assignment, which was nothing less than a crossing of the Alps to bring the war to northern Italy. In two swift campaigns, he defeated the Austrian forces. Victory was his despite the fact that the Directory neither paid his troops regularly nor supplied them. Napoleon had made up deficiencies by a policy of living on what he could requisition from the Italians, large numbers of whom saw in the Corsican a liberator.

Italy, as we have already noticed, had its own strong complement of reformers and would-be revolutionaries. The cities dependent on Venice revolted, as soon as the French forces appeared. There were also risings of the Bolognese against the Papal States and of Milan against Austria. Bonaparte reacted to this situation by tapping revolutionary support on a selective basis and setting up a Cisalpine Republic in the Po Valley. Based in Milan, the new republic was shaped on French lines. And the act of establishing it out of Habsburg and papal territories had serious political implications.

The Directory in 1797 was very much under the influence of the newly elected conservatives. Policy was to return the Italians to their former allegiances, as the condition of a peace with Austria in which the republic established in Belgium would be recognized. Thus the Directors were willing to trade off the Cisalpine Republic fashioned by a general for the Batavian Republic carved out of Austrian Belgium in 1795. Napoleon informed the Paris government that such peace terms were unacceptable to him and his army, which was by now a political force in its own right. His hand was strengthened by the fact that he had already opened negotiations with the defeated Austrians. Moreover, the Spanish had allied themselves with the ascendant French.

The determination of Britain was obviously crucial, since apart from

23. Scylla was a rock on the Italian coast, Charybdis was a whirlpool nearby; both were personified by the ancients as female sea monsters who ate sailors. This phrase thus means between two equally dangerous alternatives.

Dressed in their typical costume of long trousers and a red cap, these sans-coulottes dance around a "Liberty Tree" in support of the new republic. Pikes such as the one held by the character at left became sinister weapons during the Terror when they were used to parade heads of victims. Beyond their garb it is difficult to characterize the sans-culottes since they were an incoherent urban mob with no clear identity or goals. Their leaders, however, were professional revolutionaries seeking personal power at any cost, and they did not hesitate to unleash their followers on the innocent. Although this unruly faction was finally subdued when Robespierre sent its leaders to the guillotine in 1794, the Parisian mob persistently reasserted itself in moments of crisis throughout the nineteenth century. Bibliothèque Nationale.

sporadic Russian aid to Austria,[24] the London subsidies were essential to the Habsburg ability to fight. Britain had taken the measure of serious internal conflicts and the military reverses suffered by the Coalition. And Pitt, too, had decided to negotiate, if for no other reason than to pull the teeth of the antiwar party led by Charles James Fox. There were, however, other good reasons. Republican agitation at home had produced sharp riots, complicated by harvest failures, the suspension of *habeas corpus* and other civil liberties, an abortive assassination plot against George III (1795), and a rapid rise in the debt, induced by war expenditures.

By February 1797, there was a stoppage of payments in gold by the Bank of England. Famine threatened those unable to buy bread at high prices. Ireland was in revolt, and the French considered aiding the rebels to establish a republic. And as if the catalogue of woes were not long enough, the navy, the backbone of the British war effort, mutinied at Spithead.

Pitt had sent a team to Lille to negotiate terms with the French. A peace plan was hammered out, in which Pitt was willing to cede Belgium republican status under French tutelage. In return, Britain would get Ceylon, the Cape of Good Hope, and Trinidad. All parties were willing to give what belonged to others in advancing their own interests.[25]

At home, the Directory was of two minds. The peace party consisted of the royalists primarily. They would gladly end the republics of Batavia and Cisalpina as the price of restoring monarchy to France. The government had in it a good number of republicans, however; and they protested that the Batavian Republic was guaranteed by the Constitution itself—which indeed it was. As tensions between the two blocs grew throughout the summer, the republicans feared a royalist coup. The Directory therefore annulled the spring elections,[26] after bringing to Paris a large concentration of troops. Thus a preventive coup was carried out on September 4, 1797, or 18 Fructidor in the revolutionary calendar.

Fructidor was the Republic's penultimate agony. Britain at once broke off negotiations for peace. Austria read Pitt's intentions at Lille to reveal what Europeans called Britain's unreliability. Britain would sacrifice allies for the increase of its empire. Hence the Austrian emperor empowered his agents in Italy to accept what terms of peace Napoleon would give. And Paris, which had asked Napoleon's aid for its republican coup, was even less able to control the General. Bonaparte had sent one of his key subordinates[27] to buttress the reconstituted Directory. Meanwhile, at Campo Formio, on October 17, he concluded peace with Austria on his own terms. France kept the left bank of the Rhine, the Batavian Republic, and also its satellite Cisalpine Republic. The Austrians annexed Venice and most of the Venetian mainland in compensation.

Fructidor and Campo Formio were more far-reaching in their implications. Napoleon returned to Paris in December 1797 the greatest hero of the Republic. His policy of spreading republicanism in Italy had won. A general had been able to maintain a policy compatible only with an expansionist government firmly seated at home. The meaning of this for Europe began to show itself at once in 1798 in Italy. Under French patronage, revolution-

24. Which began in 1795.
25. Belgium was Austrian, not British; and the French were bartering territories that belonged to the Dutch (Ceylon, the Cape) and Spanish (Trinidad).
26. That is, the three "republicans" did so: Rewbell, Barras, and Larevellière-Lépeaux. They exiled the royalist François de Barthélemy and Lazare Carnot, the old hero, whose crime had been to try to prevent the split within the Directory.
27. General Pierre Augereau (1757–1816).

aries in the peninsula established republics at Genoa (Ligurian Republic) and in the Papal States (Roman Republic). The deposition of the pope from his temporal sovereignty was matched in the south by the abrogation of kingship in Naples, where the Neapolitan Republic[28] was set up. To the north, the French cooperated with the Swiss reformers to establish the Helvetic Republic.

Outside of Italy the consequences of Napoleon's political victory were also great. The petty German princes of the left bank of the Rhine were

28. Also named the Parthenopean Republic.

One of Napoleon's most daring military stratagems involved leading a fully equipped army of 40,000 through the Saint Bernard Pass of the Swiss Alps onto the Italian plains. There he joined other French forces and eventually triumphed over the Austrian army. The exhausted French troops emerge from the pass in this drawing by Müller. Much like modern war photographers, artists always accompanied Napoleon on his military expeditions to record the action. Musée de l'Armée.

The Expansion of France to 1799

French Republic

Dependent Republics

dispossessed by the terms of Campo Formio. The treaty promised compensation out of Church lands east of the Rhine. And in 1798 the French began to supervise the dismemberment of the influence of the Church and with it the Holy Roman Empire, at least in western Germany.

Except for Britain, which was still at war with France, Europe accepted a peace which in effect made all of Western Europe either republican or under the control of France and its satellites. With regard to Britain, France was prepared to fight. Napoleon gained the command of an army for an invasion of England. Instead, however, the general convinced the Directory to attack indirectly, through the British Empire, by a campaign to cut the lifeline to India and so dismember Britain's prosperity. After evading a fleet of British interceptors, Napoleon seized the Nile in Egypt. His manifest intention to control the Ottoman Empire alarmed both Russia and Austria, if for different reasons. The Russians had their own plans for the Turks. And the Austrians knew that any defeat of Britain in the East would clear the way toward an even stronger French thrust into Germany.

Thus Austria, Russia, and Britain announced a new alliance—the Second Coalition. English sailors led by Lord Horatio Nelson (1758–1805) defeated a French naval expedition at Aboukir. The Austrians and Russians, with

Napoleon's army cut off in Egypt, ranged westward. An army commanded by the Russian Marshal Suvorov (1729–1800) reached Switzerland and Italy, where it broke up the Cisalpine Republic.

The reverses abroad matched a decline in the Directory at home. In 1798, the more radical republicans made electoral gains, but were subjected to nullification, as the royalists had been a year earlier. The two legislative councils now feared the Directory more than even the revived Jacobin clubs. They therefore voted to reconstruct the executive, keeping only Barras from the old Directory, and putting in harness with him: Sieyès, the old partisan of the third estate; Roger Ducos, a republican of the Girondin faction; Jérôme Gohier, a minister of justice; and General Moulins. The most skilled politician was perhaps Barras. But the most active was Sieyès, who correctly attributed the Directory's weakness to the constitutional system, which since 1791 had distrusted strong executive powers.

Sieyès argued that what France needed now was a vigorous executive committed to republican ideas. The repository of strong republicanism he found in the army, the one institution with no loyalties to the Old Regime and with no leanings toward a restoration of the monarchy. The views of Sieyès were exactly those of Napoleon himself, who left his command in Egypt in mid-1799. Once in southern France, he was in contact with Sieyès and Ducos, who saw in Bonaparte the key to a coup d'état. The three conspirators planned to win power by naming a Jacobin plot. On 18 Brumaire (November 9, 1799), Sieyès and Ducos prevailed on Barras to resign. The other Directors were imprisoned. The legislative councils had been called into session beforehand, but now lacked an executive.

At this critical moment Bonaparte came to the councils, where he spoke to denounce the Jacobin "plotters" and asked for a vote of emergency powers. The army, he said, had always saved the Republic in the past. Now, it was the duty of the councils to give him power to use the army for that purpose again. Unable to meet a challenge about the evidence for the supposed Jacobin plot, Napoleon relied instead on troops under friendly command. These were called into action by another Bonaparte, Napoleon's younger brother Lucien,[29] who told the troops that Napoleon wanted only to save the Republic (and the army) from its enemies. The legislature was closed, after being driven from the hall at Saint-Cloud.

A small number of sympathetic deputies from both councils made the coup of Brumaire "official" by giving to Sieyès, Ducos, and Napoleon Bonaparte the power to govern as "temporary consuls."

Thus ended the Directory, which had in four years enjoyed stunning victories abroad and a mixed success at home. Its greatest achievement was simply to have endured for four years. Finance was a disaster after 1795, with the assignats falling to only 1 percent of their face value in 1796. New paper money based on nationalized lands—the mandats—lost 90 percent of its value within a year. The restoration of metallic currency in 1797 helped revive business. But the temporary end of war in 1797 was more basic to sound finance and debt control. This interval was incompatible with the basic expansionism favored by the republicans, however, and Napoleon therefore inherited a problem of finance which had weakened royal and republican governments alike. The most glittering achievement of the Directory was Campo Formio—the Austrian peace. This, however, was more Napoleon's work than that of Paris. And now the man on horseback had come home to manage politics directly.

29. Who had earlier been named president of the Council of Five Hundred.

NAPOLEON, FRANCE, AND EUROPE: AN OVERVIEW

The understanding we gain of the Consulate and Empire under Napoleon must derive from what we think of Bonaparte himself and how we read his intentions in 1799. If we judge from his actions in France in 1795, or, better yet, from what he did in Italy in 1796 and 1797, we may well hail him as a devout republican. After the reaction of Thermidor, he protected the Revolution from royalists, which he had refused to do some years earlier in the Vendée. In Italy, his republicanism had seemed radical, rather than merely a mask for other ambitions. The Convention and the Directory enforced social equality in the Batavian Republic and in Switzerland. In Italy, however, Napoleon's settlement had gone further. The Cisalpine Republic refused to recognize the validity of religious vows. Marriage was made into a civil ceremony. And Bonaparte set in motion free presses, so that in Milan over eighty newspapers came into being within five years of Campo Formio.

Was Napoleon republican by heritage? He was the son of an impoverished Corsican noble. Yet he was by birth French, for Corsica had been ceded to France (by Genoa) one year before Bonaparte's arrival in the world. His youth was spent in French military schools on state scholarships. The young would-be soldier excelled in history and geography and early showed a passion for tactics. At sixteen he won a lieutenancy in the artillery, where he found that the nobility of 1785 regarded him as a "foreigner." Discouraged about promotion, he welcomed the events of 1789 wholeheartedly in Corsica, where he had returned and joined the patriots working for Corsican independence under Pasquale Paoli.

Bonaparte fell out with Paoli, an event which led to the exile of the whole Bonaparte family. Providence, Napoleon later said, had flung him back toward France, where his "destiny" waited. He became a Jacobin, a follower of Robespierre out of favor after his idol's fall. Despite his service at Toulon, he was arrested as a Terrorist and stripped of his rank. Then, Providence again pointed the way up. The service of 1795 brought him a new general's commission[30] and the political education available to the leader of the Army of the Interior. The year 1796 saw him married to Josephine de Beauharnais (1763–1814), the seductive widow of a guillotined military aristocrat. Napoleon adopted her children, in return for which he could expect only love. Josephine had no wealth. Indeed, her situation is hard to reconcile with any image of Napoleon painted in the tones of fortune hunting. At least in marriage he was no mere adventurer in 1796.

He married two days *after* his appointment to command the Italian invasion. He was then what he must have been only a few months later, when Count François Miot de Melioto (1762–1841) met him in Italy; in the Count's words, he was a man

below the middle height and of an extremely sparse figure. His powdered hair . . . reached down to his shoulders. He was dressed in a straight coat, buttoned up to his chin . . . and he wore a tricolored feather in his hat. At first . . . he did not strike me as handsome, but his strongly-marked features, his quick and piercing eyes, his brusque and animated gestures revealed an ardent spirit, while his wide and thoughtful brow was that of a profound thinker. He made me sit near him and we talked of Italy. He spoke in short sentences and, at that time of his life, very incorrectly.[31]

30. He had been made a general in 1793, after his service at Toulon.
31. Melioto's description is in *The Norton History of Modern Europe,* gen. ed. Felix Gilbert (New York: W. W. Norton & Co., 1971), p. 825.

Next to David, Baron Gros was the greatest interpreter of the Napoleonic legend. In his famous battle pictures and portraits of the Bonaparte family he strove to authenticate their imperial pretensions by endowing the Emperor with superhuman qualities. Shown here is one of the several flattering portraits which he painted of the empress Josephine. Napoleon deeply loved this beautiful widow whom he married while still a young general in 1796, but eventually he divorced her when she was unable to produce an heir to the throne. He subsequently married Princess Marie-Louise of Austria, while Josephine retired to Malmaison, her château outside Paris. Musée National de Malmaison.

Throughout his career, Napoleon used artists to glorify his achievements. No one was better equipped to serve him than the former revolutionary Jacques Louis David, whose imagination was fired by the military daring of the young General Bonaparte. This unfinished portrait of 1797–98 shows Napoleon as the energetic genius of the battlefields, and was a sketch for a larger, though never executed work where David intended to show Napoleon looking at the Alps from the Rivoli plateau. During the Empire David assumed the powers of a virtual artistic dictator. He continued his outspoken support for the Emperor even after his fall, and was eventually forced into exile in Brussels. Louvre.

What Melioto captured in words the revolutionary painter David (1748–1825) captured in the great unfinished portrait of Napoleon, *The Consul.* The overall impression is of strong energy, even passion, near the surface, yet under control.

Contemporaries agreed that Bonaparte had the attributes seen by Melioto and David. They also agreed that the qualities seen in him immediately after Brumaire by Jean Chapal (1756–1832)[32] were the keys to his success: clarity of vision; forcefulness in argument; the ability to grasp detail precisely, without sacrificing broad views; sagacity beyond his years despite his small experience of administration; and above all, incredible stamina. These were the basic elements of his command of men and situations. In military affairs, the successes others attributed to insight and genius, Napoleon himself chalked up to exact planning and the mastery of detail. He was a careful student of history's greatest commanders,[33] and, like them, he believed in himself—his destiny. But he said that "chance" could not bring victory, only "system" could do that.

Another side of the questions which cling to Napoleon concerns the principles and attitudes he held. Historians have hailed him as the last of the enlightened despots. For some he crowned the Revolution by his domestic reforms, even though these were brought about after he himself had dissolved the Republic. Others have seen in Napoleon a continuator of changes begun under the constitutional monarchy, whose program he revived. Still others have said Napoleon was a man of no principles or ideas, simply an egotist who used people and institutions to satisfy his threefold mania for power, rationalization, and controlled systems—a sort of superior compulsive personality with a gift for leadership.

What an examination of Bonaparte in power from 1799 to 1814 indicates is another matter. Viewed from this perspective, he seems a mixture of Enlightenment beliefs and revolutionary action. He loved Voltaire, and reforms he made in Italy derived from the rational approach to religion he found in the *philosophes.* Like most of the *philosophes,* Napoleon disliked Rousseau, for whom he had had great regard until he took his lieutenancy at the age of sixteen. Indeed, Napoleon seemed to distrust emotion and professed openly his belief in reason and science. He extended his regard for science to government, which he said ought to be reduced to a single set of ideas and principles throughout the West, from the Atlantic to the Urals.

Napoleon constantly wrote and preached about the common goals all men must share and, in this context, criticized liberals who wished to see only that harmony of "interests" which would reconcile the profits of merchants with the conditions of labor in a society. Bonaparte was impatient with the traditions of the Old Regime and avid to abolish servitude. This was chiefly because he seems never to have abandoned Robespierre's idea that in a good state no hierarchies should come between a leader and the people.

Yet the First Consul—and later the Emperor—was not entirely out of sympathy with the idea of "interest" as determining in politics. The crucial thing was that interest did not mean for him what it meant to the statesmen in the countries making alliances against France. Napoleon was in this regard truly a child of the Revolution: the interests he wished to harmonize were those defined in France by the Revolution itself. He made policies for France which kept much of the substance of the social and economic

32. A close friend and loyal minister of the interior, Chapal described Napoleon as first consul in 1799.
33. Especially Alexander, Caesar, and Charlemagne.

reforms achieved from 1789 to 1799, while keeping at least the *forms* of electoral process and representative government. And where French armies reached in Europe, the same forms and substance followed.

This assertion seems to us the key to understanding the impact of Napoleon on France and on the European West as a whole. His passion for uniformity of institutions informed the empire he built. The French Empire was above all else a cosmopolitan state system in which the supreme interest was France—the France of the Enlightenment and the Revolution. The rest of Europe had to identify itself with what Napoleon thought was the essence of France.

In this forced act of identification, which reproduced on a large scale the identification Napoleon had been forced to make with France after his expulsion from Corsica by Paoli's adherents, the key to Napoleon's unlovely side lies.

The Empire was the natural culmination of Napoleon's respect for birth and his real regard for equality of opportunity. An upstart soldier in a revolutionary army, he was an early convert to centralized authority and the disciplinary value of violence. A small man, Bonaparte was a lover of force; and the lure of despotic power finally won the struggle for his soul. But this was no new thing in 1804, when he proclaimed himself emperor. In 1794 Bonaparte had been a supporter of Robespierre and Saint-Just and their dictatorship and Terror. That, too, after all, was part of the Revolution, as was the desire to compel men toward *virtue*. And the combination of authoritarianism, respect for reason, efficiency, and brute force characterized Napoleon's government of France.

FIRST CONSUL AND EMPEROR: NAPOLEONIC FRANCE

On the day after their coup d'état, the three provisional consuls took an oath to suppress civil war, negotiate a lasting peace in Europe, set finances in order, and reconstitute France. Reconstitution was to be effected by codifying law, after first adopting a new instrument of government drafted by Sieyès and approved by Napoleon.

The Constitution of the Year VIII established the Consulate (1799–1804). It also made Napoleon the first strong executive with "constitutional" powers since Louis XIV, as Robespierre and his friends had ruled without ever putting into force the democratic constitution of 1793. Sieyès had retired from office as provisional consul, along with Ducos. Under the new regime Napoleon was first consul, and he ruled with two others he had picked.[34] Nominally, the consuls had been elected for ten-year terms by the Senate, the eighty-man upper chamber of the three-house legislature. This Senate was not elected, however. It had been nominated by Sieyès and Ducos—in effect by Sieyès, with Napoleon's approval. Chosen for life terms, the two-thirds selected by Sieyès and Napoleon were then empowered to fill up the Senate itself. This they were to do from lists supplied by Napoleon and the members of the other two houses of the national legislature, the Tribunate and the Legislative Body.[35]

In practice this arrangement gave Napoleon and Sieyès a subservient Senate, since it, like the Tribunate and Legislative Body, had been nominated by Sieyès. The Constitution provided for elections by universal male suffrage for legislatures after the first one. But this, too, was a democratic form only. Actually, the electors chose "notables," from whom the

34. Jean Jacques Régis de Cambacérès (1753–1824) and Charles François Lebrun (1739–1824); both were essentially passive.
35. Which had 100 and 300 members, respectively.

Talleyrand's mercurial personality is strikingly captured in this portrait drawing. Always an opportunist, he moved with consummate adroitness through the political upheavals of his time. He recognized Napoleon's potential greatness from the very first and helped engineer his rise to power. Awarded the post of foreign minister for his efforts, Talleyrand soon grew weary of the Emperor's campaigns and longed for a European peace. When the end of the Empire was apparent, he did not hesitate to promote the Bourbon Restoration and vigorously defended French rights at the Congress of Vienna. For these services he was richly compensated with honors and a large pension by Louis XVIII. Cabinet des Dessins; Louvre.

senators (who all now had life terms) named the new members of the other two houses. The importance of this complex masquerade rested in the relationship between the executive and the legislature. Under the Constitution, only the consuls could initiate legislation. They did this by submitting proposals to the Tribunate, which, after debate, sent everything to the Legislative Body for passage. The Senate acted as a court to pronounce on the constitutionality of acts. The national legislature was therefore composed of one house which debated but did not legislate, another which legislated without debating, and a Senate picked by the executive which charged it to pass on the legality of measures wholly initiated by the consuls.

The Consulate was thus by no means a dictatorship. But it was not a democratic government responsible to electors with meaningful controls over either the executive or the legislature. The Consulate was a strong executive government, made stronger yet by another power. This was the consuls' right to name ministers. The consuls themselves were given control over raising money and making all expenditures, while the ministers in turn were in charge of departmental funds. Ministers were accountable to the lower houses, but since these had been picked by a Senate itself nominated with Napoleon's approval, this accountability was little more than a screen for executive control. Finally, the first consul appointed the Council of State to advise on policy and lawmaking.

Having approved this arrangement by an ostensibly democratic method—a plebiscite that brought in a majority of 3,011,007 to 1,562—France surrendered itself to the First Consul's care. In attempting to solve the pressing problems of government in France after 1799, Napoleon had to work with the two traditions he took over from the Revolution. On the one hand, there was the bourgeois republicanism of values represented by Sieyès. And, on the other hand, given the fact of the continued wars (which grew out of the clash between the First Consul's own annexationist ideas and the rest of Europe's resistance to *any* French hegemony, republican or royalist), there were the sentiments of the organizers of victory who saw the need for a powerful executive. This need was also nourished by the social conservatives, who saw in a strong executive the only means toward the social stability they desired.

The more radical republicans tried to establish priorities, which for the most part concerned codifying revolutionary gains in legislation. The pro-war party resisted conservative pressures for peace, which was essential for those who wanted to consolidate national finances and put down the last remnants of popular agitation. Napoleon belonged to no party or group, however, and he showed himself determined to pursue a combination of policies across the lines of the various factions.

Toward these mixed ends he relied on men and legislation. He put into high office able persons, regardless of their political past. Perhaps the most remarkable example of this Napoleonic opportunism was his placement of Charles Maurice de Talleyrand (1754–1838) as foreign minister. Talleyrand, the son of a nobleman, had been bishop of Autun and also the main Agent of the Clergy in charge of Church finance. He had sided with the third estate in 1789; supported the Civil Constitution of the Clergy in 1791, for which he was condemned by Rome; and sought refuge in America in 1793, after the execution of Louis XVI. Only after the end of the Terror and the Directory's establishment did he return to France, where he became foreign minister in 1797, a post he resigned to help the coup-masters of Brumaire.

No less remarkable were others whose careers we cannot sketch in so much detail: Fouché, the police minister, had been an Hébertist and extreme Terrorist in 1793.[36] The war minister was Marshal Berthier (1753–1815), a successful general. Others in the top offices were Abrial as minister of justice, Forfait in charge of colonies, Gaudin as finance minister, and young Lucien Bonaparte as minister of the interior.

These men helped push through the first reform measures of the Consulate. Late in 1799 and early in 1800 there were laws reversing the harsh antiroyalist measures of earlier years. Napoleon needed amnesty to pacify the Vendée. He also needed a reform of local government, to insure some measure of central control. The Local Administration Act of 1800 took over the *département* system geographically, but dispensed with complicated forms of elected local government. The new local agents were centrally appointed bureaucrats, and even the local councils of assistants were named in Paris. This arrangement of prefects (*département* heads), subprefects (district chiefs), and mayors of communes survives today, embodying still Napoleon's rejection of federalism and his preference for centralized bureaucracy over the revolutionary system of provincial decentralization. Few measures are as clear as Napoleon's reform of local government in showing how he worked along the lines of enlightened despotism.

Another illustration of the centralizing tendency was Gaudin's work in finance. The Directory had issued new paper money and had also struck a blow at government credit by repudiating two-thirds of the debt. Gaudin embodied Napoleon's wish to centralize finance and restore solvency. In 1800 he chartered the Bank of France, to provide credit, stabilize currency, and help pay bondholders, thus bringing France abreast of the practice already more than 100 years old in Britain and Holland. The tax base of government was also radically centralized and transformed—a thing monarchy had failed to do and the Revolution had not attempted. In place of municipal elites making tax rolls, Napoleon instituted a new system. A general director in Paris appointed bureaucrats (deputy directors) in *départements.* They had assistants at the next levels,[37] and these agents helped to levy taxes on all wealth, eliminate evasion, increase receipts, and assure harsh justice against the corrupt.

The other great measure of the year 1800 was the beginning of the committee work which in 1804 produced the Civil Code. It marked emphatically the return to conservative social values, by stressing ties of family, while also embodying four revolutionary achievements. The Code insured civil equality; it provided free choice of profession and labor; it made clear the supremacy of the lay-oriented state over the clergy; and it also guaranteed liberty of conscience. It gave very little more than civil liberty to the proletariat, however. Despite the moderate character of these provisions, there was opposition to putting the Code into operation in 1800, even though it was widely known how close to Napoleon's heart the matter was. The First Consul had presided over about half of the drafting sessions.

Opposition to Napoleon in 1800 and 1801 took other forms. There was a bomb plot against his life on Christmas Eve in 1800, which was the work of royalists. But Napoleon blamed it on "radicals," especially the Jacobins, and used it as a pretext to purge and deport over 100 republicans, many of whom were critical of the Code for its conservatism and also were against Napoleon's negotiations to end papal opposition to the ecclesiastical policies of the Revolution. The more annexationist republicans had also disliked Napoleon's foreign policy. The First Consul had severely defeated

---

36. Joseph Fouché (1759–1820) had been a representative on mission at Lyons, dismissed for excessive brutality.
37. Inspectors and assessors.

the Austrians in Italy in June 1800, crossing the Alps in person to triumph at Marengo. While republicans pressed for new extensions of revolution, Napoleon signed at Lunéville a peace confirming the Campo Formio treaty of 1797. In 1802 he extended its terms to Britain,[38] thus ending the war of the Second Coalition.

He had thus redeemed five promises given on the day of the coup.[39] This accomplishment he made the lever for lifting himself to a position above even the remaining opposition. Alleging plots and the need to carry on unfinished business, especially the reform of law, education, and commerce, the First Consul secured the alteration of the Constitution. A new "organic ordinance"[40] of the year X extended to life Napoleon's term as first consul, only a short while after Napoleon had ended the split with Rome, by signing in 1801 a *concordat,* or agreement, with the Vatican.

This concordat was vital to the centralization of control Napoleon wanted. Before 1801 the French Church was in turmoil because some fifty *émigré* bishops were said by the papacy to be the true governors of that Church. Napoleon wanted to have men of his own choosing governing the French Church. Hence he was willing to end the struggle by compromise. In return for placing the existing clergy under the disciplinary control of the Holy See in religious matters, a measure against which Jacobins agitated, and also in return for allowing Catholic seminaries and public religious processions again, as well as the pope's right to depose bishops,[41] Napoleon got more than he gave. While the concordat declared the fact that a majority of Frenchmen *were* Catholic, toleration gained papal consent. The republican principle of religious freedom was recognized, since Napoleon now put Protestant ministers as well as Catholic priests on the equal footing of state-salaried officials. The Vatican conceded that tithes and Church lands could not be restored to clerical hands, which protected the new holders. Avignon was made wholly a French territory.

The net effect was to pull the teeth of radical claims, especially that Napoleon had "reestablished" Catholicism. Protestantism was no more firmly "established" than it had ever been under Henry IV's Edict of Nantes (1598); and Louis XIV's return to persecution of religious dissent, by his revocation of the edict, was obliterated. Politically, those who had profited from the confiscation of Church property were now secure in possession, even at Rome. Moreover, conservatives could no longer say that Napoleon was an infidel, at a point in time when Catholic ideas were gaining ground in France again.

Armed with new powers and at peace with his former enemies, secular and ecclesiastical, Napoleon turned again to domestic matters during the "peace" of 1803–1804. Before turning to the further development of policy at home, however, we must notice an event in the year XII, 1804.

The popular pledge of gratitude given the First Consul in 1802 by plebiscite no longer satisfied in Napoleon what had become a monarchical appetite. In order to prepare the people for a frank assumption of a crown, Napoleon used agents abroad to "provoke" a coup. They convinced royalists in British pay that they were sympathetic to a restoration of the

38. In the Peace of Amiens.
39. Promises to bring about peace, establish a new constitution, bring civil war to an end, stabilize finance, and reform the law.
40. Again passed by plebiscite, with a huge majority: 3,568,885 to 8,374.
41. This had the formal meaning of ending the "Gallican" liberty of the prerevolutionary Church, by which medieval monarchs had won control over the bishops. Napoleon also recognized the Papal States, but did not return lands by then incorporated into the Cisalpine Republic.

Bourbon line. In France itself a prominent civilian politician, Georges Cadoudal (1771–1804), was implicated. More shocking was the revelation that two Napoleonic commanders were also involved.[42] Certain evidence seemed to point to the duke of Enghien (1772–1804), a prince of the house of Condé living in Baden,[43] as the conspiratorial "heir." French troops violated Baden's neutrality to seize Enghien. Brought to trial in Paris, he was executed, even though Napoleon knew the charges were false.

The upshot was a proposal by the Senate to proclaim Napoleon emperor and also to make the title hereditary in the Bonaparte family. The justification was to protect the Republic against false claimants. Probably Napoleon grasped how the new title would satisfy the growing taste for a stable social order in which new dignities might emerge. A plebiscite again confirmed the proposal, and Napoleon took part in a crowning on December 2, 1804. Like Charlemagne, the new emperor put the crown on his own head; and, again like Charlemagne, he had as witness a pope.[44] The gesture by Rome undercut the Bourbon pretenders by making the Bonaparte line "legitimate" in the Church's eyes. Finally, the Constitution was altered. The legislature remained in being, but its powers passed into the emperor's hands. Napoleon issued laws as decrees with senatorial approval,[45] while retaining power to amend all laws himself.

The results of this legislative monopoly appeared in a string of new reforms, some of which completed initiatives begun earlier. In education, for example, as early as 1791 the principle of free public schools had been established, both at primary and secondary levels. Little was ever done on the elementary level,[46] despite some successes in starting a secondary school system in the *départements* and in Paris.[47] In 1802, Napoleon had abolished this secondary system, substituting for it a series of *lycées* under direct government patronage and supervision, which meant in fact curriculum design, teacher appointments, and patriotic, military rules and uniforms. These *lycées* were supplemented in 1808 by a decree establishing a centralized *université,* which meant a system of schools culminating in what we should call universities. Thus Napoleon took control of training for citizenship in the new Empire, where, he said, the status of a man should be achieved by merit, not ascribed to him by birth.

On another front Napoleon now had the power to move unobstructed toward consolidating the gains of the liberal revolution. With the Council of State acting as a body of ministerial experts, the Emperor revived his favorite reform—the *code* of laws. The new "father" of the French people put into effect the Civil Code, strengthening the power of fathers over wives and children.[48] And he added to its guarantees of civil liberty other codes which completely rationalized the tangle of law. The codification embraced the Civil Code of 1804, known as Code Napoléon, and three other parts: Civil Procedure (1806), Commercial Law (1807), Criminal Procedure and Penal Law (1810).

In general, the codification was authoritarian and completed the centralization of French government. While keeping in being the revolutionary

Although enormous in size, the Crowning of Napoleon *is remarkable for its brilliantly detailed likenesses of the Emperor, his court, and family. Establishing the legitimacy of his regime was a major problem for Napoleon, and this elaborate ceremony, in the presence of the powerless Pope Pius VII seated at the Emperor's left, was an effective propaganda measure. At the actual coronation Napoleon placed the crown on his own head, but the event has been modified by David and the Emperor crowns the empress Josephine instead. From the balcony at the center of the work the Emperor's mother, Madame Mère, watches Napoleon and her other children who stand at left. Louvre.*

42. The famed generals Charles Pichegru (1761–1804) and Jean Victor Moreau (1763–1813); Pichegru was executed, but Moreau was allowed to go into exile in America.
43. A German state.
44. Pius VII came to Paris to bless the event.
45. In imitation of Roman practice these were called *Senatum consulta.*
46. In 1813 only 12.5 percent of all students attended state-supported elementary schools.
47. Eighty-eight schools were established in all: five in Paris, and one in each *département.*
48. Divorce, for example, was allowed by mutual consent, but hedged about with restrictions protecting the family as a unit.

"equality" already summarized, the new set of laws was strict in spirit. Penalties were prescribed for political offenses in a way which some said was that of the Old Regime. More important, as a matter of procedure the revolutionary laws had presumed innocence, until guilt was proved. Napoleon's revisions reversed this assumption, and the presumed guilt of defendants weighed the whole trial procedure in favor of the state.

This subordination of the individual to the state offended the heirs of the *philosophes.* Yet it cannot negate the supreme achievement of Napoleon's domestic policy. The Code was brief, clear, and a rationalized mixture of Roman procedure, French custom, and revolutionary concepts. The Code complemented the educational system, by helping to assure that status was achieved, not ascribed. It embodied the bourgeois order of opportunity, private property, and equality before the law. And the Code was exported to Louisiana and the satellite republics in Europe.[49] It, more than anything else, showed the nature of Napoleon's policy in marrying the Revolution to the Empire—an alliance he boasted about in making coins after 1804. New issues bore the legend *République Française* on one side and *Napoléon Empereur* on the other!

Yet some argued that Napoleon's Empire at home was antirepublican. The press and the theater were heavily censored to insure that ideas detrimental to official policy would receive little public exposure. Fouché organized a very repressive police force, making wide use of provocateurs[50]

49. As well as to the later French colonies in the imperialism of the period 1870–1914.
50. Agents used to provoke illegal acts and thus to trap "criminals."

and surveillance of the lives of citizens beyond reproach. Arbitrary detention was reintroduced, and state prisons bulged with political prisoners. Elitism was reborn in 1804, as Napoleon re-created certain "orders" to recognize the exploits of his generals and relatives. The marshals of France[51] acquired more than medals: large estates were given to them on conquered soil—some called them fiefs. And Napoleon's brothers became kings. The Emperor argued that this did not violate republican ideas, for the new status had been achieved, not ascribed. The new princes, like Joachim Murat (1767–1815), who had married Caroline Bonaparte and became king of Naples in 1808, were often of peasant or petty bourgeois origins, true. Yet they became princes and rulers of Europe.

NAPOLEON AND EUROPE

Like Napoleon himself, the new nobles of France and Europe had risen on the tide of republican victories. It was therefore of great interest in the European chancelleries that Napoleon took advantage of the "peace" of 1803–1804 to change his title, putting down the consular rank and taking up the crown of empire. The last emperor of the French to crown himself—Charlemagne in 800 A.D.—had pushed Frankish armies deep into the heartland of central Europe.

Europeans did not have to wait long to know whether Napoleon's settlement of the Revolution at home might signal a new intensification of revolution beyond the boundaries of France. Seizing on every pretext of threats to the already established satellite system, from 1805 until 1812 Napoleon extended *la grande nation française* to the gates of Moscow.

Our main concern in considering Napoleon and his impact on the European state system is not with the details of his campaigns, however. The main victories and their victims we will state rather baldly, in order to pass to the central issues of Napoleonic warfare: the effect of the victories on the structure of European politics; the organization of the new French empire; and the so-called Continental System, by which Napoleon tried to break Britain, the stubborn enemy.

During the peace years, Napoleon gave evidence that he was not content to have defeated Austria and forced British recognition of his achievements. He intervened in the Caribbean and threatened to make a bid to use Louisiana[52] to challenge the British regime in Canada.[53] Napoleon had also revised the satellite system, making himself president of the new Italian Republic.[54] He had assumed control of the Swiss states, as "mediator" of the Confederation of Switzerland. The consolidation of the left bank of the Rhine was also pushed by Talleyrand. He used the duchy of Württemberg as the nucleus of a cell of French dependents which by 1810 had made a vast state centered on Stuttgart. The main object was to disrupt the majority of the small Catholic states so as to dissolve the prospect of any future Catholic electoral triumph in the Holy Roman Empire. Napoleonic policy was by 1803 so successful that the major Protestant states were all enlarged, thus forcing on Habsburg Austria increasingly unfavorable balances of power vis-à-vis Prussia and the other kingdoms.

Two immediate consequences of these French initiatives appeared. The British began to woo the Austrians and Russians into the Third Coalition. And the Austrians declared an Austrian Empire, recognizing *de facto* in 1804 the dissolution of the Holy Roman Empire which Napoleon pro-

51. Davout (1770–1823), Masséna (1758–1817), Ney (1769–1815), and others.
52. Ceded by Spain to France in 1800.
53. Lost by France at Paris in 1763.
54. Based on the Cisalpine Republic.

Trafalgar was a bittersweet victory for the British, since it cost the life of one of their greatest naval heroes, Lord Nelson. J. M. W. Turner's poignant vision of the event shows Nelson dying in the arms of his men under the mast at center. Around them the battle continues in full heat, brilliantly depicted with the confusion of billowing sails and swirls of cannon smoke. The viewer is not allowed to objectively survey the goings-on from a distance, but rather is thrown in the center of the action. The captured French flag at Nelson's feet indicates that the tide of battle has turned in favor of the British. The Tate Gallery, London.

claimed *de jure* in 1806. The addition to the Coalition of the czar Alexander I (1801–1825) gave it new luster. The Russian ruler had a liberal reputation, and he had plans to restore constitutional monarchy in Poland. Moreover, he cast himself in the role of a humanitarian champion of peace and reform, in opposition to the French threat to German liberty. Despite their skepticism, many Europeans, who saw in Alexander the reincarnation of Russian expansion westward earlier practiced by Peter the Great, embraced the new ally: any stick to beat a dog.

The allies agreed on certain roughly sketched war aims: to end French dominance in Italy and Germany, to make a Belgian-Dutch buffer against France in an independent Netherlands, to allow Prussia to expand westward to the Rhine as a check on French movement eastward, to grant England territories overseas as compensation for its efforts against Napoleon, to stabilize Poland under Russian supervision, to divide the Ottoman Empire to Russia's advantage in the Balkans and Britain's in the Mediterranean. Britain was less enthusiastic about "freedom of the seas," which Alexander advocated. But a treaty was signed providing British money for Russian soldiers, in recognition of what both major parties had in abundance.[55]

The results were disastrous. In the fall of 1805 Lord Nelson decisively beat the French naval forces off Cape Trafalgar on the Spanish coast. This great victory established beyond question the supremacy at sea which Britain enjoyed until 1914. But it cost Nelson's life. What was disastrous was not this, however, but the land war. Napoleon crushed the Austrians at Ulm and then did the same at Austerlitz to the combined Russian-Austrian armies. The Prussians had kept out of the Third Coalition in 1805, chiefly because Napoleon had bribed them with the bait of acquiring Hanover from Britain. Instead, the French now made kingdoms of Bavaria and Württemberg, as dependents in a Confederation of the Rhine. Prussia now entered the war alone, since Russia had pulled its forces back into Poland, and Austria had signed a separate peace, granting Venice to France.[56] Late in 1806, Napoleon caved in the Prussian armies at Jena and Auerstädt. And in 1807, Napoleon audaciously pursued the Prussians eastward to get at Alexander's Russian forces in Poland. These he beat in detail at Friedland in June.

The Treaty of Tilsit[57] signed by Alexander and Napoleon was agreed to by Prussia. The basic terms of this peace left England alone, since Alexander became Napoleon's ally. The French were to have a free hand in Western Europe, including Germany, in exchange for their support of a scheme to establish Russian hegemony over Turkey, Persia, Afghanistan, and even India—when Britain's empire was seized. Napoleon occupied Berlin and took all of Prussia's western lands to strengthen Westphalia, another satellite kingdom in the Confederation of the Rhine.

Even before Tilsit, Napoleon had decided on a strategy to defeat Britain. Since he could not defeat its navy at sea, he would reduce Britain's commercial economy to ruin. Since 1806, the French had been in effective control of the Continent. At Berlin Napoleon had issued the Berlin Decree (1806), which announced the closing of European ports to British goods and shipping. This was part of the Continental System, whereby Napoleon thought he could defeat a nation of shopkeepers by inducing a depression in British trade. With Britain unable to sell its wares in Europe, unemployment

55. Britain paid £1,250,000 for every 100,000 Russian men.
56. Which Napoleon needed; the Venetian shipyards rebuilt his fleet after Trafalgar.
57. Actually signed on a barge in the Niemen River, near the border between Russia and Prussia.

Francesco Goya saw the Napoleonic military campaigns in a radically different light from those artists who glorified the battles. Traveling throughout his native Spain during the Peninsular War, Goya sketched the atrocities of both sides and later made a series of powerful etchings, The Disasters of War. In "Was it for this you were born?" Spaniards brutally mutilate the bodies of slain French soldiers in the presence of passive observers. Goya was the first of many great artists who have used their talent as a weapon of protest against the cruel stupidities of modern warfare, though none since have surpassed him in eloquence. New York Public Library, Prints Division, Astor, Lenox and Tilden Foundation.

and bank failures would ruin the British economy, bankrupt the government dependent on customs or taxes on trade, and so cripple the will to resist. At Tilsit Russia and Prussia adhered to the decree and, along with Austria, declared war on Britain. To prevent Danish adherence, a British fleet bombarded Copenhagen, thus provoking the result Britain had hoped to avoid. Only Portugal and Sweden refused to adhere to the decree but they were invaded and subdued.

Early in 1808, therefore, only Spain stood outside the system. And this defect Napoleon remedied by diplomacy and force. The Bourbon king Charles IV abdicated under pressure. Napoleon made his brother Joseph king of Spain, with a huge army at his back. In September 1808, Napoleon was apparently in control of the West, emperor of an empire never before equaled in Western history insofar as Europe was concerned. Joseph Bonaparte ruled Spain. Louis Bonaparte was king of Holland. Jerome Bonaparte was king of Westphalia. Caroline Bonaparte ruled Naples, in consort with Murat. Napoleon himself was king of Italy.

Yet there were cracks in the facade. Spanish partisans offended by French anti-Catholic atrocities began a guerrilla action. The British aided them, by sending an army to the "Peninsular War," under the command of Arthur Wellesley (1769–1852), later the first duke of Wellington, a tough Irish soldier seasoned in India since 1796 and with battle experience against the French in the Netherlands in 1794–1795. He had also defeated Danish forces in the 1807 campaigns to force Denmark into opposing Napoleon. We shall soon have more to say about this Irish commander of British troops sent to oppose French soldiers commanded by a Corsican.

Now, we must focus on Napoleon's reaction to this spark of resistance.[58] The Emperor called a conference in September 1808 at Erfurt in Saxony, where he tried to coax Alexander to join in an attack on Austria. The Czar was disinclined to do so, both because Napoleon had meddled in Polish

58. In 1808 Wellington repeatedly defeated the French armies, until Napoleon took personal command late in the summer.

affairs[59] and because Talleyrand had urged secret refusal. Russian aid against Austria would offset the problem in Spain, and Napoleon's former foreign minister, Talleyrand, now betrayed the Emperor, perhaps because he felt France overextended, perhaps because his own traditional loyalties were to a balance of power in Europe, not a monopoly.

Thus stiffened, Russia refused to cooperate. An anti-Napoleonic sentiment gripped Germany. France now wore the mask of tyranny, rather than liberation. Austria began a "war of liberation" in the spring of 1809. Alexander remained neutral, as did the German princes, who stood to profit from a new defeat of the Habsburgs, even if the German popular mood was anti-French and so somewhat alienated from princely policy. Napoleon swiftly defeated Austria, taking from it Polish territory acquired in the various partitions and also some Balkan lands. These he used to strengthen the flanks of the French imperium along its borders with the eastern empires.[60]

Perhaps some already suspected, from the outcome of the Austrian war of 1809, that sooner or later France must deal with Russia. For the moment, however, Napoleon at forty years of age was the master of Europe. In Austria defeat had brought to power a new minister, Klemens von Metternich (1773–1859), a Rhineland prince in exile from lands annexed to France. In Austrian service, this aristocrat saw the Habsburg interest to be a policy of cooperation with Napoleon, with whom he had had a good relationship as ambassador in Paris. Such a policy bought time, and Metternich viewed this as wise in the light of the fact that Napoleon had no heir. Considering Russia, the neighbor of Austria on the Danube, to be the long-range threat to his adopted homeland, Metternich proposed to Napoleon a new marriage alliance. And in 1810 Napoleon divorced the childless Empress Josephine[61] to marry Marie Louise, a niece of Louis XVI's queen, and the daughter of the Habsburg emperor Francis II. She quickly produced a son, styled King of Rome in the tradition of Holy Roman emperors. The Revolution had become absurd when the French were ruled by a man who was by marriage the nephew of Louis XVI!

Yet even this anomaly did not keep Napoleon, who was in 1811 at the zenith of his power, from spreading revolutionary ideas and institutions. All Europe was composed of either France and its satellites or France and its allies, Britain alone excepted. The Continental System had required annexation of the major ports from Rome to Lübeck, after the armies had done their work of conquest. The French Empire was therefore a crazy quilt of directly ruled states, republics, puppet provinces, and confederations. Regardless of the constitutional forms prevailing, the empire was run on the model of French *départements,* either by native satellites or imperial-family rulers.[62]

Constitutions were made embodying the idea of civil equality. This Napoleon did in the firm belief that his conquest was meant to give to the Germans and Spanish and Italians the liberal system of the Enlightenment, from which they had been kept by despots and arbitrary rulers. In practical terms, this meant abolishing feudalism, legally privileged classes, estates, manorial jurisdiction over peasants, along with tithes, fees, and fines.

59. Setting up the Grand Duchy of Warsaw, despite the Tilsit recognition of Russian influence in Eastern Europe.
60. In the Grand Duchy of Warsaw and the newly created Illyrian Provinces along the coast of Dalmatia.
61. Childless with Napoleon, that is. One of the Beauharnais sons, Eugene, had been made viceroy in Italy.
62. Never in Poland or Spain, for reasons of diplomacy and resistance, very effectively. But elsewhere the system described was operative.

The peasants paid for their new liberty by supplying compensatory sums to the landlord class, everywhere but in those territories directly incorporated into France.[63] And in Eastern Europe Napoleon made certain compromises, as in Poland for example, where the now freed serfs did not get enough land to set up as free farmers. Therefore, despite letters Napoleon sent to his puppets and brothers, urging them to govern "constitutionally," he expected them to gain the support of the politically valid classes.[64]

He also expected the Europeans to pay the cost of their own conquest and the continuing struggle to bring Britain to heel. Along with the abolition of established churches, and religious toleration as a policy newly established, Napoleon imposed a modern, uniform tax system. Land was the base for assessment, and collection was made directly by the imperial government. Along with guild restrictions, which were eliminated, town oligarchies and the class of tax farmers were dispossessed. Free trade within the empire was also a carrot given to offset the stick of the forbidden trade with Britain. For Napoleon's imposition of liberty, reason, equality, even the standard weights and measures of the metric system, was the means toward the political end of complete mastery. Europe paid tribute to France.

This is not to challenge the Emperor's sincere addiction to the values of the bourgeois revolution. He was modernizing the West by force; and he believed that the "progressive" people would welcome his reforms. Pro-Napoleonic movements blossomed, even in Prussia, as the new model state brought the dreams of the *philosophes* out of studies and into the council chambers of Europe. But all would be in vain if Paris could not put down Wellington in Spain, settle affairs with Russia, and make the Continental System work against Britain. Napoleon's remodeling of the structure of European politics and society could not settle, unless an end of the tribute system came and relieved growing doubts about "liberation." And that settlement London would fight to the death.

Facing the prospect of an endless war with Britain, Napoleon again decided to win it on the land. He would subdue Russia and threaten Britain's economy yet more seriously, by commanding the passages to India through Afghanistan and Persia. With the East won, the West must follow.

BIBLIOGRAPHY

BRUUN, GEOFFREY. *Europe and the French Imperium.** New York: Harper & Row, Publishers, 1957. A good survey of the Napoleonic hegemony.
CONNELLY, OWEN. *Napoleon's Satellite Kingdoms.* New York: Free Press, 1965. The best introduction to the organization of the French Empire as a series of satellites.
HECKSCHER, ELI. *The Continental System.* Gloucester, Mass.: Peter Smith, 1964. A reprint of the classic work on Napoleon's "mercantilist" system of warfare.
LEFEBVRE, GEORGES. *Napoleon.* 2 vols. New York: Columbia University Press, 1969. Completes the vast work on the period 1789–1815.
————. *The Thermidorians and the Directory.* New York: Random House, 1964. Continues LeFebvre's classic for the period 1795–1799.
PALMER, R. R. *The Age of the Democratic Revolution.* 2 vols. Princeton: Princeton University Press, 1959–1964. An attempt to relate the American Revolution to the European upheaval in a grand synthesis of the collapse of the Old Regime in the West.

Asterisk indicates a paperbound edition.

63. That is, Belgium and the Rhineland.
64. In Poland, the old landed aristocrats, who lost lordship over the body of serfs but remained landlords.

May 5, 1789
Estates General meets at Versailles

June 17, 1789
Third estate declares itself National Assembly

July 9, 1789
The name of the National Assembly is formally changed to the Constituent Assembly

August 17, 1789
Declaration of the Rights of Man and Citizen

July 12, 1790
Civil Constitution of the clergy

September 3, 1791
Constituent Assembly passes French constitution (Constitution of 1791) limiting monarchy

October 1, 1791
First Legislative Assembly meets

August 10, 1791
Legislative Assembly suspends monarchy

September 20, 1791
National Convention meets and declares the Year One of the Republic (September 22)

June 24, 1793
Second (Jacobin) constitution drawn up but not promulgated

August 22, 1795
Third French constitution drawn up

October 26, 1795
Convention dissolved

November 3, 1795
Directory established

November 9, 1799
Directory overthrown; Napoleon establishes Consulate and promulgates the Constitution of the Year VIII

August 2, 1802
Consulate modified to give Napoleon life term

May 18, 1804
Empire proclaimed by Senate and Tribunate

December 2, 1804
Napoleon consecrated emperor by the pope

April 11, 1814
Napoleon abdicates as emperor; Bourbon Restoration and "liberal charter" proclaimed

March 2, 1815
Napoleon restored

June 1, 1815
Champ de Mars; Napoleon issues liberal constitution, the Acte Additionnel

June 22, 1815
Napoleon's final abdication and Louis XVIII's return to Paris

July 7, 1815
Louis XVIII returns to Paris

5

THE REVOLUTIONARY HERITAGE AND THE EUROPEAN REACTION

THE COLLAPSE OF THE FRENCH IMPERIUM

Before we examine the European reaction to the Revolution in terms of political "reaction" or the realm of ideas, we must look again at Napoleon's empire and relate the circumstances of its collapse.

We have seen how by 1811 it embraced 130 *départements* extending in an arc from Rome to the Baltic and also across Europe from Portugal to Warsaw. And we have also noticed that in 1811 the dynasty seemed secure, when Marie Louise gave Napoleon a male heir. There were, however, also troubles to notice: the Spanish problem, tension between France and Russia, and Britain's stubborn struggle against the Continental System. Moreover, we have pointed out that even Napoleon's former foreign minister, Talleyrand, had in 1809 seemed to doubt the permanence of the Napoleonic empire. This newly minted prince[2] had advised Alexander I not to help increase French power. The pope had reached the same conclusion in 1809, and Napoleon had imprisoned him for resisting the formal incorporation of the Papal States into the French Empire.[3]

The imprisonment of a reigning pope by a French ruler alienated serious Catholics throughout Europe. In France itself, this act fed discontents already fanned by a strong economic recession in 1810 and 1811. In Europe, common cause was suddenly made by Catholics, patriots who resented the taxes imposed to support French aggression, young revolutionaries who protested Napoleon's repression of radical associations, and many bourgeoisie, for whom the Continental System was economically disadvantageous.

The Continental System after the defeat of Prussia in 1806 was not a real blockade at sea. Napoleon's

1. Quoted without attribution in R. R. Palmer and Joel Colton, *A History of the Modern World*, 3rd ed. (New York: Alfred A. Knopf, 1965), p. 407.
2. Napoleon made Talleyrand prince of Benevento in 1806; he resigned his ministry in 1807.
3. Pius VII was moved from jail to jail in Italy until 1812, when he was moved to France.

navy was not able to oppose the British one in its own element. Consequently, Napoleon's Berlin Decree was a paper blockade designed to give French goods the European markets banned from trading with Britain. The system was thus the material counterpart of ideological liberalism, a dual French answer to Britain's eighteenth-century mercantile supremacy and constitutionalism. However Europeans felt about exported French ideas, they often had only contempt for the paper blockade. The British had in effect a real blockade by 1807, a picket line of ships meant to starve Napoleon's allies of any share in Europe's strategic import trades.

By weakening the continental economies in their trading sectors, Britain's merchants fought Napoleon's system on its chosen ground. And they had the advantage. Britain was keeping military supplies out of Europe while encouraging smuggling of British goods which were of little military value but in demand among European consumers.[4] Napoleon tried to counter the advantages of English cheap goods, some of which were already made in truly industrialized workshops, by stirring resentment among the less developed states' ruling classes. But on balance we can say that this propaganda failed.

So, too, did the general policy, buttressed in 1807 by the Milan Decree, which declared a French right to seize neutral ships in European ports if these ships had touched a British port. The chief neutral affected was the United States. Presidents Jefferson and Madison negotiated with France and Britain, which had issued its own Orders in Council in 1807.[5] The Presidents' purpose was to gain a concession from one of the powers threatening American trade. Napoleon granted such a concession, asking in return American resistance to British search and seizure policies. Abetted by home sentiment for taking Canada from Britain, the United States eventually went to war against Britain in 1812.

But by then the German states were thoroughly disenchanted with Napoleon's grand schemes for developing European resources. The inadequacies of overland transport encouraged smuggling, in order to avoid trade depressions in the satellites. It has been estimated that nearly 40 percent of all European imports from 1807 to 1812 were smuggled goods. Moreover, the British responded to the partial loss of markets in Europe by supporting the bid for independence of the Spanish colonies in America. Exports to Latin America rose from about £300,000 to £6,300,000 between 1805 and 1809! As industrialization leaped forward in Britain, the income of the people rose from about £225,000,000 in 1805 to £335,000,000 in 1814.

The Peninsular War also went sour. There, Napoleon's armies failed to break the guerrillas and Wellington. Believing this was due to command deficiencies, the Emperor took charge personally for a time. He took Madrid in 1809, but negated the force of the victory by announcing reforms[6] that consolidated Spanish opposition to Joseph Bonaparte's kingship. When Napoleon returned to Paris en route to Erfurt, Wellington dug in to protect southwestern Spain. And the English decided to raise at Cadiz a provisional government of "patriots." Thus London became the first political center to adopt the advice of Gneisenau quoted in the epigraph to this chapter. Wellington's army allowed a national assembly to draft a constitution for Spain, mobilizing Spanish sentiment on the popular level against the French invaders.

4. Especially cheap cotton cloth, tea, coffee, domestic utensils, dyestuffs, etc.
5. Stating that neutrals could enter European ports only if they stopped first in Britain, loading British goods.
6. Especially the disestablishment of the Church.

The revolutionary era had begun with a show of French nationalism.[7] Spanish national resistance turned this force against France. But it was in Germany that resistance to Napoleon's "France first" policies provoked the keenest nationalistic opposition. Patriotic politicians and writers contrasted the French imperium, which was international in character, with the "national" interests of Germans. Conservatives argued that Napoleon obliterated native traditions. Radicals, once in the vanguard of enthusiasm for the Revolution, argued that only a turn toward "national" representative institutions would relieve the Germans of the French interference with self-rule. Thus the force of nationalism took different forms in Spain and Germany, and also in Italy and England, Poland and Belgium.

But by 1812 this force was everywhere in evidence, as Napoleon once more put his armies in motion across Europe. In Italy republican agitators called Carbonari resented the enlarged kingdom. In Poland, old soldiers like Kosciusko and younger pro-Russian advocates of freedom protested what they feared would be a march to Moscow. Even the Prussians recognized that a French conquest of Russia would be an effective answer to Britain's resistance. The shock dealt to Prussia by the unprecedented defeat of its armies by Napoleon in 1807 had spurred reforms.[8] But the reconstruction of Prussia's political and social system was in its infancy in 1812, and Napoleon had forced some of the reformers into exile several years earlier.

Thus all of Europe was concerned to know what Napoleon intended in 1811 and early 1812, when he amassed an army of over 700,000 men—the Grand Army—on German and Polish soil.[9] Russia had withdrawn from the Continental System on December 31, 1810, resuming trade with England. Statesmen knew Napoleon would not allow this open challenge to go unanswered. The question was whether Alexander would be drawn to fight on Polish soil, which Napoleon hoped would happen, or whether the Czar would force on Napoleon a campaign across the vast expanse of Russia itself.

RUSSIA, LIBERATION, AND THE GRAND COALITION

Alexander had reasons enough to attack the French forces, should he so desire. Russia had drawn few, if any, benefits from the Treaty of Tilsit. France had allowed no aid to Russia in its Turkish wars. Russia's annexation of Finland in 1809 was offset by French control of Poland. The French-Habsburg alliance engineered by Metternich seemed a loaded gun pointed at Moscow. Native Russians of the upper classes clamored for war, and so did foreigners of "liberal" backgrounds who had sought refuge from Napoleon in Saint Petersburg.[10] Thus the anti-French elements everywhere urged on Alexander the task Britain's navy and wealth could not do and their own patriotism was helpless to effect: the defeat of Napoleon on land and the destruction of the army which was the backbone of his empire.

Alexander bided his time, however, and Napoleon, characteristically, seized the initiative. In June 1812 Napoleon invaded Russia, as nearly 130 years later Adolf Hitler was to do, when he too saw Britain and Russia as the last obstacles to an unchallenged hegemony in the West. Russia had few allies, but Sweden had pledged aid in exchange for support in its bid to

---

7. See later in this chapter for a discussion of this term in the focus of intellectual history.
8. See Chapter 6.
9. The army was made up of about 250,000 French troops, an equal number of Germans drawn from the satellites and also including small Austrian and Prussian groups, nearly 100,000 Polish soldiers, and over 100,000 in smaller contingents from all Europe.
10. The Prussian Baron Stein most notably.

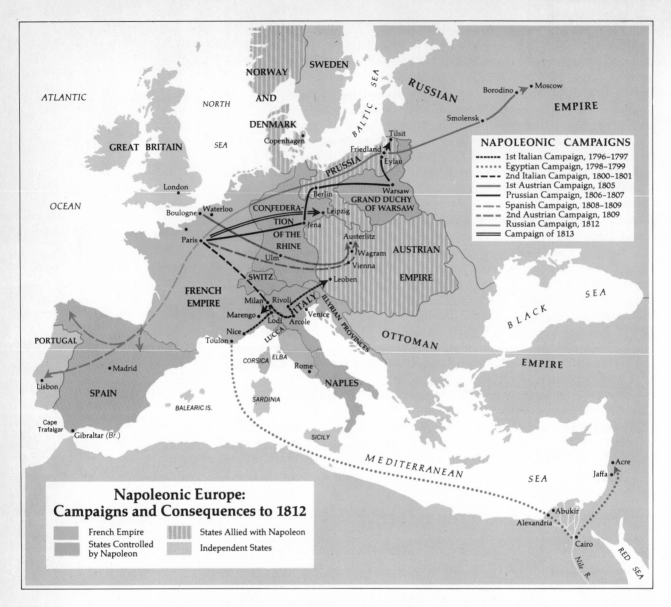

NAPOLEONIC CAMPAIGNS

- ‑ ‑ ‑ ‑ 1st Italian Campaign, 1796–1797
- · · · · · Egyptian Campaign, 1798–1799
- – – – 2nd Italian Campaign, 1800–1801
- ——— 1st Austrian Campaign, 1805
- ——— Prussian Campaign, 1806–1807
- –·–·– Spanish Campaign, 1808–1809
- –··–·· 2nd Austrian Campaign, 1809
- ——— Russian Campaign, 1812
- ≡≡≡ Campaign of 1813

**Napoleonic Europe:
Campaigns and Consequences to 1812**

| French Empire | States Allied with Napoleon |
| States Controlled by Napoleon | Independent States |

annex Norway.[11] The significance of this Swedish decision was not lost on Europeans. The ruler of Sweden was Crown Prince Bernadotte,[12] a man who had risen to fame as one of Napoleon's generals before being offered the throne there by the Estates. But like Hitler, Napoleon soon discovered Russia was easier to enter than to subdue—or to leave. Alexander had allied himself with Britain and had ended hostilities with Turkey, in order to welcome Napoleon.

The French plan was to turn Alexander's division of his forces into a decisive advantage. First, Napoleon intended to isolate and defeat the southern forces and then spend the winter in Smolensk. This isolation was to be achieved by driving in a large force to cut off the southern troops from the northern Russian army. Then, early in 1813, Napoleon planned to take Moscow, if by that time Alexander had not accepted peace on French terms.

The Russian general Kutuzov,[13] luring Napoleon toward Smolensk with-

11. Which was under Danish control.
12. Jean Baptiste Jules Bernadotte (1763–1844), one of the victors in the campaigns of 1805, elected king of Sweden in 1810.
13. Mikhail Kutuzov (1745–1813), the commander who took over from Barclay de Tolly, the designer of the strategy of retreat.

out giving him battle, refused to fight. All during a hot summer on the Russian plains Napoleon moved in pursuit, stretching his line of supply, losing men to hunger and heat, with no compensatory gain in the form of a crushed Russian force. Kutuzov abandoned Smolensk itself in August, and this caused Napoleon to change his plans. Confident he could catch the whole army of Russia in a defense of Moscow in 1812, the Emperor decided to take that city in September.

Meanwhile, Kutuzov had given the fateful order to his men: they would stand and fight to defend Russia at Borodino, a city about 100 miles southwest of Moscow.[14] On September 7 the armies met, taking about 70,000 casualties, both dead and wounded. No clear victory was won by Napoleon, but Kutuzov retreated. When Napoleon reached Moscow on the fourteenth, the city stood deserted, and it was rapidly being consumed by fires deliberately set to deny Napoleon its resources.

Every military object had been accomplished in less than the planned time, with one significant exception. The Russian armies had not been crushed, though they had been mauled. And the political objective had not been achieved at all. Alexander refused terms. Napoleon sat in Moscow, which had burned to the ground. Five weeks went by, and the Grand Army began to fall apart from a combination of inactivity and short supplies. With neither victory nor peace, Napoleon realized he could not winter in Moscow, far from his own stores of food, clothing, arms, and replacements. On October 19 the Emperor began the most famous retreat in the history of warfare, across the Russian plains toward central Europe, denied the easier southern road by Kutuzov.[15]

The Russians were now out of hiding. They had cut across the short

14. Directly on the main road from Smolensk, which was about 250 miles to the southwest of Moscow.
15. Kutuzov allowed Napoleon to reach Smolensk, but by a long route; and he prevented a retreat across southern Russia.

Amidst flames that lasted for four days, the Kremlin towers loom alongside the Moskva River in this engraving of the burning of Moscow. The origin of the fire was never completely explained— probably it was set by Russian patriots— but when it died out little remained of the city except the Kremlin, which miraculously had survived. The fire caused Napoleon to waste precious time while his army lost all sense of discipline in a mad rush to loot the city, and it allowed the Russians to reorganize in the countryside and cut French supply lines. When the violent Russian winter finally struck the retreating French army, it proved a more deadly enemy than the czar's troops; Napoleon at last knew defeat. Giraudon; Bibliothèque Marmottan.

southern route with part of their force, while Kutuzov himself tore at Napoleon's heels. The purpose was to keep Napoleon around Smolensk until November, when the fierce winter might then become Kutuzov's ally. Kutuzov's plans succeeded brilliantly. Napoleon lost tens of thousands of men on the march when, late in November, Kutuzov gave battle again, as Napoleon tried to cross the Berezina River. The Grand Army was cut to pieces by the Russians. When its units crossed the Niemen River on December 18, reaching Polish territory, fewer than 100,000 men remained under the Emperor's command. Napoleon had lost over 500,000 either dead or taken prisoner.[16]

The Emperor had in fact fled the scene of the disaster, anxious to reach Paris before the full extent of the failure aggravated the political situation at home. With the demonic energy he always showed in adversity, he recruited 350,000 new troops to hurl against Russia and Britain. But these were green men, not the veterans of Jena and Friedland. And the situation in Europe was changed also. The specter of Napoleon in defeat, of his armies starved, frozen, mired in mud, battered into a mass of disorderly fugitives, had drawn together his European enemies.

Prussia and Russia now joined in a new coalition. Bernadotte of Sweden had accepted a British subsidy and agreed in return to supply an army of good troops. The first battles between Napoleon and his enemies[17] were fought to a draw in the spring. An armistice in June gave Prince Metternich time to negotiate terms of Austrian entry in return for British subsidies and participation in a "Grand Coalition."[18] Metternich had hoped that the prospect of fighting Europe's main powers all at the same time, which France had not had to do before, would lead Napoleon to accept terms. But the Emperor refused to disband his empire and return to the old system of a balance of power among the great states.

Napoleon attacked the allies near Dresden in August 1813, winning there his final victory on German soil. In the fall he suffered the withdrawal of his "allies" from the war;[19] they soon went to war for the Coalition. The result was a number of battles near Leipzig, where Europe defeated the French in what was then called the Battle of the Nations.[20] The Emperor again returned to Paris, just in time to learn of the wave of "wars of liberation." The Dutch revolted to restore the house of Orange. The Austrians aided Italian insurgents and defeated Beauharnais's forces. Wellington drove Joseph Bonaparte out of Spain and pushed into France. The main allied forces crossed the Rhine early in 1814.

Trapped, and with about 100,000 troops to command against the massed armies of Europe, Napoleon fought brilliantly to defeat the forces of Austria and Prussia, under the command of General Blücher[21] and Prince Schwarzenberg.[22] But the main Coalition armies took Paris itself, under the leadership of the Prussian king Frederick William III and Czar Alexander. Upon their entry into Paris on March 31, 1814, Napoleon's marshals advised the Emperor to cease resistance. Talleyrand called the Senate into session and got from it a proclamation that Napoleon and his line no longer had a claim to France's throne. Napoleon abdicated and after a period of refusal applied this decision to his son.

16. He took 611,000 into Russia; 400,000 died and about 100,000 were prisoners of war.
17. All but Britain were former allies!
18. One or more of the great powers had stayed out of each of the first three coalitions.
19. The troops of the Confederation of the Rhine.
20. October 1813; this victory for the Coalition dissolved the satellite system of the Rhine's Right (eastern) bank.
21. Gebhard von Blücher (1742–1819).
22. Karl Philipp Fürst zu Schwarzenberg (1771–1820).

In this crudely drawn recollection of the crossing of the Berezina River, an anonymous artist has captured the panic of the nearly obliterated Grand Army attempting to flee. Huge crowds press forward on two hastily constructed wooden bridges, while others too frightened to await their turn try to swim the icy river. Russian artillery shells exploding in their midst and the collapse of one bridge further added to the terrible French casualties—some 25,000 in the crossing alone. The few thousand pathetic survivors who did reach the opposite bank suffered starvation and freezing, and many went mad. Leaving his disintegrated troops under the command of Murat, Napoleon dashed to Paris to raise a new army to salvage his empire. Musée de l'Armée, Paris.

Born the count of Provence, Louis XVIII gained a reputation in his youth as a witty bon vivant, who frequented the best salons and admired Voltaire and the encyclopedists. The Revolution forced him into exile, and the execution of his brother Louis XVI and the death of the dauphin made him the Bourbon pretender to the French throne. For over twenty years he patiently awaited his return to France, which came with the abdication of Napoleon. Old, corpulent, and suffering from gout, Louis XVIII is shown in his moment of triumph, sitting at the Emperor's desk in the Tuileries palace. With the exception of Napoleon's return during the "Hundred Days," Louis ruled until 1824, but his moderate tendencies were increasingly thwarted by ultraroyalists within his entourage. Musée de Versailles.

Napoleon was exiled to the small island of Elba,[23] where he was conceded "sovereignty."

THE HUNDRED DAYS AND THE PEACE OF 1815

While Napoleon's army had fought its desperate battles, Talleyrand in Paris had negotiated the restoration of the Bourbon monarchy. Louis XVI's brother, the count of Provence, was named Louis XVIII,[24] and the new king pledged to rule within a liberal, constitutional framework. The powers helped a disgruntled French people toward acceptance of this arrangement by giving easy peace terms in the Treaty of Paris on May 30, 1814.

What remained in doubt was how much that had resulted from twenty-five years of revolution and expansion would be undone by the results of fifteen months of defeat and collapse. The worst fears of liberals seemed realized when Louis XVIII's constitutional ideas were made evident. The Charter of 1814 was said by the King to be his "gift" to France, made in the nineteenth year of his reign. This claim, which thus dated his reign from 1795 and also presupposed an uninterrupted line of French monarchs (with Louis XVII nominally ruling from the execution of his father in 1793 to his own death in 1795), ignored both the Revolution and the Napoleonic era. Moreover, by pretending that the years 1789–1814 had not been legitimate, the King also passed over in silence the achievement of popular sovereignty. Despite the incorporation into the Charter of elements of civil liberty and administrative reform,[25] French liberals were alarmed.

23. Off the western coast of Italy.
24. As mentioned in Chapter 4, Louis XVI's son had been counted as Louis XVII, but he had died in prison.
25. The heritage, respectively, of the 1789 Declaration of Rights and the imperial codes of Napoleon.

With only about a thousand followers, Napoleon escaped from his exile on Elba in February 1815 and began a heroic quest to regain his throne by marching across France. Gathering recruits and momentum along the way, this adventure at first caused no concern to the Bourbon government. At Grenoble the garrison joined the fallen hero's crusade, and in Lyons, where his triumphal entry is shown in this drawing, Napoleon dissolved the Bourbon parliament. The exiled Emperor had realized that his only hope lay in a spontaneous acclamation by the common people, and this he received. In mid-March Louis XVIII quickly fled Paris, and Napoleon regained the Tuileries the following day. Bibliothèque Nationale.

They had good reason to be. Louis XVIII was far more attuned to compromise with the liberals than was his influential brother, Charles Philippe (1757–1836), the conservative count of Artois, leader of the ultraroyalists. The Ultras wanted absolutism and the Church fully restored, alienating intellectuals and the partisans of enlightenment in government. The army cadres were out of work and thus hostile to the Restoration. The disbanding of the high tariff walls of the Continental System struck a blow at the bourgeoisie, who now faced British industrial competition again. And peasants were stirred to wrath by the return of "nationalized" lands to aristocrats and other *rentiers*.

News of disaffection reached Napoleon on Elba, where in February 1815 he slipped away from careless guards. With some loyal aides he landed in France at the beginning of March, moving northward from Cannes rapidly. Far from meeting resistance, the "eagle" (as his troops had called him) found soldiers rallying to his last flight. Napoleon reached Paris on March 20, to find the Bourbons had fled to Belgium. In Paris Napoleon proclaimed the Empire restored, thus beginning the "Hundred Days."

Reading the disaffection in France rightly, the Emperor made sweeping reforms in his old system. He extended the franchise, revived and revised the Constitution of the Year VIII to make the ministry responsible to the people, rather than merely to the emperor, and dismantled the apparatus of censorship. Napoleon also put out propaganda to show that the restrictive nature of his earlier empire had been necessitated by the allied wars against the Revolution.

Yet he knew that these changes were no substitute for victory. So, too, did the allies who were gathered at Vienna, trying to work out a system of mutual security for Europe. Shocked though they were by the news from Elba and France, they agreed at once to Metternich's suggestion for a new joint war effort by Austria, Russia, Prussia, and Britain. An army of about 700,000 was levied to oppose Napoleon's forces, which stood at about 200,000. These forces engaged in Belgium, where Napoleon crossed the border on June 14 to strike directly at Blücher and Wellington.

Napoleon adopted a favorite tactic. He planned to split his enemies' larger forces and then to defeat them in turn. Pouncing on Blücher's Prussians first, he forced them to retreat, pursued by a large detachment from Napoleon's own main force. The Emperor then went to aid Marshal Ney,[26] one of his favorite soldiers, who had deserted the Restoration. Ney was facing Wellington's army near the small depot of Waterloo when Napoleon gave support to his marshal for an attack. Wellington, himself a great soldier filled with respect for Napoleon's brilliance, had dug in on the high ground, where he concealed his very large force, in accord with a military maxim of his own:

All the business of war . . . is to endeavor to find out what you don't know. . . . That's what I call "guessing what was on the other side of the hill."[27]

Napoleon made a melancholy discovery. Blücher had not been defeated, and the Prussians appeared on the field, attacking Napoleon's right flank, adding their force to Wellington's already superior force. Within a space of nine hours the Emperor saw his forces pulverized by Wellington's cannon,

26. Duke of Elchingen (1769–1815), a peer of France under the Restoration; executed in 1815.
27. Quoted from *The Croker Papers* (London: H.M.S.O., 1885), 3: 276.

Confident of victory, much of English society flocked to Brussels to be near their troops when they met Napoleon's army. One eyewitness later carefully painted his impressions of the duke of Wellington (hat in hand at left-center, mounted on his favorite horse, Copenhagen) giving orders to his staff in the midst of battle. Far from the easy triumph they had imagined, the allies nearly lost the day and were saved only by the incredible feats of the English infantry. The carnage of Waterloo left Wellington a deeply saddened man. Although the English people revered him as a hero for the rest of his life, he never displayed pride or arrogance, insisting "I am but a man." Bibliothèque Nationale.

an action described by the Irishman as "hard pounding." Despite Wellington's own view, that Napoleon's presence on a field was worth 40,000 men, the French collapsed and fled. The Duke commanded tough veteran forces, forged in the crucible of the Peninsular War, beaten into shape by harsh discipline. In Spain he had confessed to being more frightened of his own ragtag forces than was the enemy. At Waterloo, this force took over 30,000 casualties, but obeyed the call to charge again and again. When Napoleon left the field to return to his final abdication,[28] Wellington saluted him in a famous victory message: "Nothing except a battle lost can be half so melancholy as a battle won."[29]

The fallen monarch of Europe was sent to permanent exile under British guard on the South Atlantic island of Saint Helena, there to write memoirs and build himself his own version of his fight to preserve the French

28. On the twenty-second of June.
29. Attributed to Wellington on the field at Waterloo.

After the defeat at Waterloo, Napoleon was forced to abdicate and flee a second time. His first scheme was to escape to the United States, but he was prevented by circumstances and surrendered to the English instead. They placed the ex-Emperor aboard the Bellerophon, *which in this engraving is anchored off the coast at Torbay in Devon where the curious English came in rowboats to catch a glimpse of their former enemy. Napoleon remained captive aboard the ship for several weeks until he was informed of the decision to exile him to Saint Helena. His violent protests failed to alter his fate, and he was transferred on August 7, 1815, to the ship* Northumberland *for the ten-week voyage to exile and political oblivion.* Bibliothèque Nationale.

Revolution. He might well have said of this six-year captivity what he said to the Polish ambassador De Pradt after the disaster at Moscow: "There is only one step from the sublime to the ridiculous."[30]

What made plausible Napoleon's elaborate self-justification in the memoirs was less anything he had done or might say to his secretaries on Saint Helena. The actions of the powers assembled in the Congress of Vienna gave the color of truth to the Napoleonic claims. By restoring the old monarchs (or their heirs) and with them the institutions of another age still able to be resurrected, Metternich and his peers among the diplomats turned their backs on Baron Stein and the advice of Gneisenau: to use the heritage of the Revolution and consolidate the nations.

Only this fateful decision could make people forget Napoleon's real autocracy and his own often modest allegiance to republicanism, while they remembered fondly the benefits of the Civil Code, the *lycées* and *université*. Or, as the poet Lord Byron said for all who had hailed Napoleon, in marking down his less than favorable view of Wellington and Waterloo:

> Call'd "Saviour of the Nations"—not yet saved,
> And "Europe's Liberator"—still enslaved.[31]

The settlement made in Vienna in 1815 involved the whole territory once under French control. It established the principles of counterrevolutionary diplomacy which survived the new waves of discontent in the 1830 and 1848 "revolutions." It kept Europe's powers out of great wars on the Continent until 1914, by establishing a concert of powers,[32] the great "Concert of Europe." And by admitting France to the system in 1818, the Vienna congress powers sought to guarantee a reactionary peace by means of diplomacy. The aim of the Congress was not merely to settle the wars of the French Revolution. It was also the wish of the powers to insure in the future a habit of bringing grievances to the conference table rather than to the battlefield.

The Congress of Vienna met from September 1814 through June 1815. One of its first actions was to make official a treaty of alliance worked out at Chaumont in March 1814 by Viscount Castlereagh, the British foreign minister.[33] Castlereagh, who had built a reputation out of his successful work to bring Ireland into union with Britain and his advocacy of Catholic emancipation,[34] had been instrumental since 1807 in leading London's attack on Napoleon's Continental System. He had also supported Wellington in Spain, and had in 1812 conducted the diplomacy by which Russia ceased hostilities against Turkey and Sweden joined the Coalition. In 1814, he negotiated an end to the war between England and America.

Castlereagh's idea at Chaumont was to bring the four victorious powers into a "Quadruple Alliance" dedicated to settling the French wars. It was as an alliance that the Treaty of Paris was made in 1814, with its agreement to keep France strong under a Bourbon monarchy. The Treaty of Paris had given to France all territories held on November 1, 1792, including parts of Italy (Savoy), Belgium, and western Germany. But it had taken from France most of the United Provinces, the Italian states, nearly all the German states, Switzerland, and nearly all of France's overseas possessions.

30. Attributed to Napoleon by De Pradt in the diplomat's memoirs.
31. *Don Juan*, canto 9, stanza 5.
32. Britain, Russia, Austria, and Prussia.
33. Robert Stewart (1769–1822), marquess of Londonderry.
34. George III vetoed a bill in 1801 which would have granted the Irish Catholics and Catholics in England full civil liberties.

The famous Congress of Vienna met from September 1814 through June 1815 to try to rebuild European stability in the wake of the Napoleonic upheaval. The French artist Isabey captured one of its dramatic moments—the arrival of the duke of Wellington to replace Castlereagh as head of the English delegation. Wellington is shown in profile standing at far left being introduced by Metternich, who stands in front of a chair in the foreground. The brilliant French diplomatist Talleyrand sits at right with his arm resting on the table. The glittering Viennese social life and Napoleon's dramatic return to France did not prevent the Congress from partially achieving its goals. The Royal Collection, Buckingham Palace.

What the treaty failed to do, even before Napoleon upset it, was secure agreement about the fate of Poland. Alexander had seized Napoleon's Grand Duchy, and he seemed intent on keeping intact its former Prussian and Austrian lands. The Czar was influenced in this decision by his foreign minister, the Polish prince Adam Czartoryski.[35] Prussia made no objection, on the grounds of securing Saxony as compensation. Saxony had sided with the French in most phases of the many wars. Metternich would have none of it, however, and enlisted Castlereagh's support to protect Austria's interests. Britain had no wish to see Russia dominate eastern and central Europe. And this made it appear likely that the Quadruple Alliance might disintegrate into two opposing groups: Britain and Austria against Russia and Prussia.

The Congress therefore was called to make peace. France was invited, but it was clear that the power to dispose lay with the four major "victors." The smaller states confronted a closed conference dominated by Metternich, Castlereagh, and Alexander I, who attended the working meetings in person. With some dismay, the "liberated" Dutch, Bavarian, Italian, Belgian, Swiss, and Iberian representatives saw Talleyrand quickly rise to an important place in the Congress,[36] while they had to be content with small assignments in powerless special "committees."

While the assembled crowd of nobles and officers dined and danced at the expense of Austria's Emperor Francis, Metternich ran the real business of Vienna. He was both a pragmatist and a man of principle. On the one hand he recognized the Czar's sacrifices and Russian claims to compensation for starting Napoleon on the road to ruin. But too much Russian power was

35. Czartoryski (1770–1861) was the proponent of a liberal constitution for Poland.
36. In part because he posed as their champion.

inimical to Austria's own needs and Metternich's idea about Europe's future. This, he believed, would be secure only if a balance or "equipoise" of forces existed *within* states and among them. France had witnessed a loss of balance through revolution; and in consequence the balance of the European order itself had been destroyed. Effective restoration of balance domestically and internationally must therefore rest on the reestablishment of traditional institutions and the return to power of "legitimate" rulers— *wherever that was possible and wise.*

These principles Castlereagh also took as the basis for any settlement, providing only that British colonial and commercial interests were safeguarded. Then, Britain would gladly help mediate European issues in dispute, from a position of enlightened aloofness from continental problems. Talleyrand had himself accepted the balance analogy as early as 1808, as we have seen. The Prussian negotiator Prince von Hardenberg[37] was dull and also seemed handicapped by Frederick William III's loyalty to Alexander. The Czar's Polish schemes were thus the crux of the Congress, and Alexander's stubbornness gave Talleyrand a lever with which to pry concessions out of both groups within the Quadruple Alliance.

Indeed, it was Talleyrand who finally brought about a plan of compromise on Poland. By negotiating a secret alliance with Austria and Britain against Alexander and Frederick William early in 1815, he put into practice the "balance" idea. The Czar and the king of Prussia wanted no new war

37. Karl August von Hardenberg (1750–1822), shy, stiff, and nearly deaf.

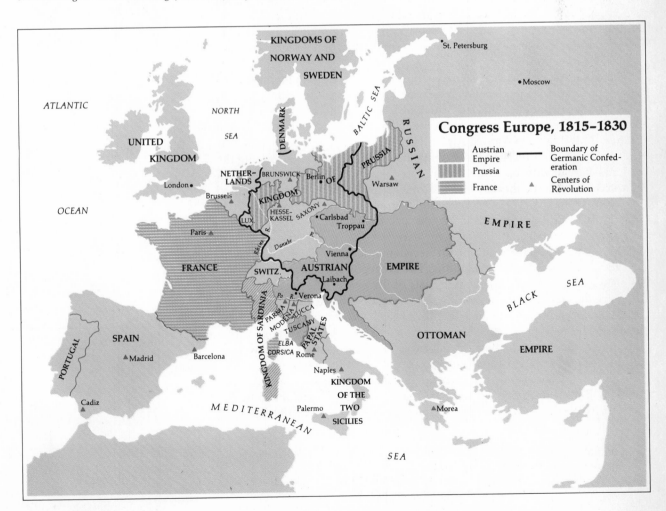

over Poland. They therefore accepted a suggestion that France join the four powers, ending French isolation and at the same time breaking the stalemate between the groups of two. Metternich then proposed an "independent" Poland, with Austria getting the province of Galicia, and Alexander the kingship of the new state itself. Alexander accepted, perhaps because he wanted to play at giving subjects other than Russians a liberal constitution. But the fact that Poland was now a heritable Romanov territory accomplished a long-range goal of Russian policy. Prussia benefited greatly; in addition to Posen and nearly half of Saxony, Prussia got large territories in the Rhineland and also Swedish Pomerania.

This agreement led to a general settlement which in many ways revived the schemes made by Pitt in 1805 and Russia a few years later. The powers gathered at Vienna thus sacrificed legitimacy to equipoise. Surrenders of territory were compensated for by additions. Prussia was allowed to expand westward as a buffer against France on the Rhine. Austria got northern Italy[38] in exchange for giving the new kingdom of Holland the Austrian Netherlands. The Alliance thus counterbalanced France to the north with King William I of Holland, contrary to the wishes of the people of the region, who since 1648 had been under different governments. France was also contained by guarantees of Swiss independence and the restoration of Bourbon rule in Spain.[39] And Sardinia was given mainland territory to hold back France on its Italian border. The more cohesive thirty-eight German states which survived Napoleon's dismemberment of the Holy Roman Empire were linked in a new Germanic Confederation. The pope regained the Papal States, while Austria became once again dominant in Tuscany, Parma, and Modena. Sweden got Norway, but was reluctantly made to allow Russia to keep Finland. Britain kept Dutch and French colonies acquired earlier in the wars.

This Final Act was actually signed before Waterloo. Certain modifications of it appeared in the Second Treaty of Paris, after Napoleon's defeat. Chiefly, these changes reflected British and Prussian debates about how to punish the French and also strengthen the Rhineland bulwark against France. The Prussians wanted Alsace-Lorraine, Savoy, and the whole Saar valley. Castlereagh resisted these demands, suggesting instead revising the original Paris treaty back to 1790, rather than 1792. The suggestion was adopted, and France thereby lost the small frontier strips of land acquired between 1790 and 1792. More significant was the addition of a "war indemnity" imposed on France: 700,000,000 francs and the cost of financing an "army of occupation" for five years.[40]

The most important result of the revision was not a change in French territory or the levying of reparations. The great powers pledged an army of 240,000 to prevent new French betrayals of the peace. They also agreed to the periodic conferences to oversee the peace already fractured once.

Alexander was not satisfied merely to seek protection for the peace, however. In September 1815, he gained Prussian and Austrian support for a far more extensive idea, the Holy Alliance. The Czar wanted the powers to renounce war entirely. Moreover, he wanted to sanction a new international order by religious ties. Castlereagh found this amusing, as did Metternich. But their rulers did not share a unanimity. England refused to adhere, while Francis II did. Other powers were excluded: the sultan of

---

38. Lombardy and Venetia as well as the Dalmatian Coast (Napoleon's Illyrian Provinces). Metternich also secured areas lost to Bavaria.
39. Ferdinand VII also was restored in Naples and Sicily (the Kingdom of the Two Sicilies).
40. The occupation force was set at 150,000 troops, cut to 30,000 in 1817, abandoned in 1818.

Turkey, on the sound basis that he was no Christian, and the pope, on the sound basis that Rome was always for the gospel of peace, justice, and charity. England, Turkey, and the Vatican were strange bedfellows, but, as we shall see, they had good reason to doubt that the Holy Alliance would bring either peace or justice in the world.

IDEAS AND IDEOLOGY:
THE REVOLUTIONARY HERITAGE

Whether the Quadruple Alliance might bring a lasting settlement to Europe or the Holy Alliance might produce a new era of peace with justice were questions for the future. What could not be doubted in the West in 1815 was that a quarter of a century of revolution had introduced a change in ideas about the words *nation, people,* and *citizen.* Europeans had been exposed directly to the democratic ideology admired at a distance, when it appeared in America, and closer to home in England, in the form of the agitations of Wilkes and his supporters. The French experience has been widely misunderstood, however, and it is still said that the Revolution was the result of democratic forces.[41] As we shall now show, the Revolution produced a democratic ideology, but was not the product of such a way of looking at the world.

When Robespierre had said he wanted to make citizens of men without property in 1789, the Assembly had answered him by saying his words were a contradiction in terms. Robespierre thought of the "people" as the whole French "nation," down to the poorest provincial, but the liberals in the Assembly seemed to equate the people with the smaller body of "citizens" who had the franchise—the *political* nation.[42] Thus Robespierre spoke of the assembled representatives of the first, second, and third estates as a "league of a few citizens against the people."[43]

Robespierre was a democrat from the beginning, therefore, and so were some others. The question is, Were the majority of men who managed the Revolution in 1789 democrats? If we judge their ideas solely on the basis of their actions, we should have to say no. The constitution they made in 1791 restricted the franchise along property lines, as we know. This, some said, was a betrayal of the Declaration of the Rights of Man and Citizen. Whether in fact the Constitution of 1791 deserted the supposedly democratic principles of 1789, we may know only by considering what the nature of political ideas and action was in 1789.

If, indeed, there was from the outset a widely held notion of identity equating citizen and nation, then we may well believe that democratic ideas inspired revolution. What we must not *assume,* however, is that this was so. For we want to discover whether terms like *nation, citizen,* and *people* were precisely formulated political ideas in 1789, rather than vague notions surrounded by a cloud of philosophical debate and heated argument. If it should be the case that the Revolution itself gave new content to diffuse political symbols, then we may conclude that the idea of universal male suffrage became a clause in the creed of democratic political ideology because of the Revolution.

A clue lies in a speech Robespierre made criticizing the Assembly committee[44] responsible for drafting the declaration of rights in August

---

41. Especially in R. R. Palmer's *The Age of the Democratic Revolution,* 2 vols. (Princeton, Princeton University Press, 1959–1964).
42. The French terms were *peuple, nation,* and *citoyens.*
43. Quoted in Palmer, *Age of the Democratic Revolution,* 1:472.
44. The famous "sixth bureau," dominated by the bourgeois "liberals" Mounier and Sieyès, Target and Malouet.

1789. The sum of Robespierre's objection to the draft was that it did not express clearly enough the rights of the "nation at large." Speaking in behalf of the "nameless masses," the future Terrorist told the Assembly its task was to make the words *citizen*, *nation*, and *people* synonymous. The issue of the Revolution's *future* was whether the nation would become a nation of equal and active citizens or one of active citizens and unequal passive "citizens." Yet even Robespierre did not define the crucial terms clearly.[45]

Nor is that strange. Throughout 1788 and early 1789 political discussion had done little to clarify the terms. Had not the privileged *parlement de Paris* said the "nation" alone could grant taxes in an Estates General—without saying what the nation was? *Cahiers* drawn up by every estate in the various committees on grievance had spoken freely about making fundamental laws for the nation, drafting a national charter, and defending national rights. But what exactly did they mean? Some bourgeois grievance makers spoke of rights belonging to the nation by social contract, echoing Rousseau. Some noble estates in the provinces seemed to equate the rights of the nation with their own customary privileges, as did many clergy. But no *cahiers* claimed that the "nation" possessing the rights listed included every Frenchman. Indeed, many drew a frank distinction between *denizens*, or inhabitants of French territory, and *citizens*.

The *cahier* makers were trying to focus vague sentiments of the thing we have learned to call nationalism, while trying to reshape French politics. But the *cahiers* were not rigorous treatises on politics. Their main characteristic was emotional fervor. Not one *cahier* defined *la nation*, nor did any approach what Marat was later to say—"The sovereign of a state is the nation itself"—thereby begging the question of who composed the nation.

This lack in the *cahiers* stemmed from a simple fact of consciousness in society. Whereas the French language in 1789 used terms like *democratic* and *aristocratic* freely, because for decades discussion had focused on them, there had been no attention given to either *nation* or *nationalisme*. The word *nation* was not widely applied as a noun synonymous with France until 1798, when the expansion of France led men to speak of *la grande nation*. So, theory lagged behind events, and as late as 1789 Frenchmen had no clearly defined association between a definite territory, its people, and the *nation*. Still less did they define *nation* ethnically. Diderot's *Encyclopédie* had not mentioned race at all in defining *nation*; and there was no article on *nationalité*.

Some *cahiers* seemed to imply a belief in "French" traits of character, or shared attitudes and even physical similarities among "Frenchmen." Others spoke of a spirit or genius peculiar to the French, while a few echoed Montesquieu by insisting that the heart of the matter lay in the way character was shaped by law, it in turn having been shaped by geography and climate. That not all people in the territory enlarged by Louis XIV shared even this mysterious identity many made clear by specifically excluding Jews and Protestants from the national community. A few *cahiers* advocated extending civil rights to the Huguenots, but none wished to so favor Jews. Fewer than 5 percent of the *cahiers* touched either racial or religious issues of nationality, however, and it is thus apparent that no doctrine of ethnic nationalism prevailed widely.

The suspicion that language tied the French together also misleads. Since 1539[46] the use of French at law and in the assemblies of the estates had

---

45. For all quotes see the text and notes of A. J. Slavin, "Democracy and the French Revolution," *Bucknell Review* 11 (1963): 53–72.
46. The Edict of Villers-Cotterêts of Francis I.

prevailed. Yet many *cahiers* in 1789 were bilingual. In a few regions a foreign language was used exclusively. And in many *cahiers* a regional *patois*[47] was preferred even by lawyers and officials. Among nearly 800 *cahiers* in print only two demanded the exclusive use of French as a "national language."

Similarly, there was yet no thoroughgoing nationalism based on either administrative or judicial practice. The grievances did express a desire for uniformity, but the provincial lawyers and bureaucrats who drafted the *cahiers* usually had less than the nation in mind. In frontier areas, especially where a provincial people spoke a foreign tongue,[48] spokesmen defended the integrity of such administrative units as *la nation provençal*[49] and *la nation artésienne*.[50] The same sense of provincial "nations" prevailed in Navarre, Béarn, Brittany, and among the Basques on the Spanish frontier. The Bretons refused to take part in the elections of 1788–1789, and the people of Navarre did not recognize the Estates General.

This survival of regional esprit de corps was not only motivated by language, religion, or military necessity among march (border) peoples. It filled the minds of men in the central government, even in the most nation-conscious areas around the Île de France. The election orders for the Estates General in 1789 specified that the right of election belonged to men of "French identity." But "French" here referred not only to men born in France or naturalized there. There were in Europe "foreigners" who held French fiefs. It was established that petty German princes with French lands were entitled to representation. Property, not nationality, ruled the councils where political revolution would be discussed. Clearly, nationality by birth and inhabitation mattered less than political privilege. Robespierre stubbed his toe on the idea that German princes counted for more than French peasants. And the early sessions of the Assembly still had their quota of Dutch and German tenants in chief of Louis XVI!

The liberals settled the issue of seating the "foreigners" in the Assembly of France in the course of the great attack on privilege which ended in the abolition of feudal and manorial structures. But we have seen that this abolition followed events of a revolutionary character, rather than being responsible for the events. And it represented a triumph for the doctrine of Sieyès, who identified the "nation" with the legally defined third estate, not with the masses.

We thus come directly to the question, How did the *cahiers* and the debates in mid-1789 represent the political nation? In retrospect, we can see that the sentiments expressed by Sieyès in the struggle over vote by head or by order were more typical than Robespierre's democratic idea. The leaders in drafting *cahiers* and shaping the Estates General into the National Assembly were liberals stressing equality of rights, not democrats. Lawyers like Target and Mounier called only for a "concord" along national lines, by a union of all classes to regenerate the body politic. The debate over voting by head or by order frustrated that concord, and this made it imperative to blur distinctions between the entire nation and the citizens. Until events "amputated" certain limbs of the body politic—the clergy and the nobles— it was better to speak generally of "a great people" bent on preserving its "national rights." This was in any event easier than defining "citizens" in a way not acceptable to the bourgeois third estate.

The liberals thus agreed to speak of the millions whose "representatives"

---

47. Or dialect of strong deviant character.
48. Spanish, Breton, Flemish, German, and Basque, among others.
49. Provence, in the south.
50. Artois, near the Netherlands.

they were. Desmoulins's *La France libre* made much of the fact that the "people" expressed their "general will" in the *cahiers*. Marat's pamphleteers cited the third estate as a "grand union" of the people. Like the street ballads in the language of the common people, intellectuals coined slogans with no clear content, at least in the sense of contributing a cohesive theory of democratic politics. The *cahiers* do not reveal a united nation on Sieyès's terms. Many aristocratic petitions say explicitly that the third estate alone cannot "constitute the nation," while the commonalty in major cities[51] often said the reverse: that the third estate was synonymous with *le peuple ou la nation* (the people or the nation).

The actual debate on Sieyès's motion to equate the third estate with the nation itself revealed a split within that estate. The liberals consistently proposed names for the verified deputies explicitly restricting the term *people*. As late as the twenty-seventh of June, when Louis XVI collapsed on the issue of vote by head, nobody had yet said that a majority favored a vote for peasants. All that was clear was that the third estate would speak for the "nation." This was no victory for democracy.

Quite the contrary, it allowed the bourgeoisie of France and the clerical and noble deserters to the third estate to develop the distinction between people and citizens in a way which split apart the concepts *people* and *political nation*. This splitting is, of course, foreign to a truly democratic ideology, in which *all of the people are equal members of the political nation*. It was precisely on this ground that democrats criticized the American Constitution, under which slavery was maintained, slaves had no vote, and each slave was counted as three-fifths of a man for the purpose of apportioning seats in the House of Representatives.

And it was on this ground that Robespierre had challenged the liberals, by asking whether there would be a grant of citizenship to men without property. The deputy from Artois condemned both the *philosophes* and the Greek and Roman thinkers who supposed manual labor was incompatible with the obligations of politics. Both ancients and moderns stigmatized the propertyless masses as "slaves" to the passions of the body. People forced to work hard for the necessities of life lacked the "mental freedom" which leisure alone could produce. Hence the education of the masses was too deficient for active citizenship, and the question of property was said to be conclusive for the quality of public participation. This, Robespierre said, was nonsense. The privileges of citizenship belonged to the uneducated masses, because they were as capable of noble political sentiments as any other people were.

Within the sixth bureau itself the Declaration of the Rights of Man and Citizen was being shaped by men who believed in the limitation of civil and social rights. *Citizen*, they argued, was not a word rightly applied in its full political sense to every man. *People* was a word referring to every *private* person, but the citizens of a nation were its *public* men, either eligible to elect men to office or be elected. There was thus no democratic idea inherent in the word *citizen*, as Rousseau himself had taught, in his praise of the Genevans who distinguished between active and passive citizens. Civil liberty meant only the peculiar virtue which recognized the inherent legal equality of unfranchised persons. The nation could then be said to be a social union in which the people were truly sovereign, but in which only the active citizens exercised the powers of government.

51. Dijon, Lyons, Marseilles, etc.

In the year following the fall of the Bastille a mood of goodwill and optimism pervaded France, and even the King, as a constitutional monarch, enjoyed a degree of popularity. Various public celebrations, or fêtes (many of them organized by the artist David), occurred during this time. To honor newly gained freedoms, "Liberty Trees" were planted throughout the country on the first anniversary of Bastille Day. As explained in the caption at upper right, the mayors of every section followed by the National Guard presided over the ceremonies to the accompaniment of a band and singers. The tricolor banners of the Revolution are everywhere, replacing the former national emblem of the royal fleur-de-lis. Musée Carnavalet; Bulloz.

Dans l'enthousiasme de cette liberté que l'on croyait
s'être donné, on imagina de planter des arbres pour
en perpétuer la mémoire, ce qui se fit dans chaque
section avec grand appareil. Les Gardes nationaux
accompagnaient le Maire, et une musique brillante
rendait cette fête intéressante.

During the debate on these ideas in the draft of the Declaration presented to the Constituent Assembly, the points made above were clarified. When certain radical democrats protested the exclusive nature of the citizenship proposed, M. Target replied.

It was strange, he said, to find in the Assembly more support for the poverty of the masses than the property of the wealthy. The majority, another liberal said, would have no commerce with democracy:

If by using the word *people* you mean that which the Romans called the *plebs*, then you admit the distinction of orders; if the word you use answers to the Latin *populus*, you signify even more than the law and the intention of the assemblies.[52]

The speaker's insistence that he knew better than the democrats the mind of the French communities provoked wild applause. Mounier, the liberal lawyer from Grenoble, went to greater lengths. He said that nobody could doubt the sovereignty of the nation. But who would argue that authority must lie with the mad dictates of the multitude? That way lay anarchy! All men had certain rights because they were men. These the

52. Quoted in Slavin, "Democracy and the French Revolution," p. 64. The *plebs* was the body of Roman citizens given the franchise by the aristocrats who controlled the Republic.

Declaration must specify. But the rights of *citizens* belonged to them only because of the definitions made within a civil society. Thus the bourgeois revolution began by making clear the difference between natural rights and civil rights.

When a few of the stubbornest democrats argued that there were precedents for enfranchising the masses—America for example—the rebuttal was swift. There, the franchise was not universal. Moreover, the parallel was inexact. America had no mass of proletarians. Happy country! It was unlike France, which had a multitude of unpropertied men with no "stake in the country." France's huge rural and urban proletariat ought not to share power with the affluent. If they did, France would have a *social* revolution, where only a *political* one was needed. When it was argued that the draft Declaration might be taken by some to guarantee true civil equality, the drafters replied that they would purge the final text of ambiguities.

This they did. The final vote gave to France a Declaration with no mention of universal active citizenship for men. The distinction was made between active and passive citizens. The moderates were a solid majority against democracy: Mounier, representative of the provincial bourgeoisie; Bailly, the scientist and mayor of Paris; Lafayette, the aristocratic hero on horseback. These men were content to avoid the claims of democrats; and when they could not, they were ready to argue against democracy.

The Constitution of 1791 was therefore nothing less than the natural fruit of the Revolution of 1789. The franchise arrangements bypassed the peasants and artisans in favor of the more limited aim of equality of right in a monarchy of law. The task set for themselves by the liberals was to unite the "nation" within the terms of constitutional monarchy, not to define it democratically. Abbé Sieyès himself never raised democratic hopes in the masses, only to cast them down in 1791. He said from the start that citizens were of two classes: the poor and incompetent who had no civil rights, and the educated and affluent who would govern.

If we ask where democratic ideas came from, we cannot say from the makers of the Revolution down to 1793. The break with the Old Regime was truly radical, even before the death of Louis XVI, however. It did superimpose a uniform set of legal rights on a once privileged social community. But beyond that there had been an unequal contest between democrats and liberal constitutionalists, at least until 1793.

Then, under the pressure of events, the Revolution was once again propelled forward. Threatened from abroad, France's newly republican government expanded its already secularized definition of the political community. The Jacobin Constitution of the June 1793 crisis committed France to universal male suffrage. Citizen, nation, and people were made synonymous. But this constitution was never put into operation. Instead, democratic anarchy took hold of France. The *enragés* and their radical allies among the bourgeois intellectuals set up in the Paris Commune and in provincial ones as well the democracies which moderates had feared to sponsor in 1793. And the moderates became the victims of the Terror, especially when old democrats like Robespierre devised democratic dictatorship as the motive force of the Terror.

The lesson learned, that the lower classes were widely and correctly feared, informed the various conservative republican constitutions from 1795 to 1804: the Directory and the Consulate in their different guises. Napoleon's imperial constitutions made no return to the promise of democracy given by the Jacobins in 1793, until the Emperor desperately needed some trick to rally France to his standard, after the mortal wound sustained in Russia. Democracy was less the commitment of the Revolution than it was the *deus ex machina*[53]—the salvation machine—whenever the Revolution was threatened by external destruction. Dictators—democratic and Bonapartist alike—picked up the tattered flag of democracy to make of it a bandage for France.

Yet the slow transformation of political ideas and *ideology,* of a certain way of regarding the social and political community, which issued in modern democracy owed a great deal to the French Revolution.

The Revolution may not have been the product of democratic thought, just as it was not the result of the ideas of the *philosophes.* But in the Revolution the French did fashion the idea of the *nation* as a political community based on certain common experiences. Nationalism received impetus from the French rejection of feudal privilege and clerical internationalism. As the Revolution developed, what was foreign to France was rejected. And even under the Empire the dependencies were made over in the image of *la grande nation*; it was not France that was made over in some foreign image.

Baron Stein was correct also to point out how the *levée en masse* marked a step on the road toward a new conception of what the nation was. He gave particular stress to how the Revolution *in the end* did put the different classes on an equal basis. Moreover, he correctly observed that there seemed to be an advantage in the Revolution, or rather two advantages, especially obvious in times of "national" danger. The newly reorganized, politically equal, people committed their energy to France as citizens in a way no monarchy's subjects did, both spiritually and materially.

The question before Europe in 1815 was therefore more complex than the questions to which the four great powers addressed the energies of the Quadruple Alliance. It was more complex still than those issues at the heart of Alexander I's mystically inspired Holy Alliance. The question before Europe was, as we can see readily from any study of literature and the arts from 1789 to 1815, whether the democratic and nationalistic ideas produced by the Revolution would lie down before the forces of reaction and the even greater force of industrialization.

---

53. Literally, "the god from a machine," a reference to a stage device in classical drama, when a god dropped from the sky to save a hero.

BIBLIOGRAPHY

GEYL, PIETER. *Napoleon: For and Against.** New Haven: Yale University Press, 1949. A brilliant collection of essays by the Dutch master.

HAMPSON, NORMAN. *The First European Revolution.** New York: Harcourt, Brace & World, 1969. Very good on the background of Napoleonic "ideas."

KISSINGER, HENRY. *A World Restored.** Cambridge, Mass.: Harvard University Press, 1957. A brilliant study of Metternich's efforts to stabilize Europe; also very good on Castlereagh.

MEINECKE, FRIEDRICH. *Machiavellianism.** New York: Praeger Publishers, 1965. Good on the German reactions to the Revolution and Napoleonic imperialism.

NICOLSON, SIR HAROLD. *The Congress of Vienna.** New York: The Viking Press, 1946. A good survey of the decade 1812–1822.

TARLE, EVGENII. *Napoleon's Invasion of Russia.* Oxford: Clarendon Press, 1942. A very good account, combining Soviet nationalism with brilliant descriptive writing.

Asterisk indicates a paperbound edition.

BOOK TWO

Industry and Politics: The Dual Revolution, 1815–1870

While Europe's statesmen sought to restore the old order following the defeat of Napoleon, new tensions were already building: demands for social and political change, a new working-class consciousness, and an awakening nationalism. Together, these forces would spread rebellion across the Continent, in 1830 and again in 1848. The German artist Käthe Kollwitz portrays a workers' revolt in The Uprising *(1899); in one edition of the etching red tones were added to highlight the flames of the burning castle in the background and the torch of the symbolic female figure hovering overhead as she calls the workers onward. Courtesy Galerie St. Etienne, New York.*

The Congress of Vienna in 1814–1815 did not achieve either the general peace or the security predicted by its makers. France was again the scene of tremendous upheavals, first in 1830 and again in 1848. New states took shape in the Balkans and in the Netherlands. The decay of the Spanish monarchy was felt in America, where the movement toward independence triumphed. Even in the most conservative states—Russia, Prussia, and Austria—the threat of revolution appeared serious; and policies of repression cast the liberals into despair in Britain, where European liberalism had hoped to make its greatest advances.

Yet the struggle against the so-called congress system after 1815 is not the most dramatic aspect of the history of the West from 1815–1870. Two revolutionary movements took hold in Europe: the Industrial Revolution and the combination of social events which together constituted the revolution in popular culture. This revolution depended on the one in production, however, and it is therefore crucial to put it in the context of the other.

The main questions of this book, therefore, are those which seek the principles of politics tending toward democracy against the background of a great social transformation: How did Britain become the first industrial society? What did urbanization mean to the working classes, with regard to standards of living and the quality of life?

Above all else, it is the purpose of this Book to tell how the "world restored" at Vienna produced the forces which, in 1848, sent Metternich into exile and Karl Marx and Friedrich Engels to press with the *Communist Manifesto*. These events in 1848 were symbolic of a shift in the center of political gravity from the western fringe of Europe toward its "German" center. And in the 1860s it was in Germany under the dual impact of industrialization and unification under Prussian leadership that events took place on a scale filled with meaning for the future.

It really appears to me to be a new discovery in the European Government, at once . . . bringing the whole bearing of the system into its true light, and giving to the great Powers the efficiency and almost the simplicity of a single state.

LORD CASTLEREAGH (1813)[1]

I met Murder on the way—
He had a mask like Castlereagh.

PERCY BYSSHE SHELLEY (1819)[2]

6

EQUIPOISE AND REVOLUTION: 1815–1830

THE TWO CHIEF SYSTEMS OF EUROPE

Two hundred years before Shelley indicted Castlereagh for the murder of the "liberal" politics of the French Revolution and its heritage, Galileo had met head on the challenge of the two chief astronomical systems of the world—those of Copernicus and Ptolemy. In Shelley's mind Castlereagh was the spokesman for the conservative, traditional European system of politics and ideas which had been vindicated by the treaty of peace of November 20, 1815. Moreover, to Shelley and Byron in England, or among the partisans of the German "revolutionary" nationalists J. G. Fichte (1762–1814) and G. W. F. Hegel (1770–1831), the two chief "systems" of 1815 seemed as irreconcilable as ever those of Ptolemy and Copernicus had been.

Without ever consciously casting the choice in such terms, those sympathetic to the revolutionary heritage comprehended "conservatism" in broad social terms and considered it a body of ideas and attitudes in opposition to "modern" ones. Certainly European conservatives were themselves aware of the tensions that existed between their own ideas and those of the "liberals," or, put another way, between what we have called traditional society and its values and the society and values clarified by the more advanced partisans of revolution after 1789.

Indeed, this tension between what was "traditional" and what was "modern" early in the nineteenth century lies at the heart of our concern here. The conservatives feared that the social foundations of traditional culture and politics could not coexist with the social foundations and consequences of the Revolution: the economic patterns of bourgeois society, the heightened conflict of social groups and classes, the atomization of society explicit in new modes of

1. Castlereagh to Liverpool, October 20, 1818; quoted in René Albrecht-Carrié, *The Concert of Europe, 1815–1914* (New York: Harper & Row, Publishers, Torchbooks, 1968), p. 43.
2. *The Mask of Anarchy*, stanza 2, lines 1–2. Although written in 1819, the poem was not published until 1832.

production and the "liberal" economic ideas serving as their rationale, or the threatened disintegration of traditional elites—especially the landed nobility and clergy.

To conservatives there seemed to be something very sinister in the sympathy shown by some thinkers toward evolutionary ideas of political development and similarly evolutionary notions of economic development. Practical conservatives like Prince Metternich and conservative theorists like his friend Gentz agreed that the combination of historicism with liberal economics had produced the virus infection of political nationalism.[3] They were also agreed as to where the virus had been encouraged and what was necessary to eradicate it.

THE PROOFS OF RESTORATION CONSERVATISM

The restored monarchical system presided over by Metternich from 1815 to 1848 was rooted in a conservative political doctrine. This doctrine embraced more than the simple counterrevolutionary wish of privileged groups to keep the power to which they had been restored, although Metternich was concerned to undo the displacement of nobilities and the Catholic Church in countries hit by revolution. And he certainly regarded the "liberal" bourgeoisie as enemies of peace, religion, privilege, and the hierarchic arrangement of society conservatives meant when they spoke the word *order*. But Metternich was also the master at giving practical form to theoretical complaints lodged against the heritage of the Enlightenment, especially the legacy of rationalism, anticlericalism, and economic liberalism, for the partisans of restoration were generally a mixed group of monarchs, aristocrats, priests, Protestant pastors, and publicists who shared the belief that "liberalism" went wrong because it dismissed traditions rooted in the sentiments of religion.[4]

Ironically, the "fathers" of post-Revolution conservatism were themselves among the chief contributors to the fund of ideas then upsetting tradition, as we see in considering four representative thinkers: the Englishman Edmund Burke;[5] the German Herder;[6] the Frenchman Joseph de Maistre;[7] and the Austrian councillor Gentz,[8] who had served as secretary-general for the Congress of Vienna.

Burke was one of the most open British friends of the American Revolution as well as a most violent opponent of the French Revolution. Why Burke took such antagonistic positions toward the two revolutions we regard as the roots of democratic politics and social equality becomes clear from a consideration of his doctrine.

We say "doctrine" advisedly, because Burke's thought about politics and the social order is rooted in certain *beliefs* about society and a *preference* for one set of social conditions over others. It is the nature of doctrinal thought to assert beliefs and conclusions drawn from them, and to defend institu-

3. *Historicism* is the general term applied to a body of historical thought characterized by three main tenets: history is the product of "laws of development," not human will; this autonomous development is incompatible with absolute, timeless value systems; it is the task of analysis to understand the "laws" of development and so to encourage social actions in harmony with the unfolding of the predetermined social order.
4. Even in Protestant states, conservatives who disagreed on theological niceties agreed on the religious question.
5. 1729–1797.
6. Johann Gottfried von Herder, 1744–1803.
7. 1753–1821.
8. Friedrich von Gentz, 1764–1832.

tions on the basis of the substantive premises derived from those beliefs. Burke, for example, believed in something called the "organic society," by which he seemed to mean a natural growth in time. Burke also believed in what he called the "necessity of authority," or a set of principles not subject to doubt by that reasoning faculty which men may apply to a set of circumstances. It was essential to the conservatives that no rational philosophy be allowed to intrude in certain areas of thought—for example, the belief in original sin or the consequence drawn from it, that men are by nature wicked and covetous.

Burke's basic doctrine may be simply stated. Society exists in the first place because men are not only wicked and covetous, which necessitates that some principles or bonds arise to prevent mutual destruction. Fortunately, God also planted in men "passions," or "organs of the mind" of two types. Passions of self-preservation arise out of a natural desire to avoid pain and danger; these are the strongest human passions making for submission to common authority to preserve peace. At the same time, however, God implanted in men "passions of Pleasure," which Burke called "the passions of society"—among them sympathy, imitation, and ambition. These passions enable us to understand what it is like to do as another does, and so to be in another person's place. They lead naturally to emulation and in due course to the chief positive bonds of society—the decent respect for the manners and opinions of others on which civilization stands.

Thus, for Burke, the idea of society itself derives from his belief that "egotistic" passions bear certain penalties, while "altruistic" passions provide natural incentives to overcome *atomism*. Men cohere in social groups because their social passions, when added to the strong emotions of fear, danger, and pain, produce over time social and political devices which are natural to mankind in the sense that they arise from a God-given "nature." Hence, not reason, the false god set up by the Enlightenment, but passion and social contrivance alone rescue us from the disagreeable yoke of reason not modulated by the fruits of experience.[9] The growth of friendship and authority is historic and organic and derives naturally from pleasure and pain. The expressions of friendship and authority in politics are consent and a sort of loving harmony whereby the prince in a commonwealth takes the role given to parents in the family.

It is this doctrine which drove Burke to accept the revolution in America and reject the one in France. The Americans were doing what was natural for Englishmen: they were claiming the bonds of amity rooted in the order, respect, privileges, and laws established by consent under William III in 1689, in the Glorious Revolution. Theirs was a *revolution against revolution*, an effort to protect what had grown up historically, naturally, organically. The goal in 1776 had been the preservation of the status quo. America had wanted nothing more than the preservation of concrete liberties, while the French radicals had tried to uproot nature and to destroy the "decent drapery of life" created over time to cover the defects of man's "naked shivering nature."[10] The French had laid aside the right rule rooted in history in favor of ideas of abstract liberty without foundation, violating authority and its fearful source in God ("the Sublime").

Edmund Burke is chiefly remembered as a statesman and political writer, although his interests were wide ranging. His particular distinction was a complete mastery of both the philosophic and practical aspects of politics. A supporter of evolution rather than revolution, Burke was sympathetic to the American position but revealed his essential conservatism when faced with the French Revolution, which he felt ignored the basic elements of human nature that had produced European civilization. Through his writings and his voice in Parliament Burke remained an eloquent Conservative spokesman until his death in 1797. Radio Times Hulton Picture Library.

9. Burke's basic beliefs and his psychology are developed in his *A Philosophical Enquiry into the Origin of Our Ideas of the Sublime and the Beautiful*; see pp. 30–58 of the critical edition by J. T. Boulton (New York: Columbia University Press, 1958).
10. These phrases occur in Burke's *Reflections on the Revolution in France*, printed in the standard revised edition (Boston, 1865–1867), 3:231–563; see especially pp. 332–333.

Government was for Burke "like the proud keep of Windsor":[11]

> The well-compacted structure of our Church and State, the sanctuary, the holy of holies . . . defended by reverence . . . rising in the majesty of proportion, and girt with the double belt of its kindred and coeval towers, as long as this awful structure shall oversee and guard the subjected land—so long . . . will we have nothing to fear from the pickaxes of all the levellers of France.[12]

Burke's reference to "levellers" in France is vital. The new wave of European conservatism was not only religious in its inspiration, it was socially hierarchic. Burke disliked especially the contrast between the elegance of manners in prerevolutionary Europe and the lack of taste and elegance in revolutionary France. This point reached deeper than personal criticism of Rousseau, for whom Burke had contempt, as if Jean Jacques himself embodied the bourgeois lack of moral taste Burke attributed to revolutionary society in general. In the eyes of Burke and the other conservatives, bourgeois mores were indelicate, overly sensual, even lewd; bourgeois youth was lacking in modesty and docility before authority; and bourgeois judgment was vitiated by levity, obstinacy, and rashness.

The defense of public morality against "Jacobin imperialism" was thus at bottom also a rejection of the social order of equality for which Robespierre had waged war. The rejection of the "new society" was made explicit:

> . . . all men have equal rights; but not to equal things. He that has but five shillings . . . has as good a right to it as he that has five hundred pounds has to his larger portion. But he has no right to an equal share in the product of the joint stock . . . .[13]

Burke's world is one drawn on the analogy of a company which guarantees harmony because it admits of few changes in status and no wholesale alterations of any sort. To maintain that society is organic is to preclude fundamental change. Indeed, it is better to preserve an unjust system which works than to risk damage to traditions of community, customs, usage, habit, prejudice, and whatever else protects established relationships in society. These ideas in English dress achieved much, for example, in the later restatements by the poet Coleridge,[14] who had contact with German thinkers. Moreover, the statesman Castlereagh was thoroughly imbued with Burke's political thought, both with regard to particular policies actually pursued before 1815 and matters of general framework for the maintenance of liberty *with order*.[15]

Also, many European thinkers shared Burke's historicist doctrine of social development and his praise of continuity. Herder especially was responsible for synthesizing ideas of harmonious development and emotional spiritualism. Like many other young Germans who were attracted by Enlightenment notions of human dignity and freedom, Herder was repelled by the role assigned to reason and intellect at the expense of passion. He

---

11. The "keep" being Windsor Castle.
12. *Reflections*, 3:410.
13. *Reflections*, 3:309.
14. Samuel Taylor Coleridge (1772–1834).
15. This has been demonstrated in detail by Stephen R. Graubard in his book *Burke, Disraeli, and Churchill* (Cambridge, Mass.: Harvard University Press, 1961), pp. 17–87, and also in his article, "Castlereagh and the Peace of Europe," *The Journal of British Studies* 3 (1963): 79–87.

was also out of sympathy with the stress on political and social atomism. Where the *philosophes* had stressed the virtue of each man's "tending his own garden,"[16] Herder had been drawn toward a different view of man as the product of society.

The *philosophes* based liberty on the individual capacity to reason, which made men equal to each other and seemed to establish a basis for supposing that men, in pursuing their personal interests, could by a happy accident thereby advance common interests as well. It could thus be said that the Enlightenment in much of Europe was simply the ideology of the classes already free. This atomism undermined the truly "individual" thing in mankind, the unique soul every person possessed, open to the world through the senses, hence an undivided seat of passion always able to respond to the peculiar qualities of any human environment. What the poet Goethe had called the inner world of a sensitive man, Herder called man's inner sentiment.[17] But where Goethe had been content with a view of sensitive man in rebellion against conventional society—and was thus once sympathetic to revolution—Herder developed ideas at odds with the fragmented world of revolutionary individualism.

He developed a doctrine of the "nation" on the basis of his interest in language and literature.[18] The "nation" for Herder was the true individual. Men were indeed shaped in their emotions by their society. But the vehicle was language, the patterns of which differed from country to country. Language itself was the cement of each *Volk*, or people, who shared a common civilization based on "culture" rather than politics. All who spoke German natively constituted the German *Volk*: transplanted intellectuals in Prague and Budapest, "French" nobles in the old Middle Kingdom on the Rhine, princes in Prussia and peasants in the Tyrol. The fact of "alien" political domination meant nothing. For each person was what he was by virtue of his growth in the natural linguistic community in which he lived.

It was therefore a mistake to suppose that the real concern for thought was a rational effort to reconstruct the political and economic institutions of the day, as the revolutionaries advocated. The real task was to understand the "spontaneous" shaping of people as members of the natural communities to which they belonged. Collective expression through the "nation" was the core of Herder's doctrine in *Another Philosophy of History for the Education of Humanity* (*Auch eine Philosophie der Geschichte zur Bildung der Menschheit*, 1774). Herder's nationalism was therefore historicist and cultural, not revolutionary, and he had no sympathy with any movement which threatened violence against the past, the sacred repository of traditions without which the *Volk* could not exist. Men were thus not only "made" by their history; they could not continue to live validly if they negated their history. This was the message of Herder's great *Reflections on the Philosophy of the History of Humanity* (*Ideen zur Philosophie der Geschichte der Menschheit*, ca. 1784–1791).

Joseph de Maistre was much less an original thinker than either Burke or Herder. But he fused their emphases on experience, history, and tradition into an amalgam important in its own right. Society and government itself

---

16. The figure is Voltaire's, in the last pages of *Candide*.
17. Goethe's phrase comes from his *Sorrows of Young Werther* (*Die Leiden des jungen Werthers*, 1774). Goethe later became a strong enemy of reform and revolution, like Burke: see Klaus Epstein, *The Genesis of German Conservatism* (Princeton: Princeton University Press, 1966).
18. He was a leader of *Sturm und Drang*, a literary movement that rejected the classical rationalism of antiquity, which dominated German writing.

were equally worthy of respect on the ground of their age. The products of slow growth, neither could be "improved" rapidly: in politics the rule was that good comes sooner to worse than to better. Institutions were in delicate balance; they were not the product of "contracts" to avoid evil but were good by virtue of being natural. And the revolutionary individual was in error on a basic point: his own happiness was not the grand object of government. The well-being of the collective of which he was merely a part was the true object of Providence. Thus the disdain of the *philosophes* for religion was merely symptomatic of a larger selfish condemnation of all authority, and of the past which was the guarantor of the authenticity of life. De Maistre made the Catholic Church the foundation of a just social order, with the idea of sovereignty derived from God, while Herder and Burke were less inclined toward absolutism than toward the more "enlightened" monarchy native to Prussia and England. But all three shared the view that religion supplied the motive for obedience, that without it there could be no "order," and that social stability could be found only in a decent respect for the traditions of a venerable past.

Similar ideas informed the writings of Metternich's friend and councillor Gentz, the German translator of Burke. Like Adam Muller a sworn foe of egalitarian and liberal ideas of 1789,[19] and also firm in the conviction that feudalism and social hierarchy were the "natural" and historical forms ideal for Europe, Gentz went even further. Despite the long tradition of government by princes and parliaments in the German world, Gentz spoke of representation of the people as an un-German thing. He pressed the view that only "corporate" estates (the Church and the nobility) were compatible with monarchy. Gentz also championed the concentration of full sovereign powers in every prince, on the ground that princes, bishops, and great feudatories were the only adequate curbs to "modern social forces," which, once represented, must undermine the state.[20]

Gentz was especially sympathetic to Burke's view that the science of constructing governments was *experimental*, by which conservatives meant a matter of historical experience and not one to be taught a priori, or by mere reason. Reason as the arbiter of politics had encouraged individualism and an atomistic notion of rights. Surer foundations for social order existed in the authority of the Church and the monarchical principle of absolutism, according to Gentz. Repression was thus the natural instrument of political order; Gentz wrote to Muller:

I continue to defend the proposition: "In the order that the press may not be abused, nothing whatever shall be printed in the next years. Period!" If this principle were to be applied . . . we should within a brief time find our way back to God and Truth. . . .[21]

On another front, Gentz attacked along a wider arc all forces of secularism. Proclaiming that the Protestant Reformation had set in motion the forces of bourgeois individualism and liberalism, Gentz traced the French Revolution to the loss of religious, moral, and political order in Luther's time. He was especially in sympathy with Burke, where the Englishman

---

19. Muller (1779–1829) was a Berliner, a convert to Catholicism, and an emigrant to Vienna. His *Elements of Statecraft* (1808–1809) was a powerful Burkean statement.
20. These ideas, together with Gentz's advice that Metternich abolish the "constitutions," triumphed at Carlsbad in 1819: see Chapter 7.
21. Quoted in E. J. Hobsbawn, *The Age of Revolution, 1789–1848* (London: Weidenfeld & Nicolson, 1962), p. 231.

had rejected the liberal economists' view of society as a machine, an *artificial* construct rather than a natural growth, and hence subject to improvement by tampering. Gentz believed that in the "old society" God put men of high and low estate in close working relationships based on the duty of the highborn to protect the base. The *philosophes*, especially the economists, had put in place of that view of personal relations the brute force of the market and an analysis of social life in terms of the exchange of commodities. Burke had seen the danger of this from the beginning, as he said in a letter to a French aristocrat in 1791: "It were better to forget, once and for all, the *encyclopédie* and the whole body of economists, and to revert to those old rules and principles which have hitherto made princes great and nations happy."[22]

SECULAR LIBERALISM: A PARADOX

The secular ideological roots of the new order were thus seen as deep in the soil of religiously sanctioned individualism, the rationalism of the Enlightenment, and the belief of the "liberal" economists that society was the sum of market arrangements which had their own logic and dynamic. Indeed, the historicism of the great English economists Adam Smith (1723–1790), Thomas Malthus (1766–1834), and David Ricardo (1772–1823) was one of the crucial elements making up the compounded revolutionary challenge.

For the "classical" liberal economists the world consisted of individuals driven by passions and drives. The tendency of these was toward the avoidance of pain or dissatisfaction and the maximization of pleasure. These results were best obtained when the "state" abstained from exercising its authority over economic events, because there were at work in nature certain "laws" of development of a sort close to those Burke found at the root of political order. Individuals in pursuit of their several interests were saved from *destructive* competition, or the "anarchy of equal competitors," as Thomas Hobbes (1588–1679) had called it, by their understanding of the advantages created by entering into "free" (voluntary) relations. Men thus constituted "natural" social groups for economic purposes, along lines of self-interest.

The conclusion drawn was that rational calculation was the law of nature in economics, that conventional morality and duty were superfluous notions, and that what the state must do was to let alone individuals in pursuit of gain. *Laissez-faire* ("allow to do") thus become the slogan of atomist economics. And the "liberal" economists agreed that freedom from interference was the only way to guarantee the result desired: the growth of capital and the rise to power of the bourgeois classes whose prophets were Adam Smith and his disciples, Malthus and Ricardo.

Smith's 1776 *Wealth of Nations* and Ricardo's 1817 *On the Principles of Political Economy and Taxation* framed the revolutionary period chronologically. Intellectually, the doctrine of the sovereign individual as the creator of the only natural social order—that is, the one in which wealth increased most rapidly—raised a red flag before the partisans of tradition. Not only was the basis of Smith's liberal order the abdication of the state and the old elites from the exercise of power. The liberals maintained that a true social division of production (labor) according to the instinct for gain insured a more just world. Traditional society was economically unequal in opportunity because it rested on the social ideal of benevolence—aristocrats treating kindly their inferiors. The most equal of all relationships in

---

22. Quoted in Hobsbawn, *Age of Revolution*, p. 247.

economics was the exchange of equivalent values in the market, whether by purchase with money or by barter. A society in which nobody depended on benevolence in economics was thus the "natural" counterpart of a political society in which all men participated on equal basis through the widest possible distribution of the franchise.[23]

From yet another direction, therefore, historical analysis buttressed by rationalism posed a threat to traditional social order and the doctrinal foundations on which it rested. Nowhere was this danger more clear than in Germany, the European region in which historicist ideas had outgrown their conservative implications and limitations under the stress of the Napoleonic Wars.

In Germany, the concern for the past and cultural nationalism had produced a spirit of revolt against alien "cultures" and Napoleon's empire. The cult of emotion favored by Rousseau had found in young Goethe[24] an avid expositor. Like Schiller[25] and Herder, Goethe focused on the development of passions in the soul in opposition to the governance of reason. At once eager to create a truly German literature and free himself from bondage to the rules of the past, Goethe made of natural emotions the key to independence of personality. He celebrated conflict within man as the hallmark of liberation. But Goethe drew from this idea the conclusion that true liberty must be won not by throwing off the leaden weight of political absolutism, but by conquering inwardly the stifling moralism of social customs.

Goethe at first welcomed the political revolution, but he never raised his voice for the oppressed. He merely espoused cultural nationalism, which had a tradition reaching back over several decades by the time of Napoleon's occupation of the Rhineland and his subsequent victories over Austria and Prussia. Goethe therefore was not a prophet for the next generation. Instead, university students and serious philosophers and politicians sought ideas not so barren of political content, concepts filled with a political sense of destiny for the *Volk* and its spirit (or *Geist*). This search was explosive when mixed with an emphasis on direct action, heroic struggle, and the idealization of genius.

Napoleon's victories were the powerful catalyst which brought German thought to a revolutionary point. If the old regimes of bourgeois radicals and petty princes could not protect the *Volk* from conquest, then perhaps the people would win freedom for themselves. A variety of "political" associations sprang up. The *Turngemeinden*, or associations of youths, led by "Father" Jahn[26] were physical fitness cohorts that espoused fanatical nationalism, anti-Semitism, and a general hostility to foreigners. They were often disruptive of university classes conducted along lines insufficiently "nationalist." Student fraternities (*Burschenschaften*) formed, encouraged by nationalist journals,[27] dedicated to the freedom and unity of the German *Volk*, and hotly against both Napoleon and any effort to restore the system he had overturned.

The various reformist groups drew sustenance from events triggered by

As a young man Goethe was part of the German Sturm und Drang *(Storm and Stress) movement. This group sought naturalistic explanations for the development of literature, art, and national characteristics. Another member was the Swiss "physiognomist" Johann Kaspar Lavater, who attempted to apply Storm and Stress theories in practice. He taught that the facial and body formations of an individual could reveal character. Paper cut-out profile silhouettes, such as this one of Goethe, became fashionable late in the eighteenth century, and they were analyzed to gain insight into the personality of the subject. Staatsbibliothek, Berlin.*

23. Ricardo and Malthus "corrected" Smith's false optimism concerning wages and supplies of food by attributing the failure of wages to rise and the pressure put on food resources to the increase in number of the laboring poor. They were, however, like Smith for free trade and against the dominance of the landed elites.
24. Johann Wolfgang von Goethe (1749–1832).
25. Friedrich von Schiller (1759–1805).
26. Friedrich Ludwig Jahn (1778–1852).
27. For example, the Frankfurt nationalist Joseph von Görres (1776–1848) published *Der Rheinische Merkur.*

the Prussian defeats at Jena-Auerstädt. In Prussia itself the state collapsed and the kingdom was stripped of its territories except for the nucleus about Berlin; and Napoleon occupied even that remnant. The huge indemnity imposed on Prussia could not be paid without a radical reordering of the economy. Hence the defeat encouraged the migration into Prussia of those who were eager to make reforms and who were also attracted to Prussia because it had resisted Napoleon and accepted defeat rather than collaborate with the "foreign" elements. Prussia became a magnet for patriotic statesmen and thinkers who were not themselves Prussians, but who saw in Prussia the symbol of the "oneness" of the German nation and people in troubled times.

Scharnhorst[28] and Gneisenau[29] reformed the army along popular lines, Gneisenau especially aware how vital it was to release the popular dynamism of German society. They believed it necessary to break military caste dominance and create a popular army to defeat the French. Baron Stein[30] and Hardenberg[31] applied the same principle to civil institutions, beginning in 1807. A new municipal code introduced self-government. The minister of education Humboldt[32] instituted reforms along humane and humanistic lines. All of the reformers hoped to shape a new constitution, providing for a legislative assembly of citizens united by culture, a sense of duty to Prussia, and the sacred cause of defeating France.

This could best be done by democratizing the system of Frederick the Great, by keeping its virtues while distributing property and opportunity more widely than had formerly been the case. Stein even went so far as to abolish the subjection of serfs to *Junkers* by giving to peasants the personal "rights" to move, to marry, and to study or take up a new trade. After Stein's dismissal in 1808, Hardenberg extended the "abolition" of serfdom to property itself. Peasants could exchange the obligations of serfdom for private property, on the proviso that they pay a fee of one-third of their land to the lord of the manor. While reform thus enlarged aristocratic economic power, it also helped lay the foundations for a modern social system through the freeing of property and people from the restraints of a custom-ridden agrarian society.

Stein's intellectual affinities are of particular interest in this context. Himself from a family of imperial knights, Stein was independent of notions of absolutism. He had been a student at Göttingen and also had traveled widely in Europe. He was under Montesquieu's influence with regard to the idea that a "balance" of powers was indispensable for a just constitution. He believed the nationalist myth that Germany had once been a community of free men only. And he thought this original "liberty" had its proudest moment in the "old" German political freedom evident in England. Moreover, Göttingen was part of Hanover, and the influence there of English ideas was great, because the ruling dynasty in Britain was the Hanoverian house of the four Georges.[33]

Indeed, it was in Stein's student days that he encountered August Wilhelm Rehberg (1757–1836), the translator of Burke, and Ernst Brandes (1758–1810), his friend and another leading antirevolutionary historicist.

In the Göttingen circle Stein acquired the doctrines he later applied. He was an opponent of popular sovereignty, but a devout believer in the

28. Gerhard von Scharnhorst (1755–1813).
29. August Neithardt von Gneisenau (1760–1831).
30. Heinrich Friedrich Karl vom und zum Stein (1757–1831).
31. Baron Karl August von Hardenberg (1750–1822).
32. Karl Wilhelm von Humboldt (1767–1835).
33. Begun in 1714 by King George I.

organic growth of national institutions. While he rejected the Revolution, he was no reactionary. Indeed, he embraced certain aspects of historicism which might lead in a "liberal" direction, especially economic reformism and the belief that there were nationalist "forms" peculiar to German life. These were ideas also important in the philosophic movement associated with the emigration of the "historical" nationalists Fichte and Hegel.

Before Jena, Johann Gottlieb Fichte had been a partisan of the Revolution. He was also an admirer of Rousseau. From the *Social Contract* he took the idea of the general will, transforming it with the concepts of German idealism. Fichte had absorbed from Kant the dialectic of spirit (*noumena*) and world (*phenomena*). But he denied altogether the reality of the physical world. In reaction against rationality and scientific laws which determined man's fate, Fichte embraced the ideas of soul and passion at work in the *Sturm und Drang* writers. He mixed individuality, spiritualism, and the denial of determinism to concoct a revolutionary creed. The right to object, to rebel, was that of the *Volk*, not the single man. Since reality consisted of the collective life of the "race," and since the individual life had value only inasmuch as it merged into the ideal existence of the *Volk*, the general will was not a count of separate wills. It was instead the realization in action of the whole destiny of the *Volk*, as this worked in history. The role of political society was not merely that of supplying the preconditions of interior freedom; it was actually a dimension of freedom itself that politics supplied.

This potentially totalitarian idea, of freeing the individual by merging him in the state, seemed, at least in the beginning, relatively harmless. What alarmed some, however, especially conservatives who heard Fichte lecture in 1804–1805, was the conclusion drawn. The "idea" working itself out in political history was nothing less than the real course of history in the sense of human destiny. The Enlightenment had served its purpose, which was to use reason to destroy authority. But the *philosophes* had opted for the inner life of reason and individual pleasure. The Revolution had exposed to view the next task: to bring into being collectives in which personal reason gave way to the reason of the people: Robespierre thus was for Fichte the prophet of right order. Jena, of course, converted the philosopher from his pro-French stance. Napoleon's despotism had shown conclusively that France was not the true bearer of the spirit needed to guide mankind to a higher stage of history.

Fichte took up the challenge directly in 1807–1808. In the latter year at Berlin he lectured to a wide audience, recalling in his title Luther's invitation to the nobility to liberate Germany from foreign domination.[34] Fichte addressed his call to the whole "German Nation," however.[35] In his new guise as a patriot, he freed Herder's *Volk* from its conservative implications. Fichte argued that the German race alone was spread wide enough in

34. Luther's 1520 *Address to the Nobility of the German Nation.*
35. *Addresses to the German Nation (Reden an die Deutsche Nation).*

Growing interest in the life of common people was manifested in the mid–nineteenth-century art movement known as realism. This was a European-wide phenomenon which started in France and England and inspired artists such as the German Wilhelm Leibl. Peasant Women in a Village Church *was painted during a long stay in the village of Berbling where Leibl observed the customs of these simple folk. The mood is one of quiet dignity and heartfelt empathy on the part of the artist who has escaped sentimentalizing the subject. As industrialization radically altered society, artists tended more and more to identify with the rural working classes who were the chief victims of that change. Photo Kleinhempel.*

Europe to bear the burden of universal liberation. The new Chosen People—the German "race"—must tie itself to the military power of the state in Prussia. Thus he transformed the mystical "people" into the race embodied in the action of the nation-state. To be part of the *Volk* was to be part of human destiny itself. The devouring flame of patriotism demanded sacrifice, for by a paradox freedom could be had only by the surrender of self to the state.

This was in part the doctrine Hegel took up in developing his own nationalist philosophy of history. The state was for him no mere convention for the satisfaction of private human wants. It was itself the "world-spirit" working historically to produce national self-consciousness. This stood Herder on his head, for now it was not folk self-consciousness which produced the state, but the ideal force of the state which produced folk self-consciousness. Morality was the proper submission of self to state. Specifically, this was the price Germans had to pay for leading mankind to the last stage of history—universal freedom.[36]

Hegel had come to this idea slowly and by various turns, beginning in the 1790s, when he was, like the poet Hölderlin and the philosopher Schelling, a divinity student at Tübingen. All three belonged to the upper bourgeois class of Swabia, where the regime of estates had produced only "liberal" freedom, i.e., the inner freedom of ideas unconnected to a broad sociopolitical liberation of men. Hegel was aware that the Revolution was itself a response to grave social dislocation, not the cause of it. Indeed, the need for revolutionary ideas was the product of the divorce of power and life. Society had no longer the power to unite men in freedom and dignity. The need was for a new argument, or dialectical tension, between the state and civil society, which it was the business of the philosopher to understand and expound. The task was to promote a revolution in bourgeois thought, so that yesterday's "liberals" would be worthy of the wider political freedom in which men's destiny lay.[37]

Neither Fichte nor Hegel ever tried to deduce from their idealism a political program with clear aims inimical to the restoration designed at Paris and Vienna in 1815. But it could not escape notice in Vienna that the new political philosophy had grown up in German states largely agrarian, but dominated by no feudal structures.[38] Moreover, converts to it were active as early as 1815 and 1817, when the Prussian press protested, and the *Burschenschaften* rioted, against Metternich's system. Revolutionary nationalism also seemed to infect student groups in Poland, Russia, and Italy. Everywhere, the romantic poets, painters, and musical composers were powerful protagonists of the cult of feeling and the ideal of universal freedom. And Metternich saw at once that his hope for peace with "order" was not likely to be realized with a watch on the Rhine alone: a wider structure of control was required.

THE CONCERT OF EUROPE

Nationalism was for Metternich a sword hanging over the crowned heads of Restoration Europe. Neither the Church nor the Holy Roman Empire had provided an adequate safeguard of unity and stability in European society before the sixteenth century. The French Revolution had called into

36. In earlier stages there had been freedom only for despots ("Oriental freedom") or for the few (as in Greece and Rome).
37. On the revolutionary politics of the early German idealists, see F. G. Nauen, *Revolution, Idealism, and Human Freedom* (The Hague: Nijhoff, 1971).
38. In Hegel's Württemberg the princes had never won victories over the "middle-class" estates of the duchy.

question the capacity of the unitary, secular nation-state ruled by "sovereign" princes, which since about 1500 had seemed the main hope for a social organization secure domestically and internationally. The 140 years after Westphalia (1648) had produced an "anarchy of sovereigns" internationally, in which aggressive and competitive states had resorted to the balance of power to protect themselves from their own appetites. Yet before 1789 war had been restrained in its objectives, as the Great Powers had seemed to agree to stop short of real destruction of national entities in their pursuit of advantage over their neighbors.[39]

The French Revolution had changed the situation radically. The *philosophes* had not "caused" it, but their concern for man and society had generated a revolutionary current of opposition to repressive rules, prejudice, ignorance, and superstition. The more "advanced" *philosophes* had spoken quite openly about the need to scientifically plan better societies in which economic, political, racial, and even sexual oppression would be alleviated.[40] But the *philosophes* had given little thought to the order of Europe internationally.[41] Nor had they paid any attention to "nationalism," even though it was true that for centuries certain local collective sentiments had encroached on such forms of universalism as papal and imperial authority and the doctrine of natural law.

The revolution of 1789 had, paradoxically, restated the case for universalism while also making clear what force there was in revolutionary nationalism. The defense of the Revolution against European reactions had consolidated both national consciousness and the wish to transform the social order beyond the borders of France. The armies of Robespierre and Napoleon had exported revolution and upset the social order. The new empire had also shown to the awakened Europeans a universalist side, and the Germans especially had revolted against the effort to unify Europe by imposing on it French political and cultural forms. Herder's *Volksgeist* and *Nationalgeist* had asserted the "national" principle of uniqueness against the cosmopolitan doctrines of the Enlightenment. And Baron Stein had prompted the humiliated and defeated East Elbean Germans to speak of a peak of "national" resistance.

This, then, was the dual inheritance of the period 1789–1815: the longing of political prophets and poets for a glorious future based on the concerns for man and society voiced by cosmopolitans; and the adaptation of that longing to the antiuniversalist framework of emerging nationalism set by the various reactions to Napoleonic imperialism. The participants in the Congress of Vienna had agreed on the necessity of condemning French expansion, but they were less united about the basic principles of the proper ordering of Europe for the future.

Metternich was conservative in a way Castlereagh was not. The Habsburg statesman rejected outright the idea of "popular" government; and he held to doctrines of absolute monarchy, orthodox religion, and the need for action by the Powers to suppress "liberal" agitation within the various states. Castlereagh reflected an equal wish to contain France, but he was after all a British statesman. And to him the defense of class rule meant the defense of British constitutionalism, with its parliamentary liberties and a fluid social order. Neither statesman shared Alexander of Russia's mystical attachment to religious universalism.

One of the ablest statesmen of his day, Prince Metternich was the Austrian minister of foreign affairs for forty years. As a young man he was appalled by the excesses of the French Revolution, and throughout his career he fought to preserve the status quo while ignoring the social movements of his time. The Congress of Vienna found him at the height of power, and the new European political system which emerged largely reflected his conservative ideas. Later Metternich fatally underestimated the power of nationalism which he helped to repress in Germany, Spain, and Italy. For many years the Prince was chancellor as well as foreign minister, but his neglect of internal policy led to the mob reactions of 1848 and the collapse of a system of diplomacy by congress. The Mansell Collection.

39. Poland provides the great exception, in the successive "partitions."
40. On the sexually repressive aspects of the Old Regime, Restif de la Bretonne and de Sade wrote voluminously.
41. Kant was an exception, as was the "outsider" Rousseau.

There was, therefore, from the beginning, the strong likelihood that the Great Powers could agree on "keeping the peace," even if this meant little more than returning to the limited objectives of competition espoused in balance-of-power politics. What was less likely was that the British "liberals" and the European *social* "conservatives" would take the same stance toward popular movements for political change and constitutionalism in Europe.

The question of broadening the basis of political life—the democratic principle which in the 1800s came to the fore in Europe—was bound to produce tensions within the Quadruple Alliance. Popular opinion, fueled by the newspaper press, might build in small states and large ones the desire for change—even movements of revolution. Demands for franchise extension might appear on the surface to be purely domestic questions; but to Metternich they might seem to be inimical, a sword to cut the means by which Europe's ruling aristocrats managed politics and maintained the structure of a stable international order. If the demand for social and political change was also fed by economic developments, as it clearly was in the movement toward industrialization, then the legacy of the Revolution would be strengthened from another quarter. The rise of working-class consciousness might become as potent a force of challenge in Western Europe as the awakening nationalist consciousness already was in the Netherlands, Italy, and the Balkan regions just then shaking off centuries of Turkish domination.

The Concert of Europe orchestrated by Metternich after 1815 was, therefore, burdened by more than the agreement to use power to maintain a stable international order. It had to deal also with the fundamental tensions arising within the individual Powers and caused by sharply differing views of what constituted a just society. Metternich supposed he could hold in check the novel social forces of the new century. Given the European interests overseas, whether close at hand in the Levant and Africa or in Asia and America, the Concert had far-reaching effects. Why this was so, we can easily grasp by focusing on certain events which took place between 1815 and 1848, each of which revealed the limits of understanding among the Powers.

The Final Act of the Congress of Vienna (and the Holy Alliance) excluded France, which was deemed the chief threat to stability. By 1818, the British were eager to see the occupation of France ended, as were the other Powers, providing that France could be brought into the "system" of peace maintenance on terms adequate to assure her good behavior. This was done by the protocol (or amendment) signed at Aix-la-Chapelle (November 15, 1818). France swore to adhere to the "System which has given peace to Europe" by means of the "intimate Union established among the Monarchs" in 1815.[42] There arose at once, however, an issue that revealed a split in the "Union," between constitutionalist France and England and the powers of the Holy Alliance—Russia, Prussia, and Austria.

In July 1820 the Kingdom of the Two Sicilies suffered a minor revolt against the Spanish conservatism of King Ferdinand I. His government was unacceptable to Sicilian and Neapolitan "patriots" who had experienced "constitutional" rule.[43] Ferdinand then gave to the rebels a new constitu-

---

42. See the Protocol and Declaration of the Cabinets, in Albrecht-Carrié, *Concert of Europe*, pp. 43–46.
43. Either in the Napoleonic variety or under British control before the Spanish restoration in 1815.

tion, perhaps under the pressure of events in America, where the Spanish colonials had been in rebellion since 1812. Castlereagh opposed Metternich's suggestion of collective intervention to repress the liberals at Naples.[44] The Habsburg minister responded by convening two conferences in 1820–1821, at Troppau and at Laibach, at which the Holy Alliance signed a protocol asserting the right of the autocratic "powers" to use force to bring any state experiencing revolution back "into the bosom of the Great Alliance."[45] The situation alarmed Castlereagh because he did not construe the alliance of Great Powers to be for the regulating of the *internal affairs of states*, viewing it rather as a means of merely extending the right to mutual security against aggressors. London and Paris agreed that no such aggressive threat emanated from Spain or Naples and that the various protocols had created no right of intervention that would admit of "a general and indiscriminate application to all Revolutionary Movements."[46]

The issue was thus squarely joined. Metternich used Austrian arms exclusively to crush the rebels at Naples, justifying his action in terms of an international mandate to defeat those who propagated revolution and confusion. His pretext was that the king of Sardinia had invited this aid, because his realm was threatened by the liberal agitators from Naples. But he was not satisfied with action alone; Metternich issued a declaration of his intention to "deliver Europe from the curse of Revolution" and the "violation of all principles of order and morality." He proclaimed "conspiracies" at the root of the agitation, and could indeed point to the underground revolutionary groups known as the Carbonari, the Veri Italiani, and others whose doctrine mixed socialism, nationalism, and revolutionary republicanism.[47]

The Spanish situation itself had not been dealt with, however, and in 1822 a new conference, the Congress of Verona, convened to consider Metternich's demand for intervention there, which Castlereagh opposed unsuccessfully. France acted in behalf of the Congress, while the chief cause for British abstention was not in Europe, but in America. The British hoped to use Spain's troubles to complete the takeover of trade in Spanish America. London supported the revolutionaries there more or less covertly. And in 1823 this prompted the United States to proclaim the Monroe Doctrine, which announced that European powers should not interfere in American affairs. The new British foreign secretary, George Canning,[48] put the British behind the right of people to choose their own governments, thus widening the rift between Metternich and the London government.

The ambiguities inherent in the congress system were fully revealed by another crisis in progress in 1821. The Congress of Vienna had pushed aside the Turkish Empire, because Russia considered the Ottoman Empire the czar's concern, and because Metternich agreed to consider the Balkans a "legitimate" area of the sultan's rule in Christendom. Yet both Napoleon's expedition to Egypt and English sea power in the Mediterranean had shown clearly how unavoidably the Ottoman Empire was a European concern. Moreover, Russia had been since 1774 "protector" of the Eastern Orthodox Christians[49] as well as a power anxious to dominate the Black Sea and the

44. Because Spain lay in France's area of action?
45. Albrecht-Carrié, *Concert of Europe*, p. 48. A revolt had happened before this in Portugal also.
46. Castlereagh's "Circular Despatch" to British Missions, January 19, 1821: Albrecht-Carrié, *Concert of Europe*, p. 49.
47. See Chapter 9, for a discussion of some of these groups and their ideas.
48. 1770–1827. (Castlereagh committed suicide in 1822.)
49. By the Treaty of Kluchuk Kainarji.

No painter better expressed the spirit or concerns of the Romantic period than Eugène Delacroix (1798–1863). The Greek struggle for independence inspired young artists throughout Europe, but Byron's poetry and Delacroix's Massacre at Chios have proven to be its most lasting monuments. This slaughter of Greeks by Turks occurred in 1822, and Delacroix soon decided to use it as a subject for a major Salon painting. He talked to survivors, borrowed oriental costumes for his models, and made numerous studies for the work. Color and dramatic movement always characterize his art, as well as a pervasive sense of melancholy which is heightened here by the quiet nobility of the victims. Although this painting was not well received when Delacroix exhibited it in 1824, it has since been regarded as a definitive work of the Romantic style. Lauros-Giraudon.

approaches to Constantinople. French interests in the Near East remained strong. Austria's own empire bordered the Balkans and included South Slav groups closely tied to kindred groups under Turkish rule.

There were thus both reasons for conflict and the occasion, but the "Eastern Question" seemed less pressing than the more limited "Balkans" problem concerning the aspirations of the Christian peoples there. Various ethnic groups existed within the Balkans, among them the Greeks, who had in the eighteenth century experienced a "revival" of consciousness of their ancient glory. This nationalist sentiment was both literary in character and political, and in 1821 it produced a revolt among the Greeks in Illyria, spurred on by those from Phanar, the Greek Quarter of Constantinople, where "liberal" ideas had taken hold. The 1821 risings led by Alexander Ypsilanti (1792–1828) failed, and in 1822 Metternich had him safely in prison. The Verona conference refused to consider the pleas of Greek representatives seeking support, but the death (on April 19, 1824) of the poet Byron at Missolonghi, where he had gone to command a regiment of "freedom fighters," fired the liberal press in London and elsewhere. Canning, however, favored the Greek cause only to the extent of wanting to arbitrate the conflict between the rebels and the sultan, thus setting the stage for a compromise.

The arbitration of 1826 set up a Greek state as a dependency of Turkey. But the Ottomans enlisted the help of the Egyptian branch of the imperial family in order to avoid such a settlement. The result was in effect an ultimatum known as the Treaty of London (July 6, 1827). This device for the pacification of Greece used feudal language to embrace political revolution. The Greeks would take possession of all "Greek" property, holding it from Turkey as a "lord paramount," with a guarantee of protection from the London powers. Should the Ottomans refuse the offer embodied in the treaty, the powers threatened "a connection with the Greeks" against the sultan.[50] When the sultan did refuse, a combined Anglo-French fleet destroyed a Turco-Egyptian one at Navarino Bay, on October 20, 1827.

Protracted diplomacy over the next three years occupied British efforts, while the Russian approach was more direct. The new czar, Nicholas I (1825–1855), declared war in 1828, and the French sent a force against the Egyptians in the Peloponnesus. The sultan was in fact battered into acceptance of terms in 1829, in the Treaty of Adrianople, the exact provisions of which were amplified by a second agreement setting up a Christian prince to rule an *independent* state in the Balkans. This Protocol of London in 1830 guaranteed the Greeks an "independent state . . . with all the rights attached to complete independence."

Austria's Metternich refused to sign this device and also another which made Prince Leopold of Saxe-Coburg king of Greece in 1830.[51] No congress of the four great powers had met since Verona in 1822. And Metternich could not countenance the use of the Concert to set up a new state born in revolutionary violence. This ran counter to Austrian action in putting down rebels in Naples and to French intervention in Spain on behalf of the Concert. Moreover, the constitution of Greece, while monarchical, gave subjects guarantees of religious freedom which extended to rights of political participation in every civil matter. These were in Metternich's eyes the principles of revolution, not those of restoration. He was even more aghast when the Greeks disapproved of King Leopold and the London powers accepted instead Otto of Bavaria, whose power was confirmed in 1832.

A monarchical state created by armed intervention *in behalf* of the Ypsilanti rebels was not Metternich's idea of the right order for Europe. Even though the new state did not modify the actual Vienna settlement, which had been silent on Balkan affairs, it did seem to Metternich a direct blow at the Restoration and an ill omen for the ability of the congress system to function closer to the Rhine, where in 1830 it was under direct assault.

1830: REVOLUTION IN FRANCE AND BELGIAN INDEPENDENCE

The Bourbon Restoration in France had put Louis XVIII in a difficult position. He stood between the liberals, who viewed the "reforms" of 1789–1815 as sacred, and the ultraroyalists, who wished to wipe out the heritage of revolution. As we have seen,[52] the Charter of 1814 had left undetermined the role of the new bicameral Assembly, which had no independent legislative power, only the right to reject royal proposals. Where a "popular" theory of politics was effective in France after 1815 was

50. For this language see the printed London Protocol, in Albrecht-Carrié, *Concert of Europe*, pp. 106–109.
51. He was a German relative of the ruling English house of Hanover.
52. See Chapter 5.

in the relationship between the royal ministers and the king. While Louis XVIII had never admitted he was bound by British notions of responsible government, he did in fact select ministers from the majority politicians in the Assembly, except in 1815 and again in 1829–1830.

In 1815 the Ultras dominated the legislature, but Louis selected his advisers from among moderates. The outraged Ultras began a campaign to repeal the reform laws and also to bring to "justice" Bonapartists and Jacobins. They failed in their attempts to restrict civil liberty and were unable to restore confiscated lands to prerevolutionary owners, but they did institute the White Terror. A system of courts backed by Ultra vigilantes arrested, tried, and executed hundreds of "revolutionaries" in southern France. Elsewhere, the victims were often guilty of nothing more than Protestant beliefs, which de Maistre had equated with treason to the dynasty. The King tolerated the purges until it became clear how extreme the measures had become. He then dissolved the Assembly.[53]

The new elections of 1816 produced a large moderate majority. Consequently, the new terror ended, and a period of new reforms began. By 1820 the electorate had been expanded to the still small number of 100,000.[54] Reform was set back in 1820, however, when an assassin struck down the son of Charles, count of Artois, Louis's brother, presumably to make certain the Bourbon line ended in the "Ultra" Count himself.[55] Louis responded by dismissing the moderate minister Élié Decazes[56] and appointing a more reactionary ministry. In 1822 the King censored the press heavily; he had already revised the franchise to restrict bourgeois political factions. His minister, the count of Villèle[57] gained support for laws repealing reform, and the reaction became truly formidable in 1824, when the death of the King brought to power Charles of Artois as King Charles X.

Now, the head of the Ultras was king of France. Charles encouraged Villèle to indemnify aristocrats who had lost lands at the expense of the bourgeois holders of government bonds (1825), by reducing bond interest rates to raise funds for compensating the landowners. The main thrust of the Ultra program was religious, however. New laws made sacrilege (as defined by Catholics) punishable by death. The bishops were put in control of the educational system from top to bottom, with the aid of the Jesuits, who were still not a lawful "order" in France.

The liberal press and political associations campaigned against what they saw as a political return to the Old Regime, attracting moderate royalists as well as liberal enemies of the new powers given to priests and nobles. New elections in 1828 showed Charles X the unpopularity of royal policy; the Assembly was even more liberal than it had been in 1816. It demanded a new ministry, but the success of Viscount Martignac (1778–1832), head of the new ministry, in relaxing censorship and diminishing religious control of education was temporary. Charles dismissed Martignac, putting in his place in 1829 the prince of Polignac (1780–1847), an Ultra so reactionary that in 1816 he had refused to take an oath upholding Louis XVIII's new charter.

Polignac's ministry was ended on the streets of Paris in three days of fighting (July 27–29) which are known as the July Revolution of 1830.

Delacroix said of the Liberty Leading the People, *" . . . if I haven't fought for my country at least I have painted for her." Although the artist was not a political radical, his* Liberty, *painted in commemoration of the July Revolution of 1830, became a symbol for French Republican aspirations. Like David's earlier works, this huge painting excited enormous public interest and marked a triumph for the Romantic artists. During a bloody Parisian street battle* Liberty, *holding the Republican flag, inspires a group of staunch combattants for the Republic, including Delacroix's friend Villot in the top hat. Lauros-Giraudon.*

53. In effect the Chamber of Deputies; the members of the upper house, the Chamber of Peers had hereditary seats.
54. In a total population of 30,000,000.
55. A frustrated hope; though the Count's son, the duke of Berry, had been killed, his wife was pregnant and produced a son!
56. Created a duke by Louis XVIII, Decazes lived from 1780 to 1860.
57. 1773–1854; in power from 1822 to 1828.

During 1829 and early 1830 Polignac had pursued the course of absolutism with Charles X's support. Assembly majorities were more moderate than ever, however, and the King clearly had embarked on a program to overthrow the nascent institutions of responsible government. As the Assembly transformed itself into an "opposition," Charles acted to dissolve it. The July Ordinances (issued July 26, 1830) dissolved the Chamber of Deputies and also abrogated the middle class's right to vote on matters of civil liberty, while imposing a rigid censorship on the press. Thus the July Revolution, although a movement from below advocating passive resistance, facilitated the resistance of the liberals to the Ordinances, which were correctly seen as the repeal of the Charter itself. When on July 28 the Paris revolutionaries took the city hall, raising once again the tricolor flag of 1789, Charles sought compromises.

The rebels would not accept either Charles X or an abdication in favor of his young grandson. They favored instead Louis Philippe, duke of Orléans and a cousin of the King; between 1789 and 1792, Louis Philippe had embraced constitutional monarchy, serving in the revolutionary army until 1793.[58] The Duke had the support of Lafayette, the hero of revolutions in America and France, an old man but also a symbol of young hopes. The Assembly offered Louis Philippe the throne on August 7, and the new king's first act was to accept popular claims to sovereignty. He revised the Charter to eliminate any suggestion that it was a royal gift rather than the

58. He left France only after the sentence was passed against Louis XVI.

birthright of Frenchmen. Louis also proudly embraced a new title. He would no longer be king of France, but merely "King of the French." This "bourgeois" monarch thereby signaled the shift from a dynastic view of the crown as property to the popular one of the crown as the representative of the people. This was the triumph of the bourgeoisie.

To Metternich and like-minded conservatives the new revolution in France confirmed the nation's inherent instability. Students, workingmen, and radical bourgeois professionals had defeated the Restoration where it most needed to endure, on the home ground of the revolutionary forces in Europe. A republic had been avoided, but only at the terrible price of admitting popular sovereignty and "responsible" ideas of government. The Orléanist, bourgeois "July Monarchy" shocked the principles of legitimacy; Louis Philippe even took as the official French flag the three-color banner of Jacobinism! He wore bourgeois "suits" rather than traditional court clothing. He abolished hereditary peerage seats in the Assembly. And he gave the franchise in the new state to about 200,000 merchants, bankers, and industrialists, the men of commerce thus being added to those of property to constitute the politically valid classes of the "legal country"—the *pays légal*.

The question on conservative tongues was, therefore, what impact the Paris revolution would have in Europe, since not even Metternich, who was too preoccupied in Italian affairs, had suggested invoking the now defunct congress system to overturn Louis Philippe's bourgeois regime. Answers were quick to come.

Once again Belgium reacted to changes across the border in France. In 1815, the Austrian Netherlands—Belgium—had been given to King William I of Holland to compensate the Dutch for losses suffered in the struggles against France. The "union" of Holland and Belgium decreed by the powers at Vienna ignored some important facts, however. The Belgians were mainly Catholics, the Dutch chiefly Protestants. Moreover, the southerners were a linguistically mixed lot: the Walloons spoke French, while the Flemings, very strong Catholics, spoke a variety of Dutch. Also, the Walloons were much influenced by liberal French ideas and had provided many of the followers of those politicians sympathetic with the 1789 revolution. King William kept alive "French" sympathies in Belgium by his clumsy way of treating the southerners as "conquered" subjects. Some "patriots" advocated autonomy, while others urged separation from the Dutch state.

The more aggressive supporters of Louis Philippe encouraged Belgian separatists. Disturbances took place in Brussels on August 25, 1830; Dutch concessions were viewed with contempt, as was the loss of control over the crowds. As Europe watched, in short order riots gave way to a "provisional government"; and independence was proclaimed in October 1830. Louis Philippe resisted pressures to intervene in behalf of the rebels, but warned the powers in Metternich's orbit also to keep hands off. Prussia agreed, despite a sentiment for action on the ground that Belgium had in it the duchy of Luxemburg—a member of the Germanic Confederation. England's government also adopted a neutral attitude, partly because a "liberal" Belgium independent of France and Holland formed an ideal market for England's rapidly developing industries. Nicholas of Russia was thus without support for his wish to aid King William, given Austria's deep involvement in Italian politics, and Russia's own preoccupation with a revolt among the Poles of Warsaw.

As soon as the Greek revolution had been concluded, therefore, the foreign ministers of Britain, Austria, France, Prussia, and Russia, at the request of King William, established a London conference to consider the Belgian situation. The Kingdom of the Netherlands was a creation of Vienna, where the Concert powers had sworn to allow no revolutionary revisions of the political map. Thus, while a mandate to act existed, the internal divisions within the Concert seemed to prohibit any effective aid to help William. The cease-fire arranged implied Belgium's separateness. And this victory for independence was made explicit in the seventh protocol of the London Conference. On December 20, 1830, the Powers urged the separation of Belgium from Holland and even went so far as to speak of the "Belgian Government," a *de facto* recognition of the rebels.

This was done on grounds which show how vain Metternich's dream of an order imposed from above was in postrevolutionary Western Europe. The Powers stated that their aim in 1815 had been to "found a just balance in Europe, and to secure . . . general peace."[59] The proper means toward the end had not been found, the Powers admitted, and therefore neither peace nor justice had resulted. Hence "liberation" was proposed for Belgium, on the terms that the new kingdom meet all the obligations of international order for which the Concert had been created in 1815. In return, the London conferees, while making arrangements for the Belgian frontiers, public debt, and whatever else pertained to a sovereign state, would guarantee the interests of William and also the Germanic Confederation in the Grand Duchy of Luxemburg.

Other protocols signed in 1831 provided for Belgian neutrality—as a buffer against France. Still others distributed the provinces between Belgium and Holland and sought to settle trade conflicts, frontier disputes, and a host of aggravated questions at issue between King William and his former subjects. After giving an ultimatum to King William, urging his acceptance of all points settled at London, the Powers reiterated the *raison d'être* of the Concert in an elaborate statement of principles issued on February 19, 1831, demanding acceptance by King Leopold[60] and King William. The statement is, in retrospect, more important than the many subsequent protocols which led to the accord at the London Conference signed between Belgium and the Powers on November 15, 1831. New causes of friction between 1831 and 1839 provoked French intervention, new Dutch hostilities,[61] and a stern British line aimed at denying France any advantage in Belgium's economy. But the doctrine of politics published in 1831 was in essence the rationale of the European political system until 1917–1933;[62] it therefore deserves special attention.

The ministers of the five courts (those of Britain, Austria, France, Prussia, and Russia) alleged some "grand principles of public law" which they called "principles of a superior order."[63] The chief tenet was that treaties do not lose their force merely because "changes may take place in the internal organization of nations." The Powers had understood this principle in 1814 when they established their trusteeship over Belgium, for the various regimes in power there since 1790 had had merely the "disposal" of Belgium, not the "sovereignty of that country." So, too, now the Powers once more had this "disposal," the purpose of which was to secure for the people—the Belgians—the "two-fold blessings of free institutions,

59. Protocol no. 7, printed in Albrecht-Carrié, *Concert of Europe*, pp. 65–67.
60. Of Saxe-Coburg; once candidate for the Greek throne, Leopold ruled in Belgium from 1831 to 1865.
61. King William did not accept the terms of the London treaty until April 19, 1839.
62. See Chapter 15, for our reasons for the date 1917–1933 instead of the usual one, 1914.
63. These quotations, and all others from Protocol no. 19, are from the printed document in Albrecht-Carrié, *Concert of Europe*, pp. 71–77.

and of a commerce fertile in wealth, and favoring the development of their industry": in other words, peace and justice.

By 1830 it was clear to all that the "union" established fifteen years before had been broken. Hence the Powers were "imperiously called" by European civilization itself to their task. It belonged to them to secure by "new combinations" the tranquility of Europe. The effusion of blood had to be stopped; and it had been. This much was truly "conservative." What was not so clearly in the spirit of 1815 was the steps to which the Powers would go to secure diplomatic and military calm in Europe. The Powers would gladly recognize new states combined on principles other than those of the Old Regime, if such states, on becoming independent, accepted the chief tenet of the law of nations: that new "governments" must honor the obligations of the "states" they control.

Solemnly, the guardians of the order of Europe announced the meaning of this "maxim." The events which give birth to a new state give it no "right to alter the general system into which it enters." Nor can an old state experiencing "changes that may have arisen" domestically authorize itself to stand absolved from earlier obligations. Delicately put! But even circumlocutions could not disguise the fact that the Powers had admitted revolutionary regimes to the comity of nations. The sole proviso was the obligation of all civilized nations to adhere to existing agreements, without which civilization would collapse.

Belgium was secure in everything her people had required: separation from the Dutch, independence, neutrality, territorial guarantees, free navigation on the rivers serving her commerce, and the "*peaceable enjoyment of her national liberties* [italics ours]."

It was momentous that the Belgians accepted the condition imposed on new states. But it was a far weightier matter that, in the wake of a revolution within a Great Power, a revolution to split a small one had been blessed by the Powers with words straight out of the rhetoric of popular nationalism. If one wanted to know when the Restoration itself became "revolutionary," one could do worse than study Metternich's inability to keep intact the "superior order" of antirevolutionary diplomacy. The new Belgium was no republic, but it was not a monarchy on the old model either. In economy and social structure it bore the look of the new-model industrial society of England. Belgium's constitution was liberal, and 1831 thus inaugurated yet another "constitutional" monarchy in Western Europe (France, Britain, Holland, Belgium) to balance the Eastern autocracies.

TWO GREAT POWERS AT HOME: ENGLAND AND RUSSIA

Ironically, Britain's internal politics from 1815 to the early 1830s reflected the violent wrench away from reform produced by the Revolution in 1789. The cry "Wilkes and Liberty" had ceased to evoke large-scale, popular support for radical reforms. The result was to turn working-class people away from the politics of reform toward either Jacobinism in the form of social revolution or narrowly defined economic improvements. For the middling groups the desire for reform became orderly, flowing in established channels of the royal and aristocratic political system. The ministry of the younger Pitt focused on administrative change, economies in government, and the crown's government of the colonies, especially the Indian subcontinent.

After 1789, the radicals who supported the Revolution enjoyed only a brief period of wider favor. The events of 1792–1794 discredited France even in the writings of the fashionable poets—Burns, Wordsworth, and Coleridge. Only the apocalyptic mind of William Blake found comfort in the

William Blake was a radical Romantic painter and poet who totally rejected the artistic conventions of the past. His religious and political beliefs were as unique as his art, and he spent his life trying to convey tormented inward visions. A prolific illustrator, Blake's imaginative genius was best stimulated by great literature such as Dante's Divine Comedy or the Book of Job. In Satan before the Throne of God, the Devil's turbulent entrance into God's calm universe forces a regeneration of divine creativity. This is a sympathetic conception of Satan's role not unlike Milton's in Paradise Lost. Job is seated beneath this heavenly drama, a biblical counterpart of Blake's own spiritual transcendence of worldly suffering. The Pierpont Morgan Library.

Republic of Virtue; and even sympathetic writers on agriculture like Arthur Young turned against France in 1793, advocating censorship of the British radical press as a guard against Jacobinism at home. Pitt's government had responded to the changed public mood quickly. And as Britain threw itself into the struggle against the expansion of the Revolution in Europe, at home a spate of statutes repressed radicalism: the Treasonable Practices Act, the Seditious Meetings Acts, acts to suspend *habeas corpus,* and the construction of a network of police informers made the much-admired "English liberties" one of the casualties of war. Real casualties in large numbers fell in Ireland, where in 1798 Pitt sent 140,000 troops[64] to put down a revolt.

When the struggle against France was won in 1815, George III's son Prince George ruled in place of his often insane father, as prince regent, until succeeding as George IV in 1820.[65] Both as regent and king this

64. Far more than England sent against Napoleon in any campaign!
65. He ruled until 1830.

George seemed less than regal. George IV's scandal-ridden life gave scope to the "party" politicians, Whigs and Tories alike. Both the "liberals" and "conservatives" were fundamentally aristocratic, although the Whigs were more in touch with bourgeois classes and Protestant dissenters than were the gentry-dominated Tories. Ideologically, the Whigs were partial to the classical liberal economists—followers of Adam Smith—and favored free trade and social reform. But the backlash effect of the war years enabled the Tories to keep parliamentary majorities. And the government of Britain from 1812 to 1827 remained in the hands of the frankly reactionary Lord Liverpool, Robert Banks Jenkinson,[66] who had watched the storming of the Bastille in 1789.

A man who embraced only two "liberal" causes—the abolition of slavery and limited concessions to Catholics—Liverpool faced a turbulent domestic situation. The end of government war spending and demobilization combined with the loss of European markets[67] to depress the whole economy. Liverpool's landlord supporters protected their narrow interests by passing in 1815 new Corn Laws, which forbade the import of cheap foreign grain until the price of English grain rose above the "basic" price of eighty shillings per quarter. This benefited landlords and their tenant farmers but was disastrous to workers, who watched bread prices rise above the reach of wages. Widening unemployment and falling standards of living produced agitation against the Corn Laws as well as a demand for the reform of the House of Commons.

Writers like William Cobbett[68] and orators of the fame of Henry Hunt[69] emphasized the unrepresentative character of the legislature. No new borough had been enfranchised since 1688, despite a rapid shift of population to industrial towns in the North after the onset of the revolution in production. There were some boroughs with no voters apart from the chief landlord-householder, who in effect nominated the members of Parliament. Some towns with the franchise had actually been washed away by the sea's erosion. There were few democratic franchises in urban constituencies; and in the county elections for "knights" of the shires contests were rare. The local gentry controlled the votes of the forty-shilling freeholders, with the aid of open pollbooks, which showed how each man voted in general elections.

But every one of more than two dozen bills to reform the structure of politics had failed in the unreformed House. Liverpool therefore viewed as very dangerous the agitation for reform, especially in 1816–1817, when extraparliamentary reform "societies" sprang up. Laws suppressing such meetings were passed, and *habeas corpus* was again suspended. The depression deepened; riots occurred; Liverpool used *agents provocateurs* to incriminate agitators. Despite bans on public meetings, these continued to be held in London and in industrial cities such as Manchester—a large town, rich, but without adequate representation for either its workers or its masters of capital. One such rally of about 60,000 had gathered on August 19, 1819, to hear Hunt speak. But local government men used cavalry to arrest Hunt; in the riot that ensued, eleven civilians were killed by troops and hundreds wounded.

Radicals took up the challenge, fashioning the slogan "Waterloo and

Widespread social unrest in early nineteenth-century England often led to confrontations and violence. In August 1819, a peaceable crowd of some 60,000 gathered in Saint Peter's Fields, Manchester, to listen to demands for parliamentary reforms and universal suffrage. Nervous officials sent in the yeomanry (a force of poorly trained businessmen) to arrest the leaders, but these undisciplined troops soon raged out of control and began to attack unarmed bystanders, many of whom were women and children. Reinforcement guards on horseback were called into the fracas, worsening the tragic carnage. Indignation at the inexcusable behavior of the yeomanry and the government's sanction of the attack was a major factor in the ultimate success of the reform movement. The Mansell Collection.

---

66. The second earl of Liverpool (1770–1828).
67. Into which contraband had flowed in defiance of Napoleon's blockade system.
68. 1763–1835; a "Yorkshire" pamphleteer, although he was born in Surrey.
69. 1773–1835; a radical, itinerant political speaker with a long history of opposition to authority, he was finally elected to Parliament in 1830.

Peterloo," designating the "Peterloo Massacre"[70] the sequel to the triumph of Wellington at Waterloo. The response of Liverpool was to rush through Parliament the Six Acts of 1819, or the so-called Repressive Acts, which broadened censorship, prohibited political associations, and in general changed the law to facilitate the convicting of "radicals."

Even these stern measures seemed justified a few months later. Arthur Thistlewood, who had already been tried on conspiracy and sedition charges,[71] plotted with thirteen other men to kill the whole cabinet at a London dinner party. Betrayed by an informer, he and others were cornered in a loft in Cato Street before putting the plan into operation. Thistlewood's scheme had also included the seizure of the Bank of England and the establishment of a provisional government. He was hanged for his Cato Street Conspiracy.

This conspiracy in 1820 marked the zenith of direct action radicalism. During the next decade an economic recovery encouraged Liverpool to broaden his ministry to give scope to "liberal Tories," and the cabinet took in advocates of reform: Canning, the foreign secretary,[72] as well as William

70. The rally had convened in St. Peter's Fields.
71. 1770–1820; perhaps an illegitimate son of a Lincolnshire farmer, the disinherited man was an ardent revolutionary as early as 1816.
72. Also leader of the Tories in the Commons.

Huskisson[73] and Sir Robert Peel.[74] All opposed parliamentary reform but were open to patchwork measures of a meliorative sort. Hence the 1820s witnessed the easing of the criminal code, the creation of London police forces,[75] as well as Huskisson's reform of the tariff system to allow cheaper imports of a variety of commodities such as sugar, tea, coffee, and wine. But the Corn Laws were not repealed. The Combination Acts which prohibited the formation of workmen's organizations (labor unions) were repealed, however. Despite harsh restrictions on bargaining passed a year later (1825), Huskisson's act of that year recognized the rights of laborers to organize for the purpose of improving wages and hours, while denying them the right to strike.

After a period of unstable ministries produced by Liverpool's death, the duke of Wellington became prime minister in 1828. His sympathies were wholly reactionary, whether the issue was Catholic emancipation, which passed in 1829 despite his obvious dislike for Catholics taking seats in Parliament and holding public offices, or the more vexed questions of the Corn Laws and the reform of the House of Commons. Shortly after seeing through the Emancipation Bill, Wellington faced George IV's death and the July Revolution in rapid sequence. The revolution shook the assumptions Wellington held about Europe. The accession of a new king forced the Duke to call new parliamentary elections. And the victory of a number of "reformers" among the Whigs created among the propertied aristocrats the choice of manipulating reform sentiments while preserving their power or perhaps suffering the fate that had just overtaken the French Ultras.

Events elsewhere in Europe made the choice seem less fanciful than it might have seemed to the victor of Waterloo and his supporters. Not only had Greece won a nationalist revolution. France had thrown out the Bourbons. The Belgians had won independence from Holland. In Poland the "nationalists" had struck hard at the czarist government of Nicholas I in 1830; and early in 1831 a Polish Diet actually dethroned the Czar,[76] who responded with a large invasion. The Western "liberals" were too distracted to protest events so far away. The result was a complete victory for Nicholas. He abolished the constitution given the Poles by his own quixotic brother, Alexander. And he absorbed Poland into his own state completely, exiling "patriots," shutting down the universities, and instituting a ferociously repressive regime. Wits in London, Paris, and Brussels said that the revolutions in Western Europe were won in Warsaw![77] Yet the fact remained that the Russian autocrat had himself dismantled a state created by the Congress of Vienna, thus exposing the hypocrisy of grand principles.

In fact Nicholas I had come to power in Russia in part because he had successfully put down a revolt there in 1825. The situation in the most autocratic of European states in 1825 was the product of the two reigns after Catherine the Great's death in 1796. Her son Paul I (1796–1801) had rejected Western ideas and reforms as threats to absolutism and his own style of divine-right monarchy. Groups of Western-oriented aristocrats plotted to murder Paul, in order to put in his place the "liberal" Prince Alexander. When the plot was carried out in 1801, Alexander I was a man of twenty-four whose mind was torn between the tradition of Russian

73. President of the board of trade (1770–1830).
74. Secretary for home affairs (1788–1850).
75. Their members called "Bobbies" or "Peelers," after Sir Robert, their creator.
76. He ruled the Grand Duchy of Warsaw as part of the settlement of 1815.
77. Because Nicholas, so busy in Poland, could not send his armies to crush rebels in Brussels and Paris, which he had the will to do.

autocracy and the values of his own humane "teachers," especially an unofficial committee of advisers of liberal views led by the French Swiss La Harpe and the Polish émigré patriot Prince Adam Czartoryski.[78]

During the truce years 1801–1805, Alexander worked on schemes for a constitution and the abolition of serfdom. It proved impossible to attack the privileges of the aristocracy during years of fragile peace, however, as any renewal of Napoleon's thrust eastward would require the loyal service of the landed classes. Hence reform moved in other directions: Western-style administrative systems, the erection of new universities, the creation of an enlarged system of secondary schools, and the issuance of a decree encouraging freedom for serfs.[79] After the resumption of war from 1805–1807, Alexander embarked on a second reform era. He entrusted great powers to Count Mikhail Speranski (1772–1839), whose main concern was to provide "constitutional" government for Russia, by means of elected "legislative" bodies at the center and at various provincial levels. Real power was to remain in the hands of a Council, however, which alone could approve laws.

Not much progress toward Speranski's goals had been made by 1812, when the invasion of Russia by Napoleon brought to an end these experiments, at least within Russia. After 1815, Alexander embraced the "superior order" ideas of Congress Europe and the Holy Alliance at home, while allowing to his Polish subjects a constitution in 1818. The contrast between Russian autocracy and the Grand Duchy's free press and speech guarantees and its elected diet irritated "liberals" at home. For there, Alexander was giving power to reactionary nobles and religious bigots who purged government and education of liberal men. Another powerful reactionary force was the institution of a system of military "colonies," which depended upon forced musters of peasants and their families under noble officers.

The greatest resentment was among the educated government officials and military men who had been imbued with Western ideas. From 1815 on they formed "secret" societies to discuss reform, the two most important of which were the moderate Northern Society and the more radical Southern Society. The northerners were chiefly aristocrats who wanted constitutional monarchy. But the southerners were anticzarists dedicated to agrarian reform and republicanism. Their plan to murder Alexander was frustrated by his natural death in 1825. The Czar had no sons but did have two brothers, Constantine and Nicholas.[80] The Northern Union plotted in favor of the "liberal" Constantine and actually persuaded troops to proclaim him in preference to the younger, conservative Nicholas, in December 1825.

Nicholas responded with force to put down the revolt in Saint Petersburg's garrison. This triggered a premature rising of the Southern Union, which Nicholas easily suppressed. These so-called Decembrist Revolt plots consolidated the new czar's hostility to liberal ideas, reform, and social change. Immediately upon gaining power, Nicholas instituted a repressive policy of executions and purges. Nobody could doubt where Nicholas stood, as he drew the line between his own personal power and reactionary mind and the liberal forces which had defied him in 1825.

78. Also Alexander's foreign minister.
79. Only 50,000 were ever manumitted during Alexander's reign.
80. Constantine was commander of the Polish army, and thus in effect that country's actual ruler. In advance of Alexander's death, Constantine had agreed to renounce the Russian throne in favor of Nicholas, but when the Czar died, he did not make clear his abdication. This made Nicholas's position in the face of opposition very awkward.

After the death of Alexander I a power struggle between his brothers Constantine and Nicholas allowed time for the Decembrist Revolt army plot to hatch. Officers desirous of constitutional reform gathered their supporters together in Saint Petersberg's Senate Square to demand "Constantine and Constitution." Nicholas met them on horseback and displayed personal courage by facing their loaded weapons for hours as he attempted to negotiate with the mutineers. Finally he consented to use force against them, ordered his troops to fire, and arrested the leaders, who were interrogated and tortured for months. The Decembrist Revolt was but one manifestation of widespread discontent within the army, and Nicholas chose to meet the threat with repression, discipline, and a new secret police force, the infamous Third Section. State Historical Museum, Moscow.

The new Russian ruler was thus from the beginning even more fanatically devoted to the Metternich System than was the Austrian himself or any of the other chief ministers in Western Europe. Nicholas won a reputation as the "Gendarme of Europe," because he was ready, if called, to intervene against the Greek, French, and Belgian rebels. At home, his chief wish was to insure the closest censorship of the press and the tightest surveillance of the schools. What was to be taught or read had to conform to autocracy, orthodoxy, and the rejection of anti-Russian (i.e., "foreign") values, art, literature, and philosophies. To achieve this result, Nicholas enlarged one "section" of the remodeled Chancery, making the "Third Section" a secret police.

Nicholas I thus consolidated at home the habit of permanent domestic intelligence work which has inhibited Russian intellectual freedom and political activity ever since. Especially after 1830–1831, when his own Polish subjects rebelled at the time of the "Western revolutions," the Czar increased the police pressure on liberals and foreigners in Russia. The chief vehicle for this pressure was the power of prior censorship of "literature"[81] given to the Third Section. And the intention was to suppress the consideration of any social or political issue regarded as contrary to autocratic order.

It was Nicholas I's misfortune, however, to reach beyond the means available even in modern totalitarian societies. Not only would technology not permit the total surveillance the Czar wanted. There was just then developing a generation of writers of genius who would not lie down before the Czar's threats. The greatest age of Russian literature had already dawned with the poet Alexander Pushkin. And Pushkin's work gave sustenance to, and was continued by, a quartet of younger men who rose to Nicholas's challenge: Nikolai Gogol, Mikhail Lermontov, Ivan Turgenev, and Feodor Dostoevski. Even the youngster of the group, Dostoevski, was old enough to be swept into prison under sentence of death in 1848, when the next great wave of revolution swept Europe. And, in the meantime, writers like Lermontov had in books such as *A Hero of Our Time* drawn an indictment of changeless Russia, a land in which even fairy tales brought suits for libel![82]

Lermontov aspired to draw a portrait of "our whole generation." And we may take this challenge up now, as we seek in the generation of people who matured between 1830 and 1848 a clue to the roots of the revolutions of 1848, looking first at the vital center, Germany.

BIBLIOGRAPHY

ARTZ, FREDERICH B. *Reaction and Revolution.** New York: Harper & Row, Publishers, 1957. An excellent general survey for the years 1814–1832.

BERTIER DE SAUVIGNY, G. DE. *The Bourbon Restoration*. Philadelphia: University of Pennsylvania Press, 1967. Very sympathetic to Catholic and monarchist principles.

ERGANG, ROBERT. *Herder and the Foundations of German Nationalism*. New York: Columbia University Press, 1931. A pioneering work in English on the rise of historicism.

HALÉVY, ELIE. *History of the English People in the Nineteenth Century.** 3 vols. London: Benn, 1949–1952. Volume 2 (1815–1830) is the most brilliant treatment of the English reaction.

HOBSBAWN, E. J. *The Age of Revolution, 1789–1848.** London: Weidenfeld & Nicolson, 1962. A brilliant Marxist analysis of the post-Napoleonic upheavals.

MAZOUR, ANATOLE. *The First Russian Revolution, 1825.** Berkeley: University of California Press, 1961. The best book on the Decembrists and Nicholas I.

SIMON, W. N. *The Failure of the Prussian Reform Movement, 1807–1819*. Cambridge: Cambridge University Press, 1955. The most acute general analysis.

TALMON, JACOB L. *Romanticism and Revolt.** New York: Harcourt, Brace & World, 1967. A stimulating effort to relate political change and the general cultural ambiance. This book continues the argument of Talmon's *Political Messianism: The Romantic Phase* (London: Secker & Warburg, 1960).

Asterisk indicates a paperbound edition.

81. Including newspapers, analytic journalism, and the whole range of published material on politics, religion, and philosophy.
82. See Lermontov, "Author's Preface," *A Hero of Our Time* (Baltimore: Penguin Classics, 1966), p. 19.

7

REVOLUTIONS WITHOUT ROOTS: 1830–1848

In my first half year at Göttingen occurred the Hambach festival, the festal ode of which still remains in my memory; in my third, the Frankfurt outbreak (April 3, 1833).[1] These manifestations revolted me. Mob interference with political authority conflicted with my Prussian schooling, and I returned to Berlin with less liberal opinions than when I quitted it; but this reaction was again somewhat mitigated, when I was brought into immediate connection with the workings of the political machine.

OTTO VON BISMARCK, *Reflections and Reminiscences*[2]

THE GERMAN SITUATION: BEFORE HAMBACH AND FRANKFURT

The 1830 revolutions produced a number of repercussions in German territories, only one of them being the Hambach gathering to which the son of an old Prussian *Junker* family referred.[3] Others worthy of note were that the Germanic Confederation had accepted the dethroning of the duke of Brunswick and the provision of the "liberal" constitutions there and in Hesse-Kassel. In the larger states of Saxony and Hanover, new constitutions were shaped by liberal European ideas of reform and also by the experiments made in certain south German states during the euphoric period (1814–1820) after the defeat of Napoleon. The chief accomplishments were some measures of tax reform, equality before the law, and the reduction of feudal power enjoyed by nobilities. In Hanover, enthusiasm for reform drew support from another connection, since the ruling dynasty there was also enthroned in England, the most liberal state in Europe.

There were, however, severe limitations on the scope of reformers of liberal and nationalistic leanings. Prussia, the most powerful of the northern German states, like Austria, the most powerful of the southern German states, was stony ground on which to sow the seeds of reform. Moreover, King Frederick William III had allied himself completely

---

1. See later in this chapter for this popular political meeting held in Hambach on May 26–27, 1832, and also for the 1833 "Frankfurt outbreak."
2. Edited with an introduction by Theodore S. Hamerow (New York: Harper & Row, Publishers, Torchbooks, 1968), p. 16. The translation used by Hamerow is derived from *Bismarck: The Man and the Statesman*, by A. J. Butler (New York: Harper & Bros., 1898).
3. Bismarck was born in 1815 on the family estate in Brandenburg, the son of an easygoing trans-Elbe nobleman and a mother from the burgher class, although his maternal grandfather A. L. Mencken had become a Prussian diplomat. His birthplace (Schönhausen) is today in the Saxony-Anhalt district of the East German Democratic Republic.

with the Emperor Francis I, of Austria, and Metternich, refusing all pressures for liberal constitutional changes. And, elsewhere in the German states, the once promising start made toward constitutional reform proved false. If Baden in southwestern Germany accepted reforms in 1831, perhaps under the influence of French and Swiss opinion, Bavaria remained antiliberal and sought systematically to remove from the region of the Palatinate French influences dating back to Napoleon's regime. Indeed, even in remote Pomerania, Bismarck, focusing on southwestern Germany, viewed with disgust the French possessions around Strasbourg,[4] while actual visits to Heidelberg, Speyer, and the Palatinate made him feel "revengeful and militant."[5] Although he had once espoused the militant liberalism of the *Burschenschaft* cause, he had on his own account come to regard nationalism in its liberal variety as foreign, utopian, and defective in a social sense.

The combination of ethnic mixture, political disunity, and social conservatism which dominated the major German states lay at the heart of the attitudes Bismarck expressed.

The Germans had made little progress toward national unity for a variety of reasons. The late medieval disintegration of the Holy Roman Empire had been furthered by the 1648 Peace of Westphalia, which had ended the Thirty Years' War by accepting fragmentation as the rule of political life. Until Napoleon's intervention reduced the number of political units radically, imperial weakness had provided aggrandizing princes an opportunity to make new political combinations. While the Habsburgs attended to the Austrian consolidation, Prussia had emerged as a power capable of playing a decisive German role.

But Prussian territorial growth, like Austrian imperial expansion, had not created a unified ethnic state. None of the other German states—thirty-nine in all[6] as a result of Napoleon's experiments—embraced the same diversity of peoples. By 1815, Austria was a multinational state in which there was a mass of Czechs, Poles, Hungarians, Serbs, Croats, and Italians who far outnumbered the German subjects in Austria's Ostmark.[7] The combination inspired in Metternich little wish to make Austria play the part of leader of a "German" nationalism. Prussia, while more German in its makeup than the Austrian Empire, and thus better suited to nationalist leadership, had its own melting pot problem. Apart from groups of Swedes and other Baltic folk absorbed into Prussia, the settlement of 1815 had ceded to Prussia the Slav populations of the East Prussia–Poland border regions, with the important strategic control of the mouth of the Vistula River and the port of Danzig.

The political consequences of the multinational character of Austria and Prussia were many. The espousal of nationalism by the subject populations in both states threatened each with dissolution. Even a purely "German" nationalist movement might raise the question of political representation for the non-German minorities, if German liberals demanded a democratic or quasi-democratic constitution. No Austrian statesman could tolerate this, for to do so might give non-German elements preponderance or, if

4. Ceded to France by the settlement of 1815.
5. *Reflections and Reminiscences*, p. 16.
6. A radical change from the more than 1,800 "states" in existence in 1650, among them 77 secular principalities, 51 imperial cities, 45 imperial villages, and 1,475 units ruled by imperial knights.
7. The old name for Austria's eastern frontier region, or march, with heavy Slav populations.

they were forbidden active citizenship, promote a move toward separatism on the Greek or Belgian model. Hence the systematic opposition to nationalism and liberalism we encounter in Metternich had profound roots in Austria's political situation, not merely in the ideas to which he was exposed or in the personal needs of his career. Similarly, for a Prussian to embrace the combined creeds of nationalism and constitutional liberalism raised the question of the eastern frontier. And no minister of Frederick William III could hope to hold power while encouraging the revival of an independent Polish state. Moreover, Prussia's western German territories were not integral, but separated from Berlin and from one another in a patchwork way. This convinced statesmen that the main task was Prussian unification, for which the tools existed: bureaucracy, a strong army, a growing economy, and the famous Prussian sense of duty.

The facts of political life after 1815 in the German world had, therefore, shaped a potential for cooperation between Austria and Prussia. The Emperor and the King of Prussia gave great stress to the dynasty as the embodiment of the state, in opposition to any doctrine of nationalism. Each rejected experimentation with political organization, especially any suggestion of popular participation, which portended an immediate reduction of power of the state and of the dynasty. Each state also had a very conservative social basis. In Prussia, the "reform era" under Stein and Hardenberg had challenged the traditional elites of land and military office. But from 1814 on, both within Prussia and from Austria, the pressures against reform grew. Scharnhorst's idea of a "popular" army was abandoned, and the chief military reforms combined a resurgence of *Junker* control with an enlargement of the army. Agrarian reform, too, was frustrated by compromises with the class of landlords, who were also military men. And the concessions made at the expense of the peasants in the countryside had consequences for the constitutional schemes of Hardenberg as well. Instead of a reform of the Estates into a genuine deliberative body with wide powers, Hardenberg settled for a merely consultative Estates, with the right to discuss matters of taxation and rights of property and person. The conservative nobility was given the dominant voice, and Hardenberg retreated from liberal ideas to the extent that what he did actually tightened the bureaucratic absolutism which had emerged in Prussia in the century before the French Revolution. The Council of State created in 1817 was an instrument of enlightened absolutism, able to check the most arbitrary uses of *Junker* power, but in itself dedicated to the economic revival of Prussia and the liquidation of crown debts.

Metternich's contribution to the Prussian reform movement was also decisive. The Austrian played successfully on Frederick William's fear of popular agitation, especially student unrest. Hardenberg was thus seriously undercut, because he had made use of the fervor of student movements after 1815. Under the guise of patriotic associations, leagues advocating various policies, ranging from national unification to the reform of academic dress codes, were put forward. To commemorate the tricentennial of Luther's revolt in 1517, students at the Wartburg had burned the works of "reactionary" writers. The reaction among statesmen was led by Metternich, who saw in nationalist student enthusiasms a challenge to the imperial authoritarian order he had made the heart of the Concert of Europe.

The students made this view plausible in 1818, when they organized a General German Students' Union (*Allgemeine Deutsche Burschenschaft*) which, unlike its predecessors,[8] adopted frankly republican politics. One

8. Karl Hoffmann's German Society (1815), for example, which had been speedily dissolved.

member of the Union, Karl Ludwig Sand, assassinated the conservative writer August von Kotzebue on March 23, 1819.

Metternich seized upon this overt act of terrorism. He urged on the Prussian king an immediate surveillance of all "liberals," especially university professors like E. M. Arndt[9] and "radical" preachers like the theologian Friedrich Schleiermacher,[10] whose chief offense was linking patriotism to the idea of a "people's church" capable of permeating public life with the spirit of reform. A meeting between Metternich and the King took place in the late summer at a Bohemian spa, where it was agreed to suppress all "demagoguery" in the schools, press, and the diets of the Germanic Confederation. A subsequent conference at Carlsbad issued the Decrees (September 20, 1819) later embodied in a federal act of the Confederation Diet at Frankfurt. The press fell under rigorous censorship; teachers with radical ideas were dismissed; and those who appeared "tainted," but susceptible to reeducation, were put under the tutelage of a commissioner to steer their teaching into the clear waters of acceptable doctrines. The "unions" of students were disbanded.

Even more important as a signal that the "era of reform" was over was an article of the Final Act of Vienna, signed in early 1820, which amended the 1815 organic law of the Confederation. On the urging of Austrians, it was declared that a state could lawfully have only one representative, its king or prince, and that other representative institutions (estates) were incompatible with the principles of monarchy. Against the plain facts of German history, it was further said that all "estates" must be of a nonpolitical character, because parliaments were un-German, a French or English invention, and without roots in the German past. Although the final language retreated a little, Metternich saw in this Article 57 a satisfactory reassertion of monarchical absolutism. The exact nature of estates was to be left to each state to decide, but in practice constitutionalism could not survive the climate of the Carlsbad Decrees. Prussia abandoned the schemes for genuine representative government prepared by Humboldt, and Hardenberg settled for the sham of a consultative body.

By 1820, then, reaction on the Austrian model had triumphed in the Prussian state. Persecution itself was in fact rather limited, but freethinking intellectuals preferred exile to silence. The result was to break for a decade the association between a deeply patriotic feeling for German unity and the ideas of both nationalism and liberalism. The army and the crown were strengthened along old lines, in separation from the mass of people. The hope for liberty came to rest more on enlightened administration than on constitutional change. Austrian ascendancy in Germany seemed assured, as indeed it proved to be for the better part of three decades, after which a new wave of revolutions swept Metternich from power and put at jeopardy his system.

THE GERMAN SITUATION: FROM CARLSBAD TO 1848

In order to understand the history of German politics and the failure of both reformers and revolutionaries in the period 1830–1848, it is not enough to account for the discouragement of nationalism and liberalism in terms of the domestic and "foreign" impulses toward conservatism among statesmen. There were also basic social and economic forces at work, some of which we may better understand after we have looked more closely at the symbols of liberalism despised by Bismarck—Hambach and Frankfurt. For by the early 1830s, spurred by the revolutionary renewal in France and by

9. 1769–1860; a German poet and historian.
10. 1768–1834.

the advent of parliamentary reform in Britain, the German opposition to the spirit of Carlsbad had itself revived; but it lacked deep roots in society.

The rise of liberalism in the Western European states rested in a basic sense on economic transformations which made popular sovereignty less of a hothouse growth than it was anywhere in Germany.[11] This was especially evident to the German political radicals who sought a social basis for their agitation after the 1830 upheavals.

In the Palatinate, for example, where French and Alsatian democrats freely met with thousands of liberal Polish émigrés forced westward by Czar Nicholas's savage repression of the Warsaw rebels, plans were made to hold a festival, in Hambach, in honor of constitutionalism. Since political meetings were illegal, the fact that nearly 30,000 people attended on May 26–27, 1832, was in itself startling. Even more startling was the open espousal of student-based nationalism, complete with the acceptance of the black, gold, and red colors of the unions, which became the banner of the popular cause. And the participation of large numbers of women—a first in German political life—also seemed to point toward a future in which politics might be reorganized radically. The "program" of the Hambach Festival was simple enough: an appeal to discard the "league of princes" in favor of a "league" of the German nation with other liberal peoples—France and Poland, for example. The vision was of a united states of Germany and a republican European confederation.

The trouble was that the bands of participants at Hambach[12] had no clear plan of action to achieve political ends. Nor did they have a solid base in the society of the states from which they came. The parliamentary leadership in southern Germany would venture little beyond moral exhortations in favor of liberty, while keeping one eye on the Germanic Confederation agents who were poised to suppress popular agitators. How unsophisticated in politics the democratic celebrants were was made clear less than a year later, when at Frankfurt the local police barracks were taken by some student revolutionaries. Few rallied to the mistaken belief that a German revolution could be made by controlling the town where the Diet of the Confederation had its headquarters.

The real power lay in Berlin and Vienna, where Metternich's influence was as great as it had been in 1819. The result of the Frankfurt *Putsch* (1833) was to reactivate the secret police and also to set in motion a wider wave of repression. Paradoxically, however, only in Hanover, with its "liberal" British connections, was an existing constitution abrogated. Elsewhere, rulers were content to let the constitutions stand, while disallowing the reforms made under them.

Yet the repercussions of revolution in Western Europe upon Germany were important, if for no other reason than the stain which 1832–1833 had affixed to the Germanic Confederation: it appeared to be a tool for Austrian reactionary policies and Habsburg domination of German politics.

There were other effects as well. Distinguished scholars protested the abrogation of Hanover's constitution and, as they were "moderates," influenced the views of a wider circle of responsible Germans. Moreover, the "defeat" of liberalism in Germany after Hambach and Frankfurt produced from the exiled leaders of a new literary movement an outcry couched chiefly in terms extolling the superiority of French and English liberal institutions. Ludwig Börne (1786–1837) adopted a radical democratic view, while Heinrich Heine (1797–1856) attacked the emptiness and formalism of German life. Both developed a journalistic prose style at once flexible and

11. See Chapter 8 on England, for example.
12. From Baden, Hesse, Nassau, Alsace, and the Palatinate, primarily.

"popular," which was probably more important for political propaganda than the specific content of their writings. In touch with the luxuriant cultural freedom of Paris in the 1830s and early 1840s, they expounded the virtues of political systems based on popular participation.

The "Young Germany" writers, cosmopolitan in outlook and many of them living in exile, were thus the partisans of social change in a world where rapid social change had made more of a mark than it had yet done in the German states themselves, although economic changes were already at work even in Germany. Although it is risky to rely on literature in order to grasp the nature of a society, the plain fact is that in German letters the "social" novel thrived after 1830. So, despite the peculiar impact of the writer's own character and social position, many novelists reflected in their attitudes toward society and politics the tensions we see at work at Hambach or in the new decrees of repression issued in 1833. One especially important aspect of the tension evident at once in overt political action and in the fiction of the social novelists is the conflict between partisans of the old, aristocratic, order and the emerging apologists of middle-class values.

The landed aristocracies were in fact the entrenched survivors of an age in which social position and political power were ascribed to persons by the accidents of birth. The aristocracies enjoyed a status based on defined legal privileges, where these had been restored in 1815 or only incompletely dismantled during the Napoleonic era. They constituted the nucleus of rigidity and exclusiveness against which the "liberals" agitated, as the partisans of reform sought to make German society more open, more mobile, more conformable to the opportunity-laden future the liberals projected, largely on the basis of foreign models.

What many of the political and literary reformers saw in France and in England was the outline of a society of *classes* taking shape, in place of the society of *statuses*. Class, in this sense, indicates the situation of persons or groups in the whole of society. All individuals in any society have given situations. In the traditional German "situation," status governed, while in Western Europe—or so it seemed to some writers—class did. The difference was that class was not ascribed at birth and legally determined; it arose out of differences in ability, but also because society guaranteed that different persons participated differently in the ownership of wealth. Where laws allowed personal mobility, people could change their class by participating differently in basic economic activities. There was thus the chance for the peasant to become an urban artisan, or even to climb higher in the social scale. And, since "situation" was the basis for every orientation, as people adapted to their circumstances, a society of classes was held to be freer, because it allowed the attainment of new standards of life, cultural and material, and so new forms of participating in political power.

In France and England, Germans observed, different classes might be as antagonistic toward each other as ever lord and peasant had been. But a society of classes seemed to offer more social and professional mobility and a wider distribution of both wealth and political power. In the German society of status, the aristocracy controlled the land and with it political power. In the "modern" societies, where industry had made great leaps forward possible, the wider distribution of different forms of property had led to the diffusion of political power. Property and its arrangements were thus seen to be central to the question of the political order; the chance to acquire wealth, which in a capitalist society was endlessly accumulating, was thus also the chance to break down the restricted distribution of power. It was thus said openly that the restrictions placed on constitutional development in Germany in 1819 were in fact a technique of the aristocracies to prevent the redistribution of land and taxes and also to forestall the development of capitalist industries, from which the aristocracies had held aloof. The Austrians and the Prussians were seen as fighting for "tradition" against the forces of "modernity."

This analysis permeated the propaganda issued by participants in the Hambach Festival long before the ideals of Hambach achieved their classic exposition by Karl Marx, the editor of the newspaper *Neue Rheinische Zeitung*, hard at work in Cologne in the revolutionary year 1848.[13] Of course, writers recognized that merchants had moved into the nobility and that there was no caste system evolved out of the system of status. But the nobles in Prussia, for example, dominated the officer corps and the upper levels of all state organs, and the higher burgher elements in government had always to yield ceremonial precedence to nobles of the same administrative rank. *Junker* ideals were portrayed in courtly literature in terms reminiscent of the Middle Ages, a movement sponsored by King Frederick William IV (1840–1861) after his accession. Installed at Sans Souci, surrounded by the trappings of its builder Frederick the Great, but filled with real hatred for his ancestor's famed rationalism, as well as for the Hambach Festival brand of democratic constitutionalism, the new king deepened the reaction.

Where in earlier decades leading writers had accepted the ideal of noble life without social limitations—Goethe in *The Apprenticeship of Wilhelm Meister (Wilhelm Meisters Lehrjahre)* advising commoners to seek harmony through personal cultivation[14]—the new generation of middle-class writers did not. Taking a leaf from the books of Lessing and Schiller, who had contrasted middle-class sobriety, modesty, and diligent honesty with noble arrogance and frivolity, such authors as Karl Gutzkow, Fanny Lewald, Gustav Freytag, and Friedrich Spielhagen pilloried the "decadent" aristocracy as useless, immoral, and antisocial.

Others, like Karl Immermann, wistfully chronicled the rise of industrial families in the Rhineland, against the background of the backwardness of the Westphalian aristocracy.[15] One character, Baron Munchhausen, an impoverished aristocrat, deceives the last in the line of the noble von Schnuck family; himself accomplished only as a liar, Munchhausen is a symbol of the future, for in order to salvage von Schnuck's economic position, the Baron compromises him, through an alliance, in principle at least, with the new "classes." Munchhausen entices the Freiherr von Schnuck into a scheme to sell condensed air at a profit of 136 percent! Von Schnuck agonizes over entering a business merely for profit, and with people of low origin. Munchhausen consoles von Schnuck, by telling him that

everyone [is] engaged in business nowadays, Count, Freiherr and Prince like the smallest shopkeeper, without harming their prestige. For the aristocratic estate, like the consecrated character of the priesthood, was immortal; a count could . . . take the bread out of the mouths of the Jews and remain none the less an unsullied Christian count as before. . . .[16]

The situation was in reality closer to the less romantic conclusion in Immermann's *The Inheritors (Die Epigonen)*. Industrial modes of production had made smaller inroads in Germany than Munchhausen supposed.

13. See Chapter 12 for Marx's travails, including the suppression of his newspaper.
14. The hero becomes a surgeon, after attempting to play different roles, i.e., literally by taking up acting.
15. In his *The Inheritors (Die Epigonen*, 1836) and *Munchhausen* (1838–1839).
16. Quoted in E. K. Bramsted, *Aristocracy and the Middle Classes in Germany*, rev. ed. (Chicago: University of Chicago Press, 1967), p. 56.

The Krupp steelworks at Essen were the symbol of rising German industrial strength. The founder, Friedrich Krupp, presided over a modest concern which upon his death in 1826 was taken over by his fourteen-year-old son Alfred. The fame of the Krupp name exploded into international prominence when Alfred developed superior cannon and weldless steel railroad tires during the middle years of the century. Enormous profits from artillery sales provided for experiments with model "colonies," or workers' villages, with recreational and educational facilities. The Krupp concern was one of the first industries to realize the advantages of providing its own raw materials by the acquisition of iron and coal mines. When Alfred died he had become the "Cannon King," and his firm has continually been associated with German military development. Friedrich Krupp.

The middle classes were weak and internally divided, and the future seemed to belong more to some yet unforeseen combinations than to either the aristocrats or the celebrants at Hambach. The heritage of feudalism and industry alike would fall to those who were neither nobles nor the captains of capital, Immermann said; in a serious prophecy, based on his belief that a class would arise less avid for mechanization and anxious, instead, either to destroy factories or to hold back the surge of industrialization, he projected a terrible struggle waged by the rural elements and the workers at machines against the master classes.

That such a struggle was taking shape did not seem irrational. German population had expanded from 25 million to nearly 35 million from 1815 to 1848. Economic production was barely keeping pace. In most German states the guilds had lost control over production. Within Prussia, only in the eastern provinces was guild control in effect. And by 1845 even these controls had been swept away by new codes facilitating the shift to factory methods. In agrarian regions, serfdom was nearly everywhere abolished in favor of peasant ownership, but manorial dues and services remained; and the economic plight of peasants worsened in a period of sharp population rise, producing serious famines in some areas in the 1840s. Everywhere, reform either displaced peasants or gave lords economic advantages over them. Some landlords suffered also, and about 33 percent of all *Junker* estates had fallen into burgher hands by 1848. There were thus incentives to social conflict and also to the migration, internally and overseas, of large numbers of Germans.

The beneficiary—if that is the right word—of such movements was the city. Berlin's population in 1847 was 403,586; in 1815 the count had been only 191,500. On a smaller scale, Breslau, Cologne, Munich, Bremen, Frankfurt, and many other cities had experienced rapid expansion. The combination of population growth and the decline of the craft guilds was not alone responsible, however. Cities grew not merely because they aggregated poor people and beggars,[17] but also because the growth of the modern factory system was slowly going on after 1815. This growth had been partly stimulated before 1815, by the large market open to German goods under French rule. Favorable tariffs against British manufactures had spurred the development of the Saar basin and also the Ruhr as well as Silesian mining. But other nascent industries were crippled by the Continental System—Prussian silk and wool clothing. And after the wars were over, the British imports proved cheaper and superior in quality to domestic production. The cities, however, did have some expansion of the industrial work force, chiefly because of the use of steam in textile production and cotton spinning.

The great impetus to the growth of new social classes given by industrialization owed most to improvements in transportation. The Congress of Vienna had guaranteed free German navigation of German rivers, but the states along the banks of the main arteries of trade often interfered, especially along the Rhine, where the Dutch levied heavy tolls, even after allowing "free" navigation, i.e., navigation without special licensing fees. However, by the 1840s freight barges plied the Rhine in impressive numbers.

It was the railroad, though, which supplied economic momentum to German industrialization. Beginning in 1835, when a small suburban spur linked Nuremberg with Fürth under the patronage of merchants, investment in this form of "social overhead capital"[18] expanded quickly. Dresden, Leipzig, and Magdeburg were linked between 1837 and 1840. Lines ran outward from Berlin to Anhalt, Stettin, Potsdam, Frankfurt an der Oder, and even Hamburg by 1846, by which time Cologne was tied to Antwerp and Berlin, and Hamburg was connected to Bremen and Hanover. Smaller lines crisscrossed the southwest. And, despite the fact that the regional centers were not yet fully linked in a complete grid or network, by 1848 Berlin, Leipzig, Munich, Hanover, Cologne, Frankfurt, and Hamburg stood in a new relationship to their respective hinterlands and to each other. And domestic producers were geared up to meet the new demand for what were then the heaviest industrial goods—iron horses and the rails on which they ran.

17. Karl Marx's *Lumpenproletariat*, a class socially inferior even to the petty-bourgeois (*Kleinbürger*) artisan and shopkeeper groups.
18. Capital necessary for the conduct of basic economic activities—also roads, canals, harbors, etc.

As elsewhere in Europe the advent of the train transformed Germany, though this charmingly naïve representation of the country's first railway linking Nuremberg and Fürth would hardly suggest the importance of the event. From this modest beginning in 1835 to the end of the century, well over 30,000 miles of lines were laid. Even though an early systematic development was planned, the variety of independent states at first impeded such an orderly progression. But as political unification was achieved the railways gradually fell under state control, and the Germans were the first to exploit the military advantages of a well-planned system in the wars with Austria in 1866 and France in 1870. Ullstein Bildautor.

The drive toward unity had other economic symbols than the puff of smoke from steam engines. Prussia had abolished all internal customs levies as early as 1818, while encouraging the import of necessary raw materials and discouraging intakes of luxury goods and foreign manufactured items.[20] The customs scheme helped to unify Prussia economically, by creating a large market which might strengthen ties across provincial lines.

Moreover, the finance minister von Motz (1775–1830) had in 1828 used customs union as a technique for linking Prussia's economic interests to other German states, both in the north and the south, squeezing resistant German states in the process. The *Junkers* regarded as the chief benefit of the enlarged union the inhibition given to native industrialists who might challenge aristocratic dominance in politics. Because the industrial goods produced in the German states *within* the customs union could now enter Prussia easily, the landlord classes hoped no impetus would be given to industrialization *within* Prussia. The scheme reached its desired end in 1834, when a Pan-German-Prussian *Zollverein* (customs union) began to operate, with only four states and the Hanseatic cities outside the "union," which embraced 25,000,000 people. Aided by powerful banks which concentrated on public finance rather than industrial development, the Prussian state was therefore moving toward a unification not motivated by the ideologies of nationalism and liberalism and also frankly at odds with the pro-bourgeois intellectuals in the Young Germany movement.

The prospects were reversed by a major economic crisis in 1846–1847, the origins of which were agricultural. A potato blight in Europe struck the crop in 1845; and in the following year both the potato and bread-grain crops were ruined by bad weather.[21] A rapid inflation of food prices ensued, despite the fact that the *Zollverein* abandoned its policy of protecting German grain from foreign competition. Famine was widespread in Silesia and East Prussia. Starvation reached into the ranks of the urban poor, as peasants unable to pay mortgages forfeited homesteads and sought salvation in the cities or in emigration overseas.[22] Food riots in Berlin took place early in 1847—the so-called Potato Revolution; and Silesian weavers revolted, looting the rich employers.

There was, however, no general rising of industrial workers. Their numbers were small in 1848, not more than 4 percent of the work force; and

19. The term (literally, the "pre-March" era) used by historians to label the period leading to the Revolution of 1848.
20. Raw materials entered free; duties on other goods ranged from 10 percent for industrial goods to 30 percent on coffee, tea, and wines.
21. The Irish famine which drove tens of thousands of Irishmen to America and Britain was another result of the European crisis.
22. Nearly 100,000 Germans came to America ca. 1846–1848.

Ankunft in Fürth

the truly mechanized factories were not hard hit by the depression. Nor were the mines. The grievances of industrial workers were not the lack of employment, but rather the conditions of labor. Wages were kept low by the use of women and children in the labor force; hours were long, factories were unhygienic and unsafe, and deductions from wages were a common feature of a system of punishments and forced purchases at company stores. Prussian social legislation, which had begun in 1839, provided faint remedies, if any, because there was no mechanism for enforcement. Yet factory workers, however miserable, were not worse off than the dispossessed peasantry or the artisan classes thrown out of work by the switch to machine production in cotton textiles.

Indeed, what the hard-pressed German proletarians agitated for in the crisis was not a revolution along the lines laid down by Karl Marx and Friedrich Engels in the *Communist Manifesto* of February 1848. The artisans especially wanted a *return* to the good old days of the guilds and the abandonment of the dehumanizing factories. The socialism and economic liberalism of intellectuals had initially no appeal for them. Nor did the workers see much hope for themselves in political liberalism and constitutional experiments. These were in their minds linked with industrial freedom and the profits of capitalists. And the workers thus did not see grounds for making common cause with the prerevolutionary middle-class spokesmen. Most German workers were—as Marx and Engels understood them to be—conservative, even reactionary, ready to strike out at every change threatening the traditions to which they looked for security, and above all else prone to seek paternalistic solutions at the hands of the old governing classes. In the minds of the workers the exponents of constitutional change were the very lawyers, journalists, and bankers who were agitating for the industrial freedom which was sweeping away the workers' security.

What finally did drive workers and liberals together in 1848, therefore, was less natural sympathy or shared convictions[23] than the stubborn refusal of authoritarian governments to reform the conditions of labor: hours, wages, and job security. From 1845 to 1848, in Prussia especially, little was done to ease the misery of the workers most trusting toward government. The result was to group the workers and the liberals, not in a positive political action, but in common distrust of the aristocrats and bureaucrats who ran the princely governments.

Together with the small number of capitalists anxious to break out of the confines imposed by *Junker* policies, workers and intellectuals joined professionals and other rejected members of society: the humanitarian and cosmopolitan reformers who saw economic nationalism as the means of unification;[24] Jewish revolutionaries excluded from public office, teaching, and other professional paths unless they converted to Christianity; and the ideological converts to Western European ideas, like Marx and Engels, who wished to see a new society founded on the ruins of the regimes of status. They were joined by rationalistic Protestants too "liberal" for Frederick William IV's repressive religious orthodoxy. The Protestant *Illuminati* were matched in Catholic circles by the followers of Johannes Ronge, a Silesian priest (1813–1887) who advocated a "German" Catholicism free from papal control.

The ranks of the disaffected had also grown as a result of the Prussian

23. There were, of course, small groups of militant socialists, communists, and democratic liberals in the working classes.
24. Their leader was the *émigré* "demagogue" Friedrich List (1789–1846), forced to flee to America in 1825, the author of *The National System of Political Economy* (1840).

After 1848 Bismarck realized that some accommodations had to be made with the rising demands of the populace. In this cartoon he is shown offering a timid German legislature two choices—socialism or dissolution. The Chancellor's strategy was to support a number of liberal programs in order to quiet discontent, while at the same time placing every possible roadblock in the way of the developing Social Democratic party. Among the reforms Bismarck championed were universal suffrage and attempts to curb the power of the Roman Catholic Church. Despite his efforts, socialism developed rapidly during Germany's period of industrial expansion and was a major force in the government by the end of the century. *Staatsbibliothek, Berlin.*

king's gesture of February 3, 1847—the "United Diet." This assembly was asked to consider certain reforms, but only within an agenda fixed by the King, without regular sessions, and with disproportionate power in aristocratic hands. When the provincial estates[25] met in April 1847, they were not content with the King's program, which was to get new taxes and loans while denying a constitution for Prussia. The King's absolutist position was challenged by a variety of spokesmen, against whom a young Pomeranian *Junker* Otto von Bismarck (1815–1898) made his mark by upholding the royal position. Although army matters and the Jewish emancipation question were debated, finance was central. The Diet refused new loans for military purposes and for railroad building when regular sessions of the Diet were not guaranteed in return. The King adjourned the parliament. And when he convoked it again early in 1848, alarmed by the French revolution taking place in Paris, the situation had changed in Prussia also.

The masses of middle-class Germans had rallied to the constitutionalist banner raised in the Diet a year earlier. Southern liberals advocated a mixed state in which monarchy and a legislature based on popular representation would limit absolutism without overthrowing the traditions of Prussia. Led by Karl von Rotteck[26] before 1840, this brand of liberalism spread knowledge of French and British constitutionalism in the northern states also, where it meshed with the ideas drawn from Hegel and others who had said that the state must help people realize their moral and spiritual freedom. Perhaps the most important publicist of moderate liberalism was F. C. Dahlmann (1785–1860), who looked to the Confederation for leadership in reform and espoused the traditions of piety and respect for the past. A third element active in 1848 was the radical one based on democratic ideas, which some held to be achievable in the present conditions of German society.

Basically, all the liberal groups agreed on what they called the *Rechtsstaat*, or government based on law, in opposition to arbitrary power. Concretely, what the liberals seemed to want was a Hegelian state, one in which law would guarantee the self-realization of the citizens by means of reforms to secure free speech, a free press, independence for the courts, the abolition of political and social privilege, and the essential elements of the

25. The Diet was composed of the members of the eight Prussian estates.
26. A professor from Freiburg (1775–1840).

NORTH SEA

SWEDEN

DENMARK

BALTIC SEA

SCHLESWIG-HOLSTEIN

Elbe R.

ENGLAND

NETHER-LANDS

P R U S S I A

RUSSIA

BELGIUM

Rhine R.

Berlin

LUX.

HESSE-KASSEL

SAXONY

Frankfurt

Prague

Paris

Seine R.

HUNGARY

Loire R.

Vienna

Budapest

FRANCE

SWITZ.

AUSTRIAN EMPIRE

Rhône R.

Novara

Milan

Custoza

Turin

PARMA

MODENA

Venice

ADRIATIC SEA

Danube R.

OTTOMAN

LUCCA

Florence

TUSCANY

PAPAL STATES

MONTE-NEGRO

EMPIRE

SPAIN

CORSICA

Rome

KINGDOM OF SARDINIA

BALEARIC IS.

KINGDOM

OF

THE TWO

SICILIES

GREECE

Naples

MEDITERRANEAN SEA

Palermo

The Revolutionary Thrust, 1848–1849

▮ Germanic Confederation

▲ Sites of Revolution

---

civil equality won in England in the seventeenth century and in France during the Revolution. To secure these things it was said that no attack on the *form* of government was necessary. Yet there were intense nationalists who advocated breaking up the existing state system. And there were radicals like Marx who saw in all "imperial" states a target for nationalist and socialist action to liberate the oppressed ethnic groups and to put power into the hands of working-class people.

The limit to which most liberals would go, however, was to explore the relationships between national unification and the achievement of constitutional freedom. Some thought the first would produce the second, while others argued that no truly German nation could be created without a settlement of the internal power question itself. On these grounds, many looked to Prussia for leadership, in the belief that the multinational Austrian state must be excluded from the future Germany.[27]

Agitation in the press for some scheme of unification and political reform had reached a high point in February 1848, when the news reached the German liberals that Paris had a new revolution in the making.[28]

27. The partisans of exclusion favored the *Kleindeutsch* idea of keeping a "little" Germany without Austria, against Austrian *Grossdeutsch* spokesmen who advocated Habsburg leadership of all Germany, a "big" Germany.
28. See later in this chapter.

Although his important contributions as a painter and sculptor have since been recognized, Honoré Daumier was famous in his own day as a political cartoonist. His savage lithographs were printed regularly in La Caricature, a publication launched in 1831 as a voice of opposition to the July Monarchy of Louis Philippe. Daumier was imprisoned for six months in 1832 after the appearance of a particularly vicious cartoon attacking the King, but he resumed his assault after his release. The Legislative Body (1834) is the artist's view of the fat and incompetent bourgeois members of the Assembly. Daumier felt that Louis Philippe owed his power to the acclaim of the people, and he never forgave his regime for selling out to a corrupt and greedy bourgeoisie. Giraudon.

Once again, therefore, an external event played a critical role in German affairs. Already in 1846 new revolts in Poland had led to united Russian, Austrian, and Prussian repression. And the Danish king Christian VIII (1839–1848) had raised nationalist pressures within Germany by putting himself at the head of the movement of Danes who wished to absorb wholly into Denmark two "German" duchies, Schleswig and Holstein, each of which had important German elements in its population. In January 1848, the new Danish king Frederick VII (1848–1863) promulgated decrees incorporating the duchies into Greater Denmark. Germans reacted to the Danish action in a *nationalistic* way. Meanwhile, the English had just intervened in Switzerland to help the cantons there form a federal state, much to the dismay of the autocratic powers.

Indeed, the constitutional agitations in the German heartland drew encouragement from the Swiss events. And, at precisely this point in time, the German struggle for reform became a part of the larger European revolutionary movement of 1848. The *Vormärz* era was over.

THE REVOLUTIONS OF 1848

In France, the "July Monarchy" of Louis Philippe had managed to suppress republicanism in 1830, without being able to relieve the tensions responsible for it. The reasons why this was the case are not obscure. In July 1830 the upper levels of the bourgeoisie had triumphed. Only large property owners had the vote. Nobility survived in the Chamber of Peers, but on a "life" basis, rather than a hereditary one. Government social and economic policies were shaped chiefly by Louis Philippe's upper-middle-class partisans, favoring the interests of manufacturers and merchants against those of the smaller tradesmen, craftsmen, and the combined

peasant-industrial work force in rural and urban France. Not only were such groups excluded from active political life; they were increasingly prone to question the benefits to themselves of such social and political changes as were occurring.

Politically, the collapse of the Orleanist monarchy during three cold days in February 1848—the twenty-third through the twenty-fifth—resulted from the desertion of Louis Philippe by the chief supporters he had counted on: the solid Parisian bourgeoisie and the National Guard. This must have come to the King as a great surprise, for from 1840 to 1848 the political questions in Paris had apparently been answered in favor of the monarchy's strongest supporters.

During the 1830s two factions among the monarchists had contested for power under Louis Philippe, within the framework of the Chamber of Deputies. One faction, called the Party of Resistance, was led by the celebrated critic, historian, university professor, and politician, François Guizot (1787–1874). He was convinced that the July Revolution had created a perfect order, in which the claims of monarchy, aristocracy, and property were harmonized. Guizot therefore resisted every suggestion that improvement was necessary. To raise one's situation in French society, one had only to get rich, because there were in France no legal barriers to upward mobility, at least none of the *status* rigidities complained about by unhappy Germans!

The original leader of the "Party of Movement" was Adolphe Thiers (1797–1877), one of the protagonists of 1830, a man anxious to hold back republicanism, but a man convinced that there must be an enlargement of the franchise before a good compromise could be effected between monarchy and popular sovereignty. Guizot believed this *juste milieu*, or happy condition, had already been achieved.

A combination of events had given power to the "resisters" by 1840. There had been a steady stream of republican agitations, but these were less important to Thiers's downfall in 1840 than some other things. Another blow to the party of moderate reform was given by Napoleon's nephew, Louis Napoleon,[29] the leader of two Bonapartist abortive coups. The second came in 1840, at almost the same time that Thiers tried to expand French interests in the Rhineland, provoking among the Germans strong anti-French sentiments. Louis Philippe had no desire to fight a war, and he used this diplomatic error made by Thiers to thrust the left-of-center politicians from power. Guizot became the effective head of government until the February Days.

Behind the facade of political differences among the bourgeois parties, however, there were more profound causes of disturbance in France, especially in the state of the economy and related social crises. The agitations for suffrage extension, law reform, free public education, and press freedom, which were often coupled with public demonstrations and riots, as well as with fierce satirical attacks on the King (especially by the artist Honoré Daumier),[30] were outgrowths of deep dissatisfactions.

Louis Philippe and the gaggle of *rentiers*, merchants, and bankers were materially secure. The majority of Frenchmen were not, a fact appreciated before the economic crisis of 1846–1847 showed itself in France as dramatically as it did in Germany. There was after 1815 a slowing down of economic activity in France. Despite the fact that foreign trade expanded by

29. Napoleon's son, the duke of Reichstadt, had died without heirs in 1832.
30. 1808–1879; Daumier, a great caricaturist, represented Louis Philippe as a pear (*La Poire*) in the opposition press—fat, corrupted, and also murderous.

30 percent from 1815 to 1848, there was at home a chronic shortage of money, insufficient growth of industry, and a failure of bankers to show much interest in useful investments at home. Their preference for foreign adventures, for commercial capitalism over industrial development, weakened the internal economy. One consequence was depressed prices; another was the failure to absorb the peasantry into the economy.

This would have been facilitated by large-scale railroad building. But in France lines were not expanded rapidly after their introduction to carry coal locally in 1823. By 1848, French capitalists had done little to extend the transportation revolution into the agrarian districts, being content instead to build small lines to serve specialized industries: coal, iron, and textiles— the silk cloth produced around Lyons or the cotton goods of Alsace and Rouen. The bankers' concern was mainly to help fix production costs at low levels and so to make exports attractive abroad.

Growth, both economic and demographic in some towns, however, was rapid. Paris apparently increased its population from 750,000 to 1,000,000 between 1830 and 1840. But the government did not seek to control this growth or to help workers or to restrict the profits of manufacturers and merchants. When the prefect of the Rhône *département* sought to regulate silk production, partly in response to a workers' disturbance in 1831, he was dismissed. By 1834 workers had organized sufficiently to seize control of several districts in Lyons, with the result that Louis Philippe ordered the National Guard to bombard the city. Daumier's great etching *Rue Trans-nonain, April 15, 1834*, recorded the results of a parallel "rising" in Paris; it shows a slaughtered working-class family—grandfather, father, mother, and child—in a bedroom where they had been bayoneted by troops.

Infuriated by a brutal army attack against totally innocent civilians, Daumier produced the Rue Transnonain, April 15, 1834. *The public impact of this simple work equaled earlier reactions to the republican scenes by David and Delacroix, and the constitutional monarchy was dealt a serious blow. In mid-April 1834, riots had broken out in the city of Lyons with serious battles between the troops and insurgents. Before sunrise on April 15 the army recaptured the rue Transnonain. Thinking they heard shots, the guards panicked and invaded a building, shooting and stabbing at random. Daumier shows the scene as daylight breaks: a man of the people and his family have been killed in their beds as the result of senseless hatreds and a shocking misuse of power. Giraudon.*

Neither Thiers nor Guizot grasped the significance of the struggles of the silk workers against their employers. The result of the Lyons "war" was, therefore, a mood of widespread repression and the imposition of severe censorship in 1835. The attitude of Guizot in particular toward the urban workers in the new factories was also evident in one "liberal" reform. In 1833, Guizot had secured the passage of the "Guizot Law," which gave elementary education the impetus Napoleon had given to the university and college system. His purpose was to morally uplift the near-savage workers and also to reduce their ignorance. The lower classes had to learn to read in order to work usefully the new machines then being introduced in certain factories. Ignorance obstructed production. Therefore, each community was to have a budget for elementary education, under ecclesiastical supervision. Attendance at these schools was neither free nor compulsory, but was pushed in urban areas where the labor problem was severe. Only 50,000 students enjoyed the benefits of this program in 1848.

The Guizot Law and the 1835 Law of Censorship[31] are equally good examples of the stifling impact of bourgeois constitutionalism on the French lower classes. At the same time, they exhibit features of French life which indicate how "progressive" French society and institutions must have appeared to people in countries less blessed with the ambiguous fruits of political and economic change.

Those who had grown up in France knew there was much material poverty to contemplate. Progress in select industries took place at a time of rapid population growth and general productivity increases. But assemblies whose deputies were upper bourgeoisie legislated the protection of French iron, silk, wheat, and beet sugar against foreign competition. The protective acts insured that cheap foreign goods would not be available to urban workers. When, after 1842, the government showed concern for building a better transportation network, therefore, the change was not dramatic enough to head off the gathering forces of industrial unrest, commercial crisis, rural unemployment, and urban poverty.

In the countryside, the agricultural day laborers and landless peasants were leaving ancient domiciles in pursuit of factory jobs. Day wages in rural France were far lower than the cotton mill wages, which amounted to some six or seven hundred francs a year. Once in the towns, however, and lucky enough to get work, the rural displaced persons found a few francs a day no fortune.

Urban working-class wages were too much to die on, but too little to live on, the Paris wits said. And in an industrial town like Lille, 20,000 of the 80,000 inhabitants were indigent. Working conditions in the "shops" were terrible: long hours, poor hygiene, crowding, differential wages for women and children. Youngsters often worked fifteen-hour days. Even liberal economists called the factory life horrible, being not altogether insensitive to the plight of a five-year-old working *under* the machinery, tending automatic looms in spaces too small even for stunted women. To the visitor, the young children of the slums were small, deformed, pale, and dirty-looking, sometimes almost naked, and so abused at work that it seemed a holiday for them to return to their living quarters, where, as in Lille, "they sleep on the bare ground, on fragments of colza chaff, on the haulm of dried potatoes, on sand, or even on the fragments they have painfully gathered

---

31. This law aimed at making prosecution of political offenses easier; it also imposed press censorship on political subjects. The middle classes wanted to move discussion wholly into the *Parlement* where the radicals were not well represented.

from the day's work."[32] The same scenes greeted the traveler to Rouen, Nantes, Sedan, Reims, Mulhouse, and Paris.

The passage of child labor laws in 1841 abridged the freedom employers had to abuse labor. The new code limited work to those 8 years old and up; it prescribed maximum hours: eight for those less than 12, and twelve for those between the ages of 12 and 16. The problem with the reform was its basic duplicity. The employers had control of enforcement; and the law did not apply to shops having fewer than twenty workers. Hence conditions in most shops were not improved, and for many workers it remained true, as was often said at the time, that to live is merely not to die.

Out on the boulevards, however, black tie and velvet gowns were *de rigueur* for attending the theater. The presses churned out stories of glamorous country life. Painters, perhaps oppressed by native life, embraced in a romantic way ancient civilizations for subjects. Daily life seemed so banal that some escape from it permeated the arts in the 1830s and 1840s. There were, however, exceptions to the rule; and in Paris, as in German intellectual circles, social critics were at work. Victor Hugo (1802–1885) had already published novels and sketches in which the misery of humble life dominated. Some theaters had working-class patrons. The novelist George Sand (1804–1876) and the historian Jules Michelet (1798–1874) rediscovered the lower classes, describing the poverty which made hypocrisy out of the French claim to have reached the *juste milieu*.

More important still was the development in France of socialist thought before 1848. Not everyone who was capable of understanding the unresponsiveness of the political system to the onset of industrialization romanticized poverty in social novels or historical accounts of the "people." Henri de Saint-Simon (1760–1825) and Charles Fourier (1772–1837) created the "utopian" thought rooted in the idea that model social communities could be founded in which the distribution of goods on equitable bases would produce just patterns of human life.[33] The utopian socialists believed that there had to occur a shift in emphasis from the production of wealth to its distribution. Saint-Simon's model was paternalistic, conceding to the capitalists "responsibility" for improving the workers' lives. Fourier elaborated a tougher criticism of bourgeois society, maintaining that capitalism itself was *irresponsible*. He drew from this analysis the conclusion that private property had to be abolished before true communistic societies— where property was held by the commune—could be established.[34]

The practical implication for politics was, of course, that the Orleanist monarchy was not the means toward the end of ever more far-reaching social reform. One of the leading French socialists after 1840, Pierre Joseph Proudhon (1809–1865), had asked whether the regime of propertied men could be trusted with the tasks of reform.[35] A working-class man himself, Proudhon had embraced anarchism by 1846, writing that in a crisis all institutions of civil society would be used repressively. The events of 1847–1848 seemed to warrant his pessimism—that only a *social* revolution would produce a new politics.

Famine and inflation had struck in 1846. Throughout most of 1847 prices had continued to rise, as food shortages worsened. The winter of 1847–1848

32. My own translation of economist Adolphe Blanqui's *Les Classes ouvrières en France pendant l'anneé 1848* (Paris: Pagnerre, 1849), p. 137.
33. Robert Owen (1771–1858) had founded such a place in Scotland in 1800 (New Lanark) before advocating it in writing in 1821.
34. Fourier did allow some differences of wealth, however.
35. In his *What Is Property?* (1840).

produced no serious rioting, however, and some decline in prices. Yet "revolution" was still predicted by some and seemed to gather momentum. What had once appeared to be a revolution of intellectuals was in fact now becoming widespread in society. In France, the keen analyst of America's revolutionary society, Alexis de Tocqueville (1805–1859),[36] warned the Chamber of Deputies not to suppose that the absence of riots indicated an absence of deep hostility. He predicted that the working classes would rebel, upsetting laws and governments, even overturning society itself. His statement that Louis Philippe was sleeping on top of a volcano soon appeared prophetic.

The more sensible politicians had advocated electoral reforms at a series of political banquets during the winter of 1847–1848. Guizot took the step of banning a banquet planned for February 22, 1848, while prohibiting also mass demonstrations for reform. On the twenty-third disorderly crowds in working-class districts erected barricades. Some National Guard units defected, causing Louis Philippe to dismiss Guizot in the hope of pacifying the opposition. In this the King misjudged the working classes. Unlike some bourgeois politicians, the Paris radicals wanted a change in government, not just a change of ministers. On the twenty-fourth even the King grasped this, but too late. The Parisians refused to allow his abdication in favor of his grandson.[37]

As Louis Philippe fled France to exile in London, the Chamber of Deputies proclaimed a new republic, at the instigation of the poet Alphonse de Lamartine (1790–1869). A provisional government was organized by the Paris rebels, by voice vote at the city hall, after a process of "election" in the Chamber of Deputies. But at the city hall the moderates led by Lamartine found themselves confronted by the "social" revolutionaries, or radicals, who had their own nominations to make. The most important nominee was the socialist Louis Blanc (1811–1882), the exponent of a radical reorganization of labor.

Blanc, who demanded attention to social reform, by which he meant the production and distribution of wealth, urged the red flag of the Paris mob on the provisional government, which consisted of seven republicans and four "social" republicans, but Lamartine carried a vote for the tricolor of 1789. Blanc also failed to carry his broad program of economic and social change to implement the "right to work," a demand pressed by the Paris mob. The government did, however, establish national workshops, though different from those Blanc had sketched in his *Organization of Work* (*Organisation du travail*). In practice these workshops were not the base of new "cooperative" worker enterprises such as Blanc had envisioned. Instead, they quickly became relief projects, in which wages earned working on state roads were the counterpart of a dole given to those not so employed. A rift was already opening between the lesser bourgeoisie and the workers, who had made common cause from February 23 to 25.

This, then, was the news from Paris which alarmed Frederick William IV sufficiently to prompt him to reconvene the adjourned United Diet, in the hope of immunizing Prussia against the new outbreak of revolutionary diseases in Western Europe. Popular demonstration had at once broken out late in February, spreading from Baden to Mannheim, Heidelberg, and Offenburg. In public meetings the various "classes" demanded of those with privileged "status" the convoking of a national parliament to make

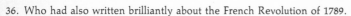

36. Who had also written brilliantly about the French Revolution of 1789.
37. The ten-year-old count of Paris.

reforms in the form of constitutions to be granted to the states individually. One after the other, rulers in the smaller states yielded to pressure.

The fate of revolution in Germany, however, depended on what happened in Austria and Prussia.

In Austria, Metternich misjudged the movement in two ways. He did not at first take it seriously and advised resistance. Street fighting broke out on March 13, 1848. Secondly, Metternich misjudged what reaction would prevail among the emperor Ferdinand's[38] councillors. Counting on the "system" he had built and the loyalty of those who administered it, he was shocked to find the council willing to protect the Habsburg dynasty by sacrificing Metternich himself, the statesman who since 1809 had guided its policies. The man who had "restored" order in Europe, for he thought of his work as nothing less than that, thus became the victim of the revolutionary forces abroad in 1848. He reached exile in England, while in Vienna students and various burgher elements took control of the city.

Ferdinand's government promised to convoke a constitutional convention, while immediately granting freedom of the press. The peasants were not satisfied by these measures; nor were the urban workers to be quieted without actions addressed to the economic issues of the day. And at the same time the "nationalities" revolted, fulfilling the prediction of those who said liberalism was incompatible with the maintenance of a multinational state. Promises of self-government were made to the Czechs and Croats. Naples and Sicily, which had experienced a revolution in January, now rejected Bourbon rule. Revolution in southern Italy endangered Austrian influence elsewhere in the peninsula. Within four months of the March riots, Austria had ceased to dominate the European Concert, and the fate of its empire was in question.

Five days after Metternich resigned power in Vienna, King Frederick William IV, on March 18, 1848, made decisions which dashed the hopes of Prussian liberals. They had supposed that the King would make compromises and so formulate a liberal Prussian state. This state would then lead the smaller reformed states and head off the more basic social and economic changes advocated by the radical revolutionaries. The German liberals meeting in the Diet at Frankfurt, now shorn of Austrian leaders, schemed to transform the movement of revolution into one for unification in Germany under the aegis of Prussia. Frederick William said no; he would not accept representative institutions but would put Prussia's monarchy in the service of all Germans. This reaction to crisis did not take into account the misery in Prussia caused by scarcity and unemployment, perhaps because food riots had not broken out again. The King showed his intention

38. He was crowned in 1835 on the death of his father Francis. Ferdinand's dates are 1793–1875.

by moving troops into Berlin, while at the same time threatening to bring the troops of his Russian ally westward to meet any threat to monarchy that might emanate from France.

The most that Frederick William would do was to proclaim an intention to reform the Germanic Confederation under the divinely inspired powers of the sovereigns. When the Berlin crowds reacted to this disappointing news by refusing orders to clear the main squares, some shots were fired, probably accidentally. The crowds became violent; and by late on March 18 Berlin was in the throes of a militant, bitter, and grim revolutionary struggle, in which students, merchants, and craft guildsmen confronted the government with a decision: either to fight or to appease.

The King tried appeasement on the nineteenth, without much success; and he then ordered a withdrawal of troops. The crowds reacted by presenting to the King the corpses of Berliners killed by Prussian soldiers, together with a demand for constitutional government. The King capitulated completely. The government formed under the leadership of merchants provided a constitutional draft for negotiation with the King. Until the new constitution for the state was finished, a Prussian parliament would have to wait. For the present only the United Diet[39] existed; and it was soon dissolved.

There thus began the ordeal of the revolution in Germany. During March and April, the smaller states and the important northern towns pursued reforms, while even Prussia and Austria sent delegates to the liberal "preliminary meetings" (*Vorparlament*) at Frankfurt. There, they discussed reforming the Confederation and also elected representatives to the National Assembly.

The German National Assembly met first in Frankfurt on May 18, just three days after Austrian radicals forced on the Habsburgs essentially democratic reforms. Hopes were therefore very high in Frankfurt. But it quickly appeared that the Prussian liberals as well as those from other German states were divided. Long debates ensued, and the resulting delays proved critical both in Berlin and Frankfurt. It is possible that swift, united action by the liberals might have led to an effective constitutional reform for Germany. As it was, the military aristocracy in Prussia and elsewhere used the period of debates to gather together its wits and formulate strategies to frustrate the liberals everywhere.

The crucial step was taken in August, when an aristocratic "parliament" (*Junker-parlament*) of soldiers and landowners met in Prussia. Led by men like Bismarck, they demanded the dissolution of the National Assembly of Prussia,[40] by force if need be. Frederick William took pledges of support during the time of debates, therefore, and in October dismissed his liberal ministers.[41] In their place he put a cabinet headed by Otto von Manteuffel (1805–1882). The Assembly was moved to Brandenburg; the popular civic guards were suppressed; and then, on December 5, 1848, the Assembly of Prussia was dissolved. The King proclaimed a constitution made wholly by himself,[42] beginning the period of reaction in Prussia which lasted until 1852.

The imposed Constitution of December was neither fish nor fowl. It

39. This was the old imperial parliament; it had few effective federal powers.
40. On May 22 the National Assembly met to consider constitutional reform in Prussia. The Assembly was one of the concessions made by the King in the grim days of the late winter risings.
41. October 31, 1848.
42. An *octroyée*, or royal act.

granted broad civil rights and also religious toleration to Lutheran, Calvinist, and Catholic believers. The suffrage rested on high property qualifications, however. The second chamber of the legislature was to be elected by three classes of voters and the upper chamber by fairly wealthy voters only. The result was a plutocratic system in which the mass of small taxpayers and nonpayers voted for as many electors as each of the other two classes. Since each group of electors then chose one deputy to the new Prussian Diet, the votes of the dissatisfied peasants, artisans, and factory workers were so diluted as to be ineffective.

This franchise was coupled with the reassertion of divine right, to stress that what had been granted in Prussia was no repetition of the popular sovereignty expressed in the Belgian constitution of 1830. Moreover, the veneer of "liberality" shown by Manteuffel's legislative program, which abolished aspects of the manorial and patrimonial land law on a provisional basis, was proved a sham. The conservative second chamber refused to accept Prussian reforms without the general German constitution then being drafted at Frankfurt. The government reacted by dissolving the new diet in May 1849.

FRANKFURT, PARIS, AND EUROPE

One of the things disturbing the tranquility of the Frankfurt sessions of the German National Assembly was the realization that the lower social classes were not mollified by constitutional debates. Up and down and across Germany peasant risings raged from early March until the middle of April in 1848. When some nobles responded with offers to liquidate feudal dues, others found allies among those liberals urging resistance to all who threatened property rights. Soldiers were used to put down the revolts, and the peasants, the most numerous German social group, withdrew from agitations in behalf of constitutional reform and national unification.

Their experience matched that of the rioting urban craft journeymen. The mass of artisans wanted to curtail industrial innovation and economic freedom in order to safeguard their traditional modes of production. Saxon textile handworkers destroyed cotton-making machinery. Boatmen thrown out of work on the Rhine and the Danube by steamships tried to burn the competition! The liberal statesmen at Frankfurt called in soldiers.

These deep splits in the ranks of the popular forces were magnified by the liberal fear of communism. The moderates saw in the popular movements the fuel for flames capable of consuming historical traditions, monarchy, and bourgeois property. In November 1847 two Germans in London—Karl Marx and Friedrich Engels—had been commissioned to prepare a theoretical and practical program for the secret Communist League. Originally this was a German-based workingman's association, but in 1847–1848 it was truly international in membership. The 1847 League Congress decision

Adolf von Menzel was a leading German painter of the nineteenth century whose works chronicled the social situation of his time. Here he observes the solemn occasion of the funeral procession for victims of the 1848 revolt in Berlin. Crowds excited by the news of revolution in Vienna had converged on the palace of Frederick William IV, and in the resulting clash with his troops there were many civilian victims. Anxious to preserve his popularity, the Prussian king called a cease-fire, paraded in the streets in a scarf of black and gold symbolizing his intention to lead a united Germany, and even praised "the glorious German revolution." Later his army crushed the remnants of the revolt, but a restricted national parliament was one positive outgrowth of the tumult. Photo Kleinhempel.

produced the *Manifesto of the Communist Party*, which was written in German and sent to a London printer in January 1848, about one month before the Paris revolution.

The *Manifesto* had no notable effect on that uprising. But a French translation of it had appeared in Paris just before the newly minted French Republic was confronted by the terrible insurrection of June 1848. The net result of the workshop scheme had been to flood Paris with "enrolled" workers for whom no work existed. The new Constituent Assembly[43] met in May and purged most of the "social" republicans, thus drawing a sharp line between the Paris masses and the less radical provincial groups. Just as in 1792, the city wanted more revolution, whereas the country did not. The Paris wage earners agitated for "factory" legislation, just as the "social" democrats at Frankfurt did.[44]

The result was an attack on the Constituent Assembly by the workers on May 15. Announcing that a social revolution must follow from the political one, the workers inspired terror in the middle classes. The liberals called in the National Guard; this widened popular resistance, which was met by a proclamation of martial law and a concession of power to General Cavaignac (1802–1857) and the regular army. From June 23 to June 26 a bloody "war of the classes" ensued, in which perhaps 5,000 insurgents were killed and some 11,000 taken prisoner. A third of these unfortunates were then deported to Algeria. Workers were thereby convinced that the bourgeois elements were their enemies.

German liberals saw a relationship between this abortive "Red Revolution" and the newly translated *Manifesto*. Karl Marx had said in the opening lines of the 1848 pamphlet that the entire world of privilege stood in terror of the "spectre" of communism:

A spectre is haunting Europe—the spectre of communism. All the powers of the old Europe have entered into a holy alliance to exorcise this spectre: Pope and Czar, Metternich and Guizot, French radicals and German police spies.[45]

Liberals in Germany had good cause to take Marx seriously. Guizot was overthrown; Metternich was in exile; a revolution at Rome had subordinated Pope Pius IX and seemed to aim at a republic. And in the German states fearful things were happening. Prague had revolted against Emperor Ferdinand. An attempted coup against the democratic leaders in Vienna had failed, and as a result Ferdinand was so discredited that he resigned the crown to his nephew Francis Joseph.

These events had gone forward while the German National Assembly had shown itself to be impotent. The "democrats" in favor of popular sovereignty were opposed by the rightists,[46] who denied to the Assembly any sovereign powers. In between were the Casino, or majority liberals, who favored Prussian leadership of a unified Germany. No group paid much attention to gaining popular support or the support of the princes. Thus the Assembly's election of a regent, Archduke John of Austria, and a ministry proved hollow when Prussia refused to pledge troops to support

---

43. Elected by universal male suffrage.
44. The social democrats were a small party of German socialists drawn from the ranks of factory workers primarily.
45. Quoted from Lewis S. Feuer, *Marx and Engels: Basic Writings on Politics and Philosophy* (New York: Doubleday & Co., Anchor, 1959), p. 6. For an analysis of Marxian ideas see Chapter 12.
46. The "Café Milani" group, a title taken from their meeting place. The democrats met in the Deutsche Hof.

the Frankfurt designs. The draft constitution hammered out and proclaimed as law on December 27, 1848, created the superstructure of a German state: a Reichstag of two houses, a responsible ministry, plus federal control of diplomacy, war, taxes, and the power to make peace. What it could not do was gain the adherence of Prussia and Austria. Nor could it regain the confidence of the masses alienated by a lack of answers to the social question of what protections would be given to workers.

Both defects were made clear early in 1849. When the Assembly elected King Frederick William IV emperor of the "united Germany" on March 28,[47] the Prussian king refused the crown. His reason was ironic; he was more *Grossdeutsch* than his supporters. Frederick William IV wanted to preserve a "primacy" for Austria in the new Germany. Moreover, only a crown of infamy could be offered by those who had no right to bestow it. The King would accept election by his fellow rulers, provided that military command in the federal Germany rested with Prussia. These demands drove Austria from the Assembly. The kings of Bavaria, Saxony, Hanover, and Württemberg refused to recognize the new constitution.

The frustrated democrats attempted to head off the reaction by armed revolution in May. And this completed the break between the liberals and Prussia. But in truth the final judgment on unification and constitutionalism had been passed in the preceding summer, when Prussia agreed to the Danish incorporation of Schleswig and Holstein and troops were used to quell the armed revolts in the southern states which followed the assassination of certain rightist deputies by republicans. Revolution had failed in Germany.

Elsewhere in Europe the fate of revolutionary groups was also a hard one. The Hungarian movement led by Louis Kossuth claimed national rights for itself which were denied to the Croats and Transylvanians, who were absorbed into a new Hungarian kingdom. The Czech revolt had been suppressed and the Pan-Slav Congress dissolved by the military commander of Prague, General Alfred Windischgrätz (1787–1862). The Hungarian kingdom was then suppressed in 1849, after a brief republican phase with Kossuth as president. This was accomplished with Czar Nicholas's aid to Austria, on the principle of opposition to all republicans.

In Italy, the revolts which had begun in January 1848 in Naples and Sicily had spread northward. Tuscany, the Piedmont, Lombardy, Venetia, and Rome received constitutions. Republican sentiment was mixed with Italian nationalism focused on ending Austrian dominance in Italy. Even the Papal States contributed troops to the army levied to drive out Austria. The curve of Italian independence and republican movements therefore followed in a general way the curve of Habsburg fortunes at home. When these arrived at their low point early in 1849, after Ferdinand's abdication, a republic was proclaimed in several states, even at Rome. And the great nationalist leader Giuseppe Mazzini (1805–1872), who had come to prominence in 1831 by founding the Young Italy[48] movement and had also embraced republicanism, sought to consolidate Italy on a new basis. He made decrees transferring Church lands into peasant hands and made provisions for public housing. The experiment in republican nation-building ended badly, however, because the reactionary regime in France under Louis Napoleon intervened against Mazzini.

We thus end where we began, with the French impact on Europe. In the

47. A victory for the *Kleindeutsch* faction; he was elected by a vote of 290 in favor, with 248 abstentions.
48. Also the name of his nationalist journal.

wake of the June Days of 1848, Charles Louis Napoleon Bonaparte (1808–1873), fresh from his exile in England, became a candidate for president of the Republic. The defender of order, as he called himself, defeated Cavaignac, and other candidates, by a huge margin. Capitalizing on the exhaustion of the liberals and the defeat and massacre of the socialists, Louis Napoleon also made good use of the sentiments his famous name evoked. It stood for unity, power, and stability in France; and his election marked the consolidation of the counterrevolution there as surely as Frederick William's rejection of popular sovereignty and insistence on divine right in Germany did.

The great battle between the bourgeoisie and the masses had revealed the aspirations of the working classes and also the gap between "social" revolution and political reorganization. The real struggle once again proved to be between different segments of the propertied classes. All Continental governments suppressed such organizations as the Communist League. And in England—even in liberal England—the workingmen's associations agitating before Parliament for political and social reforms were suppressed or frustrated in their hopes. How and why they failed in the most advanced "industrial" state in Europe raises the interesting question, Did even English radicals yet have the social basis for successful revolution?

BIBLIOGRAPHY

BERLIN, SIR ISAIAH. *Karl Marx, His Life and Environment.** New York: Oxford University Press, 1948. This standard biography and critical introduction to Marxist ideas should be counterbalanced by the more sympathetic Marxist analysis of George Lichtheim: *Marxism: An Historical and Critical Study* (New York: Praeger Publishers, 1961).

HAMEROW, T. S. *Restoration, Revolution, Reaction.** Princeton: Princeton University Press, 1958. Excellent analysis of the German political situation in terms of economic developments.

HOLBORN, HAJO. *A History of Modern Germany, 1648–1840.* Vols. 2, 3. New York: Alfred A. Knopf, 1969. The closing chapters of Volume 2 and the beginning of Volume 3 constitute the most thorough introduction to the 1848 situation in the many German states.

LANGER, WILLIAM L. *Political and Social Upheaval, 1832–1852.** New York: Harper & Row, Publishers, 1969. A masterful survey of liberal Europe and revolutionary pressures.

LICHTHEIM, GEORGE. *The Origins of Socialism.* New York: Praeger Publishers, 1968. One of the most brilliant and sympathetic accounts, worth reading in relation to Frank E. Manuel's detailed book, *The New World of Henri de Saint-Simon** (Cambridge, Mass.: Harvard University Press, 1956).

NAMIER, L. B. *1848: Revolution of the Intellectuals.** London: Cumberland, 1950. A witty, highly critical study of the German liberals at Frankfurt.

PLAMENATZ, JOHN. *The Revolutionary Movement in France, 1815–1871.* London: Longmans, 1952. A careful analysis of liberal republicanism.

RATH, R. J. *The Viennese Revolution of 1848.* Austin: University of Texas, 1957. The best and most thorough study in English.

ROBERTSON, PRISCILLA. *The Revolutions of 1848.** Princeton: Princeton University Press, 1952. Long a standard comparative account, exceedingly well written.

SALVEMINI, GAETANO. *Mazzini.** London: Jonathan Cape, 1956. The best work on the Italian revolutionary republican.

Asterisk indicates a paperbound edition.

Revolutions of 1848

January 12
Revolution in Sicily

January 20
Accession of Frederick VII in Denmark

February 10
Revolution spreads in Italy

February 23–25
Revolution in Paris

Ca. February 28
Communist Manifesto appears

March 13–15
Revolution in Vienna; Metternich resigns

March 18–19
Revolution in Berlin

April 10
Chartist Petition presented

April 27
French National Assembly meets

May 15
Communist riots in Paris

May 18
Frankfurt meeting of German National Assembly

May 22
Prussian National Assembly meets

June 2
Pan-Slav Congress at Prague

June 17
Czech revolt suppressed

June 26
Paris workers' revolt suppressed

July 22
Habeas corpus suspended in Britain

August 12
Emperor restored to Vienna.

September 7
Serfdom abolished in Austria

September 12
Kossuth proclaims Hungarian Republic

October 6
New Viennese revolts

November 12
Republic proclaimed in France

December 2
Ferdinand abdicates Austrian throne

December 5
Prussian constitution granted

December 10
Louis Napoleon elected French president

December 27
German "declaration of rights"

8

ENGLAND AND EUROPE: THE NEW PROMETHEUS

In this work I have to examine the capitalist mode of production, and the conditions of production and exchange corresponding to that mode. Up to the present time their classic ground is England. . . . The country that is more developed industrially only shows, to the less developed, the image of its own future. . . . In all other spheres we, like all the rest of Continental Western Europe, suffer not only from the development of capitalist production, but also from the incompleteness of that development. . . .

KARL MARX, *Das Kapital*[1]

THE PROBLEM OF 1848

In his great critique of political economy Marx noticed that the "social statistics of Germany and the rest of Continental Western Europe are, in comparison with those of England, wretchedly compiled." The English data rested on government activity, because periodically the ministry and parliaments appointed commissions to inquire into economic conditions. Marx praised the commissioners as unbiased professionals, a mixture of factory inspectors and medical reporters who investigated the conditions of public health, the work of women and children, and the housing and food of the urban workers in factories.

On the premise that "one nation[2] can and should learn from others," in order to lay bare "the economic law of motion of modern society," Marx examined the English experience. For he found in that experience the evidence that society was constantly changing, as shown especially in the factory legislation by which the politically active classes made the adjustments necessary in law to facilitate their own maintenance of power. His conclusion was that the English political classes had dangled before the working classes the "alms bag" of reform, seeking by a series of acts of charity and relief to steer the consciousness of working men and women away from their true destiny—socialism and the formation of a political "party" independent of the Whig and Tory parties then monopolizing power.

Marx therefore raised the problem of the relationships between economic systems, political systems

1. The quotation is from Marx's "Author's Preface" to the first edition of *Das Kapital*, of which volume 1 appeared in 1867. The translation is by Samuel Moore and Edward Aveling, Marx's son-in-law, and is printed in Lewis S. Feuer, *Marx and Engels: Basic Writings on Politics and Philosophy* (New York: Doubleday & Co., Anchor, 1959), pp. 134–138. All other unannotated quotes derive from this source.
2. The Germans, to whom the first edition of *Das Kapital* was addressed.

and events, and the struggle of the working classes to achieve self-determination. He had already concluded that the "failure" of the Continental revolutions in 1848 arose out of the fact that the bourgeoisie compromised with the aristocracies to suppress the lower classes in order to safeguard all property, confident that in the end industrial capital would win the battle against aristocratic (feudal) landed property. Moreover, the "socialism" of 1847–1848 was for Marx "utopian" in character and not rooted in the experiences of the industrial working people. The basic flaw found in the thought of Fourier, or that of the British reformer Owen, was this. The bourgeois socialists had looked to government and the educated classes to tinker with conditions, to relieve misery and social grievances by means of "political revolutions." The more penetrating socialists, the "communists," those who arose from within the working classes, saw the necessity of a "total social change" by which the emancipation of the working class would emerge from working-class consciousness and working-class actions.

Because Britain was the most advanced industrial nation in the world in 1848, indeed in many respects the only one with a mature industrial economy and the social changes attendant on such an economy, we may, like Marx, focus on it in order to answer tentatively the questions arising out of the "success" of reform in England and the failure of revolution in Europe. We may begin by sketching the work of "reform" in England from 1832 to 1848. And, on the basis of that sketch, we may then propose some further questions about why reform in England took the course it did.

ON THE SURFACE: REFORM IN ENGLAND, 1832–1848

When last we looked at English political events, we saw the duke of Wellington calling new parliamentary elections.[3] He did this after heading a government which had sketched in legislation the outlines of Tory reform: the abolition of many capital crimes; the reduction of tariffs; other measures tending toward free trade; the repeal of "test" laws, which had prohibited dissenters from the Anglican Church from holding office under the crown; the repeal of restrictions on Catholics. What no Tory government had been willing to do was to repeal the Corn Laws protecting the rent-rolls of the classes represented in Parliament or to tackle the reform of the unrepresentative Commons.

The new Whig ministry led by Earl Grey (1764–1845), the Whig (or liberal) prime minister who took office under King William IV, sought power on the promise of reform. Early in 1831, Grey brought into the Commons a bill to redistribute seats, apparently to recognize the shifts in the distribution of population which had accompanied the onset of industrialization and the growth of great urban complexes in the "cotton" districts of the Midlands and the north of England. The Commons rejected the bill, however. The Tories, with the July Revolution in France fresh in mind, refused to form a government. Grey secured a dissolution of Parliament and in a bitterly fought election gained a new majority. He therefore resumed power, introducing a second reform bill. The Commons passed the bill, but it was now defeated by the House of Lords, where Wellington's followers acted in the manner of Guizot's French adherents, the "resisters."

Against their assertion that England had a perfect political system, the mass of urban Englishmen rose. Mobs roamed the London streets. Bristol was in the hands of the rebels, while in Derby, Nottingham, Liverpool, Manchester, and York crowds rioted, burned, and looted. Their agitation

3. See Chapter 6.

A combination of fateful circumstances and the determined leadership of the Whig prime minister Lord Grey (at right) finally resulted in the passing of the 1832 Reform Act. Shown with Grey are Lord Brougham (left) who argued for the act in the House of Lords, and Lord Russell (center) who presented it to the House of Commons. Despite their persuasiveness, only the prospect of civil war in late 1831 and early 1832 overcame the opposition Lords. They abstained when King William IV threatened to swamp their House with newly created pro-reform peers. Grey continued a tradition of pragmatic English statesmen: in his youth he had protested efforts to infringe upon the interests of the landed class, but in his old age he recognized the tide of history favored such reform, and he swam with it, saving the country. By courtesy of the Trustees of the British Museum.

centered on the reforms turned down in the Commons in March and in the Lords in October 1831.

Grey now saw the means to secure passage of the "Great Reform Bill." He convinced William IV that the combination of industrial depression, civil disorder, and Tory lords who frustrated the popular will foreshadowed a revolution in England. To forestall it, Grey advised the promise by the King to create enough new lords pledged to reform to defeat the diehards in the House of Lords. The reasoning was apparently this: the members of the House of Lords, faced with certain defeat if the King carried out his threat, would choose to support the reform bill instead and thereby preserve their present, unadulterated, numbers in Parliament's upper chamber. The bill reintroduced in May 1832 secured passage on June 4, 1832.

Before commenting on why the bill passed or what its intended impact on politics and society was meant to be, we may state its major provisions. The act disfranchised 56 pocket and rotten boroughs[4] and took from 32 others one of their two seats. The remaining pool of 143 seats in the Commons was then distributed among the counties, where the narrow franchise of the 40-shilling freeholder[5] had held sway before 1832, and also among some boroughs not represented at all before 1832. Sixty-five seats went to the counties, while 22 large boroughs received two seats each and 21 other boroughs one seat apiece. There were also eight seats given to Scottish boroughs and five to Irish ones.

The act also reformed the franchise for all constituencies. In the counties, the vote went to the old 40-shilling freeholders again, but to their ranks were added many who did not *own* the land they farmed. Persons holding long leases[6] worth £10 or more a year, or those enjoying copyholds[7] in that amount, got the vote. The franchise was also now given to short-term leasees and copyhold tenants who held land worth £50 a year or more. In all boroughs, where a bewildering variety of qualifications had once existed and favored substantial propertied men, the franchise came to all males *occupying* premises for which a rent of £10 or more per year was due.

The net result of the act was, therefore, to substantially alter the size of the electorate, which increased in number from about 478,000 to 814,000. The smaller renters in towns, chiefly working-class people, were still excluded, as were the masses of rural day laborers and poor tenants. In some towns enjoying democratic franchises before 1832, numbers of workers were actually disfranchised—e.g., London and Westminster. And those who had voted in the disfranchised boroughs were now able to vote only as residents of their counties. On balance, therefore, the measure enfranchised mainly the "middle classes" in the towns and the more prosperous small farmers in the counties: merchants, doctors, lawyers, brokers, and the comfortable dependents of the rich county landowners.

Despite the fact that the act was, therefore, not laden with direct benefits for the working classes of town and country, historians have agreed upon its greatness. They argue that the capacity for the unreformed House of Commons and the Lords to vote political reform held out the hope of social reform as well, thus heading off revolution. The masses could hope that

---

4. Before the reform bill, a pocket borough was one whose Parliamentary representation was controlled by an individual or family. A rotten borough was one that had very few voters, yet was still represented in Parliament.

5. Freehold was a nonmilitary (feudal), nonservile tenure of land also called socage. Freehold land could be divided among heirs at will; it could be freely bought and sold. Males with land in freehold worth 40 shillings net per annum had had the right to vote in the counties since 1429.

6. Sixty years or more.

7. A customary form of tenure, an outgrowth of manorial usage, now the equivalent of a lease.

Supporters of Grey's Reform Act chop away at a tree symbolizing the rotten borough system, while the vested interests on the right seek to maintain the status quo. In addition to greatly increasing the number of enfranchised citizens, the Reform Act chiefly sought to establish an equitable plan of representation in Parliament. This was achieved by taking seats away from over-represented rural areas and distributing them among the new industrial centers and Scotland. No radical piece of legislation, the act left many still unsatisfied, as shown by the growth of the Chartist movement in following years. However, it did establish the principle that such basic changes could be brought about peacefully by law. Radio Times Hulton Picture Library.

they, too, would soon come to participate actively in politics. And, so the argument goes, now that the solid middle classes were represented, especially the captains of industry, perhaps the more liberal temper of the capitalists would help reduce the privileges so long enjoyed by landed wealth. Indeed, the orthodox view of the 1832 Reform Act is that it marks the beginning of the modern period in British political history, the point at which industry and the more liberal elements in the landed classes joined hands to set in place the keystone of the "democratic" constitution. Even though only one man in five had the vote as a result of the reform, and the franchise still represented a balance of property *against* numbers, many historians profess to see in Earl Grey a prophet whose motive was to embrace the future!

Did the ministry of 1831–1832 have in mind paving the way for the triumph of economic liberalism and industrial society? Or were the Whigs only seeking some means to cure the ills of society and so avoid revolution, by concessions to other propertied classes than the large landowners? What in fact were the premises of the first act of reform? And, regardless of what the reformers intended, what were the immediate and distant consequences?

Even a cursory look at the record of reform from 1832 to 1848 seems to warrant the idea that what came after 1832 was the natural unfolding of the rational political schemes of the reformers. For, if the Whigs had intended to transfer political power from the old aristocracy and plutocracy into the hands of the middle classes, the barrage of acts passed in the next sixteen years looks like the means to that end.

These further acts of reform must be listed, with only brief comments. In 1833 the reformed legislature abolished slavery in the British Empire. A year later, the new Poor Law Amendment Act made radical changes in the relief of the poor. This "reform" was opposed by the "beneficiaries," however, and did not achieve the end of abolishing outdoor relief completely. But it did force the able-bodied poor to accept work in the poorhouses ruled by over 600 "unions" and supervised by three commissioners.[8] And it ended the provision of unearned relief for all except the aged or infirm. In 1835 the Municipal Corporations Act reformed local government by putting uniform administrative and electoral councils, selected by "ratepayers" (taxpayers), in place of the nearly 200 old urban oligarchies. The new councils gained control of police work, local justice, jails, and the rudimentary systems of public health.

These measures, each of which tried to come to grips with an aspect of an increasingly urban society, were followed swiftly by others. In 1836 the Commons allowed its debates and votes to be reported in the newspapers. This step opened government processes to the scrutiny of the literate public. There were measures of church reform in the same year, especially touching the incomes of the poorer clergy and general financial abuses.

The combined force of these various measures was an invasion of the traditional Tory strongholds of local government and the Church of England. And the Tories, not to be outdone, threw their weight behind "Tory radical" advocates of factory reform, perhaps with a view to stunt the growth of industry as much as to remedy the conditions in the new industrial centers.

Parliament had first asserted responsibility for the protection of workers in 1802 when it regulated the use of pauper children who were rented out to cotton mill owners. The next achievement in this line came in the Factory Act of 1819, for which the socialist Robert Owen had lobbied. This act forbade the employment of children under 9, while allowing those between 9 and 16 to work up to twelve hours a day. Night work had been forbidden. The difficulties of enforcement were great, however, since local magistrates in league with industrialists evaded the laws. New agitations peaked in 1833, and Lord Ashley[9] gave expression in Parliament to the ideas of the radical reformers J. Wood and Richard Oastler. The Factory Act of 1833 affected all textile mills,[10] limiting children under 11 to a forty-eight-hour week, but allowing those 11 to 18 to work up to sixty-eight hours a week. More important was the provision of a group of bureaucratic supervisors, the factory commissioners Marx praised, inspectors responsible to the central government.

If the Factory Act of 1833 had teeth, this was the result of testimony on the conditions of labor in the factories which had been published in the "blue books," or reports, of parliamentary and ministerial commissions of inquiry. These "blue books" also raised by implication issues concerning health, safety, pay, and other conditions of employment affecting the mass of industrial workers. But the industrialists stubbornly fought all efforts by Shaftesbury and his friends[11] to widen the scope of reform. The chief achievement was the 1842 act regulating employment in coal mines, which

8. The poorhouses were put under a Poor Law Board, with a cabinet minister's supervision, in 1847.
9. Anthony Ashley Cooper (1801–1885), seventh earl of Shaftesbury, a Tory radical who joined the Whigs in 1847.
10. Excluding the small silk-textile industry.
11. Especially those campaigns waged by the journalist Michael Sadler (1780–1835).

Lord Shaftesbury, a leader in the agitation for a ten-hour work day, also helped focus Parliament's attention on conditions in Britain's coal mines. He told of children as young as four and five sent to work in the pits; their task, as shown in this illustration from the report of a British commission of inquiry, was to drag sledge tubs through tunnels too small to admit grown workers. A chain from the tub was attached at the child's waist. The reports of such abuses led to the 1842 Mines Act, which put an end to the employment underground of women and girls, and of boys under ten. Nine other acts were to follow, from 1850 to 1911, further regulating the coal industry and providing for the safety of its workers. Radio Times Hulton Picture Library.

prohibited work underground of women and girls, and boys under ten. Then, in 1844, a new act further reduced the hours of women and children, while abridging the freedom of employers at least to the extent of requiring the fencing of machinery as a safety measure.

This seemed most pernicious to the "liberal" economists who preached the virtues of noninterference. For, if the laws regulating hours of labor threatened to rob industry of the work it needed for prosperity, the 1844 act actually dictated that industrialists were to take part of their profits and invest them not in new production but in devices to safeguard the bodies of the surplus laborers! Industry survived, however, and continued to expand, even in 1847, when the reformers won their greatest victory—the Ten Hours Act. This act stipulated a "day" of not more than ten hours for women and children in all textile industries. The reformers hoped to achieve a ten-hour day for men, too, by this act because of the close coordination of the labor force. What they underestimated was the ingenuity of industrialists. Managers had resort to a "relay" system. By law factories employing child and female labor were allowed to operate between the hours of 5:30 A.M. and 8:30 P.M. By splitting the work of the regulated laborers, and by gearing men to the split force, workers could still be made to labor up to fifteen hours daily.[12] This practice was not eliminated until 1850, when an amendment to the Ten Hours Act required factories not to operate more than twelve hours per day.[13]

Whether the factory acts represented an antagonism between the Tory landowners who were defeated in 1832 and the "victorious" capitalists must be understood in the context of another agitation—that to repeal the Corn Laws. According to the "explanation" of reform already mentioned, it was the wish of the industrialists to maximize their profits by cutting the cost of wages. This could best be done by lowering the protective tariffs on foreign bread and cereals raised by the Corn Law of 1815. This act, as amended in 1828,[14] was meant to insure reasonable profits for landlords, by prohibiting the import of foreign wheat until domestic prices reached a level determined by law. Allegedly, the agitation to repeal the Corn Laws provided a common cause for workers and capitalists—cheap bread. The slogan of the liberals was thus "free trade," while the landlords favored protection. Ideologically, these positions also seemed consistent with the split over factory acts. The "liberal" free-trading industrialists wanted no state interference with the natural workings of the economy. The Tories favored "protection" for farmers and for workers, through government regulation of prices for grain, hours of employment, and other industrial conditions.

This placed the working classes in an ambiguous position. They sided with the capitalists on the issue of free trade in cereals, but with the farmers who wanted to regulate industry to the benefit of the workers. Similarly, rural laborers were said to favor protection of English agriculture in order to safeguard their jobs. But this meant that their "politics" also helped to drive up the cost of living, by keeping basic food costs high.

The history of the repeal of the Corn Laws throws doubt on this neat division of interests. In 1839 advocates of free trade in grain had organized an Anti–Corn Law League, which had the support of the most prominent "liberal" manufacturers in Manchester,[15] especially John Bright (1811–

12. The women and children worked only ten hours (say 5:30 A.M.–3:30 P.M. for one shift; another from 10:30 A.M.–8:30 P.M.), making up overlapping partial forces. The men worked 5:30 A.M.–8:30 P.M. (fifteen hours) as a complement force to assure full staffing.
13. In both 1850 and 1853 "compensation" was provided to the owners, however, in the form of an *extension* of the total hours women and children could work.
14. Huskisson abolished the fixed price of eighty shillings in favor of a sliding scale.
15. The greatest of the "cotton" towns.

After decades of tremendous population growth which far outstripped increases in production, Ireland was unable to cope with the problems of the potato blight which swept Europe after 1845. Despite active relief work, many died from starvation, and nearly two million fled the country after 1847; most came to America. Some of those preparing to emigrate are shown awaiting steamship passage. In many cases their weakened health and the appalling conditions aboard ship led to heavy casualties during the crossing. The general misery of the Irish people gave strength to the Home Rule movement, which sought political freedom from England. Radio Times Hulton Picture Library.

1889) and Richard Cobden (1804–1865). Opponents of the repealers argued that to let down the barriers in order to help industrialists lower wages, and hence manufacturing costs, would make English goods more competitive overseas at the expense of agriculture. Thus the profits of capitalists and any boom in factory employment would come at the expense of the landed classes on the one hand and the rural laboring poor on the other, thrown out of work by the contracting market for domestic foodstuffs. There was, however, no direct conflict between capitalists and aristocrats, but an attempt on both sides to mobilize the as yet unfranchised masses of workers.

In this effort the repealers had great success. The "Manchester Liberals" used their headquarters there to link together groups in other towns. Operating in the manner of a modern political party, with a great "campaign chest" and solid phalanxes of public speakers and pamphleteers, the Anti–Corn Law League organized opinion. It also conducted mass meetings so as to create pressures of an unprecedented kind: an appeal by one parliamentary class to those not represented in order to change the "balance of the constitution," the Tories claimed, and upset also the balance of the economy. For seven years the Tories stood firm against the pressure. Then, in 1845, the first failure of the Irish potato crop caused widespread misery in that country under British government. The spread of the threat of famine to the rest of Britain in 1846 proved conclusive.

The government in England had since 1841 been headed by Sir Robert Peel (1788–1850), a politician distrustful of the Tory resisters ever since their opposition to his reforms of the police in 1822. This distrust had enlarged in 1829, when the Tory squires opposed the bill for Catholic emancipation brought in by Peel. In 1834 Peel had been made prime minister by William IV, in a minority government from which he resigned early in 1835, "retiring" to opposition and the reformation of the progressive wing of the Tory party into what he preferred to call a Conservative party. Called back to power in 1841, Peel showed in his own actions over the next five years that reform was not a straight fight between parties or economic interests.

Sir Robert carried reform budgets from 1842 to 1845, each designed to reduce the load of indirect taxation, making up sums for government out of an income tax. This direct tax on wealth he supplemented with a program of tariff reductions. And, by 1845, Peel had abolished duties on 605 items and

reduced those on 1,035 others. He argued, correctly, as the trade figures will illustrate, that the increased consumption of goods generated by the reductions would assure England's commercial supremacy in the world. Peel also reformed credit institutions, including the Bank of England. Moreover, he wanted to lighten the burden of British government on Ireland. This he was prevented from doing by the famine there and the crisis engendered in the English food supply by efforts to relieve it and by the spread of crop failures in England itself. He drew from his own experiments with tariffs the logical conclusion, recommending to his cabinet measures to repeal the Corn Laws in slow stages. The refusal of his ministers to support Peel forced his resignation on December 9, 1845, but he resumed office eleven days later, when the Whig Lord John Russell failed to form a government.

Peel carried a cabinet proposal to repeal the Corn Laws, with the dissent of only two lords. Early in 1846, a bill to repeal the import duties on cereal and also reform the customs system was before Commons. In it total free trade was to come by 1849. Peel, after being defeated in the Commons[16] on another matter,[17] left the government. But on the same night, June 26, 1846, he had carried repeal of the Corn Laws, even though Benjamin Disraeli[18] had led more than 300 "protectionist" Tories into the lobbies to vote against the bill. Thus splitting the Conservative party, Peel spent the rest of his life supporting the Whigs, without joining them. Devoted, as Wellington had once said, only to justice and truth, Peel had urged on the country an intelligent conservatism, in the face of the revolutionary agitation then at work in Europe and in England.

IDEOLOGY, REVOLUTION, AND WORKING-CLASS POLITICS

Peel's behavior raises again the question we have already asked: What had been intended in 1832 by those who reformed the franchise? Clearly, by 1846, the acts of Parliament militated against the view that the Whig "plan" had worked. If it had done nothing else, the new franchise had brought to power members who restricted industry by legislation; they had also added to the other reforms the repeal of agricultural protection. This the Whigs had not intended, because most of Earl Grey's supporters in 1832 were in fact landlords. The Whig and Tory parties had in their ranks large cadres of big landowners. Moreover, if the Whigs saw the reform of Parliament as a measure to secure for themselves and their industrialist supporters political power, they had failed miserably. From 1832 through 1848 it was Peel's party which enjoyed office almost constantly, not the party of Grey and Russell. And, finally, the "alms bag of reform" had not prevented the rise of a truly radical working-class consciousness in Europe's first industrial society.

First, the question of the 1832 act; then the failure to head off a working-class politics.

Recent studies[19] of the Reform Act have explained *how* the unreformed House of Commons made possible the reform many thought impossible for its members. Briefly, the Tory farmers were encouraged to support reform because they were led to believe that the new constituencies could be drawn in ways to reinforce, rather than to dilute, the landed interests in the House

16. The Lords having sustained him!
17. Irish reform.
18. 1804–1881; the future prime minister.
19. Especially those by D. C. Moore: "The Other Face of Reform," *Victorian Studies* 5 (1961): 7–34; "Concession or Cure: The Sociological Premises of the First Reform Act," *Historical Journal* 4 (1966): 39–59.

of Commons. Historians preoccupied with the new borough arrangements have failed to notice in the act provisions regulating the rights of borough freeholders to vote in the counties and also the rights of men who did not reside in the boroughs to vote in them. The effect of such provisions, and also the way in which boundary commissioners drew the lines around the new, expanding, boroughs, was to gerrymander constituencies to enhance the landed interests. The fact that Tory and Conservative governments were returned by the new electorate indicates that these disregarded aspects of the act did enable the landed classes to continue to dominate elections. The effect produced by gerrymander tactics was further enhanced by the assignment of "reformed" seats to the counties. Of the 143 saved seats, 65 were given to the landed interests in the counties.

Thus the Grey ministry appealed to the moderate Tories, not to transfer political power from the aristocracy and gentry to the middle classes, but to find a way to accommodate the new urban "magnates" in their boroughs while also arresting the loss of political power traditional elites were then experiencing in England and the rest of Europe.

On this reading of the Reform Act, its consequences look less like a master plan for the triumph of the bourgeoisie than a miscalculation by aristocrats frightened by the specter Marx publicized in 1848 in an extreme form. That the problem of the legitimacy of the political order in a rapidly changing society was in Grey's mind in 1831 we know from speeches ministers made about their "remedy" for the nation's grievances. The nation could be preserved only by measures which did not recognize class interests, which did not separate "the Members of this House [Commons] into two distinct and hostile parties" on behalf of commerce and agriculture. A House so divided would fall before the pressures of the lower classes. This, it was argued, must be manifest to all who grasped the meaning of two related movements: the declining respect for members of Parliament in the communities they represented, and the weakening of traditional channels of social discipline. What else did the history of the English people indicate in the decades since Wilkes had raised a challenge to Parliament? What other sense could ministers make of the *demands* for reform, and the riots (by the unfranchised classes) behind those demands?

Thus the business of reform was to draw up a new political structure capable of putting the members of Parliament in closer touch with the different communities they represented. The elites of town and country would thereby be once more *legitimized*, because they would represent more closely the interests of their newly drawn constituencies.

In essence, Grey, Russell, and Peel, above all others, stood for a theory of harmony of interests among the elites. The slogans of "protection" and "free trade," and the ideologies of unrestrained economic activity versus regulation, were to statesmen less the issues at the heart of the matter than the effort to defeat the *antagonistic*, class view of politics which seemed to grow up in an industrializing society.

The sociological premises of reform, therefore, derived from a recognition that the preponderance of the landed interests in hierarchic communities was being weakened by the development of new social structures. Clearly the cotton mill towns threw suburbs into the countryside at a reckless rate, encouraging new forms of organization attractive to the working classes themselves. These men were for the most part not attracted by Anglican religion; they belonged more to the "chapel" than to the "church."[20] And they seemed more unwilling than artisans and peasants

---

20. The "chapel" signified the Nonconformist meeting halls of dissenting Protestants, while the "church" referred to the established Anglican Church.

had been to defer to their "betters" in political and economic matters. Unless new community lines were drawn, and quickly, English politics would cease to have the structure it had always exhibited: a unified group of communities dominated by elites hallowed by tradition. It would become instead an aggregation of individuals who, if they had any "identity" at all, would see themselves as members of *classes* determined by their situation with regard to the means of production.

There is some evidence, so far ignored, which gives substance to the fears we have called the sociological premises of reform. The onset of industrialization in England had undermined social cohesion. The thing remarkable about the new towns and enlarged old ones was that the "natural state of society"[21] failed to operate in them. This "natural state" gave to the fittest persons, who were fit by birth, wealth, and the leisure necessary to a liberal education, the power of government. The transition to industry had destroyed old habits of social trust and social deference. Men and women from the lower classes seemed unwilling to concede to their betters the right to think for the common people. Indeed, so far were working-class people from the old habits that common folk exhibited a tendency to seek cohesion in society in horizontal "classes" or layers, rather than through the ladderlike and supposedly natural hierarchy of deference to one's "betters."

One movement which thrived between 1838 and 1848, that of Chartism or the People's Charter,[22] proves the point. The tale can be briefly told. For, unlike the situation in France, where socialism and republicanism dominated the very small segment of the total work force we may call industrial labor, or that in Germany, where the social democrats were an even less visible revolutionary force, in Britain the political climate was such that social revolutionaries among workingmen melded socialist ideology with agitations for parliamentary reform.

In 1835 a witness before a parliamentary committee was asked to say whether his fellow workers were satisfied with the provisions of the 1832 Reform Act. The worker, a handloom weaver, gave this reply:

I do not think they are. They viewed the Reform Bill as a measure calculated to join the upper and middle classes to Government, and leave them [workers] in the hands of Government as a sort of machine to work according to the pleasure of Government.[23]

Three years later something was done to remedy the note of resignation found in the 1835 testimony. Prompted by discontent arising from economic depression and the failure of government to respond to working-class aspirations, some workers had in 1836 founded a London Workingmen's Association. Leading members in 1837 formulated six demands to be put to Parliament: universal manhood suffrage, the secret ballot, payment of wages to members of Parliament, abolition of property qualifications for members of Parliament, equal constituencies, and annual parliaments. While most of these demands speak for themselves, the fifth needs to be understood in terms of the Tory-inspired gerrymandering of constituencies we have spoken of earlier. Workingmen understood the meaning of the 1832 Reform Act well enough. And the ballot demand can be understood

21. The phrase was John Stuart Mill's, from his essay *Spirit of the Age.*
22. The Chartists did not finally break up until 1858, but their importance was small after 1848.
23. Quoted in E. P. Thompson, *The Making of the English Working Class* (New York: Random House, Vintage Books, 1966), p. 832.

only if we realize that, in the agitation for factory reform legislation, workers had been convinced of the values of secrecy.[24]

In 1832 in the industrial city of Leeds antiregulation forces had bullied the unfranchised workers into intimidating the reform candidates[25] in the first post-Reform election:

We could name more than a dozen mills, all the hands of which have received positive orders to be in the Yard on Monday, and to hold up their hands for the Orange candidates . . . in pain of instant privation of employment.[26]

Such experiences of the fruits of the Reform Act pushed the authors of the six parliamentary demands to seek support among disaffected workers in the provinces. The Birmingham Political Union joined hands with the Londoners. So did the Leeds supporters of the radical Irish demagogue Feargus O'Connor.[27] The several groups drafted a parliamentary bill, which they published in 1838 as *The People's Charter*. Amid increasing economic distress and the harsh work requirements of the 1834 Poor Law, mass demonstrations for the Charter took place in 1838–1839. These sometimes ran to nearly 200,000 people. A "National Convention" was held in London early in 1839, where, in the atmosphere created by this conscious use of a French revolutionary title for the assembly, threats of a general strike and armed violence were subordinated to a petition to Parliament. This cry for redress of grievance bore more than one million signatures, but was rejected.

Some sporadic strikes and one insurrection followed, but the government effectively suppressed the "physical force" Chartists. Holding to Lord Russell's interpretation of the 1832 act, and also Earl Grey's, Parliament put an end to hopes for the six demands. Again, in 1842, the reorganized National Charter Association controlled by O'Connor presented its petition, now bearing 3,317,702 signatures, or about half the adult males in a population of about 19,000,000. The Commons rejected the demands, 287 votes against, only 49 in favor. A new wave of strikes and riots proved short-lived, however, and the movement declined. Lovett devoted his attention to education reforms; Attwood attached himself to Peel's currency and tax reforms; O'Connor took up the issue of general land reform. Others devoted themselves to the factory acts, while a few sought to meet the demands of tactics by joining their economic enemies, the liberals agitating for the repeal of the Corn Laws.

Chartism was revived by the deep distress of 1847–1848 and also by the European revolutions. The net result, however, was a new wave of mass demonstrations and the presentation of a third Chartist petition. The House was more united than ever against the "threat to property" posed by political democracy. Despite the alleged six million signatures and a new convention, or perhaps because of them, the government commissioned the aged duke of Wellington to restore order. He swore in 70,000 special constables to control the "physical force" Chartists. Drills were being held by the Chartists and arms distributed; and there is evidence of a radical plan for systematic terror and the barricading of parts of London. Meanwhile

24. Previously voters had made an open declaration in a poll book.
25. Michael Sadler. The Orange (Whig) candidates were the industrialist Marshall and Lord Macaulay.
26. Quoted in Thompson, *English Working Class*, p. 825.
27. 1794–1855. The most prominent London leader was William Lovett (1800–1877), a cabinetmaker, while in Birmingham Thomas Attwood (1783–1856), a radical banker, was the leader.

there were clashes at Liverpool, and in London the Commons coolly dismissed the petition. Resolute against the specter of "Red Revolution,"[28] Britain's ruling elites broke up the Chartist movement with seeming ease. And this prompted Marx to comment bitterly about the morally degraded English workers, deceived by the carrot of reform and intimidated by Wellington's stick.

Marx and his English followers[29] underestimated the impact of the organized working classes, however. The Chartist movement, despite having leaders who were often exploitative and not from within the working classes, showed the existence in England of a self-conscious *working class*. Out of the many groups of workers—weavers, tailors, miners, smelters—the human experience shared by those who labored in industrial towns had created a common sense of *relationship*. This relationship, that of belonging to the working class, led millions to articulate the identity of interests they felt to be uniquely their own.

We can most satisfactorily investigate the roots of the sense of relationship, of belonging to a class, by *examining the experience* shared as well as by pointing, much as we have already, to evidence that this experience had become part of the consciousness of workers. For the class consciousness arose out of experiences that were inflicted on workers, not chosen in a voluntary way. And the experience was basically that of working in mechanized shops and factories. In other words, we cannot get at the social and cultural roles the Chartists played, or those played by men who organized the early English "trade" unions, without first getting at the reality of the revolution in working-class lives produced by industrialization. Examining the "Industrial Revolution" in Britain is, therefore, the essential task for anybody concerned with understanding the era of reform and how the British political structure survived intact the era of revolutions in Europe.

INDUSTRIALIZATION: CONCEPTS AND TIME SPANS

In order to deal effectively with the Industrial Revolution and not to misconceive its nature (for it was, like the Scientific Revolution, not the sum of mechanical inventions and technological discoveries), we must first offer some basic definitions. The Industrial Revolution was a European phenomenon, but it happened first in Britain, in the century from 1750 to 1850. It involved both economic *change* and economic *growth*. Indeed, certain economic changes we have already discussed as taking place in preindustrial Britain were very long-term "causes" of the specific economic growth we call the Industrial Revolution. By economic growth we mean the *increase of output per head of population*. The sustained and substantial increase in per capita output which came about from the systematic application of machine technology to production is what we call the Industrial Revolution.[30]

This compact definition is explicit about growth and the means by which it came. Implicit in the notion of the Industrial Revolution, however, are questions of its background, the economic and social processes which produced and sustained it, and the general consequences for society of industrialization. There is abundant evidence in the preceding pages that

28. The slogan was actually used by militant Chartists, in emulation of Louis Blanc's "red flag" cohorts in Paris. See Chapter 7.
29. Helen MacFarlane translated the *Manifesto* into English and published it in G. J. Harney's periodical, *Red Republican* (London, 1850).
30. See R. M. Hartwell, *The Industrial Revolution and Economic Growth* (London: Methuen, 1971), p. 46: "It is necessary to think of the Industrial Revolution primarily as economic growth through industrialization."

industrialization coincided with, and was the root cause of, social, cultural, and political changes in Western life. It is therefore insufficient to treat the revolution historically, as if it were only the sum of changes in population growth, technology, the accumulation of capital, and the utilization of resources. For the revolution produced a complete restructuring of the communities it affected; it was the maker of *modernization*, which means that the Industrial Revolution marked the great discontinuity of European history.

It is not too difficult to point to changes that took place and so transformed the growth and structure of economy and society in the century after 1750: the proportion of national income given to investment doubled; the part of the total work force employed in manufacturing and its related services reached modern proportions; population and output per capita grew at rates never before approached in history; real income[31] per person doubled. Both the standard of living among working-class people and the quality of their lives improved, despite much misery, social insecurity, and the sense of exploitation we meet in popular movements for reform.

What is harder to do is to explain the change and growth, which was unprecedented as to rapidity, scale, and scope. Yet this is what we must attempt to sketch: the social processes by which a number of independent variables[32] in preindustrial society combined to promote and sustain industrialized growth. Only then can we return to questions of consequences: whether living standards rose or fell for the masses of people, and whether or not the way of life, "the quality of work and the living environment, the quality of human relationships"[33] in urban society improved.

For the purposes of explanation, we discuss industrialization within three artificially constructed phases of the growth process: in the two sections immediately following we treat the preindustrial phase, from about 1100 to 1760, which we can only summarize, as it has been treated at length elsewhere in this history; and the "onset," from about 1760 to 1815, a period during which the new social order began to appear in clear outline. Because the period 1815–1850 provides important evidence of the measure of industrialization achieved, such data is considered there also. But before 1850 there was no great flow of benefits to the mass of the population; and it is in the period 1815–1850 that the organization of an industrial society becomes apparent. The remainder of this chapter considers social reorganization, especially with regard to the standard of living and the quality of life in an industrial society.

INDUSTRY, TECHNOLOGY, ENTERPRISE, AND SUPPLY

Economic growth before industrialization had gone on in Europe since the eleventh century, with setbacks and spurts, to produce economies in the eighteenth century more "advanced" than those anywhere else in the world. And England took the lead in Europe, with a very long-term growth that rested on a combination of techniques, resources, entrepreneurial types, and institutions—economic and political in kind. European levels of real income, or what economists and historians call real product per capita, were the highest in the world. Moreover, in the factors we call *endowments*, or resources, Europe was superior; and, within Europe, England: in terms of supplies of agricultural land per capita, for instance, or the crucial raw material of industry, coal. During industrialization coal was essential to the

31. The actual purchasing power of income measured in money; it expands and decreases even when money is constant in value.
32. Population, capital, technology, etc.
33. Hartwell, *Industrial Revolution*, p. 55.

Rapid improvements in the spinning and weaving equipment of England's cotton textile industry laid the base for the first large-scale factory production. Expansion was so rapid that by the mid-nineteenth century more than a million workers were employed in textile factories. Many were poorly paid women and children working long hours in dismal conditons, and their inhuman treatment spurred reform and socialist movements. This engraving depicts a loom shed in Derby with two rows of sophisticated jacquard looms at left. These complicated patterns were quickly mass produced by the perforated cards above each machine which varied the weaving patterns. The Mansell Collection.

new technical processes that made iron production and other manufacturing techniques cheaper and more abundant. The industrial map was a map of coalfields; and England had pioneered this mining industry in Tudor times.

But neither accumulations of capital nor endowments make for growth automatically. Some countries elsewhere in the world had adequate savings and abundant resources. What they lacked, and what England had more completely than any other European country around 1760, was the bundle of variables apart from the "heavy" factors or basic variables of capital and population. The Western societies had a heritage of institutions favorable to growth, and England especially had a rich technology and an arsenal of those institutions and organizations favoring growth. We mean not only steam engines and navigable rivers and passable roads, although Englishmen had more of these per capita than other peoples.

European history had insured a general supply of banks and commodity markets in all Western countries. But in some these were more developed, especially in England. And in none were there fewer inhibitions on economic activity. High literacy, religious toleration, flexible social structures and political institutions, a legal system strongly protective of property, and a general climate rewarding to innovators were important British heritages. In England more than in any other country during the Old Regime the investment preferences of society had changed from country houses to factories, and from cathedrals to machines, from conspicuous consumption to commerce.

There was more in this than the worship of Mammon. There was a mixture of values deriving from the Renaissance and Reformation, and also from the growth of science and rationalism as well as from the political theories of Locke and the Enlightenment. There was less of what Thorstein Veblen[34] once called the "imbecile institutions" of society, which gave to the cake of custom and all tradition a sacredness inimical to any change, let alone the rapid change of growth through industrial applications of new power sources and technical processes. Exceptional skill and entrepreneurial daring arise easily in societies where neither law nor custom impose social or legal restraints on property. Together with the usual variables of land, capital, and labor, the English had institutions with superior potential

34. 1857–1929; American economist and sociologist.

for innovation, as did to a lesser degree in 1760 other Western Europeans. The mercantile classes whose rise we have traced were as essential to industrialization as coal.

Yet in 1760 the "improvement" of society had not transformed it. Imports and manufactures were significant mainly to the top levels of society, reaching down to the tradesmen perhaps. The chief popular benefit was the improvement of diet, as agriculture after 1730 improved steadily and provided even wage earners with more meat, dairy products, and fruit and vegetables. Clothing had also improved, owing to technical changes cheapening woolen cloth. And there were complaints from the rich that the poor were idlers, drinking tea, coffee, and chocolate. But the mass of people were appallingly poor, without the amenities of modern life, including the availability of decent medical care. Indeed, inasmuch as the first factories brought people to cities in larger numbers than they could be absorbed, disease, violence, and death may have combined to lower living standards about 1760.

Then, as the second half of the eighteenth century passed, a series of inventions transformed the manufacture of cotton, giving rise to the factory system, a new mode of production which transformed other industries also. The innovations fell into three distinct patterns: the replacement of human energy by that of machines, regular, tireless, and rapid in operation; the replacement of animal power sources by inanimate ones, chiefly engines transforming heat into work; the increased use of mineral raw materials in place of the less abundant animal or vegetable ones—for example the use of coal as a fuel instead of wood from declining timber stands. Each substitution made possible new gains in the conversion of energy into work. And the result was a rise in productivity without precedent, self-sustaining, faster than parallel population rises, and therefore capable of putting back into the cycle of expansion savings previously absorbed in the demands of consumption.

In order to see how the speedup at one stage of production strained productive capacities in other phases of an industry, calling into being innovations to redress imbalance, we may look at cotton textile production.

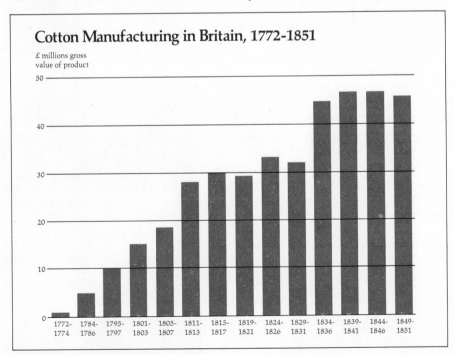

Cotton Manufacturing in Britain, 1772-1851

£ millions gross value of product

The fly shuttle invented by Kay in 1733 enabled weavers to make cloth more quickly in the woolen industry, for which it had been developed. Because spinners could not increase yarn production rapidly enough, the innovation did not catch on until the 1750s and 1760s. And when it did take hold, it was in cotton manufacture, where the supply of raw material was a plant fiber more easily expanded than the animal fiber, wool. New machines for carding fibers were made, preparatory to spinning. Then, in 1765, Hargreaves produced the spinning jenny,[35] which was followed quickly by the water frame (1769) and the mule (1779), each of which increased yarn production sharply.

The jenny had a productivity from six to twenty-four times that of the best hand spinner on the wheel. But within a decade of its invention, the mule,[36] driven by external power, produced several hundred times the output of the old wheels. Hence in less than ten years the jenny, which had replaced the spinning machines used for centuries, itself became an antique. Machine-spun yarn was finer, more uniform, and stronger than any produced by the best spinners in the world. Between 1770 and 1800 cotton consumption increased twelvefold, and new weaving devices were of necessity developed, now to keep pace with yarn making. Arkwright's power loom (1787) was decisive: one boy could control two looms and on them produce fifteen times as much cloth as the best artisan.[37]

In 1793 America contributed to the self-sustaining effect of innovation when Eli Whitney's gin increased the speed of extracting raw fibers from plant cotton, thus radically altering the supply of raw materials for English carders. Other techniques from other industries contributed to the expansion of cotton textile production. Finishing processes were transformed to keep up with the faster ginning, carding, yarning, and weaving. There was too much cloth to bleach in the sun or on open ground with urine extracts. The chemical industry solved the problem by extracting chlorine from hydrochloric acid, before Charles Tennant invented bleaching powder in 1797, by absorbing chlorine in slaked lime. Also, alkalies, used in fulling cloth, were in scarce supply naturally until the French chemist Nicolas Leblanc produced sodium carbonate by combining salt cake[38] with coal and calcium carbonate.

It was, however, true that to make attractive, multicolored, and patterned cloth from the bleached stuff, some process of printing had to be used. The old hand block or trip-hammer block machine was too slow for the rest of the industry. But in 1783 cylinder printing had been devised, by London artisans and engineers who used engines to convert the up-and-down motion of a piston driven by steam to circular motion, similar to that in the "rolling" presses of modern newspaper plants. Obviously, therefore, the final product of gay cotton cloth fabrics depended not only on innovations internal to the cotton industry but also on the growth of chemical industries and the related developments in mining, metallurgy, and engineering which produced coal-burning engines to run cylinder presses made of purified iron. The steam engine first developed in 1705 had by the late 1700s been transformed into the high-pressure devices driving factory wheels geared to machines. These devices, in turn, had depended on improving iron making by introducing coal and coke as fuels for smelting ore and then

35. Although Hargreaves invented the spinning jenny in 1765, it wasn't until 1770 that he actually patented it.
36. Combining a jenny with a power-driven (water, then steam) frame—hence the name, derived from the animal crossbreed!
37. The ratio went to 20:1 in 1833 because of new loom features.
38. Salt cake is sodium sulfate, converted by treating salt with sulfuric acid.

Coal was the primary fuel used to power the industrial explosion. Plentiful supplies were found in several areas of England, and by mid-century many peaceful rural landscapes had been devastated. The Percy Colliery, Northumberland, shown here, is typical with its monstrous towers and smoking chimneys constructed at the head of the pit. Numerous mine disasters prompted a number of parliamentary actions, most importantly a bill brought in by the earl of Shaftesbury in 1842 prohibiting the employment of women and small children below ground. Britain maintained her lead in coal production throughout the century, but the United States and Germany increasingly challenged her position. The Science Museum, London.

refining it. The availability of coal and iron ore, however, had been increased only because earlier applications of steam power, especially in pumps, had enabled men to get at deep-lying sources of mineral wealth in shaft mines.

We cannot treat the technology in detail here, but we must give some rough indications of the discontinuity in the scale of production brought about by the technological advances of the Industrial Revolution.

In 1760 Britain imported 2.5 million pounds of raw cotton to feed an industry dispersed in the Lancashire countryside. In 1787 cotton imports ran to 22 million pounds, and in 1837 some 366 million pounds of fiber were required to feed the factory-oriented industry. The price of yarn fell to one-twentieth of the 1760 price by 1837, driving out of competition even the cheapest Hindu hand-produced goods and opening the whole world market to British textiles. The number of power looms operating increased from 2,400 to 250,000 between 1812 and 1850. There was a corresponding fall in the number of handloom weavers, from about 250,000 around 1810 to fewer than 3,000 late in the 1850s. The woolen textile industry was not easily transformed because the organic fiber was less amenable to the speed of the machines, and in 1856 there were only 6,275 power looms for wool in Yorkshire, where 352,298 such looms were employed in cotton.

Similar statistics of growth in other industries exist. In 1750 Britain used 10 or 11 pounds of iron per person,[39] importing twice as much iron as was made domestically. By 1815 Britain exported five times the amount imported; and the total exported, 1,036,000 tons in 1852, coupled with home consumption of another million tons, gave a production *twice* that of the rest of the world combined! Driven by the demand for metal goods for engineering, plant construction, agricultural implements, railroad engines and track, and also pipes for water and gas lines in the growing cities and nails to build houses, the output of pig iron alone had risen from 17,350 long tons[40] to 1,998,568 between 1750 and 1848. Coal production for industrial and domestic purposes had leaped from the level of 11,000,000 tons in 1800 to 44,000,000 in 1845.

This coal was vital to steam technology, the motivation of which was efficiency, or the increase of the amount of work in the form of energy output for every unit of energy input. There were no more than 1,000 engines[41] in use in 1800, but their combined output of 10,000 horsepower had been increased to 1,290,000 horsepower in 1850. Bleaching powder rose in output from 57 tons in 1799 to 13,100 tons in 1852, while the cost of production per ton fell from £140 to £14 per ton. Synthetic alkalies were produced in hundreds of tons in 1810, at an average cost of £59 per ton; in 1852 Britain produced 140,000 tons, and the price per ton was down to £5 10s. The chemical industries employed only 9,172 adult workers in 1851, but other industries could not have expanded in scale without them—metallurgy for example, or cotton manufacturing, or the building trades; and these employed respectively 152,205, 292,340, and 390,000 workers, according to the 1851 census.

Another way of regarding this revolution in productivity, before we try to account for it in classic terms of supply and demand, lies in the energy equations which separate "cold" societies relying on animal (including human) power from "hot" ones using minerals and machines. Engines are

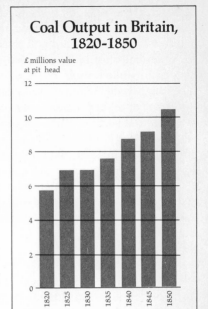

Coal Output in Britain, 1820-1850

£ millions value at pit head

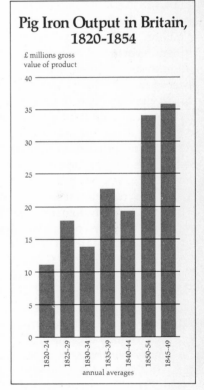

Pig Iron Output in Britain, 1820-1854

£ millions gross value of product

annual averages

---

39. This figure was derived by dividing Britain's iron use by its population. Moreover, this figure was far in advance of the rate in France (5 lbs.) or elsewhere in Europe (2 lbs. on the average).
40. A long ton is equal to 2,240 lbs.
41. Average horsepower output about 10.

not subject to fatigue in the same sense that animals are. Moreover, devices using mineral fuels to provide motive force are far more efficient than animals, at least in relation to the fuel supplies required. In 1870 the British were annually using 100,000,000 tons of coal. The food intake equivalent needed to stoke human furnaces would have been over 800 billion calories, or enough food to supply the needs of 850 million adult male workers for one year, or all of the needs of a population of about 215,000,000 people in a preindustrial setting. Britain's population in 1850 was about 31,000,000, of which about 6,000,000 were in the work force on a regular basis. Put yet another way, in 1870 coal produced steam energy equivalent to the work of 40,000,000 adult males or 6,000,000 horses. Britain produced about 110,000,-000 bushels of wheat in that year and would have required about triple that harvest to feed a work force productive of the steam energy available from coal. Coal was the bread of industrialization![42]

INDUSTRIALIZATION:
SUPPLY, DEMAND, AND ORGANIZATION

Why, and how, did the revolution in productivity take place? What forces combined in what ways pushed the national income of England and Wales from £130 million in 1770 to £525 million in 1850? Or how can we account for the fact that of the 2,600 patents for inventions given in Britain from 1700 to 1800 over 50 percent were registered after 1780? What produced the growth of the British cotton industry so that by 1850 it employed nearly half a million workers in all of its branches and accounted for 40 percent of British exports and 50 percent of total industrial production? Why did coal become the first raw material in human history measured in *millions of tons*? How did Britain have the advantage over the rest of Europe to such an extent that by 1830 it produced 75 percent of Europe's mined coal, 50 percent of its cotton goods, and over 90 percent of its steam engines?

What forces were great enough to produce a drastic break with past methods of production and the organization of work? Why did entrepreneurs redistribute their capital from the cottage-industry system to that of factories? In the domestic, cottage, or putting-out system of cloth production, raw materials and labor were the chief investments, or costs of production. When demand was slack, entrepreneurs simply stopped supplying yarn to the cottage families who did weaving. It was possible to cut risks by halting production. In the factory system, however, the entrepreneur was a "prisoner of his investment."[43] Buildings and machines were a heavy load of *fixed* capital demanding work around the year and markets able to take a steady flow of goods.

From the side of the worker, the change was as great. In cottage industry, recipients of raw materials produced piece goods to order at their own pace, within the family organized as a unit of production, without supervision. In the factory the machine separated the worker from the means of production. He owed his livelihood to the owner; he had become a hand, not an artisan, tending a tireless machine, without the comfort of home and family, compelled to toil in unison with other workers under overseers who inflicted punishments, both financial and physical, for tardiness or slackness. The factory was a jail in which the clock was the warden. Why, after resisting, did workers accept the new order?

It is easy to say the obvious: that such changes would not have taken

42. For the energy data and their interpretation, I have borrowed from David Landes, *The Unbound Prometheus* (Cambridge: Cambridge University Press, 1969), pp. 94–99.
43. Landes, *Unbound Prometheus*, p. 43.

place *unless the old modes of production had been proved inadequate.* But what made them inadequate, apart from the artisans' resentment of their dependency on the merchant who supplied raw materials, or the merchant's wish to escape the artisans' habit of producing enough to achieve the customary living standard, without seeming to care about increasing production in times of high demand? How were supply and demand factors important to industrialization? Since we have already made some comments on the supply side, in terms of technology, we may well begin with the demand for more goods.

Clearly, demand for increased production may arise within an economy (endogenous growth) or because of some external stimulant (exogenous growth), or from a combination of external and internal pulls and pushes. Just as clearly, all growth expressed in terms of demand for goods may result from either an absolute growth of population or a rise in living standards within a fixed population, or from combinations of population change and variations in real wages or purchasing power.

Demographic theory[44] and the empirical study of population history indicate that in the past the expansion of population and the rate of growth have not been independent of economic conditions. Both growth and its rate tend to adapt to food supplies and the need for labor. Obviously, the eighteenth-century British economy, which we have shown to have been the most expansive in Europe *even before industrialization*, affected population growth. By 1730 at the latest, English harvests had benefited from capital invested to improve them by persistent innovations. Good harvests after 1730 lowered grain prices, and this had the effect of increasing the real incomes of food buyers, freeing part of their money for the purchase of manufactures and goods from America. Foreign markets were also expanding rapidly from about 1740. The combination of good harvests and both internal and external market expansion was great enough to make the decade 1750–1760 effectively the onset of industrialization. Higher incomes and profits encouraged investment in roads and canals to move the commodities into new areas of increasing demand and to bring goods for export more cheaply to docks.

As the ability to save was spurred by the incentive to invest, the accumulation of capital increased the rate at which profits could be plowed back into production, in order to help meet the new demands placed on industrial capacity. The growth of country banks, which were 100 in number in 1780 but 370 in 1800, is a rough index of the spread of profits and investment. Therefore, it was investment and profit on a broad front—in agriculture, trade, communications, and finance itself—which set the stage for technical breakthroughs. These breakthroughs, a response to population growth in a dynamic economy, gave a new impetus to growth (output expansion); and the Industrial Revolution had begun. But none of this would have taken place without the agricultural improvements which by 1760 had raised wheat yields by a factor of three as compared to yields in 1600. From 1700 to 1801, when the first official census was taken, population had grown by 50 percent, from 6 to 9 million in England and Wales. From 70 to 90 percent of the whole gain came after 1750!

The growth of the home market cannot be measured effectively because early statistics concern chiefly exports. What is clear, however, is that the growth, coupled with the fact that British labor costs were twice as high as those in France and still greater than costs east of the Rhine, put a premium on all factors cheapening production. Transport improvements helped. So,

44. Hypotheses to explain how populations, human or otherwise, grow.

too, did the *concentration* of markets. By 1800 about 25 percent of the British population was in cities with more than 5,000 people; the French population was much more rural. The greater British concentration of demand was a basic force of modernization, because the leading English cities especially—Liverpool, Manchester, Leeds, and Birmingham—were nodes of economic activity in close contact with the suburban economies and the labor pool of the countryside.

The rising demand, therefore, put pressures on cottage industry which it could not meet. In order to spur cottage workers to greater productivity, what could entrepreneurs do? Pay higher wages? Demand more work per day? Wages were already a drawback to the competitiveness of some goods in Europe. Control over labor would be possible in a declining market in which artisans faced work shortages, but not in an expanding one. Moreover, embezzlement of raw materials, always a problem, rose with larger stocks given over to the artisans. Without control over his labor force, therefore, the merchant-manufacturer faced sharp limitation of productivity increase. Nor could he easily augment his labor force, since textile production was located in areas already benefiting from large immigration and natural increase of population. Raising the piece rate without controlling hours had the effect of producing fewer clothes, because, as we have said already, the facts show that workers had little acquisitiveness. They seemed to have a rigid notion of the living standard, preferring leisure to affluence beyond a certain point.

There were thus manifest needs for increasing production from the demand side, but hindrances to doing so. The condition was not peculiarly English; it existed in Normandy, Westphalia, northern Italy, Saxony.

What did not exist outside of Britain was the capacity to solve the problem from the *supply* side. This capacity depended on two things Britain had in abundance: the invention of laborsaving devices, and conditions favorable to the application of such devices industrially. The general developments in the society—in law, education, technology, etc.—insured for Britain a higher level of technical skill, a greater interest in machines, and their diffusion, than existed in any other European country. One of the strongest arguments for this *intangible* combination is this: in the decades after Britain produced the harvest of machine industry, countries with rapidly growing demand[45] did not effectively imitate the British achievement. Perhaps in Britain guilds had broken down faster. Certainly there was less stigma attached to manual labor and trade than in Spain and Prussia, even in France.

There was also a greater penetration of arithmetic knowledge and literacy among craftsmen, without which the tools and dies required for machine production could not have been made in large quantities. Additionally, we may cite the structure of law which allowed the free transfer and conversion of property from one use to another. Many early "factories" were sheds or cottages in which a few jennies worth six pounds each and a dozen workmen produced huge quantities of yarn. Property leases were so flexible in England that they allowed prospective tenants to rent parts of a large textile mill; this subdivision rental scheme permitted a "captain of industry" to begin with very little capital indeed. Noteworthy among early "mill" owners were many merchants who deserted cottage industry, driven to experiment with fixed capital by the facts we have recited. More than half of the 110 cotton-spinning mills established in the period 1770–1800 were

45. The population rise after 1750 was general in Europe, but other countries did not become industrial. Demographic growth—demand itself—cannot explain industrial revolutions.

opened by merchants in hosiery, drapery, and other branches of the fabric trades.

It is therefore wide of the mark to attribute industrialization to men with vast fortunes; it was the habit of small investment for gain that opened the way toward spectacular fortunes, not, initially, the investment of huge sums that simply compounded themselves to the benefit of rich industrialists. Recent studies have shown the importance of yet another variable, also intangible, on the supply side. Many Nonconformist businessmen, suffering serious restrictions of opportunity because of religion, were trained from childhood toward achievement based on diligence, thrift, rationality, and competitiveness. Thus, child-rearing patterns created in English groups a potential for innovation and initiative greater than that in other, more religiously uniform, countries.[46]

All of these factors seem more important to the Industrial Revolution than were capital accumulation and investment. The ratio of new capital formation to national income was probably never above 6 percent around 1760, or 8 percent about 1800. Not until the railroad boom of the 1840s did it rise above 10 percent. Modern studies commonly show rates above 12 percent in newly industrializing societies.

Our conclusion is, therefore, that the role played in "causing" the Industrial Revolution by the great (heavy) variables—land, labor, and capital—was great, but that the growth depended on technological skills and the mental habits of entrepreneurs and workers also. Without the mixture we have analyzed, the complex new order of the factory would not have displaced the old order. The marriage made the revolution possible; it created as its offspring a new order.

That the factory system called into being a new social order we cannot doubt. Machines not only replaced hand labor; investment in them could be justified only by their concentration. Factories were places where the resistance of the old order was broken, where the power of machines triumphed over the power of men. And in the factories new habits of time consciousness and precision, of standardization and repeated motion, showed in outline the potential of mechanization. The button stamped by machine[47] is the ancestor of the television set.

The creation of the factory system links the economic causes of growth to the social costs, precisely because in factories there was a shift in the balance of the factors of production, from labor to capital. Factories assembled large numbers of workers in one place to work under discipline. Factories therefore stood in the closest relationship to the supply and character of labor and the circumstances of work. By this we mean not only discipline, fines, rules—the whole apparatus by which hundreds of thousands of men, women, and children were ruled. We mean also the relationship between work on the land and in the city. We mean the cooperation of the state in supplying cheap labor, by conscripting the children of the poor, who had to work as "parish apprentices." We mean the disruption of families, as mothers, sons, and daughters entered the labor market outside the family framework.

We mean the facts shown by the 1851 census. Agricultural and handicraft workers were still more numerous than industrial ones. But the speed of the shift to the new modes of production and the growth of the cities in which it

---

46. See David C. McClelland, *The Achieving Society* (Princeton: Princeton University Press, 1961). His stress on English Methodists has been criticized, however, by those pointing to similar patterns fostered by the Quakers and the Congregationalists.
47. The steam hammer or "punch."

prospered was increasing. In 1849 one iron plant already employed 7,000 men. And the men in the plant knew they had experienced a transformation of their lives, without being clear as to whether they had benefited from it.

THE STANDARD OF LIVING: THE QUALITY OF LIFE

Again, a satisfactory approach to the vexed question of the social cost of the Industrial Revolution lies through statistical materials and an analysis of them more than through impressions gathered from literature or propaganda pamphlets. To begin with, before 1800, about 25 percent of all Englishmen lived in poverty. The poor were stimulated to crime by low wages, a harsh Poor Law, bad living conditions, depressions, and harvest failures. When things were very bad, especially as the population began to grow at a rate of 10 percent a decade after 1780, the prisons could not accommodate the social criminals. From 1788 to 1850 over 150,000 convicts were sent to populate Australia. Amazingly, the transported convicts had a higher standard of living there than the noncriminal *poor* had in Britain. What, we may ask, was the course of living standards at home in the same period? What was the quality of life for the factory workers? Did the laborers live in poverty and crime, the shadows cast by the pleasure and wealth of the capitalists?[48] Or was there a clear improvement in their lot?[49]

The question takes on real importance not only because the poet Wordsworth once hailed factory chimneys as beautiful harbingers of the future but later joined Shelley, Coleridge, Dickens, Arnold, and Ruskin in condemning the ugliness and squalor produced by the lust for gain, "the master idol of the realm."[50] The question of living standards is important for another reason. Nobody doubts that the growth of the British economy was enormous between 1760 and 1850. Yet many suppose that popular living standards fell during the same period, either because population grew faster than output per capita, or because the net wealth produced was distributed in a fashion biased against workers.[51] In an age like our own, when nonindustrialized peoples put their hope for the future in economic growth through industrialization, it becomes especially valuable for us to determine whether or not the first industrial revolution did indeed deepen the misery of its labor force.

We begin with basic facts. The population that stood at about 6,750,000 in 1750 climbed to 9,000,000 in 1800, and from that level to at least 18,000,000 fifty years later, with the maximum rate of growth in the 1820s and 1830s. This growth was once attributed primarily to medical advances which decreased death rates. We no longer believe this to be true, because available evidence does not show a change in medical practice sufficient to lower the death rate substantially; nor is there good evidence for a rapidly increasing birthrate. Hence we are driven back on the conclusion that advances in the standard of living were responsible for lowering death rates.

This large growth of population would not have been possible without expansion of the food supply. Apparently, the domestic supply did not keep pace from about 1760 to 1800. At least it is clear that England became an

---

48. This was the judgment of John and Barbara Hammond in *The Skilled Labourer* (London: Longmans, Green, 1919), pp. 1–4.
49. The chief critic of the "immiseration" of the workers is R. M. Hartwell: *Industrial Revolution*, pp. 6–9, 13–17.
50. *The Excursion*, bk. 8.
51. That is, that expropriation, or forced savings taken from the workers, financed the Industrial Revolution.

importer of grain during this period, where once it had been a European granary. Consumption of wheat per capita fell from 1.5 pounds per day to 1.0 pounds. The proportion of a laborer's budget spent on food rose from about 40–50 percent in 1760 to 50–60 percent by 1800, as bread prices rose. Meat, cheese, beer, and milk gave way to tea, bacon, and bread in working-class diets thus giving evidence of some decline in diet standards early in the period of industrialization. The years of the Napoleonic Wars gave a boost to agriculture, however, when the blockades caused Englishmen to divert capital toward improving home food supplies. Yields were kept at high levels, and the acreage under the plow increased dramatically. From about 1810 production was up by about 2 million quarters of wheat a year, and bread prices retreated from the highest levels. By 1850 yields were up from 20 bushels per acre to about 30.

Data about output and consumption of nonfoodstuffs in the period 1760–1815 support the idea of stagnation in living standards among workers.[52] Output jumped enormously per capita in total production. But the bulk of the gain was in export commodities, not in the home market. There were gains per capita in textile consumption, in metal goods like table knives and nails, and in cheap pottery utensils. But the most basic industry other than food did not keep pace with domestic demand: house building. Domestic brick production, for instance, did not rise over the fifty-five-year span, despite enormous population growth. The national income was up from £130 million in 1770 to about £290 million in 1815, but most of this rise was from the industrial sector. And it did not translate into a distributed per capita change on anything like a proportional basis. This was due to four things: a share of the increase went back to industry in investment; a share paid for food imports and the protection of English agriculture; a share paid for the wars in America, India, and Europe; and another share went out in overseas investments—the colonization of Australia, for example.

Moreover, the increase was not evenly distributed among the classes. Real wages[53] stood at 125 in 1790, but only 121 in 1815. Building-craft wages fell from a level of 62 to one of 49 between 1761 and 1815 for people remaining in their old jobs. Transfers to new jobs around the year 1815 brought improvements for agricultural workers who went into coal mines, or handloomers who got factory work. But it would be impossible to suppose that more people benefited than lost if for no other reason than that poor relief expenditures quadrupled between 1760 and 1815. The war years especially seem to have impoverished workers, while transferring income to landlords, bondholders, farmers, and industrialists. The income tax returns from 1802 to 1814 reveal increases in those categories ranging from 66 percent to over 100 percent. The government itself showed per capita annual income for the whole population falling from £13.5 to £12.2 in the period 1761–1801.

The overall picture, then, for the first half of the first industrial century, or even the first sixty years, is stagnation. Before 1760, output growth was absorbed in home consumption; from 1760 to 1815 it was absorbed in laying the foundations of an industrial state and in colonial and commercial wars, as well as in the great struggle for mastery in Europe.

The living-standard issue therefore resolves itself into a question of what happened in the long interval of peace between 1815 and the revolutionary

52. Before 1810, diets in workhouses maintained by public authorities were frequently described as superior to the diets of the common wage laborers.
53. Figures here represent weekly wages, with the base year (arbitrarily set at 100 percent) being 1800.

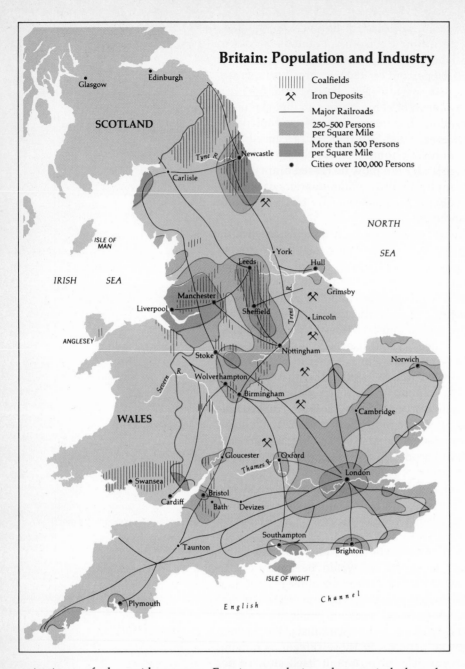

Britain: Population and Industry

Coalfields
Iron Deposits
Major Railroads
250–500 Persons per Square Mile
More than 500 Persons per Square Mile
Cities over 100,000 Persons

SCOTLAND

Glasgow
Edinburgh
Tyne R.
Newcastle
Carlisle

NORTH
SEA

ISLE OF MAN
IRISH SEA
York
Leeds
Hull
Manchester
Grimsby
Liverpool
Sheffield
Trent R.
Lincoln
ANGLESEY
Stoke
Nottingham
Norwich
Wolverhampton
Severn R.
Birmingham
WALES
Cambridge
Gloucester
Oxford
Swansea
Thames R.
London
Cardiff
Bristol
Bath
Devizes
Southampton
Taunton
Brighton
ISLE OF WIGHT
Plymouth
English
Channel

agitations of the mid-century. For it was during that period that the *proportion of the population* engaged in agriculture declined from about 40 percent to 21 percent. And it was in those years that urban growth was fantastic. London's population increased from about 900,000 in 1800 to 2,362,236 in 1851. In 1800 only fourteen towns had populations over 20,000; by 1851 there were fifty-four cities ranging from 20,000 to 100,000. The shift in population to the new giant cities[54] traced the shift in employment. By 1851 more than half of the people in Britain were town dwellers.

The growth of capital did not fully compensate for the change, although there can be no doubt that the standard of living rose for most working-class people. There were large drains abroad still, in the form of investment. There were huge sums from the output growth put into factories,

54. Those over 100,000: Birmingham, Bristol, Leeds, Bradford, Liverpool, Manchester, and Sheffield—all in the Midlands or the North, around coalfields or ports.

railways, docks, and other basic social overhead not immediately yielding consumer goods. But of the growth in the period, from a national output in England and Wales of about £290 million to one of about £525 million, much went to improve life.

This was the first great age of house building in cities, and the construction of streets, waterworks, municipal buildings, and other amenities of urban life. While the annual rate of population increase was about 1.37 percent, the index of brick production showed an average annual increase of 1.9 percent.

Unfortunately, most urban houses built produced "side effects" on the quality of life, even where the standard was technically high. Crowding made it impossible for municipalities to keep up the amenities of sewerage, paving, water supply, and recreation grounds. Terrace building and back-to-back houses spawned slums, as builders cut costs by increasing housing density. The parliamentary reports on the housing and sanitary conditions of the laboring population[55] outlined conditions so deplorable that, for example, in 1842 town dwellings were described as worse than prison quarters. In the large industrial cities poor persons who fell ill were sometimes moved to prisons for care and cure! The current state of research indicates that housing standards in the large cities fell, while rural standards rose. Urban residential quarters lagged behind overall productivity increases and held down general living standards, which seemed to increase in every other area.

By 1850, lowering costs and rising incomes became the rule, so that real wages at last moved steadily upward among all classes. Output per capita rose in food production and in all other categories of consumer goods. The annual rate of increase per capita in all categories from 1815 to 1845 was 1.5 percent compounded, or in terms of national product, a rise per capita from £13.2 to £21.3. Taking 1840 as a base of 100, we find that real wages which stood at 94 in 1815 had climbed to 110 in 1850.[56]

Not all groups entered into the boom in the same way, even in the working classes. The agricultural workers lost ground. So, too, did the older type of handicraft workers. Workers in the newer "crafts" did better, especially the miners, factory laborers, machine-tool makers, engineers,[57] and precision-tool makers. By 1840 the gain in real wages showed up in diet standards. Working-class people did now get more tea, tobacco, sugar, potatoes, ham, bacon, pork, fruits, and vegetables. But there is no evidence for more red meat in diets, or milk and cheese. Surviving budgets from the 1840s made for groups of workers considered "respectable and steady" support diet improvement. Yet in the industrial town of Oldham, in the bad year 1847, 41 percent of the total population was in poverty; and in 1849, a good year, the rate was still 15.5 percent.

The overall impression is thus one of bad housing, better food of greater variety, as well as better clothing, cutlery, earthenware, and transportation. There were, however, great pockets of poverty, and prosperity was not evenly spread within the occupationally distinctive working classes. If this is true, and the overall picture favored factory workers, why was it the case that the textile workers especially were so vocal about their "misery" in the age of Chartism? The answer depends on what we think of the quality of life in the cities; and it takes on urgency in proportion to the great social unrest of the decades of legislative reform.

55. 1840, 1842, 1844–1845.
56. The difference between the real wage calculation and the national product increase, which was larger, is due to the part of growth not used for consumption.
57. Machinists, in American terminology.

There can be no question that more people survived childhood and found jobs as adults around 1850 than had a century earlier. Nor can there be any question that the enlarged population consumed food and other goods on a larger scale per person, which in turn led to better health. The Industrial Revolution cheapened production costs through the exploitation of new sources of power. It spurred the rise of a scientific technology, deepened the demand for public education. After 1815 the growth was balanced, or as effective in meeting domestic *demands* as it had been before only in raising *supplies* for various purposes. By 1848 the patterns of income distribution had shifted toward a fairer share for workers. Life expectancy in 1850 was higher than it had been in 1780. Infant mortality rates were sharply lower.

What needs to be pointed out, however, is that neither increased consumption nor greater life expectancy necessarily makes for a *high* standard of living, as opposed to merely a higher one than had earlier existed. Also, the quality of life may deteriorate while at the same time quantitative measures of living standards rise.

On the negative side, industrial slums, unlike poor areas in market towns in an agrarian society, tend to be isolated from the experiences of the urban middle classes. The very fact that blue books had to be written to inform citizens of the wretchedness in these slums reveals the alienation and isolation of the working classes from the rest of society. Before the 1840s, legislation did not help the poorer classes significantly. The Poor Law of 1834, for example, was intended to make the life of those on relief more unattractive than that of those even in the worst jobs. Protective health measures, effective factory hour laws, and expanded education all belong to

Gustave Doré was a French painter and engraver who enjoyed enormous success in both France and England. Although he primarily executed highly imaginary book illustrations, Doré's one series of contemporary, realistic drawings —London—is paradoxically considered his masterpiece. Dudley Street, Seven Dials (above), and Over London by Rail (right) are horrifying evidence of the squalid environment of London's poor. The artist toured the slums accompanied by a plainclothes detective and made preliminary sketches which he later reconstructed from memory. Doré's impressions carried so much conviction that they were introduced as factual evidence in government reports, and their widespread distribution did much to arouse public consciousness about the intolerable conditions. The Mansell Collection (above); Prints Division, The New York Public Library, Astor, Lenox and Tilden Foundations (right).

the second half of the nineteenth century, when workers had both the vote and the freedom to organize unions, powers lacking in the 1840s.

Then, there was insecurity. The "opportunity" to move is not always a gain, even when the move is upward. Periodic mass unemployment hit workers in factories, and they no longer had kitchen gardens to see them through. Hence fear of unemployment and the uncertainty of employment promoted anxiety in an age that also witnessed the alienation of workers from the tools of production. There was, in addition, the breakup of the old social patterns, *before* effective new ones were built. Rootlessness in 1851 was profound: 60 percent of all people in England's sixty-two largest towns were recent immigrants. In only three large towns were more than 50 percent of the people natives. The result was to create large populations devoid of political and social identities, in towns which were not communities but merely places where factories happened to be.

The consequence was restlessness. The family was no longer as stable; nor was it now a primary work unit. Like local groupings based on the land, which also lost their power to balance social relationships, the family had part of its authority usurped by the factory. "Social orphanage"[58] was the result, on a large scale, before new associations for workmen helped to build social cohesion and influence for laborers.

All of these aspects of industrial life weighed heavily in the mental

58. The term is Sidney Pollard and David Crossley's invention: see *The Wealth of Britain* (London: Batsford, 1968), p. 209.

balance of the working classes, often overwhelming the sense of material gain. Yet, the gathering of workers in urban slums had a positive side as well.

The working classes did mix to become *the working class*, self-conscious and politically organized. Rapid change raised disturbing problems, but it also liberated workers from the hierarchy of servility in rural society. Despite pressures on them to defer to their betters, they organized and achieved a solidarity, as the Chartist movement reveals, that enabled them to argue forcefully for their own political, economic, and social interests. It was the working-class experience in factories that promoted protective organizations among workers. Moreover, if the machine broke some ties between parent and child, it also began the liberation of women, by putting them in situations in which a political consciousness might develop apart from that of their husbands. The factory meant higher wages for women, and thus a measure of independence. This was not true in cottage industry, where paternal authority was unchallenged and derived from economic activities on a family scale.

On balance, therefore, we may conclude that, by 1848, industrialization was a mixed blessing. But the mixture was nonetheless changing life for the better, if perhaps too slowly. The machine created rising expectations, before people had enough experimental knowledge of the new social order to satisfy them. Europeans, like Marx, grasped this, and said Europe had much catching up to do.

BIBLIOGRAPHY

ASHTON, THOMAS S. *The Industrial Revolution.** Rev. ed. New York: Oxford University Press, 1962. This revised edition is a classic pro-capitalist statement of the "benefits" of the revolution to the working classes.

BRIGGS, ASA. *Chartist Studies.** London: Macmillan, 1959. One of the best sets of essays on the movement for the People's Charter.

CHECKLAND, S. J. *The Rise of Industrial Society in England.* New York: St. Martin's Press, 1964. Very valuable on social developments ca. 1810–1850.

DEANE, PHYLLIS. *The First Industrial Revolution.** Cambridge: Cambridge University Press, 1965. An analytic study of the period 1750–1850, based on modern "growth" analysis.

HARTWELL, R. M. *The Industrial Revolution and Economic Growth.** London: Methuen, 1971. This collection of essays embodies the life work of a leading opponent of socialist critiques of industrialization; critical also of the analysis of growth in W. W. Rostow, *The Stages of Economic Growth* (Cambridge: Cambridge University Press, 1960). Hartwell is especially unsympathetic to Eric J. Hobsbawn and John and Barbara Hammond, who wrote pioneer studies of town and village workers.

HAYEK, F. A. VON. *Capitalism and the Historians.** Chicago: University of Chicago Press, 1954. The most ferocious attack on the socialist "immiseration" theories; very much an ideologically inspired book.

LANDES, DAVID. *The Unbound Prometheus.** Cambridge: Cambridge University Press, 1969. A very complex, empirically elaborate comparative study, very strong on England.

MCCORD, NORMAN. *The Anti–Corn Law League.* London: Allen & Unwin, 1958. The best modern study of the repeal agitation from 1838 to 1846; should be read with Norman Gash, *Politics in the Age of Peel** (London: Longmans, 1963), a very brilliant book.

MINGAY, G. *English Landed Society in the Eighteenth Century.* London: Routledge & Kegan Paul, 1963. Essential on the agrarian transformations in preindustrial England.

Asterisk indicates a paperbound edition.

9

THE BIRTH OF NATIONS: 1848–1871

THE LEGACY OF 1848

In 1848 the forces of liberalism, republicanism, socialism, and nationalism had been weakened by the revolutionary failures. Yet, within the European states and in the relations among states, 1848 provided an important legacy.

Constitutional government and constitutional liberty were not the principles of the Great Powers. These things were secure only in small states: Denmark, Holland, Belgium, and Switzerland. The peasants had been lucky, however, even in the most conservative large states. In the German states and the Austrian Empire the abolition of serfdom and manorial custom was not reversed. Socially, this was the chief victory. Masses of peasants in central Europe became mobile and thus able to enter the labor market at precisely the point in time when industrialization became important in Germany. The freedom of peasants was not a challenge politically. Not only were they conservative for the most part; they were in league with other propertied classes by 1850, anxious to protect the prosperity of the postrevolutionary economic boom. They were also good material to be exploited by politicians who focused on class hatred and sentiments of resentment against foreigners.

In the Habsburg Empire, the defeat of insurgency in Bohemia, Italy, and Hungary enabled Prince Felix Schwarzenberg (1800–1852) to dissolve the revolutionary parliament at home early in 1849. A centralized and repressive new constitution emerged, buttressed abroad by the promise of Russia to help Austria control radicalism in Bohemia and along the course of the Danube. In France Louis Napoleon consolidated his regime between 1848 and 1852, in two stages. On December 2, 1851, the anniversary of Napoleon's victory at Austerlitz and his coronation as ruler of the First Empire,[2] Louis dissolved the

1. Ed. Theodore S. Hamerow (New York: Harper & Row, Publishers, Torchbooks, 1968), pp. 141–142.
2. In 1805 and 1804, respectively.

republican Assembly and crushed popular republican resistance to his proclamation of himself as prince-president. One year later, on December 2, 1852, he proclaimed the Second Empire, in the name of order, authority, progress, and social justice—the Bonapartist program as he embodied it. He took for himself the imperial title Napoleon III.

In Germany, the liberal-national millennium had not arrived, despite a promising start. National union and responsible government on a democratic basis had once seemed possible, but the promise faded. Frederick William IV had betrayed national feelings in the Schleswig-Holstein affair. Moreover, his scheme for imposing unity from above on the German states failed. The Prussian king had not acted decisively in the Council of Union or in the Parliament of Erfurt, which met to revise the union scheme in 1850. This had given Schwarzenberg and Francis Joseph I of Austria time to reassert Austria's primacy among the German states, by a revival of the old Confederation. Frederick William compounded his problems in 1850, therefore, when he relented in the face of the direct Austrian challenge to Prussian leadership.

A diet had met and had voted to help the elector of Hesse-Kassel put down a rebellion within that state in Prussia's absence. This put Prussia in great difficulty, because Hesse was one of the states in the abortive Prussian Union. Moreover, through it passed two Prussian military roads, reserved exclusively for the transport of Prussian troops. For a time Frederick William seemed ready to go to war against Austria. The Russians, however, supported the Habsburgs, and at Olmütz, on November 29, 1850, Prussia gave way: Frederick William allowed the intervention of the diet in Electoral Hesse; he formally dissolved the Prussian Union; he also agreed to settle the Schleswig-Holstein question in concert with Austria. Finally, Prussia agreed to the full reestablishment of the Diet of the Confederation, under decrees dating from 1815 and 1820.

The Schleswig-Holstein affair, part of the settlement at Olmütz, requires a closer look if we are to understand the relationship between the failure of "nationalism" in the German states in 1848 and the impact of this failure on the balance of power in Europe. For it was the question of the two Elbe duchies that determined the shape of central Europe.

The system of Metternich was rooted in the alliance of the three conservative monarchies: Russia, Austria, and Prussia. The system stood against changes in the frontiers decreed in 1815 and also against constitutional changes. Toward those ends, the three states had renounced nonintervention, especially in areas where "the revolution" seemed to threaten common interests: Poland, the Balkans, and the Rhineland. Their resistance to nationalism derived from their belief that France was the leader of states accepting that principle of revolution. While 1848 did not altogether surprise Metternich and his partners—there had been risings in 1846 in Poland and unrest in Italy—the conservatives were nonetheless ill prepared for the fall of Metternich and the proclamation of Lamartine's "greater Revolution" at Paris. As revolution spread to central Europe, therefore, the system of 1815 collapsed. German liberal feeling supported the revolt of Sardinia's king, Charles Albert, against Austria. And Russia held aloof from any challenge to the revolutions in the various German states, being willing to intervene only if Austrian Poland (Galicia) or Prussian Poland (Posen) became threatened.

Since Lamartine's new revolutionary manifesto did not raise a Polish issue, Czar Nicholas was content to watch. Britain wished to remain neutral, except in Italy, where any weakening of Austria might promote British power in the Mediterranean.

The Schleswig-Holstein affair upset all calculations and further revealed

Bismarck's first important test of the strength of the new Prussian army came during an 1864 conflict with Denmark over the territories of Schleswig-Holstein. Here his troops attack the fortress of Düppel in North Schleswig, where the Danes had previously defeated Germanic Confederation troops in 1848; but this time the results heavily favored the well-equipped Prussian army. The easy success and obvious ambitions of their powerful northern neighbor prompted the fearful Austrians to declare war on Prussia. Known as the Seven Weeks' War, this bloody conflict also ended in a Prussian victory. With Austria no longer a power in German affairs, Bismarck was able to forge a role for Prussia as the leading member of the 1867 North German Confederation. Staatsbibliothek, Berlin.

the bankruptcy of the old Concert. In Denmark Frederick VII's 1848 constitution sought to incorporate the duchies. Holstein was a member of the Germanic Confederation; Schleswig was not but had in its southern half many Germans. Moreover, in the last century, Britain, Russia, and France had "guaranteed" treaties securing the duchies as Danish possessions. When Prussia promised support for the independence of the duchies in 1848, the Danes retreated, demanding only Schleswig, thus recognizing the rights of Holstein as a Confederation member. Prussian troops invaded, driving the Danes out of both territories, only to be frustrated by a joint Russian-British demand that the balance of power in the Baltic and the North seas not be upset by Prussia.

It was that demand to which Prussia bowed in the armistice concluded at Malmö, thereby exasperating the partisans of liberalism and nationalism. The Danes were no more content with the truce than were the Germans, however. Frederick VII denounced it in February 1849. A new round of fighting produced a similar result: German victories, Russo-British pressures, and another truce. This second truce, however, produced a peace treaty, then the London Protocol of 1852. In the Protocol, Schwarzenberg, who had no wish to support *nationalism* of any sort, even German nationalism in the duchies, effectively left the duchies to the Danes. With the support of Austria, Prussia, Britain, and Russia, the integrity of the Danish monarchy was declared as well as the right of inheritance to all heirs, male or female, in the Danish line. This blotted out the rights of Duke Christian Augustus of Augustenburg, the Prussian candidate. Moreover, Holstein and Schleswig were declared to be "in personal union" with Denmark, but no machinery was ever set up to guarantee local self-government for them. Austria had prevailed upon Prussia (both states acting as Great Powers) finally to disregard the Germans in the duchies and the sentiment for them at home.

Domestically, the Danish question showed clearly how little regard Frederick William had for the principle of nationality. In no state within the

Prussian orbit had liberalism triumphed either. There was not a single government responsible to electors. Hence many patriots drew the conclusion there could be no "liberal" unification of Germany, if for no other reason than that Austria had not been excluded from Germany. The multinational state was the enemy of German nationalism. It was this realization, combined with the dreamy, reactionary, character of the 1850s in Prussia, that shaped the future. The government at home strengthened the *Junkers* and reshaped education in conservative ways. From these events Bismarck drew the right conclusion. Germany must conciliate Russia, in order to balance Austria and France. The Czar's national interests were in the East, while those of Austria and France were in the same area of Europe in which Prussia must seek its strength.

The problem posed for Prussia at Malmö, and again in London in 1852, was, How could German unification under Prussian aegis take place without a duel with Russia? The answer was to exclude Austria from Germany, while convincing the Russians that the Habsburg Empire posed a threat to the land of the czars.

To think along such lines was to throw overboard the old system and seek for some new means to balance power in Europe. The great states recognized nothing beyond their own self-interest; and even Metternich's system acknowledged that fact. Alliances were born out of the fear that one Great Power might subdue the rest, as statesmen thought Philip II and Louis XIV had tried to do, and as Napoleon had nearly done. The Concert had fought revolution by means of an elaborate balance of power, opposing traditional conservatism to the new ideologies born between 1789 and 1815. The year 1848 had ended one phase of the balance of power by revealing how much at odds Prussia, Austria, and Russia were over certain vital questions. The Czar had remained aloof, except to intervene in Hungary for Austria. The Austrian Empire had nearly crumbled; it had come into serious conflict with Prussia. And Prussia had shown itself torn by political factions ranging from radical to reactionary, on every question of foreign and domestic policy.

By 1852, the chief problems of diplomacy over the next two decades had therefore been clarified. No *political* aim could be achieved without some realignment of the Great Powers. The Italian question was obviously tied to Austria's strength. The power Austria wielded was the vital element in any Prussian effort to reconstitute the German state system. Russia's interest in keeping Poland quiet, and the balance of power in southeastern Europe in its favor, had obvious significance for Austria, Prussia, and Britain—with Russia's great commercial interests in the East. Finally, France had come under the rule of a schemer and dreamer, Louis Napoleon, who embodied the imperial tradition of adventure throughout Europe, especially in Italy, along the Rhine, and on the Russian-Ottoman flank of Europe.

THE FRENCH DECADE: THE CRIMEAN WAR

Although Lamartine had not included Poland in the Manifesto of March 4, 1848, or indeed any other part of the "eastern" state system, France had traditionally been sympathetic to the Polish nationalists, just as Russia had promised to take up arms in 1812 if France interfered in Europe east of the Vistula River. In fact, the socialist republicans in France loved "all the oppressed nations"[3] but were unwilling to fight their way across Germany to help the Poles. Before Louis Napoleon's rise to power, however, the

3. Lamartine, *Three Months in Power* (*Trois mois au pouvoir*), as quoted in A. J. P. Taylor, *The Struggle for Mastery in Europe, 1848–1918* (Oxford: Clarendon Press, 1969), p. 10.

Assembly in Paris had outlined a policy which the Bonapartist pretender pursued, its main objectives being fraternity with Prussia, a free Poland, the liberation of Italy. French and other European statesmen gave credence to the program because they overestimated France's power, just as Louis Napoleon did.

The adventurer was therefore immediately at odds with his own diplomats. They viewed French superiority as being founded on national unity, drawing from this the idea that France ought to promote the division of the great "races" in Europe. Louis Napoleon started from the same premise, but drew different conclusions: Napoleon I had failed *because* he had not acted in harmony with the nationalism of the Italians and the Germans!

Louis Napoleon was a romantic who early sought to bolster his stature by writing *Napoleonic Ideas (Des idées napoléoniennes)* in 1839 in order to show how he was the man to unite the French in pursuit of his uncle's legend. At home this required marrying authority with democracy; abroad this required boundary adjustments to revise the Act of the Congress of Vienna of 1815. The son of Louis Bonaparte, king of Holland, Louis Napoleon was frail, moody, reflective, quiet, even genial, without the dynamism of his namesake. He was also by nature a plotter and lover of intrigue who had passed his youth in exile and spoke French with a German accent. He had fought for Young Italy in 1831. Louis had also seen America, after a second exile in the wake of an abortive coup in 1836. When his second coup failed in 1840, the British cartoons in *Punch* took him to be absurd. Consigned to jail, Louis had turned his trial into a national cause, saying in the dock: "I stand before you the representative of a principle, a cause, a defeat. The principle is the sovereignty of the people; the cause is that of the Empire; the defeat is Waterloo."[4]

Before he slipped away from jail in 1846, disguised as a worker, Louis Napoleon had studied military tactics and socialist doctrines. He had also put behind him the comic-opera coups of 1836 and 1840, seeing that the way to power was through the use of his name and the Bonaparte legend in ordinary politics. Now, in 1852, having come to power and been proclaimed emperor of the French, he embarked on his campaign to revive national glory. To do so, he had to accomplish two things: win the trust of the Great Powers, and rid himself of a embarrassment in Italy. In 1849 he had sent an expedition to Rome to safeguard Pope Pius IX. This had alienated Italian republicans without pleasing French Catholics, as Louis had hoped it would. France had also alarmed Russia in 1849 by taking the Turkish side in a dispute over prisoners captured in Hungary and revolutionaries who had gained asylum in Turkish possessions.

England, too, had acted to prevent Russia from jailing Polish and Hungarian rebels. A joint movement of the Western fleets caused Nicholas I to withdraw his demands. But this was the beginning, not the end, of the Near Eastern crisis. Russia and France were soon estranged over a more basic issue. Louis Napoleon demanded Turkish recognition of France as the legal protector of Catholic pilgrims en route to Palestine. France cited treaties giving duties of upkeep to Latin religious orders in exchange for the privileges of worshipping on Turkish soil. Since 1758, however, the Latins had in practice conceded the protectorate to Greek Orthodox orders under Russian patronage.

By the end of 1852, Napoleon III's search for prestige had revived the claim of the Latin monks. The Turks, convinced that France was more powerful than Russia, gave concessions to Napoleon III, thereby offending

---

4. Quoted in Brison D. Gooch, *The Reign of Napoleon III* (Chicago: Rand McNally & Co., 1969), p. 12.

An early photograph shows a heavily damaged Russian gun emplacement after the fall of Sevastopol in 1855. At the beginning of the Crimean War Russia was considered an almost invincible force, but that delusion was soon shattered. By the autumn of 1854, allied troops had besieged Sevastopol, and the stalemate that developed throughout the following winter proved a hideous ordeal for all. The sufferings of the British troops were avidly followed by an aroused nation at home. French and Russian troops endured equal hardships. Two out of every three Russian recruits sent out from the interior died along the way from sickness or starvation, and, when the allies finally entered the burning, deserted city in September 1855, the departed Russians had lost over 100,000 men. Victoria and Albert Museum.

Nicholas I's religious prestige in Eastern Europe. Indeed, Nicholas, the archconservative, saw French intervention as part of the dark plot he called the "Revolution." After all, the Turkish decision was a revision of 1815. Nicholas therefore sought to convince Turkey that he was more to be feared than the French fleets, while at the same time showing Britain and other Europeans that he still stood for the settlement of 1815.

Britain, meanwhile, had no wish to see a stronger Russian presence in the Near East, where Britain's own commercial supremacy was then being consolidated throughout the countries between India and Europe. The Czar demanded concessions at Constantinople in 1853, while suggesting to the Great Powers a partition of Turkey in exchange for support against France. The response was dramatic. The French and British fleets cooperated in maneuvers near the Dardanelles. Moreover, Austria was facing a Turkish threat to the South Slav province of Montenegro. Turkey bowed to a Habsburg ultimatum to disperse the troops, because Austria posed no threat to the Ottoman Empire. Russia could not, therefore, count on automatic Austrian aid in the event of a war with France. Nor, as it turned out, was Berlin ready to help. Austria depended on the Danube for trade and could not welcome Russian victories there. Prussia remained aloof, having no vital interest at stake and not wishing to become a highway in the event of a Russo-French war.

Clearly, the Holy Alliance was dead. Nicholas could not call upon Austria and Prussia, the conservative powers, to contain France and England, the liberal ones. The Austrians would not rise even to the bait of free access to the western Balkans. Thus isolated, Russia had to meet, late in 1853, a declaration of war from Turkey, encouraged by the French and British naval presence. This frightened Napoleon III, who saw the situation as an easy opportunity to gain prestige. When Russia destroyed a Turkish fleet off Sinope on the Black Sea, Britain and France rallied to protect Turkey by bottling up the Russians at Sevastopol.

Thus, in 1854, Nicholas I asked open aid from Prussia and Austria, or at least armed neutrality in Russia's favor. Austria answered that it could not be neutral in Eastern affairs. Prussia used the emergency to get from Britain a promise of good will toward a Prussian hegemony in Germany, in exchange for help against Russia. Thus the Crimean War began, fought against Russia, not for Turkey, and in a sense to avenge Russia's role against revolution in 1848. For what was really at stake in the 1854–1856 war against Russia was the disposition of central Europe, the corridor running southward from Denmark's troubled duchies through the German heartland and into Italy.

The proof of this lies in the treaty settlement, which came after two years of fighting in which 500,000 were killed and the Russians defeated. The

The poet and art-critic Charles Baudelaire immortalized Constantin Guys by praising him as "the painter of modern life." This title resulted from Guys's brilliant sketches of many facets of mid–nineteenth-century life, including costumes, street life, horse races, travel, and military scenes. An English magazine, The Illustrated London News, *sent Guys to cover the Crimean War, and this drawing of French officers was among his dispatches. Since photography was still in an embryonic phase, artists who could work rapidly under stress were much in demand as illustrators. Their drawings were engraved and rapidly disseminated in periodicals which enjoyed a burgeoning success throughout the later part of the century. Musée des Arts Décoratifs, Paris.*

victors (Britain and France) had laid down their goals or war aims in the so-called Vienna Four Points: Russia would concede the protectorate in the Holy Places to Europeans; the Russians would cede to Europeans the protectorate over the principalities at the mouth of the Danube (Moldavia and Walachia); navigation of the Danube was to be free; conventions regulating the Dardanelles and Bosporus straits were also to be revised in favor of the Europeans. These points were the basis of the Treaty of Paris signed in 1856, where Napoleon III posed as the arbiter of Europe, secure in the role because his French troops had been superior to the British armies in the joint actions. Moreover, Russia had been humbled and revenge had been taken for 1812. Also, Rumania had become *de facto* a new nation, created from the principalities of Moldavia and Walachia.[5]

Even during the Crimean War, the central European interests for which it was a cover had surfaced. Austria, unselfishly aided by Nicholas in 1849 when he marched against the Hungarian revolutionaries, had paid back the Czar in the coin of duplicity.

The reasons for the betrayal lay deep in the soil of Habsburg policy. During the upheavals of 1848–1849, France and Britain had both intervened, pressing Austria to make a settlement with the revolutionary regimes in Lombardy and Venetia. Each outside power sought to check the influence of the other, while weakening Austria. This they hoped to do by securing Lombardy for the Piedmont kingdom, despite the victory Austria had won in the field. Austrian councillors saw no reason to be so accommodating; after all, they had won the war.

The relationship between the Italian problem and Austria's policy toward Russia derived from Francis Joseph's reaction to his benefactors. He had personally requested Nicholas's aid in crushing the rebels, and Nicholas had complied for more than just idealistic reasons. A Hungarian state based on the "national" principle—that is, on revolutionary principles—might pose a challenge to Russian subjection of the Poles. Nicholas also distrusted Prussia over the Danish questions and schemed to neutralize any Prussian ambitions. If he could restore amity between Russia and Austria, the Austrian emperor might satisfy Habsburg ambitions through the creation of a Greater Germany of seventy million people. Nicholas understood any diversion of Habsburg power into central Europe as a victory for Russia, guaranteeing the Czar a free hand in the Near East and in the Balkans. Thus Nicholas saw himself as a patron able to help Austria in Germany and Italy in exchange for a united front against France.

The error Russia made was in not understanding Francis Joseph. He had lived through the crises in Vienna, Milan, and Prague, where nationalism had threatened to destroy his empire. He drew the conclusion that Austria must use its power in the Metternich way: maintain a balance of power, cooperate with Prussia, uphold dynasty and state as inseparable, yield no territory unless *defeated* in war. A practical man, self-disciplined, tactful, and courteous, the young emperor looked on Napoleon III as a threat to Habsburg Italy. But this would not drive him automatically toward Russia. A free hand for Russia in the Balkans might produce convulsions among the Slav peoples in the Austrian Empire. When Russia occupied the provinces of Moldavia and Walachia, the danger seemed immediate, all along the line of the Danube. Finally, if Austria did aid Russia in the Crimean struggle, it seemed certain that France would bother Austria in Italy, by supporting the Piedmont king Victor Emmanuel's bid to "free" all Italy. On the other hand, an alliance with France to protect Italy opened the prospect of a

5. In 1861 Moldavia and Walachia were officially united as Rumania.

Russian war against the Habsburg lands facing southeast. Finally, *any* active role, whether for France or for Russia, might encourage Prussia to try a new scheme of union without Austria.

When every action had dangerous implications, Francis Joseph saw advantages only in neutrality. What Francis did do was sign a secret treaty with Prussia, giving mutual guarantees of territorial integrity and the promise to go to war against the Czar if he pushed across the Balkan Mountains. With Prussia pledged to secure Italy against French interference, Francis Joseph gave Russia an ultimatum: Get out of the Danubian principalities! A mobilization of the Austrian army in June 1854 convinced Nicholas he had to give way to this Habsburg treachery. Vienna could best contain France in Italy if Russia lost in the East and posed no threat there. The Vienna Four Points were, therefore, a victory for Austria at Russia's expense. A new Austrian ultimatum to Russia, delivered in December 1855, promised entry into the war unless Russia surrendered.

Austria had been too clever by half, however, as it soon appeared. When the Paris peace conference (the Congress of Paris) opened on February 25, 1856, all the belligerents humiliated the emperor. The Piedmont prime minister, Cavour,[6] was a brilliant liberal statesman. He earned the right to sit with the Great Powers by sending troops against Russia, in close concert with France. Given a chance to speak to the Congress, Cavour denounced Austria's occupation of the Danubian "states" and Austrian rule in Italy as parallel to Russian suppression of Eastern nations. Russia made no protest, for obvious reasons. Prussia enjoyed the Austrian dilemma. France had already agreed with Cavour to promote Italian unity. And Britain had nothing to lose from any move against Austrian power in the Mediterranean or the Balkans.

The Crimean War thus had important consequences for Austria. Russia emerged as a dissatisfied power, anxious for revisions of the treaties taking away control of the Black Sea. In order to gain strength for revenge, Russia retreated from Europe's conservative alliances, entering into an alliance with France and a period of internal reform. And France under Napoleon, in order to shield the wounded Russian bear, pushed "revision" along the Danube and in Italy. Austria's diplomacy had isolated it from Prussia and Russia, while confronting Vienna with an enemy—France—willing to use nationalism for its own purposes.

The initial victory of the national principle at Austria's expense seemed to come in the Danubian principalities. In accordance with the Paris agreements, in early 1857 Habsburg forces withdrew. Unable to dominate the area directly, Francis Joseph favored an Ottoman restoration, hoping to hinder national movements in that way. In Moldavia some great aristocrats favored this solution, because the nationalists were also liberals and a threat to quasi-feudal rights. The nationalist forces were more powerful, however, and agitated for unification with Walachia, the nomination of a foreign prince,[7] and independence from the Turks. Napoleon III favored this program; so, too, did Russia. The Habsburg and Ottoman diplomats were opposed. Britain thus held the balance and could tip it. Initially, Britain did so in favor of the Turks, by cooperating with fraudulent elections to determine popular sentiment. Britain forced France to abandon unification but could not overawe the Rumanians. The people nullified "separation" of the two principalities by electing Alexander Cuza governor in both provinces, with Franco-Russian encouragement, in 1859.

Vienna reached new standards of opulence during the reign of Francis Joseph, who was personally rather austere; he is shown here in an early portrait by the German artist Franz Winterhalter. The first years of Francis Joseph's reign were marred by misfortune, and he was manipulated by reactionary forces. The autocratic young monarch had no faith in constitutional government, but difficulties with his subjects eventually forced him to accept some reforms. Like Queen Victoria in England, the Emperor's reign was unusually long, spanning a sixty-eight-year period from 1848–1916. Kunsthistorisches Museum, Vienna.

6. Camillo di Cavour, 1810–1861.
7. Along the lines of the earlier creation of national monarchies in Greece and Belgium.

Vienna could do nothing to reverse the *de facto* unification of Rumania, because its forces were totally occupied elsewhere. The French had helped Cavour's program for Italian unification, with the result that war broke out in Piedmont in the spring of 1859.

THE FRENCH DECADE: ITALIAN UNIFICATION

The Italian question was Napoleon's great obsession. Not only had he begun his political adventure there in 1831; his uncle had also. Moreover, Italy was an area of great strategic importance for the balance of power. Also, in 1857 France was in the grip of a severe economic crisis which challenged the stability of the Second Empire. Floods in the major farm areas in 1855–1856 had ruined harvests, driving up food prices in the rapidly growing industrial cities. Government-sponsored relief was inadequate. The justifications of arbitrary rule under Napoleon III had been order and glory. With prosperity gone and order threatened by elections (May 1857) which returned important opposition elements to the Assembly, Napoleon III decided to avoid political concessions at home by offering the French a striking success abroad. A revolution in Italy was more attractive than one at home!

What was lacking was some spectacular "event." This was provided on January 14, 1858, when Felice Orsini, an assassin hired in England, made an attempt on the Emperor's life. Sentiment at home consolidated in favor of the regime. And there was an additional bonus. Orsini, before being executed, wrote a letter to Napoleon begging him to liberate Italy and thus redress the harm he had done in 1849 by occupying Rome. Napoleon saw his chance. He published the Orsini letter, while urging Cavour to do so as well. Events had combined to make Napoleon III redeem his pledge to "do something for Italy."

What he did was to arrange a meeting with Cavour, secretly, at Plombières, on July 20, 1858. The Italian was one of the great realists and had drawn from the failure to unify Italy in 1848 the proper conclusion. The boast of the Sardinian king[8] Charles Albert that Italy would "do it herself" was hollow. Cavour knew that unification was a problem of diplomacy, not domestic affairs, as the radicals assumed. He had concluded as early as 1852 that what Italian nationalism needed was an ally with ground troops, not a navy.[9] Italy could be unified by exploiting rifts among the Great Powers. All efforts made by Cavour since he became premier in 1852 had tended in that direction: to find an enemy of Austrian predominance who was willing to fight. Then, and only then, could Cavour convert his domestic gains to good purpose.

Cavour was a reformer who used parliamentary techniques to make Piedmont a model of reform. Employing statistics to convince, or at least to overwhelm, opposition, he had reorganized the economy and the army. Economically, his chief achievement lay in the reform of the tax system at home and the success he enjoyed in attracting foreign investment. Loans helped to finance highway building programs and also the elaboration of a system of canals and railroads. Cavour also developed harbors, stimulated agricultural reforms, and prompted the reform of laws to make it easier for banks to extend credit for development. In fact, these policies were em-

---

8. The state about which nationalist movements formed was the kingdom of Sardinia, ruled by the house of Savoy and including both Savoy and Piedmont. Because the kingdom's capital for much of its history was on mainland Piedmont, the state is often referred to as Piedmont.
9. Britain favored unification, but would not supply troops.

The Unification of Italy

- Kingdom of Sardinia, 1815
- Territories Gained, 1859–1860
- Territories Gained, 1860–1870

braced by Cavour for their own merit. But in part Cavour saw in them the means to develop the revenues to equip a modern army, which he deemed essential to the protection of the independence of the state he led. Also, prosperity was the key to the system of alliances Cavour aimed against Austria.

He had supported the states dependent on Austria whenever they tried to escape Austrian hegemony—Milan in 1853 for instance. His program *within* Italy, however, posed only a marginal threat to Austria, which had troops and treaties up and down the peninsula. Popular discontent over Habsburg rule was necessary, but not enough. Therefore, ever since 1856, in recognition of the estrangement of Austria and France, Cavour had hoped Napoleon III would come out openly against the Habsburgs.

At Plombières Cavour and Napoleon III struck a bargain. The French promised to help Piedmont in a war against Austria, but only on the condition that a good pretext could be found to cover aggressive intentions, and on the further condition that "revolutionary" means not be employed. The agreement reached divided Italy into four parts: a northern kingdom under the house of Savoy, including Piedmont, Venetia, Lombardy, Parma, and Modena as well as part of the Papal States; a papal state comprising Rome and its suburbs; a central kingdom based on Tuscany and the adjacent papal lands; and the Kingdom of the Two Sicilies. Cavour was willing to accept this scheme, which provided not total unification but rather a confederation of states under papal presidency. He understood Napoleon's need to placate Catholic opinion in France. And he found the "compensation" requested acceptable: the provinces of Nice and Savoy, parts of Piedmont adjacent to France. While Cavour sought a respectable cause for war, Napoleon was to tour Europe in order to isolate Austria diplomatically. To further cement the alliance, Princess Clotilde of Piedmont married Prince Napoleon, the son of Jerome Bonaparte.[10]

While Cavour tried to provoke Austria, Napoleon gained Russia's benevolent neutrality. He also tried to placate Britain, which favored mediation. The price Russia exacted was French agreement to revise the Treaty of Paris of 1856 as it touched the Black Sea and its region. To England Napoleon promised certain trade concessions, the exact form of which became apparent less than two years later. On January 23, 1860, the Cobden-Chevalier Treaty reduced tariffs on English manufactures. This "free trade" agreement, some said, opened French markets at the expense of industrial development in France.[11]

Only Prussia remained. There, Frederick William IV became mentally incompetent, and Prince William[12] was regent. A German "liberal," William favored an alliance with England, in order to protect Prussia against encirclement by France on the west and Russia on the east. He also was favorable to Prussian nationalist feelings, which regarded Austria as German. Austria therefore approached William, hopeful that the old alliance could be rebuilt. William put a high price on aid: the forces of the Germanic Confederation were to be divided, giving to Prussia everything north of the river Main. This command, centered on the Rhine, would protect Prussia from France and seemed reasonable. Francis Joseph refused, however. Just as the Habsburgs would not yield in the Rumanian case to protect interests in Italy, they would not yield in Germany to protect the Italian hegemony. Austrian stubbornness was thus the insurance policy France and Cavour required; the Habsburgs remained isolated.

Cavour, meanwhile, acted in an increasingly provocative way. He mobilized the Piedmontese army in March 1859. Austria sent an ultimatum on April 23 demanding demobilization in terms too blunt to be accepted. Cavour therefore had what he wanted, knowing that his rejection would bring Austria to the attack, thus activating the French alliance as a defense of helpless Victor Emmanuel II, king of Sardinia.[13] There was thus a cause for war, but no excuse. On May 3 Napoleon said he would aid his ally, in response to the Austrian invasion of April 29. Thus began a war unique in modern history, because it did not have its origin in mutual fears. Both sides mobilized in the *hope* the other would attack.

Austria proved ready to go to war, but not prepared. Military leadership was incompetent. Little trust could be put in the Italian and Hungarian elements scattered through the Habsburg armies. Cavour and Napoleon stirred the Hungarian circle of Louis Kossuth to make a new revolution and so distract Austria's energies. And Russia had put an army on the border of

10. The brother of Napoleon I; he lived until 1860.
11. The "compensation" was easier entry into Britain of French silks, wines, and brandies—a bad bargain. See the details in Chapter 11, which suggest that the treaty did not inhibit French industrialization as much as it was once supposed. This treaty came at the beginning of a period of intense mechanization of French industry.
12. King of Prussia, 1861–1888; emperor of Germany, 1871–1888. He was the King's brother.
13. The son of Charles Albert, he was king of Italy after the unification. Italians give his dates as 1849–1878, to stress the origins of the state in the revolution of 1848.

Galicia, to make sure that any nationalist rising of the Poles in Austria's partition area did not spread to Russian or Prussian Poland.

In need of quick victories, therefore, to prevent the Austrian Empire from coming apart, the Habsburgs found only quick defeats. The French invaded Italy on May 12, with Napoleon III in command. Widespread insurrections followed throughout the peninsula. Defeats were inflicted on Austria by the French at Magenta and Solferino. Napoleon was not satisfied, however. Cavour had violated the agreement by encouraging the revolutionaries throughout Italy. France was not prepared to campaign against Austria in the great fortresses of the Italian north if the result would be a wider Italian kingdom than that planned at Plombières. Moreover, the Prussians, alarmed over French intentions, had begun to mobilize their army along the Rhine. This was clearly a threat motivated more by Prussian self-interest than by any wish to aid Austria. Britain and Russia were now also in favor of mediation. Austria, too, saw the advantage of peace, even if a bit late, considering the threats to Habsburg rule elsewhere.

Francis Joseph met Napoleon III at Villafranca in July 1859. The terms made to end the war involved an Austrian cession of Lombardy to France, which would in turn convey it to Piedmont. Austria would keep Venetia and the four northern fortresses, which were called the Quadrilateral. Rulers displaced by insurrection were to be restored and a confederation of Italian states established. Britain reacted with hostility, arguing for a unified and independent Italy. Cavour, proclaiming that he had been betrayed by Napoleon, resigned from office. He would accept no congress to ratify such terms.

Whether Napoleon had really betrayed Cavour is debatable. Insurrections continued throughout Italy, and France made no effort to suppress them. It was in fact Francis Joseph who had been duped. The central Italian states would not take back princes under Habsburg tutelage. A British fleet was sent to Italian waters in order to prevent any extension of French influence, which London now viewed as a threat to its commerce. This fact made Piedmont bold in support of the revolutionaries. By January 1860 new regimes had consolidated in most states and voted for unification with Piedmont. Cavour returned to power in triumph, and Napoleon had no choice but to recognize his own miscalculation. France supported plebiscites everywhere, with the result that Savoy and Nice voted to become French while the other states became "Italian."

While the annexation of Savoy was a turning point in the history of the Second Empire, signaling the shift from a policy of liberation to one of aggrandizement, the results were more profound in Italy. In the south, the republican leader Garibaldi made a revolution against the Kingdom of the Two Sicilies in May 1860, aided by Piedmontese troops from Genoa. He agreed to the incorporation of the "republican states" into a united Italy,

For centuries many Italians had dreamed of national unity, but the reality was not achieved until 1861. The most successful military leader of the unification drive was Giuseppe Garibaldi, whose men had conquered Sicily and all of southern Italy against overwhelming odds. Garibaldi (left) finally joined the Piedmontese king, Victor Emmanuel (right), in Naples where Garibaldi surrendered the dictatorial powers he had proclaimed for himself over the south. An uneducated man, fired with devotion to his ideal, Garibaldi was regarded almost as a saint by the peasants and inspired absolute devotion in his disparate group of guerrilla followers. The Bettmann Archive.

Rumania was a new nation to emerge in the aftermath of the Crimean War. Previously comprised of the principalities of Moldavia and Walachia, Rumania had, in fact, been controlled by Russia and Turkey. Here, one of the divans ad hoc *bringing together Turkish and European representatives decides the fate of the territory. Eventually all parties accepted the right of Prince Alexander Cuza to lead the country, and the union of the principalities was formally proclaimed in 1861. Cuza set about implementing some drastic and unconstitutional reforms, and he soon alienated most of his subjects. A coup d'etat forced his resignation in 1866. Bucharest Library of the Rumanian Academy.*

unlike Mazzini, who wanted a republican victory. Cavour used Garibaldi to convince Italians that Piedmont would do as much for independence as republicanism. The point was simple enough: Italians had everything to gain from a movement both national and monarchical. When Garibaldi finally understood the plan to annex Sicily and Naples, his forces were no match for Victor Emmanuel's. So, on October 26, the revolutionary saluted Victor Emmanuel with these words: "Hail to the King of Italy."

Italy had been "made." In March 1861 an Italian parliament[14] met, proclaiming Victor Emmanuel king of Italy, by God's grace and the will of the people. The British foreign minister, Lord Russell, had made a similar declaration from London, denouncing the Vienna settlement of 1815 in the name of "the people." Indeed, the unification of Italy did complete the destruction of Metternich's system. It had been made possible by Napoleon's challenge to Russia and Austria, by Russia's wish to revise the Crimean War treaties, and by Prussian estrangement from Austria over the question of hegemony in Germany. The French decision had been to go forward with a revolutionary alliance, rather than backward in league with Austria.

The Italian war, unprovoked and aggressive, had other profound consequences. While Austria was preoccupied in Italy, Cuza and the Rumanians had carried out a political, legislative, and administrative amalgamation of Walachia and Moldavia. This was complete in 1861, and five years later Cuza was replaced by an elected prince, Charles of Hohenzollern-Sigmaringen. There was in Rumania—as the new state called itself—no direct threat to the Habsburg Empire. What was a danger to the Empire was the unrest Rumania's existence might stir up among the peasants of Transylvania and Bukovina, neighboring provinces in which the people were primarily Rumanian by language and culture.

The Empire was the most populous state in Europe, apart from Russia. The main constituent parts were Austria, Bohemia, Galicia, and Hungary, with at least a dozen different nationalities or language groups in the four

14. With only Venetia and Rome not represented.

areas: Germans dominated in Austria and in parts of Bohemia; the Czechs were a majority in most of Bohemia and in Moravia; Ukrainians peopled Galicia; the Magyars were in the vast majority in Hungary. Given the success of the Italians and the Rumanians in proclaiming their independence, what means would Vienna find to control the above-named peoples and also the masses of Poles, Ruthenians, Slovaks, Croats, Serbs, Slovenes, and Dalmatians left within the Empire? Neither the Magyars nor the Rumanians were Slavs, but nearly all of the other peoples were linguistically Slavic, cousins to the Russians.

That nationalism was the fundamental movement of the nineteenth century we may debate. But there can be little disagreement that the "nationalities question" was fundamental to the survival of the Habsburg Empire. Statesmen in Vienna had to find a way to bring diverse peoples into some sentiment of harmony with Habsburg policies. The Italian struggle had made this urgent and also difficult. Austria was defeated. The failure of its armies revealed the general weakness of its government. Hence the most significant Austrian reaction was the "October Diploma" issued in 1860. This reorganized the Empire on a federal basis. Local diets gained greater autonomy; a central parliament was created. Then, in 1861, a new decree restored the unitary system, while keeping the parliament. These fluctuations reveal the tension which was then gripping Vienna—and with good reason. Prussia had shown a willingness to use Austria's problems with the "nations" as the opportunity to raise again the question of the German nation.

The Peoples of the Austro-Hungarian Empire

Germans
Italians
Magyars
Rumanians
Slavs

KLEINDEUTSCH, GROSSDEUTSCH: GERMAN UNIFICATION

If Habsburg ministers and Francis Joseph faced in Cavour a great nationalist and in Napoleon III the supreme adventurer in foreign affairs, then in Prussia they faced the great master of what Germans called *Realpolitik* (political realism). Otto von Bismarck was not a man of many illusions, either in the affairs of Prussia or in those of Europe. While Napoleon III busily negotiated trade treaties with Britain, Belgium, Switzerland, and the German *Zollverein*, and at the same time dealt with opposition at home, the Prussian situation in Europe was transformed by the conservative Bismarck's rise to power. Elsewhere in Europe liberalism seemed ascendant: the czar had emancipated the serfs in 1861; France had embraced free trade; in Vienna a parliament now sat; Italy had a constitutional monarchy. And in Prussia the death of Frederick William IV had brought to the throne the "liberal" Prince Regent William.

Before we treat in detail either Bismarck's policies in the 1860s or his achievements, it will help to put in perspective the man and his policies and values.

Bismarck, who first came to prominence at Berlin among the loyalists of 1848 opposed to constitutional concessions, was a *Junker*. The revolutionary threat had exposed his opposition to parliamentary government, his dislike of industrial cities and their radical politics, and the warmth of his sentiments about agriculture, hierarchy, and the military values of his class. In 1848 he had tried to rally the peasants on his estates to come to Berlin and fight for the King. When Frederick William IV seemed indecisive, he had argued *against* any unification of Germany which excluded Austria.

The range of his ideas expanded in the 1850s, however, as he moved up from routine posts in the judicial bureaucracy to the chief posts in diplomatic circles. Frederick William IV had sent Bismarck to Frankfurt in 1851 to head the Prussian delegation to the reconstituted Diet of the Germanic Confederation. There, he had taken the measure of Austrian strengths and weaknesses in German affairs, while becoming convinced that Prussia could unify the Germans only by giving up the romantic attachments to the medieval idea of "Greater Germany" to which his king seemed bound. Before he was called to power on September 22, 1862, as minister-president and minister for foreign affairs, he had also served as ambassador to Russia and France. In Saint Petersburg he had grasped that the new czar, Alexander II (1855–1881), was bent toward domestic reform as a result of the trauma of the Crimean War.[15] And Bismarck also understood the growth of pro-German sentiments in Russia, both out of resentment of Austria and because Russia needed a buffer against French "revolution," especially in Poland. At Paris, Bismarck had seen at once that Napoleon III had passed the zenith of his European interests, more intent now on pursuing adventures in Algeria, Cochin China,[16] Syria, and Mexico than on playing the role of arbiter of Europe.

His experience outside of the narrow limits of East Prussia had convinced him that no version of the old Confederation could meet the needs of the new society emerging in Germany, a society in which urban and economic developments dictated new political structures. Bismarck drew the conclusion that seemed necessary: intelligent conservatism could save tradition

15. Bismarck served as ambassador to Alexander II from 1859 to early 1862. He then went to Paris, before being recalled to Berlin in 1862.
16. Former name for the southernmost region of South Vietnam.

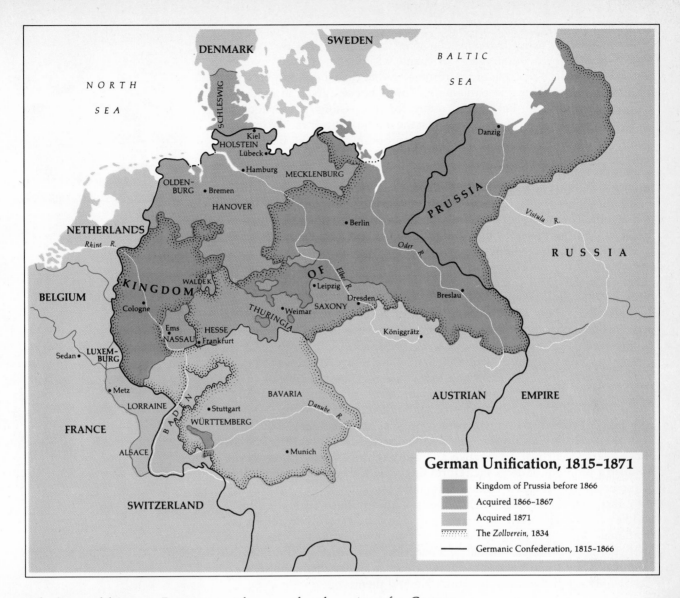

German Unification, 1815–1871

	Kingdom of Prussia before 1866
	Acquired 1866–1867
	Acquired 1871
··········	The *Zollverein*, 1834
——	Germanic Confederation, 1815–1866

only by modifying it. Prussia must become the champion of a German nationalism. If it did not, the odds were that either Austria would succeed in the same endeavor or Germany would remain weak and divided in the age of national states. The opportunity to press this view arose in 1862, out of the tangle of Prussian politics.

Frederick William IV's declining years were distinguished chiefly by reaction. There had been a vigorous renewal of liberal agitation, however, chiefly the work of the National Association. This movement drew some support from the regent William in 1859 and from other "liberal" elements at court, especially William's son Prince Frederick, who was married to a daughter of the English Queen Victoria. The most significant gesture was the dismissal of Manteuffel, the minister responsible for the humiliation of Prussia by Austria at Olmütz. By 1860, Britain was pressing William to assert Prussian leadership in Germany. Austrian weakness gave rise to an impulse in the same direction, but William believed that army reform was the basic instrument of a forward-looking policy in Germany.

He therefore proposed a reform of the military system early in 1860, in a speech to the Prussian *Landtag*, or the lower house in parliament. The architect was the general and war minister von Roon.[17] He proposed to increase the field army from 200,000 to 371,000, to extend the term of service from two to three years, to spend 9.5 million thalers[18] on new weapons, to reduce the role of the reserve, and to curtail exemptions from service. The liberals in the parliament's lower house agreed to fund this program provisionally, but only in return for concessions: a reduction in service time and some safeguards against the military power revival implicit in the new program. William would not compromise, and in this determination the upper chamber supported him. Then, on January 2, 1861, his brother's death vaulted William into the kingship. At the same time, however, democratic forces in Prussia turned toward the Progress party.

The elections of 1861 gave a strong majority to the opposition in the parliament. The new liberal majority pressed for concessions and itemized budgets. William replied by dissolving the parliament, in the hope that new elections in which government pressure was applied would produce a tractable majority. The Conservative delegation was cut in half instead! The liberal ministers and Prince Frederick advised capitulation, but William refused to abandon army reform. Taking von Roon's advice, he summoned Bismarck from Paris. William told Bismarck he could not rule without a budget, hence the alternatives were either to abdicate in favor of Frederick or to surrender to the demands of his ministers.

Bismarck analyzed the situation in compelling terms. What was at stake in the impasse between crown and legislature was the principle of sovereignty versus that of responsible, parliamentary, government. Bismarck proposed a different course: reconstruct the cabinet with Conservatives and give power to Bismarck, along with a promise that the King would not abdicate under any circumstances. He, Bismarck, would fight the liberals and preserve the royal prerogative and army reform. His method was to promise a program of domestic reform tinged with the social welfare ideas of the prominent socialist thinker Ferdinand Lassalle.

In fact, what Bismarck intended was a compromise with the liberal middle classes, in which he would give domestic reforms in return for "national" support for the monarchy's authority in Germany. In a speech on September 30, 1862, Bismarck made clear his sense of the liberals' dilemma. They could not easily oppose Prussian nationalism, which was, after all, a part of their own program. He told them:

Germany does not look to Prussia's liberalism but to her power . . . the great question of the time will be decided not by speeches and the resolutions of majorities—that was the mistake of 1848 and 1849—but by blood and iron.[19]

17. Albrecht Theodor Emil von Roon, 1803–1879.
18. About £1.5 million.
19. Quoted in E. J. Passant and W. O. Henderson, *A Short History of Germany* (Cambridge: Cambridge University Press, 1966), p. 46.

One of the many monuments erected in Bismarck's honor was this 1891 Hamburg tower where the "Iron Chancellor" is shown in the costume of a medieval knight—a reference to the nationalistic German traditions which he fostered. Bismarck realized before other leaders the political and military implications of industrial progress, and he cleverly maneuvered to establish Prussia at the head of a unified Germany and Berlin as the most important European diplomatic and cultural center. The key to Bismarck's successful strategy was his stunning victory during the Franco-Prussian war of 1870. With France totally humiliated no one could challenge the preeminent German position in European affairs. Staatsbibliothek, Berlin.

Despite the directness of the warning to the liberals, they rejected the budget. Bismarck prorogued the parliament and ruled without a budget until September 1863. Then the struggle deepened, as new elections resulted in a similar stalemate. So far from saving William was Bismarck in 1863 that it was said openly he had estranged public opinion completely inside Prussia and in the smaller, more liberal states that looked to Prussia for leadership. What saved Bismarck and William was a clumsy Austrian intervention.

As early as 1860 Francis Joseph had told William there could be no concessions of leadership by Austria to Prussia in German affairs. In 1861 Prussia had revived a scheme for leadership, and a year later the inclusion of France in commercial treaties with the *Zollverein* had pointed toward the exclusion of Austria. This step harmed Austro-Prussian relations, which Bismarck did nothing to improve. He pointedly told the Austrian ambassador to Berlin that Austria's proper focus of interest was the Danube and Hungary. Moreover, the Prussian statesman told the ambassador that Prussia was the equal of Austria in German affairs. In those circumstances Francis Joseph could have wished nothing better than the constitutional struggle within Prussia. He invited the German princes to a Frankfurt *Fürstentag*, or princes' assembly, to convene on August 16, 1863, for the purpose of discussing German reform. Bismarck countered dramatically, by refusing to permit King William to attend.

Where Bismarck's predecessors in Berlin had been dependent on William, the impasse at home and the Austrian scheme made William dependent on his minister. Bismarck justified the reversal of roles in a series of brilliant diplomatic coups, followed by three successful wars.

As early as December 1862 Bismarck had envisioned a war with Austria over hegemony in Germany. He had pointedly asked the French ambassador what Napoleon III would do if things got hot in Germany. The reply was to the point: Napoleon III favored Prussian domination, Russian friendship, and the unity of Italy. Scarcely had this reply been made when Poland exploded. Radicals proclaimed a general rebellion in Posen, Galicia, and Russian Poland. Bismarck seized the opportunity and made a deal with Alexander II. Always anti-Polish, Bismarck had the added incentive of protecting Prussian Poland from revolution. What he could not have counted on was a reversal of French opinion. A new foreign minister prevailed on Napoleon III to take a pro-Polish stance, while raising the idea of a grab at France's old playground, the southern German Rhineland.

The news alarmed Bismarck, chiefly because he suspected French intentions along the Rhine in any event. There was some comfort in the situation, however, for France could not be for Poland without alienating Russia. With Britain's forces heavily committed elsewhere, on the border between Canada and the United States,[20] the Russians need not fear British intervention. Hence the critical outcome of the Polish crisis was to reduce German worry over France; Napoleon III could not contemplate action against a Russian-Prussian alliance. France condemned Russian policy in Poland. Austria and Russia were in conflict in the Near East.

Thus Prussia was at liberty to make a strong response to Francis Joseph's scheme to force Austrian leadership on Germany. The princes would not accept any reform to which Prussia had not consented. This fact gave Bismarck a new idea. He now asked Russia for support against Austria, in

---

20. During the American Civil War Britain favored the South, chiefly because the cotton towns in England were dependent on Southern cotton. The British feared an American attack on Canada in reprisal.

return for the pledge he had given to Alexander II with regard to Poland. Speaking boldly about war in the manner of Frederick the Great, he in fact meant only to convince Russia that Prussia was its bulwark against the West. In this he succeeded completely. Russia now favored a Prussian hegemony in Germany. This would weaken Austria in the Near East and so advance the one real Russian objective: the revision of the 1856 treaty. The French blunder over Poland had, in the end, removed the one thing Bismarck feared most in 1863—a French attack along the Rhine while the struggle for Germany unfolded.

Schleswig and Holstein provided Bismarck with the opportunity he needed. On November 15, 1863, the Danish king Frederick VII died. His successor Christian IX signed a new constitution, incorporating the duchies into Denmark. This was a breach of the 1852 London Protocol. Moreover, German public opinion rallied around Duke Frederick of Augustenburg, the heir in the male line,[21] who advocated the separation of the duchies from Denmark and their inclusion in the Germanic Confederation. This view was just as much in violation of the 1852 settlement, because in London the Danish succession had been recognized along with the integrity of the Danish kingdom. Notwithstanding these facts, the National Association in Germany called for interference of the Diet of the Confederation.

Bismarck disregarded the niceties and urged William to act to increase Prussian territory as his predecessors had always done. This Bismarck did in private, since such a policy, if known, would have been considered absurd. In public, Bismarck coolly refused to recognize Augustenburg. He called instead for a joint Austro-Prussian ultimatum to Denmark, demanding observance of the London Protocol. Bismarck calculated a Danish refusal, since to accept would mean revoking the new Danish constitution. A cause for war would then exist to vindicate treaty rights. The Great Powers would not intervene against maintenance of the status quo of 1852. And the Prussian and other German liberals would be made to understand that Prussian diplomacy and military strength were the means toward unification.

Bismarck thus trapped Austria into a joint action. Vienna could not be less German than Berlin! Under the authority of a decree of execution passed before Christmas 1863 in the Confederation Diet, Bismarck and von Schmerling[22] presented an ultimatum to Denmark on January 16, 1864. Bismarck's calculations proved correct, and troops crossed into Schleswig. The Great Powers remained neutral. Denmark's army was pushed into Jutland and quickly overwhelmed. Austria and Prussia then agreed to a new London Conference, which Bismarck then made unworkable by declaring the 1852 Protocol invalid as a result of Denmark's breach of it. The war resumed, and when the Danes were again crushed the London Protocol was a dead letter. The fate of the duchies now rested with Berlin and Vienna, a fact recognized in the Treaty of Vienna in 1864.

Under its terms Denmark gave up Schleswig, Holstein, and the smaller state of Lauenburg at the base of the Danish peninsula—about 40 percent of Denmark's territory. Liberal opinion in Germany had predicted a French intervention, or a British one. When neither power did prevent the defeat of Denmark, Bismarck was clearly the victor. Not only had he waged a war to "protect" the Germans living in the duchies, he had done it on respectable grounds, as Cavour had against Austria in 1859. It now remained to settle the fate of the duchies through some agreement with Austria.

21. The Danish claimants were in the female line.
22. Anton von Schmerling, 1805–1893, Austrian minister of the interior.

Bismarck proposed that Austria surrender the duchies to Prussia, for which the Habsburgs would get compensation elsewhere. Austria demanded to know where. Bismarck proposed Italy: if a war there could be arranged, Prussia would help Austria recover Lombardy. Francis Joseph replied that Lombardy was not Prussia's to give, while Silesia, which Prussia had stolen from Austria in 1740, was.[23] Bismarck had thus maneuvered Austria into the position of refusing a settlement, on the very good grounds that Bismarck was proposing a Prussian hegemony in Germany.

The stalemate was deceptive, however. What Bismarck grasped was that Austria was still isolated. Hence Prussia was free to settle the fate of central Europe without the interference of either France or Russia. War between Prussia and Austria looked to be inevitable in 1865, when Austria suddenly took up the Augustenburg claim. This crisis eased, however, because Vienna retreated. Racked by financial problems and Hungarian nationalist movements, the Habsburg emperor agreed to a compromise. Under the Convention of Gastein (August 14, 1865), Prussia would get Lauenburg and Schleswig, while Austria got Holstein. Prussia also gained the harbor of Kiel in Holstein and the roads of a military nature in the territory. This consolidated Prussia's hold on the Elbe River, while linking its Baltic and North Sea provinces.

The Prussian minister followed this decisive diplomatic victory with a visit to Napoleon III and another to Victor Emmanuel. He left the French with the impression he would tolerate their acquisition of Belgium, or even some German land along the Rhine, in return for neutrality. The Italians got the solid advantage of a trade treaty. Austria resented the Italian overture especially and responded foolishly by reviving in Holstein the pro-Augustenburg agitation. Bismarck protested bitterly this "seditious agitation" in the duchies. To buttress his position in the event of war, he pledged to Napoleon III Venetia and other Italian territories still in Austrian control, with the understanding that France would again be Italy's patron, by handing Venetia over to Victor Emmanuel. The Italians promised to be neutral in the event of an Austro-German war over the northern duchies.

All that remained was to provoke Austria. This was done by a scheme launched on April 9, 1866, for German unification. Austria was to be excluded. Liberal opinion of the *Grossdeutsch* variety was mollified by the proposal of a national parliament elected by universal manhood suffrage. Austrian attempts to win French support failed. Then, Vienna blundered again. The Austrians proposed to the Diet at Frankfurt a federal decision of the duchies' status. This was Bismarck's cue, because the Austrian notion violated the Convention of Gastein. Prussia declared the joint administration in force again, and an army occupied Holstein on June 7. Vienna declared this an act of war and proposed a federal mobilization against Prussia. When the major states accepted the Austrian request for support,[24] Bismarck declared the Germanic Confederation at an end.

The Austrian folly dissolved the last impediment to Bismarck's war for supremacy. King William opposed aggression against Austria, but he was helpless to discourage the defense of Prussia. The Austrian mobilization decree of June 14 produced a Prussian invasion of Saxony on the fifteenth. The Austrian frontier was breached on the twenty-first from the north; and the Italians declared war on Austria, invading from the south. The war was over in seven weeks. The Austrians had managed to defeat the Italians at

---

23. Actually, Frederick the Great had occupied Silesia in 1740, but it wasn't until the treaty of Breslau and Berlin in 1742 that Austria formally ceded Silesia to Prussia.
24. Only Saxony gave major support, but Bavaria, Hanover, Baden, and others gave qualified aid.

Custozza. But the Prussians destroyed the main Habsburg force in Bohemia on July 3, at Sadowa, or what in German was called Königgratz. The French offered to mediate and Bismarck immediately accepted, proposing moderate terms.

This he did because he understood that the real feat was not to beat Austria but to make stand what had been achieved: an alteration of the balance of power in Germany and in Europe. Bismarck's calculation was again correct. Russia was too occupied elsewhere to intervene. France had committed great military resources to the senseless struggle in Mexico.[25] In fact Bismarck's greatest difficulty was in convincing his king and the Prussian army to accept the moderate peace the statesman proposed, a thing Bismarck realized was necessary if France was to accept Prussia's domination of Germany.

The Peace of Prague gave to Prussia both Holstein and Schleswig as well as a small indemnity for war costs. Saxony and the other southern states that had aided Austria were not penalized. The treaty did recognize Prussia's right to unify the states north of the Main in a new confederation, from which Austria was excluded. Prussia annexed Hanover, Hesse-Kassel, Nassau, and Frankfurt, thus giving William an unbroken territory from Königsberg to Cologne, with over three million new subjects. When the Reichstag of the new North German Confederation ratified Prussia's control over policy and military resources in the new German federal state on April 16, 1867, Bismarck had completed the first part of a stunning achievement. Not only had he excluded Austria from a share of power; he had defeated the 1862 parliamentary bid for responsible government in Germany. The legislature approved a bill to indemnify King William's war costs, in an act of liberal submission to the politics of unification. He had vindicated the crown's right to act without legislative support, thus ending one phase of the liberal agitation—for constitutional restraints on royal power.

Perhaps it is clear in retrospect that Prussia would emerge the victor. There was rapid progress in its territories in economic development. The northern railroads and ports were linked. The *Zollverein* gave Prussia economic leadership. The administration and army reforms equipped Prussia for a leading role. In every respect, Prussia had advantages over Austria, whose empire was but loosely tied together and whose varied population posed an unyielding problem of nationalism that hindered any Austrian bid to lead Germany. In the Prague peace even Venetia was taken from Austria, which had been excluded from the whole central European corridor by the events of the period 1848–1866.

Indeed, no account of either the victory over Austria or the further successes Bismarck had in unifying Germany is complete without a discussion of the nature of the social and economic advantages Prussia enjoyed over Austria.

As early as 1848, it had become clear to Austrian statesmen that exclusion from the *Zollverein* was weakening the Habsburg position in Germany. This was of central importance to the imperial ministers, because without a solid German position it was difficult to maintain control over the subject nationalities within the Empire. In the 1850s Schwarzenberg and Bruck, the ministers of commerce, had grasped the facts and had tried to modernize the economy by eliminating internal tariffs and improving communications. While these efforts contributed to internal growth, they did not win

25. Where the popular leader Juárez had been overthrown by Maximiliam, a puppet with French and Habsburg support.

entry into the German customs union. Nor did they persuade the smaller German states that the advantage to them lay in alignment with Austria.

That Bismarck understood Prussia's economic position we cannot doubt. Not only did he stress the advantages of the Prussian-led *Zollverein* in his diplomacy within Germany; in 1865, on the eve of the Austrian war, he shook the economic foundations of loyalty to Austria among the German states. In that year he successfully negotiated a tariff agreement with France and persuaded the other German states of its advantages. This Prussian-French treaty excluded Austria from the reciprocal customs reductions on the wide variety of goods covered. And the result was to exclude Austria from Germany economically *before* the political exclusion of 1866.

Thus the legacy of 1848, when Prussia had been humiliated within the Confederation, was not simply the weakening of liberalism, nationalism, and socialism within the German world. It was also the realization among some Prussian statesmen and parliamentary leaders that the social foundations of German unity were of necessity economic. The German middle classes were alarmed by the growth of a threat from the "left," especially among the radical new working classes. But they were just as hostile to what they deemed the reactionary social basis of Habsburg power. Bismarck understood this and fashioned his victory over the liberals on constitutional questions that arose from the ambiguities of the situation. On the one hand, he embraced the popular goals of nationalism, which the liberals had advanced in 1848, only to be frustrated by the Prussian monarchy. On the other, Bismarck's domestic policies proved favorable to a "liberal" economic structure, as we shall soon demonstrate in detail. In exchange for the middle-class aims of unification and industrialization Bismarck exacted full payment. He secured political power for the aristocracy in the new state, which stood on the social alliance of the *Junker* elite and the elites of trade and industry.

THE NEXT STEP

There were still unresolved questions in 1866, however. These concerned the exact nature of the enlarged North German federal state, the impact of another defeat in Vienna, and the fate of the Germans south of the Main, whose independence had been guaranteed by the Prague arrangements.

Bismarck presided over the reorganization of northern political life. In the states not directly annexed to Prussia, the King's supremacy was established by virtue of his presidency of the North German Confederation. Ministers were responsible to him, not to the parliament. The monarch also had control of military and foreign affairs. The two-chamber legislature consisted of a *Bundesrat* and a *Reichstag*. The first had in it delegates sent by the member states without popular elections. In the Reichstag, however, the representatives were returned by universal male suffrage. The four states south of the Main were in alliance with the Confederation, both offensively and defensively; they were also in the *Zollverein*.

Francis Joseph was far from accepting these arrangements as final. With Beust,[26] he began internal reforms designed to restore Habsburg strength for a new round with Prussia. The major step taken was to strengthen the loyalty of Hungarians. In 1867 the *Ausgleich*[27] divided the Empire into two units, one called Austria, the other called Hungary. The parts shared a

---

26. Frederich Ferdinand von Beust, a Saxon, was chief adviser to the Emperor from 1866 to 1871.
27. A compromise settlement between equals.

common ruler and the ministries of foreign affairs, war, and finance. In Hungary Francis Joseph was king, while in Austria he retained the title of emperor. Economic agreements provided common arrangements for tariffs, railroads, currency, and banking. There was also a legislative body, meeting alternately in Vienna and Budapest, with powers to supervise budgets and also the shared ministries. At the same time, reforms internal to the two states were made. The Austrian regime was more liberal than the Hungarian one, but in Austria the German-speaking minority[28] dominated the nationalities. The Magyar leaders of Hungary completely controlled that country. Not surprisingly, therefore, the other nationalities were dissatisfied with the *Ausgleich*, which was in fact a victory of Magyar nationalism only.

The *Ausgleich* proved to be another blunder by the Habsburgs. The Magyars were preoccupied with Russian and Turkish power, being hostile to the Czar and in favor of the Ottomans. Also, in order to serve their purpose, which was to divert Austria toward southeastern politics, the Hungarians were pro-Prussian. They were thus a force opposed to any more concessions to nationalism and at the same time prone to look favorably on new Prussian attempts to integrate the four southern states— Bavaria, Baden, Hesse-Darmstadt, and Württemberg—into the North German Confederation.

Bismarck had this in mind, if only he could be assured that France would not be able to make war effectively to prevent the total unification of Germany. Too late to do anything about the Prussian victory of 1866, the French emperor now saw one last chance to diminish Prussia's strength. Napoleon instructed his diplomats to demand as compensation for neutrality the parts of Bavaria and Hesse west of the Rhine. Bismarck refused. The French countered with a demand for Prussian approval of a takeover in Belgium and Luxemburg. Meanwhile, Bismarck played on the fears of the south Germans by leaking the original demands for compensation. Having gained support in these states from treaties giving to Prussia command in wartime, Bismarck next refused to countenance the *purchase* of Luxemburg by France. Russia was neutralized in 1867, by promises of a free hand in the Black Sea and the threat of Prussian support of Polish nationalism.[29]

Bismarck had repeated the brilliant diplomacy which had isolated Austria before its war with Prussia. Now it was France left in the lurch, as Bismarck let the British know about Napoleon's design on Belgium.

Napoleon was also weak at home. The retreat from the Luxemburg demand in May 1867 humiliated the Emperor. Throughout the 1860s opposition had mounted over domestic issues also. Despite measures to make a "Liberal Empire" in a series of decrees in 1860, Catholics, republicans, and a variety of powerful urban-based politicians were dissatisfied. The liberal politician and writer Thiers had marked the cause: what the French wanted was not enlightened despotism a hundred years after Voltaire, but ministerial responsibility, the full restoration of civil liberty, an end to rigged elections, and that kind of diplomacy that had helped produce a powerful and aggressive German state across the Rhine. France's wisest observers realized that since 1863 the appearance of French power in Europe had no longer accorded with the reality. The belated compensation claims were proof of ineptness. So, too, was the absurd affair of the Belgian railroads, a Napoleonic effort to usurp Britain's lead in economic aid there.

28. A majority, if one reckons without Galicia.
29. Russia was also preoccupied in the Balkans, where Crete had rebelled against Turkey in 1866. Bismarck intervened diplomatically in 1868, against Russia's Greek clients.

In the end, Prussia and Britain forced a suspension of French leases to run Belgium's railroad system.

From 1868 on, the opposition press in France condemned the Emperor's despotism. Victor Hugo attacked Napoleon in pamphlets; the republican Leon Gambetta demanded in 1869 the separation of church and state, free secular education, the suppression of the standing army, and elections for all public offices. The May elections in 1869 produced 45 percent of the vote for antigovernment candidates. Under this pressure Napoleon III decided to grant ministerial responsibility, the system by which the legislature could force on the Emperor a new set of ministers in a no-confidence vote. New elections early in 1870 heartened the government, which got three million more votes than it had in 1869.

Time had run out, however. Spain had experienced a revolt in 1868, against the person and policies of Queen Isabella II, an absolutist whose private life was a scandal. When a Spanish provisional government formed, the Queen had fled to France. The provisional government then offered the crown to Prince Leopold of Hohenzollern-Sigmaringen,[30] the brother of the prince who became King Carol of Rumania. Bismarck had urged the nomination. Paris reacted violently to the prospect of Hohenzollern encirclement from the Rhine to the Pyrenees. The French informed William of Prussia that the situation could not be tolerated, because it amounted to a revival of Charles V's empire! While French newspapers called for war, King William advised Leopold to decline the Spanish crown.

The French were ecstatic. A great victory had been won over Prussia. The duke of Gramont, the foreign minister, was not content with that. He wished to humiliate King William; and on July 12, 1870, Gramont sent a telegram to his ambassador at Ems, where William was vacationing. An assurance was demanded that Leopold's candidacy would not be renewed. William was annoyed and refused politely, relaying his own draft telegram to Bismarck at Berlin. Bismarck had been disappointed over his sovereign's initial concession, probably because he wanted war with France.[31]

He now seized this second chance, altering the King's "Ems Dispatch" by omissions and then giving the reduced, blunter, Prussian "ultimatum" to the newspapers. Authority to release the telegram had come with the message. But Bismarck altered it to arouse public opinion. And he did so after putting to General von Moltke

a few questions . . . as to the state of his confidence in the extent of our preparations, especially as to the time they would still require in order to meet this sudden risk of war. He answered . . . he expected no advantage to us by deferring its outbreak . . . he regarded a rapid outbreak as, on the whole, more favorable to us. . . .[32]

The Paris press reacted with cries of war. Thus it was that France actually became the aggressor, duped by Bismarck into a declaration of war on July 19, 1870. No greater miscalculation was made by any power in the nineteenth century. Napoleon thought his armies would cross the Rhine and get support from the south Germans, as well as help from Austria and Italy. The south Germans sided instead with Prussia. On July 20 Austria declared

---

30. A Catholic branch of the Prussian royal family.
31. In his *Reflections and Reminiscences* (pp. 184ff.) he wrote that he had decided to resign. While Bismarck was at dinner with Generals von Roon and von Moltke, the dispatch came in cipher.
32. Bismarck, *Reflections and Reminiscences* pp. 185–186.

neutrality. Italy sought unsuccessfully to persuade Austria to join in aid to France, after a brief delay for preparations. Thus Italy too was officially neutral on July 20. Meanwhile, the war minister Leboeuf, who had bragged that France could mobilize 400,000 men within two weeks, could do nothing of the kind. The French mobilization was chaotic; and, when the Emperor arrived at Metz to command the thrust across the Rhine into south Germany, reality caught up with him.

The Prussian army was superior in numbers, equipment, and leadership. Supported by Bavaria, Baden, and Württemberg, the main force of King William repulsed attacks at Saarbrücken, before crossing the Rhine and bottling up the main French force at Metz. After heavy losses in Alsace and Lorraine, the main army under Napoleon and Marshal MacMahon surrendered at Sedan, on September 2, 1870, barely six weeks after the war had begun. The Emperor was captured along with 106,000 troops. At Metz 170,000 surrendered. Revolution broke out in Paris in September, where the Third Republic was declared. Patriots under Gambetta fought on for a few months, but an armistice offered by Prussia was signed at the end of January 1871. On March 1 the National Assembly accepted the peace terms, by a vote of 546 to 107.

The swiftness of Prussia's triumph over France stunned Europe, while denying to Italy and Austria the time needed to prepare an effective intervention. Britain had thought France the stronger party. And Russia was pleased by the events; in October the Czar declared the 1856 treaty clauses about the Black Sea null and void. Bismarck was able to dictate terms: a cession of Alsace and eastern Lorraine to Prussia and a French payment of five billion francs to indemnify Prussia for war costs, with an occupation of certain provinces in eastern France as a guarantee against payment of the debt.[33] To cap it all, Bismarck staged the crowning of William I as kaiser, or emperor, of Germany, having already gained the adherence of the southern states to the new federal constitution on January 1, 1871. The ceremony of coronation took place in Louis XIV's Hall of Mirrors at Versailles. Austria now had no choice but to pledge cooperation with the victor.

Europe, recovered from the paralysis induced by the terrible swiftness of the Prussian victory, now had to make sense of what had happened and why.

Certainly, an epoch in European history had ended. The myth of French power had been shattered. A new balance of power existed. France could no longer master central Europe by playing off Prussia and Austria. Nor could Prussia and Britain use the "balance" of France and Prussia to make the Rhine a pivot point for European security. The victory at Sedan in 1870 had set the seal to the superiority demonstrated in 1866 at Sadowa. France now faced the problem of defending its territory against the most powerful country on the European continent. Moreover, the defeat of Napoleon III overthrew the French Second Empire.[34] France reverted to republicanism as a consequence of the war between nations; and the new Paris radicalism re-created in the monarchies a fear that 1848 would come again, thus helping Bismarck. Thiers was unable to gain support for a conference to "mediate" the harsh peace terms.

33. Some regard the peace as Bismarck's great error. The demand for Alsace-Lorraine, in their view, made France Bismarck's irreconcilable foe and forced on him the diplomacy needed to contain French "revenge."
34. Formally dissolved on September 4, 1870. Napoleon III went to exile in London, where he died in 1873.

The ultimate blow to French pride and the culmination of the German nationalist movement was the proclamation of the German Empire in the Hall of Mirrors at Versailles on January 18, 1871. With Paris beseiged and Napoleon III a prisoner in Germany, William I presided over the creation of the Second Reich, while Bismarck and the military theoretician Helmuth von Moltke stood at his feet. Although William concurred with Bismarck's authoritarian ideas, they both incorporated many liberals into the government, and significant social progress was achieved. Until his death in 1888 the Emperor was content to leave government affairs almost entirely in Bismarck's hands. Staatsbibliothek, Berlin.

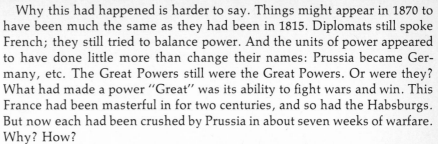

Why this had happened is harder to say. Things might appear in 1870 to have been much the same as they had been in 1815. Diplomats still spoke French; they still tried to balance power. And the units of power appeared to have done little more than change their names: Prussia became Germany, etc. The Great Powers still were the Great Powers. Or were they? What had made a power "Great" was its ability to fight wars and win. This France had been masterful in for two centuries, and so had the Habsburgs. But now each had been crushed by Prussia in about seven weeks of warfare. Why? How?

The answer lies in sets of statistics about changes in population and measures of economic resources and the degree to which political structures were altered because of developments underlying such data. Until the twentieth century, the basic strength of a country was in its infantry, despite the rapid deployment of artillery. For reasons we shall demonstrate soon, Prussia—Germany in 1870—had done more to "catch up" in the race of industrialization than the other Continental powers. Germany's infantry was therefore better equipped for war than were the ground forces of the other European states.

Before turning to the shifts of economic organization in Europe, however, we may well ask whether the period of national unification and revolutionary unrest did not coincide with the shaping of a new culture as well.

BIBLIOGRAPHY

BINKLEY, R. C. *Realism and Nationalism, 1852–1871.** New York: Harper & Row Publishers, 1935). A now dated synthesis, still useful for quick survey purposes. A more fragmented but modern survey is in Volume 10 of the New Cambridge Modern History: *The Zenith of European Power* (Cambridge: Cambridge University Press, 1964), covering the years 1830–1871.

CRAIG, GORDON A. *The Politics of the German Army.** Oxford: Clarendon Press, 1964. Chapter 6 is essential for an understanding of Bismarck's era.

GOOCH, BRISON D. *The Reign of Napoleon III.** Chicago: Rand McNally & Co., 1969. A good brief treatment of France in the second imperial era.

JELAVICH, BARBARA. *The Habsburg Empire in European Affairs, 1814–1918.** Chicago: Rand McNally & Co., 1969. See especially Chapter 2 in this outstanding survey of a difficult subject.

KANN, ROBERT A. *The Multinational Empire.* 2 vols. New York: Columbia University Press, 1950. The standard English work on the Habsburg "nationality" questions.

PFLANZE, OTTO. *Bismarck and the Development of Germany.* Princeton: Princeton University Press, 1963. A good survey of the period of German unification; should be read together with H. Friedjung, *The Struggle for Supremacy in Germany, 1859–1866* (New York: Russell & Russell, 1966), and also Michael Howard, *The Franco-Prussian War* (London: Rupert Hart-Davis, 1961), an exciting military history.

SETON-WATSON, HUGH. *The Decline of Imperial Russia.** London: Methuen, 1952. Especially good on Alexander II.

SMITH, DENIS MACK. *Cavour and Garibaldi.* New York: Cambridge University Press, 1964. A major revisionary work contrasting two leaders and two styles of political action in the struggle to unify Italy; see also Smith's *Garibaldi* (New York: Alfred A. Knopf, 1956).

TAYLOR, A. J. P. *The Struggle for Mastery in Europe, 1848–1918.* Oxford: Clarendon Press, 1969. The first 200 pages of this brilliant and provocative book are basic to our narrative.

WILLIAMS, R. L. *Gaslight and Shadow: The World of Napoleon III.** New York: The Macmillan Company, 1957. A very favorable view of the Emperor.

Asterisk indicates a paperbound edition.

10

SOCIETY AND THE STREETS: THE NEW CULTURE

Living in the nineteenth century, in a time of universal suffrage, democracy, liberalism, we asked ourselves whether what are called "the lower classes" do not have a right to the novel; whether these lower depths of society, the "people," must remain under a literary ban. . . . We began to wonder whether tragedy, the traditional literary form of . . . a vanished society was really dead for all time; whether, in a country without castes and a legal aristocracy, the sufferings of the poor and humble . . . could make us cry as easily as those [tears] which are shed on high. . . .
EDMOND AND JULES DE GONCOURT, *Germinie Lacerteux* (1864)[1]

THE SHIFT IN PERSPECTIVE: CULTURAL REVOLUTION

The French brothers Goncourt wrote history, art criticism, plays, novels, literary diaries,[2] and newspaper accounts of Parisian life. They were patrons of men like Turgenev and Émile Zola, who heeded their call to abandon stories that "pretend to take place in 'society'" and write about what "comes from the streets." The Goncourts' reasons for issuing the challenge to change the perspective in literature derived from their belief that artistic work must be rooted in social reality—indeed, that all forms of culture must be so rooted. And they assigned to the novel, which was then mature as a form but growing and expanding in its influence, the task of "social inquiry." Artists and writers—all serious intellectuals—must make efforts to reveal to the world at large what the orders of Catholic nuns saw every day in the slums, hospitals, and almshouses of Europe.

The preface to the novel *Germinie Lacerteux* was thus a manifesto of the *realism* which after 1848 successfully displaced Romanticism as the dominant mode of thought and expression in Europe. The Goncourts' demand that the novel assume "the methods and duties of science" reveals also the prestige scientific method had among Europeans in the 1860s. And it stood in the sharpest contrast to the tone of Romantic revolutionary ideas, for example those of the young Russian emigrant in Paris Alexander Herzen (1812–1870).

A voluntary exile from Russia, Herzen had arrived in Paris in time to see the savage slaughter of radi-

1. From the authors' preface, as quoted in Roland S. Stromberg, *Realism, Naturalism, and Symbolism* (New York: Harper & Row, Publishers, Torchbooks, 1968), pp. 69–70.
2. The famous Goncourt Journal. Edmond left most of his fortune to found the Académie Goncourt, which annually awards a prize, the Prix Goncourt, still one of the great honors in French literary life.

cals during the June insurrection.[3] In despair, Herzen cast aside his "last illusions," compounded of hopes and faith, and asked what would be the outcome of this new madness. He ventured a prophecy:

The world which stands in the way of the new man, preventing him from living and establishing the future, will fall. And this is splendid! So, long live chaos and destruction! *Vive la mort*! And let the future come![4]

To base a scientific view of the future on a disciplined analysis of the past and an adequate description of the present was the challenge given to thought and expression by the revolutions of the nineteenth century. The political challenge matured in 1848, when the outlines of industrial civilization were already clear in England. Herzen understood that no man "can remain the same" after the blow struck against the working classes of Paris by the republicans. But Herzen could not yet perceive the future, and he advised against the search for quick answers to the puzzles put before people by reality. His chief conclusion was that writers "must fight against the specific falsehoods" encountered in daily life.

This was a creed not too distant from the rule of writing adopted by the novelist Charles Dickens. Nor would Engels have disagreed in 1844, when he studied the condition of the English working class and wrote a great descriptive account of life in the first industrial society.[5]

There were, of course, some who went beyond realism, beyond description and analysis, to philosophy: the French scholar and man of letters Ernest Renan (1823–1892), who made science his religion, deriving from it a certain sense of the moral and physical foundations of civilization; and the German refugee working in London, Karl Marx, who drew from his critique of bourgeois society and capitalism a doctrine of what alienated human beings from the order of industrial society. Socialism is therefore as important an element of nineteenth-century thought and expression as Romanticism and realism.

The socialism of Marx looked to the streets for a hearing, as did the works of writers like the Goncourts. And the change in viewpoint marked a decisive break with all concepts of "culture" confined to aristocratic courts or bourgeois salons. Elitism had always been part of the ambiance of the dominant art forms, especially painting, sculpture, and music. The novel was one of the chief products of popular culture. So, we intend no slight to the other arts if here we concentrate chiefly on literature, in order to get at the culture of the majority of people.[6] Moreover, we must pay attention to working-class culture as well as middle-class culture. Indeed, the development of these two "cultures," in competition with surviving aristocratic patterns of taste, thought, and expression, was as revolutionary in the history of expression as democracy and industrialization were for government and the shape of society.

To speak of a cultural revolution, however, poses some problems to which we must address ourselves. The democratic ideology produced as a result of the eighteenth-century revolutions in Europe and America transformed Western politics everywhere by 1870. Neither violence nor fraud, much less the weight of tradition, could keep peoples from experiments

3. June 23–26, 1848.
4. *From the Other Shore*, as quoted in Stromberg, *Realism, Naturalism, and Symbolism*, pp. 8–9.
5. *Conditions of the Working Class in England*, published in 1845.
6. The roots of modern art in the nineteenth century are discussed elsewhere; so, too, the roots of modern music, which remained the most "courtly" art: see Chapter 14.

with self-government. In a similar way, industrialization transformed the nature of economic life and social patterns related to how people get and spend. As we shall soon show, the transit of the economic revolution to the European continent had implications for the democratization of life there. While the relationship is complex, there can be little doubt of the significance of the new economy in shaping forms of organization that stressed mass participation.

Nor, we think, can there be well-founded doubts that the widened circle of politics and the needs of the new industrial organization of society transformed ways of looking at the world. The extension of education, especially literacy, more widely in society was essential to the new politics and the new economics. Limited groups no longer dominated either the creation or the consumption of thought and expression. The changes in basic institutions produced by industrialization reached into the family and the school, creating new demands for entertainment, edification, and the basic equipment of social mobility in an industrial democracy: literacy. The net result was a revolution in culture, a basic change in the character of consciousness.

In this chapter our objective is to indicate some aspects of this transformation. Perhaps the most basic one concerns the genesis of what critics call realism or, often, the new realism.

Western thought and expression in the Christian era had been dominated by three main notions of creativity: that art imitated the mind of God, or embodied some ideal beauty or "form" imitated by the artist, or expressed human feelings about visible nature. Medieval arts used allegory or other symbolic means to express divine imitation. The doctrine of creativity based on the imitation of ideal beauty dominated classical art and its various revivals, whether in the classicism of the Renaissance or that of the Enlightenment. The tendency to add to the observation of visible nature human emotion, with a purpose to show things not as they are but as they *ought to be*, had its main influence spread over several centuries. The principal phase of the "Romantic" movement began in the last quarter of the eighteenth century and reached its apogee in the 1830s.

The main thrust of Romanticism was to moralize, to stimulate exemplary feelings, and to instruct the passions. But, unlike the earlier modes of expression, Romantic art and literature relied on the creative activity of the mind itself. It did not look either to the divine world or to some "idea" outside human thought, but instead expressed the creative imagination of artists, giving a free reign to their feelings, making their inner world prevail over any external one. How—and why—Romanticism gave way to realism is, therefore, the central concern here.

ROMANTICISM: THE LAST PHASE

Before the rise of the realism called for by the Goncourt brothers, the reaction against Enlightenment consolidated the style of Romanticism. In the first generation (ca. 1780) Rousseau, Goethe, Wordsworth, and their followers clarified their distrust of reason and abstract thought. The mood in literature and in painting was one of self-exploration. Romantics wished to express their feelings and toward that end cultivated solitude and reverie. The key to a better world was introspection, and the Romantics had little impulse to analyze the new society already outlined by 1800. Egoism flourished, and so did historical nostalgia. Artists and writers who found the world of political and economic revolution unacceptable created in their works a melancholy sense that the past, especially the distant past, was more "natural" than the present.

There is a quality of escapism in Romantic creativity, a preference for illusion, even delusion, in place of ordinary reality. In a sense, therefore, Romanticism still clings to the *supernatural* reality beyond ordinary experience. Ordinary men and women, with only the ordinary power of seeing, describe reality as it appears to be. Artists, in Romantic doctrine, have exceptional perceptions, and depict a superior reality.

For the work of artists, the insistence on superior perception, on communicating what ought to be, had practical consequences. Romanticism was basically an elitist movement in literature and painting, intended for audiences of the upper classes well enough educated to grasp what lay behind the surface of things. Romantic painters, for example, show a preference for subjects taken from the romances of medieval chivalry. Even though they employed an idealized style based on natural-looking representations, they generally ignored subjects familiar to ordinary people from everyday life. The subjects favored were those with grandeur, scenes able to inspire virtue and nobility of sentiment, or at least able to conjure up the sense of a past better than the present.

Moreover, Romantics drew their inspiration from verbal sources, from a heritage of literature, often mythology, rather than from visual sources. Appreciation of Romantic works therefore depended on one's recognition of their often ancient sources, or on one's familiarity with the history of a distant society. The Romantic style derived its meaningfulness to a large extent from the appeal it made to well-educated people, themselves perhaps wistful and concerned about the decline of aristocratic grace before the rise of industry. Because the arts in general are intense forms of communication, every element in a work which is not part of ordinary experience, or which requires special learning for its understanding, restricts the audience for whom active appreciation is possible. Some examples will make this point clear.

A Romantic painter might depict a ruined classical temple, perhaps to suggest the frailty and pathos of what was once a place of worship. Distance made a thing exotic, while also making it sublime in contrast to modernity. The same sensitivity showed itself in architecture; rich men put up ruins, because the picturesque linked the present to a past less ugly, less corrupted by technology. The English landowner and industrialist William Beckford built a "medieval" castle called Fonthill Abbey in 1800, but it was poorly constructed, falling to pieces a few years later. Beckford was pleased, however, because the ruin seemed to connect him to the past he had lost. This love for revivalism was also typical of the Romantic style.

Concretely, we may see the mood cultivated in works by the painters Turner,[7] Runge,[8] and Delacroix,[9] and also in those of Blake[10] and Friedrich.[11]

Turner was at first a watercolor artist who lived by making pictures of landscapes and architectural monuments with stress on picturesqueness. By 1799 he had begun experiments with light and the effects of space on the atmosphere of paintings. The shimmering, haunting quality of his technique found its perfect Romantic subject in Venice and the architectural remnants of its grandeur. His taste for drama and emotion also found good material in the powerful suggestions created in scenes of war and disaster: a

7. J. M. W. Turner, 1775–1851.
8. Philipp Otto Runge, 1777–1810.
9. Ferdinand Victor Eugène Delacroix, 1798–1863.
10. William Blake, 1757–1827.
11. Caspar David Friedrich, 1774–1840.

line of fire ships perceived through a haze, or a shipwreck. In his seascapes Turner's Romanticism is most obvious in the dramatic, luminous way he makes the forces of nature visible on canvas.

The German painter Friedrich was a landscape painter whose canvases had a haunting, ethereal, and melancholy quality that contemporaries found disturbing. Friedrich seemed to worship nature, while giving to objects in it a personal grandeur capable of dwarfing man. His paintings often have in them tiny human figures in the foreground, sometimes with their backs toward the viewer. We see mysterious mountains shrouded in mist or illuminated by a hidden moon or dominantly present rainbow; and we know that the figure in the picture sees what we see more fully. The attitude of people is rapt, for example, in Friedrich's *Man Looking at Mountains, with Rainbow*.[12] The emotion aroused is one of awe at nature's grandeur and the cosmic insignificance of man. The thought was expressed in verse by Coleridge:

> O dread and silent mount! I gazed upon thee,
> Still thou, still present to the bodily sense,
> Didst vanish from my thought: entranced in prayer
> I worshipped the Invisible alone.[13]

12. Turner did the same sort of thing: e.g., his *Buttermere*.
13. As quoted in Lord Clark of Saltwood, *Civilization* (New York: Harper & Row, Publishers, 1969), p. 276.

Turner's atmospheric style in which the physically concrete world dissolves in a flood of light was perfectly suited to capture the mystery of Venice. The Dogana and Santa Maria della Salute *was painted late in his career when his technique was most radical. Although many laughed at his colorful canvases, Turner's observations were not lost on later innovators such as the impressionists who felt similar motivations. Politically impotent and physically decayed, Turner's beloved Venice was a favorite city of Romantic and Victorian artists and writers. The critic John Ruskin, who devoted much of his life to defending Turner's art, sought solutions for the ills of his contemporary industrial world by studying the art and society of medieval Venice. National Gallery of Art, Washington, D.C.*

Romantic egoism often dwelt on purely personal attitudes of yearning to know the infinite. Philipp Otto Runge's *Four Phases of the Day* tried to put man in a changing natural setting in order to suggest in painting what Coleridge's poem is explicit on: one man's relationship to the universe. Blake, the English visionary poet and artist, in words and on canvas, showed the Romantic love of mystery, ruins, and the *personal* experience of truth. He claimed that the illustrated poems he printed were revealed to him by his dead brother Robert. He also said his work clarified the fact that sense experience was sham, the mystical envelope which hid from the uninitiated the spiritual reality concealed within. Using color and form unrealistically, as in *Shadows of Men in Fleeting Bands upon the Wind*, Blake elaborated the ultraesoteric view that art departed from ordinary experience and depended on people with visionary understanding.

Delacroix's work also illustrates the main features of all Romantic art. The French painter was the successor to Géricault,[14] who had used conventions of form and color borrowed from Renaissance masters—Raphael and Michelangelo especially. But Géricault's themes—shipwrecks, madmen, slaves—were treated in a rhetorical manner which was entirely Romantic and intended to arouse emotional responses. So, too, Delacroix's subjects were typically Romantic. His first painting of any consequence was *Dante and Virgil Crossing the Styx*, a theme at once literary, Gothic, and mythological.[15]

Like so many other Romantics, Delacroix also painted "revolutionary" subjects: *The Massacre of Chios*, an episode in the Greek struggle for independence, is a good example. What Delacroix painted, however, was no document of social realism; his work is instead a wistful, compassionate statement of liberalism, the sort of sentiment Romantic poets like Byron and Shelley made in verse, and the kind of emotion Beethoven wished to stimulate in his opera *Fidelio*, in which political prisoners are freed from a jail in the final scene.[16] By 1830, Delacroix's hope for liberty had taken a new direction. In response to the July Revolution, he executed a painting of National Guardsmen and also one entitled *Liberty Leading the People*. The allegorical figure of Liberty dominates the scene, while the dying fighters merely serve as stepping-stones for her advance.[17]

From 1830, however, Delacroix withdrew from the bourgeois, materialistic society of Paris. Like so many other Romantics, he found the age he lived in unacceptable—too crass, too common, too dedicated to the ordinary. Escapism dominated his work, which was now thematically based on the poetry of Shakespeare, Byron, and Scott, the sublime animals of the

14. Jean Louis Géricault, 1791–1824.
15. Based on the myth of the river Styx, crossed by the dead, and on Dante's *Divine Comedy*.
16. Géricault painted a "liberation" scene; Turner painted the slave trade.
17. See Chapter 6 for this illustration.

German Romantic painting reached its apogee in the work of the landscape artist Caspar David Friedrich. Like Turner in England, Friedrich completely overturned past artistic conventions, as is obvious in his masterpiece of 1821, The Wreck of the Hope. *The scene refers to an actual shipwreck in the Bering Strait, but this factual incident is merely a pretext to make a universal statement of man's condition. Whereas earlier painters might have concentrated on the ship itself and the pathos of the victims, Friedrich delineates every inch of the jagged, inhuman ice floe and shows only a glimpse of the sinking ship. Contemporaries were stunned by the artist's new vision, and one viewer compared the experience to having one's eyelids cut away. Kunsthalle, Hamburg; Photo Kleinhempel.*

The theme of a tiger attacking a horse was a favorite of the great English animal painter Stubbs, and his work, along with fighting animal scenes by Rubens and Gros, may have inspired Delacroix to develop the subject in numerous versions including this watercolor. Delacroix's profound feeling for the graceful beauty of the animal world was heightened by his trip to Morocco in 1832, an event which lasted less than six months but crystallized the artist's vision for the rest of his life. In the strong light of North Africa the painter witnessed ferocious horse fights which he recorded in his sketchbooks for future reference. Louvre.

Paris zoo, or the emotions inspired in him by the Arabs of Morocco.[18] His *Lion Hunt* is representative of late Romantic subject matter; so, too, is his picture *Attila*, where the barbarian king is shown trampling on the classical civilization of the West.

Delacroix showed in this work the estrangement, the despair, of the Romantic artists, who needed to escape the corruption they saw in Europe. For, to them, the coming age of industry was a blight on humanity, incompatible with dignity, nobility, and serenity. Delacroix's later contemporary, Paul Gauguin (1848–1903), actually made the break physically, seeking in Tahiti the refuge from modern times which Delacroix found in poetry, animals, and the simple, natural Arab life of North Africa.

Early nineteenth-century painting offers evidence of the gap opening between the aristocratic legacy of culture and the new culture of the middle classes who were coming to power. Their lives and their scale of values were more earthbound, embracing as they did the new materialism of industry and profit. And their lives and values found artistic expression in the developing realism we see first in satirical works: Daumier's observations of Louis Philippe and the Paris bourgeoisie, or Gustave Doré's lithograph[19] *Men Setting Their Watches by the Noon Gun*. The middle-class concern for time contrasted with Delacroix's sense of timelessness. Romantics looked on the new men as barbarians or philistines, but we need not accept their view of the new energy let loose in society.

18. Which he visited in 1834.
19. A print made from a stone on which the subject is drawn.

The poet Robert Burns saw the great ironworks at Carron[20] and compared the sight to hell:

> We cam na here to view your works,
> In hopes to be mair wise,
> But only, lest we gang to Hell,
> It may be nae surprise.[21]

Others, however, saw a terrible and fierce beauty in the mills and in the things made from iron and steel. The painter de Loutherbourg made the great works at Coalbrookdale, belching fire and smoke, a matter for art. The painter Wright of Derby[22] painted classical subjects, but he also did a work entitled *Experiment with an Air Pump*. And one of the great English portraits of the eighteenth century is his almost photographic picture of Arkwright, the inventor of the spinning frame, sitting near the symbols of the new age—a rack of white cotton spools. Moreover, if in the sixteenth century Vasari wrote *Lives of the Painters*, in the industrial century Samuel Smiles would write *Lives of the Engineers*.[23]

It is difficult to deny to the great engineers the honor of having created beautiful things. The painter and poet in Thomas Telford (1757–1834)

20. Founded in 1780.
21. Quoted in Lord Clark, *Civilization*, p. 321.
22. Joseph Wright, 1734–1797.
23. Smiles was a writer on morals, business, technology, and the general round of middle-class life; he lived from 1812 to 1904.

The Third Class Carriage of 1862 is typical of Honoré Daumier's finest work in which he freely explored the character of working-class people; his perception and sympathy is comparable to Rembrandt's mature period, which Daumier greatly admired. The artist has captured the mood of an anonymous modern crowd in which each individual is withdrawn into a private world. The rough, sketchy quality of this painting was daring for the time and increases its strong visual impact. The Metropolitan Museum of Art, the H. O. Havemeyer Collection. Bequest of Mrs. H. O. Havemeyer.

would never have earned fame, but his drawing of the design for London Bridge (1801) predicted the grace of iron arching over water, a feat Telford achieved in 1820 when his Menai Bridge became the first suspension bridge, a form not yet superseded. Telford's bridges, in combination with the tunnels of Isambard Kingdom Brunel (1806–1859), not only inspired artists who admired the new realities.[24] Bridges and tunnels brought the railroads from London to the most distant, hitherto inaccessible, provinces. So, too, did Brunel's steamship *Great Eastern* (1858) revolutionize ocean travel to America, by freeing travelers from the winds. And in America the engineer Roebling in 1867 made his design for the magnificent Brooklyn Bridge, in which the poet Walt Whitman saw the shape of the new age, long before painters created in it "modern art":

> Shapes of factories, arsenals, foundries, markets
> Shapes of the two-threaded tracks of railroads,
> Shapes of the sleepers of bridges, vast
>   frameworks, girders, arches.

THE CULTURE OF THE WORKING CLASSES

One feature of the new culture deserving special attention is the relationship between its development and the existence of the working classes.

As early as 1868 the English painter Ford Madox Brown (1821–1893), who had earlier done such Romantic works as *Bringing Harold's Body to the Conqueror* (1844), painted *Work*. The center is filled with the activity of ordinary working men, digging a hole in a London street, while flitting about the edges are the elements of the city's diverse society. In France, the lives of working-class people were seized on by the French founders of social realism in painting: Gustave Courbet (1819–1877) and Jean François Millet (1814–1875). Both painters had been revolutionaries in 1848. In 1849 Courbet painted a stone breaker at work, and in 1850 he did his famous *Burial at Ornans*, in which social hierarchy disappears. Ordinary people stand in a row, all on the same plane, grieving together. Millet made unsentimental drawings of the French workers, urban and rural, with no effort to place them in a scene. The impact derives wholly from the subject, the common man or woman, in the round of daily life.

The realism of common people in everyday life had thus entered the tradition of the painter again.[25] Even earlier, as we shall soon see, working-class lives had become the subject matter of writers, especially Dickens. But before we examine the new realism in bourgeois literature, we must try to place working-class culture itself, as it developed in the industrial age which had begun.

Quite apart from any literary culture to which the laboring classes aspired, in preindustrial European society working people exhibited certain forms of traditional collective behavior. Industrialization and the rise of popular education came at the expense of these forms of collective action, but not without producing often violent resistance to preserve traditional ways. Then, as industrialization and literacy pointed the way, workers' violence shifted from *protest* and "primitive" rebellion to the actual *contest* for power itself. The curve of change spanned the French Revolution on one

---

24. The celebration dinner given at the halfway point in Brunel's Thames Tunnel was painted.
25. It had flourished in Brueghel and Bosch centuries before, as well as in eighteenth-century genre painting.

By the sheer force of his boisterous personality, Gustave Courbet did more than anyone else to force realism into the public view and conscience. Shaken by the revolutionary atmosphere of the late 1840s, Courbet left Paris for his small hometown of Ornans where he sought to renew his self-identity. Burial at Ornans of 1850 is his greatest work from this period, and it shows his audacity for daring to elevate a common event to the level of great art. Although it appears to be a straightforward and rather naïvely composed scene, the artist actually makes subtle borrowings from folk art, which was just beginning to influence the realists. Beneath the placid surface appearance of unity, these stone-faced mourners seethe with the tensions which were growing in rural France. Bulloz.

side and the 1871 Paris Commune on the other, with the shift itself becoming pronounced in the 1840s.

Indeed, as late as the 1840s the main forms of collective violence by workers in France were traditional; they were also reactionary: the tax revolt, food riots, resistance to military drafts, machine breaking by skilled handicraft workers anxious to protect craft jobs, and peasant invasions of fields or forest preserves to protest against aristocratic ownership. These violent protests existed side by side with nonviolent working-class agitation, but we get more evidence when the protesters against coercion employ violence than in other circumstances. And by the second half of the nineteenth century the character of the agitation had changed sufficiently to warrant the view that protest had organized itself to the point of becoming a purposeful contest for power.

In other words, one of the most important shifts observable in popular culture is in the types of expressions of discontent among workingmen. The most primitive forms of behavior were brawls among rival groups of artisans, feuds among the followers and dependent peasants of powerful landlords, and simple fights among villagers or members of small communal groups. The emphasis here is on the *communal* character of the behavior because people tended to identify themselves with primary communities in the centuries before nationalist mass movements appeared. Indeed, it was the growing power of "national" monarchies which often provoked the "reactionary" forms of violent behavior already enumerated. The struggle for sovereignty over large polities enlarged the framework of resistance to change—from the opposition to local leaders to that directed against royal tax gatherers, conscription masters, and economic administrators advocating a shift in the use of land and other resources.

Faced with the deployment of large-scale forces threatening the traditional forms of social organization—by railroad building, for example, or a state policy of land enclosure—resisters had to abandon mere communal behavior. It became necessary to organize artificially, by voluntary association, across the lines of village or neighborhood. Thus, the era of industrialization was also the era in which the maximum threat to tradition existed.

The railroad might bring cheap grain into a region and introduce manufactured goods imported from abroad at prices lower than the products of local handicraft industries. The old experiences based on family, religious congregations, and community were giving way to secret societies, "trade" unions, and even political "parties." Increasingly, we read of early-nineteenth-century "associations," where once we encountered only communal groups.

The change corresponds to a massive shift in the routine of working life. Before the onset of industrialization and the bureaucratic state, the behavior of laboring people tended to center on the natural rhythms of small communities—local market days, harvesttime, churchgoing. These focuses of collective peaceable behavior had therefore served to rally violence, when it was deemed necessary. But it was in the nature of these collectives that they were spontaneous, undisciplined, and also unscheduled. Perhaps the food riot on a market day is the best example, or resistance to the collection of a church tithe at harvesttime. Between such behavior and the planned, disciplined "marches" of the English Chartists a gulf yawns, with regard to scale, setting, and purpose.

Industrialization and urbanization produce the contests of associations slowly, however. This is because both processes transfer large numbers of people *out* of their traditional collectives where communal agitation required no organization. Once in the strange new setting of the city, the forever agricultural laborer or craft worker took time to acquire a new collective identity. The factory did not at once seem a boon, nor did the mine or the neighborhoods in which working-class people were packed. In time, however, the process we have sketched in England appeared everywhere.

It is obvious that in France the factory, mine, and neighborhood had encouraged new collective identities by the 1830s and 1840s. Common conditions of work and living fashioned a sense of common interests and also encouraged the setting up of voluntary associations to express common needs through joint actions. In fast-growing towns like Paris, Nantes, Bordeaux, and Lyons the result was evident in organized demonstrations. But these same towns also show how slowly the new organizations come to play a leading role. In the revolutions of the 1830–1848 period, especially in the Paris insurrections, most violent people were drawn from the small workshops and the handicraft classes.

If the immediate effects of the movement toward *associations* were felt only slowly in the city, perhaps because the rise of literacy was a requirement for effective organization, it was true in the countryside that the early nineteenth century was a period of "primitive" rebellion. The increasing urban demand for food drew off rural stores into the prosperous cities. Communal rioting against the withdrawal of food from local markets was prominent among the problems the French government faced in the 1840s. The road to the age of *strikes* and urban revolt was paved with cobblestones torn from village squares by hungry rebels! It is especially significant for understanding the rise of the urban popular culture, then, to grasp what lay behind it.

This was nothing less than the transformation of peasant society. Industrial culture required that land be treated as a mobile commodity, that it pass into the hands of men willing to destroy local communities in order to "farm for the market" in towns, and that both these ends be accomplished at the expense of peasants. Long-range trends which we have already discussed at length had weakened precapitalist landed elites over much of Europe. State policy helped reduce the class of small peasant proprietors into rural wage laborers, especially after 1770 in Britain, France, Prussia, Ireland, and most of the rest of Europe.

This was done in part by the revolutionary relaxation of "feudal" restrictions on personal freedom and mobility, beginning with the voluntary Danish abolition of the 1780s and stretching down to the 1860s in Russia and Rumania. The repeated failure of crops in the 1840s and the inability of small farms to sustain a growing peasant population completed the task. And the mass migration of peasants and handicraft workers overseas after 1848 was one movement produced by the developments also responsible for the new mass culture.

It is not surprising, given the foregoing, that often the earliest view we have of the mental life of the working classes is in scenes of violence. We catch the Parisian sans-culottes in 1793–1794, decked out in their red woolen caps, hunting down the aristocratic relics of feudalism. They insisted on the language of equality, preferring *citoyen* (citizen) to *monsieur* (mister), and the familiar *tu* rather than the polite *vous* in speech. The sans-culotte existed on a mental diet of proletarian pamphlets, but the reading skills of most must have been rudimentary at best. In their political clubs the sans-culottes appointed literate persons to read publicly from Rousseau, the radical pamphleteers, and the daily newspapers. While it may be true that the presses could not keep up with the demand for cheap papers, the implication of the existence of public readers seems to be widespread illiteracy.

Yet the literacy of some workers clearly was important in generating what we may call working-class consciousness among French workers. In the working-class riots of the 1830s the evidence for popular literacy is again vague. But the fact that students played a leading role in the rebellion of 1834 in Lyons may suggest again the "leadership" role of the literate over the illiterate, or what the police called the "madmen" led by "badmen" in the 1830–1831 riots. Occasionally, a worker was arrested with a well-thumbed "manual of the duties of a republican" in his pocket.[26] In 1849 about 87 percent of all adult males in Paris were illiterate. By 1850, however, the crowds in French riots took on a distinctly *ideological* cast, especially among industrial groups; and this may be in part a response to a widening literacy among workers.

This does not mean that the "common man" came to power in the mid–nineteenth century. But it does mean that the mental culture of workers was being transformed along with their economic circumstances. In 1848 the most concentrated arrest records in the June insurrection were among the most advanced industries: of 11,744 workers arrested, there were 1,045 clothing workers, 1,334 metal workers, and 2,077 construction workers. These were the insurgent workers in France as a whole again in 1871, and it thus appears that the semiskilled workers were both more literate and more discontent than the less skilled industrial laborers.

Across the Channel in England the literacy of the working classes is easier to evaluate. Qualitatively, the self-taught workers were not as well educated as the school-taught. But as early as 1800 there is plenty of evidence in the inventories of books among property left by workers to support the view of a rapid spread of literacy. Although "readers" and "orators" were frequently appointed by clubs and associations, and the common ballad singer and "patterner" were still important sources of

---

26. See the analysis in Charles Tilly, "How Protest Modernized in France," in W. O. Aydelotte et al., eds., *The Dimensions of Quantitative Research in History* (Princeton: Princeton University Press, 1972), pp. 192–255.

information among English industrial laborers, the book and newspaper were becoming the main source of mental life for laborers in England long before literacy became widespread among the working classes in the rest of Europe. It is therefore important to look closely at the rise of literacy and its relationship to culture in the first industrial society.

As soon as we do this, we learn how misleading mere literacy can be if used as a guide to the role men and women play in shaping mental culture. The 1870 act establishing school boards to complete a network of elementary schools in Britain led in 1876 to another act making universal elementary schooling compulsory. These acts were in turn amplifications of the 1862 Revised Code. This code applied to tax-supported schools, providing payments to them according to the *minimum standards* attained by students in them. These minimum standards involved reading a simple newspaper paragraph, writing such a passage from dictation, and demonstrating basic knowledge of the arithmetic of sums and fractions. What this standard meant in practice by 1870 we may estimate by two related facts. Most children left school before they were eleven years old. And, as recently as 1861, of the 2,500,000 children in minimum standard schools,[27] the average duration of attendance was about two years.

The problem of working-class literacy is thus one of rudimentary skills in a society which reserved further education for other classes. Even having the skill to read and exercising it were different matters. Not only was there no training in handling abstract ideas and consecutive argument for working-class children. Most workers could not spend money to buy extra candles for night reading, before gas-lighting came to slum houses. Children at work during the daylight hours were thus not able to practice reading. Letter writing was also expensive, and the price of postage inhibited the working classes from exchanging ideas or even ordinary greetings. The cost factor also entered the learning situation directly. The children of the slums could not often afford slates or practice pads. English, French, and German sources frequently show poor youngsters tracing out their alphabets in the sand.

Yet even pitmen in the northern coalfields of England exhibited their hard-won skill—sometimes in ways teachers could not have intended. A Sheffield laborer might have brought a smile to the mouth of a Sunday school teacher, when, despite the difficulties arising from having broken his pair of spectacles, he wrote of the "four vollams of the Missionary Register witch give me grat satisfaction. . . ."[28] A coal miner must have caused consternation, however, when he recounted in 1831 how he and some mates had broken into a supervisor's home during a riot:

I was at yor hoose last neet . . . I see ye hev a greet lot of rooms . . . I naw some at yor colliery that has three or fower lads and lasses, and they liv in won room not half as gude as yor cellar. I dont naw very much, but I naw there shudnt be that much difference. . . . I dinna pretend to be a profit, but I now this . . . that wer not tret as we owt to be . . . But weve just begun to find that oot, and ye maisters and owners may luk oot. . . . [29]

Moreover, despite the imposition of tax stamps on the cheap newspapers so welcome among urban workers, reading laborers showed keen interest in their situation in society. By 1828 one tale of a worker-hero's death had

27. Out of a population of about 2,750,000 children under eleven years of age.
28. E. P. Thompson, *The Making of the English Working Class* (New York: Random House, Vintage Books, 1966), p. 715.
29. *Ibid.*

sold over 100,000 copies.[30] Radical teachers had prepared a "Bad Alphabet" with which to catechize the young: *B* was for *Bishop* and *Bigot*, *W* for *Whig* and *Wicked*. The Church of England and the liberal industrialists were thus early put down as enemies of labor. The message circulated in penny newspapers for adults also, especially in London, where popular "educational" weeklies sold as many as 40,000 copies—*The Voice of the People* and *The Working Man's Guardian*.

Working-class people were creating and consuming what we may well call a counterculture. In addition to the literature about the workers written by romantics and realists, liberals and Tories, there was coming into existence a genuine working-class literature.[31] The poet Joseph Swann was arrested in 1819 for having written these lines, which we may cite in lieu of many others:

> Off with your fetters; spurn the slavish yoke;
> Now, now, or never, can your chain be broke;
> Swift then rise and give the fatal stroke.[32]

The danger to the social order from class consciousness was, therefore, already apparent thirty years before Marx urged workers of the world to unite, because they had nothing to lose in rebellion but their chains. In order to appreciate the implications of cultural democratization, however, we must turn to the ways in which the images societies have of themselves are reinforced by educational systems and by the values they instill in the young.

CULTURE, EDUCATION, AND SOCIETY

If we wish to examine broadly the "culture" of England, say in the 1840s, by which time the industrial economy had matured, we cannot do so by supposing that this culture is identical with the tradition of literature taught in colleges and universities today. Time is selective. When we think of English writing between 1840 and the year 1870, we think in terms of writers already productive in the Chartist age and deservedly famous since: Dickens, Thackeray, the Brontë sisters, Arnold, Carlyle, Mill, Ruskin, Tennyson, Rossetti, and perhaps Disraeli. We think also of the great daily newspaper the *Times*. Yet the most-read papers were weeklies like *News of the World* and *Bell's Penny Dispatch*. And the best-selling authors recorded by the chain bookseller W. H. Smith[33] are not so familiar today: Lytton, Marryat, G. P. R. James, Miss Sinclair, Haliburton, Mrs. Gaskell.

30. *The Confessions and Executions of Corder.*
31. See, for example, Shelley's poem "Song to the Men of England."
32. Quoted in Thompson, *English Working Class*, p. 731.
33. Founded in 1848.

In this portrait by their brother Branwell, Anne, Emily, and Charlotte Brontë convey the brooding melancholy which permeates their writings. The Brontë children grew up without a great deal of supervision near the remote moors of northern England, and their isolation and stark environment profoundly agitated their vivid imaginations. Emily's Wuthering Heights *best reveals these early influences. Charlotte's masterpiece,* Jane Eyre, *deals with the horrors which she and Emily had experienced at a girl's school. All of the Brontë's died tragically early deaths, Branwell, Emily, and Anne all perishing within a year of one another in 1848–1849. Only Charlotte lived to be married, but her happiness lasted only a year and she died following childbirth in 1855. The Brontë's have come to typify the spiritually tormented existence of the Romantic artist. Radio Times Hulton Picture Library.*

Popular taste ran to *Bell's*, the subtitle of which was *Sporting and Police Gazette, and Newspaper of Romance*. The headlines were far from sedate—"Daring Conspiracy and Attempted Violation"—backed by an illustrated story. Against the 60,000 copies sold by the quality dailies, *Bell's* and its imitators sold 275,000. Even the most popular of Dickens's books, *Pickwick Papers*, which sold 70,000 copies, was no rival to the leading lights in the "Parlour and Railway Libraries" series, with forty-seven titles by G. P. R. James[34] in print at the same time—1849.

The purveyors of high culture noted that Bulwer-Lytton's *Last Days of Pompeii* and *Scalp Hunters* were books whose sale was not confined to the degraded poor. Even people of the "better classes" read them with relish, along with the pornography produced in London in very large quantities. This popular literature is therefore a better guide to ordinary thought than is the small body of great writing about philosophy, history, economics, and religion, or the first-rate poetry and novels of the age.

For the popular press in its rise traced the arc of a wider popular culture. There were also periodicals combining romances, recipes, household hints, and "advice" to correspondents. These were edging out the cheap "educational" periodicals, just as the music halls were competing with the serious theaters. The new technology of steam printing, rotary presses, railroads, and gaslights was creating new needs for entertainment and new places for the distribution of culture—the railway station bookshop, for example. Moreover, the organization of popular culture was not motivated solely by commercial considerations. Together with legislation beginning public museums (1845), parks (1847), and libraries (1850), the inexpensive journalism was intended to control the development of working-class opinion. For this purpose the "family magazine," the predecessor of our own women's journals, was safer than the serious journal of comment and criticism. What opinion makers wished to stimulate was a particular set of social ideas and values helpful to the preservation of the class structure of society as it existed.

The age was shot through with the tensions behind free trade, Chartism, the Ten Hours Act, the new Poor Law, the Public Health Act of 1848, and with agitation against the Church by the Chapel, even opposition to the spread of railways. British cultural institutions responded to the pressures of the "industrial economy" with new styles in journalism, because there were new publics to be reached. But the popular writers and the writers of the "literary tradition" reflected the social changes in literature in an interesting way. Dickens's *Dombey and Son*, Carlyle's *Past and Present*, Kingsley's *Alton Locke*, and Disraeli's *Sybil* and *Coningsby* share a set of assumptions.

Each writer assumes that a class society exists, in which status is defined by attained place rather than by birth. It is also assumed in the society that the poor are poor because of their personal failure; the truly virtuous are able to rise above poverty, goaded by the punitive Poor Law, which imposed a frugal diet, separation from family, and hard work on slackers. Hardship is also held to teach courage, humility, thrift, sobriety, piety, and duty. Marriage is sacred; the family is the chief cement of society, threatened with dissolution by adultery.

The social *character* expected of the working class is projected down toward it by the dominant groups in the society. And this character was that of the properly moral and industrious business classes. Other character models were of course available: from the aristocracy, where birth mattered

34. 1799–1860; a specialist in historical romances.

more than money, and where play mattered more than work, while sobriety and chastity were marks not of the good man but the dull one. The redeeming feature of aristocratic values for the worker was the insistence on charity, which the bourgeoisie equated with contributions to the weakness of the wicked. To balance the advantage, there was the natural habit of the aristocracy to sanction brutal repression and to conceive all relations as those of master and servant.

Against the popular culture and its value schemes, we see the laboring poor building a different morality, rejecting repression, punitive rehabilitation through the poorhouse, and the combination of money and birth set at the top of the ladder of middle-class and aristocratic values. But the tools with which to build the values of an open and free society of equals were hard won. The Ten Hours Act was as much a victory for working-class culture as for working-class bodies. It was necessary to winning *leisure*, without which a wider mental life is impossible. Also, the sense of fraternity we see in Chartist propaganda is based on cooperation and mutual aid, in flat rejection of the society of birth and success with money. But Chartism failed!

It is this sense of conflict of values which we see in even the literature of the great tradition, as realism crowds out Romanticism. The struggle of working-class people against middle-class repression, as in Dickens's *Hard Times*, has counterparts in the family instability and debt which pervades life in the better classes. In Disraeli's *Sybil*, the "nations" of rich and poor "meet" because an aristocrat falls in love with a Chartist girl, a poor heroine. The problem is resolved by the discovery that a secret legacy belongs to the girl, who is really a dispossessed aristocrat! In *Coningsby* Disraeli also arranged a union of classes: the young aristocrat marries the daughter of a Lancashire industrialist. He is then elected for the industrial seat in Parliament, where he reconciles conflicting groups. Less charitable, but sympathetic, critics of the new society dealt more harshly with the conflict. Mrs. Gaskell's *Mary Barton* stains working-class associations with murder plots. And Kingsley sends the Chartist hero of *Alton Locke* to Canada.

The themes of legacy and migration are themselves revealing about the character of English society, as this was projected in literature. Dickens's orphans and victims of fortune are saved by a sort of magical intervention, as in *A Christmas Carol*. Disraeli's heroine is an heiress. Truer to life was the "magic" of Australia, America, Canada, New Zealand, South Africa, and the other "white" colonies, where black sheep[35] and the desperate honest folk of Britain sought relief from the social conflicts and divisions at home. Emigration stood at 90,000 per year by 1840; and a decade later 270,000 Britons left for overseas.

Putting people on a boat was more consistent with the prevailing social attitudes than was the notion that some general solution to the social problem could be found. By insisting on exile the writers of *Alton Locke* and *Vanity Fair*[36] not only reflect the character of society. By their art they also create new perceptions of the reality, which was that those who had wealth and security generally wished to keep down those who had not. The exotic colors and feelings of Romantic writers could no longer disguise the bleaker reality.

This reality was managed by the dominant classes, by equipping working

35. Australia was settled between 1780 and 1830 by over 150,000 transported convicts.
36. Thackeray's great book about Becky Sharpe, the social-climbing orphan girl turned governess.

people for the social roles they were expected to play. Every pattern of culture is built up out of the individual responses people make in relating themselves to the system in which they exist. And it is this fact that makes our earlier attention to education important, the point to which we must now return.

The organizers of industrial society wished to teach "approved" things to those organized, and it was toward that end that the public education movement was dedicated. The "self" of working-class people had shown a dangerous independence in the 1840s, which led to ameliorative laws that in turn needed the support of other cultural institutions.

The Western system of education had always expressed the values of dominant classes; and it had always been organized to instill the desired social character in the leaders: a bundle of attitudes about loyalty, authority, justice, and the general purpose of life. Together with this social system of values, education always transmits general knowledge and the elements of skill essential to earning a living and upholding the welfare of one's community. Schools dominated by Churchmen did this in one way from the sixth to the sixteenth century. The schools dominated by the classically educated, humanistic gentlemen did so from the Reformation until the onset of industrialization.

In neither system, however, was it considered important to educate large numbers of people. There were perhaps 500 grammar schools in Britain in 1530, or one for every 5,625 persons. The working people were accounted for at home or in the education for crafts and trades known as the apprentice system. The assumption of the system was that most people had no need for any intellectual skill beyond that needed for useful work. Higher education was restricted to the gentry, poor boys very gifted and so marked for academic training and then the clergy, and the sons of the elites of town and country. The Reformation reorganized most grammar schools under the auspices of some secular trust or corporation. Yet very little else changed on the level of academic education. The main development was at the elementary level, where petty schools multiplied between 1530 and 1800 to teach the ABCs, sums, and the rudiments of religion. There was no widening of the scope of education for the lower classes. In 1864, therefore, there was one grammar school for every 23,750 people, a serious decline in opportunity in an enlarged population! The Charity School Movement was unable to keep pace with demand, and in such schools the training was chiefly moral instruction to uplift the poor.

In this "system" the Industrial Revolution could not be accommodated. In 1816, a British survey showed that 12,000 parishes existed: 3,500 had no school, 3,000 had endowed schools, and 5,500 had unendowed schools of varying quality. These schools were under the supervision of justices of the peace, members of the local elites, who wished to instruct the poor only to read Scriptures, which would make them submissive. Further education would make the poor restless and "disrelish . . . the laborious occupations of life."[37] Education early in the 1800s was restrictive, class determined, with higher education the monopoly of the governing classes. Only "moral rescue"[38] education was deemed suitable for the poor, to rescue them from their own degeneracy.

The vehicle for the rescue was the industrial school, which combined

37. Quoted in Raymond Williams, *The Long Revolution* (New York: Harper & Row, Publishers, Torchbooks, 1961), p. 135. I owe a great deal to Mr. Williams's great works on English culture and society.
38. A popular phrase in the nineteenth century.

manual training and elementary reading for proletarian youngsters. The Bible was the sole approved reading fare given along with the skill needed in the factory, in a system that provided what popular writers called the union of the "Steam Engine and the Moral World."[39] It has been estimated that in 1835 1,450,000 working-class children in a population of 1,750,000 attended such schools; and it was this education that was mandated by the 1862 code already discussed. At the same time, the elite grammar schools were experiencing the curriculum revision sponsored by Thomas Arnold of Rugby,[40] the purpose of which was to consolidate a value structure suitable for a society of Christian gentlemen. The chief effect of this, and the examination system coupled to the curriculum, was to make it practically impossible for a laborer's child or one of lower-middle-class parents to enter a university or the professional schools of law and medicine.

The class system of education was then further consolidated in the 1860s. The nearly 2,000 grammar schools functioning in 1868 were grouped so that nearly two-thirds of the English towns had none. The Public Schools Act of 1868 modernized the curriculum again, but "public" here was a euphemism for privately endowed grammar schools nominally open to everyone, but in fact dominated by the middle classes under arrangements supervised by the National Headmasters' Conference.

By 1868 the system had three tiers: one for the upper and upper middle classes, keeping boys until age eighteen, preparing them with a liberal education for the universities and older professions;[41] the solid middle-class level, keeping boys for nine years, to age sixteen, before sending them to the army, the newer professions,[42] and the civil service; and the lower-middle-class schools, where boys were kept until age fourteen, by which time they were suitably molded to be tenant farmers, small tradesmen, and the better sort of craftsmen. Provisions were made to "pass" bright boys

The English satirist George Cruikshank caricatures an eighteenth-century schoolmaster thrashing a pupil to the taunts and amusements of his peers. Cruel and often brutal treatment was frequently a condition of English school life throughout the early nineteenth century, particularly in the "public schools," which were in fact private schools for the upper classes. Industrial development and social unrest during this period revealed the need for a national system of day schools, but despite much discussion real progress was made only through a series of reform bills later in the century. Not until 1902 was compulsory attendance and free education a reality for all. The Bettmann Archive.

39. See the discussion in Williams, *Long Revolution*, p. 136.
40. Reflected in the 1857 book *Tom Brown's School Days*.
41. Clergy, law, and medicine.
42. Engineering, accounting, etc.

from the elementary schools to the third-grade secondary schools, but not generally beyond.

The Taunton Commission of 1867 had not minced words in establishing the system. The three "grades" of secondary schooling could admit only ten children per thousand of the whole population, or a mere 1 percent! Moreover, the division put eight of every ten children admitted in schools of the third grade, roughly 256,000 in a total school-aged population of about 4,000,000. Only 64,000 were to be admitted to schools of the two best grades, or .016 of the child population of Britain. The Commission freely acknowledged its purpose: "These distinctions correspond roughly . . . to the existing gradations of society."[43]

The democratization of education was only partial, therefore, and did not yet extend to the laboring masses. The new system, and the new culture reflected in novels, music halls, and newspapers, had not yet reached beyond the classes with the vote. And the 1867 Reform Act had given the vote in the counties to small copyholders and leaseholders (£5) as well as to £12 "occupiers"; in the boroughs the £10 householders and rent payers were enfranchised, the better-off workers primarily, not the rank-and-file workers.

THE MIDDLE CLASSES AND THE NEW REALISM

The practical point of educational reform in France, England, and in other industrializing states was the same: the upper classes who extended the franchise not only wanted their new "masters" to know their letters. The ruling groups wanted to make certain that the cultural *content* of this spreading education would reinforce prevailing cultural values and patterns of social organization. The industrial "trainers" prevailed with regard to the working classes in mid-nineteenth-century reforms. Therefore the shadow of class attitudes lay over the technical, narrow, training deemed suitable for workers and the more liberal education provided for even the mass of lower-middle-class people. Morality took the place of politics in a system not designed to stimulate criticism from within.

In France, the middle classes also had to cope with the voice of an aroused, excluded working class. The utopian socialists had spread a body of thought throughout the working-class organizations before 1848. Working-class literature thrived in Paris in 1840. In addition to such papers as *Le Globe* and *Le Producteur*, wholly dedicated to socialist doctrine, the monthly *L'Atelier* was written and edited by printing-house workers. The men and women of *L'Atelier* refused to accept bourgeois collaboration, proudly denouncing liberals as enemies of democracy, while maintaining that only workers know working-class needs. Like the Chartists in England, they advocated universal male suffrage and the regulation of industry. Guizot

43. Williams, *Long Revolution*, p. 139.

Auguste Rodin freed sculpture from its past just as Courbet liberated painting. When he was commissioned to make a public statue of Balzac, Rodin conceived one of his most daring ideas and presented the novelist wrapped in a shroudlike cloak with only his carefully delineated, tormented face thrusting out of this giant, unarticulated mass. The effect is an overpowering vision of Balzac as a genius looming above lesser men. Indeed few writers have equaled his output or surpassed his goal, which was to present a profound psychological study of all levels of French society. At first Rodin's work was refused as inappropriate, but later it was cast in bronze and placed at the head of a busy Parisian boulevard where Balzac seems perpetually to observe the city he knew so well. Bulloz.

was so alarmed by *L'Atelier* that he brought suit against it for provoking hatred between the working classes and the bourgeoisie. What was equally troubling to Guizot, as it was later to Bismarck—the bourgeois politician and the *Junker*—was the insistence of the articulate workers that they must speak for themselves, across national lines wherever possible, in a sort of "international" of proletarians.[44]

With respect to education, the basic parallel to the class controls imposed in England in 1867–1868 had appeared in France earlier. Thiers supported Louis Napoleon's 1850 "reforms" which put the clergy back in charge of all public elementary education. Thiers said frankly that such education *must not be within everybody's reach*. Education was the gateway to affluence; and wealth was not intended by Providence for everyone. Most men, certainly the lower orders, were put on earth to suffer. The challenge to this doctrine, which was embodied in the notorious Falloux Law[45] of 1850, was given by the sympathetic realist Victor Hugo:

Compulsory education is the child's right. . . . Not a commune without a school! Not a town without a college! I reject your law. I reject it because it confiscates Elementary Education, because it lowers the level of knowledge, because it debases my country. . . . [46]

During the Second Empire, however, the new Napoleon gave his support to repression and to the subordination of the working classes in France. Yet in 1863 the Paris labor movement was strong and dedicated to radical socialism. Observers in the monarchist press noticed the militancy of the workers' interest in education and their founding of schools to encourage a culture contrary to the bourgeois "realism" of the novelists. In 1864 French workers won the right to strike; the same year saw French and English socialists band together to form the first workers' international.

Side by side with the spokesmen of the revived working-class culture, which had been silent for a decade after 1848, the literary realists among the bourgeoisie drew indictments of the new civilization.

Flaubert's *Dictionary of Current Opinions* pilloried the crassness and stupidity of the new empire, in which middle-class men masqueraded in imperial uniforms. Beyond complaint, however, there was in realism in literature a profound impulse toward objectivity. Writers seemed anxious to make literature do with words what photographers were just then able to do with chemical emulsions and light: to be photographic, to translate to paper a real slice of life. The novelist Zola wrote books which he called "reports" on the Second Empire. Balzac, decades earlier, had "drawn" somewhat romantically the world of middle-class morality and the never-ending concern for money which motivated it in *La Cousine Bette*, *Le Père Goriot*, and *Eugénie Grandet*. The greatest of the realist novels, however, was Flaubert's *Madame Bovary* (1857).

Flaubert hated the middle class to which he belonged socially and economically. In some works he indulged in romantic escapism, indirectly criticizing the society he lived in: *Salammbô*, for example, or *The Temptation of Saint Anthony (La Tentation de Saint-Antoine)*. In *L'Education sentimentale*, he had shown the decadence of Romantic rebellion, through the weakness of his main character, Frédéric, who "observes" the 1848 revolution. Then, in *Madame Bovary*, realism wins out. The story of Emma

44. In 1841 the *L'Atelier* group was in contact with English Chartists.
45. The code repressing speech, newspapers, public secular education, etc.
46. Quoted in Georges Duby and Robert Mandrou, *A History of French Civilization* (New York: Random House, 1967), p. 477.

Bovary is the tragedy of a respectable woman, unloved, caught in the smug conventions of bourgeois life, and strong enough to defy them, only to become the victim of two worthless lovers in turn.

French writers of realistic, documentary, novels thus led the way on the Continent, soon after Dickens had been joined in England by Thackeray. *The Pickwick Papers, Hard Times, Nicholas Nickleby, Henry Esmond, Vanity Fair* were all in print, and many translated into French, before 1857, when Flaubert's masterpiece appeared. Then, in the late 1850s and in the 1860s as Dickens continued to describe urban life in an industrial society— he detested London—the Continent began to "catch up."

The way was led not only by the French, but by a quartet of Russian writers of genius: Goncharov, Turgenev, Dostoevski, and the heroic Count Tolstoi. Goncharov's *Oblomov* (1858) exposed pitilessly to view a decaying, bankrupt Russian absentee landlord. Turgenev (1818–1883), who spent much time in Paris and was part of the Goncourts' circle, returned to Russia periodically in the 1860s, but never to live in the country from which his writing showed such profound alienation. His despair over Russia's "backwardness" took shape in *Fathers and Sons* (1862), in which the central character, Bazarov, is a *nihilist*, a man who believes in nothing.

This stance is not strange in a Russian artist familiar with the West. There, the bourgeois society which workers found so repressive was positively free for *émigré* intellectuals in comparison to czarist censorship, persecutions, and suppressions. Turgenev and the other great novelists of Russia saw in realism a sword and in literature not a pleasant vocation but a promise of guidance, even of deliverance. This attitude toward the novel matured fully in Dostoevski, however, rather than in Turgenev.[47]

Dostoevski (1821–1881) did for Russian life what Dickens did for English society: he took the lid off. The son of a murdered father and a mother who died when the son was still a boy, Dostoevski was himself an epileptic and the victim of nine years in Siberian prisons for his part in "conspiracies" in 1848;[48] he knew the world of rapists, gamblers, drunkards, and murderers firsthand. This knowledge was put to use in his indictments of traditional society in Russia, for example in *The House of the Dead*, which complained that youth was buried within the walls of the prison that was czarist Russia. The society which looks indifferently at such phenomena, Dostoevski said, is already doomed, contaminated, divorced from reality. Dostoevski expounded in his writing the antithesis between Russian spiritualism, decadent and oppressive, and Western materialism, where men were free but suffered from a spiritual anesthesia. His massive novels,[49] and also his *Notes from the Underground*, constitute the most impressive combination of realism, psychological depth, and social criticism in contemporary European literature.

In these works the life of man in society is subject to the most minute examination, along with families, love, work, and pleasure. The same can be said about the achievement of Tolstoi (1828–1910) in *War and Peace* and *Anna Karenina*. Tolstoi was himself a landed aristocrat, a count, whose view of Russian society connected him to a *populist* movement based on sharing the conditions of peasant life. Yet his greatest work, *War and Peace*, concerns the total life of the Russia invaded by Napoleon in 1812, as seen realistically through the eyes of aristocrats. In *Anna Karenina*, Tolstoi took

Leo Tolstoi's life was centered around his country estate, where he worked in the simple study shown in this photograph. Brought up during the last years of serfdom, Tolstoi was long on the verge of an inner crisis over his own exalted position in life, but this was postponed for many years as he found contentment in his domestic life. About 1876 he again felt his old sense of guilt. After first turning to orthodox Christianity he later developed his own creed stating that the Christian's first duty was to avoid the organized violence of the state and living off the work of others. As he began to dress like a peasant and engage in manual labor, his wife became increasingly hostile, making the writer's last years extremely difficult and bitter. The Bettmann Archive.

47. The central period of Turgenev's work, 1856–1862, included *Rudin, A Nobleman's Nest, On the Eve, Fathers and Sons*.
48. Turgenev was arrested in 1848, Dostoevski a year later.
49. *Crime and Punishment, The Idiot, The Possessed,* and *The Brothers Karamazov*.

up the documentary realism already familiar in France and England. The novel is based on the real death of a woman who had committed suicide on the estate of a neighboring landowner. Tolstoi's creation of the tragic heroine Anna marks in Russian literature the sort of documentary breakthrough in depicting a woman's life that had been achieved by Flaubert in 1857.

There is nothing in German literature to set beside the work of the realist masters of England, France, and Russia. Nor is there much in European fiction elsewhere of anything like equal stature. American writers were just then beginning to have an enormous impact in Western Europe—Nathaniel Hawthorne and Herman Melville particularly, whose greatness was recognized in *The Scarlet Letter* and *Moby Dick*.

It was in drama, however, that other countries contributed most to the movement toward social and psychological realism. There was in this a certain appropriateness, because the multiplication of small theaters was one of the most important *institutional* developments of the new culture. The middle classes at first demanded only "entertainment" in the theater, not wanting illuminations of real life when they paid for tickets. Indeed, the popular theater audiences, especially music hall audiences in England, France, and Germany, the chief industrial states by 1870, seemed to want only an escape from reality.

The magical reaction between audience and stage in theater scenes such as Melodrama (1856–1860) *was one of Daumier's favorite subjects. Like most of his paintings the milieu represented is decidedly lower middle class, and the artist concentrates on their awkward manners and believing naïveté. The melodrama was an early–nineteenth-century invention which grew out of Diderot's notions about the theater—it should be neither drama nor tragedy, but something in between that dealt with actual situations in contemporary middle-class life. The burgeoning number of theatergoers in Daumier's time showed a clear preference for overwrought drama and stage histrionics. Bayerische Staatsgemäldesammlungen, Munich.*

At first, therefore, realism invaded the new theater only in stage effects. The simple backdrops of classical theater[50] were abandoned in the small theaters, and realistically constructed "sets" were used. The box set spread rapidly in the 1860s, from Moscow to London and from Rome to Oslo. Not only were furniture and property put on stage; in an outdoor scene set in autumn, falling leaves were blown on stage, or snow was sent howling into the scene by the stage manager's wind machines.

Where realistic methods went, the realism of situation and character soon followed. Ibsen, Strindberg, Hauptmann, and Chekhov—a Norwegian, a Swede, a German, and a Russian—transformed stage realism into the theater of modern times. But this was chiefly a development of the 1880s, in Paris's *Théatre Antoine*, Berlin's *Freie Bühne*, and London's Independent Theatre. We may discuss it with greater profit in the context of the age that ended in 1918.[51]

In 1867, when Ibsen's *Peer Gynt* first played, however, Karl Marx published the first volume of *Capital*. Eight years earlier Charles Darwin had brought out his theories of evolution, in *On the Origin of Species by*

50. Shakespeare, Racine, Schiller, etc.
51. See Chapter 14.

In this lithograph and watercolor of the playwright Henrik Ibsen sitting in a café in Christiana, his fellow Norwegian Edvard Munch has emphasized the suffering which the old man had endured in his struggle against a narrow-minded milieu. Munch was trained in the symbolist art circles of Paris and Berlin and was naturally sympathetic to Ibsen's use of universal themes explored in a symbolistic manner. A favorite device of the artist was to isolate the head of his subject in an area of somber color to emphasize the feeling of distortion and suffocating loneliness. Munch avoided the overt drama of apparitions or theatrical settings favored by some Symbolist painters, instead probing life's deepest dramas in simply constructed everyday situations. Munch-Museet, Oslo.

Means of Natural Selection. In 1863 a group of radical Paris painters whose work had been refused a showing in the Salon of the Academy of Arts—the impressionists—put on a show of their own in what they called the "Salon of the Rejected."[52] A year earlier Herbert Spencer, the English philosopher, had published a "scientific" and "positive" account of progress, the *First Principles* of his ten-volume *Synthetic Philosophy.* And in Germany Wagner, who in 1849 had published *Art and Revolution*, the herald of his music-dramas, transformed opera and profoundly influenced orchestral music.

Darwin, Marx, Wagner, Manet, Spencer, and Ibsen did not immediately transform the culture of the West. But their work pointed toward a future in which the perception of society and natural reality was again to shift radically, not merely among small classes of leaders, whether of opinion, taste, or politics, but among the vast masses of people concerned about the nature and quality of life in the West.

BIBLIOGRAPHY

BRAMSTED, E. K. *Aristocracy and the Middle Classes in Germany.** Chicago: University of Chicago Press, 1964. A provocative study of social types in German literature, 1830–1900.

CLARK, SIR KENNETH. *The Gothic Revival.** New York: Holt, Rinehart & Winston, 1962. A clear analysis of the "medieval" revival that was part of Romantic art. This can be read in the context of the more general study by Maurice Raynal, *The Nineteenth Century: Goya to Gauguin* (New York: Skira, 1951).

EINSTEIN, ALFRED. *Music in the Romantic Era.* New York: W. W. Norton & Co., 1947. The standard text on the composers from Berlioz to Tchaikovsky.

LEVIN, HARRY. *The Gates of Horn.** New York: Oxford University Press, 1964. A stimulating discussion of the French novelists.

MORAZÉ, CHARLES. *The Triumph of the Middle Classes.** Cleveland: World Publishing Co., 1966. The most provocative Marxist analysis of bourgeois society.

OLLMAN, BERTELL. *Alienation: Marx's Concept of Man in Capitalist Society.* Cambridge: Cambridge University Press, 1971. The best book in English on this crucial subject, using techniques of language analysis to clarify Marx's critique of capitalism as alienating.

PECKHAM, MORSE. *Beyond the Tragic Vision.* New York: Braziller, 1962. A very good treatment of the nature of ideas in European literature.

ROHR, D. G. *The Origins of Social Liberalism in Germany.* Chicago: University of Chicago Press, 1963. Argues that German liberals reacted to the social problems of industrialization in England by urging ameliorative programs in Germany.

SIMMONS, E. J. *Dostoevsky.** New York: Random House, Vintage Books, 1962. The best introduction to the writer and to the Russian literature of his period.

THOMPSON, E. P. *The Making of the English Working Class.** New York: Random House, Vintage Books, 1966. The best book on the development of working-class consciousness.

WILLIAMS, RAYMOND. *Culture and Society, 1780–1950.** New York: Harper & Row, Publishers, Torchbooks, 1958. This brilliant critical study of social values in English literature is especially good on the nineteenth-century writers critical of industrialization. It should be read together with Williams's *The Long Revolution* (New York: Harper & Row, Publishers, Torchbooks, 1961) because the earlier work provides additional support for the argument that a true popular culture emerged as a result of a "long revolution" in favor of democratic values. Williams's work is especially good on the popular press and the literacy of common people.

Asterisk indicates a paperbound edition.

52. *Salon des Refusés.* Manet's *Luncheon on the Grass* (*Déjeuner sur l'herbe*) was the main work in question.

BOOK THREE

The Crisis of Liberalism, 1870–1918

After 1870, industrialization spread beyond Britain and Belgium, making rapid gains in the rest of Europe, in Japan, and in the United States. It was an age of industrial machinery, steam power, electricity, coal, and steel. Automobiles and airplanes appeared on the scene, creating new demands for oil. Thanks to new technology, engineers blasted great tunnels through the earth and carved canals between oceans. The German artist Max Schulze-Sölde depicted the new civilization in this 1925 work, The Age of Technology: *technology, whose symbols dominate this scene, was king indeed—but who, then, were the servants? Stadtische Kunsthalle, Recklingshausen.*

This book begins with the consolidation of Bismarck's political and diplomatic achievements after the Prussian victory over France in 1871. The focus, however, quickly shifts to an account of how the Continental states and the United States caught up with Britain in the race for industrial supremacy. We place special emphasis on the nature of industrialization as a social process. These concerns lead necessarily to a consideration of the increased power of the state over economic life and the rise of social policies designed to alleviate conditions of squalor in large cities. The processes of democratization and the struggles for constitutionalism occupy our attention, therefore, but not as ends in themselves.

We are concerned to discover the roots of the politics of social welfare and to explore the territory in which mass politics transformed nationalism. Where once the idea had been a "liberal" one, late in the nineteenth century it loomed as the creed of expansion-minded Europeans. Sometimes the refurbished doctrine fired conflict within European states, for example, within the dual state of Austria-Hungary, which encompassed a dozen or more "ethnic" minorities eager for independence. At other times the doctrine supplied the emotional basis to unite scattered classes within a state in pursuit of national glory, either by defeating rival Europeans or by the easier process of subjecting "colonial" peoples in new empires carved out in Africa and Asia.

The expansion of Western power, politically, economically, and militarily, was not a steady march toward final triumph. Tensions among the states exploded in global war in 1914, bringing to an end the "liberal era." Long before 1914, however, on the plane of art and ideas, the advent of cubism, atomic physics, a new theory of evolution, and Freudian psychiatry had heralded the twentieth century's violent concern over space, time, and human emotion.

11

CATCHING UP: THE INDUSTRIALIZATION OF THE WEST

The deepest problems of modern life derive from the claim of the individual to preserve the autonomy and individuality of his existence in the face of overwhelming social forces. . . . In addition to more liberty, the nineteenth century demanded the functional specialization of man and his work . . . the person resists being levelled down and worn out by a social technological mechanism. An inquiry into the inner meaning of specifically modern life and its products, into the soul of the cultural body, so to speak, must solve the equation which structures like the metropolis set up between the individual and the super-individual contents of life. . . .
GEORG SIMMEL, "The Metropolis and Mental Life"(1900)[1]

AN OVERVIEW: THE PHASES OF INDUSTRIALIZATION

Economic historians disagree about the chronology of the transformations by which "traditional" economies and societies became "modern"—i.e., industrial—ones. That is to say, they disagree about when new productive activities reached a level able to effect massive and progressive changes in the economic and social structures of the countries in which industrialization occurred. Some would date the "takeoff" as follows for the earliest such transformations: Britain, 1770–1800; France, 1830–1860; Belgium, 1835–1860; the United States, 1840–1860; Germany, 1850–1870; Sweden, 1870–1890; Japan, 1880–1900; Russia, 1890–1914. Others, looking at the periods of most rapid growth rather than onset, would shift the dates, so that we have this pattern: Britain, 1820–1850; Germany, 1870–1890; Sweden, 1890–1920; etc., with periods of rapid growth extending for some twenty or thirty years and taking place immediately or some decades after periods of onset.

But, by any reckoning, there is little disagreement that several Western nations, especially Germany and the United States, had by the early twentieth century overtaken Britain. We see elsewhere the same ceaseless expansion of production and trade, the steady growth in the amount of power used, the voracious appetite for raw materials, and the provision of more and better consumer goods. Moreover, we see also the displacement of once dominant industries by others: textiles yield to iron and steel, then to electricity and its associated industries.

1. Trans. Kurt Wolff, in M. Cherniavsky, A. J. Slavin, and S. Ewen, *Social Textures of Western Civilization: The Lower Depths* (Lexington, Mass.: Xerox College Publishing, 1972), 2:261–262.

Factories dot the Belgian countryside in a late–nineteenth-century painting entitled
The Black Country *by Constantin Meunier. Between 1846 and 1900 tiny Belgium*
became one of the most heavily industrialized areas of Europe with enormous
increases in the number of workers and the amount of power produced. This
transformation coincided with the birth of the modern Belgian state which dates
from the establishment of a constitutional monarchy in 1831. The first king, Leopold
I of Saxe-Coburg, took measures to promote economic development by abolishing
protectionism, establishing a national bank, and signing commercial treaties with a
number of countries. His successor, Leopold II, was an ardent capitalist who
acquired the African Congo almost as a personal property and used it to supply raw
materials for Belgian industry. Musée d'Art & d'Industrie, St.-Etienne.

Of course, in different places the internal chronology of development is
different. The coal industry of Belgium led the way there until about 1900,
when it declined. In Germany and the United States, however, coal
production was in a phase of growth in 1900. What each industrializing
nation in the West shared—and before World War I only Japan outside the
West had the "revolution"—was the nature and impact of the experience of
modernization through the diffusion of new technologies.

There is, therefore, no point in giving here a detailed, internal, "history"
of the Industrial Revolution as it transformed each Western country or

region. The problem is rather one of relating economic and social changes and their causes to the broad political and cultural developments that occurred in the West before 1914, when a world war set the seal to those changes and pronounced a death sentence on some aspects of the prewar world.

This chapter, indeed this Book, has as its purpose, therefore, to provide a way of looking at "modern" history in the West. Our problem is to understand how the traditional societies based on agricultural production followed Europe's western fringe into the modern world. We must also be alert to the impact of industrialization on the social and political face of the West, as well as on the character of its mental life. Moreover, we cannot afford to forget that wherever economic changes produce social and political shifts in a society, conversely, political and social processes peculiar to different societies may determine how economic forces appear at work in modernizing that society. It made a great difference to the character of life in industrial Germany that the Prussian political system had triumphed there over the Austrian. And it made a greater difference still that the German drive beyond "takeoff" toward maturity came at a time when Russia and France seemed determined to reverse the losses symbolized by the treaties of 1856 and 1871.

Moreover, we must be clear at the start about the nature of the great transformation itself. In traditional societies, there is a ceiling on levels of output, due in part to the manpower needs of agriculture and the hierarchic social system, in which products are confiscated for the support of elites. In the traditional societies, centralization of power was usually one of the preconditions for industrial growth. Another was the expansion of markets. A third was the growth of science. A fourth was the combination of possibilities created by governmental support for enterprises of the kind capable of radically altering social habits, social values, and the balance of political power between urban and rural groups. Clearly, seen in this light, the political revolutions in England (1642–1689), France (1789, 1830, 1848, 1871), and Russia (1905, 1917), as well as the unification of Germany (1848–1871) and the Union's victory in the American Civil War (1861–1865), illustrate how political events contribute to a society's potential for modernization.[2]

Governments play a tremendous role in determining whether factory workers are mobile enough to supply industrial needs, whether property law is modified to allow the transfer of rural capital to industrial systems, and whether the modernization of agricultural production will provide the basic energy requirements of expanding urban populations. The defeat of the slave system in America and the abolition of serfdom in Russia (1861) in the same decade were essential aspects of the long-term process of modernization. Without the political results thus obtained, there would have existed inhibitions to the requirements of modern efficient production.

Finally, in every example of modernization through industrialization—and there has been no successful modernization in a nonindustrial society—mature economies move beyond the phase of *primary* industry (coal, iron, railroads, machine tools, chemical industries, electrical industries, and military production) into a condition of consumerism.[3]

2. That is, by bringing to power politically social groups sympathetic to nontraditional economic and technological practices.
3. It has been maintained that in the eighteenth century the Netherlands became "modern" without benefit of industrialization. Other historians have coined the phrase "proto-industrial society" for this development. In any event, the case hardly negates our argument. The exception is a small one, and the Netherlands subsequently experienced industrialization and the modernization associated with it.

What has characterized the mature economies of the industrial West has been the ability to choose what will be produced in order to satisfy demands for a "better life." It is fashionable today for Americans, Swedes, and other Western people to deride the notion that consumerism, the mass consumption of a wide variety of personal goods, is necessarily making a good life. But in countries where real income per capita has not yet risen to Western levels, and where the structure of the work force has not yet freed labor from subsistence living, there is much less doubt on this matter.

The Western societies became "modern" en masse between 1870 and 1914.[4] The basic pattern of availability of food, shelter, and clothing was transformed for working-class people. Urban populations rose at the expense of rural populations. And even the former dominance of factory work gave way to the rise of new "service" work forces, especially those of office workers in modern, technologically sophisticated states. On the eve of the First World War, the Western societies had the capability to produce both political security and social welfare, as well as the capacity to diffuse widely the basic laborsaving devices essential to leisure and culture. In this chapter we shall discuss the shaping of Europe's economic opportunities down to 1914. In those which follow we shall trace political and social developments during this period and the complex series of international events that eventually embroiled Europe in war.

THE LAG OF INDUSTRY IN EUROPE BEFORE 1850[5]

Europeans aware of Britain's lead in manufacturing flocked there after 1770, in order to study, and if possible to emulate, the leader. Part of the same civilization, the other Western countries were slow to catch up, even slow to emulate the British achievement, despite often abundant resources, a good scientific base and an adequate technology, and great incentive in governing circles. The reason lay in the structure of continental economies.

Elsewhere there were poorer transport networks than in Britain, beset by numerous toll systems, themselves a reflection of the many political divisions before the age of the unification of nation-states. Even France suffered in this regard before the Revolution of 1789. Belgium's access to trade, for example, lay through the Dutch-controlled ports. There was also a critical dependence on foreign supplies of raw material—wool for textiles for instance, which the British produced in abundance at home or in their Australian colonies. Also, the demand for goods in the rest of Europe was sluggish by comparison to the British pressure, and this was a function of the more hierarchic structure of income distribution in other European societies. There were weaker commercial and financial services available, especially in France and the German-speaking countries. Moreover, the drain of capital into nonproductive outlets—especially land, office, and the outward display of aristocratic status—endured longer in continental Europe than in Britain.

In business itself inhibiting practices were also stronger in continental Europe: the residue of guild control; the prevalence in France, Germany, and the Low Countries of family enterprise with limited capital stocks; the subordination of trade to the war-oriented policies of the land-based powers; the destruction of social overhead capital[6] in war; the power of local authorities to restrain trade in local markets; and the social contempt

---

4. These dates are, of course, a shorthand for a more complex chronology of change: see later in this chapter.
5. This account rests on David S. Landes, *The Unbound Prometheus* (Cambridge: Cambridge University Press, 1969), chapters 3 and 4, both for the main illustrative material and for the data samples.
6. Roads, bridges, port facilities, etc.

of the aristocrats for the commercial classes. All of these features of continental life slowed industrial development there.

The net result was an economy of small markets, striving for self-sufficiency rather than wider profits through large-scale operations. Of course, there were industries with a wider focus gathering strength from about 1750–1850: woolen clothing in Flanders, Normandy, Saxony, and Languedoc; cottons in Switzerland, Normandy, and south Germany; iron in Silesia, eastern France, and Styrian Austria; several metal industries around Liège; and coal throughout Belgium. These were usually industries without state support, however, and the industries actually developed by the crown in France, Prussia, and Austria before 1800 lagged somewhat, or were at best only moderately successful. This was often the result of two facts: monarchs seemed indifferent to capital accumulation, and they preferred the wrong products. Frederick the Great wanted power, not an industrial revolution, from his Silesian mines. And the French Gobelin tapestry works and Saxony's Dresden porcelain factories were labor-intensive in luxury production, promoting both monopoly and restricted consumption.

The breakthrough on the Continent came elsewhere, in manufactures free of the kind of state control that was producing bottlenecks of supply unable to meet expanding demand. In Germany, for example, the scarcity of water supplies was dispersing ironworking. Also, merchant clothiers met growing demands for labor in the Belgian towns once part of northwestern Germany, where guild control was weak in heavily populated rural areas around Aachen, Limburg, Monschau, and Verviers. Yet even in spinning yarn the incentive for radical technical adjustment was small. The cost of labor in continental Europe was less than it was in Britain, because population growth was at a rate in excess of industrial capacity. The steady growth of a very poor rural proletariat, a sure sign of economic backwardness, encouraged labor-intensive solutions to demand pressure. Abundant labor inhibited technological applications. Thus, in Flanders' cotton industry, the fly shuttle was not introduced until about 1810, many years after its invention and application in Britain. In France there were only 900 jennies in use in 1790.

Continental Europeans thus knew Britain's superiority and the reasons for it around 1800. But they did little—or could do little—to catch up. There were exceptions, of course. French officials encouraged the use of new metallurgical techniques in the 1780s. German entrepreneurs adopted the water frame in cotton spinning as early as 1794. Belgium made use of the rotary steam engine in a spinning mill in 1801. German engineers built and employed steam-driven machines in the Rhineland as early as 1791. What finally made continental Europe more open to industrial experiments, however, was a series of political events: the French Revolution and the Napoleonic Wars.

As fighting over wide areas put new premiums on certain sorts of mass production, in France in the 1790s, and in the areas subordinated to France under the Napoleonic Continental System, vast changes began to affect the European economies. The need to create substitutes for overseas imports stimulated chemical industries and led to the invention of beet sugar. Small industrial economies suddenly were placed in the wider framework of a continental European market. In central Europe, to cite one example only, the textile industry was mechanized in some areas. But a balance was struck in Saxony, where the cotton industry suffered from the blockade imposed by England. Perhaps the greatest effect of the Napoleonic Wars was institutional and social, however, rather than directly mechanical.

A Gas Workers & General Labourers union membership certificate stresses the goal of an eight-hour working day. Trade unions were outlawed in England until the second quarter of the nineteenth century; after which they expanded rapidly and became an integral part of the industrial system. Coal was the basic source of energy for early industrial expansion, and its use in the production of gas is illustrated on this card. At left, bags of coal are being unloaded from a ship, and the gas is extracted from the burning fuel at right. The final product was stored in the tank at center known as a gasometer. The coal-gas process, which was invented around 1800, was first used as a source of light and later for heat. Trade Union Congress; R. B. Fleming.

The spread of the French Revolution had removed some of the traditional restrictions on the mobility of both capital and labor, restrictions which in any case were already weakened by population expansion. To give but one example, the famous 1791 Le Chapelier Law in France *abolished* guilds, and similar laws followed French armies into the Low Countries, Italy, and western Germany. In the immediate postwar years, however, industrialization in continental Europe also experienced some peculiar inhibitions. British technique had not stood still. By the 1820s, in textile manufacture, for example, the British were using mules worked by steam and encompassing a thousand spindles. Each machine cost over £1,000. And similar advances had been made in iron production, chemical industries, etc. Continental producers were often unable to use the latest machines and technology, either because legal barriers and consumption patterns made it difficult to do so, or because the capital required was too great. Moreover, continental Europe had not the same access to raw materials in South America, Africa, and Asia as was enjoyed by Britain. The result was a mechanization in the 1820s and 1830s *without the latest equipment.*

Britain's competitive advantage was thus assured throughout the first half of the nineteenth century. Even where cost factors and productive functions did not inhibit catching up, there seemed to operate a "voluntary obsolescence."[7] The gap in technique widened; and the educational, social, and economic patterns within the other European states remained "backward" by British standards. Only when the diffusion of the new technology had created new cultural institutions, especially educational systems to train the new cadres of "mechanics" in France, Belgium, and Germany, could the

7. The phrase is from Landes, *Unbound Prometheus*, p. 147.

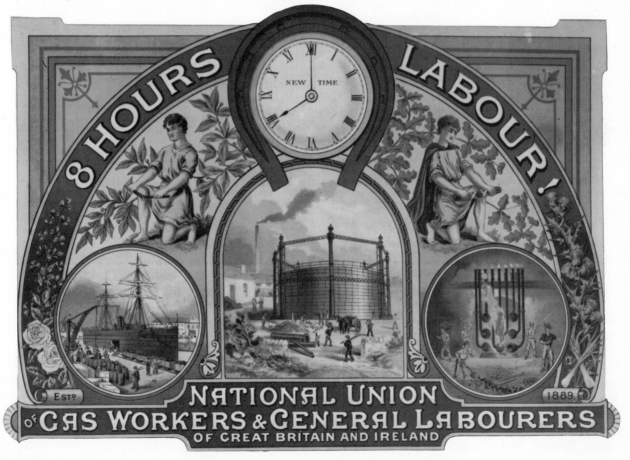

rest of Europe truly catch up. That the need was felt we know from some data: in 1825 about 2,000 technicians from Britain had jobs on the Continent; and in 1840 the British treasury was trying to stem the illegal export of machinery, while the legitimate shipments already were worth £600,000 per year!

Britain was supplying the aid Europe needed, but often against the will of a government determined to protect the industrial and commercial supremacy of the British Isles. Neither laws nor spies could halt the flow of knowledge and technique. In the 1840s machinery from England was being set up in factories as far away as Poland. Moreover, the continental governments had begun to support the creation of a hierarchy of special schools to train native industrial cadres; in France the *École Polytechnique* and its affiliates for mines and bridges, in Germany the Berlin *Gewerbe-Institut* and the Prussian *Hauptbergwerks-Institut*. And in both countries there developed also a whole array of mechanical training schools. In Germany especially the governments were determined to spend what was necessary to catch up. The discovery, so important in our own time, had already been made: that education of a special sort was a cure for backwardness.

This felt need, to reduce the gap between Britain's prosperity and "progress" and continental Europe's own "backwardness," does not alone explain industrialization on the Continent, any more than supply without demand explained the revolution in Britain. From the demand side there was also pressure of another kind. The following figures show estimated population in three countries in 1801 and 1850: France, 27.5 million and 35 million; Germany, 23.5 million and 33.5 million; Belgium, 3 million and 4.3 million. Growth in numbers was matched by increasing facility of movement for goods and people. The Rhine estuary was opened to German shipping; the Belgian railroad network was essentially complete by 1850; the 1834 *Zollverein* forced on member states lower tariffs. Although the great railroad networks of France and Germany did not mature until the 1850s and 1860s, even in the 1840s railroad construction created unprecedented demands for iron and the various materials needed for cars and stations—wood, glass, furniture, leather, stone, etc. One immediate effect was an increase in pig iron production in the 1840s. Prussian output rose only 13 percent, but this was because of large imports from Britain and Belgium. In France the make of charcoal pig iron rose from 246,000 metric tons to 339,000 between 1835 and 1847, which amounts to an increase of 38 percent.

The impact of these changes in other areas of the economies affected was striking. Cheaper and faster materials and transport lowered prices as supplies rose. This was true in agricultural production especially. The new populations were fed by increased yields from lands cultivated by new methods and held, at least in part, by new owners thanks to changes in land tenure which favored the peasants. Yields per acre and per worker increased in France between 1815 and 1850 by over 50 percent for wheat and 150 percent for potatoes. The fact that agriculture did not need new, massive, capital inputs to meet the food needs of the people meant that savings could be mobilized for investment. At first investors preferred state bonds, but first in France and then in Austria railroad building proved attractive.

The continental countries had less capital to work with than Britain, however. And it has even been said that the capital demands of railroad booms starved certain sectors of agriculture in 1845–1846, thus contributing to the harvest crises of those years. Be that as it may, in the years around 1850, French, Belgian, and German investors pioneered the joint-stock

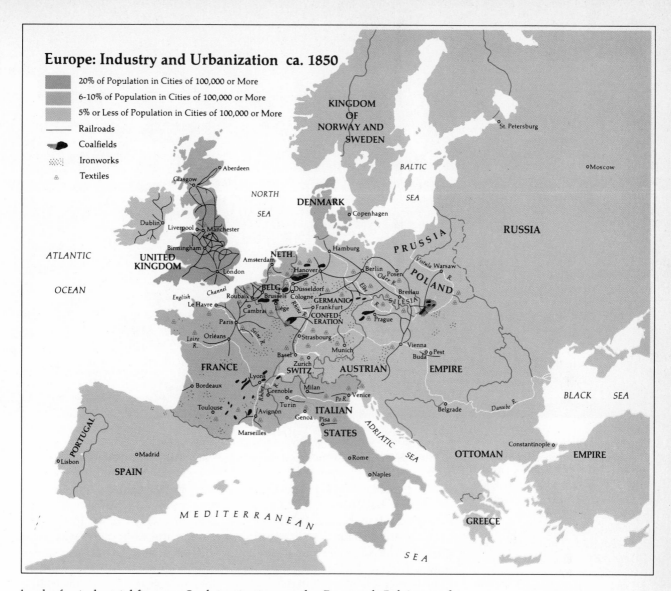

Europe: Industry and Urbanization ca. 1850

- 20% of Population in Cities of 100,000 or More
- 6-10% of Population in Cities of 100,000 or More
- 5% or Less of Population in Cities of 100,000 or More
- ⎯⎯ Railroads
- Coalfields
- Ironworks
- Textiles

banks for industrial finance. Such institutions as the *Banque de Belgique* and the Prussian *Seehandlung* played a leading role in development. Perhaps as important was the readiness of British capitalists with huge accumulations to seek profits from a flow of funds to the rest of Europe, at first to France, but increasingly to central and eastern Europe.

The net effect was to put on the European map around 1850 a number of industrial centers, with specialized competence. French cotton, for example, centered in Rouen, Lille, and Alsace; by 1850 France was consuming more raw cotton than Belgium and the *Zollverein* countries together, while still far behind Britain.[8] The Belgian industry was centered around Ghent, where handweaving disappeared. The German centers were in the Rhine valley, Saxony, Bavaria, and Silesia; Switzerland developed a very "modern" industry by 1850, in Basel and Zurich. Important industrial centers for woolens existed also around 1850: in France at Reims, Elbeuf, and Roubaix, as well as in Sedan and Paris; in Belgium at Ghent and Verviers, also in Liège; in Germany at Aachen, Reichenbach, Silesia, Augsburg, Vogtland, and Cottbus.

8. The figures in metric tons were 59,273 (France), 7,222 (Belgium), 17,117 (*Zollverein*), and 222,046 (Britain).

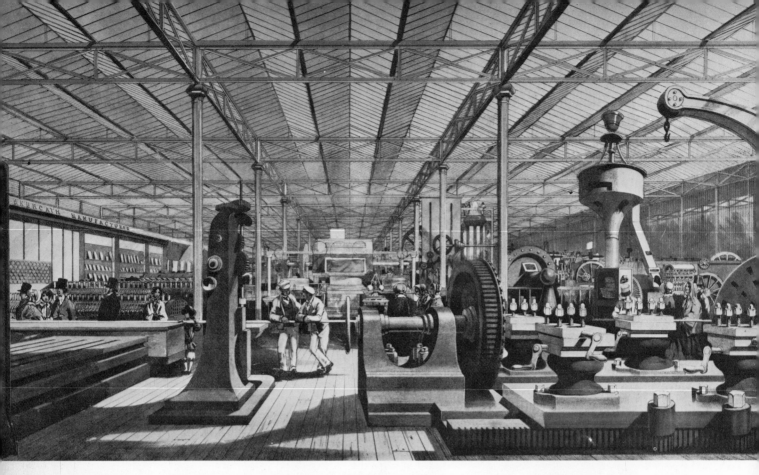

Housed in a giant pavillion of wood, iron, and glass known as the "Crystal Palace," London's Great Exhibition of 1851 was a tribute to the progressive ideas of Queen Victoria's husband Prince Albert. His goal was to bring together the finest new products and inventions from all over the world to serve as an invaluable educational experience and to stress the growing unity of all people which industrialization signified. Despite bitter conservative opposition, the exhibition was an enormous success. The most astounding exhibits were the new machines, such as these tools invented by Joseph Whitworth. His lathe for forming railway wheels (right foreground) was a vital contribution to railway development. Elsewhere the finest continental decorative arts, luxury goods, and exotic products from faraway colonies vied for the public's attention. New York Public Library.

In the heavy industries, iron and coal, slow growth began to show results in the 1840s. The French output of coke pig iron rose from 5,000 tons in 1820 to 187,411 tons in 1846. Great works grew up at Vienne, Charenton-Le-Pont, and Le Creusot. The Belgian industry grew on the basis of German demand in the 1830s and 1840s. In Germany, progress was slower in pig iron production before 1850, because of tariffs which gave an edge to Belgium and Britain. Yet in the Rhineland and the Ruhr there was some growth. The scale was small, but fine steel was being made also in the newer forges. Indeed, at the Great Exhibition of 1851,[9] the German industrialist Krupp exhibited a two-ton block of cast steel, thus illustrating the advantages a late start might produce in the form of the goods of a modern plant. Germany, with a productive capacity far less than that of the British in 1851, was already in the vanguard in technical processes. Moreover, the Silesian mines were slowly gearing up to the tasks of a modern iron industry.

The net results, however, showed up in statistics for mining, pig iron production, and the use of steam engines. In 1850 no country in continental Europe had furnaces able to produce the output of the average British works, 90 tons per week. The best on the Continent were Belgian, at 60 tons per week, while the French top effort was about 18, the German only 14 tons per week. Belgium was the only country using impressive amounts of steam power. Britain used 42.2 horsepower per thousand people; Belgium 8.76; France 1.5; and Germany only .76. Waterpower was still more important than the steam engine in French iron manufacture in the 1840s.

There were also important engineering firms everywhere: Schneider in France, Cockerill in Belgium, Egells in Germany. But these were not yet specialized, as the machine tool industry was in Britain. And a firm like

9. For which the famous Crystal Palace, a huge structure of glass, iron, and wood, was erected.

Egells made locomotives as well as lathes and distilling equipment for chemists. There was little standardization possible, therefore, and the lack of standard parts inhibited the large-scale development of reliable machine tools, which required interchangeable parts. Similarly, chemical industries were not yet *rationalized*, even where, as in Belgium, they were well supplied by nature with raw materials. In the 1840s Belgian inspectors noted how unsystematic conditions were, compared to those in the best British plants. The French industry was slow to grow, and in Germany it was not until the 1840s that a start was made at all. What distinguished the nascent chemical industry there, however, was its firm base in science, firmer than that of the other nations.

In summary, therefore, we can say that by 1850, the task of catching up was still in its first phase. Half of the English population was urban in 1851; only 25 percent of the French and German peoples lived in towns. Only 25 percent of the British worked at farming in 1851; in Belgium, the most industrialized of the continental states, half of the people worked in agriculture. In Germany a balance was not struck until 1895! There were as yet few concentrations of industrial workers in huge cities. The putting-out system was still vital to manufacturing in continental Europe, as outside of Eastern Europe the pattern of land distribution still favored small peasant proprietors willing to supplement farm incomes by weaving and spinning. Conservatives congratulated themselves on guarding against the rise of the working class and other perils of the new order, especially in France and Prussia after 1848. But the low cost of nonindustrial labor was also an index of poverty and weakness, as France was to discover when the paternal social order of the Second Empire crumbled before Prussia's armies.

CLOSING THE GAP: 1850–1873

In the period 1850–1873, which ended in a spectacular Western economic depression extending across the Atlantic to America, the continental nations caught up with Britain. Growth was rapid, with rates of increase in production in certain key measures[10] running at 5–10 percent per year. Technical maturity was also reached: handlooms gave way to powered ones; mineral fuels replaced vegetable ones; steam edged out waterpower; machine production took the place of handicraft in making nails, paper, cutlery, etc. Innovations piled on innovations: the steam hammer came in the wake of the engine; electricity entered the plant; the gas motor appeared; refined steelmaking techniques[11] were developed; and the chemical industries grew very rapidly.

The explanation of this remarkable growth falls into two quite distinct parts: on the one hand, a series of internal and external stimuli to growth appeared in the economy because of social and political events; and, on the other, a pattern of technological and organizational change struck production itself. The net result was to make Germany the main challenger to Britain's industrial supremacy. The following table illustrates this, while at the same time presenting the most striking evidence of the success of Bismarck's aggressive policy of unification in the 1860s. The new wars were won by industry rather than by infantry!

The Industrial Revolution broke the back of traditional restraints on freedom of enterprise, but it also required a steady transformation of

10. Railroad mileage, coal output or consumption, steam-power capacity, pig iron production, raw cotton consumption, etc.
11. The Bessemer and Siemens-Martin hearths for removing impurities.

TABLE 1 *Economic Development in the Third Quarter of the Nineteenth Century*

	Railroad Mileage (Statute Miles)	Coal Production or Consumption (× 1,000 Metric Tons)[a]	Steam-power Capacity (× 1,000 Horsepower)[b]	Pig Iron Output (× 1,000 Metric Tons)	Raw Cotton Consumption (× 1,000 Metric Tons)
Germany					
1850	3,639	5,100[d]	260	212	17.1
1869	10,834	26,774	2,480	1,413	64.1
1873[c]	14,842	36,392	....	2,241	117.8
France					
1850	1,869	7,225	370	406	59.3
1869	10,518	21,432	1,850	1,381	93.7
1873[c]	11,500	24,702	....	1,382	55.4[e]
United Kingdom[f]					
1850	6,621	37,500[g]	1,290[h]	2,249	266.8[h]
1869	15,145	97,066	4,040[h]	5,446	425.8[h]
1873	16,082	112,604	....	6,566	565.1[h]
Belgium					
1850	531	3,481	70	145	10.0
1869	1,800	7,822	350	535	16.3
1873	2,335	10,219	....	607	18.0

SOURCE: Landes, *Unbound Prometheus*, p. 194.

a   For Germany, production; for the United Kingdom, France, and Belgium, consumption.
b   Estimates for 1850 and 1870 (on 1869 lines) only.
c   All German figures for 1873 are swollen by the annexation of Alsace-Lorraine; conversely the French achievements are diminished.
d   An estimate based on extrapolation of a ratio of Prussian to German output.
e   A bad year; consumption in 1872 was 80,257 tons.
f   Comprised of England, Scotland, Wales, and Northern Ireland.
g   By extrapolation from post-1854 figures.
h   Great Britain, rather than United Kingdom.

commercial and civil law for its success. The agrarian societies of the West were bound by traditions to *community*-oriented legal standards of economic behavior. Britain had led the way toward a legal order that was individualistic and mobile, hence useful to the rational application of capital to production. The law, which always reflects spiritual values as well as material needs, economic interests as well as morality and social prejudice, therefore affected economic development. In the third quarter of the nineteenth century, changes in law within nations and in law governing relations among nations gave a powerful impetus to the modernization of society in Europe.

These changes were profoundly influenced by railroad building. As the major European networks were completed in the 1850s, the implications of cheap transportation became clearer. Not only were there gains in output; the least efficient shops, no longer protected by distance, were forced to streamline production or go under. Competition became a profound incentive to cut costs; so, too, did crises of credit and prices under the new conditions of enlarged markets. Producers sought relief from inhibiting institutions and prejudices. By the end of the 1860s, guild rules regulating the labor force had been swept away by legislation over most of Europe—in the North German Confederation, for example, in 1867.[12] Similarly, laws

12. The legislation was extended to the southern German states in 1870–1872.

restricting the formation of joint-stock companies were either abolished or evaded, as the demand for larger pools of capital developed.

Generally, industrialists put pressure on governments to make it easier to form companies and limit the liability of the individual members or stockholders. Laws to that effect were passed in Britain in 1856 and then in France (1863) and Germany. In Germany before unification there had been some legal tolerance for insurance companies, and also for transportation and utilities combines, but not for banking companies or manufacturers. From 1850 to 1870, when the law was changed to permit automatic registration of companies of all sorts, only 295 firms had been formed, with a capital of 802,000,000 thalers. Between 1870 and 1874, 833 new firms were formed, with a capital of nearly a billion thalers!

Other important legal changes affected the climate of commerce and industry. Prohibitions against usury[13] disappeared, again, first in Britain (1854), then everywhere: Holland (1857), Belgium (1865), Prussia (1867). Similarly, checks were legalized, bankruptcy and debt laws became less punitive, and new laws allowed foreign businesses to set up in competition with domestic ones. This last change was a signal of the general rush toward free trade. From 1857 to 1870 levies on river and maritime traffic were reduced or removed on the Danube, Rhine, Elbe, and Scheldt rivers, on the Danish Sound (Skagerrak and Kattegat straits), and in the North Sea and the Baltic. Another vital legal shift consolidated the complex currency systems left over from the age of petty states, beginning with the German "union thaler" in 1857 and extending to the "Latin" money treaties among France, Belgium, Italy, and Switzerland in 1865.

These shifts were all part of a political and intellectual climate change motivated by the needs of states and of businessmen. The French-British free trade treaty of 1860 (Cobden-Chevalier Treaty) was vital to Napoleon III's diplomacy over the Italian question.[14] But a general mood of prosperity and optimism lay at the heart of the wider series of trade treaties reducing tariffs: France-Belgium (1861), France-Prussia (1862), France-*Zollverein* (1866), Prussia-Belgium (1865), Prussia-Britain (1865), and Prussia-Italy (1865). The revolution in production was sweeping away the root assumption of the age-old economies of scarcity: that one nation's gain was another's loss. The prospect of plenty encouraged the idea of mutual profit. Protectionism was defeated between 1860 and 1870 by the fact of mutual growth and prosperity, as trade encouraged the retooling of inefficient producers and the general desire to be competitive.

The desire was essential, but not sufficient. There were also material forces at work beside transport improvement—especially new energy sources and new raw materials, most notably from colonies;[15] an increase in the supply of money; and entrepreneurial creativity.

Railroads were built in this period by the British outside of Europe, especially in Egypt, India, and North America. Within Europe, 50,000 miles of new line were laid from 1850 to 1870, compared with 15,000 miles before 1850. French capital financed construction in Spain, Switzerland, Italy, Russia, and the whole Danube valley. The Prussians, meanwhile, concentrated on building at home, with very important consequences for the distribution of power in Europe. Together, the British, French, and German thrust of railroad construction made this the leading sector of the industrial advance, which once had been led by textiles.

The search for energy sources and raw materials accelerated, both within

13. Giving loans at interest.
14. See Chapter 9.
15. See later in the chapter.

Europe and overseas.[16] Internally, some of the most important effects were spread from Sicily to Norway, where the sulfides necessary to acid production were mined. More central, however, was coal production. The exploitation of mineral fuel fields leaped ahead in France around Calais in the northwest, in the German Ruhr Valley, and in Scotland. French production quadrupled in two decades, while German extraction increased more than 500 percent between 1850 and 1871.

All of the new economic activity required increased money supplies, only part of which came from gold rushes in America and other overseas areas.[17] More important was the waning of distrust of paper money, the issue of which tripled in France and increased more than 900 percent in Prussia! "Easy money" lowered interest rates and helped expand the credit available to industries with huge appetites for capital. Bankers did, of course, ration credit to protect profits in the form of interest and the fees taken to "place" loans. But bullion reserves were growing in all central banks in the 1850s and 1860s, and credit expanded steadily, especially in three "booms": 1852–1857, 1861–1866, and 1869–1873.

The financial revolution brought with it a steady inflation, as Europe began to experience that upward march of the general level of prices which, even allowing for "busts" or depressions (1873, 1929), has characterized all industrial economies. The expansion of money supplies went hand in hand with daring innovations in the organization of banking, as the clientele for banking services widened among consumers and also among industrialists. One manifestation of the first demand was the rise of personal checking accounts and ordinary consumer credit—buying on time and the start of "savings" banks for small producers, tradesmen, and even better-paid laborers.

More important to industrial growth, however, was the organization of gigantic international joint-stock banks to finance industrial development. The corporate finance company had roots in the 1820s in Bavaria and in the 1830s in Belgium. But it was in France in the 1850s that the *Crédit Mobilier* (1852) gained government support as a balance to older financial interests. The industrial banking movement then spread to Germany, where Bismarck needed capital for army reform in the period of the budget crisis; and in the 1860s investment banks were formed in Austria, Spain, Italy, Holland, and Scandinavia.

What the investment banks did was to channel wealth into industry, seeking clients for their funds, and therefore promoting industrialization in an active way in order to maximize their own profits. Specifically, "mobile credit" banks speculated for profit on internal and overseas development,

16. As earlier it had in response to textile production: Britain drew on American and Indian cotton, Australian wool, etc.
17. Australia, South Africa. The timing of these "rushes" in the years before and after 1850 is thus not accidental, but a necessity.

Rudimentary stock exchanges were first established late in the eighteenth century, usually as informal gathering places where securities might be bought and sold. But as the capitalist system grew increasingly more complex the necessity of regulated trading and a formal manner of operation became apparent. London's exchange was built in 1802, with New York following fifteen years later. In Paris a handsome exchange was built during the Napoleonic era where trading was carried on under strict government regulation. In this mid-century drawing of the Paris bourse Gustave Doré's sharply satirical eye was trained on the spectacle of men grabbing for wealth. Enormous fortunes were made and frequently lost during this freewheeling period in international capitalism. Bibliothèque Nationale.

risking capital in "backward" economies on the assumption that industrialization was the irreversible wave of the future. Even banks that had, in the past, financed only already *established* commerce began in the 1850s to mobilize technology in new areas in order to expand what was already being called the business world. Receiving deposits, they lent for long terms in a cycle of assistance and reinforcement for growth. These "great banks" (*Grossbanken*) experienced huge gains, but in periods of sudden deflation—1873, for example—also suffered huge losses, with the side effect of bankrupting businesses which had in turn invested capital for growth in banks.

The net result of this combination of "negative" and "positive" developments was to spur the concentration of production in ever-larger units and to promote urbanization, with its attendant social developments (appearing now in continental Europe as they had in Britain): worker agitation, the rise of the "social cost versus standard of living gain" question, and other side effects—such as the increased noise of city life, with the psychic strain thus imposed on urban populations. Moreover, industry was "rationalized," by a process of relocation near major raw materials and energy sources. Thus, not only did new social patterns emerge; the patterns emerged in new places, as cities grew up where none had been before. The extreme example, of course, is dramatic: the gold-rush towns in the American West. But even more important was the rise of the industrial regions, or groupings of industrial towns.

France had always had cotton and other textile "regions," around Rouen in Normandy for instance. And Germany had in the southern region (Bavaria, Baden, and Württemberg) an important textile center, even in the days of handicraft and waterpower. In the age of iron and steel, however, Belgium became the seat of vast, sprawling industrial regions in the district around Liège; the German Ruhr Valley witnessed unprecedented increases in the scale and concentration of industrial operations. New regional patterns of life emerged to recast the map of Europe in terms of spatial concentration and also in terms of *new* centers of production.

One example must suffice. The Ruhr Valley, as noted above, experienced the most impressive change during the decades considered here. Westphalia in the 1790s, when Hegel had begun to form his notions of historical development, had been an agrarian region primarily. In the 1870s deposits of coal and iron, developed with German, French, and Belgian capital, made of it a densely populated industrialized area. In the district of the city of Dortmund alone 421,000 tons of pig iron were made in 1870, twice the output of all Germany in 1850, and thirty-five times the local production two decades earlier. Between Dortmund and Bonn creeping urbanism had begun, and two-thirds of all Prussian iron output took place there. The prevalence of cheap coal in the region had also encouraged other industrial growth: metalworking, engineering, the production of hardware. The scenery in an age of steam and speed had been transformed. Now one saw factory smokestacks, the big hoists above the coalpits, and the soot which so covered the region around Birmingham in England that it was known as "the Black Country."

Indeed, by 1870, the European industrial map already had the shape it bears today. Only the Balkan oil complexes and the Scandinavian mining regions experienced large-scale development *after* the third quarter of the nineteenth century, in terms of heavy industry. The newly industrialized areas there had not yet matured. But they had entered the era of the Industrial Revolution. And they had experienced the onset of the forces which broke apart the traditional social and political organization of Europe.

The history of economic development in Europe and the "colonial" areas which with it constituted the West between 1870 and 1914 falls into two nearly equal divisions. From 1873 to 1896, there was in the judgment of contemporaries as well as of modern-day analysts, a bust, deflation, and depression. This was followed by a period of tremendous boom and expansion, which in the eyes of contemporaries was a glorious epoch—*la belle époque*, as the French called it. It was widely held then, and is still maintained now by some historians, that the great war of 1914–1918 was alone responsible for closing this era of prosperity and optimism coupled with freedom—the "liberal era," in which the West extended its control over most of the world.

Here, we can do no more than characterize the economic development of the whole period to 1914, while pointing out how this development was itself shifting power away from Western Europe even before the world war began. For this will enable us to depict the power shift *within* Western Europe, from Britain to Germany, and also to comment on the rise of those countries which were to challenge successfully the European hegemony: Russia, the United States, and, in the Far East, Japan. In our brief, twofold account, we will trace the maturation of the Industrial Revolution in Europe and relate to it the acquisition of the new empires overseas, without concentrating on a narrative of imperialism.

The first thing requiring comment is the deflation, or decline of prices, in Europe between 1873 and 1896. Unlike the great depressions of the past— say from 1350 to 1450, or again in the first half of the seventeenth century—which were linked to serious setbacks in production and popula- tion, the late–nineteenth-century deflation took place in a period of great growth, in both population and production. Indeed, it was the gain in output per capita caused by industrialization, even in the face of the population rise, which lowered the prices commanded by goods of every sort. Real costs dropped steadily for food and for industrial commodities. Despite the fact that different national economies grew at different rates, the overall pattern was one of growth in a *world market* served by European goods.

Among the industrial countries only Britain showed a decline in the rate of growth; and this was a function of its early start. Britain exhausted the potential for increased growth from 1870 to 1890, at least in the old leading sectors. Newer industries show rapid expansion even there, however— steel, for example. Then, after 1900, what we call the Second Industrial Revolution produced another leap forward in the British growth rate; what lay behind this was a cluster of innovations: electric industries and motors; synthetic production of new materials from organic chemistry; the internal combustion engine and automobile; and, above all else, the introduction of the assembly line for standardized, precision manufacturing. Also, the new strikes of bullion in South Africa (1887), Western Australia (1887), and the Alaskan Klondike (1896) gave money supplies a boost, the effect of which became apparent in a new wave of inflation before the outbreak of World War I.

The overall result was that Germany, after a period of setback in the 1870s, rapidly resumed a very high growth rate. France responded more slowly, as did Belgium, probably because these countries had used up more of their early growth potential than had Germany. But France, so much more "down" from 1870 to 1900, had a sharp upturn from 1901 to 1913. So, too, did Belgium. And even in the so-called period of deflation impressive gains were registered in countries not effectively industrialized in the 1860s.

Sweden and Denmark showed strong growth from the 1870s, in total output and in productivity per capita. Elsewhere, the movement was more piecemeal: in Russia, Hungary, Austria, and Italy, for example. In these countries industry remained inhibited by legal and political structures, yet even in them the *rate of growth*, starting from a smaller base, was generally larger than the rate even in Germany.

Certain market considerations affected the overall pattern. First of all, demand rose sharply because of steady rises in population. The overall European population grew from 290 million to 435 million between 1870 and 1910. France and Germany had a combined rise from 72 to 110 million.[18] This population spurt meant a jump in domestic demand. Moreover, this demand was widely distributed; national incomes doubled and tripled in the most advanced economies. There is also much evidence to support the conclusion that worker living standards were rising throughout the West, although not at the same rate.

Furthermore, there was a great push from the colonial markets. Britain had consolidated both formal and informal control over important populations in India, North America, South Africa, and Oceania before 1870. From the 1850s on, the industrializing states emulated the British in imperialism also. Imperial dominion, which is discussed elsewhere in this chapter, vastly expanded the demand for European goods. From 1876 to 1914, the Western colonial powers annexed over eleven million square miles of territory, completing the expansion of Europe, which had in the medieval centuries reached the Eurasian plains and extended downward into Iberia (with the expulsion of the Arabs), before spilling over into America and Asia from 1492 to about 1610. Yet even this expansion was not all gain. The British exported their technology as well as their products, first to India, then to China and Japan. One result was the rise of local competition. The British cotton export to China fell 90 percent between 1885 and 1913. India and Japan invaded Chinese markets in addition to taking over the supply of domestic needs.

In part, this rise of competition, both among the European powers and between the Europeans and non-Western peoples beginning to industrialize,[19] benefited the people at home. The rise in per capita income made it attractive to compete for the domestic demand, by offering a larger variety of consumer goods. This was especially evident in food consumption. Cheap transport, both by rail and by steamship, brought into Europe great quantities of relatively cheap foods from overseas: Argentine beef, Australian lamb, Canadian and United States wheat, fruits and nuts from tropical places. A side effect was the encouragement of cost reductions in specialized European food production to meet the competition of colonial foods. Danish pork and dairy foods, French and Swiss cheeses are good examples of the impact of competition on the rise of Western food industries.

Together, cheap transport, which lowered production and distribution costs, and the new urban population densities made it profitable to raise food on industrial principles of cost efficiency and mass markets. From the standpoint of the ordinary consumer in the working classes, one of the most important effects of the Industrial Revolution before 1914 was the rise of the food-store chain and the miscellaneous goods shop or department store. Another was the advent of taste making through advertising and the

18. French figures were relatively stable—a measure of France's decline as a great power.
19. Especially Japan; its export of yarn and cloth in 1913 was twice that of Germany and 40 percent of the British total!

development of catalogue sales stores (the ancestors of Sears Roebuck) providing merchandise even in rural areas. The goods available at cheap prices also multiplied, as sewing machines and electric lighting encouraged the "spin-off" demands for yarn, cloth, wooden stands, and reading materials.

Some by-products of market competition were, perhaps, inevitable even if less desirable. Beyond producing goods to satisfy the needs created by advertisements, competition, together with the world trade depression, fired the retreat from free trade in the 1870s. The French, aware of the lag in their own industrial growth, blamed it on the free trade treaties of the 1860s. After decades of French agitation for the "protection" of domestic markets from British and German goods, in 1892 higher tariff walls were erected. Bismarck was anxious to court industrialists in the new German Empire, and in 1879 he initiated the repeal of the low duties. Other countries followed suit: Austria and Russia in 1874–1877, Spain between 1877 and 1891, Italy in 1887, and America in a steady stream of acts after the Civil War.

Another development, within the industrial countries, was the formation of *cartels*, or combinations of major producers to control the domestic supply and price of key commodities: coal, iron, chemicals. This trend was naturally enlarged in all countries by the general advantage in productive efficiency of large units over small ones. But in Germany large combinations to control trade fitted well with the legal structure, which was less individualistic than elsewhere, and also with the psychology of entrepreneurs hostile to the competition of nations which now appeared at an advantage in the race to acquire overseas colonies—a race Germany was late to enter. France had some traditional restraints on competition; Britain's law forbade the restraint of trade. While the legal, economic, and political situation in Germany favored cartelization the most, British "combines," nonetheless, were common in the cotton and alkalai industries, in response to German threats to dominate those fields. Moreover, in some cases—plate glass sales especially—the cartels were truly international and tended toward monopoly.[20]

Viewed in the long perspective of the history of industrialization, therefore, what the new situation represented was the adjustment of the West to the decline of the British "monarchy" industrially and the onset of Western "oligarchy," the shift to multinational domination after a period of one-nation rule. The features of the shift reflected the alteration in the balance of political power and contributed to further changes in that balance. A period of fruitful interaction on a cooperative basis gave way to a period of growth based on nationalistic economic competition. This shift was not historically unique, realizing trends already at work during the period when Britain established its commercial supremacy, before the Industrial Revolution. Moreover, the shift now appears to have been only the first of several in modern industrial history. Another was the shift of dominance to America, which was apparent after 1918. Yet another is going on now, in our time, as the growth of the Russian and Japanese economies has made non-Western societies effective challengers to American preponderance.

Before summarizing the reasons why the shift took place, we may state briefly the chief new materials, methods, energy sources, and organizational modes apparent between the late 1890s and 1914.

20. The Plate Glass Convention of 1904 involved Britain, Belgium, Germany, France, Italy, Austria-Hungary, and Holland.

The chief new materials and processes appeared in steel and chemicals. In heavy industry steel replaced iron, because of its great strength in proportion to weight and volume, and its greater plasticity. Pig iron is harder, but more brittle and less susceptible to hammering, drawing, cutting, stamping, and drilling. The use of steel industrially derived from the techniques of refining iron in crucibles which could also pour the molten metal into molds. The Bessemer and Siemens-Martin processes[21] lowered costs from one hundred pounds per ton in the 1860s to about ten pounds per ton by the 1890s, while improving the quality greatly in the crucial aspects. Britain at first dominated production; but by 1879 German output was increasing more rapidly. Total European production rose from 385,000 tons in 1870 to 32,020,000 tons in 1913—a gain of 8300 percent, at a rate of annual increase of 10.8 percent per year compounded.

The impact of the age of steel was spectacular. Steel rails, for example, endure six times as long as iron ones. Steel enabled armored ships to be built on a huge scale. In Germany the steel cartel formed in 1903 was four times as large as its British competitor. The new military application increased mechanization of production and also the division of labor, which in Germany imitated the methods pioneered in American mills. Automation introduced the "rolling" of the poured, formed metal, a successful technique which encouraged new intensive uses of capital and the growth of precision engineering. The German industry moved rapidly toward standardization; it also perfected the economy of reusing waste, both steam condensed and recycled and also oil drippings. The result was that by 1910 German iron and steel exports surpassed those of Britain. A similar shift in leadership overtook Britain's chemical industries. By 1914 Krupp Steel and I. G. Farben Chemicals were acknowledged as leaders in the industrial world.

Meanwhile, work in science and technology were assuring a similar transit of leadership in the conversion of energy into work, in the form of the distribution of petroleum fuels and electrical energy. The British inventor Charles H. Parsons perfected the use of the kinetic steam engine by coupling a jet of steam through turbines in 1884. He developed the dynamo or generator, capable of running at speeds of 18,000 revolutions per minute while putting out an electric current with the energy equivalent of 13,400 horsepower. Applied in ships, the new energy was sufficient to enable "engines" to develop 68,000 horsepower and propel a vessel of 50,000 tons at speeds of 25 miles per hour. The world was shrinking.[22] Even more striking was the invention of the internal combustion engine burning oil-based fuels, or "gasoline." The supply of Baku oil to Russian experimenters in the 1870s had proved the cheapness of the new fuel, which by 1910 dominated Russian steam production. The West depended on the opening of the Pennsylvania, Texas, and East Indian[23] oil fields before accepting for land use the new energy and the new engines burning the new fuel. But by 1914 the automobile was a familiar sight in Europe, despite atrocious roads.

The combination of electricity and the automobile completed the industrial transformation of the West. Goods and people could now traverse in a day distances measured earlier in weeks, if not months. The steam locomotive had been joined by the steamship, the automobile, and even the

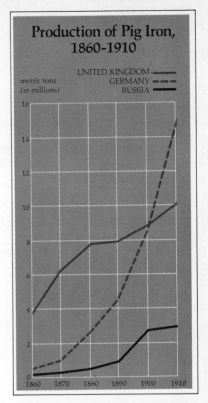

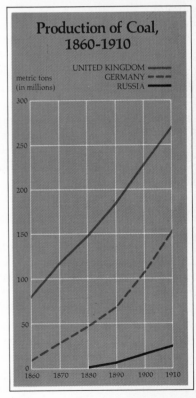

21. This last was the combined development of the German brothers Frederick and William Siemens and the Frenchman Pierre Martin.
22. In 1906 the *Lusitania* was launched.
23. Javanese and Bornean, for example.

One of the most innovative figures to explore the possibilities of the automobile was Karl Benz, a German engineer. By the time of this 1887 photograph, which shows him behind the controls of a triwheeled vehicle, Benz had developed a high speed, four-stroke engine, invented electrical battery ignition with spark induction, and discovered the differential. At this same time a number of inventors were making rapid automobile advances, and the exact chronology of events is often hard to trace. In general the search for a truly practical automobile continued until about 1910, after which the efficient production and marketing of the vehicle became the main concern. Deutsches Museum, Munich.

airplane—there having been rapid studies in flight using the new light materials and the radically more powerful internal combustion engines. Electrical generators lighted houses and streets, moved machines, sent messages over wires[24] and even by "wireless," without the benefit of metal conductors;[25] Bell had perfected the telephone in 1876. The Germans in the Ruhr pioneered the use of "current" for industrial and domestic consumption, producing 388,000,000 kilowatt hours in 1915, a level not reached elsewhere in Europe for more than another decade.

Indeed, by almost any measure, in 1914 Germany had gained industrial leadership within Europe. There was not yet a motor car in every garage or a refrigerator in every house, nor even a Gramophone; but there were many electric irons in use. The German Empire produced almost six times as much steam power as Belgium in 1907 and more than twice as much as France. German coal consumption in 1913 was equal at last to Britain's, two and a half times that of France, seven times that of Belgium. German industry was the most mechanized, the most productive, and the most specialized in terms of labor. The trend in Germany toward increase in scale of industry and toward concentration regionally was also more advanced than elsewhere, with the result that the efficiency of German labor could not be matched in Europe, nor could German power. Shortly after the world war, and despite great losses of territory by the 1918 treaty, Germany was producing 21,186,825 horsepower in its generating plants, compared with only 16,808,700 in Britain. In electric generators the German output in 1925 was 13.3 million horsepower, as compared with 8.5 million in Britain.

Despite the strides forward in industrialization, however, there was still disharmony in many quarters. The German handweavers in Silesia bitterly resisted mechanization. Workers everywhere complained of the boredom of

24. Electromagnetic telegraphs spread from Britain (1837) to America (1866).
25. Marconi began his work with wireless telegraphy in 1895.

special-purpose machine tending on assembly lines. But they were caught between these discontents and their desire to maximize their wages by overworking, since in most industries that produced small articles piece wages were more common than time wages. Laborers also were hostile to the new analyses of production sponsored by managers, in which workers were looked on as animate machines.[26] The insistence that reason take the place of habit in order to "maximize the product" was a natural sequel to mechanization; but men were not machines. And in their trade unions and in their politics they showed hostility to the ceaseless demand for speed and "standards." The marriage of science and technology might be raising living standards but seemed also to be undermining the quality of life.

This feeling of proletarian outrage was, as we know, reflected in literature—for example in Zola's novel about miners, *Germinal*, and also in Erich Maria Remarque's *All Quiet on the Western Front*, where the hatred of war was mixed with distaste for industrialism. Earlier, Dickens's *Hard Times* had included a chapter[27] about the gearing of minds to industry, in which Thomas Gradgrind, "a man of facts and calculations," seeks to destroy fantasy and imagination in Sissy Jupe, a child of nature whose father trains horses in a circus and doubles as a clown. Stefan Zweig's *World of Yesterday* had discussed some of the sexual consequences of industrial cities like Vienna, where the "steady demand" for easy sex called into being an "infantry . . . of roving prostitutes," women sexually exploited by the bourgeoisie, who supported free trade in sex also. But perhaps the most telling image of the new monotony and the debasement of love was created in Maxim Gorky's short story of 1899, "Twenty-Six Men and a Girl":

> There were six and twenty of us—twenty-six animated machines, cooped up in a damp basement where, baking butter pretzels . . . we kneaded dough from morning till night. . . . Our boss had iron-barred the windows in order to make it impossible for us to hand our morsels of bread to beggars or those of our comrades who were out of work and starving. . . . All twenty-six of us would be singing. . . . But, besides our songs, we *possessed* [italics ours] something else that was good, that we loved, that was, perhaps, a substitute for the sun . . . Tanya, a sixteen-year-old housemaid.[28]

Tanya, the innocent from the gold-embroidery shop on the second floor, who is at first never the object of lewd talk, becomes the test of the reality of the bakery-prison. The "inmates" pit their fantasy of her virtue against the seductive wiles of a handsome soldier. A game is played with Tanya as the stake. When she appears to have slept with the soldier, the bakers insult her and try to degrade her. She, in turn, calls them "convicts," in a word summarizing the contrast between her freedom and their fettered reality.

THE SOCIAL COSTS: IMPERIALISM

We cannot tell the whole story of the revolution in Western economy and society in terms of production factors, domestic demand, or even charts summarizing the shift in the balance of power within the West. Nor can we tell that story simply by looking at the changing social policies of governments, although it is essential that we do so to some extent. And, although

26. Such analyses were called Taylorism, from the writings of the American pioneer of "scientific management," F. W. Taylor, a Pennsylvanian.
27. "Murdering the Innocents."
28. This passage, and others from works of Zweig, Dickens, and Zola, are quoted from the selections in Cherniavsky, Slavin, and Ewen, *Social Textures*, pp. 130–139, 144–156, 156–166, and 166–172.

we must treat the social costs and cultural responses to industrialization in the West, it is true that even that account will not compass the full impact of the Industrial Revolution. The reason is this: part of the cost was defrayed in the non-Western world, as the "new imperialism" of the industrial nations colored the globe with the tints of the flags of Europe.

The Industrial Revolution initiated a new phase of "world history" as well as a new era of Western history. The people of Europe—from the Atlantic to the Urals and from Norway's North Cape to the southern Balkans—spilled beyond Europe's edges. In so doing, the white Europeans gave much to the world, but took much as well. If Europeans dispersed millions of people overseas, provided banking services to a world poor in capital, conquered distance itself, and diffused European technology everywhere, the Europeans down to 1914 had not done so to plant *self*-sustaining economies of growth. Instead, their purpose was often to feed the self-sustaining industrial economies of the West at the expense of economies of *survival* elsewhere. In much of the world colonized in the new empires founded in the nineteenth century, the intangible values of the old civilizations were ruined, without the benefits of rising living standards which in Europe compensated people in part for the traditional society lost in the process of industrialization.

European civilization was materialistic and filled with a sense of "mission," both heritages of its own Graeco-Roman and Christian past. This sense of mission often expressed itself in gospel terms, those of *raising humanity*, presumably from the lower depths of African or Asian "barbarism" as this was understood in Europe. But raising humanity to what? Chiefly to the mixture of God, greed, glory, the gospel, and gunpowder which the Europeans carried wherever they planted their flags. In 1884–1885, the international Berlin Conference of the European powers, called to mediate disputes at home and in the empires overseas, expressed clearly this view of colonial empires—that they existed to spread the "liberal" order of the West universally. Aggrandizement and allusions to Christ in glory were both more and less than hypocrisy then, but what is certain is the reach of Europe everywhere.

Space allows us here only the merest chronological sketch of the new expansion of Europe, with nothing more than dates, places, and the appropriate "mother" country listed, with Asia considered first and then Africa.[29] And the first thing to record about the new imperialism is this: while it made progress before 1850, it was a creation of the period 1850–1914, with the real "scramble" taking place after 1870.

Britain exercised the first and greatest influence in Asia. By the end of the 1880s, India, Burma, certain coastal areas of eastern China, the Malay Protected States, North Borneo, Sarawak, Malacca, Singapore, and part of New Guinea belonged to Britain. The British were joined in China after the 1880s by France, Prussia, Germany, the United States, and Japan. British and Russian interests had clashed in an eastward moving arc from Afghanistan (1839–1842, 1878–1879) and Persia (1884), until fear of German intentions in the region prompted a division of southwest Asia into spheres of influence in 1907.[30] Blocked in the southwest, Russia expanded to the Pacific, until 1905, when Japan defeated the Russians in a war for control of Manchuria.

The French had consolidated their interests in Cambodia by treaty in 1787 and used Catholic missionaries to penetrate Vietnam. Saigon had been

29. The Americas had been partitioned by the European powers before 1800, along with parts of Oceania.
30. Russia controlled the north, Britain the Persian Gulf "lifeline" to India.

occupied in 1858; and in 1887 a French force defeated China in a contest to control the whole region, which came to include Laos in 1893. British influence in Siam (Thailand) forced a division of spheres there in 1907. The Dutch were successful in controlling much of Java, Sumatra, Borneo and Bali after 1859.

Something of what the so-called Treaty Powers wanted from Asians can be seen in the origins and resolutions of certain conflicts. The Chinese emperors had prohibited the trade in opium in 1808, but a series of Opium Wars forced a reopening of the trade in Indian opium, managed by the British to drain bullion from China. In 1842 "treaty" ports and a huge indemnity were stripped from China by the Nanking Treaty. The concession of trade rights in the ports provided the pattern on which other Europeans created markets for Western goods and opportunities for Christian missionaries. The Opium Wars were also a model, in that they set the pattern for new wars to "correct" Chinese violations of treaty rights, with, subsequently, new treaties to expand those rights: 1856, 1858, 1860, 1895. The result was that Western countries and Japan assumed control over Chinese trade, customs, and provincial governments in some cases. Also important was the fact that in the 1890s competition for markets in China caused serious tensions among the Europeans, especially Britain, Germany, Russia, and France, while America, in 1899, pronounced the "Open Door Policy" to provide itself with an equal opportunity to invade China and provide markets for its own capital, skills, and goods.

From 1899 to 1905, with the rise of Japanese and American imperialism in the Far East, the European Great Powers were confronted there with the consequences of Japanese and American industrialization. This fact, plus the growing estrangement of the powers *within* Europe on the eve of the First World War, foretold the future. By 1910 the Western nations were unable to oppose the Japanese annexation of Korea. America was not yet ready to flex its muscles there. And the result was an opportunity for Japan. The Western influence in Asia, which suffered enormous setbacks after the Second World War—the British withdrawal from India (1947) and the defeat of the French in Indochina (1954)—had already begun to wane before the First World War.

During 1884 French and Chinese troops battled to control what is now North Vietnam. A Chinese artist painstakingly recorded a battle between the two powers, with the French occupying the two forts on the top while their battleships attack the Chinese troops maneuvering along the river from the right. Although the French won this battle they lost several subsequent encounters, and their victory in the area was only achieved by an 1885 negotiated treaty in which they agreed to evacuate Formosa and the Pescadores. The treaty left France in charge of all of Indochina which soon saw a large influx of European colonials and the establishment of a bureaucracy and government based on French models. Musée de la France d'Outre-Mer, Paris.

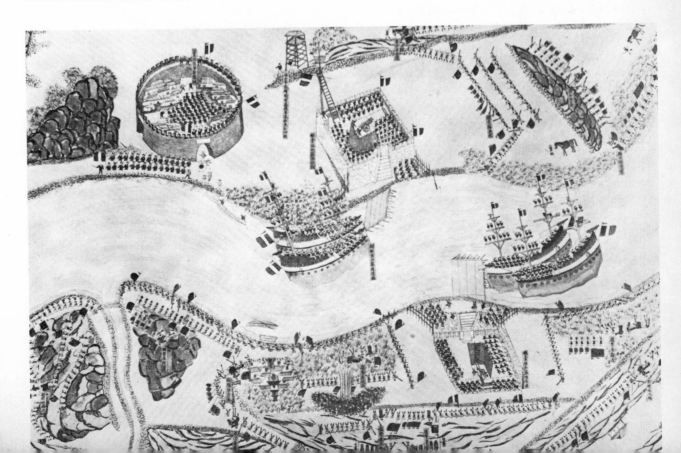

The stepping-stones of Oceania were also acquired by the Europeans, for strategic value[31] and as sources of raw materials and outlets for goods made in Europe: Britain took Australia in 1788, then New Zealand (1840), Fiji (1874), Papua (1884–1887), the southern Solomons (1893); the French took the Marquesas (1842), New Caledonia (1853), the Loyalty Islands (1864), Tahiti (1880); in 1884 the Germans took both northeast New Guinea (the western region had been in Dutch hands from 1828) and the outer islands proudly dubbed the Bismarck Archipelago! Starting late, the Germans made up for lost time: the Marshall Islands (1885), the Marianne and Palau islands (1899), with part of Samoa.[32] The United States was not outdone: it acquired Alaska and the Aleutians (1867), Midway (1867), Wake (1900), Hawaii in 1898, and Guam and the Philippines in the same year. Earlier, of course, the United States had defeated Mexico and seized a huge part of its people and territories (1848).

Africa was, of course, closer to home for Europeans and even more tempting. The coastal regions had been occupied steadily from the fifteenth century, first by the Portuguese, then by the Dutch and the English. From about 1760 to 1840 Ethiopia and the course of the Niger River had been well explored from North African bases. But it was the work of David Livingstone[33] from 1841 to 1873 which opened the era of feverish European interest in Africa. A missionary-explorer, "Bula Matari" (Rock Breaker) as Africans called him, Livingstone crisscrossed north central Africa many times, tracing the Nile and Zambesi, finding the great lakes[34] and falls, and bringing in his wake the journalist Stanley,[35] whose reports in 1871 of meeting Livingstone in "darkest Africa" caused a sensation.

The partition of Africa had started in earnest somewhat before this publicity, however. France had the largest share, a territory larger than Europe in fact, moving southward from Algeria (1830) and eastward from Senegal. By 1914 the French had acquired these areas: North Africa, West Africa [Senegal (1883–1888) and French Guinea (1895)], the French Congo (1880), Tunisia (1881), Somaliland (1884), the Ivory Coast (1889), Dahomey (1890), and a spreading northern empire in Morocco (after 1906). Belgium had annexed part of the Congo in 1908. Before that time, Britain had carved out the second great African empire, building on its southern bastion of the Cape Colony. Before 1880 Britain had taken over Sierra Leone (1808), the Gold Coast (1874), and Gambia (1843), as well as the Lagos coast (1861). In the next phase "protectorates" were declared over Somaliland (1884), Bechuanaland and Rhodesia (1885), the backcountry Gold Coast and Ashanti (1886), Zanzibar (1890), Nyasaland (1891), and Nigeria (1900). By defeating the Dutch Afrikaners (Boers) in 1902, Britain consolidated its control over South Africa.

By 1914, only Ethiopia and Liberia remained free of European control. The Portuguese extended their power in Angola and Mozambique. The Spaniards continued in control of parts of Morocco and Guinea. The Italians, late arrivals in the race, made a settlement on the Red Sea in 1885. But their real interest lay in Ethiopia, which they tried to absorb, only to be defeated in 1896 at Adowa. Turning northward, Italy "proved" the superiority of Western arms at the expense of the Turks, taking Tripoli and Cyrenaica in 1911–1912, christening the lands Libya.

31. As ports, fuel depots, and dry docks for navies, etc.
32. Germany's control in Samoa began in 1879 with a treaty securing the harbor of Apia for Germany. In 1899, after disputes, Britain ceded its possessions, leaving the United States and Germany as the only colonial powers.
33. 1813–1873.
34. Nyasa, Tanganyika, Bangweolu.
35. H. M. Stanley, who explored the Congo.

It remains only to chronicle the German achievement. Like Italy a late starter, Germany under Bismarck did enter the race for overseas territory in 1884. At the Berlin Conference, which had been convoked to settle Great Power disputes arising out of the scramble for Africa, the Germans determined to gain colonies. In 1884–1885 the acquisition of Togoland and the Cameroons began. By 1892 contiguous territories had been seized to fashion German Southwest Africa; and seven years earlier German East Africa had been established.

What the Europeans wanted in this partition of whole continents in the late nineteenth century is sometimes evident in the place names they had earlier given to some regions: the Gold Coast and the Ivory Coast. But West Africa, where these coasts lay, was not in the ultimate analysis the most

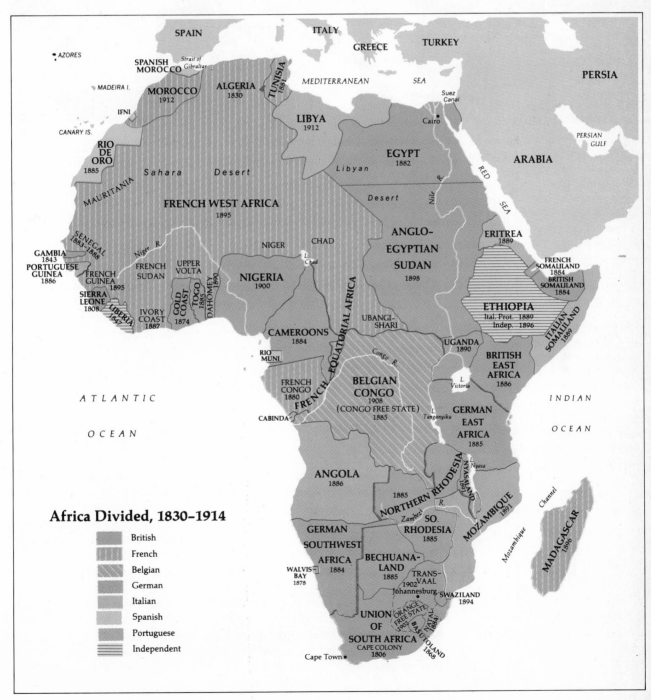

Africa Divided, 1830–1914

- British
- French
- Belgian
- German
- Italian
- Spanish
- Portuguese
- Independent

A German cartoon of 1896 mocks the "efficiency" brought to Africa by a German officer. Trees, animals, and natives stand at rigid attention as the representative of the new ruling class inspects his troops. Because of her preoccupation with the struggle for national unity, Germany entered the colonial land rush later than her European neighbors. As implied in the cartoon, the rationale of colonialization was partially built on the belief that the "civilized" societies of Europe were obliged to uplift the nonindustrial, nonwhite, "primitive" areas of the world. Behind this pious explanation lay the thinly veiled greed of the industrially advanced nations for the raw materials and commercial trade awaiting them in Africa and Asia. By courtesy of the Trustees of the British Museum.

attractive area, either economically or as a place for colonies of settlement. It was in North Africa, South Africa, and East Africa that the great colonial regimes were built and large European populations established. In the Congo and South Africa diamonds and gold dazzled Europe. The British wanted control over Egypt, as did the French, because the Suez Canal, built from 1859 to 1869 with French capital, was the great trade route bringing Asia closer to Europe. Elsewhere, the "industries" most attractive to Europeans were either the raising of food for human needs or the mining of metal to feed the even hungrier mouths of machines. Africa became the supply depot of Western wants: oil seeds, cotton, coffee, tobacco, cocoa, sisal, maize, timber, rubber, and those other "foods" for machines to feed on and to make new machines—iron, tin, copper, and rarer metals.

There were other forces at work than economic ones within the states eager to paint the map of the world in their own colors. Imperialism was in some cases a political necessity and a popular way of integrating social classes otherwise pulled in different directions by the stresses of industrial and urban life.

It is wrong to suppose that the primary social benefit to a mother country came directly from the removal into "colonies" overseas of surplus population, however. From 1851 to 1914 nearly 40,000,000 Europeans emigrated. But the vast majority[36] settled in the United States, Canada, Australia, and Latin America. The British dominions of New Zealand and South Africa were also popular destinations, because of the availability of cheap land and the demand for labor. But these countries were not "victims" of the new European imperialism after 1850. All were stable areas with essentially independent governments. Argentina, for example, absorbed nearly 6,000,000 emigrants from Europe between 1857 and 1930, while Cuba, Uruguay, and Mexico together took perhaps 2,000,000. Fewer than 1,000,000 white Europeans had settled in northwest Africa even as late as 1960! In the heavily "colonial" areas of central and eastern Africa the European population was very small in 1914: perhaps 35,000 in Rhodesia, less than 5,000 in Kenya, with even smaller groups in Uganda and Nyasaland. Indeed, in all of Africa fewer than 10,000,000 Europeans were settled in 1910 and only 6 percent of all emigrants from Europe settled there after 1870.

36. Nearly 30,000,000.

The chief "European" movement to Asia has been that of Russians into Siberia. From 1860 to 1914 about 6,000,000 Russians moved eastward, but this total is hardly ever reckoned in the context of European imperialism, although it has been the one substantial movement of settlement by Western peoples in Asia, and it has been a migration now grown to massive proportions—about 25,000,000 in all by 1970. The Russian case is a useful reminder that the "economic" motive used to explain imperialism is hardly adequate. Perhaps three-quarters of the early migrants were peasants in flight from poverty and oppression, and the majority of the labor "settlers" were either prisoners or exiles or persons forcibly resettled for reasons of state policy.

Thus, while the lands overseas did provide relief from the pressures of population within Europe, this relief was not had primarily in the areas we associate with the late-nineteenth-century "scramble." The classic lands properly associated with European imperialist ambitions after 1870 provided relief from tensions at home more directly, within the political process.

Napoleon III was one of the first European leaders to understand the potential of empire as a channel for the manipulation of popular forces. After his election in 1848, he had moved cautiously toward the restoration of the French Empire, which he accomplished in 1852. Thereafter, he sought to divert domestic grievances through a succession of adventures to restore French glory: in the Crimea, in Italy, in Mexico, and in North Africa. His pose as the champion of Italian nationalism must be understood in the general context, however, which was one of extending French influence and bringing together on that issue classes otherwise sharply divided.

Because the political strength of states was becoming increasingly dependent on the measures of industrialization, which were producing societies of many classes with diverse interests and widely divergent economic statuses, the assumptions of politicians were changing. On domestic issues

After a decade of construction, the Suez Canal was opened in 1869 under the auspices of the French empress, the Austrian emperor, and the German crown prince. Their presence indicated international recognition of the canal's vital importance in linking African and Asian colonies to Europe. A French diplomat—Ferdinand de Lesseps—was the main promoter of the canal scheme and actively supervised its progress. After early opposition to the project England also realized its potential and by 1875 moved to purchase a large percentage of the shares. Early construction on the hundred-mile-long waterway was dependent on forced native labor, but after vigorous protests from Egyptian officials the working force was greatly reduced and new mechanical and engineering methods of construction were devised. Staatsbibliothek, Berlin.

it was increasingly clear that the "classes" were at odds over economic interests and that these clashes were expressed politically. Some workers were saying there could be no economic improvement without a radical redistribution of political power—even through revolution. Within the "middle classes" there was no homogeneity either economically or in broader terms of education and outlook. Unlike the preindustrial bourgeoisie linked in guilds or a limited number of professions, the new middle classes consisted of a mixture of small artisans, shopkeepers, wholesalers, salaried managers, white-collar workers, free professionals (doctors, lawyers, and academics), engineers, scientists, ministers, writers and other artists and intellectuals, plus many grades of civil servants.

Naturally, such people had different views on key questions—for example, the extension of systems of higher education, state intervention to regulate the economy, franchise reform, and social welfare legislation. Increasingly, therefore, the original constituencies of "liberal" politics were fragmented. And politicians anxious to reconstitute them often did so only at the cost of stressing elements at odds with the original tenets of liberalism. Indeed, not only did they often encourage hostility to proletarian "revolutionists," they often accepted racist ideas, economic exclusivism, and more limited notions of how trustworthy the "masses" were with regard to the franchise.

Within Europe, this combination produced a politics we shall examine in the next chapter. Here it is crucial to notice that notions of "superiority" and racial ideas were tied together in doctrines of aggressive nationalism. Early in the century, nationalism had been a doctrine of liberation, emphasizing human brotherhood. In the hands of the imperialists, it became a racist doctrine justifying the subjection of the non-white world.

Perhaps the clearest expression of this lay in the deeds of Cecil Rhodes (1853–1902). He stressed the growth of British power through alliances with other "superior" races. The most immediate expression of this was the Anglo-German division of certain regions of Africa, which Rhodes hoped would take place on a cooperative basis. A more remote expression was in his will, in which the founder of Rhodesia provided funds to bring members of the "superior" races (Germans, subjects from certain British territories, and Americans) to Oxford University. It was Rhodes's idea that a nation's commercial and industrial classes must rely on the power of the state if that nation was to succeed in the competition for primacy among the Great Powers. But to do this, politicians must exploit the forces of nationalism in the world overseas. As "foreign affairs" ceased to be the concern only of the military and diplomatic elites, the basis of successful policy lay in diverting popular domestic tensions in the direction of the struggle for world power.

The two most outstanding examples of politicians who understood this are Joseph Chamberlain in England and Bismarck. Chamberlain had begun political life as a reforming urban official, advocating social welfare, general humanitarian ideas, and free trade. Under the intense pressures of national politics in the 1880s and early 1890s, in the age of mass parties, strikes, and the fear of socialism, Chamberlain became the leader of the British school of "liberal" imperialists. From 1895 to 1903,[37] he advocated the expansion of the British Empire, not only because of the economic advantages, but because of the opportunity such a policy offered to exploit the ultranationalist prejudices of the working class and so to limit the appeal of socialist parties which were strongly anti-imperialist.

37. His years as colonial secretary.

Bismarck constantly played on the old military and imperial heritage of the German aristocrats to win support for his colonial policy in the 1880s. In exchange for the growth of the German Empire, he argued the necessity of economic concessions to the middle classes and social welfare policies for the workers. On such terms, he sought to unify the people around the idea of Germany's national "destiny."

How exactly these compromises of policy in the national interest arose in each state is the issue to which we must now turn. But it is worth noting here that Bismarck in 1887 was able to control the Reichstag, which since 1881 had been recalcitrant on economic and fiscal policies, by raising the flag of national unity in the face of the threat of war with France and Russia.

BIBLIOGRAPHY

CADY, JOHN F. *The Roots of French Imperialism in Eastern Asia.* Ithaca: Cornell University Press, 1954. A very important work.

CAMERON, RONDO. *France and the Economic Development of Europe.** Princeton: Princeton University Press, 1966. This abridged edition treats in detail the mobilization of French capital.

CLAPHAM, J. H. *The Economic Development of France and Germany.* Cambridge: Cambridge University Press, 1930. Dated, but still a valuable introduction.

CORCORAN, THOMAS, and MILLER, W. *The Age of Enterprise.** New York: The Macmillan Company, 1949. A stunningly written account of American industrialization after 1860.

FEIS, HERBERT. *Europe: The World's Banker.** New Haven: Yale University Press, 1930. A classic now reissued; still valuable, especially for colonization from 1870 to 1914.

GALLAGHER, J. T. and ROBINSON, R. *Africa and the Victorians.* New York: Doubleday & Co., 1968. Challenges the assumption that the "scramble" for Africa was economically inspired; sees the basic consideration as political and strategic.

HENDERSON, W. O. *The Industrial Revolution in Europe.** Chicago: Quadrangle, 1961. A very good survey to supplement David S. Landes's *The Unbound Prometheus* (Cambridge: Cambridge University Press, 1969).

———. *The Zollverein.* Chicago: Quadrangle, 1959. The standard authority on the origins of economic unification in Germany.

LANGER, WILLIAM L. *The Diplomacy of Imperialism.* New York: Alfred A. Knopf, 1935. The classic study of European expansion after 1870, from the viewpoint of international relations.

LAUE, THEODORE H. VON. *Sergei Witte and the Industrialization of Russia.* New York: Columbia University Press, 1963. A careful account of the modernization of czarist Russia.

MAY, ERNEST R. *Imperial Democracy.** New York: Harcourt, Brace & World, 1961. A very good study of American imperialism.

MUMFORD, LEWIS. *Technics and Civilization.** New York: Harcourt, 1934. A prophetic quasi-Marxist, quasi-Freudian study of the alienating potential of technology.

PRATT, J. T. *The Expansion of Europe into the Far East.* London: Sylvan, 1947. Though dry, a good, useful introductory survey.

SCHUMPETER, J. A. *Imperialism and the Social Classes.** New York: Meridian, 1955. An anti-Marxist critique of Western enthusiasm for empire.

SINGER, CHARLES J. *A History of Technology.* Oxford: Clarendon Press, 1954–. Volume 5 is essential for developments in the West in the nineteenth century.

SUMMER, B. H. *Tsardom and Imperialism, 1880–1914.* Hamden, Conn.: Shoe String Press, 1968. A reissue of a classic on Russian expansion in the Middle East and the Far East.

WRIGLEY, E. A. *Industrial Growth and Population Change.** Cambridge: Cambridge University Press, 1961. A good introduction to demographic history in relation to industrialization.

Asterisk indicates a paperbound edition.

12

STATE AND SOCIETY: 1870–1914

As the seige of Paris dragged on into a months'-long stalemate, the Germans and the French finally agreed to a cessation of hostilities while a new French government was elected. A historian and right-wing intellectual, Adolphe Thiers, emerged as the head of a government pledged to end the war, and after six days of bitter negotiations with Bismarck he agreed that France would give up Alsace and Lorraine, pay an enormous indemnity, and allow the newly crowned German emperor, William I, to lead his troops in a victory march through Paris. The shame of the Parisians is expressed in this cartoon where Thiers kneels and hands the keys of the city to William. The Germans remained in the city for only two days, departing as soon as the French Assembly ratified the Thiers-Bismarck treaty. Éditions Robert Laffont, Paris.

From the time when the Revolution brought down to the masses its Gospel . . . of the Rights of Man—ever since it proclaimed that all men are equal, that all men are entitled to liberty and equality, the masses of all European countries, of all the civilized world . . . began to ask themselves whether they, too, had the right to equality, freedom, and humanity. . . .

MIKHAIL A. BAKUNIN, *On Socialism without the State* (1871)[1]

In our tactics one thing is thoroughly established for all modern countries and times: to bring the workers to the point of forming their own independent party . . .

FRIEDRICH ENGELS TO KARL KAUTSKY (September 4, 1892)[2]

THE QUESTION OF SOCIAL DEMOCRACY: TACTICS AND IDEOLOGY

In the defeats the French experienced at Prussia's hands in 1870 the Second Empire collapsed like a house of cards. The French armies had been either encircled or captured. The Paris legislature had constituted itself a "government of national defense," and a group of deputies had proclaimed a republic, the Third French Republic, on September 4, 1870. In its emergency the Assembly asked Thiers to wield supreme executive power, because the liberal statesman was alone among the old leaders in one respect: he had emerged from the politics of the 1860s with a reputation for probity and also had shown great skill in parliamentary affairs.

As Thiers sought to consolidate a new republican regime, he had to do so at a great disadvantage, however. The Prussian troops had entered Paris on January 27, 1871. A preliminary armistice had been signed the following day at Versailles. Some army elements[3] had seized forty artillery pieces meanwhile and seemed determined to continue the struggle, from the high ground of Montmartre and Belleville above the city. The new Assembly, elected in February to make peace and design a new republican government, contained many monarchists who would support only a "conservative republic." French intellectuals were shocked by the defeat of 1870, and many Catholic thinkers debated the issue of the catastrophe in terms of national decadence,

1. Quoted in Massimo Salvadori, ed., *Modern Socialism* (New York: Harper & Row, Publishers, Torchbooks, 1968), p. 139. Bakunin (1814–1876) was a Russian, upper-class, anarchist socialist.
2. From the letter condemning English "Fabian socialism" (the doctrine of the "gradualists" who advocated democratic, slow movement toward socialism) in Lewis S. Feuer, *Marx and Engels: Basic Writings on Politics and Philosophy* (New York: Doubleday & Co., Anchor, 1959), p. 446.
3. National Guard troops.

bad institutions, and the shortcomings of the educational and spiritual system within France. The ex-priest Ernest Renan (1823–1892) consolidated the sense of unease in his *Intellectual and Moral Reform,* calling for a new elitism while criticizing the hierarchic Catholic Church and comparing French education unfavorably with the German system. The climate of defeat thus revealed splits in the army and in the Church over responsibility for it.

The cannon seized by Guardsmen provided the occasion for the other major disaffected groups to express themselves. Thiers was determined to force the Parisians to give up the guns. The mayor of Montmartre was adamant against a show of force. This man, Georges Clemenceau (1841–1929), who later became premier and led France in the great war against Germany in 1917–1918,[4] warned Thiers that riots would follow any move against Montmartre. On March 18, 1871, Thiers sent troops anyway. Riots ensued, generals were assassinated, and the citizens of the capital proclaimed a commune, a revolutionary government established on March 28. Thiers massed the armies for an assault against the "Communards," who were bitterly divided among themselves.

There was some who saw the "civil war" as the first shot in a world revolution against royalists and the liberal bourgeoisie. Others sought only

Enraged by the humiliating news that Napoleon III had been taken prisoner at the battle of Sedan, the Parisian mob once again became a crucial factor in determining the flow of events. On September 4, 1870, crowds broke into the National Assembly demanding the proclamation of a republic. As they awaited news of the new Third Republic, the fashionable crowds strolling outside the assembly on that day must have shared the general sentiment that victory over the Germans could now be achieved. In fact, only two weeks later enemy troops completely encircled the city and began a four-month seige that was to bring acute shortages of food and general misery. Parisians responded magnificently to the challenge, and launched a heroic defense of their city. Musée Carnavalet; Bulloz.

4. At the beginning of the war the premier was Viviani; Clemenceau achieved power during the war.

to extend the social democratic system of communes throughout France, by means of a Declaration issued on April 19. This document stated the grievances of suffering workers and declared that the Republic alone was a regime compatible with human freedom and the hope for a decent society. In a more doctrinaire socialist vein, the Declaration asserted that public policy had to be based on community control in worker hands, without which there could be no freedom of individuals, conscience, or work. Further, the Declaration condemned the "unity" imposed on the masses from the top by "Empire, the Monarchy, and Parliamentarism," which were castigated as "nothing but despotic centralization." In the new dispensation governments would be popular, "experimental, positive and scientific." The old world, with governments based on clericalism, militarism, bureaucracy, stockjobbing, monopolies, and privileges, must cease to exist, and with it the servitude of the proletariat.[5]

Here, indeed, was another explanation of the defeat of 1870. Social distress produced by an unjust system had caused both defeat and revolution. Karl Marx, then living in London, had produced a similar analysis of the civil war in France within two months of its outbreak; on May 30 he read a treatise to the General Council of the International entitled *The Civil War in France*. In his view, the Paris Commune of 1871 was the signal for an era of proletarian revolution. Yet, only the day before his reading, the last commune (Vincennes) had fallen to Thiers's troops. Moreover, only in a few large towns had effective revolutionary communes been set up: Marseilles, Lyons, and Saint-Etienne. Elsewhere, the risings had been crushed swiftly and completely: in Toulouse, Narbonne, Le Creusot, and Limoges. Indeed, not until 1968[6] would barricades in Paris again threaten a violent revolution in France.

The real legacy of 1871 was a blow to both socialism and the working-class organizations of France, a setback which kept the left weak for a generation. During the 1870s even the Republic itself was not securely established. Thiers fell from power in 1873, before the soldier Marshal MacMahon (1808–1893), a rightist president who resigned in 1879, after having exercised nominal power during the crucial years. The German occupation ended in 1873; the new Constitutional Law officially created the Third Republic in 1875; conservative republicans gained control of the legislature in 1877. In a half-dozen years France had passed through successive stages of monarchy, revolutionary war, and republican constitutionalism based on the responsibility of the executive to the Assembly. In fact, a cabinet system emerged in which a premier, or chief minister, and his working colleagues at the main ministries exercised power because they

5. See the text of the Declaration in David Thomson, *France: Empire and Republic, 1850–1940; Historical Documents* (New York: Harper & Row, Publishers, Torchbooks, 1968), pp. 186–187.
6. In the student revolution of May 1968.

One of the artists to experience the brutal last days of the Commune was Edouard Manet, who captured the carnage in drawings and lithographs such as The Barricade. *The Commune built over one hundred barricades to use in a last-ditch, street-by-street defense of the city. When Thiers's troops finally invaded Paris on May 21, the Communards met them with fierce resistance that lasted for several days. Both sides committed atrocities, and countless innocents were shot by firing squads such as the one in* The Barricade. *When the Commune was finally crushed, over 25,000 Parisians were dead and vast areas of the city, including some of its most priceless monuments, were destroyed. Yale University Art Gallery, Meeks Fund.*

had the support of a parliamentary majority. But unlike the situation in Britain, where two parties divided the seats of the legislature, in France many existed,[7] necessitating coalition politics or alliances (blocs), with the result that parliamentary politics in France were not as stable as they appeared to be across the Channel.

Marx had therefore made a serious error of prediction in 1871, perhaps even of diagnosis. The repression of the Paris Commune had reinforced the lessons learned in 1848. A revolutionary coup from below, aimed at toppling a modern state by frontal assault, seemed an impossible adventure. A modern military machine in the hands of a willing government, even a defeated army and a government without deep roots, was too much of an obstacle to overcome. The advantages in material, transport, and communications were on the side of government. Engels, who had a keen military sense, grasped this and in the 1890s wrote to caution socialists against *premature* revolutionary actions; insurrections and street fighting were not games to be played unless the conditions insuring success existed.[8]

The defeat of 1871 was thus part of the general dilemma facing communists, socialists, and nonideologically-oriented working-class elements in the West. Was history on their side? If it was, what was the correct disposition of workers who wished to cooperate with the "future" before it happened? Was the proper stance to "help" the revolution which Marx predicted? Was it to seek a nonrevolutionary solution to the problems of inequality, through the politics of independent labor parties of the sort Engels praised? Or was it better to aim at social democracy in alliance with bourgeois liberals—to ride their coattails, so to speak?

Marx had given a clear analysis in favor of a revolutionary stance. The supreme reality in life is matter. All emotions and ideas arise out of the material conditions, or economic circumstances, of life. The natural social units are "classes," collectives of people who share the same relationships to the means of production and exchange. In the system of industrial capitalism, laborers serve the interests of others who control the tools of production and take the profits (surplus value) created by the active producers or workers. Laborers are thus alienated from control over the means of production and from the distributed benefits of their own work. They stand in an antagonistic relationship to capitalists, as once servile peasants did to lords in feudal regimes. All social and political reality derives from the dialectical opposition, or tension, between antithetical interests.

Historically, therefore, the class struggle is a manifestation of the law of the universe in human affairs. The workers are left only with the means to subsist by the parasitic capitalists. There is thus engendered in the workers the will (class consciousness) to replace capitalism with socialism, then communism—in other words, to replace the system of private ownership of property with the system of public ownership. Competition thereby gives way to cooperation, production for profit gives way to production for service. The means are *necessarily* violent revolution, because of the tension produced in proletarians by their misery.

Marx, in his general theory of production, had "explained" history as the result of the conflicts engendered among the alienated victims of economic systems. In every area of life, man is the object of manipulation by others. He is told when, where, and how to work, what to buy, and which things to

7. More than a dozen.
8. See the analysis of those conditions in our next chapter. Engels expressed himself clearly in the 1895 edition of Marx's *The Class Struggle in France.*

believe. Moreover, by asking the question, Why does everything in modern society have a price, Marx had dramatized the fact that work was expressed as the value of a product—abstractly in profit terms, rather than in terms of the basic conditions of workers' lives. Marx had said that it was labor which created value in the first place. And he had asked by what right capitalists laid claim to any part of it. The whole thrust of Marxism was to encourage workers to see capitalists as useless and harmful, and to overthrow them. Marx thus did for socialism what Rousseau had done for liberalism: put the capitalist on the defensive as once rulers had been put on the defensive.

To some of the intended victims of this analysis—the capitalists—the obvious answer was to act in such a way as to keep the workers from realizing their situation. To some of the historical victims—the workers— the future looked more pleasant from the perspective of liberal-labor cooperation than from that of class war. And, as we shall see, most workers acted other than Marx had said they would. The years after 1871 were those of the "constitutional" flowering of liberal democracy and the "welfare" politics of social amelioration. They also witnessed the political organization of labor along lines suggesting that Marx had little real knowledge of factory workers' consciousness, whatever we may think of Marxism as an explanation of reality. The politics of modernization simply did not conform to the Marxist model.

A NARRATIVE VIEW

Before pursuing in detail the relationship of economic change to either the constitutional order of the Western states or the problem of social welfare or that of the status of labor, it may be helpful for us to have in mind a brief narrative sketch of events in the main nation-states.

Britain was ruled from 1837 to 1901 by Queen Victoria and from 1901 to 1910 by the flamboyant Edward VII, a dour mother and a son notable chiefly for his love of good race horses, attractive women, and the motor car. It was good of Victoria to sponsor charities and for Edward VII to be the patron of the Automobile Club of Great Britain, but political life was centered in the ministries responsible to Parliament. After Peel's fall in 1846, the great pace of reform abated as the Liberals and Conservatives seemed equally disinclined toward new policies. The dominant politician was Henry John Temple, Viscount Palmerston (1784–1865), a man at home in foreign affairs and dedicated to domestic peace. This he hoped to achieve mainly by means of improved administration and a minimum of reform: Jewish emancipation, the establishment of a civil service commission, budget changes, and some new factory acts.

In 1867, however, a new period of major reform began. The dominant figures were the Liberal William Gladstone (1809–1898), who as a young member of Parliament favored slavery and imperialism, and Benjamin Disraeli (1804–1881), the young radical who became a great Conservative prime minister. Under successive ministries each party pursued a combination of constitutional and social reform programs down to 1885. The range of new measures touched the franchise, education, Church disestablishment, land law in Ireland, further civil service reforms, the reorganization of the courts, introduction of the secret ballot, public health and urban living standards, including as well a vast array of new acts to give the government regulatory powers over many aspects of ordinary life. Successive governments failed to ease the problem of Ireland, however, as Parliament would not endorse the principle of home rule for the Catholics there.

Benjamin Disraeli, Lord Beaconsfield, was the only Jew to become prime minister of England, and he held power in 1868 and from 1874 to 1880. Something of a dilettante, he began his career as a lawyer, then turned to writing, and was finally elected to Parliament as a Tory in 1837. His foppish appearance and theatrical manners caused his fellow members of Parliament to laugh him down during his first speech. Later he gained their admiration and became the nation's foremost Conservative spokesman, declaring himself "a Conservative to preserve all that is good in our constitution, and a radical to remove all that is bad." An ardent imperialist, Disraeli was a favorite of Queen Victoria whom he had crowned empress of India. National Portrait Gallery, London.

If the British in the 1880s and early 1890s found the question of a repressed minority in Ireland troublesome, they were subsequently to become embroiled in another troublesome question—that of labor and its position in the political structure. After a period of rapidly alternating governments—1885–1895—the Conservatives held power for ten years under the lead of two members of a powerful family,[9] the marquess of Salisbury (1830–1903) and his nephew Arthur Balfour (1848–1930). The Conservatives and the Liberals were equally parties of the upper landed and industrial classes, insofar as leadership was an issue. And both parties had embraced a combination of liberalism and imperialism, seeming to retreat from questions of social change after 1884. A serious economic crisis gripped Britain after 1893, however, and the working classes grew increasingly restive under the pressure of unemployment and a sense of political powerlessness. The organization of labor parties dates from this period, and from 1893 to 1906 the leading politicians like Joseph Chamberlain[10] watched with alarm this new development.

In 1906 a new government, based on a Liberal-Labour alliance—the Lib-Labs—initiated a new era of domestic reform, as young liberal politicians seized on the issues of imperialism and democracy as the keys to the kingdom of popular politics. David Lloyd George (1863–1945) was the brightest star, as the Liberals held power for a decade, but there were others, including the young Winston Churchill. The crucial challenge to the old order was Lloyd George's 1909 budget, which proposed high inheritance taxes and sharp levies on *unearned* income. The new revenues were to be used for social purposes. A terrific fight ensued in which the Lords repeated the error of 1831—defeating a bill popular in Commons. After two years of crisis, a Parliament Bill was passed, under threat of new peerage creations, providing for an end to the Lords' absolute veto power. The passage of the act which diminished the Lords' power was thus tied to a budget promising sweeping changes in social policy. But by now, as Britain girded for the possibility of a new European war, the problem of Ireland and the domestic constitutional crisis had sapped the strength of liberalism and raised grave questions about the future of conciliatory parliamentary politics.

Across the Channel in France questions of an even more serious nature had been raised. The Republic had been uncertain of survival in 1877, when MacMahon and the Orleanist duke of Broglie (1821–1901) flirted with Napoleonic methods, manipulating the central government's machinery to secure tractable Deputies. They failed, however, and in 1879 MacMahon lost the right to dissolve the Chamber of Deputies. A year later the seat of government was returned to Paris from Versailles, and the revolutionary "Marseillaise" was made the national anthem. The real republicans won control of the government, led by Leon Gambetta (1838–1882), the organizer of resistance in 1870 and the architect of the victory over Broglie in 1877. His hope was to unite moderate republicans against both the left, which favored attacks on the army and the Church, and the right, which was composed of clerics, industrialists, and other conservatives hostile to reforms.

Gambetta's defeat and subsequent death in 1882 opened a new period of tentative reform, directed mainly against the clerics. The Jesuits were expelled from France and primary education was reformed. But pressing economic problems preoccupied the government, especially the sluggish state of agriculture and the preference of investors for overseas adventures

9. The so-called Cecil gang.
10. A Birmingham industrialist, 1836–1914.

instead of industrial development at home. Moreover, radicals wished to reform taxes, to democratize the 1875 constitution, and to weaken the Church, while demanding revenge on Germany. The Monarchists also seemed threatening, as they rallied around the count of Paris as pretender. When danger came, however, it took the form of General Georges Boulanger (1837–1891), the war minister who in 1886–1889 rallied the "malcontents"[11] and the working classes. Dismissed from office in 1887, Boulanger capitalized on threats of war in the Balkans, and in 1888, now dismissed from the army, he stood for election.

This campaign for a coup of ballots not bullets worked in 1889, when Boulanger won election in a Paris radical district. But a planned coup d'état based on the popular mandate failed when Boulanger apparently turned coward and fled. New elections produced large moderate majorities. The threat of Bonapartism, of which Boulanger was the shadow, remained to plague the Republic, however. Corruption was widespread. Then, in 1894, a Jewish army officer, Captain Alfred Dreyfus (1859–1935), was convicted of treason in an atmosphere of rampant anti-Semitism. Zola and other writers gathered evidence pointing to the guilt of another man, but the army reacted peculiarly. A staff officer forged evidence to confirm Dreyfus's "guilt," with the support of anti-Semites, royalists, militarists, and a segment of the clergy. Dogged effort on Dreyfus's behalf exposed the fraud in 1899; a pardon was obtained for the prisoner on Devils Island.[12] The socialists and radical republicans who had championed Dreyfus's cause used the victory to punish opponents, namely in the army and the Church.

By 1906, therefore, a stark confrontation existed between two Frances, that represented by journalists like Zola, the Dreyfusards, and that represented by Charles Maurras (1868–1952), the leader of the emergent right, an apostle of monarchist revival, Church, and army. Abetted by others like Maurice Barrès,[13] a racist-nationalist who integrated anti-Semitism with a militarist advocacy prophetic of facism, the rightists had launched street attacks against known Dreyfusards, especially the politicians Clemenceau, Briand, Caillaux, and the Jewish socialist Léon Blum. In France, therefore, in the decade before the First World War, the Republic and liberalism were in place but also besieged. Relations with the pope had been broken in 1904. From 1906 strikes crippled industry. Schemes for tax reform failed, while more was spent for military purposes than liberals and socialists believed proper. Most notable in his opposition was Jean Jaurès, parliamentary socialism's leader, who fought relentlessly against Clemenceau's "war" budgets, which to Jaurès seemed to predict the new war with Germany which revenge-minded republicans appeared to want.

Affairs in Germany were on the surface more orderly. The empire Bismarck had established was dominated by Prussia. Within that state, the king ruled in cooperation with the noble military-bureaucratic class. Prussia had a veto in the new Federal Council, and the three-class franchise in Prussia assured conservative domination in the elected *Landtag*. In the smaller states monarchies existed. Bismarck had thus protected Prussia against "merger" with the rest of Germany as well as against the democratic constitutionalism he distrusted. Responsible to the kaiser, he was imperial chancellor in Germany and minister-president in Prussia, a combination of offices held until 1890, when a rupture with the new ruler William II (1888–1918) forced Bismarck from power.

---

11. Bonapartists, Monarchists, aristocrats, and extreme radical republicans.
12. Full exoneration was made in 1906.
13. 1862–1923; author of *Les Déracinés* (1897).

During the years of Bismarck's dominance, there were two weaknesses in his system. Power depended on the kaiser's good will and also his character, his willingness to exert himself in government. Secondly, the dominance of the army and Prussian *Junker* class within Prussia was a direct reproach to the Prussian liberals. The elections for the federal Reichstag were based on universal manhood suffrage. This not only made it difficult to justify the system within Prussia. In the empire it meant that Bismarck had to rule in alliance with the National Liberals.[14] For a few years the Chancellor's policy seemed acceptable to the compromise-minded liberals, especially in 1872, when Bismarck abolished the remnants of manorial jurisdiction. Indeed, Bismarck may be supposed to have accepted "liberal" programs early in the 1870s for practical reasons. The termination of French indemnity payments in 1873 coincided with the onset of a worldwide economic crisis. This had been predicted by some economists who had viewed the great boom of the sixties as unhealthy. But Germans had all but ignored the crash of the Vienna stock exchange in May 1873. Then, in October, the major German exchanges fell from the dizzying heights to which they had earlier risen under the stimulation of many fraudulent operators. The depression begun in 1873 lasted until 1895, and in its first stages caused much soul-searching about the benefits of industrialization. But Bismarck, reacting slowly, had by 1876–1877 decided on a course of economic and social reform.

He began the passage into law of many significant measures. These touched coinage uniformity, commercial law, reform of the criminal law and the courts, and the establishment of a national bank and railroad bureau. Paradoxically, the most important reform measures touching the working classes were enacted from 1883 to 1889, in what historians regard as the high-water mark of the "conservative" system established in 1881.

Neither characterization—that of the 1870s as a liberal period or that of the 1800s as an era of conservative policy—is entirely secure. The 1870s were marked by numerous antiliberal measures. Bismarck launched an attack on the Catholic Center party, because it accepted the doctrine of papal infallibility declared as an article of faith in 1870. But Bismarck also had as a motive in this *Kulturkampf*, or cultural struggle, the protection of the "Old Catholics" who rejected the new papal claims. From 1871 to 1874 legislation repressive of the pro-papal groups was passed, and then, in response to protests from Protestants alarmed by abridgments of free worship, even more harsh legislation took shape, compelling civil marriage and abolishing cloisters within Prussia. Bismarck thereafter made a slow retreat, and laws passed in 1880, 1882, and 1883 restored Catholic rights.

During the same so-called liberal period of the 1870s Bismarck deserted the National Liberals on the free trade issue. Moreover, an assassination attempt against William I in 1878 rallied conservative forces in support of repressive measures against radical parties. Bismarck struck hardest at the socialists in the Social Democratic Workingmen's party in 1878 by passing acts outlawing socialist meetings, publications, and fund raising. These measures were renewed periodically until 1890. The acts were accompanied by the "state socialism" reforms of the 1880s, but even ameliorative acts could not disguise the nature of the system already in place in 1881, a system which lasted unchallenged until 1918, except for a brief period under General von Caprivi.[15]

This system was in essence what the later socialist leader Karl Liebknecht

14. And the pro-Bismarck Reich party conservatives.
15. Chancellor, 1890–1894.

(1871–1919) called a "night-watchman state." Reforms as "bribes" to workers were intended to encourage their loyalty to Bismarck and imperial Germany in a regime of paternalism. Power rested with an alliance of Prussian conservatives, industrialists among right-wing National Liberals, and some centrist elements—all adamant against responsible government. Along with an elitist system of higher education, the government rested on press control, the police, the army, and the bureaucracy. The dominant outlook was that of the *Junker*-militarists who protected agriculture and the cartel-oriented big industrialists who supplied the army's modern needs.

The characteristic policies suppressed the national minorities (Poles, Danes, Alsace-Lorrainers), stultified party life, encouraged imperialism, and enshrined the principle of "divide and rule" at home. William II was by disposition a "liberal," and he clashed with Bismarck over repressive laws. But it is a mistake to suppose that William's "new course" after 1890 was really liberal. Caprivi conciliated the masses by dropping the antisocialist laws and extending social welfare, but there was no move toward democracy. The Kaiser pushed hard for aggressive military, naval, colonial, and diplomatic policies which isolated Germany in Europe. And by 1912 something like a crisis had occurred in the Reichstag, where the restored Social Democrats controlled one-third of the seats. Although Marxist, the SDP was also reformist, agitating for political democracy within the German Empire and especially in Prussia, with the support of other "progressive" parties. A constitutional crisis loomed even before 1914, when the war intervened.

In the three chief Western states—England, France, and Germany—the triumph of liberalism was therefore incomplete. England was the most liberal state; France was in some ways more radical, but much less stable; and the German Empire blended political conservatism with a variety of welfare measures, while disallowing any idea of responsible government.

Elsewhere in Europe a similarly wide array of political situations had taken shape between 1870 and 1914. In Austro-Hungarian life the great fact was Francis Joseph, who retained the dual monarchy from 1867 to 1916. Within each state there were responsible legislatures, but on military and diplomatic questions the Emperor was not effectively restrained. His government rested on the clerical support of the Church and Catholic politicians, and it was not uncommon to have a cardinal archbishop as chancellor. Socialism was under the burden of repressive legislation and the same sort of state welfare measures Bismarck had designed to secure worker loyalties. As in Germany, policy toward the "nationalities" (Czech and Slav especially) was repressive. Yet there was in 1907 a concession to political democracy, in the form of universal male suffrage. This was bitterly denounced in Hungary. There, the Magyars were worried by the prospect that the Slav majority might use the vote in one of two ways: either to revolutionize the country or to shape movements of "national" secession. The result was the withdrawal of the extended franchise in Hungary.

At the eastern end of the West, Russia had passed through a phase of liberalism, followed by one of severe reaction, and then a period of revolutionary agitation. The liberal experiments were made under Czar Alexander II (1855–1881), who nonetheless was wont to resort to the by now familiar tactics of Russian autocracy, governing through edict, police action, and the power of the army.[16] Equally characteristic of the Russian system was the rural regime of serfdom, in which some "owners" were paternalistic but many were brutal and not effectively limited by public law.

16. The Rumanian regime remained without any vestige of democracy or responsible government also in this period, indeed down to 1914.

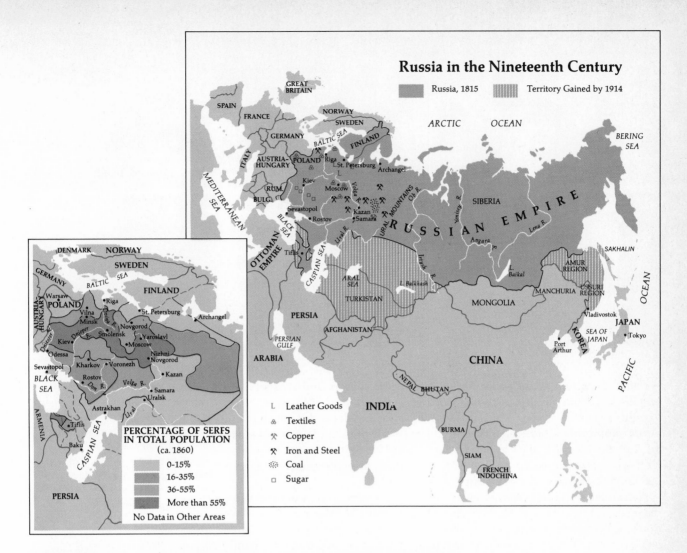

Russia in the Nineteenth Century

▨ Russia, 1815   ▥ Territory Gained by 1914

PERCENTAGE OF SERFS IN TOTAL POPULATION
(ca. 1860)

- 0-15%
- 16-35%
- 36-55%
- More than 55%
- No Data in Other Areas

L Leather Goods
⚶ Textiles
⚒ Copper
⚒ Iron and Steel
▦ Coal
▢ Sugar

Alexander's reforms were sponsored by the pro-Western intellectuals, or *intelligentsia*, and directed at reforming serfdom and the methods of both local and central government. Serfdom was abolished by a decree of emancipation in 1861, which made the peasant a subject of the government, not of the former owner, and ended the institutions of forced labor and manorial jurisdiction. But the gentry kept about half the cultivated land, and the half the serfs received had to be bought by the freed serfs, who also had to compensate their former lords for the abolished dues and services.

The long-term result within village society was the establishment of a rural social structure of peasant classes within the *mir*, or commune. Very prosperous peasants emerged, as well as wretchedly poor ones unable to take advantage of their new mobility or the other reforms Alexander set in motion. An edict of 1864, for instance, had reformed the courts of law, providing for public trials and the right to counsel as well as an appeals system. An edict of the same year established provincial and district councils of self-government also—*zemstvos* with powers to supervise education, relief, and the provision of the basic amenities of community life.

The revolution of 1863 in Poland had set Alexander II against the idea of a liberal government at the center, however, and he suppressed agitators for representative government who called for a parliament.[17] This campaign

17. A duma, or *zemsky sobor*.

presided over by a secret police force[18] persecuted writers and a variety of socialists, including the anarchist followers of Bakunin, Marxists, and disciples of the less radical Herzen. In 1880, however, Alexander relaxed the police suppression, restored a measure of press freedom, and went so far as to propose elected bodies to advise the Council of State. A year later the Czar was assassinated by an anarchist member of a secret terrorist society called *Narodny Volya*, or the People's Will.

Alexander III (1881–1894) restored a regime of suppression against not only revolutionaries but liberals also. These years set the stage for the renewed agitations of the period 1894–1905, at which time Russia's defeat by Japan triggered an abortive revolution and new experiments with reform. But these developments may be discussed more fruitfully elsewhere, by way of introduction to the revolution made by Lenin in 1917.[19]

In Italy, which was the other major state in the Western system, the legacy of unification was not a good one. The national government of Victor Emmanuel (1861–1878) met with bitter papal opposition over the loss of temporal power forced on Pius IX. Moreover, Italy was a poor country, especially in the south, where no industrialization had occurred. The southerners resented the Sardinian dynasty, with its "modern" policy of centralization. Victor Emmanuel also had to combat the aggressive patriotism of men like Mazzini and the politicians who favored "redeeming" the territories held by France and Austria but regarded as Italian.[20] There was also no clear-cut party system to manage legislative and political life. The lack of an educated public inhibited traditions of responsible government and encouraged political corruption. Italy's political life settled into a moderately incompetent pattern of efforts to transform the country, under the liberal Agostino Depretis (1813–1887), the leading politician from 1876 to 1887.

But he and his successor Francesco Crispi (1819–1901) enjoyed only

Gustave Doré scorns the callous treatment of Russian serfs by their owners in this cartoon of nobles betting their peasants in a card game. Russian intellectuals who were in contact with the West strongly agitated against the barbarism of Russia's agrarian economy. Finally, under the threat of a peasant revolt in 1861, Czar Alexander II freed some 40,000 serfs. However, the terms of their liberation were less than generous, and the serfs were forced to pay their former masters for their lands and abolished feudal rights. The basically conservative Alexander made concessions only under duress, and the later years of his reign were marked by harsh terror; he was assassinated by revolutionists in 1881. Prints Division, The New York Public Library, Astor, Lenox, and Tilden Foundations.

18. The infamous Third Section.
19. See later in the chapter.
20. *Italia irredenta*: the Trentino, Trieste, Istria, Fiume, and parts of Dalmatia.

limited success as exponents of *trasformismo*. Italian politics produced a baffling array of short-lived coalition governments based on Depretis's principles of transforming opponents into allies by bribery. *Trasformismo* thus came to mean a method of political manipulation which more than adequately implemented laws changing social structure or raising the level of education, prosperity, and political consciousness. As Italy moved into the twentieth century, little had been done to modernize agriculture or reduce inflation. Less had been done to make the tax system fairer. But protectionist policies had helped the growth of some industries—especially silk, rubber, textiles, and armaments.

Crispi had diverted badly needed energies into imperialism and war in Africa. Then in 1898, the temporary dictatorship of General Luigi Pelloux (1839–1924) grew out of the acute unrest caused in the northern industrial areas by unemployment. His failure was significant, however, because King Humbert was assassinated in 1900 for the support he had given Pelloux.

The next decade was marked by industrial strikes, which produced strong support for repressive measures against workers among the moderates. Electoral defeats of the left did not still the fears of revolution among moderates, however, and the rise to power of Giovanni Giolitti[21] signaled two things: a realignment in politics and a decision for modernization. Pope Pius X encouraged Catholics to enter politics to support moderation. Giolitti was determined on industrializing Italy on a broad democratic basis, which included franchise reform and cooperation with nonrevolutionary socialists. His schemes required Catholic support, however, and by 1912 this had raised the question of the stability of the social experiment in which success depended on the reconciliation of hostile interests: anticlericals with Catholics, socialists with the great "feudal" landlords of the south, the mass of illiterates with the elitist partisans of restricted educational opportunity.

Thus in the great states, the impulses toward modernization given by constitutional reform and industrialization in different combinations had produced tensions encapsuled by the label "the social question." It was only in the small states that the road to modernity seemed less rocky. Switzerland accepted universal manhood suffrage in 1874 and enacted much social welfare legislation afterward. The same thing may be said of Belgium after 1893, the Netherlands after 1896, and the Scandinavian nations[22] after 1898. In North, Norway was able to establish its independence from Sweden by peaceful means in 1905, in a "nationalist" revolution without precedent elsewhere in Europe. Even in the so-called backward states of Iberia and the Balkans[23] outwardly constitutionalist democratic regimes existed in monarchical form on the eve of the First World War.

The politics of modernization seemed to work best in the less advanced states, therefore—a proposition gaining in strength from the example of the emerging colossus of North America, the United States. Its Civil War (1861–1865) was in large measure the test of strength between an industrializing democracy in the North and an elitist, quasi-feudal slave power in the South. It is hard to imagine a sharper formulation of the "social question," with its integration of issues touching the franchise, the status of labor, and the actions of governments in the area of social welfare legislation.

How the politics of modernization worked in the large, more industrial states of Europe must now be our main concern.

21. 1842–1928; three times prime minister between 1903 and 1914.
22. Norway (1898), Sweden (1907), and Denmark (1914–1915).
23. Spain, Portugal, Greece, Bulgaria, and Serbia.

THE POLITICS OF MODERNIZATION:
PROLEGOMENA

In the preindustrial societies of the West the dynamic force of growth supplied by economic changes had many social and political transformative effects.[24] The economic growth represented by the Industrial Revolution wholly transformed productive processes in the advanced Western societies by 1870–1890, however, and with the productive processes social and political equilibriums as well. There were now new problems, new institutions, new men, as well as the new technologies, affecting educational needs, the media capable of forming consciousness, and the very movement of peoples in space. Even in the most conservative political systems— in Russia for instance—we have seen how phases of passivity and government reformist activity alternated as leaders sought appropriate responses to challenges often but half-understood.

As the shape of society is transformed, political leaders face policy issues of unprecedented complexity. And the complexity derives in part from the fact that rapid growth and social change outstrip the ability of the political system to adjust to the political sentiments of vital new constituencies. Sometimes, these "constituencies" enjoy the franchise and agitate for such directly modernizing objectives as the construction of the transport network and commercial law codes essential to growth. Sometimes the pressure comes from groups not yet "constituencies" in the formal political sense of having the vote—for example, laborers who seek the right to form trade unions long before they contemplate an active political role either by obtaining the vote or by organizing working-class political parties.

The politics of modernization in the West were, therefore, characterized by a variety of pressures which we may subsume under three headings: the direct constitutional question of the franchise and the distribution of political power; the economically induced issue of social welfare for the masses; and the related matters of colonial expansion and war, which were organic components of the expansive needs of industrial states. In the remainder of this chapter, we shall focus on the constitutional and welfare questions, relegating to the next chapter in this book the issue of imperialism and security in the industrialized West. The main burden of our argument here, in a selective comparative analysis, will concern the vote and the struggle for democratized, responsible government.

THE POLITICS OF MODERNIZATION:
CONSTITUTIONAL CHANGE

The basic constitutional challenge posed by industrialization was that of wider participation in the political processes of the state. Specifically, the question was whether justice could be obtained in an industrial society on the political bases of that society's preindustrial organization. And, if it was supposed that a just society could not be had on such bases, then there was a further question: Could order itself be maintained within a society perceived to lack justice? There are many aspects to each question, but two related ones concern us here. Within the new economic framework, what changes in electorates were made? And what was done to accommodate within the law the desires of working-class people to organize associations to advance their interests? To answer these questions we shall draw on data from Britain, France, Germany, and Russia primarily.

With regard to the electorate, Britain had made the decisive change toward democratization in four stages. When the 1832 Reform Bill became

24. See chapters 8 and 10.

law, only 25 percent of the people lived in cities. In 1867 about 55 percent of the British were town dwellers. This shift was recognized in the Reform Bill of 1867, with which Disraeli intended to win urban voters to the Conserva-tive party. The act increased the electorate from 1,359,000 to 2,456,000 voters, with most of the new franchise in the hands of urban workers. A further Reform Bill in 1884 was promoted by the radical Liberals, largely in the hope of making Gladstone's party the home of labor. This bill democra-tized the electorate, adding about 2,000,000 new voters. No further reform took place until 1918, at which time universal male suffrage was introduced and women over thirty were given the vote. The government was widely based and responsible to the majority of elected representatives in Parlia-ment.

The French electoral laws of 1871 and 1875 had provided the essentials of a universal male suffrage, with about 10,000,000 voters, although women remained without a voice throughout the period we are here considering. In France there was also responsible government after the failure of Mac-Mahon and Broglie. This constitution emerged after protracted struggles between widely separated factions, however, and the result was, as we have seen, factional parties and an instability of ministries, there being ninety-nine different governments in office from 1871 to 1940. Moreover, gerry-mandering produced a situation in which one urban vote cast by a worker had less weight than one rural vote. French political life was therefore both fragmented and distorted under the Third Republic, facts which made the solution of welfare questions difficult despite genuine constitutional democ-racy.

The German Empire resolved the constitutional issue in 1867–1870 in favor of electoral democracy. The imperial franchise for the Reichstag was universal male suffrage. On the state level, however, there were sharp differences between the southern states and the northern ones; the former adopted universal male suffrage, while the Prussian "class" system was favored elsewhere, with strict requirements based on property and tax payments. The purpose of these state restrictions was to limit the represen-tation of urban workers in rapidly industrializing states like Saxony and Prussia, and so to minimize socialist influences at the state and local levels. Within the class system the first-class constituency of 300,000 Prussian conservatives returned 143 legislators; the same number of socialist voters in the third class returned none! It was generally conceded that each vote in the first two classes counted as much as 100 third-class votes. To illustrate the point, we may consider the Berlin Social Democrats. In the 1903 city elections, their party won every seat in the Reichstag, but in the Prussian *Landtag* the party was practically unrepresented.

Even on the federal level, however, the democracy was deceptive. Bis-marck had ignored the Reichstag in 1862, and at critical moments other chancellors followed the precedent. Indeed, in 1890 Bismarck had openly urged reducing the powers of the Reichstag, which in any case could not hold a chancellor responsible for the policies of his government, forcing his dismissal. Nor could it protect from dismissal a reforming chancellor like Caprivi, who fell in 1894, a victim of William II's surrender to the *Junkers*.

The relative impotence of the German legislature was also a result of political fragmentation as well as of a formal lack of powers. From 1884 to 1912 there were never fewer than seven parties represented, and these parties were more concerned with special interests and ideology than with the coalitions that might have made constitutional responsibility possible. The *Junkers* favored an authoritarian monarchy to shield their own class interests, and the upper bourgeoisie leaned in the same direction to hold off the rise to real power of the workers. The overriding political fact, there-fore, was that the socialist and liberal "progressive" parties used up energies in campaigns for electoral reform and responsible government. Riots over these questions, breaking out first in 1906 and 1908, became common thereafter, and only the First World War eased the suffrage agitation, before sweeping away the German Empire itself.

Similar riots plagued the regimes in Belgium and Hungary, in 1902 and 1912 respectively. Belgium suffered a new wave of electoral violence in 1912. Meanwhile, the constitutional issue was decided in favor of democracy in Austria in 1907 and in Italy in 1912, in each case tying literacy to male suffrage, for those over twenty-four in Austria and those over twenty-one in Italy. In all of the Western states, therefore, unresolved ballot issues existed, because only Denmark in 1914–1915 had given the vote to all citizens, male and female, on the sole requirement of being twenty-five years of age.

Electoral reform and the principle of responsible government lay at the heart of political consciousness among the majorities in all states—even in Russia, where the Revolution of 1905 protested against outmoded autocra-cy, bureaucracy, and the utter failure of the system to adjust to the onset of the Industrial Revolution there. Czar Nicholas II (1894–1917) granted a new constitution in 1905. By its terms a constitutional monarchy was created, with an elected duma. From 1907 a prime minister and a council had the cooperation of a relatively free press, legal parties, a parliament elected on a broadened franchise, and a ruler sufficiently frightened to go to the extreme of legalizing trade unions at the urging of his premier, Peter Stolypin (1862–1911).

The Russian government had suffered a defeat in war in 1905, and this had called into question its legitimacy, just as Napoleon III's empire had to

answer for the defeat of 1870. Foreign intrusions could, therefore, be as transformative—more so—for a constitutional system as domestic industrialization had been elsewhere. Military defeat had even produced the redress of worker grievances in the form of legal unions and the right to strike, things won elsewhere without war.

Within the framework of the constitutional order of the West, the status of organized labor was a crucial one. Briefly, the situation in the West before industrialization had been such that "trade unions" were outlaw organizations, on the premise that collective working-class activity was always a conspiracy to restrain the freedom of enterprise. In Britain the basic legislation was passed in medieval times, and various guild law codes had enforced similar restrictions in the many states and free cities on the Continent. The rise of industry caused new vigilance, however, and industrial labor relations became a vital part of the problem of justice and order.

Within Britain the Combination Acts of 1799, 1800, and 1825 maintained the marginal character of worker associations. A repeals act of 1824 had not fully liberated workers from legal restraints, and the 1825 act, while being repressive had allowed some union activities. Within the narrow framework of legal unionism there had been a rich growth of unions by 1867. As the industrial economy matured after 1850, the problem of defining in public policy what workers could and could not do deepened. The basic problem was the organized strike, the weapon used to advance the expressly lawful purposes of securing better wages and shorter hours. The Amalgamated Society of Engineers had been a model for other skilled workers after 1851, and in 1868 a Trades Union Congress had organized nationally to agitate for labor reform. The chief problem was to repeal on 1859 act restricting picketing and prohibiting strikes.

With the political power created by the 1867 Reform Bill had come another legal blow. A royal commission in that year had investigated union "violence"; and a court decision had withdrawn legal protection of union funds against damage suits. Between 1871 and 1876 various statutes relaxed restrictions on strikers and legalized picketing and forms of "collective" bargaining. The struggle for justice then shifted to the plight of unskilled workers in the 1880s, as trade unionism spread to their ranks. The successful strike of the London dock workers in 1889 stressed the militancy of unskilled labor, which seemed less persuaded of the benefits of liberal reformism. The fear of socialism revived among industrialists and intensified in 1893, when workingmen formed their own political party, the Independent Labour party, under the lead of Keir Hardie, a Scottish miner.[25] When in 1900 the socialist Ramsay MacDonald[26] helped to form the Labour Representation Committee,[27] the conjunction of the strike and the socialist "labor" party seemed to many to threaten the liberal dominance of parliamentary politics and the satisfaction of grievances in behalf of workers, but not by them.

One result of the new climate was the Taff Vale decision of 1901. The Taff Vale Railroad successfully sued for strike "damages" the Amalgamated Society of Railway Servants. An award of £23,000 was made against the union, thereby revealing a new weakness, the lack of immunity at law of union funds. It had been thought that the 1871 reforms had protected such treasure chests. When the Lords upheld the decision on appeal, the result was a transformation of working-class politics. Labor representatives in

A series of Japanese victories over Russia during their war of 1904–1905 had immense political repercussions inside Russia. After several general strikes, mobs swarmed toward the Winter Palace in Saint Petersburg to demand reforms from Czar Nicholas II. Palace troops fired on the crowd, killing over 1,000 people. During the tense period following this "Red Sunday" there were student protests, military mutinies, and the assassination of the Czar's uncle by anarchists. Finally Nicholas's minister, Count Witte, negotiated a treaty with Japan and soothed the Czar's irate subjects by promising them a constitution. Here, marchers in Odessa carry a picture of the Czar after his concessions. Culver Pictures, Inc.

25. 1856–1915; the first Labour member of Parliament.
26. 1866–1937; later the first Labour prime minister.
27. The forerunner of the Labour party (1906).

Commons pressed Parliament to reverse the decision, while outside parliamentary chambers the Labour Representation Committee saw a growth in its membership from 376,000 in 1901 to 881,000 in 1903!

In the 1906 general election 50 Labour candidates stood, 40 with varied labor union support, and 10 supported by the ILP. Bargains were struck with Liberal candidates to have 32 of the 50 unopposed by Liberals, making for a straight fight in those constituencies against Conservatives. In that election 29 Labour members of Parliament were elected, with 377 Liberals. The back of the Conservative rule had been broken, and the immediate consequence was the reversal of the Taff Vale decision by the new Lib-Lab Parliament. A new age for labor had begun.

On the Continent working-class combinations had similar traditional restrictions. In France laws passed in 1791 had made unions illegal. The Civil Code of Napoleon had outlawed unions and had given a master's word greater weight at law than a worker's. A law of 1834 reinforced bans on picketing and strikes, and in 1849 the new republic of industrialists again outlawed unions, after the revolutionary "freedom" granted in 1848. Some relaxation came in 1864, when the law making combination a crime was abolished. Then, in 1869, the double standard regarding testimony in courts which prohibited workers from giving evidence against their employers was abolished. The Commune of 1871 set back labor tremendously, however: 38,000 workingmen were arrested, some 20,000 executed, and 7,500 deported to New Caledonia. There was no amnesty until 1880, and freedom of association was delayed in France until 1884.

The long-term result was to slow the growth of unions and also to insure that in them socialists would gain a more attentive hearing. When the first French Labor Congress met in 1876, there were already 130 unions represented. But in 1914 the total membership of such unions in France was about 1,000,000, less than a third of the total for Britain. Within union ranks, in the CGT,[28] or General Confederation of Labor, there were sharp divisions. Some saw the law of 1884, which forbade freedom of association in labor unions, as opposed to association in political parties which were transitory, as a mandate for cooperation with parliamentary radicals. They rallied to the reform programs of Clemenceau in 1906, which promised social justice in the shape of a welfare package.

Others learned to think of *direct action*—the general strike and the barricades—as the only hope for French labor. Jean Jaurès led the "political" socialists, while Georges Sorel (1847–1922) supplied the arguments of the *syndicalists* with writings on the "general strike" and the role revolutionary elites would play in fomenting class war in France. But efforts at such strikes failed, while the unified Socialist party in 1906 had elected fifty-four deputies. This sharpened the question as to whether working-class hopes lay in the path of parliamentary action, just as the 1906 elections in Britain had given an edge to the "political" working class there.

The contrast between France and Germany was arresting. Industrialization in Germany was associated with an annual population growth at the rate of 1 percent from 1840 to 1914. The output growth rate was 3.8 percent per year, compared to 2.6 percent for Britain and about 2.5 for France. French population was stagnant. And in 1914 urbanization in Germany was much more advanced than it was in France, 60 percent to 44 percent. These impressive growth statistics lay behind the political dilemma caused by the failure of Germany's dominant classes to recognize the just demands of labor *politically*.

28. *Confédération Générale du Travail*, formed in 1895.

The same paternalism that had showed itself in industrial and constitutional development prevailed in the organization of labor. Until 1848, the guilds had retained control over labor conditions. The Prussian laws in 1849 consolidated the old system in the face of the agitation for shorter hours, higher pay, freedom of movement, the right to unionize, and some form of political representation. Not until the 1860s did the thrust of industrialization force the abolition of the old legal structure. Then, between 1878 and 1881, Bismarck's repression of socialist groups in politics produced two results. It strengthened the hand of the Marxists among German workers, and it gave a powerful impetus to union organization, which the new laws allowed, while prohibiting direct labor participation in political life. Growth until 1895 was steady but not spectacular. Then, the problem of inflation put new pressure on the laborers' living standards, with the result that workingmen turned toward union action to redress the imbalance of prices and wages. From 1895 to 1914 union membership grew from about 250,000 to nearly 3,000,000.

The problem faced by the now numerous trade unionists was the age-old tactical one that divided their French brethren. From 1875 the bulk of the politically conscious working class had been represented by the Social Democrats, who had dominated a congress held at Gotha. As early as 1863, the Lassallean socialists in Germany[29] accepted the idea that the "liberal" political system would work to labor's advantage if universal suffrage were incorporated in it. Lassalle's Universal Workingman's Association discounted the possibilities of socialist revolution on Marx's model, preaching that parliamentary democracy was the sure road to socialism's goal of a just order. The skeptical Marxist socialists called the Lassalleans Social Democrats (*social democratie*), and in 1869 the believers in the identity of interests among democrats and socialists formed the Social Democratic Workingmen's party. Their doctrines were accepted in 1875 as the Gotha Program, which Marx criticized as mistaken in its belief that all wage earners were "socialists" and that industrial wage earners would ever be a majority of voting citizens.

Thirty years later, Marxists could point to the accuracy of the critique made in 1875. In that year a Central Union of German industrialists was still refusing even to allow collective bargaining with unions. The bulk of the voters were bourgeois, if not in fact, at least in their distrust of the Marxists, with whom they identified even Social Democrats. Moreover, even in 1912, when in a Reichstag of 391 members the Social Democrats had 110, while the next largest party had 91, a liberal policy on the matter of constitutional government—that is, a responsible ministry—could not be made effective.

The Social Democrats had combined with the Center Catholics (91) and the leftist National Liberals (42) to make a majority of 243 votes. But they

29. Led by Ferdinand Lassalle (or Lasal), the radical son of a wealthy industrialist (1825–1864).

No artist was more sympathetic to the plight of working classes and their struggle for social justice than Käthe Kollwitz (1867–1945). Conspiracy, an etching by the German woman artist, shows a furtive conversation among workers planning a revolt. Like other Germans influenced by the advent of psychology and the symbolist movement, Kollwitz sought highly emotional subject matter. Undernourished mothers and children were a favorite theme, passionate antiwar statements another. She worked until her death, always faithful to the humane ideals she had formed in the Socialist circles of late–nineteenth-century Berlin. Courtesy Galerie St. Etienne, New York.

could pursue no common policy for long, and in 1913, when they censured the chancellor[30] on a minor scandal involving the army, this vote of no confidence made no difference. The Kaiser kept Bethmann-Hollweg in power; and William II personally decorated the officers who had dispersed a crowd at Zabern in Alsace with a bayonet charge![31] The growth of the workers' political power had not produced the essential democratic concession of responsibility, which the Czar had conceded to Stolypin in Russia in 1907. This was so despite the mushroom growth of the Social Democrats in the Reichstag. In 1890 they had held only 35 seats; in successive elections, however, their numbers were 44 (1893), 56 (1898), 91 (1903), 43 (1907), and 110 (1912).

The working-class politicians in Germany in 1914 had settled for what the Marxists contemptuously called "revisionism" and "reformism." Revisionism was the doctrine of Eduard Bernstein (1850–1932), who, under the influence of English parliamentary socialists,[32] revised Marx's propositions about the anarchy capitalism produced in industrial states. Bernstein observed a growing capacity in capitalist systems to avoid major crises and also to distribute goods more equitably. He held this to be the result of the "common" interests prevailing among proletarians and bourgeoisie. And he urged workers to avoid all actions upsetting the capitalist order. After all, Bernstein said, did not the history of the liberal states show progress toward social justice by the democratic means of responsible parliamentary government, trade unionism, and the "municipal socialism" that provided cheap public utilities?

Officially, the German Social Democrats, like their counterparts in many countries, rejected the doctrine that "gas and water" socialism would produce a socialist society. The theorist Karl Kautsky (1854–1938) wrote an official refutation of Bernstein in 1899.[33] And early in the new century the "orthodox" revolutionary doctrines of Marx were pushed by radicals[34] and incorporated into new party programs. But various local leaders in southern states[35] adopted reformism *in practice*, paying lip service to doctrine but trading support for the military budget in return for welfare legislation. After all, before 1905, when the Russian liberals won concessions *by revolutionary means*, the debate on tactics had seemed academic. Progress in the major states had come through parliamentary means.

THE POLITICS OF MODERNIZATION: THE SOCIAL WELFARE PROBLEM

That is not to say that reformism had succeeded everywhere. In some countries with major programs of welfare legislation antagonisms between classes remained at the flash point—Germany for example. In others, France especially, welfare legislation lagged behind the codes passed elsewhere in the major states. And in the Balkan states no industrial codes had been enacted.

Yet over most of the West there was a pattern of law governing the labor of women and children, the development of natural resources, the expansion of systems of tax-supported education, conditions of safety and sanitation in factories and urban dwellings, plus a package of "social security"

While by no means an invention of modern times, urban planning gained new emphasis late in the nineteenth century as a result of chaotic conditions caused by industrialization and rapid urban growth. One proposed solution was the "garden suburb," featuring modest houses in well laid-out settings with open spaces and trees. The west London suburb of Bedford Park was the first such project (1876), and it soon became fashionable with middle-class intellectuals. Similar planned communities were built throughout Europe and later in the United States, but they did little to halt the helter-skelter development of the inner cities. Collection of T. A. Greeves, London.

30. Bethmann-Hollweg.
31. The censure of 1913 was over the Zabern incident.
32. The Fabians.
33. *Bernstein and the Social Democratic Program.*
34. The party chairman August Bebel (1840–1913) and "Red" Rosa Luxemburg (1870–1919), among others.
35. Especially in Bavaria and Baden.

legislation providing some measure of health care, compensation to injured or unemployed workers, and death benefits. These codes represented a major diversion of legislative effort and budget resources, away from the traditional issues of *relieving* misery and toward positive standards of welfare. A policy recognizing industrial growth and the society shaped by it had emerged.

In Britain before 1850 the issues had been relief of the hunger of the poor and "factory" laws, and the characteristic acts were the Poor Law of 1834 and the Ten Hours Act of 1847, as well as the repeal of the Corn Laws. The third quarter of the century had been notable chiefly for municipal reforms, culminating in the codes of 1882 and 1888, which consolidated the control of local services and public utilities in the enlarging cities. Joseph Chamberlain, who began his political career as a radical mayor of Birmingham, had led the way in the fight to meet the urgent needs of urban growth and city life. He was instrumental in the movement to clear slums and improve parks and transportation facilities, and so to go beyond mere minimum safeguards in standards of urban life.

This movement for municipal reform in Britain drew on the extensive chartered powers given by Parliament to town councils in 1882 and 1888. In Germany, town governments had similar sweeping powers. The pattern was set by the Rhineland city of Düsseldorf, which initiated restrictive zoning laws to prevent developers from building structures harmful to the environment of working-class residential areas. Düsseldorf also led the way in providing police and fire protection, schools, public assistance for the needy, street railways publicly owned, and also municipal gas, water, and electricity, as well as markets, baths, and hospitals. The town council there initiated a broad band of other services, some economic, some cultural: hostels for workers, low-cost mortgage banking, city pawnshops and cemeteries, and also a concert orchestra, libraries, museums, and theaters.

The Düsseldorf achievement had created before 1914 the idea of a city as the gathering point of the full cultural potential of a whole people, not merely the traditional upper-class culture open only to those with wealth. Enthusiastic crusaders for urban reform studied the British and German developments,[36] praising the socialism of the cities.[37] In Austria the reforming mayor of Vienna Karl Lueger (1844–1910), who held office from 1897 to 1910, won fame and built the platform of his later career as the anti-Semitic hero of the middle-class Christian Socialists on his rehabilitation of the city. Elsewhere in Europe, especially in France, Belgium, and Italy, the achievements of the local councils were less complete, despite expanded powers. The French cities were distinguished for their provision of cultural facilities, but behind in social services and health care. The movement for reform made much more progress in Scandinavia.

But Germany and England then retained a lead in the area modern Scandinavia now considers its special achievement: town planning. In England the "garden city" movement produced between 1898 and 1914 more than three dozen new towns, really suburbs for the most part, which contrasted sharply with the central cities resulting from the nineteenth-century expansion. Industrialists built Port Sunlight near Liverpool[38] and also Bournville near Birmingham.[39] There were similar well-designed

36. The American F. C. Howe wrote *European Cities at Work* in 1913, with a chapter entitled "Düsseldorf and Municipal Socialism."
37. That is, the public ownership of such things as street railways and utilities.
38. Lever Brothers, the soap and chemical house.
39. Cadbury, the chocolate manufacturer.

and cheerful "greenbelt" towns in Germany near Dresden, Nuremberg, Frankfurt, Karlsruhe, and Munich.

The main problems of social welfare were beyond government at the municipal level, however, in the great industrial states. The economies of the industrial system moved rapidly up and down in terms of wage-price relationships because of trade cycles and other factors producing sharp, short-term fluctuations in the demand for certain goods. It was therefore the case that workers' real wages and the provision of employment itself were less stable in the new society, both issues dramatized by the economic downturn or deflation from 1873 to 1896 and the rapid inflation of prices early in the twentieth century. There were downward pressures of real wages on a working class by then well organized, protected by law, and politically active.

Bismarck was remarkable in reacting to the new environment. Despite his true conservatism on constitutional questions and his reputation as a militarist, he initiated a social reform policy which shaped the spending of public revenues from 1870 to 1914. There was throughout the period a steady rise in public expenditure as a percent of the gross national product.[40] During the whole period expenditure rose an average of eighty-one deutsche marks[41] per capita. Of this new expenditure only 20 percent went for military use, or about 5 percent of the GNP. Educational services absorbed as much, while the government spent more than 33 percent of the increase on social reform and an additional 12 percent on urban improvement.

This investment in social welfare began with Bismarck's tenure of office and produced enduring monuments: insurance against accidents (1871, 1884), sickness (1883), old age and the plight of invalids (1889). At first the benefits flowed to a narrow range of industrial workers, but by 1913 the system was codified and extended to domestics, agricultural workers, casual workers (i.e., not regularly employed), and salaried office staff also. The year after Bismarck's resignation, the industrial code of 1891, based on British experience, established safety protections in factories, maximum hours, and the other aspects of factory regulation agitated for by workers. Together with the social insurance codes of 1911–1913, these laws made German workers the best protected in the world. German social services and insurance required nearly 7 percent of the GNP, a level not equaled elsewhere. Measured in DM, the German expenditure per capita in 1908 for nonmilitary purposes dwarfed that of other nations: Germany, 25; France, 14.6; Austria-Hungary, 13.9; Italy, 7.8; Britain, 5.7.

The bill was paid by indirect taxes levied by the Reichstag[42] and by income taxes within the states of the federal system. Germany had no income tax on the federal level, but was not alone in this: France, Hungary, Belgium, and the United States had not gone to this direct tax to finance expanded services. Nor had they yet adopted the array of other taxes needed for social welfare: inheritance taxes (death duties), estate taxes, taxes on business transactions, and augmented taxes on luxury goods (excises). All of these new levies, including the income tax, had been accepted before 1914 in Austria, Italy, Spain, Switzerland, Denmark, Norway, the Netherlands, and Japan. But acceptance of the income tax in England in fact was not matched by other budget reforms until 1909, and this helps to explain the relatively low level of social service expenditure there until 1909.

40. Hereafter referred to as the GNP.
41. Hereafter called DM.
42. Customs for the most part, as well as direct contributions by workers.

It was Lloyd George who broke the back of resistance to social insurance in 1909, in the great budget crisis. Before that time, Britain had moved to modernize its social system in many ways: the Balfour Education Act (1902) extended elementary and secondary schooling greatly, the Trade Disputes Act (1906) protected union funds, meals for needy children were provided in 1906, as the new Lib-Lab parliamentary majority redressed long-standing grievances. From 1907 to 1909 Parliament enacted a program of school medical inspections, provisions for the eight-hour day, minimum wage laws, housing and town planning statutes, and other useful measures.

But in 1908 the Lords balked at a scheme for old-age pensions.[43] Then, in 1909, as chancellor of the exchequer, Lloyd George used a report on poverty produced by a commission appointed by Conservatives to warrant a National Insurance Bill. He based his scheme on the German laws of the 1880s, providing for contributions by the state, the worker, and the employer. His bill provided insurance against sickness and partial unemployment benefits, financed by a new tax on land in the form of a death duty. In the constitutional crisis that followed,[44] the new principles carried.

The result was to legitimize what had been to that time a moral revolt against the consequences of industrialization. This gave heart to the parliamentary socialists in the Labour Party, as the turn from economic agitation to politics produced the results revolutionaries had said were impossible. In 1891 expenditure for the social welfare of workers took less than 2 percent of the British GNP; in 1914 the proportion of state revenues so spent was 4.1 percent. The intervention of the state was apparently able to hold society together in Germany and in England, on different bases, since the two systems were constitutionally quite dissimilar.

There was still some question, however, as to what measure of justice had been achieved in Britain and in Germany. In Britain, for example, wages and salary as a proportion of national income had actually fallen between 1890–1899 and 1905–1914, from 49.2 percent to 47.2 percent. Profits and interest had risen from 38.8 percent to 42 percent. Radicals said openly that the social insurance programs were a bribe paid to disguise the increasing maldistribution of the profits created by labor.

This charge was more credible in France than in the other leading industrial states. We have already noted the many failings of the French political system, France's stagnant population, the lower level and slower pace of industrialization there, and the limitations in law on trade union politics. This combination of forces naturally produced a weaker response to the questions of working-class welfare also. In France the same reform ideas existed, but the tax system before 1914 was prone to *transfer* resources from one sector or population group to another, without redistributing income. Primary reliance remained on excise taxes rather than on the

43. Because it required contributions from employers; the Lords accepted noncontributory schemes in that year.
44. 1909–1911; see above.

The problems of providing for the old-age and welfare needs of salaried workers received increasing attention late in the nineteenth century. The newly powerful workers' unions and the various socialist movements pressed governments and industries to concern themselves with public welfare. Germany under Bismarck developed an advanced program of social assistance in the 1880s as part of the Chancellor's program to kill socialism with kindness. Reform in Britain was further behind, with the first old-age pensions distributed in 1909, as shown here. Despite these improvements, benefits were minimal and the struggle for just compensation had far to go. Radio Times Hulton Picture Library.

progressive income tax or schemes of contribution by workers and employers. The poor fiscal base was as great an impediment to social welfare as the split within working-class ranks between advocates of political action and those favoring direct action.

There were some measures, though, however modest in comparison to the German scheme of social welfare or the British regulation of industrial life. The chief benefits were free medical assistance to the poor (1893), old-age and invalid pensions for miners (1894), compensation for work accidents (1898), factory hour laws (1900), an eight-hour day for miners (1905), and the six-day week (1906). In 1901 a broad pension scheme to embrace nine million workers failed to win legislative approval. In 1910 the CGT itself opposed old-age insurance for non–mine workers. No broad programs of social welfare were passed until *1936*, by which time France had the largest Communist party in Western Europe!

The nation responsible for the revolution in politics in 1789 and the pioneer socialist thought of Fourier, Saint-Simon, and Babeuf was retrograde in social democracy. Even czarist Russia had "factory" acts (1882, 1885, and 1897) and limited workmen's compensation (1903). And across the world in Japan 10 percent of all public outlay was for education by 1900, far above the French proportion. The Japanese also achieved broad programs of social insurance before France did, by a series of acts passed between 1921 and 1927. Turkey had more liberal labor laws and benefit provisions by 1936. Likewise, Austria, Denmark, Italy, and Switzerland had accepted more of the German system of social insurance, much of the "seventeen-point program" which Clemenceau failed to carry in France, with the predictable result: the French working classes drifted away from parliamentary democracy and still shared some hostility toward it in the 1960s.

RETROSPECT

The impulses for social change through political process, or what we have called the politics of modernization, had not produced uniform results in the West. As the shape and structure of society altered, the middle classes consolidated control of constitutional government in some countries. But this control was often an illusion, as in the case of Prussia. Mixed results were also obtained by the industrial working classes, both in gaining rights to political participation and in securing protection against the harsher aspects of the factory regime and life in industrial cities. The same may be said with regard to social services. The new allocations of power and resources produced a smoother modernization in Britain than in France, but not as comprehensive a program as in Germany. This fact alone fueled the debate over tactics among socialists and conservatives, because Germany was, paradoxically to the socialists, politically more repressive than the other industrial powers west of Russia while being more advanced socially.

Doubtless the path toward modernity in each country was determined by the larger setting of its preindustrial history. We cannot dispute the impact of the past on the democratic "compromises" of the pre-1914 period. The early tradition of free speech and responsible parliamentary government in Britain had shaped that country's lead in the Industrial Revolution and provided the political basis of the successful "Labour" politics supported by Lloyd George in the crisis of 1909–1911.

But it is impossible to predict what further developments there might have been toward social welfare in France or responsible government in Germany, and toward some combination of the two elsewhere in the West, under conditions of peace. The Great War of 1914 intervened, directing energies to the third task of government—security—and away from considerations of the constitutional order and welfare. Moreover, the world war itself created situations profoundly affecting the constitutional order, and hence the response to social questions, throughout the West. What the First World War did not do, however, was to begin the "modern" world. Industrialization had done that, along with nationalism and the politics of democracy and welfare.

BIBLIOGRAPHY

BRIGGS, ASA. *Victorian Cities.* London: Oldham, 1963. Good on bourgeois life patterns in English towns.

GAY, PETER. *The Dilemma of Democratic Socialism.** New York: Columbia University Press, 1952. The best book on Bernstein; other good studies of "revisionists" are Harvey Goldberg, *Life of Jean Jaurès* (Madison: University of Wisconsin Press, 1962), and Henry Pelling, *A History of the British Labour Party** (London: Macmillan, 1961).

HANHAM, H. J. *Elections and Party Management.* Cambridge, Mass.: Harvard University Press, 1959. Politics in the reform era dominated by Disraeli and Gladstone.

HAYES, C. J. H. *A Generation of Materialism, 1871–1900.** New York: Harper & Row, Publishers, Torchbooks, 1961. This survey is ably continued in Orin J. Hale, *The Great Illusion** (New York: Harper & Row, Publishers, Torchbooks, 1971), on the period 1900–1914, in the Rise of Modern Europe series.

HORNE, ALISTAIR. *The Fall of Paris.** New York: St. Martin's Press, 1965. A vivid account of the 1871 Commune and its defeat.

JENKS, W. A. *The Austrian Electoral Reform of 1907.* New York: Columbia University Press, 1950. This detailed study should be read together with Arthur May, *The Habsburg Monarchy* (Cambridge: Cambridge University Press, 1951), and chapters in the works of Taylor and Kann.

LANDAUER, CARL. *European Socialism.* 2 vols. Berkeley: University of California Press, 1959. The best comprehensive survey.

MEDLICOTT, W. N. *Bismarck and Modern Germany.** New York: Harper & Row, Publishers, 1968. This fine study is the best brief account; but see also the abridgment of the three volumes by Erich Eyck: *Bismarck and the German Empire** (London: Allen & Unwin, 1950).

ROSTOW, W. W. *Politics and the Stages of Growth.* Cambridge: Cambridge University Press, 1971. Extends the argument of Rostow's *The Stages of Economic Growth* concerning democracy, security, and welfare.

SALOMONE, W. A. *Italy in the Giolittian Era.* Philadelphia: University of Pennsylvania Press, 1960. The basic study of the democratic politics of the Giolitti government.

SCHORSKE, CARL E. *German Social Democracy, 1905–1917.** New York: Harper & Row, Publishers, Torchbooks, 1972. A brilliant, complex study of the Marxist parties in the context of Germany's bid for European hegemony.

THOMPSON, DAVID. *Democracy in France since 1870.** New York: Oxford University Press, 1964. A gracefully written analysis of the politics of the Third Republic.

VENTURI, FRANCO. *Roots of Revolution.** New York: Alfred A. Knopf, 1960. A sympathetic and brilliant study of the "radical" Russian intellectuals and revolutionaries; very well complemented by Robert F. Byrnes's work on a reactionary leader [Sergei Sergeyevich Poboedonestev] *Poboedonestev* (Bloomington: Indiana University Press, 1968).

WEBER, ADNA F. *The Growth of Cities in the Nineteenth Century.** Ithaca: Cornell University Press, 1963. This reissue of an early-twentieth-century classic is well worth reading.

WEBER, EUGEN. *Action Française.* Stanford: Stanford University Press, 1962. Extremely good on the French right in the Dreyfus era and afterward.

WHYTE, A. J. *The Evolution of Modern Italy.** Oxford: Blackwell, 1950. Very good on "liberal" politics at the turn of the century.

Asterisk indicates a paperbound edition.

13

IMPERIALISM, WAR, AND REVOLUTION: 1870–1918

This war [Franco-Prussian] represents the German revolution, a greater political event than the French Revolution of the last century. . . . There is not a diplomatic tradition which has not been swept away. You have a new world, new influences at work, new and unknown objects and dangers with which to cope. . . . The balance of power has been entirely destroyed. . . .

BENJAMIN DISRAELI (1871)[1]

THE PROBLEM OF PERSPECTIVE

Allowing for the exaggeration in this statement by Disraeli, who was in 1871 no longer Britain's prime minister but an opposition politician after Gladstone's job,[2] we can still find much that is revealing in his analysis of Bismarck's victory over France. The French Revolution had unified the French people by making the nation and the state identical for political purposes. It had turned loose in Europe the forces of democracy and nationalism. But it had also turned loose the force of imperialism. The expansion of "the great French nation"[3] had followed its unification. Would German unification now produce the same result? Would Bismarck, who was no friend to democracy, accept the other third of the French trinity? Would the Germans now seek to incorporate into their Reich the German peoples in Europe who were not part of the new state but were culturally part of the German nation?[4]

The questions reveal a problem of perspective we must settle if we are to orient ourselves toward the *totality* of the Western experience between 1870 and the end of the First World War. There has been a historical custom to treat the world war as the end of an era. Many historians look on the modern world as the creation of 1914–1918. They see in the conflict itself the conditions responsible for the global politics of our own age, in which Russia and the United States vie with the Oriental giants, China and Russia. They see also in the war the end of European world supremacy, indeed of Western world dominance. And they often attribute these results to the German appetite for expansion, which after 1870

1. Abridged from Felix Gilbert, ed., *The End of the European Era, 1890-Present* (New York: W. W. Norton & Co., 1970), p. 1206.
2. Disraeli had resigned in 1868 and was out of power until 1874.
3. *La grande nation française* in the revolutionary language adopted by Napoleon, meaning the French people.
4. There were large German elements in Denmark, Switzerland, Belgium, the Netherlands, Baltic Russia, and the Habsburg Empire.

produced the diplomacy and the military aggression responsible for the stumble into disaster.[5]

By our account of industrial and political development, however, the modern world took shape well before 1914. From the perspective of the shape of society, not the fate of dynasties, the First World War clarified the outlines of the modern world. But it was not responsible for creating it. In the next chapter we shall examine how the chief cultural and intellectual characteristics of the modern world may be said to show the same thing. In science, art, literature, technology, indeed in the chief aspects of mental and material culture, the half century *before* 1914 was fundamental in outlining Western civilization as we know it in this century. Democracy, socialism, welfare economics, relativity of time and space, quantum physics,[6] the automobile, and the airplane: these had already transformed the civilization based on liberal philosophy and Newtonian science.

Yet the First World War did sweep aside some of the main political structures of the West: the Habsburg Empire, the Ottoman Empire, the Russian Empire of the czars, and the German Empire of Bismarck. In doing so, however, it confirmed the importance of the forces which had challenged empire *within Europe* since 1789. What the great conflict from 1914 to 1918 made clear was the final defeat of the conservatism Metternich had advocated between 1815 and 1848 and Bismarck had revived from 1871 to

On the eve of the Franco-Prussian War a French cartoonist took this despairingly droll view of European affairs. Austria lies prostrate, completely dominated by Prussia, who is about to be challenged by an angry France. The newly nationalistic Balkan states are awakening after a long slumber, posing further problems for Austria. To the east Russia hulks as a sullen giant looking westward, but is pursued by a pack of wolves. England is involved in her own problems as she struggles with a recalcitrant Ireland. The key to the map is a bayonetted rifle symbolizing the struggle for military superiority which was taking place on the Continent. Bibliothèque Nationale.

5. For examples, see Barbara Tuchman's best sellers, *The Guns of August* (New York: The Macmillan Company, 1962), *The Proud Tower* (New York: The Macmillan Company, 1966), A. J. P. Taylor's *The Struggle for Mastery in Europe* (New York: Oxford University Press, 1971), and the standard text by R. R. Palmer and Joel Colton, *A History of the Modern World*, 4th ed. (New York: Alfred A. Knopf, 1971).
6. The basic revolution in physics behind the harnessing of the *atomic* energy.

1890. In order to see the validity of this view, we must look at the politics of the "Age of Imperialism" from the vantage point of the state system. It was experiencing a change as fundamental as that experienced at the end of the Middle Ages, when the old empires and free cities gave way to the emerging dynastic states. The war had not initiated this change; nor, as we shall discover, did it mark the end of the transformation. We are living with it still.

CONFLICT WITHOUT WAR: THE AGE OF BISMARCK

During Bismarck's tenure of power in Germany, perhaps his greatest accomplishment was the reassurance he gave Europe that Disraeli's fears were pointless. The Iron Chancellor had achieved power for himself and for Germany by war. And he grasped the fact, quite clearly, that both could be maintained only by peace.

Germany was the middle term in Europe's state system in 1871, in both a physical and a political way. Physically Germany stood between France and Russia, as part of a central corridor which together with Italy formed an alternative axis of power to either the Western states or the Slavic East. Of course, the powers poised on the edges of Europe might seek satisfaction for their ambitions outside Europe: France in overseas expansion, Russia in Asia. But the French *had* crossed the Rhine during their drive for empire in the period of Napoleon. They also had long-standing economic and political interests in Italy and the Mediterranean. And the Russians *had* not been content to contain the French Revolution on the Polish border either in 1807 or in 1812, after driving Napoleon back from Moscow. The czar's armies had crisscrossed German territory, even if only for defensive reasons. Hence, by necessity, every German statesman had to think in continental and not simply national terms. As the man in the middle, Bismarck had always to worry about a drive into Germany from two directions. His system of diplomacy rested on measures to minimize the realization of that menace.

Politically, Bismarck's Germany was also in the middle in another sense. To the east there were great empires as neighbors, potential rivals, often friends: Turkey, Austria-Hungary, and Russia. They were the traditional opponents of the "French" politics of nationalism and democracy, the sworn enemies of revolution. To the west lay the territory of the nation-state, as distinct from the dynastic, multinational empires. There Germans saw the integration of independent peoples politically as the basis of the state: Britain, France, Spain, Italy, Belgium, and the smaller nation-states.[7] In Germany, however, there existed both a nation-state and an empire: Prussia-Germany, the result of unification and the home of nationalistic Pan-German sentiment.

Moreover, in Prussia-Germany the nation-state was not wholly Western in character. The state was dynastic, like the Eastern empires, not democratic in the Western sense. As we know from our discussion of German political and economic development, the structure of German society was ambiguous. Industrialization was shaping a society more advanced in some ways than any other, but political structures were those left over from another age. Bismarck had encouraged nationalism only to the point of German unification; he had never encouraged democracy.

Both by circumstance and preference, therefore, Germany was a political

---

7. In the Balkans some nation-states had emerged but were "clients" of one of the three empires or existed independently only under Western guarantees.

compromise between two worlds. The old military aristocracy and great bourgeois industrialists refused to put the state on a popular basis. Germany's natural affinities after 1871 were thus with the Eastern empires politically, against revolution, nationalism, democracy, socialism—the greatest forces shaping modern politics. Germany was also by military victory and industrial prowess the strongest European power. How the German government would behave and what would be its policy were questions of the greatest importance, therefore.

Answers were not long in coming. From 1871 to 1878, Bismarck pursued a peace policy that was truly European rather than narrowly dynastic or national. The policy of those years was centered on Eastern Europe and matured in the Congress of Berlin, but it had sprung from the inescapable necessity of finding allies to prevent the French from so doing and launching a war of revenge. Germany's participation in the international events of 1871–1878, therefore, was in large measure the result of the legacy of the Franco-Prussian War. Following the Congress of Berlin, Bismarck worked to consolidate further his Eastern policy, until he viewed it as stable, in 1881–1882. From that point on, Bismarck sought the diplomatic means toward a similar stability in Western Europe. The methods he used were those of aristocratic diplomacy; the ends he had in view were the preservation of the balance of power achieved by Germany's victory over France and the safeguarding of the monarchical order east of the Rhine. To do both he had to reduce the threat of war over the Balkans and Constantinople, which had put Russia and Austria on an uneasy footing after the Crimean War, a threat fed by Russia's fury over Austria's menacing neutrality during that episode. Moreover, he had also to prevent any power from gaining a clear supremacy in the Turkish regions of strategic importance as links between Europe and Asia.

Bismarck's first step was to revive the league of conservative empires sworn to preserve the domestic status quo. By the end of 1873 he had concluded understandings for that purpose with Austria-Hungary and Russia, in what was called the Three Emperors' League. Italy was sympathetic to this league, although it did not adhere to it formally. When the League was tested, it was found defective. In 1875–1876 Slav nationalism produced revolts in the Balkans against Turkish rule. Germany had no direct interest at stake there. This was not true of the other powers. The Balkans were Russia's road to Constantinople and warm water, Austria's path for economic expansion eastward, the gateway for both powers to challenge the hold Britain and France had on the Middle East, where the Suez Canal had been opened in 1869.[8]

Germany exerted pressure for a peaceful partition, but Russia supported the Slavs in Serbia and Montenegro against Turkey. Assured of Austria's willingness to stand by as a neutral, Russia defeated Turkey in 1877 and gained an imposed treaty in 1878.[9] The terms were unacceptable to Austria, however, because Russia required the creation of a vast Balkan state (Bulgaria) extending from the Black Sea to the Aegean. Nor could Britain and France accept this Russian access to the Mediterranean, which undid the results of the Crimean War.

Vienna therefore invited the other powers to a conference to revise this peace, in what became the Congress of Berlin. Before this Congress met from June 13 to July 13, 1878, under Bismarck's presidency, Russia made secret agreements to protect its gains. In exchange for "guarantees" of its

8. Linking the Mediterranean and the Red Sea, cutting the distance from London or Bordeaux to India by 40 percent!
9. San Stefano, March 3, 1878.

eastern satellite in the Black Sea region, Russia promised Britain to give up its Aegean outposts, which threatened the Mediterranean supremacy of Britain. But the Black Sea concessions still posed a Russian threat to the British in the Middle East, hence in Asia. The British therefore guaranteed Turkey's Asiatic territories, in return for the island of Cyprus, an ideal naval base.[10] The British then completed their deception of Russia by agreeing with Austria to disallow the creation of any large Balkan state.

When Bismarck entertained Europe's foreign ministers, chancellors, and

10. In the eastern Mediterranean, strategically located with regard to the Dardanelles strait, the Suez Canal, and the Aegean.

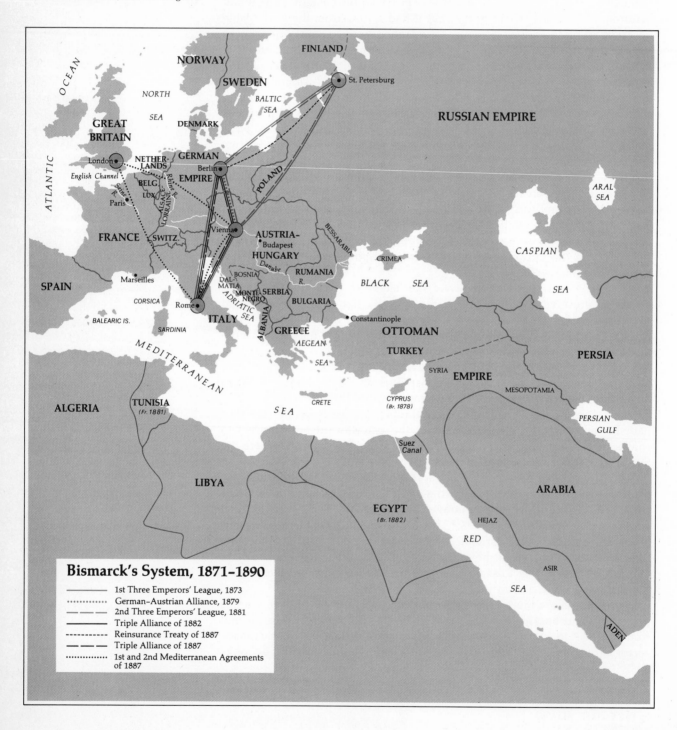

Bismarck's System, 1871–1890

————————	1st Three Emperors' League, 1873
··················	German–Austrian Alliance, 1879
— — — —	2nd Three Emperors' League, 1881
————————	Triple Alliance of 1882
- - - - - - - -	Reinsurance Treaty of 1887
– – – –	Triple Alliance of 1887
··················	1st and 2nd Mediterranean Agreements of 1887

ambassadors in Berlin, therefore, it was not to dictate terms, but to preside over the ratification of agreements. Turkey was in fact dismantled as a *European* empire. Serbia, Montenegro, and Rumania were made completely independent. The large Bulgarian state was divided into three new states. Austria occupied Bosnia and Herzegovina and a wedge of territory between Serbia and Montenegro, all nominally Turkish dependencies. Russia was left in control of southern Bessarabia. The Turks enjoyed some power over eastern Bulgaria (Eastern Roumelia) and were left in control of the Aegean borderlands. Britain got Cyprus. France and Italy got nothing directly, but were given to understand there would be toleration for a French move against Tunis[11] and Italian "redemption" of the Dalmatian coast.[12]

Germany got no territory, but was perhaps the major gainer. Bismarck had gained recognition for Germany as a Great Power; he now became Europe's "honest broker," the peacemaker. Moreover, Bismarck did not have to choose between his two allies in the Three Emperors' League. The Balkan question seemed settled. The other powers now appeared to believe the claim that Germany was a satiated power, indifferent to any drive to expand, and hence itself no threat to the status quo. Even more important was another set of "facts." The French seemed to be diverted from European to overseas concerns, while the Russians had been pushed toward an eastern focus—in the Balkans and in Turkey. Bismarck had apparently solved the problem of being in the middle.

But there was agitation beneath the surface of this European "solution." The Turkish Empire was beset internally with revolutionary tensions between reactionaries and the "Young Turks," angered by the rape of Turkey. Within Russia, Pan-Slav ambitions were frustrated by the retreat from San Stefano, and many said the humiliation came about because Germany had not supported Russia against Austria. The Balkan region of Macedonia caused a war in 1912, after being a source of tension for a generation. And Bosnia stuck in Austria's throat, finally to choke the Habsburgs in 1914, when an incident there produced a crisis that triggered the world war itself.

But that is hindsight. To Europeans, 1878 could not be seen as the lever of a great war. Rather it cemented the foundation for thirty-four years of peace,[13] as it ended the three decades of major wars set in motion by the 1848 revolutions. The Congress of Berlin produced circumstances in which Europeans could travel from London to the edge of Russia without a passport: "Europe had never known such peace and unity since the age of the Antonines."[14]

From 1878 to 1890 Bismarck worked to keep it that way. In Eastern Europe he forged a defensive alliance with Austria against Russia. His purpose was to control Habsburg ambition in the Balkans; Vienna could not go to war without Berlin's support. This alliance worried Russia into seeking the renewal of the Three Emperors' League. In 1881 this was done, secretly, providing for spheres of influence in the Balkans,[15] a defensive alliance against Turkey, and a pledge of neutrality in the event any partner went to war against a fourth power other than Turkey. Austria followed this

---

11. In Turkish North Africa.
12. The *irredenta* land of Albania.
13. 1878–1912, when the Macedonian war broke out.
14. Taylor, *Mastery in Europe*, p. 255. There were, of course, minor wars: Serbia-Bulgaria (1885), Turkey-Greece (1897).
15. East (Russia) and west (Austria-Hungary).

agreement with pacts to tie Serbia and Rumania into an area of amity open to Austrian capital (1881–1883). Bismarck also supported the Austrian extension of influence into Bulgaria, until 1885, when war threatened. He then tried to draw in the reins, but Austria succeeded in making Alexander of Battenberg (1857–1893) independent of Russia.[16] By 1890, Germany had bound Austria to its side, thus guarding against any renewal of Habsburg alliances with France and Britain, a combination always worrisome to Germany.

The other danger was that Russia might ally itself with the anti-German elements in France, as politicians in both countries harbored motives of revenge against Germany. Since it never seemed probable that Bismarck could make the French forget the loss of Alsace-Lorraine, his aim was further to divert the French, while neutralizing Italy. He had launched the strategy at Berlin, by encouraging French imperialism in Africa, in Tunis.

Within France the revenge-minded politicians did not rise to the bait. But the "colonialists" did, led by Jules Ferry (1832–1893). They seized Tunis and consolidated control over it in 1881, by the Treaty of Bardo. The trouble was that there were already 20,000 Italians there and only 200 Frenchmen. The Italian finance capitalists were building railroads there, and this worried the French, who did not want a threat to their neighboring Algerian colony. Nothing suited Bismarck's diplomacy better. Italy turned again to Germany, renewing the tie as old as the medieval Holy Roman Empire, estranged now from France, which had been the patron of Italian unification. Some Italians welcomed the reversal on other grounds. Bismarck was no friend of the papacy[17] and would keep it from recovering its temporal power, which the French under Napoleon III had protected.

The immediate dividend was Italy's entry into the Triple Alliance of 1882, with Germany and Austria. This was an affirmation of monarchy and the social order against domestic enemies and also a defensive alliance against France, Britain, and Russia. Renewed at five-year intervals, this understanding protected Austria in the event of a war with Russia, and Germany in the event of war with France. It was also aimed against various British combinations, which, while not posing European threats, might lead to colonial conflicts. This last "danger" was not to Germany, but to its allies in the Three Emperors' League, each anxious that Britain not gain more power in the Far East and the Middle East.

Britain had done just that, however. The rulers (*khedives*) of Egypt were dependents of Turkey politically, but in fact they were deeply in debt to French and British financiers. When a sale of Suez Canal stock shares[18] in 1875 did not stabilize the bankrupt government's finances, a joint Anglo-French control was established in 1876. Six years later, resentful of this mortgage on their government in behalf of foreign capitalists, army men revolted and established a new, national government. In that year 80 percent of the shipping passing through the Suez Canal was British. London therefore replied to the revolution with a bombardment and invasion, ordered by the "anticolonialist" prime minister, Gladstone. He thought national freedom every man's birthright, but placed a higher value on financial regularity: Gladstone called bankruptcy "the greatest of political crimes"![19] Thus the British occupied Egypt, from which they had expelled Napoleon in 1802. While promising to stay only long enough to restore order, they remained influential until 1952, when Gamal Abdel

16. Russia forced Alexander to abdicate in 1886 but did not regain control there.
17. See Chapter 12 for his *Kulturkampf.*
18. By Khedive Ismail.
19. Taylor, *Mastery in Europe*, p. 288.

Nasser got rid of the last vestige of their control in his revolt against King Farouk.[20]

The British seizure of Egypt played into Bismarck's hands. Neither France, which had been Turkey's ally in the Crimean War, nor Russia, which had been Turkey's enemy, had since gained much land once in Ottoman hands; but Britain now had Cyprus and Egypt. Bismarck had encouraged this, in order to estrange England from France and Russia, as earlier he had encouraged French-Italian competition over Tunis, in order to assure estrangement between them. This policy came to maturity in 1890, when there was an Anglo-German defensive agreement, secured by the English cession of Heligoland[21] in exchange for Zanzibar and tolerance for a German entry into the colonial race.

Meanwhile, Bismarck continued to encourage Ferry and the French imperialists, both politicians finding that colonial adventures were useful issues in domestic politics, because they were popular with the nationalists and the democrats.[22] Ferry and Bismarck engineered a new Berlin conference in 1884–1885, ostensibly over disputes in the Congo. Its main outcome was to suppress the African slave trade and to establish the doctrine of effective control over a colony before ownership might be claimed. In addition, the French agreed to German expansion in Africa in return for the consolidation of French colonies there.[23] Britain was now isolated in Europe, while France was diverted from it, apparently making Germany secure in the West: France and Russia had conflicts with Britain.

The price for this achievement since 1871 was suspicion among the conservative emperors. Russia distrusted Austria more than ever and would not renew the Three Emperors' League in 1887. Bismarck had now to conciliate Russia *without* abandoning Austria. Britain was the key. Bismarck told London he would join with Austria in encouraging Russia's Mediterranean hopes, unless Britain would help contain Russia. Germany thereby encouraged an alliance based on Austria, including Italy, Turkey, and the Balkan states, but *excluding* Germany. The First Mediterranean Agreement[24] achieved this guarantee of the status quo there, leaving Germany free to make a separate approach to Russia. The renewal of the Austria-Germany-Italy Triple Alliance served the same purpose.

Bismarck capped the diplomatic coup with the Reinsurance Treaty of 1887. This secret agreement with Russia pledged each power to neutrality in the event of a war involving the other, except that Russia would aid Germany if France attacked, and Germany would protect Russia against an Austrian onslaught! Bismarck reduced the chance of a Franco-Russian alliance—the war on two fronts he dreaded—by helping Russia against an Austrian threat which Bismarck had *created* and could control. Germany leaked the thrust of the 1887 agreements, but not the elaborate dovetailing achieved in Berlin.

By a series of conjuror's tricks Bismarck had guaranteed the status quo in the Balkans, in Italy, in the Mediterranean, and in central Europe. The leaked information discouraged warmongers in every country. And there were warmongers: Frenchmen who wanted back Alsace and Lorraine; Italian irredentists; German militarists eager to try arms with France and Russia; Pan-Slavs; Austrians eager for Balkan dominance. Bismarck's

20. From 1882 to 1922 Britain made sixty-six promises to get out; it is doubtful that the British stayed that long to "restore order."
21. A strategic island naval base in the North Sea.
22. Who were thereby encouraged to suspect England; otherwise they might have looked there for support for liberalism.
23. See Chapter 11 for the "scramble" for Africa.
24. 1887. A Second Mediterranean Agreement was signed later in the year.

system not only kept noblemen employed; it mitigated the danger that general staffs would get to play real war games, with Europe as the victim and the prize. Instead, the French fought in Indochina, the British in the Sudan and South Africa, the Italians in Ethiopia, the Russians in eastern Asia. In Asia and Africa there was no status quo. It was an imperial age.

THE TWO FACES OF IMPERIALISM

The Berlin Conference to settle the fate of Africa had not produced a new imperialism; it had merely directed the energies of an old practice, while admitting Germany to the competition. European imperialism was of two kinds, however: the overseas empire variety, and the dynastic imperialism within Europe. This latter variety had blocked in Eastern Europe the principle of national self-determination, the political idea dominant in Western Europe since 1789, out of fear that the eastward spread of that principle would ruin the Habsburg, Romanov, and Ottoman empires. The Romanovs and Habsburgs had been instigators of the nationalist upheavals in the Balkans, however; and their complicity had ruined the Ottomans.

The other "domestic" empire, the Hohenzollern German Empire, had not shown any such appetite in southeastern Europe under Bismarck. But it

Europe: Diplomacy and War, 1891–1914

1891–1904

- The Triple Alliance Renewed, 1887
- Franco-Russian Alliance, 1894
- Anglo-French Entente, 1904

The Balkans, 1900

- Independent Balkan States
- Ottoman Empire

A – Independent, 1908
B – To Greece, 1908
C – Annexed by Austria–Hungary, 1909
D – New State, 1912 (ALBANIA)
E – To Italy, 1912 (DODECANESE IS.)
F – To Montenegro, 1913
G – To Serbia, 1913
H – To Bulgaria, 1913
I – To Rumania, 1913
J – To Greece, 1913

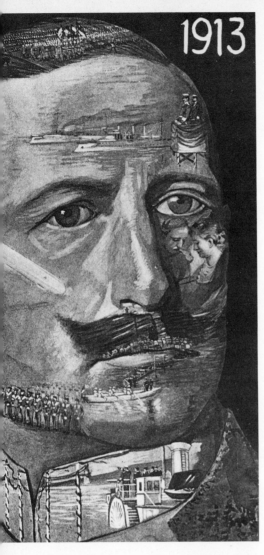

1913

This special postcard was issued in 1913 to commemorate the jubilee of Kaiser William II's reign. At the moment he was about to lead his nation into war, nationalistic and military images are superimposed on the ruler's face. As a haughty young man William had removed Bismarck from power and personally guided Germany through a prosperous period of industrial expansion. The Kaiser aggressively built up the German Empire and attempted to frighten the world with displays of military might. In 1918, after the war, the Kaiser was unceremoniously deserted by the military, and he went into a long exile in Holland where he died in 1941 fully approving of Hitler's new attempt to restore German superiority. Altonaer Museum, Hamburg.

had embarked on adventures overseas in the 1880s and also promoted imperialist rivalries among Russia, Britain, Italy, and France. However, as we shall now see, the dismissal of Bismarck in 1890 changed the significance of this policy. When William II became kaiser (1888–1918), he abandoned Bismarck's policies as well as Bismarck. Where the old chancellor had used Germany's strength to maintain the European balance of power and the peace advantageous to Germany, the Kaiser used German power to overthrow the balance. Germany took up the modern form of imperialism with a vengeance.

From 1890 to about 1911 William II set in motion a new policy. This new course put a general in Bismarck's place,[25] signaling in foreign policy the determination not to renew the Reinsurance Treaty with Russia. Czar Alexander III hoped to remain friendly with Germany, but in 1891 and 1893 he invited exchanges of visits between the French and Russian fleets. The Kaiser compounded this danger with a pro-Polish stance bound to alienate Russia. In 1893–1894, therefore, Russia negotiated an alliance with France. This Dual Alliance broke the back of Bismarck's system, by again creating the conditions in which France and Russia, two states wanting to limit British power and harboring grudges against Germany, but of supposedly incompatible political principles,[26] buried their ideological differences.

William II was not content merely to alienate Russia. He gave support at home to the apostles of expansion, setting the scene for leagues and propaganda associations of an ultrapatriotic nature: the Eastern Marches Association, the Colonial League, the Naval League, the Pan-German League, and others supported by the combination of military landowners and industrial imperialists. The industrialists contributed funds to promote expansionist ideas and also Pan-German links with Austrian anti-Semites; they encouraged the aggressive mood of "protectionist" landowners and the military bureaucrats. They gave support to Habsburg initiatives in the Balkans, at Russia's expense. Most of all, however, they advocated the policy of which William II finally became the spokesman and the prisoner. Germany must pursue a *Weltpolitik*, a global policy to acquire territory by diplomacy or threats of force. By 1898 the net effect was to challenge Britain's naval supremacy and launch a campaign for control of the Middle East, by dominating Turkey and the Balkans.

The result was a splitting of Europe into two systems of powers cutting across the old lines. On one side stood Austria, Germany, and Italy, the old Triple Alliance, in which a nationalist and democratic state (Italy) joined the two empires whose territories were held together by force, military codes, religious beliefs, and dynastic loyalties. On the other side stood a similar empire, Russia, and its Western partner France, itself holder of an empire built on the power of capital invested overseas. Britain was outside the two systems in 1894, isolated from European affairs, which it considered a nuisance, but also eager to short-circuit any challenge to its worldwide network of colonies, trade, and capital investments.

The key to German security lay in Britain's keeping, therefore. A prudent course to follow was the conciliation of London to maintain British neutrality. British adherence to the Dual Alliance, for any reason, would complete the division of the great powers into two blocks pitted against each other: the Triple Alliance against what was later called the Triple Entente.[27]

25. Caprivi; William II originally favored the more militant successor to von Moltke, General von Waldersee.
26. French radical nationalism and democratic republicanism versus czarist autocracy.
27. Germany, Austria, and Italy against Britain, France, and Russia.

Bismarck's system had linked the powers across various lines to avoid any such suggestion of opposed armed camps.

There was in 1895 some hope that the Dual Alliance powers might cooperate with the Triple Alliance. One year earlier Japan had challenged the Western imperialists over China. The Japanese won a short war against China in Korea, demonstrating their industrial superiority with their modern weapons. The result was the Treaty of Shimonoseki of 1895, by which Japan got Formosa and the Liaotung Peninsula;[28] Korea's independence was also secured. This successful adventure by Japan caused William II to warn of the "Yellow Peril" to civilization. More significant was the impact on Russia, which had just pushed its Trans-Siberian railway (begun in 1891) toward Vladivostok. Manchuria divided Siberia from Vladivostok; Japan's control over it would therefore endanger Russia's Eastern interests. Nicholas II (1894–1917) secured French agreement to join with Germany, which now had interests in China, in a demand that Japan give back the Liaotung Peninsula to China. Japan yielded, thus setting the stage for its war with Russia in 1904; and China responded by "agreeing" to the various treaty concessions which the Western powers made the price of their protection against Japan. Britain resented the intrusion of Germany into its "concessions" area.

Africa provided a more important series of incidents, illustrating cooperation across the old alliance lines. France, Germany, and Russia opposed Britain's power there. The first instance concerned Egypt. France and Britain were in conflict over access to the Nile and over railroad building southward from Egypt. Germany supported French expansion in the region and also a plan of the United States to thwart a British railroad that would connect the Cape[29] to Cairo. British forces clashed with French ones at Fashoda in 1898. The Germans were anti-British in this crisis. Two years earlier, the Kaiser had alienated London by expressing support for the Boer Republic in South Africa, which was trying to establish a Dutch-based state independent of Britain. In 1898 German warships had intervened against the British in a dispute over some Portuguese territory near Delagoa Bay.

These provocations were resented in London and officially regarded as interference in Britain's imperial affairs. Lord Salisbury retaliated for the earlier incidents in 1897, when he refused to renew the 1887 Mediterranean Agreement for the status quo there. William II seemed to believe that Britain could not reach any understanding with the Dual Alliance (France and Russia); at least he seems not to have relented in Germany's policy of provoking London. Moreover, Britain was unhappy at the economic penetration of Turkey by the German Bank[30] and felt especially uneasy over the building of the Baghdad Railway. The railroad threatened both British and Russian interests in Persia and India, a fact made more obvious by the domestic propaganda of the Pan-German League for an alliance with Turkey.

Then, from 1898 to 1902, Germany sought better relations with Britain, perhaps alerted at last to the danger of the course being pursued. Conventions were signed to settle colonial problems.[31] More important, however, was the withdrawal of the Kaiser's meddling in South Africa. The Boer War between Britain and the Dutch settlers raged from 1899 to 1902. The Boer

28. Thrusting southward from Manchuria into the seas dividing China from Japan.
29. That is, the Cape of Good Hope (Cape Town), South Africa.
30. The *Deutsche Bank*, under the patronage of the secretary for foreign affairs, Marschall.
31. In Samoa, in Africa, and in China.

president (Kruger) sought German aid. While William II did little to stifle a press hostile to England, he gave no help of any sort to the Boers.

This short period of, on the surface at least, better relations had been undercut, however, from the very beginning. In 1898 the real meaning of *Weltpolitik* became clear in a way directly challenging to Britain. The Reichstag passed a Navy Bill, the first in a series down to 1914. This had been instigated by von Tirpitz,[32] who became naval secretary in 1897, with the support of the Colonial League and the Naval League. The goal was a building program to achieve effective parity with Britain. British efforts to reach an arms limitation agreement with Germany failed in 1907–1908. William II was indifferent to the effects of the tax burden at home; and as early as 1901 he had said Germany's "future is on the water."[33]

A full-fledged naval arms race was in progress from 1898, therefore, and it spread among the other Great Powers. By 1900 Germany was spending more on "army estimates"[34] than any other Great Power. And, by 1914, naval expenditures had risen to parity with those of Russia and to about 50 percent of the British estimates. In 1890 German naval estimates had been only one-third of corresponding British expenditures; in 1914 they had increased fivefold and were now showing an absolute gain over British figures.[35] In total defense estimates Germany in 1870 had appropriated £10.8 million, Britain £23.4 million. In 1890 the comparable figures were £28.8 and £31.4 million. By 1914, however, the Germans were outspending the British, by £110.8 to £76.8 million.

Berlin dismissed a British threat to join the Dual Alliance in 1901. In 1902 Italy made an agreement with France incompatible with the Triple Alliance. Worried over the lapse of the Mediterranean agreements, which had been Italy's incentive to join Austria and Germany in the first place, the Italians safeguarded their interests in North Africa (Tripoli) by agreeing to French freedom of action in Morocco. This secret agreement began the isolation of Germany and Austria; and its effect was shown in 1914–1915, when Italy not only failed to join the "Central Powers" in war but came in on the other side.

Unknown to Berlin at the time was the more alarming fact that in 1903 Britain had begun negotiations with France. The objective was to settle all colonial grievances peacefully. In 1904 a pact was signed to that effect; Britain had not yet joined the Dual Alliance, but was adhering to the French partner in it.

What finally turned Russia openly against Germany was the Russo-Japanese War of 1904–1905. William II had encouraged Nicholas II to "crusade" against the Yellow Peril, but in the event he provided no help. The defeat of Russia by Japan produced violent anti-German feelings in Russia as well as the 1905 Revolution. Efforts to bridge the gap failed, because of the Russian obligation to France and also what were now clearly incompatible interests in the Balkans. Russia, blocked in eastern Asia, tried to turn dissent at home into concord by focusing again on the Pan-Slav feelings of Russians for the Balkans and also on the traditional interests in Turkey and Persia. Since 1902, however, Germany had been the possessor of wide concessions in Turkey; and the Austrians, with German support, were rampant in the Balkans.

32. Head of the *Reichsmarineamt*.
33. E. J. Passant, *A Short History of Germany* (Cambridge: Cambridge University Press, 1952), p. 125.
34. The budget for land forces.
35. Taylor, *Mastery in Europe*, p. xxvii.

In 1905, therefore, Germany's only ally was Austria. The system Bismarck had designed *to control* Austria had now been ruined; and Germany had become the prisoner of the aggressive policies of its satellite and its emperor.

The effects became clear at once. Certain French demands on Morocco prompted the Kaiser to land troops at Tangier in 1905. William's goal was less to keep the French out than to cut across the lines of any Anglo-French friendship that might threaten to cement a powerful anti-German alliance. At the Algeciras Conference of 1906, called at German insistence, only Austria supported the German demand for Moroccan independence from French domination. In 1907 it became clear that this first Moroccan crisis had indeed produced the result exactly opposite to German hopes. England drew closer to France. France secured the Atlantic coast of Morocco, while the Spanish gained a "zone" of control in northern Morocco. Moreover, in 1908 British and Russian differences were smoothed over, and the Triple Entente with France took shape. The Russians helped the situation by conciliating Japan. Therefore, Germany had not only failed to gain anything in North Africa, but had emerged in a weaker position on the Atlantic, the Pacific, and the Mediterranean, thus reviving talk of "encirclement."

These facts made it imperative that the Triple Alliance work in Europe. In order for this to happen, Austria must be counted on, and Italy as well. But Italy had secretly contracted out in 1902, as we know; and Austria now showed itself too beset with problems to be an asset as an ally. The Habsburgs had for generations repressed Slav nationalism in the Balkans, since 1867 in concert with the Magyar majority of Hungary. The victory of Japan over Russia, however, had not only diverted Russian imperialism toward the Balkans again, where Slav nationalism was the natural Russian ally. The Japanese victory had set an example of the possibility of throwing off the yoke of Western power.

By modernizing on Western principles,[36] Japan had set in motion a shock wave of revolution. In 1905, revolutions began in Russia and Persia; the Persian movement was intensely nationalistic. So, too, was an outbreak in Turkey in 1908.[37] Each revolution had increased the pressure in the Balkans.

This became clear in 1908, when the nationalist movement there exploded. In that year the lands between Constantinople and the Adriatic held a few independent states: Greece, Montenegro, Bulgaria,[38] Rumania, and Serbia. The state of Bosnia-Herzegovina, nominally Turkish, was dependent on Austria, while the area of Croatia and Slovenia was wholly within the Habsburg Empire. The Bosnians, Croats, Slovenes, and Serbs were all Slavs, unified linguistically[39] and conscious of being part of a South Slav (*Yugoslav*) people or nation. By 1900 Yugoslav nationalism had pledged itself to independence, which in practice meant union with independent Serbia, long the focal point or nucleus of the hoped-for state that would include Bosnians, Slovenes, and Croats.

The revolt of the Young Turks in 1908 had a catalytic effect on the

---

36. That is, by accepting the Industrial Revolution.
37. The Asian revolution spread to India in 1909, China in 1911, and Indonesia in 1916, thus beginning the process of decolonization that eventually ended Western world supremacy: see Chapter 17.
38. Autonomous, but not fully independent of the Turks.
39. The Serbs and Bosnians used the Cyrillic alphabet, however, while the others used the Roman system.

Balkans. The rebels forced on Abdul Hamid[40] a parliamentary regime; and they vowed to challenge Austrian and Russian claims to the Balkan provinces of the Ottoman Empire. This they did by inviting Bosnians, Herzegovinians, and Bulgarians to sit in the new imperial legislature, thus threatening Russia's ambitions to hold Constantinople, Austria's empire, and the German economic interests represented by the Baghdad Railway. The Europeans counterattacked in a secret conference at which Russia and Austria agreed to support one another, especially Austrian annexation of Bosnia and Herzegovina and Russia's naval rights in the Bosporus and Dardanelles. The Serbians rejected this attack on Bosnia. France and Britain refused to accept Russia's share of the spoils, the opening of the Dardanelles and Bosporus straits to a czarist navy. At the same time, Bulgaria declared its independence from Turkey, and Ottoman Crete seceded to join the Greek state.

The result of this "first Balkan crisis" was to frustrate further the Yugoslavs and the Russians. Nicholas II was forced to back down on the secret spoils of his agreement with Austria as the price of good relations with his partners in the Triple Entente. Since the Pan-Slavs in Russia did not know the content of the secret agreement, it appeared at home that the Austrians, with German support, had trampled the "little Slav brothers" in the Balkans.

Three years later, a second crisis struck the Balkans. In 1911 Italy attacked Turkey in order to gain Tripoli and some island territories. The French and the Germans were preoccupied with a crisis of their own, the second Moroccan crisis, caused by gunboat diplomacy.[41] The British, too, were alarmed over the Morocco affair. This seemed an opportune time for various Balkan nationalists to join the attack on Turkey, given the distracted state of most of the Western powers. Bulgaria, Greece, and Serbia did so. After defeating the Turks, however, in the Balkan War of 1912, the allies fell out over the settlement. The Bulgarians wanted territory the Serbs considered "Yugoslav."[42] The result was a new war in 1913, in which Greece joined Serbia, Turkey, and Rumania against Bulgaria. Then the Greeks and Serbs fell out over Albania, which both claimed.[43]

Nationalistic passions were running riot in the Balkans, therefore, in 1913 and early in 1914. The Russians supported Serbian claims, while Austria, intent as ever on denying Russia's Slav friends access to the sea—Albania was on the Adriatic—supported the Greeks. The Great Powers grasped the potential for larger war in the new Balkan crisis; and they tried to settle it by creating an independent Albania. Neither the Russians nor the Serbs considered this a decent compromise, however, because it achieved Austria's ends: the Serbs were again denied their wishes, and Russia again had to back down from its Pan-Slav supporting role.

The consequences of the defeat suffered by Russia in 1905 were thus made even more clear. The Western powers regarded Russia lightly; Austria especially looked on the czarist empire as exhausted and too divided by the 1905 Revolution to effectively check Habsburg ambitions. Slav nationalism was at the flash point. And Turkey's demonstrated weakness encouraged the Kaiser's eastern ambitions.

40. Sultan of Turkey (1876–1909), the ruler forced to accept the Congress of Berlin's 1878 partitions.
41. The gunboat *Panther* was sent by Berlin to protect German interests in Morocco. The real purpose was to force French concessions in the Congo. The crisis was peacefully resolved with little profit to either side.
42. The disputed territory lay in Macedonia; the Greeks also rejected Bulgarian claims.
43. Alarming the Italians who looked on Albania as part of *Italia irredenta*.

As early as February 1914, William II had said that Russia and Prussia were now enemies. Diplomacy no longer seemed a guarantee of peace, but rather the expression of the fact that peace could be kept only as long as statesmen and generals did not want war. Now it appeared that Germany and Austria wanted openly to challenge Russia. The English did not want war, because they were too preoccupied at home with social questions and the challenge to their rule of Catholic Ireland.[44] The French seemed to want nothing more than to catch up in the race for industrial wealth. The Russians desperately needed peace, in view of their internal weakness.

What proved determining was the Austrian appetite in the Balkans. Bismarck's principle had been that the Habsburgs need not fear Russia, so long as Austria-Hungary was not threatening to the land of the czar. But the Russians, who wanted an independent Serbia and Rumania as a barrier between the German nations and the Straits, could not tolerate aggrandizement by the Habsburgs at the expense of Slav nationalism. Even William II recognized this in 1914, but his one secure ally was the aged Francis Joseph, and this made it possible for Vienna to engage Berlin in a war against Russia which became the First World War. Moreover, the naval professionals and industrial imperialists in Germany wanted a war against the British, while the militarists were eager for war against France.

Thus it is hard to say what was most crucial to German aggressiveness in 1914—the navy, the railroad to Baghdad, or the desire of the Prussian generals to master Europe. But it is easy to identify the immediate cause of the war. On June 28, 1914, the Archduke Francis Ferdinand, heir apparent to the Habsburg dual monarchy, was shot to death by a Bosnian-Serb nationalist in the Bosnian capital of Sarajevo. The nineteen-year-old student Gavrilo Princip was in league with five other would-be assassins, but only two got off shots at the Austrian prince and his wife when the chauffeur of Francis Ferdinand's car took a wrong turn and tried to back up. This accident put the car within six paces of Princip; and his bullets slew the prince and his wife almost instantly.

Ironically, Francis Ferdinand had been the "friend" of Slav nationalists. He had proposed converting the Dual Monarchy into a Triple Monarchy, by creating an autonomous, parliamentary Slav state under Habsburg protection. Various nationalist groups saw the danger to independence in this design, however, and had vowed to kill the prince. The chance for the six assassins came because Austrian security precautions discounted the risks of the plot, which was partially known. Moreover, Francis Ferdinand had planned to deliberately provoke the separatist-nationalists. He visited Sarajevo to review Austrian military maneuvers in honor of his wife's

---

44. The Home Rule movement was set back by the war in 1914, and a civil war loomed there; troubles in the northernmost province of Ulster (Northern Ireland) have, as we know, continued into the 1970s.

Shown here is a German artist's map of Europe at the outbreak of World War I. England is being punched in the face by German naval strength in the North Sea. Both France and Russia are forced aside by a Germany hungry for lebensraum, *and Austria-Hungary helps her ally by also turning loose forces on Russia. Turkey, which was later to join the German side, cautiously sits out the early part of the conflict. The scale for the map is indicated by a rifle which shows that two Germans equal at least eight enemies. Imperial War Museum, London.*

birthday. But his trip coincided with the "day" of the national saint[45] of the whole Yugoslav world. It was also set for the time of "national mourning," commemorating the defeat of the Serbs by the Turks in 1839, when at Kossovo the sultan subjugated an earlier generation of nationalists.

Princip's shots proved fatal to nine million soldiers and thirteen million civilians in Europe, Asia, Africa, and on the oceans of the world because of the decisions made in Europe's capitals over the five weeks from June 28 through August 4.

Diplomats in Vienna, following the lead of the Austrian foreign minister Leopold von Berchtold, acted on the assumption, never proved since, of the Serbian government's complicity in the plot. They resolved to force war on Serbia and end Yugoslav separatism. This view they presented to William II on July 5. The Kaiser and his chancellor[46] accepted Berchtold's interpretation and on the sixth issued the famous "blank check" to Vienna, saying that "Austria must judge what is to be done . . . with Serbia; but whatever Austria's decision . . . Germany will stand behind her as an ally."[47] This pledge broke Hungary's resolve to resist war, with its dangers to Magyar domination; and on July 14 Hungary gave a similar pledge. On the twenty-third Berchtold sent an ultimatum to Serbia, threatening war unless Serbia allowed Austrians to investigate the assassination and punish the guilty "nationalists." The Serbs then surprised Vienna by accepting almost every humiliating condition.

It did not matter. The Austrian minister in Belgrade had been sent instructions to *refuse* Serbia's note *before* he had received it! Austria declared war on Serbia on July 28, in haste, *before* mobilization was actually started. The necessity for haste late in July derived from delays in early July. The Habsburg and German plans for success rested on speed, since every member of the general staff assumed that a new war would be over within weeks, as Bismarck's wars had been. For this, surprise was essential. The month between the assassination and the declaration of war had worked against the plans.

As Berchtold himself had said, the diplomatic situation might change quickly; it did. The British had offered to mediate the dispute. The French, however, had sent Poincaré[48] and Viviani[49] to Saint Petersburg for negotiations with Nicholas II. The French discouraged aggressiveness, but pledged to uphold the Dual Alliance if Russia were attacked. The Russians therefore began a general mobilization, after having attempted to mobilize against Austria alone. When the Austrians declared war, however, the Czar was persuaded to call for general mobilization.

This call on July 30 suited the German militarists perfectly, and they replied on July 31 with a call for a general German mobilization. The German general staff had only one basic war plan: to precipitate a rapid thrust into France through neutral Belgium and, after putting France out of the war, to turn all available force against Russia.[50] It was thus essential to Germany that war come at once. On the thirty-first Berlin demanded an

45. Saint Vitus.
46. Bethmann-Hollweg.
47. Taylor, *Mastery in Europe*, p. 522.
48. Raymond Poincaré (1860–1934), prime minister, then president.
49. René Viviani, appointed premier by Poincaré in 1914.
50. This was the Schlieffen Plan of 1905, evolved between 1891 and 1905 by Field Marshall Alfred von Schlieffen. The main outline of the plan was complete in 1902, however, and known to the French in 1904. The earlier plans of von Moltke and von Waldersee had reversed priorities.

end to Russian mobilization and a pledge of French neutrality. When both demands were refused, Germany declared war against Russia on August 1. The German press then advertised some lurid and false stories of French violations of German territory. On August 3 Berlin declared war on France, a declaration unprovoked by any French threat to Germany.

A general war was beginning for one reason only, the demands of a military timetable. While the British continued their efforts to negotiate, events had passed out of the hands of the diplomats entirely. Germany demanded free passage through Belgium in order to follow the schedule for the defeat of France. On August 4 Britain demanded that Belgian neutrality be respected according to the guarantees of 1831–1832.[51] What London did not know was that the German ultimatum to Belgium had been drafted on July 26, two days before the declaration of war on Serbia by Austria! This is another clear indication that Germany welcomed war in 1914, when William II and his generals believed they were at the peak of their power.

The Austro-Hungarian problem in the Balkans was the occasion of the war, therefore, but not the basic cause. Against the fashionable view that Europe went to war because diplomats failed and therefore "stumbled" into war,[52] we set the view that the war came because men wanted it to happen. The war itself proved that Germany had a better chance to master Europe diplomatically than by force, however. When Britain declared war on August 4, the Germans had activated the alliance Bismarck had always feared: the Entente powers were now all at war with Germany and Austria. And, as events soon showed, no one had anticipated accurately what the war would be like.

What did happen we can make clear with a minimal analysis of the course of the war, paying more attention to its nature and its consequences. This much we can say by way of anticipation: the war was a social catastrophe for the old empires, none of which survived it by so much as a year. Secondly, the war had an effect on society in the "victorious" states which nobody could have anticipated. Thirdly, none of the original plans for the war were realized. Fourthly, the end of the war made manifest the fact that the United States had become the leader of the West, while also raising for the "liberal" states the prospect of a contest with revolutionary Russia, in which the prize would be the loyalty of the world beyond Europe.

BLITZKRIEG, SITZKRIEG: 1914–1918

The world war lasted for four years and pitted the Central Powers against the Entente Powers, or Allies. The Germans expected to march to Paris, where they would dictate peace. The French thought they would speedily regain the Alsace-Lorraine territories lost in 1871. The Russians believed they would easily move across Poland toward Berlin and across the Carpathian Mountains to seize Budapest. The Austrians were confident they would crush Serbia. The British anticipated a quiet victory over the new German fleets, which they would follow up with a blockade of the German ports. President Woodrow Wilson advocated American neutrality and did not suppose that the United States would be involved in Europe's quarrels.

All expectations were erroneous. The Germans got close enough to Paris to see the Eiffel Tower, but not closer. The French made no progress along the Rhineland. On the western front the Battle of the Marne in September

51. See Chapter 6.
52. See Palmer and Colton, *History of the Modern World*, p. 660.

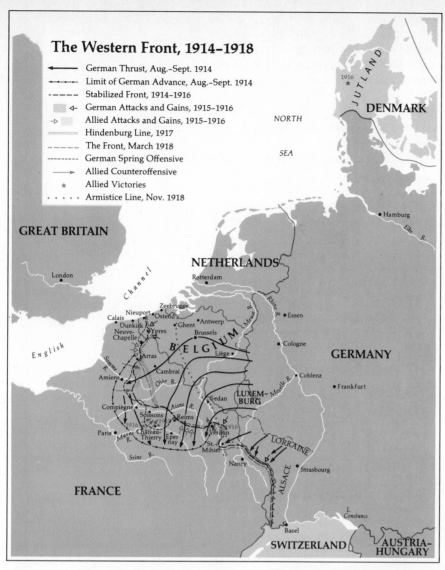

The Western Front, 1914–1918

←———	German Thrust, Aug.–Sept. 1914
+·+·+·+	Limit of German Advance, Aug.–Sept. 1914
- - - - -	Stabilized Front, 1914–1916
▨ ◁	German Attacks and Gains, 1915–1916
▷ ▨	Allied Attacks and Gains, 1915–1916
··········	Hindenburg Line, 1917
— — —	The Front, March 1918
- - - - - -	German Spring Offensive
——→	Allied Counteroffensive
★	Allied Victories
· · · · ·	Armistice Line, Nov. 1918

1914 produced a stalemate. The shovel triumphed over the "war of movement," and by September the French and Germans had carved a line of
trenches from Switzerland to the North Sea: *sitzkrieg* had replaced *blitzkrieg.*[53]

The Schlieffen Plan had failed because it rested on a false political
premise, that Belgium could be coerced without bringing England into the
war,[54] and a false military premise. The Battle of the Marne had nullified
German military hopes because of a fundamental strategic error based on
Schlieffen's miniscule appreciation of modern warfare.[55] The idea of out-
flanking France's fortified line between Switzerland and southern Belgium
by violating Belgian neutrality made sense only if the French army could be
destroyed. But the plan required the German forces to make a wide circle
through northern Belgium before crossing the Seine to reach Paris. Nearly
85 percent of the forces were committed to this wheeling operation on the

53. The "sitting war" had replaced the "lightning war" of mobility.
54. A condition *conceived in 1891* but no longer realistic in 1914.
55. Not because Schlieffen's plan was applied by his successor, the younger von Moltke, who
    lacked genius.

circumference of a large circle. And these forces were made up either of foot soldiers or of horse-drawn convoys of baggage, artillery, and supplies. The French forces commanded the short chord of the circle and could move their men and supplies *by railroad*. Modern technology (the speed of French deployment) had thus sapped the German plan of its intended advantage—surprise attack.

On the eastern front Russia got as far as East Prussia in August before losing a tremendous battle (at Tannenberg) to German troops sent from the western front, where they might have won the Battle of the Marne. The Russian southern forces never reached the Carpathians. The Austrians took Belgrade but were quickly expelled by the Serbian army, which then invaded Hungary. In 1914 the fleets remained in port, and America seemed secure at home. Before 1914 was over, however, one decisive change did occur: the Russians found they were *out of munitions* and must therefore avoid any further eastern-front offensives.

The year 1915 thus arrived with little possibility of a German victory in France or an effective two-front Allied strategy involving France and Russia in combination. Earlier, when Allied cooperation had been possible, there had been no common war plan anyhow. The Turks, meanwhile, had entered the war on the German side, afraid that the Western powers would in time partition their empire after an Allied victory. They were essentially

The War in the East, 1914–1922

1914 Boundaries
Central Powers
Allied Powers
Neutral Nations
Furthermost Russian Advance, 1914–1915
The Front, 1915
Armistice Line, 1917
Brest Litovsk Treaty Line, 1918
Territory Lost by Russia, 1918
Areas Permanently Held by Red Army in Civil War
1921 Boundaries

Russian troops suffered horribly during the war, as seen in this 1916 sketch of Russian prisoners by the German artist Max Rabes. Nicholas II's army was cumbersome, slow moving, and ill prepared to face an efficient, modernized, German enemy. Bureaucratic corruption added further woes, and after a series of disasters the Czar decided to personally assume command of his forces. He left the government in the care of the hysterical Czarina who was under the spell of a mystical priest, Gregory Rasputin. By late 1916 the entire fabric of Russian society was falling apart, and in March 1917 Nicholas abdicated his throne. A provisional government failed to recognize the public will to end the monthly slaughter of thousands of Russian soldiers, and the way was clear for the Bolshevik take-over. Bayerisches Nationalmuseum, Munich.

correct in this estimate, as we now know from the published series of the secret prewar treaties.[56]

The military effect of the Turkish entry was immediate, however. The Allies tried to turn the flank of the Central Powers, by coordinating an attack on two southern fronts in 1915. Italy had entered the war in that year, *against* the Central Powers, in the hope of gains at Austrian expense in the Adriatic and at Turkish expense in North Africa and the Near East. The Allied effort on the Italian front failed, despite a concentration of German forces elsewhere, in an attack on northwestern Russia (which took 2,000,000 Russian lives). There was a similar failure of the strategy advocated by Winston Churchill,[57] which was to attack the Dardanelles with a combined naval-military force. The Allies lost 145,000 men before abandoning the campaign.

The year had also brought Russia closer to exhaustion on the eastern front, where trench warfare had not dominated tactics. But 1915 had not altered the siege warfare in the western sector. There was one important development, however. The success of the British blockade forced Germany to declare the shipping lanes around Britain a war zone in which Allied vessels could be attacked, and also neutrals carrying contraband. The weapon used was not the surface fleet, still bottled up in port, but the submarine, or U-boat.[58] What even limited submarine warfare might mean became clear in May, when a sub sank the British liner *Lusitania*, with the loss of 1,200 passengers, of whom 118 were American "neutrals." The Germans knew the ship carried munitions for the Allies; and their diplomatic mission in the United States had taken newspaper advertisements to warn people against booking passage on a contraband conveyor. The people in the United States disregarded these facts, however, and President Wilson stirred anti-German riots with his view that the subs had committed unprovoked hostile acts.

The Germans were next forced to enlarge the submarine war at sea as a result of the one decisive action in 1916. After a long period of small-scale surface engagements between fast, powerful German "raiders" of the High Seas Fleet and the ships of the British Grand Fleet, the Germans were trapped into a major battle off Jutland in May 1916. Admiral Jellicoe[59] used his 151 ships cautiously to force the Germans back into coastal waters. His objective was neither to risk his own fleet nor to destroy the German one, but to assert British control. In this he was successful. The German command decision to move to a policy of *unrestricted* submarine warfare resulted from the strategic defeat of Jutland. Bethmann-Hollweg opposed this policy, in the belief that it would threaten the only vital interest the

56. Published by the Russian communists in 1918.
57. Churchill was first lord of the admiralty (a post corresponding to secretary of the navy) in 1915.
58. A translation of the German abbreviation for *unterseeboot*, "undersea boat."
59. 1859–1935; commander of the Grand Fleet. He took heavier losses than the Germans in this battle.

The German embassy printed this warning to American travelers who were considering booking passage on the British liner Lusitania. *Despite the notice 118 Americans were killed when the ship was sunk by a German U-boat attack in May 1915. The incident did much to hasten anti-German sentiment in the United States and was used to justify American intervention in the war. Although seen at the time as a defenseless slaughter of innocents, recently released secret documents have shown that the* Lusitania *was loaded with munitions for the Allies. The disaster made the world aware of the awful efficiency of submarines in warfare. Culver Pictures, Inc.*

The Battle of Verdun proved one of the most costly encounters for both sides during the war. H. de Groux's painting, The Assault, reflects the determined stance taken by the French defenders. From February 1916 through the summer of 1917 sporadically intense fighting occurred around Verdun. Although the Germans made progress at first, there was no victory, and territory was often traded back and forth several times in desperately close-quarter fighting. Artillery was heavily used, with appalling casualties. Finally in late August 1917 the French succeeded in driving out the enemy, their courage exemplified in the battle cry, "They Shall Not Pass." Musée des deux Guerres Mondiales, Paris.

Americans had in the war—freedom of the seas. In 1917 the politicians were overwhelmed by the generals in Germany, however.

Ludendorff[60] carried the new policy on January 31, 1917, at the same time that Bethmann-Hollweg was seeking to negotiate American neutrality. This new policy was coupled with a German attempt to exploit American involvement against Mexican revolutionary forces south of the Rio Grande border. The German minister in Mexico City had received a telegram from Berlin, urging a German-Mexican alliance against the United States. Mexico would receive back under German guarantees the "lost" territories of Texas, New Mexico, and Arizona. The intercepted "Zimmermann Telegram"[61] was published in America, where it combined with the furor against submarine warfare to bring America into the war on April 6, 1917.

The entry of the United States on the Allies' side was eventually decisive. President Wilson governed a state which in 1914 had 96,000,000 citizens, a coal production of 455 million tons, and over 60,000,000 tons in combined iron and steel output. The campaign of 1916 in France had been indecisive, at Verdun in February, where the Germans attacked, and along the Somme, where the Allies countered in July. The chief result had been to

60. 1865–1937; together with Hindenburg (1847–1934) at the top of the High Command since 1916.
61. Arthur Zimmermann was German state secretary for foreign affairs and the author of the dispatch.

bleed all armies. In the Verdun campaign there were almost 700,000 casualties, about evenly divided. On the Somme River fields there were over 1,100,000 casualties: 500,000 German, 400,000 British, and 200,000 French. The Russians had lost over 1,000,000 more men in various encounters in 1916 and were totally exhausted, without arms, dispirited, and faced with revolutionary agitation at home. New armies and supplies might be conclusive.

The German forces had not been defeated, but they had not broken any of the opposition. It thus seemed possible that a negotiated settlement might emerge. And this chance looked brighter in March 1917, when the Russian troops in Saint Petersburg mutinied in a period of prolonged strikes and riots. The Germans thought the March risings might take Russia out of the war, but the liberals who forced Nicholas II to abdicate on March 15 were pro-Allies. By the time Wilson obtained a congressional declaration of war in April, it had been decided by the provisional government of Russia to launch a new campaign. The failure of the July offensive in Galicia coincided with two other failures among the Allies. An Italian army had been smashed by the Central Powers at Caporetto. A British-supervised offensive in Belgium cost 400,000 men without producing an advance of the front more than five miles. The net result on all fronts and at sea pointed toward a stalemate, because the United States had not yet effectively intervened.[62]

Events in Russia then threatened the Allies with defeat. In April 1917 the German High Command had permitted the Marxist Russian revolutionary V. I. Lenin (1870–1924)[63] and some cohorts to reach Saint Petersburg from Switzerland via Finland. Their hope was that Lenin would foment new revolts against the pro-Western liberals in the wake of Nicholas's abdication. Lenin was aided in his insurgency by the dispirited armies, which could not be motivated to fight after the July campaign failed. The Marxists seized power in November and promptly began negotiations to take Russia

62. As the Germans correctly guessed, the United States could not for a year after entering the war.
63. See below for the Bolshevik Revolution in Russia.

In the spring of 1918 the Germans began a series of brilliant offensives planned by Hindenburg's chief of staff, Erich Ludendorff. In this combat photograph taken from the German side the Kaiser's troops overrun British lines near the Somme and advance through a devastated landscape of corpses and wrecked homes. Ludendorff's successful strategies allowed the Germans to push to within forty miles of Paris. Partially because of the thousands of American troops pouring into France, success turned to failure and the advance became a rout. Sensing the eventual outcome, Ludendorff forced the resignation of the civilian government in Berlin and requested an armistice. Later he decided the fighting should continue, and his opposition to peace resulted in his fleeing to Sweden. UPI.

By 1918 American soldiers were arriving in Europe en masse in time to engage in some of the bloodiest fighting of the war. At Belleau Wood 6,000 American marines, out of a total force of 8,000, were killed. The most crucial engagement was at Château-Thierry, where the Americans endured a savage German attack and won the battle on July 2, 1918. After that the Germans were on the defensive, and the safety of Paris was secured. In this photo Americans man a machine-gun nest on the western front in 1918. National Archives.

out of the war, which Lenin condemned as an affair of capitalist imperialists, not one of the Russian people. Early in 1918 the Bolsheviks accepted a harsh peace settlement,[64] acknowledging the national independence of Poland, Finland, the Ukraine, Estonia, Latvia, and Lithuania. This apparent German espousal of revolution and nationalism shows how little ideological concerns motivated Berlin.[65]

More important was the fact that the eastern German armies could now be transferred to the French theater. With these forces Ludendorff launched a spring offensive, using massed artillery, poison gas, aerial bombardments, and more than a million troops. On May 30, 1918, German armies were on the Marne again, within forty miles of Paris, where they had been four years earlier. The year America needed for full mobilization had elapsed, however, and on July 18 the Supreme Allied Commander, the French Marshal Foch,[66] counterattacked, using nine American divisions from the total force of 3,500,000 now ordered to fight by President Wilson. With further divisions from the United States, then coming to Europe at the rate of 250,000 fresh troops per month, the Allies launched a major offensive in September. The Germans admitted the need for peace, and an armistice was arranged on November 11, 1918, to avoid a march into Germany by the combined Allied forces. A war in which there were 30,000,000 military casualties had ended, with 21,000,000 maimed by gas, tanks, planes, machine guns, and the old-fashioned rifle and bayonet, and the rest dead.

64. Brest-Litovsk; a similarly harsh pact was forced on Rumania.
65. In reality, of course, a German occupation force in the new states secured allegiance to Germany.
66. Ferdinand Foch, 1851–1929.

The nature of the war had been as unprecedented as its effects. Twenty-eight countries had fought over the face of the globe, even in China. The statesmen and generals who made the war believed in 1914 that even an unsuccessful war might benefit a people by at least protecting its vital interests from surrender. In the past, this had seemed to be true because wars were limited in scope and consequences. The first global war had come to people operating with the assumption that war was a rational extension of diplomacy, with calculable prices to be paid as part of an acceptable risk. Even the germ of the Schlieffen Plan was twelve years old when the war began! And it was based on the premise of a short encounter with limited death tolls.

The failure of Germany's slow-moving western *blitzkrieg* made obsolete all ideas about war. The trench and the machine gun dominated in fact. There were rarely advances of more than a few miles on any part of the western front, until the breakthrough in the Marne in 1918. Even on the eastern front, where movement occurred, the losses were beyond expectation; the Russians lost one million in dead and wounded in 1914 at Tannenberg and the Masurian Lakes.

There is no evidence that any major commander grasped the nature of the impact which industrial technology had on warfare. The airplane, for example, was at first thought of only as a superior means of reconnaissance. Then its use was extended to the classical aerial combat with synchronized machine guns. By 1918, however, the rapid development of bombs led to the deployment of dozens of planes to bomb troops, and also civilians in industrial cities. The idea had dawned that modern war was total war, against troops and the workers who supplied them with factory-produced weapons. Thus the principle of the old naval blockade, denying food to civilians and strategic imports to the military, was extended on new lines.

There were other new weapons. Poison gases that paralyzed, burned, and killed were used from 1915, first against the French, then by the Allies. Technical defenses were devised, especially the gas mask. The British introduced the tank in 1916, and it eventually terrified and overcame the

The American painter John Singer Sargent observed these victims of a poison gas attack as they were led to medical aid. The use of gas in warfare and defenses against it were unknown at the beginning of the war, but the Germans soon struck upon the idea of using gas to drive their opponents out of entrenched positions. From 1915 onward both sides rapidly developed new chemical attack methods, including the famous "mustard" gas, which was responsible for the majority of casualties and had the added effect of lingering for a long period in the soil. Many complications arose from such weapons including the necessity of respirators and other special equipment. Imperial War Museum, London.

toughest infantry; but the German automobile makers were as good at producing tanks as the British, with the result that the tank was not a decisive advantage to either side. The dominant new weapon was the machine gun manned in a fortified place and in command of the open ground between trenches. In combination with long-range artillery it accounted for more casualties than the other new weapons. Nothing proves the stupidity of the generals more than their persistent delusion that a charge across open ground against opponents dug into trenches and heavily armed would succeed. In the American Civil War General Robert E. Lee had made the error at Gettysburg, after earlier having done so at Malvern Hill. Nothing seems to have been learned by the Europeans since 1863. At Verdun the only strategy was slaughter; and there were one million dead to testify to the fact.

This war, then, erased the line between soldier and civilian; and it made all combatants, in and out of uniform, the victims of so-called statesmen who submitted to history as their achievement the 21,000,000 dead, ground to pieces in butchery aided by machines. Gone was gallantry, except among those knights of the sky who saluted their victims in air squadron dining rooms. Meanwhile, propaganda machines at home convinced the population that the 42,000,000 Allied men under arms and the 23,000,000 troops of the Central Powers were locked in a struggle for freedom and civilization itself.

The aim of propaganda was often to dehumanize the "enemy" and so justify the slaughter. The English were pictured as people without a soul, shopkeepers who were ignorant of Mozart, while the Germans were portrayed as a new wave of Huns, barbarians in the service of "Kaiser Bill," the beast of Berlin.

Something had to be done to justify the cost in lives and wealth,[67] the strafing of troops from the air, and such events as the air raid on London made on June 13, 1917, by fourteen German bombers, killing 162 and wounding 432. The bombardment of undefended towns by any means had been banned by the war rules adopted at the Hague Conference of 1899. Germany had not signed, however.[68] By the war's end, Britain, which in 1914 had only 113 military aircraft, had 3,300 planes capable of dropping on German towns "blockbuster" bombs weighing nearly one ton apiece.

Some total, radical, war aim seemed necessary to explain the life of the trenches to the men who lived it, amid rats, frogs, mice, mud, the hand grenades, trench mortars, gas-pipe bombs, rotten bacon, rum, steel helmets, telescopic sights, pillboxes, and the dazzling magnesium flares used to illuminate enemy charges against the armies of that long night of four years' duration.

For it was clear to the poets on all sides that the blinking light of many dawns brought to view no objective worth gaining at the cost paid "to take some cursed wood."[69] The soldier prayed less for victory than for a minor injury that would at least send him home alive:

> O Jesus, send me a wound today,
> And I'll believe in Your bread and wine,
> And get my bloody old sins washed white![70]

67. Perhaps $350 billion in old dollars.
68. Nor had France, Italy, Russia, or Japan.
69. Siegfried Sassoon, "At Carnoy," in *Collected Poems, 1908–1956* (New York: The Viking Press; London: Faber and Faber, 1957), p. 22.
70. Sassoon, "Stand-to: Good Friday Morning, 1916." From *The Old Huntsman and Other Poems.* Copyright 1918 by E. P. Dutton Co. All rights reserved. Reprinted by permission of The Viking Press, Inc.

Dehumanizing, jingoistic propaganda was widely exploited by all sides in World War I. The Threshing Floor of Europe is the title of this poster where the Kaiser's enemies—France, Russia, and England—receive a sound beating from his troops, while other smaller nations ponder the situation in the background. While overt appeals to nationalistic feelings were nothing new (Napoleon had been an able master of propaganda), they had never been so widespread or effective. Signs asking the public to purchase bonds or subscribe to loans to underwrite the cost of the war as well as recruitment posters were common sights in every participating country. Altonaer Museum, Hamburg.

The world war had unloaded hell step by step, and the combatants required a promise of salvation.

For the Allies this "salvation" emerged clearly during the war itself, in the course of the diplomacy of the war. It was the policy of identifying the war as the people's war, the war for democracy, national self-determination, and the utter defeat of Germany. When the conflict began, no power had any aim but traditional ones of victory. As the stalemate developed, there was a period of intense diplomacy aimed at the limited objectives a victory had not produced. But a German offer to withdraw from Belgium was rejected by the British in 1914, on the ground that Britain must be secure from future attacks from Germany. France and Russia agreed to this idea.

But the idea of total security demanded the total defeat of Germany, even its destruction as a great power. Germany was thus condemned by the Allies for using its power; the Allies were condemned by Berlin for obstructing the course of a superior civilization.[71] The German idea of domination was therefore countered by the notion of a war to make the world safe for democracy. Of course, the British wanted to destroy the German fleet; the French wanted Alsace and Lorraine; Italy wanted to control the Adriatic; Russia wanted to reduce the Habsburg Empire. And all the Allies talked of ending German militarism.

To gain such limited and chauvinistic ends, the Allies in 1915–1916 resorted to secret diplomacy. The network of agreements among the Allies, which could be realized only by a total victory, thus inhibited a compromise peace based on any return to the 1914 status quo. President Wilson had feared this impasse late in 1916, and asked the Allies to define their war aims. This they did in January 1917. Officially, those goals were to restore Serbia and Belgium and to evict the Germans from France, Russia, and Rumania. Secretly, many other agreements had been reached: Italy was to get its *irredenta* lands and the Turkish territory of Adalia in Asia Minor as well as Libya and Somaliland in Africa, while the French and English would divide Germany's African colonies; the further division of the Ottoman Empire was to produce a Jewish state in Palestine, Russian control of the Black Sea Straits, British control over Mesopotamia, and French control over Syria; Russia was to get Armenia and Kurdistan.

Wilson, who was adamantly opposed to secret imperialist agreements, was told that the Germans must never get back their colonies overseas and that Austria's hegemony over the Balkan Slavs must end. This opened to Wilson an ideological path to make the war acceptable to the United States. From about 1851 to 1911 over 34,000,000 Europeans had emigrated from Europe. Nearly 25,000,000 had come to the United States. Until 1880, British, Irish, German, and Scandinavian immigrants had dominated; after that year the major part of the new wave of immigration came from the Austro-Hungarian Empire, Poland, Italy, and Russia—9,000,000 people from 1905 to 1914. In the American cities the various European ethnic groups, often with considerable access to funds and to the press, exerted pressure in favor of a war of liberation against Germany. Wilson's acceptance of Balkan national self-determination was thus a critical point; it could be achieved only if the Allies were really free to dismantle the empires of Austria-Hungary, Germany, and the Turks. The United States' entry into the war sealed the fate of the Central Powers in more ways than one, therefore.

By the end of 1917, with the Russian withdrawal, most of the ideological

71. See Chapter 14 for a discussion of doctrines of racial superiority.

elements required by the victors were in place. So long as the Allies included czarist Russia, a democratic and nationalist peace was not in the cards. The Bolshevik Revolution in Russia, however, fundamentally altered politics within the alliance states. The socialists in France and Britain now had a cause to oppose the war (opposition to all imperialism) and a goal in peace (freedom for all peoples). The rise of domestic antiwar sentiment led to a new logic, based on the principle of freedom for all peoples through self-determination. President Wilson, taking a stand against the antiwar socialists, argued that there could be no free, self-determined peace without a total victory over the *old* imperialism and on that ground justified America's entry into the war, on the condition that the Allies give public support to this American ideology of self-determined peace. The program Wilson had in mind he made public in the Fourteen Points early in 1918.

The American president's goal was not only to rescue the Allies; he wished also to prevent the socialists from looking to the new Russian state for moral leadership. His chief "points" were these: European imperialism within the Continent would come to an end; there was to be self-determination for all states, without regard for the historic rights of the contending powers; countries independent before 1914 would be restored; France was to have Alsace and Lorraine; but Poland was to be free, along with all Balkan nations and the diverse peoples within Austria-Hungary; there was to be absolute freedom of navigation upon the seas; there was to be no more secret diplomacy; and a League of Nations must be created to replace the balance of power as the principle of peace-keeping. Any peace on these lines would necessarily mean the disappearance from the map of all the old empires. This would be followed by disarmament.

Russia had already disappeared; and when the Allies treated for peace with the Central Powers at Versailles, so had the Hohenzollern Reich and the Habsburg imperium. Charles I[72] abdicated on November 12, 1918, and within a few days republics were proclaimed in Austria and Hungary and also in Rumania, and Yugoslavia. The Czechs had proclaimed a republic even before Charles's abdication.

In Berlin the Kaiser had tried to save his dynasty from the consequences of defeat in October by conceding the program of the national liberals—a parliamentary, responsible government. But the Kaiser was regarded as a force inhibiting peace, a view encouraged with indecent haste by the industrialists and the aristocratic militarists who scrambled to shift the blame for defeat on Charles I and the "traitors" at home—Jews, socialists, and democrats. There was much talk of abdication, even before November 3, when the fleet at Kiel mutinied. A general strike on November 9 followed a socialist demand that either William II abdicate or they would go into opposition and so bring down the new responsible government.[73] William II fled to Holland that day.[74] The Weimar Republic began to take shape under the pressure of accepting the defeat.

Of the twenty-eight combatant states, only twenty-seven assembled at Versailles. Russia was the absentee, hated by the liberals for its new communism and for having taken itself out of the war. It quickly became clear to Wilson that Lloyd George, Clemenceau, Orlando,[75] and other Allied diplomats were not convinced by the Fourteen Points. Britain would

The Allied leaders Wilson, Clemenceau, and Lloyd George are seated together in the Hall of Mirrors in Sir William Orpen's painting of the signing of the Treaty of Versailles. On the near side of the table the two German delegates are presented with the terms already agreed upon by their victors. The treaty was an extremely harsh one for Germany: she was stripped of much of her territory including all overseas colonies, forced to pay enormous reparations, and severely limited as to the size and nature of her military forces. By basing their demands on past hatreds rather than trying to work out a peaceable future, the Allies themselves laid some of the groundwork for the internal strife and discontent which plagued Germany in succeeding decades and resulted in Hitler's rise to power. Imperial War Museum, London.

72. 1916–1918, the last Habsburg emperor.
73. The socialists were the most numerous single group in the parliament.
74. He lived there until 1941.
75. The Italian prime minister (1860–1952), V. E. Orlando.

not accept freedom of the seas. France wanted a Carthaginian peace,[76] with a heavy German reparations penalty. Wilson accepted these modifications and assured the German democrats at Paris that peace would be made within the general framework of his program. But Wilson was deceived by France, Britain, Italy, and Japan.[77] They refused to accept his League of Nations until he agreed to new demands.

These new demands were essentially five in number. The French insisted on Anglo-American guarantees against new German aggression. This they tied to French control over the German coal mines and the demilitarization of the German Rhineland for a fifteen-year period, both guaranteed by an

76. After its victory over Carthage in the Third Punic War, Rome decreed that Carthage be annihilated. Thus, a Carthaginian peace is a treaty of peace so harsh that it means the virtual destruction of the defeated foe.
77. Japan had joined the war on the Allied side to gain the German territories in the Far East.

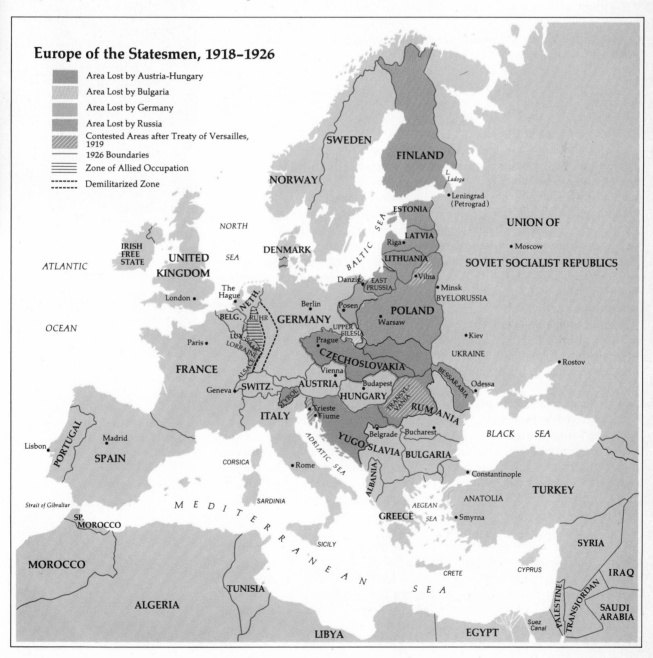

Europe of the Statesmen, 1918–1926

Allied military occupation. Secondly, the German populations in Poland, Silesia, Lithuania, and Bohemia were not to be joined to the new, reduced, German republic. Thus secret treaties, a military occupation, and a denial of self-determination for the German "nation" cut the ground out from under some major elements of the Fourteen Points. The Allies cut off Austria from the sea and made the new German republic tiny and weak, while destroying the old Germany.

A third compromise concerned the German colonies. The best Wilson could manage for open colonial adjustment was a fiction. Instead of a simple distribution of the German colonies to the victors, the colonies were made "trusts" of the new League of Nations, which gave "mandates" to govern them to the victors. Curiously, Italy was excluded, while France, Britain, and Japan divided the major mandates. To guard against any new maritime threat from Germany, a fourth requirement was the surrender of all German warships to the Allies. Loyal sailors sank the ships instead; the victors then "sank" the German army. The Versailles Treaty required the German forces in the future to be fewer than 100,000 troops, without annual drafts, heavy artillery, or airplanes.[78]

Wilson's dream of disarmament thus applied to the Germans only; the Allies were busy sending troops and supplies to Russia to overthrow the Bolsheviks. Churchill, the British minister in charge of demobilization, asked Parliament to send 900,000 men to crush the Soviet threat to civilization!

Finally, there was the issue of reparations and war guilt. Wilson agreed to indemnities in principle, but even he was staggered by the bills presented. The treaty set no limit on the debt, a matter left for future decision. In practice this was a blank check drawn against Germany's ability to pay. Indemnities were tied to the war-guilt clause of the treaty, and the Germans, without a hearing, were forced to accept unspecified damages, on the theory that such an enormous crime must require enormous penalties. This was the peace to which the Weimar representatives were made to affix signatures in June 1919, after the original delegates refused to accept the treaty in May. A German blank check had begun the war; another one ended it.

It is impossible to estimate the total cost, in men, material, and in human suffering, of the First World War brought about by repressed nationalism and by a lethal combination of militarism, imperialism, and folly. But the Allied insistence that Germany pay the war's monetary cost provides one clue to the financial picture. Before the war the United States had been the largest debtor nation in the European network of debtors. In 1918 the European credits in America had been nearly eliminated by the sale of European assets to pay for the war. The United States had become the chief source of international funds; all the European countries had become debtors, Germany the biggest of all. The American debt to Europe had increased fivefold from 1900 to 1914; European investments in America were worth about $6.5 billion, about 14 percent of all international indebtedness. It was the cost of this liquidation, beyond the actual war damages, that the Allies passed to Germany.

The war was therefore an element in the redistribution of power *beyond* Europe, not merely within it. The roster of small new states was in the future to exercise less influence on Western history than was the emergence of Russia, Japan, and the United States, the first ideologically and politically, the latter two, in every sense, as great powers. In 1919, when "peace"

78. Submarines were banned from the German fleet.

No previous war had so devastated wide areas of earth. Incessant artillery barrages and the use of chemicals laid waste much of northern France leaving scenes such as the one confronting Paul Nash when he painted his bitter We Are Making a New World. *Even in view of more recent holocausts the losses occurred in World War I seem staggering. England, France, Germany, and Russia each lost almost an entire generation of young men. European economies lay in ruins, contributing to the inflation and financial crises of following years. But perhaps the greatest loss of all was the common failure to learn from the experience that such conflicts must be avoided at all costs in the future. Imperial War Museum, London.*

was made in Western Europe, the anti-Bolshevik crusade grew out of the anti-German one. Europe had in fact ceased to be the center of world power, even if it was still the center of Western civilization—although even that was subject to question. The war had begun with a German challenge to the European Great Powers. It must therefore rank as one of history's greatest ironies that, having beaten that challenge, Europe now faced the prospect of domination by either Russia or America, or both.

BIBLIOGRAPHY

The literature on the prewar diplomacy, the war itself, and its consequences is too vast to be satisfactorily sampled. Two general works on European history provide good background material: George Lichtheim, *Europe in the Twentieth Century** (New York: Praeger Publishers, 1972), and J. M. Roberts, *Europe, 1880–1945* (New York: Holt, Rinehart & Winston, 1967). Beyond these surveys, we consider the following basic to an understanding of the period:

DEHIO, LUDWIG, *Germany and World Politics in the Twentieth Century.** New York: W. W. Norton & Co., 1959. A very provocative collection of essays.

FELDMAN, GERALD D. *Army, Industry and Labor in Germany 1914–1918.* Princeton: Princeton University Press, 1966. Valuable on the whole subject of the economic impact of the war on government in Europe.

FISCHER, FRITZ. *Germany's War Aims in the First World War.** New York: W. W. Norton & Co., 1967. A revisionist work by a German accepting German "responsibility" for the war.

HOLBORN, HAJO. *The Political Collapse of Europe.** New York: Alfred A. Knopf, 1951. A humanistic historian looks at the Great War in pessimistic terms.

KING, JERE C. *Generals and Politicians.* Berkeley: University of California, 1951. An excellent book on French civil-military relations.

———. *The First World War.** New York: Harper & Row, Publishers, Torchbooks, 1972. A very well done documentary history.

LA FORE, LAURENCE. *The Long Fuse.** Philadelphia: Lippincott, 1965. A very sound review of the "origins of the war" problem and the vast literature; basically a digest of Luigi Albertini's three-volume classic on the same subject.

LANGER, WILLIAM L. *Explorations in Crisis.** Cambridge, Mass.: Harvard University Press, 1969. Continues the discussion begun for 1890–1902 by Langer's *The Diplomacy of Imperialism*; focuses on the dozen years before the war.

MAY, ERNEST R. *The World War and American Isolation, 1914–1917.* Cambridge, Mass.: Harvard University Press, 1959. The standard account of the American entry into the war.

STAVRIANOS, LEFTEN S. *The Balkans, 1815–1914.** New York: Holt, Rinehart & Winston, 1963. An excellent and lucid account of a difficult subject.

TAYLOR, A. J. P. *The First World War.** New York: G. P. Putnam's Sons, 1964. A good brief history; see Taylor's *The Struggle for Mastery in Europe* (New York: Oxford University Press, 1971) on the prewar diplomacy and the crises.

TUCHMAN, BARBARA W. *The Proud Tower.** New York: The Macmillan Company, 1966. The European political world before 1914; markedly anti-German, but well written. See also her *The Guns of August** (New York: The Macmillan Company, 1962) on the opening days of the war.

WOLFE, BERTRAM D. *Three Who Made a Revolution.** New York: Dell Publishing Co., 1964. Together with Adam B. Ulam, *The Bolsheviks** (New York: The Macmillan Company, 1965), the best short account of Lenin, Trotsky, and the 1917 coup.

ZEMAN, Z. A. B. *The Breakup of the Habsburg Empire.* New York: Oxford University Press, 1961. A useful analysis.

Asterisk indicates a paperbound edition.

14

TIME
AND
MOTION

Bergson[1] has shown us what a paralyzing influence static conceptions of reality have had upon the history of philosophy and how futile have been all attempts to represent movement by rest. The scientist of today thinks in terms of motion. All modern thought is assuming kinetic forms and we are coming to see the absurdity of the old ideas of immutability and immobility. A similar revolution is impending in art. . . . But we need not speculate as to the future of the motion picture. . . . There are very likely at this moment more people looking at moving pictures than there are reading books. . . .

"The Birth of a New Art," The New York *Independent*, April 6, 1914[2]

IMAGES IN SEQUENCE

Four years before printing "The Birth of a New Art," the *Independent* ran an editorial entitled "The Drama of the People." Its anonymous writer hailed the "cinematography," or moving picture, as an advance doing for drama what the printing press had earlier done for literature—"bringing another form of art into the daily life of the people."[3] His article hailed celluloid film as the medium which brought quality drama to even the poorest people, by virtue of the cheapness inherent in mechanical multiplication of prints. Sunshine and clouds from the Carpathian Mountains, or some other shore of the world than the Atlantic one hemming in New York, were suddenly produced on the silver screen, together with *Camille*.

The result was that "first-night performances" by the world's best actors and actresses were no longer the privilege of a favored few. Drama no longer consisted of the nightly repetitions of a given production, but was transmitted instead as the instantly captured essence of the original performance. The new art form had all the permanence of a painting, and it created a better illusion of reality than the stage play because at the end of a film the slain hero does not rise from the dead to take curtain calls. The *Independent*'s critic, who obviously found the motion picture valuable in proportion to its *realism*, confidently predicted the final triumph of realism. The cinematographer would someday make the

1. Henri Bergson, the French vitalist philosopher of evolution.
2. Reprinted in Lewis Jacobs, ed., *Introduction to the Art of the Movies* (New York: Farrar, Straus & Giroux, The Noonday Press, 1960), pp. 45–46; Jacobs's anthology explores motion pictures as art from 1910 to 1960.
3. Jacobs, *Art of the Movies*, p. 41.

ultimate conquest, by showing that other shore to us in a "stereoscopic colored speaking moving picture drama. . . . "[4]

The struggle to escape the limitations of time and place in art of every sort and in thought about the natural world as well as the inner world of human consciousness had succeeded between the 1850s and the end of the First World War.

Darwin had radically altered the time scale of human life and its interpretation with the appearance in 1859 of his work on evolution and the origin of species through the *process* of natural selection.[5] The impressionist painters had brought to realistic art a sense of time, in opposition to the static quality of a view fixed once for all time. Perhaps the most familiar example of this aspect of the new style in painting lies in the work of Claude Monet (1840–1926), who from 1892 to 1894 painted a series of views of Rouen Cathedral at different times of day in different lights. By 1912, however, the "modernist" painter Marcel Duchamp (1887–1968) had gone to the extreme of depicting in geometric forms the successive motions made by a nude walking down a staircase over some period of time.[6]

The motion picture was born in 1889, with a demonstration of Thomas Edison's picture machine. Within little more than two decades, "movies" had become big business, in 1916 ranking fifth in the nation (behind railroads, clothing, iron and steel, and oil, but ahead of the automobile industry). In the early days, movie fans, like these outside a Brooklyn movie theater, paid five cents admission; the coy young girls they paid to see on the screen were earning five dollars a day. By 1916, though, the opening of a lavish new movie theater was a gala occasion, and Charlie Chaplin was earning almost seven times as much as the president of the United States. Brown Brothers.

4. "The Drama of the People," The New York *Independent*, October 8, 1910, as quoted in Jacobs, *Art of the Movies*, p. 44.
5. The first essay drafts of the material in *Origin of Species* date from 1842, however.
6. His *Nude Descending a Staircase* was actually done in 1911, exhibited but withdrawn in 1912, and then became the sensation of the 1913 New York Armory Show.

The idea of serial pictures was not new with Duchamp. The photographer Eadweard Muybridge had made experiments with serial photographs of closely related actions in 1872, in order to help Leland Stanford win a bet.[7] The governor maintained that a running horse had all four feet off the ground at some point in its stride, but artists had never represented this, apparently because they could not see it. Five years later Muybridge won the bet for Stanford by making a moving picture. In fact what he made was a short-interval series of stills with a simple apparatus. Across the experimental area of the track trip wires were stretched, too weak to deter the galloping Occident[8] but strong enough to pull the triggers of the battery of cameras Muybridge had set along the course. Muybridge perfected "chronophotography," as it was then called, and in 1881 exhibited pictures to the impressionist painter Degas,[9] himself a horse-lover and ardent still photographer. The link between Duchamp's cubism, which combined a series of separate actions into a single geometric image, and both still and serial photography was a long one, and it passed through the space occupied by Degas's paintings of nude bathers and his bronzes of horses.

7. Stanford, the railroad tycoon, was then governor of California. Muybridge died in 1904; the bet was for $25,000!
8. Stanford's favorite horse.
9. Edgar Degas (1834–1917). Degas favored horses, races, dancers, bathing scenes, and other ordinary subjects showing spontaneous movements.

In other aspects of thought and expression, the rapidly changing understanding of time and motion produced even more revolutionary results. The Viennese physician Sigmund Freud (1856–1939) overturned traditional doctrines of psychology. His psychoanalytic view depicted the unconscious as a dynamic force shaped by events in time and drawing its energy from instinctual drives long ago repressed, or kept below the level of consciousness. The writers Marcel Proust (1871–1922) and James Joyce (1882–1941) had broken with the social novel of realism to develop a concept of time as a personal, vital experience which alone gave meaning to life. Philosophic thought had also taken a turn toward stressing the fundamental role played by time in shaping existence.

This was true of speculation influenced by the doctrines of biological science, particularly evolution, as Henri Bergson (1859–1941) worked out his idea of "felt duration" as the core of his *vitalistic* thought. On the side of the physical sciences an even more radical departure from tradition was made by Ernst Mach (1838–1916) and the physicists influenced by him. The most important of them was Albert Einstein (1879–1955), the mathematician who totally rejected Newtonian mechanics and the timeless, static universe predicted by classical physics. In place of the old ideas Einstein put the concept of a nature composed entirely of bundles of energy transformed in the flux of time. The law of the conservation of matter was overthrown.

Even in music the imposing structure of melody, harmony, and rhythm was displaced from the central position it held in composition. The generation of composers beginning with Stravinsky[10] and Schönberg[11] gave stress to the element of rhythm, expanding the dominance of intervals of time and the emotional qualities of rhythm. While composing in the Romantic tradition continued in certain "national" schools, Vienna and Paris, the very nerve centers of the Romantic tradition from Berlioz to Brahms, became centers of modern music.

There was no significant area of mental culture left untransformed, no aspect of thought and expression in which the old certainties of Romanticism, realism, and scientific positivism remained intact. The decades before the First World War were those in which what is characteristic in modern culture first emerged.

THE CULTURE OF LIBERALISM

Four aspects of the culture of the last half of the nineteenth century were representative of the flowering of liberal realism and scientific positivism: impressionism, the drama of democracy and women's rights, the vision of a "positive" science of society, and the incorporation of Charles Darwin's doctrine of evolution into social thought. These developments may be said to have reached maturity around 1890, almost precisely at the point in time when the discontent with the culture of liberalism gathered the force needed to relegate scientific positivism and artistic and literary realism to the scrap heap of history.

The impressionists owed their name to an unfriendly critic. In 1874, at an exhibition held in a photographer's gallery, Claude Monet exhibited a painting entitled *Impression: Sunrise.*[12] Monet's painting was in the Romantic manner, depicting as through a haze of light blue shot through with the rising sun's pink a scene of sky, water, and boats. Monet painted

10. Igor Stravinsky (1882–1971).
11. Arnold Schönberg (1874–1951).
12. Painted in 1872.

Although he was a friend of the impressionists and learned much from their experiments, Edgar Degas remained more closely tied to artistic concerns of the past which he restated in inventive ways. The Tub (1886) is one of a series of pastel drawings prepared for an impressionist exhibition in 1886. The radically foreshortened bather shows a knowledge of both Japanese prints and the newly developing art of photography. What is most strikingly different about the work is the artist's point of view, which departs completely from the posed, idealized, classical conception of the female nude. Here the observer seems to be peeking through a keyhole catching a glimpse of everyday life. There is seldom an emotional involvement with Degas's figures; rather the artist observed them in a scientific way, analyzing their formal qualities with complete detachment. Louvre.

reflections with a few sharp, short, and broken strokes, suggestive of the ephemeral and momentary character of his subject. Academic Romanticism had often attempted similar subjects, but without giving up the realistic sense of permanence deemed important for art. The experiment in rendering a fleeting impression prompted the critic to call Monet's "impressionistic" work outrageous.

"Impressionism" thus entered the art vocabulary as a term of derision. But the artists themselves took the name for their movement, gathering the support of a few critics and dealers and also that of the editor of a paper dubbed *L'Impressioniste*. Originally, they had exhibited as the "unknowns,"[13] after the Salon rejected pictures by Monet, Renoir,[14] Pissarro,[15] Cézanne,[16] and Sisley[17] in 1873. But in subsequent shows they used the term "impressionists." Édouard Manet (1832–1883) was the elder statesman of the group, which had begun to form in the 1860s, shortly after the rejection of Manet's *Luncheon on the Grass (Le Déjeuner sur l'Herbe)* in 1863. This painting was based on the respectable example of Giorgione's *Fête champêtre*. Where the Renaissance master had painted nymphs and shepherds relaxing in the woods, however, Manet had depicted his own world: two bohemians after a picnic. Critics complained of the obviously "dissolute" scene but were just as outraged by Manet's conviction that artists had to paint realistically the things of their own experience.

The critics also disliked the technique. The painting was relatively flat, abandoning the effort to create an effective illusion of depth, a central element in all Western styles of naturalistic painting since the Renaissance discovery of perspective. Moreover, Manet had also given up the minute brushstrokes used to create a smooth surface. He employed broad strokes to define large masses and sketch colored shapes. He did not try to make an exact image, probably because the invention of photography had made it pointless for painters to strive for effects better achieved with the new tool. The same departures were condemned as "excesses" by the critics of Manet's "erotic" nude, *Olympia*, his *The Races at Longchamps*, and his celebrated portrait of the novelist Zola. It was pointed out that the "accessories" were not in perspective, departed from tradition, and were cluttered. Moreover, the pants worn by Zola were not made of cloth, but paint!

In trying to explain the impact of Manet and his friends, it is not enough for us to cite the negative effects produced by the camera. Western artists had used tools as aids to perception at least since da Vinci's experiments with the science of optics and the employment of the *camera obscura* by Giambattista della Porta (1541–1615). The early use of optical tools in art was intended to aid in copying lines and shapes exactly, to which color would later be added. The impressionists, and also the sculptor Rodin[18] and the American painter Thomas Eakins,[19] took up photography to master movement scientifically and also to help them understand reality, especially how to convey the effect of accidental and chance dispositions of things. In regarding impressionism as the last stage of realism, therefore, we see that the camera discouraged one form of "realistic" painting while helping painters achieve a sense *impression* of the immediate aspects of a subject, not its timelessness.

Claude Monet's Cap Matin near Menton *(1884) represents his mature impressionist technique. Monet's lifelong artistic ambition was to study the reflection of light striking landscapes. Rather than working in a studio, he set up his easel outdoors to make direct observations of nature, as in this scene of the French Mediterranean coast. More than anyone else, Monet broke with the tradition of a slick, "finished" manner of painting, preferring instead obvious, sketchy brushstrokes of pure colors. When seen at a distance these lines fuse in the viewer's eye and convey a more realistic and scientific impression of light sensations than traditional methods. Courtesy, Museum of Fine Arts, Boston.*

13. "Société Anonyme."
14. Auguste Renoir, 1841–1919.
15. Camille Pissarro, 1830–1903.
16. Paul Cézanne, 1839–1906.
17. Alfred Sisley, 1839–1899; he was born in Paris of English parents.
18. Auguste Rodin, 1840–1917.
19. 1844–1916.

But it is not enough to say that the artists who adhered to impressionism[20] created a refined realism based on a more sophisticated view of natural reality. The impressionists went beyond the notion of momentary time as a solvent of fixed images to explore the qualities of light. These artists saw the colors of nature anew, breaking with the blacks and browns favored by the academics who painted indoors. By going out to their subjects, the impressionists gave to us the rainbow palette we admire in Renoir, the sunburst of giddy blues, yellows, greens, reds, oranges, and whites we know to be in things.

Thus the "movement" rejected the false realism of the studios for a superior realism. But they also rejected social realism. Manet's bohemian romp was followed by a turn toward splashed colors in landscapes devoid of social comment. Also, there was a total break with Romantic ideas and subjects. The purpose of art was not to convey the emotional excitement of the artist, but to render reality in dynamic terms. This meant giving up mythological and historical subjects in favor of the dancers, bathers, seamstresses, and café habitués we find in Degas, Renoir, and Manet. The new palette, the broken line, the broad stroke, and the use of a complementary color to paint the shadow of the main colored object combined with gay subjects to create a comfortable, happy art in which exact modeling with outlines gave way to impressions of pleasure. It was as if the triumphant bourgeoisie had found the art style most in harmony with its own new realism, at once confident and optimistic.

20. Including Frédéric Bazille (1841–1870) and Berthe Morisot (1841–1895).

*Paul Cézanne once explained his painting as "redoing Poussin from nature."
Although he was a friend of the impressionists and learned much from their
experiments, Cézanne felt that art must have structure and be logically
coherent—characteristics exemplified for him by Poussin. At the same time he
realized that a direct reaction to nature was the great artistic contribution of his
contemporaries, and he wished to combine this with an eternal, timeless beauty.
The Turn in the Road shows how a geometric, highly organized composition can
merge with a loose, impressionist brushstroke. Cézanne's achievements were the
basis for cubism and of all modern painting which emphasizes form and structure
over content. Courtesy, Museum of Fine Arts, Boston.*

In the 1870s and 1880s certain artists influenced by impressionism began
to challenge its main concerns, however. Cézanne insisted that what
mattered was the formal relationships of objects, which he viewed as
combinations of pure geometric forms. Georges Seurat (1859–1891) carried
the concern for scientific treatments of color to the extreme of *pointillism*, or
the building up of images by optically arranged dots or points of color on
utterly "flat" surfaces. Toulouse-Lautrec[21] pushed his work in the direction
of flat designs, treating space as two-dimensional, in the manner of the

21. Henri de Toulouse-Lautrec, 1864–1901.

Forsaking the life of privilege to which his aristocratic birth entitled him, Henri de Toulouse-Lautrec chose to frequent the cabarets and brothels of Montmartre, which he immortalized in his drawings and posters. The artist suffered from a congenital bone disease that left his legs shriveled and misshapen, and this may have prompted him to seek acceptance in a bohemian milieu. Divan Japonais *is an advertisement poster for a cabaret of that name, and the colors and flat, stylized two-dimensional figures reveal the artist's intense interest in Japanese wood-block prints. Lautrec learned to appreciate the prints from Degas, who in turn had discovered their strange aesthetic charms from Manet and the impressionists. By using posters as a medium of serious artistic expression Toulouse-Lautrec opened the way for many twentieth-century avant-garde developments. Collection, The Museum of Modern Art, New York.*

Japanese prints he studied and emulated. Together with Gauguin[22] and van Gogh,[23] these neo-impressionists or postimpressionists went to extremes in freeing color from line. They thus pointed away from realism entirely, toward the new representations of reality called expressionism and cubism, and also toward entirely nonrepresentational styles such as abstraction. A period of radical realism in painting generated the movements destructive of realism itself.

In the theater, the triumph of realism had also produced a tension between the artist and ordinary perceptions of social reality. Anton

22. Paul Gauguin, 1848–1903.
23. Vincent van Gogh, 1853–1890.

The Dutch artist Vincent van Gogh first painted gray, gloomy interiors of coal miners' houses, but after a trip to Paris in the mid 1880s he was overwhelmed by the impressionists and sought to drench his works with intense sunlight. In search of strong light conditions he settled in the southern French city of Arles. Because of a highly unstable personality, van Gogh was in and out of mental institutions, but his powers of creativity at this time were never greater, and most of his masterpieces date from the last months of his life. House at Auvers *is one of a series of almost hallucinatory paintings done just before his suicide. Courtesy, Museum of Fine Arts, Boston.*

Chekhov (1860–1904) in Russia was the heir to the techniques of realistic production. But he used his plays to depict the vast panorama of Russian life in critical terms which went beyond the boundaries of mere realism. His great plays[24] centered on independent people at odds with society, struggling for self-understanding as the condition necessary for understanding the social role one had to play. In a realistic framework, therefore, Chekhov explored *subjectivity*, the psychological reality of human character, rather than the more *objective* social situation only.

And when Chekhov did center attention wholly on the values of society in the familiar sense of realism, it was often to pass sentence on that society, as in the prophetic speech of Baron Tusenback in *The Three Sisters:*

The time has come, an avalanche is moving down on us, a mighty, wholesome storm is brewing . . . and soon will sweep away from our society its idleness, indifference, prejudice against work, and foul *ennui.* I shall work, and in some twenty-five or thirty-five years everyone will work too.

Chekhov's sense of the necessity to transform reality (by bringing to Russia the values of the work-oriented and liberal Western European society) permeated other playwrights in Europe's marginal states. We see it in Strindberg of Sweden,[25] who moved from the realism of *The Father* to the mystical, religious, and psychological concerns of his *Dream Play.* Unlike Strindberg, who was in fact a victim of bourgeois society, a man with a violently distorted life, the Austrian Schnitzler[26] and the Norwegian master Ibsen (1828–1906) had no actual mental breakdowns. Schnitzler was a Jewish writer, oppressed by anti-Semitism, a doctor, excessively concerned with death, a man sympathetic with the impressionist search for change and fascinated with the idea that personal insight holds the key to transforming reality.

In Ibsen we meet the perfection of the use of realism as a warrant for both social change and personal liberation. The son of a merchant who went bankrupt, Ibsen had studied medicine and been a stage manager as well as director of the Norwegian Theater. In 1866 he produced his first masterpiece, the play *Brand*, which he followed a year later with *Peer Gynt.* These early plays established Ibsen as the master of realism, because in them he developed the technique of presenting people whose lives were in crisis without giving explicitly the *history* of the crisis. Ibsen presented in unrelieved form the intense dilemmas of middle-class life, of people haunted by money worries and by lost opportunities for self-expression, people sexually frustrated and stifled by the narrow conformity demanded by bourgeois morality.

Ibsen was a realist in his social criticism and in the artistry with which he pictured Norwegian society. But he was more than an advocate of women's liberation[27] and the democratization of industrial society.[28] The appearance of strict realism was in Ibsen meant to serve another purpose: it was meant to convey the subjective drama of the divided *self.* Ibsen's great rebels— Brand, Peer Gynt, Nora (the heroine of *A Doll's House*)—protest the alienation of the individual from society and the alienation of the self. The unfulfilled women in his plays are in rebellion against their cramped lives, organized for them by the subordinate role they must play because they are

---

24. *The Cherry Orchard, The Seagull, Uncle Vanya, The Three Sisters.*
25. Johan August Strindberg, 1849–1912.
26. Arthur Schnitzler, 1862–1931.
27. In *A Doll's House* and *Hedda Gabler.*
28. In *Rosmersholm, The Master Builder,* and *Pillars of Society.*

tied to men—inevitably less strong and self-willed than they are themselves. Against the optimism of liberal realism Ibsen set his ideas of individualism, an antibourgeois set of values and guides to behavior. His work rejected the money god which had rejected his father.

Playwrights like Ibsen and painters like Manet were thus already at odds with the results of liberalism, while at the same time reflecting its supreme articles of faith: that progress is possible, that human effort tends toward improvement, that reality is "rational." This "positive" approach had drawn strength from scientific rationalism and, after the struggle to resist Darwin's ideas, from the social interpretation of his theory of evolution.

Positivism was less a philosophy than a set of confident assumptions about the industrial society. The new industrial technology had borrowed from the physical sciences many of their methods, but even more important was the central belief in a world of objective laws. The idea that nature was governed by unalterable "laws" not subject to variations encouraged the belief that men could master those laws and so achieve progressively greater control over the real world. Scientific realism therefore involved the assumption that the predictable, regular, behavior of things in nature made possible progress in the sense of *social* improvement based on the manipulation of nature.

Even before the publication of Darwin's *Origin of Species* gave new support from the side of the biological sciences, the idea that society itself was organic and had regular processes had made important converts. The whole school of Marxist socialism had developed out of the general socialist belief that social institutions were the result of regular forces, just as the ideas of the liberal economists from Adam Smith to Bright and Cobden had embodied such doctrines as the "law" of supply and demand and the "iron law" of wages, or Thomas Malthus's "law" that populations increased geometrically while food supplies grew arithmetically.

The French positivist Auguste Comte (1798–1857) had formulated a law of the three stages of human progress. Mankind had passed through theological and metaphysical ages, which Comte viewed as dominated by the imperfect "sciences" of religion and philosophy. The "positive," or scientific, stage had been reached under the impact of industry and republican politics, however, and in it the science of society (sociology) had matured. Earlier, the "natural" sciences had flowered; now, sociology dominated the hierarchy of sciences. And it was leading mankind toward even greater (progressive) refinements, culminating in a scientific "religion" of humanity.

Comte's doctrine of social evolution disturbed many scientists because it seemed to abandon empiricism. The scientists were especially critical of the organic analogy, or the doctrine that society was a sort of biological organism. In Comte's time, despite the development of evolutionary ideas held by geologists who believed that fossil evidence told against the biblical account of *specific creation*,[29] there was as yet no clear formulation of biological evolution. It therefore seemed a double presumption to suppose that societies evolved in stages in an organic manner, when it was not generally accepted that animal species changed over time.

It was Darwin's achievement to consolidate the ideas of his predecessors and his own research into a coherent theory of evolution. In place of *eternity*, the timelessness of Christian thought about creation, scientists and "natural" philosophers had already announced that the world was a changeling thing too varied to be explained by the story of the ark captained

29. The doctrine in Genesis that God had created all living species of plants and animals once
    for all time.

by Noah. Time itself had produced the mountains in geological upheavals, had worn away shores and canyons wherever water had free play, and alone accounted for man himself. Earlier observers had said that the variety and distribution of landscapes and creatures could not be explained on the static assumptions of Genesis. But the hold of religion on thought had not abated sufficiently to allow the acceptance of an evolutionary world view. Nor had a powerful enough mind come to grips with the natural data, bringing out of masses of observations a convincing, overarching theory to account for reality, bringing together the living record and the fossil record of old life forms.

Darwin's essential achievement was to link the present life forms to past ones by extrapolating into the past of fossil organisms the anatomical similarities observed in living species. Comparative anatomy convinced Darwin that the gradations and complexities in nature could not be explained by specific creation. Organisms past and present seemed too obviously related in a great chain of being incompatible with creation theory. Not only had some forms become extinct; others seemed to be still changing! This suggested to Darwin that the higher forms of life, man for example, stood in a different relationship to apes than the one allowed by the Christian "chain of being," which saw man and apes created in their present order by God, as eternal monuments of a static world.

Against the old world view, Darwin set two related concepts: time on a vast scale, and the mutability of forms. The terrestrial and marine forms, including man, had evolved from simpler life forms. The nature of this change over time was clearly stated in the first edition of *Origin of Species*. All living things faced the challenge of adapting to their environments. Some features of the organism proved more valuable to its survival. Therefore, over time, as the species reproduced biologically, there was a mysterious process[30] of "natural selection" of the characteristics vital to survival in the struggle of nature. Evolution was a drama of conflict, a competition to survive in which some living things arrive at a "higher stage of perfection, or dominating power" than others. Some unknown mechanism, according to Darwin, enables those fitted for survival to pass on the fortunate adaptations to their offspring. The fittest survive, therefore, by means of biological reproduction.

Darwin had thus raised the sexual activities of all living things to the creative place once held by the Deity! Extinct forms known from fossils represented the losers in life's competitions, while man obviously represented the biggest winner, the highest form of adaptive life. Biological evolution thus challenged the churches on the one hand, while on the other providing new fuel for the mills of positivism. Not only did animals evolve; mankind had evolved from lower forms to its present high estate. Life was progressive.

The long battle against Darwinism by the churches is not yet over.[31] And in Darwin's own time social thinkers immediately grasped the importance of his work. If the order of nature was not eternal, but progressive, tending toward the evolution of higher forms of life, then the idea of social evolution was better founded than its critics supposed.

This was the point made by the English positivist Herbert Spencer (1820–1903), who was for the English-speaking world what Comte had been earlier in Europe. Beginning with his *First Principles* in 1862, Spencer

If Charles Darwin had rocked the worlds of science and religion with the 1859 publication of Origin of Species, *he was to arouse vehement controversy once again when in 1871 he published the* Descent of Man, *in which he elaborated his evolutionary theory in regard to human beings.* The Hornet *magazine, reflecting popular scorn for the theory that man was descended from the ape, derided the new "unnatural history" in this 1871 cartoon: the body is that of an orang-outang, the face is that of Darwin. Thames & Hudson Archives.*

30. Darwin had no knowledge of genes or their elements as determinants.
31. Even in the 1970s the state of California has found itself embroiled in a controversy over textbooks, because of a demand that the biblical "theory" of creation be given equal space with the theory of evolution.

championed the natural history of society. The sociologist's task was to discover the causal laws behind social evolution. Mixing together biology, psychology, ethics, economics, and politics, Spencer's sociology had two basic principles: individual evolution produced better social types, and these individuals by cooperation produced better societies. Progress was necessary, determined by cosmic evolution!

Reality was not only "rational"; its social course was predictable. For the Marxist theorist Engels, evolutionary positivism became part of the explanation of the inevitable triumph of the proletariat. For anti-class-war socialists like George Bernard Shaw (1856–1950) and Sidney Webb (1859–1947) in England, the faith in limitless progress was the basis for parliamentary democracy. For H. G. Wells (1866–1946), the idea of progress was essential to his creation of a science fiction literature rooted in the creed of technological elitism: the best of the human species would create a global state governed by scientific rationalists.

The marriage of evolution and positivism also produced ideas destructive of the scientific rationalism of Spencer and at odds with the view that the processes of evolution were wholly benign. Henri Bergson accepted the idea of evolution, but rejected the scientific rationalism reinforced by it. Introspection and intuition were the real modes of biological self-realization, not the spurious determinism taken over from the physical sciences. Life evolved, but it was unlike other matter in doing so. The creation of higher forms of life turned on the organism's own creative force (or *élan vital*), an irrational, psychologistic force, intuited and not subject to scientific investigation. Bergson's repudiation of mechanistic notions of progress doubtless owed something to his own alienation from the culture of French society in the Dreyfus period. He was born a Jew in a society permeated by active anti-Semitism. But his distrust of rationalism owed more to the manifest failure of harmony in French society. Formal learning had little social utility.

Useful knowledge was found not in systems, but in successful actions. And successful actions were understood only in the course of doing them,[32] because instinctive force alone directed us to "comprehend" what was useful. Evolution, like individual life, was motivated by blind, irrational forces. Successful actions, moreover, were the product not of harmony but of conflict. Georges Sorel (1847–1922) produced several works on that theme,[33] in which he declared that useful transformations in society were achieved only by violent means; peaceful, evolutionary progress was an illusion.

The exaggerated evolutionary irrationalism of Sorel and Bergson was not as isolated from the mainstream of Darwinian social realism as may appear at first sight. Darwin's theory of evolution easily gave rise to ideas of violence and racism. Superior organisms in nature had their social counterparts in superior peoples and classes. The survival of the fittest by the displacement of the weaker had its social parallel in the belief that the stronger industrial nations had been "selected" by a natural process for world dominion. Applied to nations rather than to individuals, this meant not only the ideology of the white man's burden in Asia and Africa, where Europeans would dominate and "civilize" the inferior peoples. Within Europe Social Darwinism had sharpened antagonisms within classes and between nations. Anti-Semitism had part of its foundation in the doctrines of racial superiority spread by the "superior" Anglo-Saxon theorists and

32. Bergson shared this "pragmatism," or belief in truth as successful action, with the American thinkers William James, C. S. Peirce, and John Dewey.
33. Especially his 1906 *The Illusions of Progress* and his 1908 *Reflections on Violence*.

their Latin counterparts. The *Herrenvolk* (master race) idea flourished in writers like Houston Stewart Chamberlain, Julius Langbehn, Paul de Legarde, Édouard Drumont, and Charles Maurras. It also had a solid grip on rulers like William II and on political organizations in France, Prussia, Austria, Poland, and Russia.

Thus around 1900 the culture of success—liberal realism—had revealed things not easily reconciled with the optimism of Spencer. These elements of Western culture were, moreover, obviously direct outgrowths of its most celebrated accomplishments, while at the same time seeming to pose a threat to liberal values, ideas, and taste. The modern age somehow had gone off the rails of rationality, progress, and harmony.

SCIENCE AND SOCIETY

It is an error to overstress the negative implications of the new scientific revolution, however. The Darwinian idea of the mutability of species produced a great deal of anxiety, but also much enthusiasm for reexamining the assumptions of science in general. For every prophet of despair like the tortured neurotic Friedrich Nietzsche,[34] who challenged liberalism and positivism by celebrating irrationality and aggressive egoism, there were others less eager to embrace the "survival" ideology of power.

William James (1842–1910), for example, accepted the challenge of philosophical unrest in a more pacific way. A psychologist by profession, James regarded "action" less egoistically than either Bergson or Nietzsche. James took what he called a "pragmatic" view of social reality. No principle mattered as much as the actual consequences of an action. Man in motion —and James's age was the age of the motorcar and the moving picture— required one test of an action: Was it useful? Men participated in the "evolution of reality"[35] by repudiating determinism and regarding as worthwhile only the experimentally useful things advancing their desires. Living was more important than thinking!

This was a more acceptable variety of egoism, because it carried with it the corollary that the utility of actions was not to be judged without regard to their impact on others. Nietzsche's irrationalism had ended in a demonic stress on the will to power without regard to consequences. Yet pragmatism, which some regard as the perfect ideology of American industrial society, with its emphasis on what works, might also encourage irrational experimentalism. The Italian socialist leader Benito Mussolini (1883–1945) was an admirer of pragmatism, and by 1912 he had drawn the conclusion that the failure of parliamentary reformism in Italy proved the bankruptcy of liberal democracy. He was later to become a Fascist "man of action" who judged deeds wholly in terms of the future they might produce for his revolutionary movement. The dangerous notion of national regeneration by means of a bloodbath was already current before 1914.

The new stress in society, and in social thought, on change was no longer hemmed in by the rational tradition. It had turned instead toward intuition, sentiment, personality, and the purposively antirational style of leadership, harmless in Nietzsche's literary fantasies but not so in politics. If truth was action, it was also said that truth was internal, psychological, and not objective.

This gloomy conclusion was resisted by a new generation of sociologists,

34. 1844–1900; the son of a Lutheran pastor, he was for a time a professor of Greek; after 1889, when he suffered a mental breakdown, Nietzsche bordered on insanity.

35. The phrase is from James's "Pragmatism: A World of Poor Experience," *Journal of Philosophy* 1 (1904): 533–543.

among whom the greatest were Émile Durkheim,[36] Max Weber,[37] Vilfredo Pareto,[38] Gaetano Mosca,[39] and Robert Michels.[40] What linked these men from different countries and widely differing backgrounds[41] was a fundamental commitment to rational science, hostility to Marxism, and a lack of confidence in democratic liberalism. Yet all were in agreement with the Marxist notion that a valid sociology could be built only on an integration of economics and politics in a broad historical synthesis. The new sociologists were thus in the scientific rationalist tradition, while rejecting the *conflict theory* of Marxist socialism. In place of that "irrational" element, the social scientists put a more positive synthesis: that social systems were self-regulating organisms capable of adjusting conflict in order to maintain a stable, self-perpetuating social order.

Their emphasis on stability, relations within systems, order, and conflict avoidance produced different results in each case, but there was a basic community of thought. Durkheim emphasized the necessity of collective conscience, or shared sentiments which transcend conflict; without such beliefs, societies became *pathological.* Pareto was not optimistic that such shared beliefs were possible. This doubt arose from his conclusion that *all* gradations in society[42] arose out of natural differences determined by human heredity.[43] Pareto developed the elitist ideas of Mosca, a theorist who condemned democratic and socialist egalitarianism as utopian. Like Michels, the Italian sociologists accepted the reality of conflict, but drew from the struggle the very "biological" notion that the fittest in every society dominate the rest. All social change tends toward the recirculation of elites, not the genesis of classless societies.

Weber, a German nationalist disenchanted with sham democracy, labor movements, and liberalism, focused his ideas on the rise of economic individualism and the development of bureaucratic rationalism. His sociology took shape between the two poles of repellent, frustrated German middle-class values and the lure of nationalist power. The founder of modern empirical sociology in Germany had more than a little Social Darwinism in his intellectual baggage. He confidently predicted that history would give Germany a third chance—after the failure of Bismarck's *Realpolitik* and William II's *Weltpolitik.*[44] Twenty-four years earlier he had warned students that what they had to pass on to their heirs was eternal struggle and the improvement of the German national stock. And in 1914, with Europe at war, he had warned Germans that they would be held responsible if civilization itself fell before the onslaught of Russian commissars and American ingenuity!

This dark view of civilization, and the hint that it might fail, was familiar in Europe after 1900. Catholics had been encouraged to accept industrial progress by the liberal Pope Leo XIII, who in 1891 issued the great encyclical on social justice, *Rerum novarum.*[45] But Pius X (1903–1914) purged from Catholic thought every facet of "modernism," by which he meant materialism, secular values, ideas of social change, socialism, and support for any movement working-class people might regard as tending to

---

36. 1858–1917.   37. 1864–1920.   38. 1848–1923.   39. 1858–1941.   40. 1876–1936.
41. Durkheim was the son of a Lorraine rabbi, Weber the son of a prominent German National-Liberal party politician, Pareto an aristocrat turned academic economist, Mosca an engineer, and Michels an Italian citizen born of French and German parents!
42. That is, economic classes, social hierarchies, political elites.
43. The genetic basis of heredity was fully grasped by 1916, when Pareto's *Treatise on General Sociology* appeared.
44. Remarks made in 1918, quoted in Carlo Antoni, *From History to Sociology* (London: Merlin Press, 1962), p. 135. Weber did not live to see the Third Reich!
45. (On new things); Leo's pontificate was from 1878 to 1903.

improve their lot. This repudiation of the twentieth century was unmatched in Protestant circles, where broad accommodations to modern thought were made. There was a popular trend toward a focus on the historical Christ, which seemed to sweep aside all obstacles to liberal and humanistic Protestantism, until the gloomy Alsatian theologian and physician Albert Schweitzer condemned religious rationalism in a famous book: *The Quest of the Historical Jesus*.[46]

Early in the twentieth century, however, religious interests were less binding on the loyalties of people in industrial societies than in the more "backward" rural areas of the West. While very few middle-class people actually separated from the churches through formal acts of disavowal,[47] the conservatism of the established or state churches, which were hierarchic and politically dependent, put off workers. Their lives were centered on political parties, unions, sports clubs, and the pub or music hall.

For the most alert, the secular "religions" of progress—socialism and positivism—were more attractive than Christianity. Marxism and scientific realism promised relief from bondage and oppression; and both positivism and socialism were by 1914 well equipped with a sort of "clergy" and an official body of ideas (scriptures?) to interpret. The prophetic leaders who promised a classless society seemed more attractive to the masses than the older clerics.

For a smaller coterie of well-educated people in Europe and America, there was a younger "science" with profound importance for the self-conception of men and women in the modern age. The Viennese physician Sigmund Freud (1856–1939) had formulated a broad analysis of human culture and civilization with the aid of a clinical tool of his own invention—psychoanalysis.

Freud's personal roots were in the German-Jewish culture of Moravia, but he was raised in Vienna in an irreligious family. His intellectual and ethical life did owe a great debt to the strict teachings of certain Jewish sects, but his most obvious philosophical and scientific affinities were to the philosophy of Edmund Husserl[48] and to the developing science of experimental psychology.

The similarity of Freud's view to that of Husserl lay in the concern of both to describe essentially the objects of consciousness. Husserl's system[49] was descriptive phenomenology, the insight he had into the nature of phenomena, or events in nature. Reality, he said, is knowable only in the sense that we apprehend the significance of things in our consciousness. The consequence of this stress on consciousness is to shift inquiry away from objective ideas of reality, toward the description of things in the mind. Husserl thus broke with the reliance of natural science on static, empirically derived notions.

Freud, who said his purpose was to describe behavior as he found it, was on that account still in league with the traditions of scientific realism. He allied himself with the long line of psychologists who thought that the truth of all psychological statements could be empirically tested. But he was especially interested in inner mental life, or psychic reality, not in experiments on sense perception,[50] the measurement of intelligence,[51] or condi-

---

46. Published in 1906.
47. In Germany fewer than 20,000 annually between 1909 and 1914.
48. 1859–1938; also a central European Jew.
49. Published in 1900–1901 as *Logical Investigations* (*Logische Untersuchunger*).
50. Pioneered by Wilhelm Wundt at Leipzig and his students, who developed experimental psychology.
51. The classic work was that of the French researcher Alfred Binet (1857–1911), who in 1905 published his studies on intelligence quotients and mental age.

tioned reflexes.[52] Freud was concerned with mental perception itself, imagination, and the motivations of behavior not obviously reflexive in nature. And in these areas nobody had yet solved the problems created by the fact that people were able to perceive their own mental acts. Human beings were constantly confronting internal acts whose origins were not obvious and could not be approached like the causes of external phenomena. While accepting the physiological basis of all thought—there was no "mind" without a physical brain—Freud confronted *as consciousness* things which he could not explain empirically. Like the phenomenologist Husserl, Freud needed to get beyond conventional science. He became the Darwin of psychology in his efforts to do so.

Where Darwin made sense of time as the essential determinant of the nature of things and discovered the principle of mutability, Freud attacked another part of the traditional static world view. He made a map of the unconscious, pointing out that time in the individual life accounted for more than physical "maturity" and emotional growth. Time laid down in the inner recesses of every person's psyche a veritable atlas of the emotional past. His discovery of the unconscious produced a coherent explanation of behavior hitherto unexplained and held to be inexplicable even by psychologists.

Freud's basic discovery was that in psychic processes *unconscious* impulses were at work, energized by instinctual needs or drives. These drives or bundles of energy (*libido*) were often unacceptable in conscious life, where the *ego* had the job of governing behavior in the world to maximize pleasure and minimize pain. The ego thus was like a policeman, forcing back below the threshold of consciousness drives both shocking to the person who had them and unacceptable as behavior in society. The constant struggle to repress instinctual behavior, or repression, took a severe toll in some people, who suffered psychological disorders called neuroses. The task of the psychological analyst (psychoanalyst)[53] was to bring the unconscious processes to the conscious level. Freud believed that mental health could be restored by rationalizing the unconscious.

Freud's approach to the problem of the relief of neuroses stemmed from an early collaboration with the physician Josef Breuer (1842–1925). Together, by means of hypnotic suggestion, they had relieved symptoms of hysterical paralysis[54] in patients who had no physical cause for loss of motion or sensation. Their cathartic method, or *purge*, was based on bringing to consciousness "forgotten" (repressed) experiences. Freud had witnessed such cures in Paris, where he was especially impressed by the relief of the paralysis of a young railway worker who had once failed to secure a coupling between cars of a train. In a resultant accident a comrade had his legs crushed. The paralytic had completely repressed the "accident" and had no memory of it; he simply could not walk himself! Under hypnosis the young man recalled the experience and walked freely.

This technique of encouraging patients to recall a traumatic "forgotten" past was soon replaced in Freud's practice by that of "free association," or the art of encouraging unhypnotized patients to follow their own stream of consciousness in response to questions from the analyst. Freud maintained a posture of neutrality, avoiding even eye contact with the patient.[55] Much

---

52. Chiefly the work of the physiological psychologist Ivan Pavlov, a specialist in glands and digestion, who won the Nobel Prize in physiology in 1904 for his famous work on dogs.
53. Freud used the term as early as 1896.
54. And other disorders produced by psychological causes.
55. The use of the shaded room and the couch was thus essential to the technique, not a form of mysticism, as is sometimes charged.

to his initial concern, Freud's hysterical patients, whether in the free-association state or in recounting dreams, especially recurring ones, revealed a barrage of sexual material as the disturbing factor. He was reluctantly driven to conclude that his patients' disturbances had their origin in sexual fantasies already active in very early childhood. Neuroses were the price people paid for acting in a civilized manner, or for not acting out the "primitive" drives forced back into the unconscious.

Freud was driven to his radical conclusions by the logic of his own work. Since he did not believe that any psychic phenomenon was meaningless, the often terrible battles fought in the night landscape of dreams were obviously related to the neurotic diversion of psychic energy. Repression directed the flow of memory to protect the person; that much was certain from the clinical evidence. So, too, was the sexual content of the repressed. It must be the case that repressed sexual drives were the common basis of psychological disturbances.

Between 1900 and 1905 Freud put forward these findings in his three most basic books: *The Interpretation of Dreams, The Psychopathology of Everyday Life,* and *Three Essays on the Theory of Sexuality.*[56] Anti-Semitism, prudery, and obstinacy among physicians delayed public acceptance of Freud's basic findings. Not one of his books had sold a thousand copies by 1910. Even the more "popular" works, in which he extended his views on the origins of neuroses to explanations of creativity as a redirection of blocked sexual energy,[57] or the more general works on the way in which individual psychology pointed toward a theory of social conflict, violence, and war[58] failed to attract a wide public. People at large simply could not accept the universality of the *Oedipus complex,*[59] much less the speculative idea that primitive societies were shaped by the rebellion of a cohort of brothers who murdered their father.[60]

Freud's influence was therefore at first confined to psychoanalytic circles, which he organized with great energy, and to introspective artists, especially writers. The idea that in sleep the censorship of conscience was held at bay, allowing the free play of instincts, provided much encouragement to the stream-of-consciousness novelists Proust and Joyce, as well as to analysts of mythology and drama, anthropologists, folklorists, and other socially-oriented researchers.

Freud's lasting importance does not depend, however, on what people then thought, or what we now think, of psychoanalysis as either a diagnostic tool, a therapeutic device, or a general theory of culture, conflict, and personality. Freud discovered the hitherto unexplored territory of inner psychic reality, a voyage as perilous to him as Columbus's and as profitable to us as Newton's mechanics or Darwin's theory of evolution. He brought sex from the shadows where it had been obscured by churchmen into the light of scientific study. He exposed to view the idea that sexual energy could be diverted into other forms of gratification, many of them as harmful[61] as healthy sex is beneficial. Freud was the pioneer of sex education and a child psychology based on tolerance for the libidinal needs of the infant. He began a revolution in the Western climate of opinion when he said that mankind had a life other than a conscious one, where instincts

56. Published in 1900, 1904, and 1905, respectively.
57. *Leonardo da Vinci* (1910), *Moses and Monotheism* (1913).
58. *Totem and Taboo* (1913), *Civilization and Its Discontents* (1929).
59. The myth of Oedipus generalized: boys direct their first sexual wishes toward their mothers and have violent fantasies of murder against the fathers.
60. The main thesis of *Totem and Taboo.*
61. For example, mass sadism or war.

were quantities of energy in search of release and as susceptible to disciplines of a destructive nature as to beneficial uses.

In physics the inner world of the atom was being explored at the same time. The years around 1900, in particular the decade around 1895–1905, as we now know, witnessed a revolution in the Western attitude toward reality. Traditional apprehensions of space and time were shaken to the foundations by the rejection of the Newtonian model of the physical universe, with its three-dimensional view of timeless space and continuous motion explicable in mechanical terms. In the year 1895 the first discoveries of X rays and the observation of radioactive transmutation of elements were made. And in 1905 Einstein's special theory of relativity depicted a four-dimensional universe in which time and space were interchangeable. Within the next decade, Ernest Rutherford (1871–1937) and Niels Bohr (1885–1962) had developed the theories about atoms which saw them as divisible bundles of energy. In 1919, Rutherford had broken apart atomic nuclei, creating the entirely new science of nuclear physics and starting man on the path that would lead to, among other things, the destruction of Hiroshima and Nagasaki in 1945.

This new scientific revolution, like that of the seventeenth century in physics, grew out of an awareness among workers doing normal scientific work that Newtonian concepts of time, space, and motion were no longer adequate. But physics had not yet had its Darwin to reconcile the anomalies in scientific work by means of new theories of reality. The Austrian Ernst Mach in 1883 had condemned Newtonian absolute time and absolute space as *metaphysical* concepts not confirmed by sense experience. His trust in the old world view had been shaken by the facts of electric technology, by the wireless and other devices derived from the discoveries of Michael Faraday[62] and James Clerk Maxwell.[63] The two British scientists had contributed the basic data and the theory of the propagation through space of "waves" of energy capable of action at a distance, but unlike Newton's gravity. Mach recognized in the work of Maxwell the solvent of classical physics.

So, too, did Henri Poincaré in France, as well as popularizers of doubt about the doctrines no longer harmonized with sense experience. In 1900 a new edition of a book called the *Grammar of Science*, first published in 1892 by Karl Pearson, generalized the discontent. Pearson asserted that Newtonian time and space had no real existence, and were merely the modes under which we perceived material reality.

One reason for this discontent was Maxwell's discovery of the radiation in space of electromagnetic waves. After his death much work was done to explore radiation. But it was not until 1895 that Wilhelm Roentgen began the revolution. The Würzburg physicist noticed that a cathode-ray tube under high-voltage pressure glowed on its surface, and that in the course of glowing seemed to produce an energy release he called X rays.[64] He further discovered that this invisible energy penetrated dense objects and left impressions of them on photographic plates. Physicians realized the medical applications at once. Then Henri Becquerel discovered that uranium gave off rays, in 1896. One year later the English physicist J. J. Thomson, in his laboratory at Cambridge, identified the source of invisible energy as the

62. 1791–1867; the discoverer of the electromagnetic "lines of force" responsible for the attraction of iron filings to magnets, and other magnetic properties of electricity.
63. 1831–1879; the deviser of the kinetic theory of gases and the "field" theory of electromagnetic energy.
64. Others had noticed this production earlier.

electron, the small bit of matter able to imprint objects on a photographic plate in a totally dark room.

Marie Curie and her husband Pierre, a chemist-physicist team, measured the actual electrical current produced by the unknown energy source in the element uranium in its unrefined state—pitchblende ore. In the course of their work they identified two hitherto unknown elements, *polonium* and *radium*.[65] In 1903, Becquerel and the Curies shared the Nobel Prize in physics, for their theory that radioactivity was a property of atoms and not a chemical reaction of some sort.

While this work was going forward, Thomson and his student Rutherford had observed that X rays in a gas tore off from gas atoms small particles of negatively charged matter. They reached the conclusion that the gas atoms were not *indivisible*, and were not therefore the tiniest constituent parts of matter, as classical theory maintained. Within *divisible atoms* there were "electrons." The experimental evidence forced the conclusion on a reluctant pair of observers: subatomic particles existed! In 1902 Rutherford published a paper on the nature and cause of radioactivity, with the theory that the elements uranium, radium, and thorium,[66] far from being indestructible matter, as classical theory maintained, disintegrated and gave off energy while doing so. New matter was actually created as atoms of one element broke up, giving off a charge of electrical energy, leaving behind a new atom. The radical nature of the transmutation theory was that it violated yet another central "law" of physics, that of the conservation of energy. Matter could neither be created nor destroyed without some visible input of chemical energy—fire, for example. But the radioactive elements did give off energy and transform themselves *without any* energy input.

Rutherford pushed this theory further between 1903 and 1911. He said that the energy locked up in the atom was far greater than the energy released in chemical reactions like oxidation. He related radioactive disintegration to physical evolution by supposing that over billions of years basic energy transformations took place and accounted for the development of life itself. He identified other subatomic particles scattered by radioactive elements. On the basis of these new discoveries, in 1911 Rutherford built a model of the internal structure of atoms, which Niels Bohr developed and refined in 1914. Bohr worked with the simplest atom, hydrogen, which he showed to have a very heavy nucleus to which a single electron was attached.

As research into radioactivity and the divisible atom mounted, the Newtonian "laws" no longer satisfied either observation or the basic requirement that they predict physical behavior accurately. Doubts multiplied, and the mechanical world view fell into disrepute. It was at that point of crisis that the theoretical physicists entered. Max Planck (1858–1947) was very concerned about the distribution of energy in the normal spectrum of radiant heat. This seemed to be uneven, where physics taught that energy release was even and continuous in all reactions. In 1900 Planck published a paper in which he said that in all energy releases, *quanta* (plural of the Latin *quantum*, "how much") of energy or "action" were radiated. Under heat, for example, energy was emitted in bursts, discontinuously, in small packages. Planck failed to extend his argument to all radiation. Others did claim that the electrons in some atoms were more loosely bound to the nucleus than they were in others. Natural radioactive decomposition freed quantities of energy as electrons became detached from the nucleus. It

65. In honor, respectively, of Poland, Marie's homeland, and the radioactive source of the energy.
66. Another recent discovery.

Antonio Frasconi's woodcut engraving of Albert Einstein as an old man captures the famous bushy hair and moustache of one of this century's greatest intellectual figures. As a young man in his mid twenties, Einstein had already presented his theory of relativity. Following the work of Max Planck, Einstein next spent many years pondering the problems which might be solved by the quantum theory. Although he was a natural optimist who felt that his work was beneficial to mankind, the great scientist could not escape the political upheavals of the 1930s. Like so many of his fellow German academics, Einstein was forced to flee to the United States because of his Jewish background. Princeton University Library; by permission of Antonio Frasconi.

was this notion that led Bohr to picture electrons as in orbit around the nucleus. And it was this notion which led Rutherford (in 1919) to bombard the nucleus of apparently stable atoms with small physical particles in order to smash the atoms and release their energy. But the basic theory was Einstein's.

Einstein took up Planck's line of speculation and in 1905, in one of the three great papers he published in that year,[67] established that light rays were a radiation phenomena produced by the release of *quanta* of energy from substances under excitation—for example, when a beam of ultraviolet light struck a metal plate, forcing the release of electrons. This discovery doomed the Newtonian wave theory of light and put in its place the idea that light consisted of energy bundles moving at fantastic speeds. Thus light was really an event, a relative happening in time, not a fixed property of physical matter.

In his light experiments Einstein had discovered that the *photons*, or energy bundles in light, vary with the color of the light, being greater in violet light than in red, for example. Quantum physics thus made the universe less determined or fixed, by opening up the view of reality as a series of related events. Scientists watching the radio-transformations of elements achieved the same awareness of instability and mutability. These

67. On photoelectric effects, on the movement of particles in fluids and gases, and on electrodynamics.

results undermined mechanical determinism and the idea of causality itself. The new physics worked, but defied common sense. Things now seemed to have bearings only in relation to other things, not in a fixed way, as for instance any object in a moving train. A glass on a table in the dining car is usually said to have a fixed position. But this is obviously true only in relation to other immobile objects *within* the car. In relation to remote bodies the position of the glass obviously changes every minute—every moment—during which the train goes down the track. Thus *position* is a relative thing. So, too, is motion, which we can understand if we suppose that one train passes another going in the same direction, while on a third track another train goes by in the opposite direction. One train, the third, appears to us to move faster than its own actual speed. Its motion is relative to the motion of other moving things.

Newton had grappled with relative motion but had in the end considered our "space" as a fixed frame of reference in which we witnessed the absolute motion of the stars. Space was thus finite, stationary and immovable, and real, a notion developed into the ether theory of space, which postulated the existence of a medium called ether through which waves of matter moved. This idea was exploded in 1881, however, when scientists sent two beams of light into the supposed ether stream surrounding the earth, one beam against its "current" and the other beam with it. Since the speed of light was known to be 186,282 miles a second, and the velocity of the earth around the sun is 20 miles a second, the velocity of the two beams of light was expected to vary by the total amount of the help or hindrance provided for the beam by the motion of the ether stream.[68] The measured velocities were identical, however.

It was this further dilemma Einstein resolved in 1905, in his Nobel Prize paper, "On the Electrodynamics of Moving Bodies." Because of the velocity experiments, Einstein began by rejecting the whole ether theory and, with it, the fixity of space. It appeared that the velocity of light was a universal constant, without regard to the earth's motions, or those of any other body in the universe. The conclusion from this was that the laws governing moving bodies were the same for all uniformly moving systems, moving relative to one another. This simple formula, which said that movements can be described only in relation to one another, meant that space offered to us no fixed basis for comparisons to establish "true" velocities. Space is only the order or relation of things among themselves. We must stop looking for any fixed frame of reference in physical reality, which has neither directions nor boundaries.

Einstein further pointed out that we must scrap absolute time along with absolute space. Time is not an abstract, uniform flow with a reality of its own. It is, instead, like the colors we see in photoelectric changes; we have a sense of time, a perception of it, and it is, like space, simply the way in which we confer order on the things we observe. We merely define associated events with the aid of clocks; but the events are part of our subjective perception. And it is a gratuitous assumption to say that time exists objectively in nature because we use clocks! The "year" is in reality simply the relative measure of the earth's progress in orbit around the sun, not a thing of any relevance to observers differently placed in the universe. Mercury, were it inhabited, would have different "time," because it goes around the sun once in eighty-eight days and turns on its axis only once during that time!

The "special theory of relativity" was soon confirmed by a variety of experiments with light within the terms of equations devised by Ein-

68. Like a swimmer in a current: 186,282.

stein. These experiments established the relativity of motion, distance, space, and time, allowing only the velocity of light as a constant. One of the simplest experiments showing the relativity of time did not require light and was done by fixing a clock to a stationary system and another like clock to a moving system; the two clocks immediately began to run at a different rhythm! Similarly, a measuring rod, which we think of as physically constant, can be shown to *shrink* in the direction of any rapid acceleration. But we do not perceive the changes if we are in motion with the clock or rod. A stationary observer, i. e., stationary relative to the moving system, would, however. We are thus forced to conclude that even size and rhythm are not mechanical properties fixed in nature. A clock traveling at the speed of light would stop completely; and a rod moving at 90 percent of the velocity of light would lose 50 percent of its length.

The assumption of classical physics that objects have fixed dimensions at motion and in rest was as unfounded as the ideas of absolute time and space. The quantum theory overturned the idea that small particles behave in the manner of large particles visible to the eye. The theory of relativity unfolded the differences between the fast world of light and the slower world of gross reality. These achievements in theory deepened the crisis in short-run terms, especially among nonscientists as the results became known in popular form. The composition of matter was not what it seemed; the atom and radiation revealed a new world; celestial mechanics, gravitation, linear space, time itself were transformed. The submicroscopic world of atoms reproduced in miniature the old model of the solar system, with the properties of things no longer being those of ordinary experience but determined by the relationships of electrons and other particles to the nucleus. The physical world was one of energy levels and events, where states changed more magically than alchemists had ever imagined. If base metals did not become gold, rare ones like radium degenerated into lead. Visual experience was no guide to reality. The flux of time governed everything.

THE NEW VISION: ART AND REALITY

The age of modern science had arrived, and its central proposition was that in order to represent physical reality correctly scientists had to disregard appearances and common sense. Invisible waves of electrical character now carried messages across space. Planck had asserted that both matter and energy were discontinuous in their structure. Einstein had shown that time was the "fourth dimension" of reality, and in many ways the most important one. The once eternal definitions of time, space, and matter had become temporal, as surely as the theory of creation had bowed to temporal evolution. The generally accepted vision of the world, the view of reality, had been completely transformed. Where once science had posited an objective reality indifferent to the presence of man, it was now held that reality was a continuous "becoming" in which man the observer was the one presence always necessary.

It is hardly possible to maintain that the new modes of music, painting, and literature which flourished around 1910–1914 grew up without obvious interaction between the consciousness of artists and the changing world picture.

In painting the relationship is immediate. Wassily Kandinsky (1866-1944), the first abstract painter and founder of the Munich "Blue Rider" group in 1912,[69] acknowledged that the discovery of subatomic reality

69. This group also had in it August Mache, Paul Klee, and Franz Marc.

caused him to rethink the relationship of nature to art. He, Klee,[70] and Miró[71] painted subatomic worlds. Cubism had obvious affinities to the shapes of the machine age, and the poet Guillaume Apollinaire[72] related the experiments of cubist artists to their interest in the "fourth dimension" of science. The composer Claude Debussy (1862–1918) and the great radical Stravinsky confessed that the dissociation of time and motion in science affected their work. In it harmony and melody were dissociated from rhythm, the energetic pulses which, for example, dominate Stravinsky's *Rite of Spring* and take from the music the sense of continuous motion from one section to another.

In the history of the novel the new psychology and the new physics stand behind the work of Marcel Proust (1871–1922), especially his monumental *Remembrance of Things Past*. His *Swann's Way* appeared in 1913, and in it chance happenings begin to evolve the "forgotten" past in a pattern of discontinuous memories which reveal Swann's "self" as well as the total past present in every sense experience. In Joyce's *Ulysses*, the action of which is all in a single day,[73] the stream of consciousness alone supplies the

70. Paul Klee, 1879–1940.
71. Joan Miró, 1893–.
72. 1880–1918; the "press agent" for Picasso, Braque, Juan Gris, etc.
73. June 16, 1904. Joyce's dates are 1882–1941.

In Picasso's pencil Portrait of Igor Stravinsky *(1920) the great innovator in twentieth-century painting depicts his musical counterpart. Far from appearing radical, the drawing points out the classical training which provided the foundation for Picasso's art and reemerged at various times throughout his career. The artist was particularly fond of Ingres's pencil portraits, and from them he learned to capture the sitter's personality with only a few simple lines. Picasso and Stravinsky knew one another in Italy in 1917 when they were both associated with Diaghilev's Russian Ballet. Together they discovered Naples and its colorful local theater, and their impressions were later used in a collaboration for the ballet* Pulcinella *for which Picasso designed the sets. The Bettmann Archive.*

Celebrated as the first painter to develop totally nonrepresentational art, Wassily Kandinsky attributed his discovery to a chance event. As he returned to his Munich studio one night in 1910 the Russian artist saw a painting lying on its side, and suddenly he was struck by the power of design and color when not related to subject matter. Although Blue Mountain *(1908) was done two years earlier, an emphasis on the independent existence of various forms and patterns is already apparent. Many of Kandinsky's ideas about the emotional connotations of color derived from the French symbolists. Later he was a member of the Munich-based "Blue Rider" group, whose members combined a knowledge of cubism with highly charged expressionist subject matter. The Solomon R. Guggenheim Museum.*

continuity in a book the form of which breaks completely with the realistic novelist's convention of real time and the serial technique of telling a story. Joyce's great work itself took seventeen years to complete in book form, having its origin in 1905, the year of Einstein's revolution. Its explicit sexuality, free-association technique, and discovery of time itself as discontinuous put Joyce firmly in the disoriented world of 1905.

To approach the problem of the "modernist" movement in the arts, however, we may learn more from a clear view of a major figure than from a hurried survey of the whole. Moreover, because we shall return to modernism later, in order to give a historical overview of it, in music, literature, painting, and the motion picture art, it seems in order to select for consideration here the greatest artist of recent centuries, Pablo Picasso (1881–1973). This son of the Spanish artist José Ruiz Blasco and Maria Picasso has personally influenced the development of every movement in visual art in our century. And he shows clearly the link to the schools of the late nineteenth century, especially postimpressionism and expressionism.

Picasso was classical in his training, a superb draftsman with a firm grip on every aspect of technique in the tradition of the Spanish schools of realistic composition. From 1895 to 1900 he painted mainly in Barcelona, and then in Paris as well as in Spain, from about 1900 to 1904. His early works show little concern for anything but plastic representation, combining emotional intensity and social realism. He drew social outcasts and melancholy people in the "blue period," but the bullring was also a favorite subject. Perhaps the most famous painting of Picasso's adolescence is *The Girl with Bare Feet*, and it is characteristic of his somewhat flat surface technique. A change entered his vocabulary of painting in Paris. His preference for flatness received support from his study of Toulouse-Lautrec, and we can see in his earliest Paris works a postimpressionist bias, for example in his *Travesty of Manet's Olympia* and in the self-portraits of 1901, as well as in *The Embrace*. Even his subjects now imitated Lautrec: *Can-Can*, *Bal du Moulin*, and other famous works.

The Embrace (1900) also revealed the impact of Cézanne and Gauguin in the simplicity of shapes and abandonment of a naturalistic palette. In this period Picasso also used blue as a color for skin, when it suited his mood; and in *The Embrace* Picasso shows us his psychological interests. The couple want to come together, but they cannot; there is no warmth between them. As the years 1901–1904 unfolded, Picasso was feeling his way toward a style divorced from those he had learned or imitated. He clearly no longer accepted the idea that painting imitated nature. He had concluded that only a spontaneous return to nature itself could reinvigorate art in an age of photography. Imitation was dead when no amount of invention could improve on photographs. The challenge for painting was not to conform to the old world view, but to make a translation into art of the new one just unfolding. Primitive peoples had not created a mechanical leg to move things; they had made the wheel. This was not imitation of reality; it was an inventive improvement on nature.

Picasso now went quickly beyond naturalism and social realism. His *Destitute Woman* (1902) uses blue tones to force on us the sadness of the subject *within herself*. The sharp angularity of *The Woman Ironing* (1904) made observers ask a similar question: What is the meaning of life for this gaunt creature? Her broken body carries us away from every form of naturalism, including impressionism. The mood is closer to that created by the mentally unstable Norwegian artist Edvard Munch (1863–1944), who read Nietzsche and Freud while putting on canvas the despair of the

During 1904 when he painted The Woman Ironing *Picasso was living in extreme poverty in Montmartre. His art from this "blue" period is filled with empathy for a suffering humanity, and the recurring themes of work-worn women, blindness, unhappy lovers, and destitute mothers haunted him for several years. Although Degas had previously represented the same subject, Picasso's exhausted, angular woman more intently exploits the pathos of the situation. His emotive use of color to evoke a mood had been explored by the symbolists Gauguin and van Gogh who left their imprint on Picasso's early work. The painter was described by his friend Guillaume Apollinaire as having looked at "the human images floating in the blue of our memories." Picasso later rejected oppressive subject matter in favor of an art concerned with formal aesthetic problems. Justin K. Thannhauser Collection: Courtesy of the Thannhauser Foundation, The Solomon R. Guggenheim Museum.*

The Norweigian Edvard Munch studied in Paris from 1889 to 1892 and was familiar with the often tormented art of the French symbolists. Building on their example, he carried the artistic probe of the psyche to new depths. He knew of Freud's experiments, and works such as The Death of Marat *give visual expression to radical new ideas about human nature. There is an ironic reference to David's famous work of the same title, only here the political event has become merely a metaphor for the destructive battle of the sexes. Brutally slashing brushstrokes and livid colors aid the painter in conveying the mood of this somber tale. Munch struggled with this canvas for more than twenty years (1905–1927). During this time he suffered a nervous collapse, and in his late work he was increasingly concerned more with a perfection of style than psychic subject matter.*
Munch-Museet, Oslo.

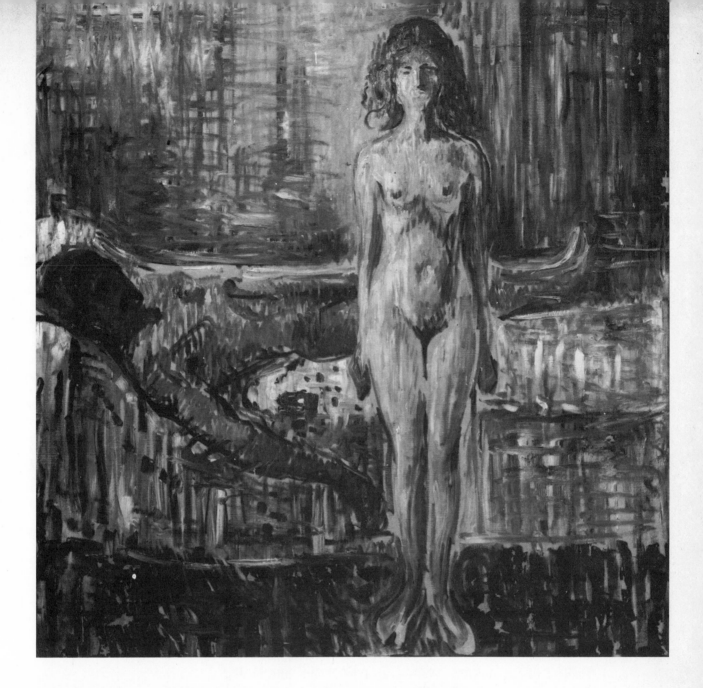

sickroom and death. There is thus an affinity with expressionism[74] in this period, which changed mood in 1904, when Picasso took a studio in Paris and apparently took also a new lease on optimism. His "rose period" canvases explored the new techniques, but the palette was cheerful even where the subjects remained somber, as in the *Family of Saltimbanques* and *Young Girl on a Ball*, both 1905 pictures. Also, in 1905 a painting like that of the Saltimbanques family abandoned the snapshot scale for one expressing unlimited space and time. The critic Apollinaire[75] noticed this at once, suggesting that the young genius was on the verge of a breakthrough in relating on canvas "the universal aspects of the world."

Picasso now began to experiment with nudes, employing as his model his mistress Fernande Olivier. What is clear in the 1906 *Nude with Hands Joined*

74. An artistic movement in which forms derived from nature were distorted or exaggerated and colors were intensified for subjective spontaneous expression.
75. In a review published May 15, 1905, in *La Plume*.

is a new treatment of color and shapes. There is an effort to paint *volume*, a three-dimensional presence on the two-dimensional canvas. Picasso complained to friends that with paint you could not achieve a sense of thickness the way a sculptor could. One could walk around the sculpture and view it from different angles. This lack of a third dimension was to Picasso as disconcerting as anomalies in science were to Darwin or Einstein. He read feverishly in art history and studied African art, especially the angular, almost geometric tribal (negroid) masks brought to Paris by anthropologists. He concluded that perspective painting was false. He also said that to achieve concreteness one would have to paint as if the subject had been previously sculpted. What was required for a truly stereoscopic painting was not to reproduce on canvas a single photographic view but to reassemble the plastic perceptions of successive instants, as if we could see simultaneously from different angles.

Picasso thus invented for painting a new language of masses, forms, and *durations*. Cubism, which he invented in 1907 in his startling *Young Ladies of Avignon*, created a new sort of artistic reality. The departure from tradition was greater than that made from academic painting by impressionism. Manet and his friends had exhausted the visual analysis of color in order to capture the impact of the passage of time on objects. Picasso created on canvas movement itself. Renaissance artists, employing perspective as a trick, broke through the flatness of medieval paintings. Picasso's figures recorded movement, both in the subject and in the observer, in a kind of *cinemascope* which did what still cameras could not do. Photographs were flat in the manner of medieval work.

Ironically, *The Young Ladies* remained rolled up in Picasso's studio until 1920. But it was not unknown. Georges Braque[76] saw it there in 1907 and joined Picasso[77] on the road to cubism, by way of primitive art. Picasso had grasped that the *Nabis*[78] who had championed linear distortion, and the *Fauves*,[79] who followed Matisse into decorative abstraction, were imposing a conceptual scheme on reality, not imitating it. But, where the other "primitives" were in revolt against modernism, Picasso looked to African and other primitive art as a conceptual achievement from which moderns could grasp the nature of the industrial reality itself. This was especially true of the cave artists of Spain whom Picasso studied in 1906 and the black sculpture he pored over in 1907. The impact of primitive abstraction and African sculptural masks is apparent in *The Young Ladies* and in the other early cubist masterpieces of 1907–1908: *The Dancers of Avignon, Nude with Drapery, A Young Lady of Avignon*. We see eyes left blank, the oval elongation of faces, sharp accent lines which seem to rotate the face.

But it is with *The Young Ladies* that everything matured first. The scene is a brothel in the Avinyo[80] alley of Barcelona. The arrangement resembles that of Cézanne's *Bathers*, which Picasso may have meant to memorialize (Cézanne died late in 1906). The girls in the center stare full-face at us, but we see some of their ears *frontally*, from a different viewpoint, just as in the central one of the five figures the body is tilted to the right. We thus see this figure from three different vantage points simultaneously. Asymmetry and discontinuous experiences of reality were thus amalgamated to provide the third dimension of sculpture in a painting. From geometric forms Picasso had made *planes*, rather than a single planar view. This breach with the

Perhaps the most revolutionary painting of this century, Picasso's Young Ladies of Avignon *(1907) not only created a style which no one could at first comprehend, but also shifted the whole concern of painting away from subject matter to the aesthetic qualities of the work of art itself. The painting was started in a relatively conventional style and gradually metamorphosed as the artist realized the significance of such "primitive" art forms as Catalan frescoes, Iberian reliefs, and African sculpture. Through his insight gained by studying these objects Picasso was able to move beyond traditional Rennaissance perspective and find an entirely new structural logic for his art. In his attempt to start over again from scratch Picasso worked in complete isolation. The painter Georges Braque was the first to understand what he had accomplished in the* Young Ladies, *and together they developed cubism through its various phases. Collection, The Museum of Modern Art, New York, Lillie P. Bliss Bequest.*

76. 1882–1963, earlier influenced by Cézanne.
77. As did Juan Gris (1887–1927) in 1910, also earlier devoted to Cézanne.
78. From the Hebrew word for "prophets"—Pierre Bonnard, Édouard Vuillard.
79. The "wild beasts" grouped around Henri Matisse (1869–1954), among them Georges Rouault, Raoul Dufy, Maurice de Vlaminck.
80. The Avignon of the title.

spatial and temporal fixity of classical perspective painting allows us to see at once what we know we can see in reality: the backs and sides of things.

Picasso thus also introduced time into painting in a far more radical way than Monet did in making several images of Rouen Cathedral on separate canvases to show the effect of season and daytime lighting. Moreover, Picasso's human beings, like Darwin's species, are no longer "creations" fixed for eternity in God's image. They are the product of a vision shaped by Darwin, Freud, and Einstein. It was this "intellectual" character that caused Matisse to say Picasso's new style was a loss to French painting! For Picasso, however, the time had come to represent things correctly, and he lived in a four-dimensional world. The cubist style grew out of one man's need to depict volumes, not plane surfaces, and to convey to us the whole series of perceptions we might have of a head if we spent time walking around it. By fracturing the ordinary painted view of things in one plane, Picasso, moved painting into the modern world.

It was not until 1909 that a critic derisively coined the term "cubist" for the work Braque and Picasso were doing. The years before 1907 had belonged to Cézanne in Paris, where a memorial of his work showed the influence he had on Picasso: Cézanne had tried to reduce reality to the abstract forms of the sphere, the cone, and the cylinder. Where Cézanne had tried to put geometry in perspective, Picasso had destroyed perspective, however. His cubist experiments in 1908–1909 had already produced the

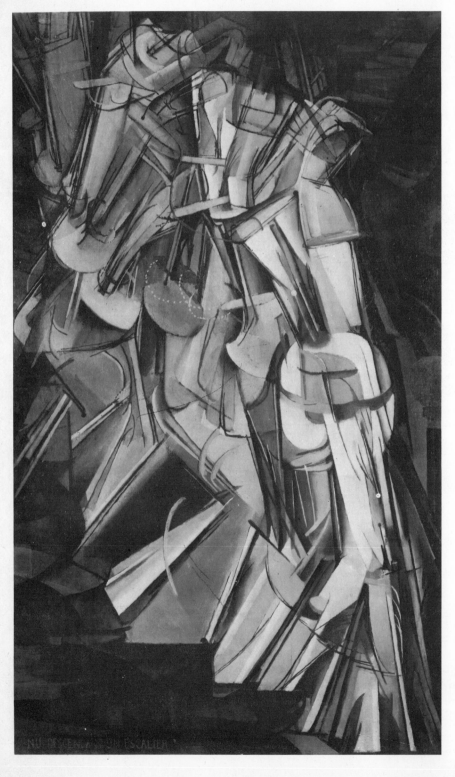

When it was exhibited in the New York Armory show of 1913, Marcel Duchamp's Nude Descending a Staircase *(1912) was vilified in the press as incomprehensible and offensive. The mechanistic appearance of the figure even upset some of his fellow artists, who found it dehumanizing. In terms of style the* Nude *represents an advanced, unorthodox interpretation of cubism which relies on violent, heavy brushstrokes and a repitition of the image to achieve its sense of movement. By 1915 when Duchamp moved to New York from Paris he was hailed as a celebrity, possibly because his bleak view of humanity seemed more feasible in the midst of a global conflict. Louise and Walter Arensberg Collection, Philadelphia Museum of Art.*

stunning cubist portraits of the art dealers Kahnweiler and Vollard. A year earlier his *Three Women* had shown a mature art, a truly plastic art. At the same time, Braque was painting cubist landscapes, rejected by the Independent Salon on Matisse's advice, because they were composed of little cubes.

Together, Picasso and Braque made the breach complete in 1909 and 1910: Picasso with the great masterpieces *Nude Woman, Horta de Ebro, Girl with a Mandolin;* Braque with his *Road near L'Estaque, Violin and Palette, Guitar and Compote.* The foundations of cubism are also clear in Picasso's sculptured bronze *Head of Fernande* (1909) and the painted *Portrait of Braque.* The way was thus open to Duchamp's great *Nude Descending a Staircase* (1911), but it lay through the agony of the men who made the leap. Concerning this Braque made a comment which is fitting for all the pioneers of modernism, from Darwin to Braque, from Planck to Picasso:

The things that Picasso and I said to one another during those years will never be said again, and even if they were, no one would understand them anymore. It was like being roped together on a mountain.[81]

BIBLIOGRAPHY

BARNETT, LINCOLN. *The Universe and Dr. Einstein.** New York: Bantam Books, 1957. Einstein himself supported this clear explanation of his work.

CHASE, C. T. *The Evolution of Modern Physics.* Princeton: D. Van Nostrand Company, 1947. A useful survey of developments in the fields of wave theory, quantum mechanics, and subatomic particle physics.

DAIX, PIERRE. *Picasso.** New York: Praeger Publishers, 1965. The best brief introduction to the man and the work.

EISLEY, LOREN. *Darwin's Century.** New York: Doubleday & Co., Anchor, 1961. The best introduction to the rise of modern evolutionary ideas; strong on geology, biology, and anthropology.

HELLER, ERICH. *The Disinherited Mind.** New York: Farrar, Straus & Cudahy, 1957. Excellent on the "irrationalist" philosophers.

HUGHES, H. STUART. *Consciousness and Society.** New York: Alfred A. Knopf, 1958. The best work on the reorientation of social thought in Europe after 1890.

LANG, PAUL. *Stravinsky: A New Appraisal of His Music.** New York: W. W. Norton & Co., 1963. A collection of essays on the master of "modernism" in music.

MASUR, GERHARD. *Prophets of Yesterday: Studies in European Culture, 1890–1914.** New York: The Macmillan Company, 1961. A very well done introduction to the major figures shaping modern thought and expression.

NISBET, ROBERT A. *The Sociological Tradition.* New York: Basic Books, 1967. This general study leads easily to particular ones on Durkheim, Weber, etc.

REVEL, JEAN FRANÇOIS. *On Proust.* New York: Library Press, 1972. A very convincing analysis of Proust in the context of psychology and politics, the matrix of the "deeper self" Proust sought to reveal.

REWALD, JOHN. *The History of Impressionism.* New York: Museum of Modern Art, 1962. A standard work; so, too, is Rewald's *Post-Impressionism* (New York: Museum of Modern Art, 1956).

RIEFF, PHILIP. *Freud: The Mind of the Moralist.** New York: The Viking Press, 1969. A good brief "biography" of Freud's thought; for the fullest life, see Ernest Jones, *The Life and Work of Sigmund Freud,** 3 vols. (New York: Basic Books, 1953–1961), abridged in one volume also.

Asterisk indicates a paperbound edition.

81. As quoted in Pierre Daix, *Picasso* (New York: Praeger Publishers, 1965), p. 82.

BOOK FOUR

An Age Like Ours, 1918-Present

For all the progress that the twentieth century has witnessed, it has also been a time of unparalleled death and destruction. Two global wars engulfed the world, the first taking some 10,000,000 lives and the second an estimated 40,000,000. In an age marked by unspeakable brutality and by weapons whose strength is measured in overkill, it is perhaps not accidental that the sculptor turns from polished marble to welded steel. Here, Leonard A. DeLonga expresses the century's anguish and anger in a 1970 work, Rage against the Dying, not the Living. *Leonard DeLonga, courtesy Kraushaar Galleries, New York, on loan to the De Cordova Museum.*

The final Book of this history is, of necessity, not an ending, nor is it a judgment. Certainly, if we consider the enormity of the history of an age like ours, we might conclude with Lenin: "Optimism is the luxury of fools; but hope is necessary for the struggle." For this Book begins with the First World War; traces the rise of totalitarian regimes out of the hopes of the Versailles peace; considers how and why the Second World War came to pass and what have been its consequences; and treats in detail how precarious has been the civilization salvaged from the ashes of 1945.

Those ashes were not only the residue of ruined regimes. They were the ashes of other hopes; for example, that a League of Nations would stabilize the world's politics, instead of umpiring a twenty years' crisis (1919–1939). And they were the ashes of nearly six million Jews incinerated in the name of "racial purity" and the hundreds of thousands of Japanese reduced to dust by the atomic bombing of Hiroshima.

One aspect of recent history dealt with here is the emergence to world power of four great powers not originally comprehended in the Western industrial tradition: the United States, Soviet Russia, Communist China, and Japan. Especially noteworthy is the fact that two are "capitalist" superstates and two are "socialist," two European and two Asian powers, opposed in their traditions as well as in their immediate global objectives.

Thus the last Book of *The Way of the West* marks a path trod; but it also points to a wilderness uncharted. In our closing chapter we raise major questions and doubts as to whether any ideology or political tradition will be able to master the material forces of production and a runaway technology. For we have reached the threshold of an age in which mankind has the capability for universal destruction. And we also stand face to face with a future in which the Westernized societies have a potential for material plenty denied everywhere else in the world.

15

THE LIBERAL AGONY: DEMOCRACY BETWEEN THE WARS

What we actually see is that the Western world strikes up a still more rapid tempo—the American tempo—the very opposite of quietism and resigned aloofness. An enormous tension arises between the opposite poles of outer and inner life, between objective and subjective reality. Perhaps it is a final race between ageing Europe and young America . . . to cheat the laws of nature of their hidden might and to wrest a more heroic victory from the sleep of nations. . . .

C. G. JUNG, *Modern Man in Search of a Soul*[1]

THE WAR AND MODERN MAN

The Swiss analyst and culture critic Jung in 1931[2] looked at modern man "in search of a soul"—in a depressed state produced by the First World War and its aftermath. Barbed wire and poison gas had underlined for Europeans, but not so much for Americans, who escaped without seeing the war at home, the futility of supposing that modern men and women were the culmination of historical "progress." World War I had produced evidence that science, technology, and "superior" forms of political organization might be catastrophic as well as beneficial. And by the time Jung wrote, it was obvious some statesmen still believed that preparation for war was the only safeguard for peace.

It had not been enough that Europe had gone to ruin, wrecking in the world war its global leadership and raising the sharpest questions about the Christian ideal of human brotherhood. The great economic unrest of the 1920s had culminated in the "crash" of the stock markets in 1929 and the onset of a worldwide economic depression. Moreover, high tariff barriers to the free exchange of goods belied the old liberal idea that there was some solidarity of interest among industrial nations. International social democracy, once the hope of socialists everywhere, was manifestly failing. The Soviet regime in Russia had been treated with disdain by Western nations after the armed intervention by the Allies in 1918–1919 had failed to restore the pro-Western liberals, or "white" Russians.[3]

And within the European states a tremendous political struggle was going on, to determine whether the liberal democracies would survive. Although we shall treat the rise of the "totalitarian"

1. Trans. W. S. Bell and Cary F. Baynes (New York: Harcourt, Brace, Inc., 1933), p. 254. Carl Gustav Jung attacked Freud's reliance on rationalist and sexual drive theses, after breaking with Freud's movement.
2. The original publication date.
3. See below.

states in the next chapter, here it is important to note that in 1922 the Fascists in Italy had overthrown parliamentary democracy, the Nazis in Germany were in 1933 the most numerous party in the Reichstag, Spain was already in a state of civil war,[4] and the Soviet Union had lost the bloom of its revolutionary youth. Stalin was fashioning a totalitarian dictatorship as Lenin's heir to power.

For these reasons, many besides Jung had drawn the conclusion that European life now bore a fatal psychological scar, or at least had suffered a near fatal shock. Jung would not say what Oswald Spengler (1880–1936) did,[5] that the white races were doomed by some fatal disease and that Western civilization itself was on the verge of collapse. Jung was a physician trained to see diseases, but also trained not to see them where they did not exist. And this distinction he made was essential, between the First World War as a *catastrophic, scarring event* and the war as the *symptom of a fatal malady.*

Against the prophecy of doom, many set the idea that the West was experiencing a profound spiritual and social crisis. But this was no new thing in the history of the civilization. There had been crises as great: the fall of Rome; the new age of invasions by Saracens, Vikings, Magyars, and Slavs; the Black Death; the Reformation; what some historians call the "general crisis" of the seventeenth century; the wars of the French Revolution; even the social upheaval of industrialization itself. It was arguable, however, that each challenge evoked a response which had strengthened Western civilization while also transforming it.

The question was whether the great new spiritual, social, economic, and political upheaval was one the West would survive, whether Europe or America could wrest a heroic victory. We can answer the question only by examining the liberal agony between the world wars, from 1918 to 1939, focusing domestically on the European democracies and the West's American partner on the other shore of the Atlantic.[6]

THE WHEEL OF FORTUNE, 1918–1939

The world war had ended what liberal economists used to call the "free enterprise system." Beginning in 1914, there was set in motion a related train of events which, seen in retrospect, invited progressively more systematic state regulation of the production of wealth and the distribution of income. The prewar era had produced broad secular "boom" trends in world trade, population growth, capital formation, and technological advance, at different rates in the advanced industrial societies. People were encouraged in the belief that economic growth was a one-way process. Part of the progressive optimism of the pre-1914 period derived from the economic miracles wrought by industrialization and by the modernizing politics associated with it. Then, as the war came, and with it stalemate, Europeans looked back on the decades before 1914 as a golden age. The economist John Maynard Keynes (1883–1946) pictured a prewar European sipping tea in bed while on the telephone, who would order

4. The republican government established in the 1931 revolution against the monarchy was insecure, although the full-scale attack on it by Spanish reactionaries which we call the Civil War did not begin until 1936.
5. In his two volume study *Decline of the West* (*Der Untergang des Abendlandes*) which appeared in 1918–1922.
6. The developments of diplomacy are treated in Chapter 17, where the Spanish Civil War is also discussed in the context of the struggles between dictatorships and democracies.

the various products of the whole earth, in such quantity as he might see fit, and reasonably expect their early delivery . . . and by the same means adventure his wealth in the natural resources and new enterprises of any quarter of the world . . . and would consider himself greatly aggrieved and much surprised at the least interference. But, most important of all, he regarded this state of affairs as normal, and permanent, except in the direction of further improvement. . . . [7]

Keynes's point was that even the wide disparities within Europe did not weaken the argument that there was a "European" economy dominant over the world economy. This European economy was supported by low tariffs and the common gold standard for money. Moreover, the more "backward" regions were able to exchange their agrarian and other primary goods for industrial wares, while continuing to industrialize. Russia provided good evidence for this view, as it made very rapid gains, despite the occasional "downturns" of the whole European economy. Agricultural income and productivity were rising parallel to the rising rate of urbanization and industrial exports to the non-Western world. The value of world trade in manufactured goods had risen to 15.17 billion dollars from 6.96 billion between 1891 and 1914;[8] during the same period primary products traded rose from 13.013 billion dollars to 25.33 billion.

The only disturbing element, from a European point of view, was the growth of competition from the United States, Japan, and Russia. The Western European countries had accounted for over 50 percent of world manufacturing in 1900. In 1913 this share had fallen to 36.1 percent, largely because of rapid American growth. Some Europeans already understood that the "second industrial revolution" of steel and electricity was helping younger industrial powers to overtake the original giants. Thus, even before the war, economists were advising European clients to invest in new technologies or face the loss of markets, as trade looked from the old centers of coal and iron to the new ones of hydroelectric power. The failure to make the investment might produce stagnation, unemployment, social conflict, and political instability.

What the First World War did was to prevent a peaceful transition to a new economic equilibrium in Europe and the world dominated by it. The war and the political events stemming from it—the collapse of empires and the creation of new, weak states—denied to Europe and Western outposts elsewhere the opportunity to respond in a merely economic way to economic adjustment. The two decades after 1918 were decades in which technology, marketing, population, and industrial organization took a back seat to external influences. The trend began before the war, but the wartime management of economies for "defense" accelerated the divergence of the national systems. In the 1920s it became clear that the Allies and the defeated powers were on radically different economic courses; so, too, was there a wide divergence between Russia and the Western democracies. Rivalry replaced cooperation to such a degree that in truth a "European" economy had ceased to exist. Recovery from the war was nationalist in character, and so was the effort to cope with the Great Depression after 1929. From this point of view, even the extreme divergence between the "liberal" economies and the "totalitarian" ones was more a question of degree of management by states suspicious of their neighbors than a question of fundamental differences.

7. Keynes, *The Economic Consequences of the Peace* (New York: Harcourt, Brace & Howe, 1920), pp. 10–11.
8. In dollars worth 1.50463 grams of fine gold.

The mobilization for war had introduced government control over trade, food distribution, labor mobility, wages, prices, and the import and export of "strategic" goods. The war costs forced the suspension of currency exchanges for gold payments, as the belligerents confiscated foreign assets or sought to control markets to damage enemies. Inflation was severe, wiping out private savings, while forcing the states to unprecedented borrowing. Patterns of domestic consumption changed radically, in housing for example; the requisition of building materials for war made domestic shortages in housing acute, developing a pattern which in many regions was not significantly altered until the 1950s, when another catastrophic war produced a reconstruction of Europe with the aid of American gifts and loans.

World War I had other dislocating effects. In Germany, for example, the needs of military production could not be met from overseas resources. The superior German chemical industry responded to the challenge, developing synthetics as substitutes for everything from coffee to rubber. The war was also a great stimulus to radio technology, the aircraft industry, and the motor transport industries—and thus a determinant of social patterns among people accustomed to the new speed of wartime communications. Some states could not bear the burden of the struggle economically; Italy was only in part successful in converting to a peacetime economy, and Russia collapsed. But even in states successful in adjusting to the strains of war and to subsequent peacetime conditions, economies were distorted by the costs of war and the shifting patterns of trade produced by alliance systems and the Versailles peace itself.

The greatest change of all, however, was without doubt the growth of regulation. By 1917 Britain's war cabinet controlled everything: the assignment of men for iron-mining operations; the actual seizure of entire industries vital to the war effort (coal, railroads, shipping); the alteration of law to permit the growth of administrative power in the form of new state agencies such as labor exchanges, the Compulsory National Service Department, wage boards, agencies to control local food resources, war agriculture, and even one to encourage the fair pay of women. The employment of women rose from 5,966,000 in 1914 to over 7,300,000 four years later, with gains chiefly in the munitions industry, but also in shops and even in the operation of public transportation. The opening of jobs once restricted to men was a powerful force of liberation, more so than the drama of Ibsen.

In Russia the picture was similar. There was a mushroom growth of government by committee under the supervision of the Conference for the Defense of the State. The Germans formed a War Raw Materials Bureau and passed new laws to reorganize economic life within the new doctrine of "sequestration," or the right of the state to seize whatever private goods were required for the war effort. The German government confessed that people resisted this "new doctrine."[9] The French government in 1916 issued decrees under its "emergency" wartime powers, legalizing the liquidation of foreign assets in French banks to help finance the war. Technically, this mobilization of capital was a loan to the state, or a seizure for which the market price was paid to the holders of the foreign securities. What could not be disguised, however, was the fact that the war had

9. See the translation of a section of the "report" on the "unprecedented policy," prepared by Walter Rathenau (1867–1922), the industrial genius, in S. B. Clough, ed., *Economic History of Europe: The Twentieth Century* (New York: Harper & Row, Publishers, Torchbooks, 1968), pp. 30–40.

relegated the sacredness of property to the lumber room of history. The most conservative, property-minded states were as "guilty" as the Russian communists who confiscated foreign holdings in the course of their revolution.

When peace came, therefore, more than financial chaos faced weak states—Austria for example, where peasants refused to accept the republic's paper money in payment for their crops. The emperor's golden eagles were remembered with longing! Europe faced a more general crisis in production and trade. This was only in part the result of the actual devastation of the war. The Versailles Treaty of 1919, we will recall, imposed war damages or reparations on Germany. These reached beyond actual repayments of the losses of the victors, however. There were forced cessions of colonies; and future limitations on economic activities were imposed also, in the form of "damage" levies on current German production. Moreover, Germany was not allowed to keep a large merchant navy. While crippling German recovery, the peace made no adequate arrangements for the development of

As the Allies entered World War I, their standing armies and trained reserve forces (14 million men) were almost double those of the Central Powers (7.9 million). The shortage on both sides was of skilled workers to produce armaments, and this need increased as more and more men were called to the battlefield. Women began to fill the breach, working in factories such as the British munitions plant shown below, taking office jobs, even serving in Britain in newly founded women's branches of the military. In addition to altering the character of the labor force in a number of countries, the great influx of female workers produced significant changes in the outlook of women, their roles, and their position in society. Imperial War Museum, London.

Out of the debacle of World War I there arose a group of German artists who viewed their contemporary situation with exaggerated, brutal realism. Otto Dix's The Matchseller *(1920) shows a pitiful ex-serviceman—blind and missing his limbs—trying to exist by peddling in the streets. Economic survival was a struggle for all in postwar Germany. With industrial areas occupied by Allied troops, a worthless currency destroyed by rampant inflation, and a glut of unemployed workers, the country seethed with bitterness and despair. Dix's characters are people in a frantic rush—some to enjoy themselves, others merely to survive—who convey a highly neurotic social situation. Staatsgalerie, Stuttgart.*

the economies of the Eastern European states, such as Austria, which lacked access to the sea entirely.

Keynes recognized these facts as inhibitions to recovery, in a famous judgment which the years 1919–1924 did much to justify:

The Treaty includes no provisions for the economic rehabilitation of Europe— nothing to make the defeated Central Empires into good neighbors, nothing to stabilize the new States of Europe, nothing to reclaim Russia;[10] nor does it promote in any way . . . economic solidarity among the Allies themselves . . . or . . . adjust the systems of the Old World and the New.

The Council of Four[11] paid no attention to these issues . . . of a Europe starving and disintegrating before their eyes. . . . [12]

The result was quick to come. The reparations "annexes" of the treaty required Germany, among other "deliveries," to give to the Allies billions in gold marks secured by bonds, to France alone seven million tons of German coal per year, and to the Reparations Commission half of the production of its chemical industries. The German response was to predict a disaster for the new Weimar Republic, in a Declaration given to the Allies.[13]

The industrial state of Germany in 1914 maintained about 20 percent of its population of sixty-seven million people on imports of food and other raw materials. Bereft of colonies, ships, and vast resources, obliged to the "options" on resources given to Allies, and stripped of eastern territories that produced 21 percent of its basic food supply, Germany could give neither food nor work to its people. The Allied blockade of food imports had

---

10. Excluded from the Peace Conference.
11. Wilson, Orlando, Clemenceau, Lloyd George.
12. Keynes, *Economic Consequences*, pp. 226–227.
13. The reparations clauses are printed in the collection of documents for economic history in Clough, ed., *Economic History*, pp. 65–86; the Declaration follows, pp. 87–89.

produced nearly one million deaths by starvation in wartime, according to German estimates. This blockade was not lifted until the spring of 1919, despite the armistice of 1918, with the result that mass starvation continued into 1919 and 1920. There is a vast amount of demographic and statistical evidence pointing to the progressive malnutrition and emotional dehumanization of the German people after the peace. And for those who do not heed this evidence, we have the grim appeal of the etchings and lithographs of Käthe Kollwitz (1867–1945), in which she recorded the misery of mothers watching their children starve.[14]

The appeal went unheeded by the Allies, but it was not the German society and economy alone which limped away from the disasters of both war and peace. Throughout Europe the dislocation of converting to peacetime produced unstable wages, price fluctuations, serious shortages, strikes, and the use of force by governments against discontented crowds. From 1919 to 1924 severe economic disturbances endured, led by a runaway inflation. The currencies of France and Italy lost about 75 percent of their 1914 value; those of central Europe about 90 percent. In Russia, Germany, Austria, and Hungary the collapse was total. People on fixed incomes were ruined, and only debtors found much comfort in the daily decrease in the value of money. They at least could pay off their debts with bad money for good!

In Eastern Europe the disintegration of economic life followed the collapse of political structures. Famine and disease throughout the area were intense and widespread. This produced "relief missions" from Britain and America. The conditions also produced eyewitness reports from observers like the future American president Herbert Hoover. What was becoming clear was that there were not enough trains or wagons to carry coal in Austria, nor a willingness of the Czechs, Hungarians, Austrians, Poles, and Yugoslavs to pool their resources of food and fuel. And, where cooperation was tried, it often failed because of a lack of trust. This lack was critical in relations between Austrian farmers and Czech cities, where milk was lacking, as cattle could not be fed on lands that had somehow lost about one-third of their productive capacity. In Poland during the immediate postwar years the birthrate fell to about 12 births per thousand people, from a 1914 rate of about 40 per thousand. There were illicit or "black" markets in necessities like soap. And throughout central and Eastern Europe there was a lack of fluid capital, currency chaos, inadequate fuel and transport, and low labor efficiency due to poor nutrition. Unemployment was massive. No relief could be had from trade with the traditional partner, Russia, which was reckoned an "outlaw regime."

14. See especially Kollwitz's 1920 lithograph with the inscription, *Wien stirbt! Bettet seine Kinder!* (Vienna is dying! Save the children!). A Communist, she died in a Nazi concentration camp.

Russia is estimated to have lost 4 million men in World War I; losses for Germany have been set at almost 2 million—nearly twenty times the losses sustained by the United States. In some areas of Western Europe, one out of every four young men had died in the war. And the end of the fighting was to bring, for many, starvation and continued suffering, as the Allies maintained their blockade while the peace treaty was being drawn up. The German artist Käthe Kollwitz, who had so often taken as her subject the sorrows and torments of the poor, portrayed in this 1907 lithograph, Need, *the helpless misery that was to plague so many, both before the war and after. Courtesy, Galerie St. Etienne, New York.*

As Germany's economy struggled under the harsh terms of the Versailles Treaty, the Weimar Republic began to show signs of severe strain. As the year 1923 progressed, the value of the mark fell from 14,000 to 4.2 trillion to the dollar. This 1924 campaign poster of the German Democratic party promises an end to inflation, in an effort to shore up the party's flagging support. Democracy, which had earlier seemed the best route to German recovery, had lost much of its appeal; instead, socialist parties were gaining, independents were turning to the Communist party, and on the right, Hitler had already attempted a march on Berlin, in November 1923. Within ten years' time, Adolf Hitler would be chancellor of Nazi Germany. Imperial War Museum, London.

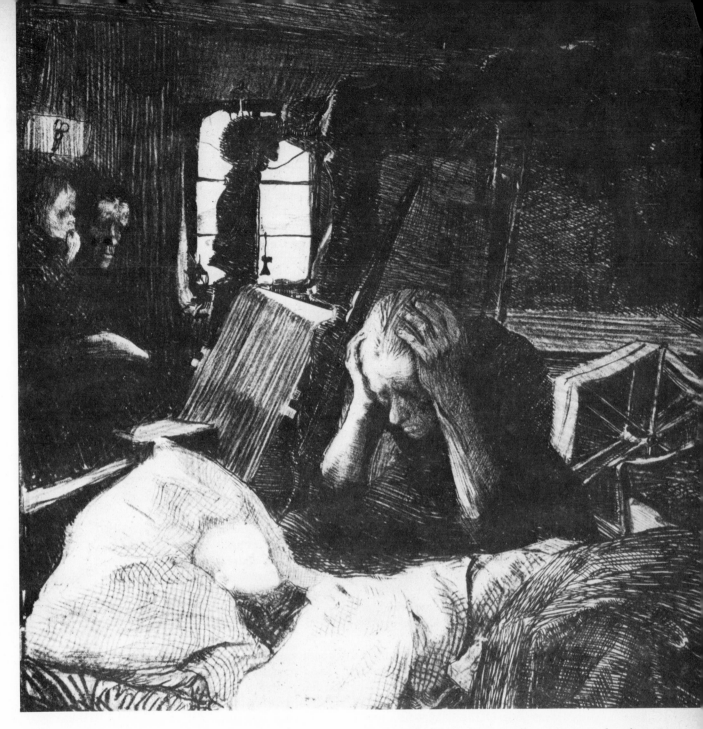

In the impoverished countryside, even large-scale seizures and redistributions of land, which took place before 1925 not only in socialist Russia but in all Eastern states, failed to provide relief. Land reform in the shape of distribution to peasants occurred in Czechoslovakia, Rumania, Hungary, and Poland. But the reforms had adverse effects in many cases because they encouraged the formation of units too small to be productively efficient and because, in general, rural overpopulation could not be relieved without a massive shift away from low levels of technology and inadequate investment capital. The payment of war debts to the Allies drained funds from the more backward countries, thus insuring the relative recovery of the already more advanced Western European states. This problem, together with that of inflation, occupied the best minds, and the League of Nations convened an International Financial Conference in 1920. But the more powerful states, burdened with great external war debts, were unwilling to relax their demands on either defeated enemies or poorer Allies.

In all countries there were vigorous efforts to reintroduce currency stability and orderly production and distribution. The League economists concluded that in the new states[15] the institutions for stability were lacking; that only Britain among the belligerents approached a balance of income and expenditure; and that even the neutrals[16] suffered from high food prices, a consequence of the inflationary flow of gold to them as a result of eager purchases of their goods by belligerents cut off from overseas markets. The severest inflations were in Russia, where in 1922 it took 290,000 rubles to buy what one ruble had bought in 1913, and in Germany, where in November 1923 it took one trillion marks in paper to purchase what one gold mark could have bought in 1913. Since the government had lost the revenues from the rich, occupied, Ruhr, it met its costs by printing more and more money. In 1923 "currency" was no longer current once the ink on paper money had dried. Businesses collapsed, especially small ones, but industrialists and others with real assets in hand grew more powerful.

Reconstruction in France and Britain meant different things.

In France, the problem was to pledge the full resources of public finance—taxation and the "damages" from Germany—to repair the ravages of war. This the government did in 1919, and by 1924 public expenditures were producing a milder brand of inflation which most people hailed as prosperity.[17] There was no replacing the 1,320,000 dead soldiers, as the birthrate continued to decline. But a good start was made toward replacing 23,000 ruined factories, 5,000 kilometers of railroad, 742,000 houses and restoring agriculture on about eight million acres of embattled ground.

Therefore, from 1924 to 1929 the French economy provided a dramatic instance of recovery. Not only was France rebuilt industrially, the reincorporation of Alsace-Lorraine brought back the most concentrated area of industrial resources in Europe. Additional input toward recovery derived from tourism and the sale overseas of luxury goods, especially cosmetics. The French gold reserves grew to a level second only to those of the United States, and the demand for labor in France led to the importation of workers from Italy and Spain. It is arguable that in 1930 the French economy had more fully recovered than any other European one, but this is misleading if for no other reason than the dependence on tourism and the export of luxury goods.

In Britain, which advocated a lenient attitude toward reparations, perhaps because it had not been a battleground and had not been devastated, the peace produced hopes for a better social order. The war had softened the rigid separation of the classes and spurred a feeling for wide reforms. But the achievement was poor. Of the 300,000 new houses required according to the government's own estimates, only 14,594 had been started before 1922. A recession in 1923 produced budget cuts which ended public housing subsidies. Labour party politicians said that the slums in 1924 were worse than those of 1914. Great conflicts arose over the issue of peacetime government economic intervention, despite the fact that free trade was dead and that the British laborer was very poorly paid. Conservative policies triumphed, but they did not relieve the depression that had set in. British exports fell steadily in 1921; 23.1 percent of the labor force was unem-

15. Austria, Czechoslovakia, Estonia, Finland, Hungary, Latvia, Lithuania, Poland, Rumania, and Serbia.
16. Denmark, Sweden, Norway, Holland, Spain, Switzerland, and Luxemburg.
17. In 1920 there was five times as much money in circulation as in 1914; prices, however, were only 350 percent higher.

ployed. Even in 1922, when improvement in trade set in, over a million were unemployed, or "on the dole."[18]

In 1924, a strong "recovery" set in for the Western European economies as a whole, lasting until 1929. This recovery was not uniform, however, and even where prosperity seemed most pronounced, it was sometimes not well founded. The peace settlement itself insured this, as did the facts of the world trade pattern shifts and the rise of new industries. Yet real wages rose strongly between 1925 and 1929; there was a dramatic surge in the construction of public works and housing. This was apparent to the ordinary people as well as to politicians and social critics, to the delight of the politicians and the disgust of the critics. The politicians welcomed any sign of prosperity as a harbinger of a new stability. The social critics saw the recovery as evidence of a crass materialism, as Europe seemed to drown the sorrowful memory of 1914–1918 in alcohol, the wail of jazz, and the roaring motors of fast cars.

What was less apparent even to economists was another series of facts set beside the rosy ones. On the plus side, industrial output was rising relative to the immediate postwar levels. This was due to absolute increases in key "new" industries—for example, the production of chemical fertilizers, rayon filament yarn, motor vehicles, and electric power. There had been a fivefold increase in chemical nitrogen production over 1914 levels by 1928 and a ninefold increase in the production of synthetic fibers. The number of privately registered autos had not been statistically significant in 1914; in 1928 there were 3.1 million in Europe, exclusive of Russia. What was also true in 1928 was that the United States *produced* 5.4 million vehicles; that the European population had reached 525 million, against only 460 million in 1914; that the world trade index, a measure of total industrial production for export,[19] showed a rise to 120, from the low of 65 in 1921. The *European* index, however, which had fallen to 56 in 1921, stood at only 103 in 1929. This meant a general European stagnation since 1913, when Europe's economic activity was considered against the world secular trend.

What the statistics indicate is that even after the postwar crisis had been overcome, by 1924–1925, Europe had done little beyond returning to the 1914 condition internally, while losing ground in world competition. The population increases were general, with only Austria showing a negative rate in the 1920s, while France lagged all other countries. Its rate of growth was only 2 per thousand; the country with the next lowest rate was Sweden, at 5.8. The fastest rates of increase were in the Netherlands, Spain, Italy, and the Balkans. Because the less-developed agrarian areas had the fastest growth rates for population and the most severe economic disturbances, they did not participate in the boom. The backward countries had an adverse effect even on the others. Slow growth and high unemployment combined with a collapse of prices in agriculture to weaken the market for industrial goods made in Western Europe among Eastern Europeans. Throughout the 1920s the price of foodstuffs and raw materials declined relative to manufactured goods. This weakened the European export industries throughout the world, especially in the areas where Britain had once enjoyed favorable trades. Weak rural demand was bad for everybody.

Again, in Britain, which we know to have been the *least disrupted* of the Western economies among the belligerents, events indicate the severity of the liberal agony. The victor seemed less prosperous in 1925 than vanquished Germany. By 1924 the Europeans had accepted the necessity of a

18. Collecting benefits under the Unemployment Insurance Act, which gave benefits for two periods of sixteen weeks.
19. With 1913 providing a base year of 100.

return to "normalcy" in Germany as the price of general recovery. A plan devised by the American banker Charles Dawes,[20] submitted early in April 1924, recommended a new system of German annual payments geared to actual productive capacity. While it did not reduce the total reparations bill, the Dawes Plan contributed to a remarkable German recovery, in conjunction with American loans and the issuance of a new currency backed by a mortgage on industrial capital and on all real property in land. These *Rentenmarks* practically wiped out German internal debt and facilitated industrial investments which triggered a boom.

Politically, the former Allies also relented, pledging themselves at Locarno to peaceful collaboration with Germany. The *quid pro quo* was an end to the occupation of the Ruhr in return for a German pledge to seek no revision of the boundaries established in 1919. In the new climate Germany was admitted to the League of Nations in 1926. In 1928 German iron and steel production exceeded the 1913 levels; and by early 1929 only the American economy was growing more rapidly than Germany's.

During the same period, things went from bad to worse in Britain. While industrial production was 10 percent above 1913 levels in 1925, more than one million men remained out of work, mostly in the old standby industries of coal, iron, steel, and textiles. Shipbuilding was in a profound crisis, in part because the peace had required German yards to rebuild the Allied fleets as part of the war damages bill! British imports were 10 percent higher in 1925 than in 1913, while exports were off by 25 percent. The Conservative government could think of nothing better to tell the unemployed "heroes" of 1918 than this: "All the workers . . . must take a reduction in wages to help put industry back on its feet."[21] This followed by two months a decision by Winston Churchill[22] to put Britain back on the gold standard, in the misguided belief that solid money would restore confidence in British goods and thus help trade. Actually, by stabilizing the pound at a high prewar rate of $4.86, Churchill raised the price of British goods to foreigners. This *reduced* exports even more. When next we meet Churchill, it is in 1926 as chancellor of the exchequer arming troops to shoot at workers who in that year launched a costly, doomed general strike. In 1929, therefore, British exports were still 20 percent below 1913 levels, while imports were now up by 20 percent. It was in these circumstances that Keynes proclaimed the economic consequences of Mr. Churchill to be as disastrous as those of Versailles!

The illusion of prosperity was not accepted by many economists. At the International Economic Conference in Geneva in 1927 under League of Nations auspices, the conferees recorded their view that recovery was a temporary phase in a more basic maladjustment due to war-induced dislocations, the nationalist tariffs, and other barriers to the flow of labor, capital, and goods. Moreover, it was understood that the relative European decline had forced Europe to renounce some of its control functions on an intercontinental scale. Even in 1927 the conference spoke of a "depression" in world trade in the goods of fixed capital, while recognizing that the production of motorcars, silk, and goods of luxury or immediate consumption was increasing in a "false prosperity."[23]

Steady and long-term high unemployment rates were holding down the

The New York stock market crash of October 1929 turned already unstable economies into financial disasters. The formerly wealthy sold apples on American street corners, and here, an investor wiped out in the stock market peddles one of his last remaining assets. Between 1929 and 1932 5,000 American banks went under. When a leading bank in Vienna failed in 1931, the financial collapse of the Great Depression spread over Europe as well. UPI.

20. Also vice-president of the United States, 1925–1929.
21. Stanley Baldwin, prime-ministerial policy speech, July 30, in George Lichtheim, *Europe in the Twentieth Century* (New York: Praeger Publishers, 1972), p. 146.
22. Chancellor of the exchequer.
23. See the "Report of the President," in Clough, ed., *Economic History*, pp. 152–163.

purchasing power of large population groups, while at the same time smaller classes were indulging in orgies of speculation on the stock market and conspicuous consumption. On a very pessimistic note the conference closed, recording the hopeful signs of change but marking explicitly the deeper roots of economic unrest, especially the diversion of trade to American control and the high level of taxation in Europe in relation to resources, a result of war pensions and armaments expenditures to preserve peace. What was needed was a new organization of Europe as an "economic unit"; what was forthcoming was the exclusive practice of "economic nationalism," in part the result of the rapid creation of new nations. No notice was taken of the Soviet economy, where government management was rapidly moving production in a positive direction, after it had reached the nadir in 1920–1921, when industrial production was about 15 percent of the 1913 level. Indeed, in 1928, the first Five-Year Plan for collective agriculture[24] and the elimination of private enterprise in some sectors broke completely with the Western pattern.

It was a Europe characterized by these conditions, which some observers correctly analyzed as those of long-term "depression," that was taken by surprise by the Great Depression of the 1930s. But both major causes of the new economic crisis—the collapse of the New York stock market in late 1929 and the instability of prices for foodstuffs and primary goods—were directly related to conditions recognized in 1927.

The New York crash reached Europe after a short delay. From 1923 to 1929 American speculators in foreign investments sent more than $3 billion overseas; so did Britain. Germany and Austria were the chief European borrowers, with more than $4.3 billion of imported capital. The sudden decline of values for shares in New York caused American and British capitalists to call in loans, in order to salvage their own positions. This

24. See Chapter 16 for Soviet economic development under the comprehensive state "plans."

strangled German and Austrian finance, and the shock wave of the attack spread to the other financial centers, as investors had to find gold to pay off overseas debts.

By 1931 the whole Western machinery of finance had collapsed: markets were closed, the gold standard had been forsaken, and governments had recourse to direct intervention. Naturally, the financial collapse caved in the market for primary goods. Production had expanded somewhat artificially in the 1920s, and by 1929 inventories of foodstuffs and raw materials were piling up in warehouses. The failure of the financial system destroyed the market for much of this "surplus." Europe suddenly faced the paradox of having food that people could not afford to buy, even at very low prices. The collapse of agriculture meant commodity exporters no longer could afford to buy industrial goods; the result was mass unemployment in the industrial states and a reciprocal failure of the ability to buy food.

The Great Depression fed on a cycle already at work in the Eastern grain-belt countries in the early 1920s. By 1931 the "scissors" cutting agriculture had closed, one blade made of declining food prices, the other of credit failures. The price for Polish wheat in dollars per hundred kilos fell from a 1926 high of $5.06 to a low in 1931 of $2.78 on the Chicago exchange. The German *Reichsbank* reserve of marks was cut in half between 1929 and 1931. Despite growing unemployment in every German region, the government protected its reserves by decreasing social expenditures, including relief, by 22 percent from 1929 to 1932. Frightened legislators reacted with a frenzy of laws to "protect" home markets. European tariffs rose 64 percent over the 1927 levels by 1931; and in 1932 even Britain "officially" abandoned free trade. Of course "protection" merely added new burdens to trade, which in the major industrial states fell in the 1930s to 50 percent of the prewar levels.

The most immediate effect of the Depression on people was the loss of jobs. As the *New York Times* index of stock shares fell from 452 to 58, from 1929's plunge to the 1932 bottom, industrial production fell off by half in America, formerly a thriving commercial marketplace, where there had been a chicken in every pot and a car in every garage and people smoked good nickel cigars. Europe had 15 million unemployed, 6 million in Germany and 3 million in Britain. The United States alone, however, had 15 million unemployed in 1933; and in 1939 17 percent of the work force had not gone back to work.

The society with the most egalitarian bias, the best suburban housing, the highest wages and worker living standards elected Franklin D. Roosevelt in 1932, because he promised to get the economy going again. The most "mature" industrial economy, built on refrigerators, cars, and suburbia, could no longer feed or clothe its people without government intervention, without a shift from the politics of Big Business to those of welfare and the New Deal. Neither could Europe, where unemployment rates reached 45 percent in Germany and hovered around 18 percent in Britain, with hardship almost as great for the "white collars" and "black coats" of the middle classes as among blue-collar workers. Europe was looking for saviors too!

THE POLITICS OF "NORMALCY": 1919–1939

In 1919 there were twenty-seven "democracies" in Europe, or at least that many states in which a variety of political parties competed for power in more or less free elections. The forms of constitutions varied; there were monarchies and republics, federal states and unitary states, conservative ones and radical ones. The Soviet Union in theory was a democratic state in

In the winter of 1930, 2,300,000 Germans were out of work, and among the rest, the greatest fear was unemployment. The misery, insecurity, and frustration of the German masses had spawned agitation, hatreds, and a bleak outlook which saw Hitler, in the words of this National Socialist party poster, as "Our last hope." Hitler became chancellor in January 1933, and in the elections the following March, over 17,000,000 Germans voted for the Nazis, giving them 288 seats and thus control of the Reichstag. Imperial War Museum, London.

which the dictatorship of the proletariat prevailed. At the other end of the spectrum, the Spanish monarchy manipulated the democratic franchise and constitutional forms to prop up a military dictatorship. Twenty years later a European trend toward dictatorship and totalitarian rule had destroyed most of the democracies.[25] Only ten survived: Czechoslovakia and Finland among the new states; and the "old" democracies of Britain, France, Holland, Belgium, Switzerland, Sweden, Norway, and Denmark.

In retrospect it is easy to say why constitutional and democratic governments in many places did not survive. The old democracies had a long inheritance of the two revolutions that had shaped the modern West—the political one deriving from France in 1789 and the industrial one, for which Britain had set the pattern. Together, the two revolutions had deeply rooted the urban, factory-oriented social systems in which the politics of liberty, equality, and self-determination struggled against whatever counterrevolutionary forces existed in each country. This successful struggle was waged only in Europe west of the Elbe, with the exceptions to the rule being Czechoslovakia and Finland. And Czechoslovakia became a Russian dependent after the Second World War, while Finland existed as a neutral state in the shadow of Soviet expansion.

The democratic states produced by the First World War had no firm historical grip on either industrialization or the politics of democracy. West of the Elbe this was true for Spain, Portugal, southern Ireland, and southern Italy, which had remained peasant societies. East of the Elbe this was true nearly everywhere; the whole area seemed "backward" by comparison with the Western European industrial region. The result for all of the underdeveloped states within Europe was the same: a sometimes heroic struggle to overcome historical "deficiencies" rapidly. The new states lacked a valid parliamentary tradition; they also had low levels of education and literacy, profound economic problems, bitter and unresolved questions of what to do with "nationalist" minorities, a critical need to redistribute land on a basis sound enough to bring the peasants into the national economies, plus strong reactionary and counterrevolutionary groups which were aided by hatred and fear of "Bolshevism." Land reform in Eastern Europe was the dominant social question, but this often involved nationalist passions directed against alien landlords and thus became more than a purely domestic issue.

The new states in the Baltic and in the Balkans faced all of these problems in a more aggravated form than those few "backward" Western states. But in southern Italy and southern Ireland there were absentee landlords, from northern Italy in the one place and Britain in the other. The Sicilians resisted the north Italian "foreigners," and the Irish Catholic "republicans" actually waged a war against British rule in the south. The outbreak of the world war in 1914 had caused the British to defer putting in effect Home Rule, voted by Parliament that same year. Irish nationalists[26] sided with the Germans, and with some support from the Kaiser rose in a bloody "civil war" in 1916. This was suppressed with savagery by Britain, but in 1919 a war for independence began; and late in 1921 the London government recognized an Irish Free State.[27]

---

25. Dictatorship was an old *historical* form of government, with its roots in the ancient city-states. It was in essence a one-man rule to tide a people over periods of unrest. Totalitarianism was a modern *social* form, permanent and extended to every human activity.
26. The Sinn Fein party, the backbone of what was to become the outlaw Irish Republican Army.
27. Without Protestant Ulster, or the largely Anglo-Scotch six northern counties.

In Spain the immediate postwar period had produced very severe political unrest from 1919 to 1923, aggravated by the alliance of the Church, the army, and the upper classes against the republicans, the Catalan "independents,"[28] and working-class socialists. Caught in the middle, the Spanish parliament lost its effectiveness. The king, Alfonso XIII (1886–1931), was also rapidly declining in popularity. He settled on the army as the one force able to restore power and in 1923 gave dictatorial authority to General Primo de Rivera. The dictator was learned and courageous but politically inept and out of sympathy with parliamentary liberalism. De Rivera attempted to arbitrate worker-capitalist grievances as well as initiate reforms of agriculture and plans for industrial expansion. During his years in power, until 1930, when he was overthrown (shortly before Spain was declared a republic, in 1931),[29] de Rivera also pursued policies inimical to his own largely mythical united Spain. He banned the Catalan language, deported opposition liberals, suppressed the anarchists, encouraged republicans to emigrate, and in general tried to solve by military means problems at bottom social and economic in character.

Primo de Rivera steadfastly denied that his methods were "Italian," but there were similarities between the Spanish situation after 1923 and that prevailing in Italy. Italians had emerged from the war deeply frustrated and divided. On the winning side, they were denied their full irredentist claims because the principle of self-determination was applied on the Yugoslav side by the Balkans, where the 1915 secret treaties had conceded to Italy the major port of Trieste. The Peace Conference in 1919 turned over Trieste, but not the city of Fiume or the rest of the Dalmatian coast. The cry of *Italia irredenta* helped to discredit the Italian parliament; so, too, did the deep economic misery Italy suffered. During the war the government had been unable to pay its costs without resort to printing paper money not effectively backed by foreign loans or domestic bullion reserves. By 1920 the lira had lost 80 percent of its 1914 value, causing serious distress to peasants, bureaucrats, landlords, and industrial laborers alike.

Over 90 percent of the peasants owned less than three acres of land apiece! Worker demands for social reform were frustrated by middle-class fears of a Soviet-type revolution. Strikes and riots became common in 1920, when the metallurgical workers and peasants occupied factories and made seizures of land. The chief benefactor of the growing unrest was the onetime Socialist politician Benito Mussolini (1883–1945), by now an intense nationalist who had broken with the Socialists because of their opposition to the war in 1914. In 1919 Mussolini had organized his militant and irredentist Fascist party, or *Fasci di Combattimento*. The Fascists grew in strength from 1920 to 1922, at the expense of the Catholic People's party and the traditional bourgeois parties of the center and the left, the Liberals and the Democrats. His Fascists campaigned against the Socialists, largely on the spurious ground that the Socialists aimed at a Soviet-style revolution. In fact, the established parties with mass support agreed on land reform and social justice for workers. Mussolini's chief support came from Church ultras and a combination of big landowners and industrialists, aided by unemployed soldiers sympathetic to Fascist violence and the idea of a campaign for Dalmatia.

Taking their cues from *Il Duce*, the "leader," the Fascists formed paramilitary groups which spread a doctrine of nationalist revival, revolutionary

28. The old kingdom of Catalonia had always been ill at ease within the Castilian-dominated monarchy.
29. De Rivera fled to Paris, where he soon died.

activism, patriotism, and contempt for parliamentary reformism. Mussolini encouraged street violence, while also exploiting brilliantly his gifts as an orator and journalist. Old political leaders who were hostile to the popular mass parties supported Mussolini's rise, because they believed he would be easily controlled in any situation of a revolutionary kind. Negotiations in 1922 had achieved an agreement to take the Fascists into government partnership. On October 27, however, Mussolini's Fascists made the famous March on Rome. The government was prepared to resist, but the king refused to mobilize the army against Mussolini's men, the "Blackshirts," perhaps because he thought them to be stronger than they actually were. This heartened Mussolini, who had remained in Milan, and on October 30 he demanded the post of premier, although the Fascists held only 35 seats in the legislature of over 500 members.

Thus he came to power, leaving behind a trail of wrecked unions, leftist party offices, and ousted Socialist and Communist town governments. He promised a restoration of peace, order, and new victories, in return for which he began an "emergency rule" of one year with a decree of dictatorial

Benito Mussolini had boldly threatened, "Either the government of Italy is given to us, or we shall seize it by marching on Rome." On October 27, 1928, Mussolini's Fascists, the "Blackshirts," made this threat a reality. Shown here are Fascist leaders arriving in the capital after the famous march on Rome. Following this, Mussolini, after accepting the office of prime minister from King Victor Emmanuel III, moved to establish a dictatorial regime. Brown Brothers.

powers *legally* granted by the parliament. Two years later, his party won a massive victory and, with over 60 percent of the vote, carried out a program to dismantle the representative democracy. The militant period of formation was over. From 1924 on Mussolini consolidated a totalitarian dictatorship on a permanent basis, backed by a new Fascist militia and a variety of programs to uproot liberal values and capitalism itself.

The exact character of the Fascist state, its ideological roots, and the many concrete programs it carried out to transform Italy will concern us elsewhere.[30] Here it is enough to notice that in the 1920s and 1930s Mussolini's example of personal and military power was followed in large measure through much of Europe: in Spain under General Franco,[31] in Germany under Hitler,[32] in Poland under General Pilsudski,[33] in Hungary under General Gömbös,[34] in Greece under General Metaxas,[35] in Portugal under the economist-president Salazar,[36] and in Austria under Chancellor Dollfuss.[37] Each of the national reactionary leaders had successors; and imitators came to power in the majority of Latin American states, as one by one the weak democracies succumbed to the pressures of the immediate postwar crisis, or the more severe stress of the Great Depression in the 1930s. In Yugoslavia, Rumania, and Bulgaria the monarchs themselves led the movement.[38]

In the Balkans especially the problems facing the new governments in 1919 were insurmountable. Not only were nationalist rivalries severe; there was acute fear of Hungarian "revisionism," the desire of Magyar politicians to relieve internal pressures by advocating gains at the expense of the boundary lines established for the Slav states at Versailles. Then, as we have seen, the capital required for industrialization was lacking. By 1924, therefore, when the more stable Western economies began to boom, and Balkan land reform was in progress, the agrarian economies were showing the weakness of imbalance, which after the 1929 crash produced the collapse of the market for Eastern foodstuffs. The underdevelopment of Eastern Europe, and of Iberia and southern Italy, was thus an essential determinant of political instability. And this instability invited the expansion of the two powers most successful in recovery from the Depression: Nazi Germany and Soviet Russia.

Only in the Baltic republics of Lithuania, Latvia, Estonia, and Finland was the decade of the 1920s more benign to new states. Created by fiat at Versailles, they occupied an area traditionally a battleground of German and Russian ambition. Now, with the decision to reconstitute Poland, which had ceased to be a state in 1795, the Baltic states were in some danger from their powerful neighbors. Pilsudski, the hero of the Polish "independents," was a Lithuanian by birth and anxious to exercise political leadership over Lithuania, which was Catholic in religion, as was Poland. The Protestant majorities in Estonia and Latvia were chiefly Lutheran and distrustful of Polish ambitions. From 1919 to 1921, Poles, Germans, Russians, and Allied forces contested for supremacy in the region, the Allies especially eager to secure the Baltic as a buffer against Communism. Pilsudski actually seized parts of the Russian Ukraine and some more

It has been estimated that during its first three years World War I cost an average of $123 million a day; in 1918 that cost rose to $224 million. The Europe that was left at the end of the war faced a long road to recovery; shown here, a Serbian peasant begs in the Belgrade streets in December 1918, one month after the armistice, and in the same month that the new Yugoslav state formed its first government. Yugoslavia, a country where agriculture accounted for 47 percent of the national income, possessed only 1,500 tractors, according to pre-World War II statistics. For every 1,000 peasant holdings, 379 had no plows, 639 had no harrows, and almost all had no implements for sowing seeds. For the peasants, little relief lay ahead, as the Eastern European agrarian economies declined while the Western states progressed and new powers rose, in Soviet Russia and in Germany. Library of Congress.

30. See Chapter 16, which deals with totalitarianism in Italy, Germany, and Russia.
31. Francisco Franco, born in 1892.
32. Adolf Hitler, 1889–1945.
33. Marshal Józef Pilsudski, 1867–1935.
34. Julius Gömbös, 1886–1936.
35. Joannes Metaxas, 1871–1941.
36. Antonio Salazar, 1889–1970.
37. Engelbert Dollfuss, 1892–1934.
38. King Alexander of Yugoslavia, King Carol of Rumania, and Czar Boris of Bulgaria.

northern border areas, including Lithuania Vilna. In Finland General Mannerheim, a former czarist commander, drove out Soviet troops and German adventurers. The outcome of the early instability was a successful Allied effort. The Baltic states became advanced democracies on the Western model, where women voted and farm cooperatives seemed to solve the agrarian problem, at least until the Depression.

In the less powerful liberal states of the West the postwar period was at first marked by enthusiasm for reform. This was true not only in the belligerent states, but in the neutrals as well. The idea of self-determination, for example, operated in Scandinavia, where the Danish government gave Iceland "national independence,"[39] though Iceland was still under the formal authority of the king of Denmark. The other import motifs of reform at work in the early twenties, or even in 1919, were universal suffrage for both sexes and the reduction of gerrymandering to give the different parties proportional representation.[40] These measures were pushed through in Belgium, Sweden, Holland, Norway, and Denmark, or perfected where earlier women had the vote.[41] In Belgium women

39. This move came on November 30, 1918, after the armistice but before the Peace Conference.
40. That is, a number of seats in the legislature proportional to the actual vote count.
41. Norway (1913), Holland (1917).

were selectively enfranchised, however, as was the case in Hungary and Bulgaria. In Switzerland women lacked the vote throughout the interwar period.[42] And only the Scandinavian monarchies took seriously the disarmament proposals of the League of Nations.

On Europe's northwestern fringe, the French and British political systems passed through quite distinct phases, roughly characterized by these motifs: the establishment and guaranteeing of the peace (1919–1924), the return to normalcy (1924–1929), and the experimentation of the 1930s, when every nation sought the means to relieve the social unrest and political doubt caused by the Depression. Dependent on one another because of their mutual distrust of Italy, Russia, and Germany, the two chief democracies of Europe were also divided by their attitudes toward reparations down to 1924. Moreover, the Greek war to drive the Turks completely out of Europe (1920–1923) also caused serious tensions. Britain supported Greece, which suffered a terrible defeat at Turkish hands, with the Turks enjoying French support. The French were determined to prevent the Greeks from consolidating control over Asia Minor, which had become the field of conflict after initial Greek successes.

Domestically, France had trouble digesting its "victory" over Germany. France had gotten back Alsace-Lorraine; a French marshal (Foch) had been the Supreme Allied Commander in 1918; the new states—Poland for example—looked to French military men for instruction and support; and Spain had reason to be grateful for French support in Morocco. The reputation of France's artists and its writers[43] made it plausible to predict a new era of French leadership in Europe. But inflation was severe; the occupation of the Ruhr diverted manpower needed at home; and peace brought back into focus the factional nature of electoral politics.

In the 1919 elections, the nationalist conservatives won 437 of the 613 seats in the Chamber of Deputies, at the expense of the left, especially the Socialists, under the leadership of Herriot.[44] This was in part an expression of middle-class hatred for the Russian Revolution. The Soviets had expropriated foreign capitalists; and France had been the chief investor there. In part, however, the vote expressed the bourgeois fear of organized labor: the CGT (*Confédération Générale du Travail,* or General Confederation of Labor) had grown rapidly during the war, doubling by 1919. Clemenceau had responded by social reform laws, which he passed just before the 1919 elections. The defeat promoted a Socialist split in 1920, into a majority Communist party oriented toward Moscow and the Socialists, led by León Blum (1872–1950). The conservative "National Bloc" therefore maintained control, until 1925. Under the leadership of Poincaré and Foch, this bloc pursued a harsh anti-German line, leading to the seizure of the Ruhr in 1923 on the grounds of the failure of Germany to pay its war debts. This policy had produced anti-French feelings in London and other European capitals, however, and it also had failed to resolve the problem of French inflation.

In 1924 the "Left Alliance"[45] turned the conservatives out. Herriot became premier, and he made the conciliatory Aristide Briand (1862–1932) foreign minister. Briand had been premier during the great campaign at Verdun. A witness to the horrors of the war, he was committed to the League of Nations. A former minister of education, he had presided over school reforms to diminish clerical influences. A former minister of justice,

42. And still do.
43. André Gide, Anatole France, Marcel Proust, Paul Valéry.
44. Édouard Herriot, 1872–1957.
45. *Cartel des Gauches.*

The Ruhr has always been Germany's richest industrial and coal-mining district. Because it had sustained the German war effort in the First World War, it was deliberately left defenseless by the Treaty of Versailles. In January 1923 France charged deficiencies in German reparations payments and occupied the entire Ruhr district. Although this poster protests that action, Germany passively resisted; the result was a total paralysis of the entire German economic structure, which made payment of any further reparations impossible. Institute of Social History, Amsterdam.

Hände weg vom Ruhrgebie

Briand had a keen sense of the need for a liberal social policy. It was therefore the case that the Herriot-Briand ministry was the French expression of the period of stabilization before the Great Depression.

This reformist regime with its internationalist policies could not arrest the real decline in French social stability, however. The 1920s contributed to the net drop in population; in 1935 deaths per thousand in population exceeded live births. Industrial growth itself contributed to social tension and a loss of confidence. The 1920s were years of pronounced shifts from agriculture to industrial employment; and the new urban concentrations were enlarging at a time of restricted government capacity to supply social services. This produced a basic sense of national decline among liberals.

In these circumstances, the Depression obscured the real economic gains made after 1926, when the reconstruction and modernization of industry became an accomplished fact. Unemployment never reached the rates prevalent elsewhere, but in 1935 production was off, nearly a million were jobless, and trade had slipped to pre-1914 levels. The leftist coalition found no remedies; Briand's death in 1932 had weakened the government. Workers spoke of the dilemmas induced by the worldwide Depression as if it were the product of either ministerial incompetence or a conspiracy of the rich to defraud labor. As morale sank, the premier Édouard Daladier (1884–1970), seemed to exhibit a genius for magnifying small crises. In 1934, for example, a network of corruption in government produced a rash of suicides and dismissals. Protest marches by veterans drew police fire, and what began as a minor matter ended in bringing down Daladier's government. This allowed the formation of a Government of National Unity under Gaston Doumergue (1863–1937), a former president, who assembled a cabinet of war heroes and ex-premiers.

But the Doumergue government was itself unable to deal with the main problems of foreign policy, Russian and German expansion, or the issues of the economy. Doumergue's foreign minister was assassinated; his efforts to increase executive power at the expense of the legislature aroused the fear that this authoritarian policy was the prologue to a broad strike at parliamentary democracy. The cry of "Fascism" was heard, and Doumergue's government fell. No new stable one was formed until 1936, when Léon Blum brought back to power the leftist parties already formed into the "Popular Front." His union of middle-class radicals, socialists, and communists was pacifist and humanitarian. But it came to power after Hitler had already remilitarized the Rhineland, after the Spanish situation had erupted in a civil war, and in the midst of a wave of strikes in which workers sat down in the factories, preventing strikebreakers from entering to take up production.

That this means succeeded in winning a forty-hour week, large pay raises, paid holidays, and compulsory collective bargaining served to underline the attractiveness of direct action. It was rapidly becoming clear that the Depression and the new German menace could not be dealt with by the old means. In France after 1936 the government nationalized the munitions industry, brought the banks under direct control, undertook to supervise relations between labor and management, and developed a series of public works programs to stimulate the economy, along the lines already pioneered in democratic America by Roosevelt and in Europe by dictators like Hitler and Mussolini. The rising curve of public expenditure weakened the Popular Front, however, by frightening the bourgeois Radical Socialists, to whom public debt was nearly as unbearable as Fascism! Blum was forced out; Daladier returned to power. And in 1938 he looked to the French right, even to the Fascists, to guard France from socialism.

The situation in Britain was similar, but more inherently stable because the parliamentary system there was essentially a two-party system, not because it was better equipped to settle the social question.

Lloyd George, the Liberal leader, had won a tremendous victory in the "Khaki Election" of 1918.[46] But his majority of 478 to 87 contained unionists opposed to Irish Home Rule, Conservatives who favored Irish self-determination, and Liberals who wanted to pursue a conciliatory policy toward Germany. The ministry also contained supporters for Lloyd George's own special programs of social reform, which the prime minister calculated would pull the political teeth of the Labour party, which was now as strong as the Liberal party. Moreover, the government contained anti-Bolsheviks like Churchill, who, despite the pressing problems of demobilization and conversion to peacetime production, bombarded his leader with schemes for an all-out invasion to rid Russia of the scourge of Communism. The result was the failure of this league of "stars" to produce any really workable policies.

Of course, some reasons for the failure lay beyond the control of British politicians—for example, French policy, the role played by the "press lords" who controlled huge newspaper chains and manipulated public opinion with them, and the world trade situation. But it was *policy* that doomed Ireland to civil war and caused a retreat from housing supported with public money. It was Conservative power within the government that dismantled the wartime controls needed to cope with inflation before 1924 and Depression in the thirties, the "hungry thirties," as British writers still remember that decade. And it was policy that used troops to break hunger marches and the general strike in 1926.

The result was a period of rapid changes of government. The electorate seemed confused in its loyalties. Working-class people before the war had begun to leave the Liberal and Conservative parties for Labour. The war itself had split the Liberals badly in 1916 and strengthened Labour. Trade union membership in 1914 stood at about 4.4 million; in 1919 it was 8.9 million. And in the First World War Lloyd George had taken labor union members of Parliament into his government, including the powerful leaders Clynes and Henderson. Not all Labour members of Parliament had supported the war, however, and this was true of the great leader Ramsay MacDonald (1866–1937), a rather aloof intellectual, but a pacifist and Socialist of solid convictions. MacDonald had hailed the Soviet revolution and said openly that someday the Red flag would fly over Buckingham Palace.

This certainly did not occur, but late in 1923 MacDonald's Labour party combined with the Liberals to oust the Conservatives led by Stanley Baldwin (1867–1947), little more than a year after Bonar Law (1858–1923) had led the Conservatives in their victory over Lloyd George. Because Labour won more seats than their Liberal allies, MacDonald formed the ministry. Thus Britain in 1923–1924 was led by a man pledged to socialism, and it seemed possible that a Western nation committed to parliamentary democracy might apply socialist policies to the problems of the post-recovery era. MacDonald's government, despite its limited scope for action,[47] pushed hard the "revision" of Versailles in practice, which in 1924 led to the phase of cooperation with German recovery. The Labour govern-

---

46. So called from the British army uniform color; in France the election was the *Horizon bleu*, from the French uniform color.
47. The effect of the Liberals on the Labour ministry, which had a minority of all seats in Commons.

ment also pushed subsidized housing and took the radical step of establishing diplomatic ties with Soviet Russia, cemented by a trade treaty. These policies alarmed the Liberals, who deserted MacDonald in the famous case of the Zinoviev letter, a forgery which purported to be the work of the head of the Soviet-dominated Communist International.[48] The published letter contained a plan for revolution in England.

The furor provoked by this scandal brought back to power the Conservatives, but MacDonald, acting as his own foreign minister, had opened a line toward normal relations with Russia and Germany. MacDonald had publicly blamed France for Germany's plight and the isolation of Russia, citing also the complicity of President Wilson. The Labour government pointed a way the Conservatives followed only partially, however. While adhering to the German policy, chiefly because German recovery was essential to a sound European economy, Baldwin's second ministry turned away from conciliating Russia and from peace with Labour at home.

The result at home was the 1926 general strike, which grew out of the miners' demands for a guaranteed wage level and a shorter work day. A commission had recommended wage *reductions* to the government along with reorganization of the whole coal industry, then operating at a loss. Baldwin's response to the general strike was to declare a state of emergency and in it to continue vital services with special volunteer corps. Hard-liners led by Churchill advocated an attack on union funds, a declaration of the strike's illegality, and military measures. The defeated workers went back to work for longer hours and lower wages, into a miserable mining life captured in 1913 in D. H. Lawrence's *Sons and Lovers* and in 1937 by George Orwell's *Road to Wigan Pier*. Politically, the Baldwin government's reaction embittered Labour. The employers had made no concessions at all; and in 1927 the right to strike was limited by new laws. Economically, the long-term result was to shape an atmosphere of utter labor-management distrust, and thus to contribute to the decay of an industrial system desperately in need of cooperative modernization.

Except for a second brief return of Labour to power under MacDonald from 1929 to 1931, coalitions dominated by Conservatives held the reins of government until the end of the Second World War. Baldwin, a rich industrialist, was premier from 1924 to 1929, surrounding himself with the Chamberlains,[49] Churchill, and a variety of aristocrats and snobs. Baldwin's political axiom was to do nothing at all until it was absolutely necessary. Churchill championed the gold standard; the Chamberlains tinkered with social security reforms. The short Labour government had the ill luck to be in power early in the Depression; and in 1931 voters held it responsible for the rise in unemployment, when in fact the free trade policy of Philip Snowden[50] had been good, if unsuccessful. The problem was a world one, not a Labour party production. But voter panic produced a defeat for Labour in 1931. MacDonald then split the party, joining a National government, together with Snowden and the union leader J. H. Thomas (1874–1949).

The split had been impending for some time, however; as a condition of support for sterling devaluation, MacDonald accepted pressure from bankers in England and America, aimed at *reducing unemployment benefits* when nearly three million British were jobless. This issue foreshadowed the

---

48. Grigori Zinoviev, 1883–1936.
49. Austen and Neville Chamberlain; Chamberlain (1869–1940) was responsible for two measures: an enlarged health scheme for Britain in the 1920s, and appeasement of Hitler in the 1930s.
50. 1864–1937; chancellor of the exchequer, a Socialist with liberal economic ideas.

struggle for budgets and taxes characteristic of the 1930s in Britain. Mac-Donald remained prime minister until 1935, presiding over the policy of benefit cuts, wage reductions, and other blows to the politics of welfare. Then, in 1935, Labour gained only 46 seats, while the Conservatives took 472. The Liberal party was essentially dead. Baldwin became prime minister for the third time, a post he retained until his resignation in 1937 in favor of Neville Chamberlain, a man also at home with the cautious policies of Baldwin.

Thus, on the eve of the new war, Britain was unable to solve the problems of the Depression. What helped was not the success of the government, but the failure of the Fascists and the Communists to make large gains among a people not friendly to ideological politics in any guise. But the mood was bitter. Out of power, Churchill warned that Hitler was a menace to civilization. And in 1936 King Edward VIII shook an already dazed and dispirited democracy when he abdicated to marry the American divorcée Mrs. Simpson.

THE LOSS OF CONFIDENCE

The crisis of the democratic tradition after the First World War is easy to see in the history of Western literature. There is an abundance of prophetic despair, of revolt against the political traditions which had produced the conflict and against bourgeois social values, and of surveys of man's fate that view the future in terms of a choice between anarchism, bourgeois complacence, and enthusiasm for the "new society" of fascism and Soviet communism. There is practically no literature affirming the liberal values of the late nineteenth century produced by writers *born after 1890 or 1900*.

There were, of course, many famous writers of another generation, born mostly in the 1860s and 1870s, who had achieved reputations early in the new century, and who lived on into the 1920s, 1930s, and beyond: Hermann Hesse, Thomas Mann, André Gide, Paul Valéry, W. B. Yeats, and Paul Claudel, D. H. Lawrence, James Joyce, Colette, Joseph Conrad, Theodore Dreiser, John Galsworthy, Thomas Hardy, Knut Hamsun, and others too numerous to mention. Among them there were some who continued the traditions of the novel of society, the comedy of manners, the family chronicle, the novel of social realism (rooted in the belief that amelioration was possible), and even the novel of romance.

Mann, for example, perhaps Germany's greatest novelist, made his name in 1901 with *Buddenbrooks*, a chronicle of the solid middle-class Buddenbrooks family. This reputation he confirmed in the smaller masterpiece *Death in Venice*, 1913 (*Der Tod in Venedig*). Yet even in *Buddenbrooks* the theme of bourgeois decay is omnipresent. In the 1924 *Magic Mountain (Der Zauberberg)*, a work especially cited when Mann received the Nobel Prize for literature, this concern had become generalized. The "magic mountain" is in the Swiss Alps, where a young German, Hans Castorp, has come to visit his cousin in a tuberculosis sanatorium. Hans himself remains as a patient, there to experience his own decay and dissolution, while discussing with two fellow patients, the ascetic Naphta and the humanist Settembrini, conflicting world views embracing art, war, civilization, and the opposition of the mountain and the "Flatlands" below.

But even in the other great writers who had won laurels before 1914, the struggle with pessimism which we meet in Mann had surfaced. Anatole France's great skeptical books were produced shortly before the war. He more than balanced Colette's easy sensualism and acceptance of life. Conrad's symbolic *Lord Jim* and "Heart of Darkness" plumb the depths of loneliness, corruption, and the struggle for self-mastery in a world which appears alternately as a hostile jungle or a terrifying sea. Galsworthy's trilogy, *The Forsyte Saga*, was a publisher's invention, a sales trick to sell books that had originally appeared separately. But in the separate books—*A Man of Property*, for example—the condemnation of upper-middle-class life turns in part on Galsworthy's idea that "liberal" men treat their wives as just another kind of property.

Even before the war, therefore, writers were saying clearly what the industrialist Rathenau sensed in the Berlin streets in 1911: "Wherever I turn, I see shadows . . . when I consider the insane way we flaunt our wealth; when I hear the . . . sabre-rattling speeches."[51]

The First World War produced one variety of writing in which the disillusionment with Western values was straightforward—the war memoir, whether in drama, poetry, or the prose of journalism or the novel. Sometimes the memory was of a promising writer swept away with those slaughtered on the western front. Those French writers who wrote about the war, Jules Romains for example, and Apollinaire, did not forget those who died in it—Alain-Fournier and Charles Péguy among others. Dozens of Englishmen wrote war poetry and novels. But there were few who glorified war, and fewer who romanticized it as Hemingway did for Americans in *A Farewell to Arms*. From the defeated came the greatest seller of all antiwar novels, Erich Maria Remarque's *All Quiet on the Western Front (Im Westen nichts Neues)*, which evoked the slaughter and inhumanity, not the incompetence satirized in *What Price Glory*.[52] The German found nothing funny in the deaths of innocents destroyed on assembly-line principles.

Yeats sensed better than most what the war meant for those just old enough to fight in it, or young enough to miss service but not too young to grasp the devastation:

> Things fall apart; the centre cannot hold;
> Mere anarchy is loosed upon the world,
> The blood-dimmed tide is loosed, and everywhere
> The ceremony of innocence is drowned;
> The best lack all conviction, while the worst
> Are full of passionate intensity.[53]

Yeats was certainly right in his insight. The worst were full of passionate intensity, for example the Italian futurist, Filippo Marinetti. His *Futurist Manifesto (Mafarka le futuriste)* had sounded one characteristic note as early as 1909, praising the "beauty of speed," while also prophesying that in the coming age there would be no beauty but in struggle: "Our praise is for the man at the wheel . . . in struggle, no masterpiece can be anything but aggressive, and hence we glorify war. . . ." And, after the war, the best did often seem to lack all conviction. The poet Rilke[54] gave up Roman Catholicism for mysticism, and his poetry traces what he called his "search for death" amidst the ruins created by his own egotism. Yet his lyrics are undeniably great. T. S. Eliot (1888–1965) published his *Waste Land* in 1922. This poem, one of the major influences on English literature between the

51. Quoted in Raymond J. Sontag, *A Broken World, 1919–1939* (New York: Harper & Row, Publishers, Torchbooks, 1971), p. 166.
52. By Maxwell Anderson, the American playwright, in collaboration with Laurence Stallings.
53. "The Second Coming," lines 3–8. Reprinted with permission of Macmillan Publishing Co., Inc., M. B. Yeats, and Macmillan Co. of Canada from *Collected Poems* by William Butler Yeats. Copyright 1924 by Macmillan Publishing Co., Inc., renewed 1952 by Bertha Georgie Yeats.
54. Rainer Maria Rilke, 1875–1926.

wars, projected a sense of drift, hopeless, helpless, filled with images of decay, sterility, and the general dissolution of society. In lines reminiscent of Chaucer, Eliot also recalled the April campaigns in France:

> April is the cruellest month, breeding
> Lilacs out of the dead land, mixing
> Memory and desire, stirring
> Dull roots with spring rain.[55]

While Eliot complained about a life measured out "with coffee spoons,"[56] Franz Kafka (1883–1924) made a different complaint. Himself the victim of tuberculosis and a patient for long stays in dreadful sanatoriums, Kafka was a minor bureaucrat from Prague. His experience of the labyrinthine government of the decadent Habsburg Empire prompted his two great symbolic masterpieces, *The Castle (Das Schloss)* and *The Trial (Der Prozess)*. His characters are pilgrims in an alien world, bound for some unknown destination, under arrest for unknown crimes, forced to deal with officials with whom they cannot communicate. Their very helplessness bears down on them relentlessly, until the full irrationality of the world breeds in them a sense of guilt for merely living. The only hope is a distant one. The women in Kafka's novels refuse to accept the nightmare as reality; being less involved, they are less corrupted. The message was similar to that of the early German horror film, *The Cabinet of Dr. Caligari* (1939). In the film the audience is asked to accept life in an insane asylum as the "normal" state, making it impossible for the spectators to discern the lunatic murderers.

For writers of Kafka's age, there were few ties to the world of *la belle époque*, especially among young Germans. In 1928–1929, Ernst Gläzer[57]— all but forgotten now—published *Class of 1902 (Jahrgang 1902)*, a novel that went through six printings in German, with sales beyond 70,000 copies and translations in twenty-five languages. This pacifist novel took its title from the author's birth year, which also defined his military-service class. Just too young for the war, Gläzer remarked that war "established no moratorium on puberty." For those too young to give their bodies, there was the "tragedy of murdered minds and souls and diseased temperaments" in the civilian social body.[58] The children of the class of 1902 grew up to sense that they had been thrown into world history too fast, unprepared, without the guidance of fathers, who were dead or at least away in France, while the boy-men either slept with women deprived of mates or entertained elaborate fantasies of guilt over food gotten for them by women who seemed to honor the boys as if they were the heroes.

The newcomers in the literary world of the 1920s and the 1930s often took society as their theme. But they had little to be nostalgic about, in the manner of Proust, who admired the decadent aristocratic life he recalled. The "optimism" we do find was itself peculiar. In France, André Malraux (born in 1901) was a Communist adventurer who fought in China against the "fascists." His *Man's Fate (La Condition humaine)* represented the struggle for socialism in Asia in heroic terms but had an odd tincture of hero-worship and fatalism, as if the author were seeking a world in which

55. *The Waste Land*, lines 1–4, from *Collected Poems*, 1909–1962 (New York: Harcourt Brace Jovanovich, 1962; London: Faber and Faber, Ltd., 1962).
56. "The Love Song of J. Alfred Prufrock."
57. 1902–1962.
58. The quotes are from Peter Loewenberg, "Psycho-historical Origins of the Nazi Youth Cohort," *American Historical Review* 76 (1971): 1493.

free will might balance the blind forces of nature and so conspire to produce something beneficial to mankind. There was in this an echo of the pre-1914 literature, of the belief in individual solutions to problems and the liberal code that the person at odds with society can actually transform it.

It became increasingly difficult to maintain this posture in the 1920s and 1930s. Writers found it hard to find meaning in life except by fulfilling Yeats's prophecy and losing themselves in the exile of "society"—in Europe, where Hemingway sought release from his memory of driving an ambulance on the Italian front, or on Long Island and in Hollywood, where F. Scott Fitzgerald chronicled the dissolute life of businessmen who cheated at everything. Personal existence was not determined by personal experience; lives were shaped instead by an unpredictable flow of events beyond human control. This attitude encouraged some to explore sensation itself: D. H. Lawrence in his erotic novels, Aldous Huxley in his tales of London rebels against restraint, Jean-Paul Sartre in his philosophical writings.

Even a Communist, the German writer Bertolt Brecht (1898–1956) expressed a taste for anarchism and cynicism in his 1928 hit *Threepenny Opera*. But Brecht was one of the few Western Communists to break through the official veneer of Soviet society's literature of uplift, called Soviet social realism.[59] His plays and criticism in the early 1930s foretold the excesses of Stalinism, the prison camps, purges, thought control. Brecht's humane socialism found an English echo in the novels and journalism of George Orwell (1903–1950): in the condemnation of imperialism contained in *Burmese Days*; in the warning against fascism as Orwell came to know it in the Spanish Civil War, which he sounded in *Homage to Catalonia* in 1938; and in his critical essays on what he saw of the Communists in Spain, where the Moscow-oriented left betrayed other socialist and antifascist groups for *tactical advantages*.

Between D. H. Lawrence's brooding portrayal of the relations among men and women and among the classes in England and the prediction of a totalitarian utopia in Huxley's *Brave New World* (1932), Western literature in the late 1920s and early 1930s seemed caught between a love of irrational ecstasies and the superrational world of bureaucratic eugenics and thought control on Pavlov's psychological model. The few who were realists were no match for the "sympathizers," however. In the middle 1930s Eliot and Yeats espoused profascist and anti-Semitic views. Liberals looked to Stalin's Russia for light and hope. And all the while the fascists and Communists were squeezing the life out of democracy in Spain, Germany, Italy, Russia, the Baltic, and the Balkans. The war was coming.

BIBLIOGRAPHY

COLTON, JOEL. *Léon Blum: Humanist in Politics.* New York: Alfred A. Knopf, 1966. Excellent on the social problems of France.

EYCK, ERICH. *A History of the Weimar Republic.** 2 vols. Cambridge, Mass.: Harvard University Press, 1962–1963.

GALBRAITH, J. K. *The Great Crash.** Boston: Houghton Mifflin Co., 1955. A very readable account of the Depression.

JACKSON, GABRIEL. *The Spanish Republic and the Civil War.** Princeton: Princeton University Press, 1965. One of the two best accounts of the 1920s and 1930s; see also Stanley Payne, *The Spanish Revolution** (New York: W. W. Norton & Co., 1970).

Asterisk indicates a paperbound edition.

59. See Chapter 18.

KEYNES, J. M. *The Economic Consequences of the Peace*. New York: Harcourt, Brace & Howe, 1920. See also the rejoinder to Keynes's anti-French view by E. Mantoux, *The Carthaginian Peace** (New York: Oxford University Press, 1946).

LEDERER, IVO. *The Versailles Settlement*.* Boston: D. C. Heath, 1960. A useful anthology of the divergent views.

LEUCHTENBURG, WILLIAM. *The Perils of Prosperity*.* Chicago: University of Chicago Press, 1958. America in the 1920s.

MASARYK, T. G. *The Making of a State*. London: Allen & Unwin, 1927. A moving book on the Czech republic.

MAYER, ARNO J. *Politics and Diplomacy of Peacemaking: Containment and Counter-revolution at Versailles*.* New York: Random House, Vintage Books, 1967. A New Left analysis, continuing the work of Mayer's *Political Origins of the New Diplomacy** (New Haven: Yale University Press, 1959).

MOWAT, C. L. *Britain Between the Wars*.* Chicago: University of Chicago Press, 1955. The best survey; especially good on economic developments.

SETON-WATSON, HUGH. *Eastern Europe Between the Wars*.* New York: Harper & Row, Publishers, Torchbooks, 1951. The best English survey on the Balkans.

SONTAG, RAYMOND J. *A Broken World, 1919–1939*.* New York: Harper & Row, Publishers, Torchbooks, 1971. A systematic, lucid, and accurate survey, valuable also for the nondemocratic societies of the West. See also the relevant chapters in Lichtheim, *Europe in the Twentieth Century* (New York: Praeger Publishers, 1972).

16
DICTATORS AND TOTALITARIANS

> *We want to glorify war—the only cure for the world—militarism, patriotism, the destructive gesture of the anarchists . . . and contempt for women.*
>
> *We want to demolish museums, libraries, fight morality, feminism and all opportunism. . . .*
>
> *We will sing of great crowds agitated by work, pleasure and revolt; the multicolored and polyphonic surge of revolution in modern capitals. . . .*
>
> FILIPPO MARINETTI, *Futurist Manifesto* (1909)[1]

A NEW VOCABULARY

In the historical study of modern Western societies we face the paradox that the age of totalitarian despotism and widespread dictatorship took Europe by surprise. Yet there is evidence that some considered several forms of despotism and dictatorship the most likely course of social order in the new century. There was the grim prophecy of Nietzsche's *The Will to Power (Der Wille zur Macht),*[2] predicting the downfall of civilization in its present form. The new order would be a benign tyranny of philosopher-kings of American and Russian origins. And the world in which they ruled would be anti-Christian and *amoral*, judged by traditional standards. But Nietzsche had no grasp of the nature of totalitarian dictatorship.

Nor had scholars of law, economics, politics, and history. Weber, Pareto, Mosca,[3] Veblen, and their contemporaries pointed out the roots of bureaucratism, the "naturalness" of elitism, the social consequences of militarism, and the often antithetical nature of economic interests among workers and the rest of society. Students of the First World War stressed the impact it had because of its irrationality, its mass slaughter, and its elimination of distinctions between soldiers and civilians. But few thought that the way toward the future lay through a total disruption of Western traditions.

There was even less reason to suppose that the feeble revolutionary regime in Russia would endanger the West. In the years 1918–1921 it was honestly doubted that the Bolsheviks could survive Allied intervention and the international boycott imposed on Russia. The Soviet economy was in

1. Quoted in James Joll, *Intellectuals in Politics* (New York: Pantheon Books, 1961), pp. 139–140.
2. Especially paragraphs 972–980.
3. See Chapter 14.

danger of total collapse in 1921; and in that year it was certain that the Baltic states had been preserved from "Bolshevization."

It would have taken a pessimism greater even than Keynes's to predict correctly the wars in Europe's three political zones: the democratic Western states, the central zone of the legitimist constitutional monarchies of Hohenzollern and Habsburg, and the third zone, that between the Elbe and the Danube. Of course, observers might easily have seen that in the first zone both stable and unstable democracies existed. They might also have noticed that in the second zone constitutional monarchy had draped no more than a cloak of democratic additions over a dual heritage of absolutism and feudalism. And even a careless observer of the third zone might have stopped to consider the viability there of constitutional democracy. Not only was Russia already in Bolshevik hands. In the Balkan states a mainly agrarian social condition prevailed, with weak industrial bases, strong remnants of authoritarian churches and landlord politics, and widespread illiteracy. Only in the Baltic provinces and Poland had the Russian populations[4] been consistently oriented toward Western conceptions of society, including socialist ones.

Without pretending to gifts of prophecy, therefore, one might easily have supposed that, in the future, the political ideals and institutions of these three zones might come into conflict along their "frontiers." The "improvised" democracies had not been planted on promising soil. And this applied to the Soviet experiment as well as to the Weimar regime in postwar Germany—not only to the small states behind the eastern frontier.

The eastern democracies lacked the intellectual traditions and the institutional basis on which the democratic order in the West rested. In 1918 all of the improvised democracies lacked experienced politicians. The older ruling classes had been defeated or stripped of power by revolutionary actions. Economically and socially, the switch from an authoritarian regime to a democratic one would have benefited from a period of transition in which valid traditions of public order and self-government might have been nourished in a setting of social welfare. In the conditions that existed, however, dictatorships arose as a functional necessity: the new states could not be kept together on any other basis.

Even if we admit this, say in the cases of Estonia and Rumania, or Poland, Latvia, and Lithuania, or yet again in the Balkan monarchies, it does not follow that the *authoritarian states ruled by dictators had to become totalitarian states*, much less states on a fascist model. Our evidence is clear on this point. In Rumania and Estonia, for example, there existed strong fascist organizations, but the states were antifascist. We may even say that certain dictatorships were in self-conception "educational"; that is, the dictators viewed themselves as caretakers, proclaiming the dictatorship would vanish when the political and social conditions of stability had been shaped. It is worthwhile remembering that, in Lenin's Russia, it was official Marxist ideology that the "dictatorship of the proletariat" put in power in 1917 and exercised by the Communist party would "wither away." Other dictatorships had no ideological warrant for this educational phase, only the practical necessity, produced by historical events early in the life of a new state.

Moreover, it is not accurate to suppose that states with the *potential for dictatorship* necessarily became dictatorships, or that all dictatorships were authoritarian in a totalitarian sense or examples of fascism.

4. Before 1918, we must recall, these provinces were parts of the Russian Empire.

Finland was a democracy on the Western model until after 1945. During the Second World War, it was the only democracy allied with Nazi Germany, a circumstance derived almost wholly from the anti-Soviet attitudes of the Finns. The Swedish minority lost power in Finland after 1918, but it was never repressed. An ultrademocratic constitution existed until 1930, when a trend toward a stronger presidency surfaced, *as it did in America* after the victory of Roosevelt in 1932. No lasting dictatorship resulted in either place, however, as we know. Once the Communist party had been dismantled with the aid of antidemocratic fascists, the Finnish government divorced itself from the fascist, largely peasant-inspired Lappo movement. In the last prewar election—1937—the Finns voted massively against the parties with totalitarian ideas.

In Czechoslovakia, it is arguable that the same trend toward a temporary functional dictatorship combined with democratic constitutionalism appeared. The founder and first president of the republic, Thomáš Masaryk (1850–1937), the son of a Slovak coachman, governed in harness with his foreign minister Eduard Beneš (1884–1948). Masaryk fashioned a very strong presidency with the aid of Czech liberals once in the Austrian government. Masaryk was often ruthless against the Slovak clergy and their fascist supporters. But this "dictator of respect" adhered to the multiparty system and free elections, even in the midst of the crisis created by Hitler's efforts to promote the Nazi movement among the German minority in the republic. This functional and limited one-man rule by Masaryk was the antithesis of the Austrian situation, where Dollfuss created an ideologically dictatorial regime by means of a coup d'état in 1933. The one-sidedness of the new politics of the "Christian Corporate State" in Austria promoted race hatred against Jews and attacks using paramilitary units against the Social Democrats.

Hence in Austria we see the course run earlier in Italy and simultaneously in Germany: the conversion of a democracy improvised as a result of war into an ideologically fascist, narrow and fanatically aggressive, totalitarian state. The model for this type of revolution was made by Mussolini out of political instability and the Italian economic weaknesses, which were permanent in the south but a product of the suffering of war north of Naples. It is therefore to Mussolini's movement that we turn first, in seeking to grasp the nature of fascist totalitarian dictatorships.

FASCISM: ITS NATURE AND ROOTS

In 1918 there were no fascist states, no fascist parties, and no fascism. In the 1920s and 1930s numerous fascist states emerged, along with some authoritarian states tinged with fascist traits. These fascist states varied in their radicalness, their bases of political support, their racial policies, even the means used by the fascist movements to achieve power. While all fascist states were anticommunist[5] and nationalist, so, too, were many other states ruled by parties on the extreme right politically. These states also shared with fascist ones powerful hatred for liberalism and parliamentary democracy. But these shared traits do not entitle us to lump all right-wing movements together as fascist. The true fascist states developed an ideology refined among the leaders of what had once been tiny fascist "movements." And this ideology, which first was incorporated in a party out of power, became the motive force of state policy.

5. And anti-Marxist in particular.

The essence of fascism[6] is the binding together of a movement, party, people, or state by means of an ideology seeking to eliminate the regimes of parties, of democratic pluralism, and to replace such regimes by an authoritarian state. This state is *corporative* in nature, which is to say that it appears to be a single body politic, a state in which the "party" based on an earlier "movement" gains control of the entire machinery of the state. The party, once in power, forges a perfect overlap or identity of membership with the actual government of the state. Naturally, not all party members become officials; but all officials must in theory be party members. Hence fascist movements were in origin elitist, fascist parties were exclusive, and fascist states were established by relatively small cadres who struggled for power. The fascists therefore were at bottom organized on the lines of select paramilitary parties, the main purpose of which was to take over a state's government and thus assume total control over the society.

The uniformed fascists[7] claimed to be in possession of a special truth about state and society. The basis for the fascists of both Italy and Germany was nation and race, or what we might properly call the "myth" on which all fascist ideology rested: that there was some racial basis for the state and that the duty of the party was to purify the state of people not racially part of the true "nation" while at the same time spreading the state to all territories inhabited by the "nation." Obviously, states with large irredentist claims—Italy, Austria, Hungary, or Germany after 1918—were states which might prove good ground for fascism. We will recall that Mussolini broke with the Italian Socialists because they originally opposed entry into the First World War; Mussolini saw in the war a vehicle for the satisfaction of Italy's nineteenth-century claims to the "Italian" Alps, the Adriatic coast, and the "unredeemed" lands Italians had colonized in Africa.

Fascist ideology, however, was not merely an amalgam of nationalism and racism. The fascist myth rested also on a vision, often wildly distorted, of a grand past—in Mussolini's case the ancient Roman Empire, from which the symbol of power itself derived. For Hitler the pure stock was not the "Latin" people but the "Aryan" race of ancient Germans, from whom he took the swastika as a symbol for his movement.[8] Also essential to fascism was the cult of leadership. Fascist movements became parties centered in a "leader"[9] to whom semidivine qualities were attributed: perfection, absolute rectitude, prophetic vision. In fact the great fascist leaders possessed amazing charisma, or qualities of personal force, which appeared to followers as a combination of demonic energy, "spiritual" presence, and oratorical skill.

This magnetism was genuine, but it was augmented by very careful publicity of the kind familiar in the saints' cults of an earlier age. Indeed, the essentially "religious" ecstasy obvious in followers at huge outdoor meetings had parallels in the gatherings of Christians who listened to the preachers of Crusade in medieval Europe and was, in fact, not unlike the spirit that prevailed among the audiences at modern music "happenings" in the 1960s. The cult-worship aspect in fascism also derived support from another element of the myth. Because the early movements were small and oriented toward street violence, "defeats" were common in the history of

6. Which Mussolini derived as a name from the ancient Roman symbol of power, the *fasces*, a bundle of rods containing an ax, banded together and carried before magistrates.
7. Mussolini's Blackshirts, Hitler's Brownshirts.
8. The swastika is basically a cross with the extremes of the bars bent at right angles. It was a geometric decorative motif in prehistoric Europe and in prehistoric America. The Nazis were in error in supposing it was exclusively "Aryan."
9. German *Führer*, Italian *Duce*.

fascism. Such defeats produced "martyrs" whose deeds were remembered in mass meetings and also supplied themes for "religious" marching songs.[10] The dead were invoked in much the way patron saints had once been urged to "march in spirit with us."[11] The fascists thus played on love as well as on hate.

The quasi-religious cult aspects of leadership and the celebration of martyrdom were two bases for the later mass appeal exhibited by fascism. But it would be wrong to attribute to mislaid religious needs the broad support for Mussolini or Hitler and the other fascist dictators. Fascism drew its followers from every segment of society, especially from people who had been uprooted or socially displaced, whether the cause of the loss of place was economic, political, or military.

In the postwar period many people in every social rank had frightening experiences of hunger, unemployment, deprivation of parents, loss of "national" identity, and revolution. Sons deprived of fathers or aware of the disgrace of defeat were eager cohorts for Nazi recruiters in the schools and universities. Leader, party, and ideological certainty attracted persons not securely rooted either personally or socially. Older citizens had a sense of loss with regard to authority. Kaisers and kings were gone; and in their place people often saw no stable political regime to reassure them that traditions of law and order could be maintained. The postwar inflation hit especially hard the lower middle classes, composed of artisans, shop-keepers, office workers, small farmers, and certain military people.

In Germany the lower levels of the officer corps and the professional noncommissioned officers had no employment or prospect of jobs, given the Versailles terms of peace. Fascism's strategy of street fighting and its paramilitary organizations provided a natural focal point for men whose world before the peace had revolved on the axis of war. The Rumanian leader Corneliu Zelea Codreanu (1899–1938) gathered his Iron Guard[12] in battles against Jews and other national "political enemies," confessing that his followers loved battle for its own sake. The fascist movements all promoted respect for old-fashioned "military" virtues—order, discipline, and leadership. Codreanu was a graduate of a military academy as well as an ardent anti-Communist. In this context it is significant that he organized his movement in 1919, in a year of strong "left" revolutionary threats to new governments.[13] The Rumanian fascist movement also had a strong basis in anti-Semitism, as did other right-wing movements. Anti-Communist agitators often pointed to the fact that Christian Europe's most obvious "national" enemies were the cosmopolitan Jews, the "stateless" and "racially unpure" people whom fascists placed at the heart of the international "conspiracy" of Communism. The practice of singling out the Jews as a focus for racist ideologies predated the Bolshevik Revolution in Russia, however; and the idea that the Jews were a threat, because of their purported association with Bolshevism,[14] was one twist in a long, tangled

10. The most famous was the German "Horst Wessel Song." Wessel was a Nazi "martyr" allegedly killed in a brawl by Communists.
11. See F. L. Carsten, *The Rise of Fascism* (Berkeley: University of California Press, 1969), p. 232.
12. Formed officially in 1926.
13. In Germany and Hungary "Soviet" republics were proclaimed, in Munich and Budapest. In Italy workers "occupied" factories in 1919 in what was the prelude to widespread strikes and riots by workers and peasants.
14. Leon Trotsky and some other Jewish Marxists did play an important role in the Bolshevik Revolution, notably Martov and other former members of the Jewish Social Democratic party, known as the Bund.

One of the most popular and imaginative artists of this century, Russian-born Marc Chagall has spent his life trying to interpret the Jewish experience of his background. The Sabbath *is an early work painted before the artist left Russia for France. An orthodox family remains quietly at home on their holy day, with only the ticking clock breaking the silence. In view of later events the painting seems metaphoric of the tragic fate awaiting European Jews. Before the rise of Hitler, Russian anti-Semitism had for generations been particularly violent; more subtle discrimination existed in the West. Jews were mistrusted as outsiders and made the scapegoats for society's ills in a variety of European countries.*
Wallraf-Richartz Museum, Cologne.

skein of European anti-Semitism and the role played by it in totalitarian systems.

It is a part of the story of fascism, however, because of the racist character of fascist ideas in general, and the availability to fascist leaders of coherent anti-Semitic traditions throughout the West. Moreover, one of the most important facets of the totalitarian era of Western history is the confluence of anti-Semitism and anti-Communism in the minds of men like Hitler. The Nazis carried out the extermination of nearly six million Jews from 1939 to 1945, under the dual pressures of the reality of the new world war and the racial myths of *Volk* made explicit in *Mein Kampf*, Hitler's political testament.

Ironically, much of fascist anti-Semitism had as its chief source book a Russian forgery from the *czarist* era. Nicholas II's police had fabricated an alleged Jewish master plan for world dominion, the *Protocols of the Elders of Zion*. After the assassination of Czar Alexander II in 1881, czarist policy became officially anti-Semitic. The immediate cause was doubtless the fact that one of the assassins was a Jewish girl.[15] But Russian anti-Semitism had existed for generations before 1881 and has survived into our own time. In 1881 the murder became the excuse for official racism and the pogroms, or

15. Hestia Helfmann. Even more ironic is her German background. The *Protocols* users always showed how Russian Jews who were Communists attacked "Western" European ideals. Marx was a German Jew by birth!

orgies of terror, slaughter, and rape, which endured until 1892–1893, before their renewal on a mass scale in 1903.

As early as 1881, therefore, a European government had introduced purposively into politics the systematic slaughter of a people. Before that time Russia's Jews had been forced into a miserable life in the so-called Pale of Settlement, in the Empire's western and southern regions. There they had lived either as a factory proletariat, chiefly in the clothing industry, or in the roles of economically marginal people: coachmen, tailors, moneylenders, and cobblers. In 1881, however, the minister Pobiedonostev decreed as the Jewish fate death, emigration, and assimilation, with one-third of the people slated for each end. His declaration was the herald of the ghetto system. Jews were not allowed to settle in rural Russia, even within the pale; they were disfranchised, barred from the legal profession, put under quotas for school admission, evicted from their homes, and forcibly "resettled." A regime under great internal stress had relieved some of the social pressure on it by introducing mob violence against the "enemies" of the "people."

Elsewhere in Europe the Jews had also been made the scapegoat for the failures of social systems. In France journals and leagues to combat "Jewish finance" flourished in the 1880s, and books like *Jewish France in Public Opinion*[16] prepared the ground for the Dreyfus Affair and the *Action Française* (French Movement). This movement identified the Jews as "anti-French" and an element of social disintegration, along with democracy, feminine weakness, Marxism, and anarchism. *Action Française* was a middle-class reaction to defeat and defeatism based on the elitist idea of the "party" making history by leading the masses toward a purer state. After 1906 street battles and paramilitary activities were an essential part of its nationalistic and racist violence against republican democracy. Under its founder Charles Maurras the movement also exhibited other fascist traits—the leadership cult, for example. Like earlier French movements of

The Russian Empire comprised almost half of the world's Jewish population by the beginning of the twentieth century. An unwanted minority, the Jews were subjected to harsh restrictions, permitted to live only in certain places, such as the poor village shown above. Riots, or pogroms, directed against Russia's Jews, and often simply watched by Russian soldiers and police, became frequent occurrences; a pogrom at Easter time in 1903 lasted three days, massacring hundreds of Jews in the city of Kishinev; a pogrom in Odessa two years later took the lives of hundreds of Jews, wounded thousands, and destroyed over 40,000 homes and shops. Yivo Institute for Jewish Research, New York.

16. *La France juive devant l'opinion* (1886), by Édouard Drumont.

its sort, however, *Action Française* was a tiny minority movement before 1914.

The small Italian Nationalist party,[17] founded in 1910, was violently anti-Semitic, but in place of the Jews (who were a minor population element) the Italian proto-Fascists concentrated on the Arabs. It was by "Arabs"[18] that the Italians had been defeated and embarrassed in North Africa in the 1890s. This party was also anxious to reunite to Italy all unredeemed lands, and its founder Enrico Corradini had fought in Ethiopia. Moreover, the nationalist movement regarded authoritarian militarism as the model form of government. Corradini pointed to German and Japanese progress toward a state based on discipline and obedience, which the party preferred to the "decadent" democratic liberalism of the West. Before 1914, the Nationalist party never had a mass basis, and in 1913 it captured three seats in the legislature. This lack of electoral support it had in common with *Action Française.*

The situation for right-wing politics in conservative Germany was dismal in Bismarck's time, until the court preacher Adolf Stoecker tied his Christian Social Workers' party to anti-Semitism in 1878. He began to gather mass support then, by striking out against the Jews. Civil liberties were enjoyed by German Jews and some were prominent in journalism and finance. Stoecker combined a simple anti-Semitism with a shrewd grasp of the social discontent among peasants, artisans, officers, and small tradesmen as industrialization took hold in Prussia, especially in Berlin, where Jews were numerous. Early in the 1880s anti-Jewish riots became frequent; and this trend drew the support of responsible people. Heinrich von Treitschke, the greatest "nationalist" historian, published anti-Semitic papers. The philosopher Eugen Dühring formulated theories of Jewish inferiority. Some writers advocated driving the Jews out of central Europe as the necessary condition for purifying the German "nation." The most important spokesman for this view was Paul de Lagarde.[19] Perhaps the most significant idea Lagarde expressed was the need to "resettle" all Jews in Palestine, while Germanizing the eastern European areas bordering Russia. His follower Langbehn advocated close scrutiny of personal ancestry as a means of protecting the German citizenship from corruption.

In the 1890s, however, the nationalist anti-Semites experienced more reverses than accessions to their strength, partly because of conflicts within the movement and partly because the general prosperity after 1893 reduced the discontent among the lower middle classes. Extreme right-wing politics required large pools of hatred and resentment; and these were not yet available. Yet the propaganda of anti-Semitism continued. Also, small "parties" existed, including the Imperial Hammer League and the Germanic Order.[20] And as early as 1903 the black swastika on a white field enclosed by a red circle appeared among such groups. This was later taken over by Hitler's Nazi party. More important than this evidence of continuity of symbolism, however, was a gradual coalescence of militarist, nationalist, racist, and antidemocratic sentiments in literature and politics.

The later fascist movements in the German-speaking world had a solid ground on which to build, where the massive social disintegration produced by the defeat of 1918 spread. Writers like the British *émigré* Houston Stewart Chamberlain, in his *Foundations of the Nineteenth Century (Die Grundlagen das neunzehnten Jahrhunderts),* summarized the view that the

17. *Associazione Nazionalista Italiana.*
18. The Ethiopians were not primarily Arabs in fact, but Libyans were. Jews constituted only 0.1 percent of the Italian population in 1910.
19. The adoptive name of Paul Bötticher, 1827–1891.
20. Formed officially in 1912.

German *Volk* was a master race, and German soil and blood the elements from which the salvation of Europe would be compounded. His book sold over 100,000 copies before 1914, and after 1918 its central theme proved attractive to the defeated and the displaced. As early as 1904 the tiny Bavarian German Workers' party[21] had based its official program on the notion that the Jews were enemies of German civilization. Fourteen years later this party changed its name to the National Socialist German Workers' party, or the National Socialists.[22]

Similar movements thrived in Vienna, by 1910 a city of two million people, nearly 10 percent of whom were Jews. In the Austrian population Jews were about 5 percent of the whole, but 33.6 percent of all students at Vienna's famous university were Jewish. Doctors, lawyers, journalists, and liberal politicians of Jewish ancestry were therefore an easy target for the discontented at a time when the Viennese lower middle classes were increasingly under pressure economically.

Anti-Semitic politics in Vienna looked back to Georg Ritter von Schönerer (1842–1913), a parvenu noble who sat in the *Reichsrat* and gravitated toward nationalist and anti-Semitic circles. Schönerer's politics were never "popular," however, and his real base was among students resentful of Jewish competition. The popular mantle fell on Dr. Karl Lueger,[23] the famous mayor of Vienna who cleverly exploited anti-Semitism in local politics, between 1895 and 1910.

Meanwhile, Schönerer developed strong Pan-German ideas and the ideology of the *völkisch* German extremists. By 1913 Schönerer's liberal Pan-German movement had been transformed into the militant DAP, the forerunner of the NSDAP, anti-Marxist, anti-Slav, anti-Semitic, and antidemocratic. In 1914 the party program reached 45,000 members in 611 local branches. The essence of this program was the appeal to frightened workers to close ranks against capitalists, Social Democrats, and Jews.

These were the ideas later taken up by Adolf Hitler, the son of a minor Austrian customs officer, born in 1889, and a youth who at eighteen arrived in Vienna. From Lueger the young Hitler learned the central place of social questions among workers and also the techniques of mass propaganda. From Schönerer he took over the militant Pan-Germanism and anti-Semitism.[24] The city politics and the right-wing ideology available to Hitler were thus as important in shaping the Nazi dictator as was Mussolini's Fascist achievement in Italy.

THE FIRST FASCIST REVOLUTION

Mussolini had first made his mark as the astute editor of *Avanti*, the official paper of the Italian Socialist party. As we have seen,[25] however, he split with his colleagues over entry into the First World War. Deprived of his newspaper post on that account, he organized his own journal, *Il Popolo d'Italia* (The People of Italy) late in 1914. This caused the party to expel him, a move fateful for Italian socialism and for the future dictator. Mussolini nourished hatred for his former colleagues; and he formed also the first *Fasci*, a group aiming to force Italy into the war. Thus, in a matter of weeks, Mussolini had gone from one side of the political spectrum to another, driven there by a taste for war and nationalist ideas as well as by what his friends had done to him. Wounded in an accident in 1917,

---

21. *Deutsche Arbeiterpartei.*
22. *Nazionalsozialistische Deutsche Arbeiterpartei,* or NSDAP. *Nazi* was an abbreviation of the first word in the party's full name.
23. See Chapter 12.
24. Lueger was, of course, also anti-Semitic.
25. In Chapter 15.

Mussolini returned to journalism. And in 1918 he was openly advocating the suppression of socialism and the establishment of a nonparliamentary regime, justifying both demands by references to the "traitors" who had undermined Italy's war effort at home.

We will not repeat here the course of events leading to the famous March on Rome in 1922, nor the capitulation to Mussolini made by the king at that time. Rather, we will concentrate on the nature of Mussolini's movement and program, as the *Fasci di Combattimento* carried out the tactics of violence and agitation which Mussolini saw as the means to power. Suffice it to say that the road led past the gutted ruins of *Avanti*, which the Fascists attacked in 1919, with a military elite[26] drawn from the total strength of 15,000 members. For these were the early victories, not the results at the polls. When Mussolini stood for election to the parliament as an independent in Milan in 1919, he got less than 5,000 votes in a poll of 268,000! The Socialists were in the ascendant, gaining over half the total vote in 1919. In the 1920 local elections Socialists gained control over more than 25 percent of all communes and 30 percent of the Italian provincial governments.

Mussolini was refining both his tactics and his program. The program was interesting in its details: it advocated support for veterans, an Italy from the Alps to the Adriatic, opposition to Marxism, and the main outlines of a *radical* social policy. This social policy was anticapitalist and filled with worker-oriented proposals: progressive taxes on capital, universal suffrage, a "national" militia, minimum wage laws, nationalization (socialization) of strategic industries, seizure of Church property. Mussolini had already grasped the fact that to succeed, Fascism must outbid the Socialists for worker loyalties. In his "military" practices, he disguised his personal hatreds, condemning his enemies only as "antinational" and defeatist when they were Socialists, as "reactionaries" otherwise. The other essential step was the alliance entered into with the *arditi*, displaced expert soldiers trained in shock-troop tactics during the war. This private army promoted the program; and the program for veterans attracted new recruits to the private army. Mussolini in 1919 had already assembled the main elements of revolutionary Fascism.

The seizure of factories and farms in 1919–1920 terrified Italians who viewed such violent acts as the herald of revolution. So, too, had the decision of a part of the Socialist party to adhere to the Communist International.[27] As the government failed to respond strongly to these threats to stability, the middle classes began to look for a strong force to put down unrest; the fear of the Red Guards[28] was especially important in urban areas. Mussolini used these circumstances to woo industrialists, landowners, and the army. One decisive action was not initiated by the Fascists, however. The minister of war published a decree giving 80 percent of regular salaries to demobilized soldiers joining the Fascists!

Thus from an early time, officials of government gave support to the revolutionary party of the right. People in the education ministry encouraged discontented students to join Fascist *squadre d'azione* (action squads). Certain street toughs with no convictions in politics joined. These accessions of strength raised the number of local *fasci* units from 108 in

26. The *arditi*, or commandos.
27. The Third Communist International, proclaimed as the vanguard of international socialist revolution in March 1919. At the Livorno Congress in 1921 the Italian Socialist party split into Communists and Socialists.
28. Communist paramilitary units in northern Italy.

mid-1920 to over 1,000 eight months later. In order to achieve a true mass base, however, Mussolini now softened his former anti-Catholic stand and also hinted at cooperation with dissident Socialists. It had become his view that a league of Socialists, Fascists, and *Popolari*[29] now could dominate elections. But in fact he put the Fascists into coalition with the ultra-conservative National Bloc in 1921, and the Fascists won thirty-five seats.

The leader of a parliamentary group must appear moderate. Always an opportunist indifferent to the fate of his benefactors, Mussolini now talked of peaceful competition for power. The local Fascist cadres would not accept the softer line toward Socialists, however, or toward democracy. In order to preserve his position, he acceded to the demands of a party congress. The old radical social policy was abandoned in favor of a potpourri of nationalism, antisocialism, anti–trade unionism, anti-intellectualism, and antiparliamentarism. Before the March on Rome, therefore, Mussolini's movement was transformed into a true Fascist party, with 320,000 members in 2,300 local branches. Using its "army" to defend law and order and to suppress strikes, in 1922 Fascism was already acting as a state within the state. The government made no move against the party, even when on October 3, 1922, it published in *Il Popolo d'Italia* military rules, the oath of loyalty to the party, and provisions to divide Italy into military zones under Fascist control. This show of strength intimidated the government.

Mussolini's formal appointment as prime minister brought to power the thirty-nine-year-old Fascist *Duce*, decked out in his Blackshirt uniform and fresh from the fourth destruction of *Avanti*.[30] Mussolini was actually in coalition with other "nationalists"; but he personally served as prime minister, minister for home and foreign affairs, while Fascists headed the ministries of finance and justice and were in control of the "liberated" provinces. The Fascists already controlled the key posts, despite adhering to constitutional forms. Mussolini went to the legislature for support of his Declaration; and he got it, 306 to 116.

What the Declaration required was not full parliamentary power invested in the premier, but a limited grant of powers to rule by decree until the end of 1923. Then, the results of the decrees touching taxes, the budget, and economic reorganization were to be audited. Also, there were no dictatorial powers to suppress parliamentary institutions or non-Fascist papers and parties. The state of emergency had produced a Fascist ministry, out of the matrix of Fascist violence and Socialist "threats." But it was essential to further developments that the army and police support Fascist violence against the left. Had the armed forces opposed Mussolini early in 1923, he could not have made his ministry the springboard to a Fascist revolution and a totalitarian state.

Over the next five years the failure of the opposition to grasp the nature of Mussolini's intention proved fatal to it. Beginning in January 1923, the Fascist attack on the state, the parties, the press, and the parliament began. The first step was significant. Mussolini decreed an end to all paramilitary organizations; but the Blackshirts were made over into a voluntary Militia for National Security, on the state payroll, while swearing an oath to Mussolini, *not the king*.[31] The Militia was in fact a party army. Next, the Nationalist party of Corradini was absorbed by agreement. Confident of a

---

29. Members of the Catholic People's party, under Church influence.
30. The defender of law and order had given the order on October 29, as he left Milan for Rome!
31. In 1925 the form of the oath was changed, and loyalty was now pledged to Victor Emmanuel III.

majority in elections, Mussolini predicted a regime of sixty years! His confidence really rested on a new electoral law, profoundly antidemocratic. It required that any party with 25 percent of the vote would get two-thirds of the seats in the parliament, if it led the poll. The liberal opposition either abstained or secretly supported the bill, perhaps in the misguided belief they could thus keep Fascism in parliamentary channels. The new National Bloc—Fascists still were in it for electoral purposes—got 65 percent of the votes cast in the 1924 elections. The government took 403 seats, while the combined opposition gained 105. The popular poll was 4,500,000 to 1,745,000 in favor of the National Bloc over the combined opposition.

Italy had voted for stability, even if it portended one-man rule. Mussolini understood this, and, after calling in *Il Popolo d'Italia* for the death of Giacomo Matteotti, a Socialist deputy who demanded the restoration of freedom, Mussolini arranged the murder.[32] The Matteotti Affair provoked the left to withdraw from the legislature. This allowed Mussolini to make "reforms" and restore legal means of action. In fact, he had the support of the Church and the King as well as all classes who feared a Socialist revival. Shrewdly, Mussolini came out strongly against those who lived for violence, in an effort to reassure the army.[33] This caused a split in the Fascist movement itself, with the "Consuls" seeking to intimidate Mussolini by further acts of undisciplined violence against the left. Mussolini used the occasion to abolish press freedom, before giving in to the extremists early in 1925.

On January 3, 1925, in a parliamentary speech, Mussolini endorsed force against all opposition. His words are worth recording, because in them we see the mature Fascist position on politics. And it was this position that led directly to the consolidation of the totalitarian one-party state. *Il Duce* began by remarking that struggle was the rule of life and that opposed forces were reconciled by force. Then, marking the end of constitutional government, Mussolini said:

I have created this political, historical, and moral climate [of violence] by a propaganda which extends from the intervention in the Great War to the present day. . . . If fascism has become a criminal association . . . mine is the responsibility. . . . Italy wants peace, wants tranquility, wants industrial calm. . . . Rest assured that in the next 48 hours the situation will be clarified.[34]

This promise Mussolini kept. The Militia was authorized to arrest suspected persons. Opposition papers were suppressed, along with parties and political clubs. Opposition newspapers were forced to suspend publication. In 1945 Mussolini, looking back over twenty years of dictatorship, acknowledged that the Matteotti Affair had laid the foundation for the totalitarian state. Within a year even the liberal opposition had been eliminated entirely from the parliament, which now became the forum for the one-party state. In 1926 formal laws took the place of the "actions" of suppression, and a revolutionary tribunal was set up to deal with crimes against the state. Persons accused before it had no right to appeal, be tried before a jury, or even summon witnesses. Terror thus became the continuation of violence. Over the next eight years the tribunal deported thousands and condemned thousands of others to penal servitude within Italy.

32. The assassins were on the payroll of the minister of the interior, Mussolini. (Mussolini reserved for himself certain cabinet posts—minister of the interior being one of them.)
33. Which was concerned over its fate should the Militia become the most important military arm.
34. Quoted in Laura Fermi, *Mussolini* (Chicago: University of Chicago Press, 1961), pp. 245–246.

The economic structure of the state was made over, as all production workers had to be members of a syndicate, or corporation, pledged to the principle that the nation stands above individual interests and rights, such as labor strikes. There was to be no legal class self-defense after 1926; and in June of that year the state decreed increased hours of labor for workers at the same wages once paid for the shorter day. From 1927, the Charter of Labor gave industrialists rights against labor, by withdrawing the state from all pro-labor industrial regulation. The strike, collective bargaining, and picketing became illegal. The "Corporate State" no longer recognized class interests as valid expressions of social processes.

Power flowed steadily to the Fascist Grand Council, which in 1928 was incorporated into the constitution of the state. Government in fact became closed to all but Fascists. The Grand Council, Mussolini said, was the symbol of the unity of party and state. As such it chose deputies for the parliament, through the office of the party secretary.[35] What one-party rule meant politically became clear in the 1929 elections: the opposition polled approximately 136,000 votes; Mussolini's Fascists got more than 8,000,000 votes.

Popular support now was available for the full Fascist program. The *fasces* became the state emblem, just as the party song became the national anthem; earlier, of course, the party militia had become the state militia. Only the Church was not subordinate to the state and its totalitarian

35. The former party boss of Cremona, Roberto Farinacci.

Like Hitler in Germany, Benito Mussolini's promise to the Italian people was that he would make their government work again. Indeed, from the moment he came to power in 1922 Il Duce applied his formidable energy to overhauling the cumbersome Italian bureaucracy, and he met with success and widespread acclaim from the people. Mussolini's dream was to return Rome to its ancient political glory, exemplified by this picture of his face superimposed on the ancient ruins of the city. Because of the essentially weak Italian military, Mussolini was forced by Hitler into a puppetlike role during the war. Museo Aeronautico Caproni di Taliedo; Weidenfeld and Nicolson, Ltd.

programs. This deficiency was corrected in 1929, when Mussolini concluded the Lateran Treaty with the Holy See. In return for mutual diplomatic recognition[36] and an end to anticlerical policies, which had plagued the Church ever since the early days of unification, pope and dictator agreed. A small papal state was set up in which the Italian state had no legal powers. This state was compensated for the property taken from it by previous governments. Moreover, Mussolini restored ecclesiastical control over education. These were the prices to be paid for Church support in a strongly Catholic country, where Fascism and the Church were equally hostile to socialism and modern liberalism. Ideologically and in fact there were no longer any viable opposition groups, and Mussolini held in his own hands the offices of *Duce* of the ruling party and prime minister in the state now identified with it. The new totalitarianism had replaced one liberal state.

THE GERMAN CASE: HITLER AND THE RISE OF NAZI RULE

The victories of Fascism in Italy provoked sympathetic reactions in Europe, in places where distress was pronounced after 1919 or where strong protofascist groups had existed before. *Action Française* published fascist literature, including a book called *Le Fascisme*; and in 1925 the French Fascist party (*Faisceau*) was formally established. And the old followers of Lueger and Schönerer revived in Austria.

It was in Germany, however, that the movement of Mussolini attracted most attention. The military hero Ludendorff had been active in Bavarian politics and was in 1923 part of a smashed plot to organize a "March on Berlin" to overthrow the "Marxist" government. He had the support of the leader of the Bavarian National Socialist party, a disaffected ex-corporal named Hitler. They drew to Munich a mixed lot of nationalists and unemployed soldiers, but local authorities recognized that the National Socialists as plotters had received a shot in the arm from Mussolini's March. Hitler's friends had said openly on November 8, 1922, "We have in Bavaria our *Duce*. His name is Adolf Hitler."[37] Other associates hailed Mussolini and the 1922 coup as the "storm signals" given to decadent liberalism. Hitler, they proclaimed, would not see Germany go under to Marxism, democracy, and anarchism.[38] But the Munich plot failed miserably in November 1923, and Mussolini ridiculed the plotters as "buffoons."

It did not matter that Mussolini regarded the National Socialists as clownish imitators; events were to prove quite the opposite. What Hitler said and thought and did had more of an effect on the world than even Mussolini's rise.

But those who knew Hitler as an alienated young man before the First World War or in the five years between 1918 and his arrest after the abortive *Putsch* of 1923 could never have predicted his historical role. He had some charismatic qualities but had not yet written *Mein Kampf*, his jail-born account of how he had formed his "world outlook" (*Weltanschauung*), and a blueprint for a totalitarian state more thorough than Mussolini's.

On the surface, Hitler's youth seems without influences capable of explaining his later conduct as a leader. His father was illegitimate[39] but

36. A papal goal since 1870, when the Vatican had refused to recognize Rome as the capital of the new Italy, after the occupation of Rome.
37. Quoted from the newspaper *Popular Observer* (*Völkischer Beobachter*), in Carsten, *Rise of Fascism*, p. 80.
38. This was the recollection of Hitler's minister of propaganda, Joseph Goebbels (1897–1945), in a 1934 book, *Fascism*.
39. He was later legitimized.

nonetheless made the transition from cobbler to customs official. Alois Hitler died when his son Adolf was thirteen, when in fact Hitler had already imbibed Pan-German history from his teachers at Linz. Hitler's relations with his father were not good, probably in part because Hitler adored his mother, a lower-middle-class woman brutally treated by Alois. It was her death in 1908, however, that cast the adolescent Hitler into the melting pot of Vienna, an orphaned and rejected candidate for entry into an art school there, where he had first gone in 1907.

It was in Vienna that Hitler later placed his real schooling, hard but thorough, as he encountered poverty, Marxism, Jews, and personal defeats. Hitler in Vienna was a proletarian, but not by choice. The meager wages he earned from doing odd jobs and designing and selling painted postcards forced his income to the point of subsistence. He therefore lived in flophouses or hostels frequented by drunks, bums, and other social rejects. Loneliness and poverty drove him to fantasies which often took the form of long monologues, later rationalized as a result of not having had people to talk with from whom he might learn anything. Hitler thus learned to despise the working-class life, while becoming addicted to oratorical politicians who manipulated the masses. In Vienna Hitler also came to hate the socialists and the Jews, while blaming their influence over Austrian life on the Habsburgs. Austrian imperialism had defiled the city by admitting to it the inferior peoples of Eastern Europe; where the worst corrupted the best, none would be good—that is, truly German. This perception drove the Pan-German anti-Semite to Munich, a real German city, in 1913.

The research of historians skilled in handling biographical data on a psychological plane has made it clear that the roots of Hitler's personal rage and anti-Semitism were planted before 1907, however, and long before he left Vienna for Munich in 1913. Anti-Semitism is a continuous thread in Hitler's development, from his childhood to the point in time at which he made it the supporting principle of a whole society. It was also the most striking aspect of Hitler's pathological personality, the roots of which lay in his homelife.[40] Hitler's first *political* act in 1919 and his last political act in 1945 voiced his demand for the elimination of the Jews from Europe. But the literature he drank in between 1907 and 1912 fed a personality need; the books did not create it. This personality need was one of requiring objects in reality to which to transfer hate otherwise focused inwardly, in a self-destructive way. And in Hitler's case the evidence is clear: he thought himself contaminated by Jewish blood, through his paternal grandfather; he thought a Jewish doctor guilty of his mother's death; and he had strong incest-fantasies, which he thought a Jewish crime. There is evidence on all these points in Hitler's own secret police files, as well as on his sexual perversions, neurotic symptoms, and need to project beyond himself the demonic source of guilt. These things he took to Vienna and Munich. What he found there channeled the energy into political anti-Semitism.

World War I disrupted the Munich stay, however. Though an Austrian citizen, he joined a Bavarian regiment, fought in Belgium, was wounded and gassed. Apparently a courageous soldier, he was later promoted to corporal and, what is unusual, given the highest military decoration, the Iron Cross, both first and second class. The defeat of 1918 Hitler regarded as the result of a "stab in the back" by the German Social Democrats and

40. On the question of Hitler's pathology see Robert G. L. Waite, "Adolf Hitler's Anti-Semitism," in B. B. Wolman, ed., *The Psychoanalytic Interpretation of History* (New York: Basic Books, 1971), pp. 193–230; and also Walter Langer, *The Mind of Adolf Hitler* (New York: Basic Books, 1972).

the Jews. Hitler's personality seemed more secure in uniform than out; and in 1919 he had not yet been demobilized. In fact, his regiment commissioned him to spy on workers' political groups in Munich and also to see whether the German Workers' party there might be a useful ally for the discontented *Reichswehr* (army), who were outraged by the peace treaty.

Thus a rootless man whose inner world was tormented and whose outer world was in collapse found purpose in his life as a propagandist of the nationalist right among workers. In 1919 he joined the party executive, bringing with him a tremendous respect for military habits of discipline and blind obedience. Hitler exhibited a typical amalgam of right-wing hatreds and a tremendous ambition to do whatever lay in his power to reverse the defeat of 1918 which he felt had been signed by Jews, after honorable Germans had refused.[41] His ideas had been sharpened before the war by voracious reading; the war had merely confirmed his existing views, by putting him in danger, according to his own account, of being "gunned down by a Jew or Negro."

As a party recruit Hitler regarded himself as that rare being, a rational "programmatic thinker" who was also a politician: "Every power that does not come out of a firm intellectual base will remain wavering and insecure. It lacks the stability which can only rest on a fanatical *Weltanschauung.*"[42]

To this intellectual capacity and his oratorical skill he credited his rise in the National Socialist party. Hitler's rise was truly meteoric; starting as the lowest-ranking member of the executive committee, he became *Führer*, or leader, in 1921. Actually, he owed perhaps as much to the *Reichswehr*, which had backed him financially from 1919, and to the Bavarian state government, the Anti-Bolshevik League, and the wealthy industrialists in Munich who had better reasons to fear socialism than Italian followers of Mussolini had.

After the armistice in 1918, the chaos into which German political life sank provided all nationalist and paramilitary anti-Semites and anti-Socialists with a good field for action. The Weimar Republic under President Friedrich Ebert[43] was beset with the hardships imposed at Versailles. But it also had internal enemies with diverse motivations. When the January 1919 elections were held to return a national assembly on a universal suffrage, the old Reichstag parties reconstituted themselves. The Social Democrats were the strongest party; but they had no absolute majority. The government was thus one of coalitions between the minority Social Democrats, pledged to *democratic means*, and the liberals of the Center and Democratic parties. The Munich-based National Socialist party returned no legislators. It obviously could not foresee a rise to power by democratic means.

Thus the drawing up of the Weimar Constitution was entrusted to the Social Democrats. The Republic guaranteed full democracy, all civil rights and freedom of expression, the right for the electorate to initiate legislation by referendum, and a quasi-federal system immune to Prussian dominance. Moreover, the new state had powers to nationalize industries and to control the economy by means of local and central councils. The difficulty was therefore not in the theory of the regime, which was a model of parliamentary democracy, but in the total social situation. Germany had no tradition of democracy. The economy was in a state of collapse. The

41. The new deputation of Social Democrats included several Jewish members. Hitler never forgot this, attributing to the first delegation, which had refused the terms, the motives of patriotism he denied to the second.
42. *Mein Kampf*, trans. Alvin Johnson (Boston: Houghton Mifflin, 1939), p. 222.
43. 1871–1925; he was succeeded as president by Hindenburg in 1925.

elections of 1919 were undermined by the terms imposed several months later at Versailles; in the 1920 elections the government coalition lost many seats. And the constitution itself also suffered from the discredit accruing to the governments formed under it. Germans who gave support to democracy early in 1919 often did so because they hoped to obtain a liberal peace and admission to the League of Nations in exchange. None of this came to pass.

The peace had reduced Germany territorially and in natural resources. Army men wanted to refuse the terms, but Hindenburg and other military leaders saw that this was impossible. Some officers continued, however, to feed right-wing discontent, alleging that Germany had been betrayed by its enemies, chiefly Jews like Hugo Preuss[44] and Walter Rathenau.[45] There were also many officials and judges who used their powers in an unconstitutional way, often to wrong people who favored the constitution.

The most powerful enemies of the Republic, however, were in the Free Corps (*Freikorps*), comprising groups of young militants financed after 1919 by the Anti-Bolshevik League.[46] The pretext in 1919 for the Free Corps was the Red risings of January in Berlin and February in Munich and also the wave of strikes across Germany. There were also hostile Polish forces on the eastern frontier. The government therefore gave tacit support to the Free Corps units, who fought in the Baltic against Soviet forces also. Military men entered the Free Corps for a variety of reasons, but above all it was an opportunity to use the only skill they had. It made relatively little difference whether the "enemy" was Soviet, Polish, Jewish, or republican. The infamous Ehrhardt Brigade refused to use the new red, black, and green Weimar flag, preferring instead the imperial red, black, and white. Significantly, a racist myth showed in Free Corps insignia: uniforms had Viking ships on the sleeve and the swastika on the steel helmets; the death's-head later taken over by the Nazis also appeared.

More important than the symbols of the German racist national myth were Free Corps actions. In Berlin, after suppressing the Communist rising, Free Corpsmen killed Rosa Luxemburg and Karl Liebknecht.[47] When Free Corps units overthrew the Munich Soviet, they executed many Socialists, anarchists, and even republican intellectuals. In 1920 Free Corps units made an abortive coup against Ebert's government.[48] Already, the Free Corps were engaged in anti-Semitic assaults; and by the time the 100,000 or more Corpsmen were disbanded, frightful persecutions of Jews had entered political tactics. By 1921, therefore, German political life had embedded in it the symbols and tactics which Hitler perfected.

As *Führer* of the National Socialist party in Munich, Hitler brought into it ex-officers and Free Corps people. Quick to respond to the lure of anti-Semitism, he went beyond mere slanders. Soon, he was using paramilitary units in the Fascist way, to beat his rivals, destroy their meetings, damage their presses, and otherwise intimidate the political left. Hitler organized "Protective Detachments" and "Assault Detachments" with the help of Captain Ernst Röhm, the head of the SA.[49] The *Reichswehr* and Free Corps were therefore instrumental in Nazi tactics, until in 1923 the Munich *Putsch*

44. Preuss was a Democrat and the chief architect of the Weimar Constitution.
45. The industrialist responsible for managing the war effort; he was assassinated in 1922.
46. The greatest industrialists were the heaviest contributors: Krupp, Stinnes, Vögler, Röchling, and others.
47. The founders of the Spartacus party, which in 1918 was transformed into the German Communist party.
48. The "Kapp *Putsch*," after Dr. Wolfgang Kapp, the head of the new government; this government fell in a few days.
49. An abbreviation of the German names for these units: *Schutzabteilung* and *Sturmabteilung*. The latter name gave rise to the popular term "storm troopers."

In November 1923 the German National Socialists tried to seize the government of Bavaria, attempting even a march on Berlin. Hitler, depicted here by a Nazi artist as he makes his plans, signaled the start of the uprising in a Munich beer hall. Firing a revolver at the ceiling, Hitler proclaimed to his Brownshirt followers the beginning of a "national revolution." Though the so-called Beer Hall Putsch was quickly suppressed and Hitler was sentenced to five years in jail, he was released within less than a year. And he had used his prison term to write Mein Kampf. Radio Times Hulton Picture Library.

failed and caused Hitler to digest its lessons, in the solitude of his imprisonment in the fortress of Landsberg.

Earlier, enormous economic disturbance and the French seizure of the Ruhr had led to the fall of the government. The new chancellor was Gustav Stresemann (1878–1929), a right-of-center Nationalist opposed to extremism of any sort.[50] Aside from the externally induced stress, in Bavaria Stresemann faced a virtual secession movement backed by civil and military elements, including Hitler and Ludendorff. In order to win Reichswehr support for the central government, however, Stresemann allowed the army to suppress the Socialist-Communist state governments in Saxony and Thuringia on October 29. This did not satisfy the Bavarians and Hitler, and on November 8, 1923, the Führer burst into a beer hall[51] to force the Bavarian premier to declare a "March on Berlin." Agreeing under duress, the premier von Kahr retracted his support once free; and on November 9 Bavarian police and Hitler's demonstrators exchanged shots. Apprehended, Hitler was sentenced to five years in prison, an incredibly mild sentence for treason.

This mildness was merely another piece of evidence showing Hitler the feeble support for the Republic; and Hitler drew certain conclusions from the Putsch. Stresemann might succeed in bringing Germany back into Europe on better terms after 1923. Indeed, as we know, he did. But Hitler in prison decided that the time for SA thrusts had not yet come. Either the Reichswehr itself must assault the state, or the Nazi movement must gain a mass base. Both were unlikely to come about in the conditions of 1924, with

50. He remained chancellor for only one hundred days. He was foreign minister from 1923 until his death.
51. The Bürgerbräu Cellar in Munich.

prosperity beckoning Germans, or in 1926, when admission to the League of Nations was granted. Hitler therefore decided to make the Nazi party a law-abiding political force. To do this, he revived the 1920 program: all Germans must exist in one state; Jews must be excluded from citizenship; parliamentary government must yield to a more stable authoritarian regime.

This was also the old-fashioned line of the conservative parliamentary German National People's party, which in 1924 had taken 95 seats in the Reichstag. What distinguished the National Socialists from the DNVP[52] was the social program. In Berlin, for example, the Nazis emphasized socialist reforms to attract workers, with the result that propagandist Goebbels and party-organizer Gregor Strasser were slowly building a politically popular party. Nonetheless, while the Nazis captured 32 seats in the first 1924 election, they fell back to 14 later that year and to 12 in 1928. The years 1924–1929, therefore, were not years of great electoral successes; they were years of internal success for Hitler in his struggle to control the party. He had gained the total support of Goebbels in Berlin; he had subordinated Röhm's SA; he had formed the famous SS,[53] sworn directly to him, as the militia members in Italy were pledged to Mussolini.

Yet in 1927 the actual party membership was about 40,000—hardly a basis for effective parliamentary action. On the plus side, Hitler had shown a genius for organization that might prove fruitful, even admitting the reluctance of the military and the industrialists to disrupt the peace and prosperity of the late 1920s. Hitler had organized effectively small groups of professionals in 1928: Nazi lawyers, Nazi teachers, and Nazi physicians, in a series of associations.

More promising was the establishment of the Hitler Youth Organization, or *Hitler Jugend,* which was later to be paralleled by a "League of German Girls."[54] The youth who were coming of age in the decade of bitter defeat had experienced emotionally traumatic childhoods. Their politics were as yet unknown, but from 1928 to 1933 6.5 million first-time voters came of age, while more than 3 million former voters died.[55] In 1928 over 30 million votes were cast, with the Nazis taking only 2.6 percent, or about 810,000, which gave them 12 seats. Some 3.5 million eligible young voters did not go to the polls, uninspired by "normalcy" and not unhappy over the state of the economy.

It was to the voters among this enormous reserve that Hitler made his emotional appeals. Nazi propaganda focused on the elders who had betrayed the German future. Party slogans stressed that old men must give place to young people, and that "National Socialism is the organized will of

---

52. The abbreviation for German National People's party (*Deutsche Nationalvolkspartei*).
53. From *Schutzstaffel,* or bodyguard.
54. *Bund-Deutscher-Madel.*
55. A net shift of more than 9 million potential voters in an electorate of about 30 million!

Like Otto Dix, Georg Grosz was another leading German realist working between the wars. Even more savagely than Dix, Grosz took as his target the corrupt, greedy elements who controlled Germany. In The Pillars of Society (1926) priests, soldiers, politicians, and businessmen are all caricatured as evil, self-serving creatures.
Perhaps most frightening of all the figures is the Nazi in the foreground: his scarred cheek and sword in hand reveal the sadomasochistic tendencies of Hitler's early followers. From his head springs a knight in armor charging forth to avenge the national honor. Grosz's painful works form one of the most stinging indictments against humanity in a century filled with artistic pessimism and despair.
Nationalgalerie, Berlin.

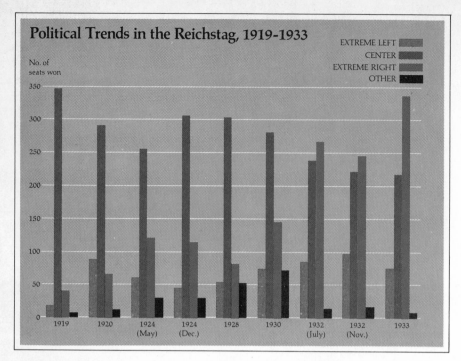

Political Trends in the Reichstag, 1919-1933

EXTREME LEFT
CENTER
EXTREME RIGHT
OTHER

No. of
seats won

350 — 300 — 250 — 200 — 150 — 100 — 50 — 0

1919   1920   1924 (May)   1924 (Dec.)   1928   1930   1932 (July)   1932 (Nov.)   1933

youth.''[56] What Hitler desperately needed was publicity, new issues, and great unrest.

The year 1929 provided all three. The publisher Hugenberg[57] gave to Hitler the support of his press syndicate for a campaign against the Young Plan. This was a proposal to exchange immediate termination of the Rhineland occupation for two things: new German guarantees of the 1919 borders and the conversion of reparations debts to a fixed amount of 110,735 million Reichsmarks.[58] Stresemann died just after negotiating this agreement, only a few weeks before the New York Stock Exchange crash. Both events weakened German political stability. Unemployment had already soared over the million mark. Hitler therefore campaigned early in 1930 against the Young Plan, the Weimar system, and the Jews and other ''criminal'' elements left over from the black days of 1918–1919. His pledge to restore old German borders promised new food supplies and new jobs for all.

It is interesting to look at the Nazi electoral success up until January 30, 1933, when ''Adolf *Légalité''*[59] became chancellor, against the background of the economics of unemployment. The percentage of trade unionists either wholly unemployed or on part time rose as follows from 1929 to 1932:

	Unemployed	Short-timers
1929	14.6	9.4
1930	24.4	16.2
1931	37.0	21.7
1932	48.0	24.2

56. G. Loewenberg, *Parliament in the German Political System* (Ithaca: Cornell University Press, 1969), p. 1469.
57. Alfred Hugenberg, leader of the Nationalists (members of the German National People's party).
58. Payable over sixty years.
59. Lawful Adolf, as the more extremist opponents on the right derisively called him.

During the same years apprentice positions for young men fell off in the steel industry alone by over 113,000. The Nazi share of the vote went from 2.6 percent to 37.4 percent. The party had held only 12 seats in 1928; in 1932 it captured 230 and was the largest single party in the Reichstag.

In March 1933, in the last free election, five weeks after Hitler came to power as chancellor, the Nazis took 17,277,200 votes, or 43.9 percent. Unemployment ran to 6,000,000. And in that election over 88 percent of the electorate voted. Of all voters, 30.1 percent were in the age group from eighteen to thirty; about 42 percent voted Nazi, a result surpassed in student elections even as early as 1930. The Nazi students were already in an absolute majority before the Nazi party broke through to hold the majority of the Reichstag seats. Among the young the program of "blood and soil," *Volk* and culture made Hitler's political investment in the young a flash of genius. He was the snail among greyhounds prior to the Depression! Patriotic oratory and unemployment catapulted the Nazis to power, with the aid of the troubled youth of Germany.

The 1930 election brought to the chancellorship Brüning, a Center party opponent of Nazism. He had Social Democrat support, but his program of cutting social benefits helped Hitler, while dividing the conservative Nationalists. Brüning ruled by emergency powers, publishing decrees, as he was authorized to do by Article 48 of the Weimar Constitution. But his policy of high tariffs and support for failing industrialists was pale beside the vivid campaign of Hitler against the Versailles Treaty. Hitler was the leader youth needed psychologically, a substitute father in the German mold, stern but loving, violent but promising rewards, and above all providing outlets for frustrations in the Wagnerian meetings, ceremonies, rhetoric, and passion. While politicians of the old parties promised economies, Hitler conjured up a vision of a "third empire," in which there would be a great German state devoid of Jews and Marxists: *Ein Volk, ein Reich, ein Führer*: One People, One Empire, One Leader! And the SA grew as fast as party rolls swelled: the one increased from about 18,000 to 600,000 from

Above, a painting by Hans Grundig depicts a 1932 meeting of German Communists. In the early 1930s Communism in Germany seemed a bigger threat than fascism. Communist representation in the Reichstag had almost doubled during the early Depression years, rising steadily from 54 seats in 1928 to 100 in November of 1932. But the left, divided internally, was no match for the Nazis, especially after leaders of business and industry threw their support to the anti-Communist Hitler. In 1933, when Hitler became chancellor, the Communist party was outlawed. Nationalgalerie, Berlin.

1929 to 1932; the other from about 120,000 to 800,000. Street fights against Communists were daily events in this period. The big industrialists were pouring money into Hitler's organizations.

The final break for Hitler was given by old Hindenburg. In May 1932 he helped drive Chancellor Brüning from office, resorting to a "presidential" Ministry of Barons lacking a Reichstag basis. This unconstitutional policy entrusted power to Franz von Papen, a Catholic allied by marriage to Ruhr industrialists. Papen overthrew Social Democrat state governments illegally. But Hindenburg and Papen wished to avoid a direct rejection of the Republic. This drove them to seek a popular mandate in July 1932; and in it the antidemocratic parties held the parliament in pawn, taking over half the seats.[60] Hitler, as the leader of the most numerous party, was constitutionally able to claim the post of chancellor. Hindenburg refused to allow this; and he had army support. This drove the Nazis into violent opposition, in the streets and in the Reichstag. A sharp division in the governing group ensued in December 1932. And after a brief period of ministerial switches, Hindenburg proposed to Hitler a "presidential" chancellorship, with military and industrial support. Hindenburg's hope was to keep Hitler a figurehead, subordinate to Papen, Hugenberg, and other anti-SA elements.

The illusions of every politician were smashed immediately. The Nazis staged mass parades in every major city the night of January 30. This was followed by a wave of SA terror, which culminated in the burning of the Reichstag building on February 27. This was blamed on the left, and Hitler's *Hilfspolizei*[61] took reprisals at will. On March 2, 1933, Hitler allowed "protective custody" measures, a euphemism for concentration camps. It was this atmosphere of officially inspired violence that governed the "free election" of March 1933, without press freedom, freedom from arrest, freedom of speech, or the right to hold public meetings.[62] On March 23 the new Reichstag under Nazi control[63] gave Hitler dictatorial powers; only the Social Democrats voted against this measure and the companion law suspending the constitution. Armed with this "Enabling Act," Hitler did in Germany in less than five months what it had taken Mussolini five years to do: on July 14, 1933, a cabinet decree made into law a one-party state.

The Enabling Act was passed by deputies either sympathetic to Hitler's totalitarian ideology or intimidated into supporting it by the SS and SA troops stationed in the streets around the Reichstag. The Third Reich was established legally, therefore, as the result of a revolution *within* the framework of a presidential dictatorship, which Hindenburg had encouraged in 1930. When this act expired in 1937, it was preserved by decree only, because parliamentary politics had ceased to exist in the interval. Under the original decree Hitler produced the policy of coordination, or *Gleichschaltung*, the German parallel to Mussolini's "corporative" policy. What this meant in practice was a rapid take-over of all state apparatus by Nazi party leaders, from Göring[64] on down. *Reichskommissars* were given control of the federated states; diets were dissolved, to be succeeded by "governors" who were usually "district bosses" (*Gauleiters*) in the party.

Germany thus ceased to be a federal state. Then, as had happened in Italy, the trade union movement was broken. The SA occupied all union

60. The Nazis took 230, the Nationalists 37, the Communists 89, in a total of 608.
61. Deputized civilians to "help" the police, i.e., Nazis.
62. Hindenburg had authorized the suspension of these rights on February 28.
63. But still not a Nazi majority.
64. Already in control of Prussia.

Mass meetings and party rallies were key means of building a unified Nazi Germany. Here, at a rally held on September 30, 1934, Hitler strides before Goebbels, minister of agriculture Darre, and General von Blomberg, commander-in-chief of the army. Nuremberg, in Bavaria, became a Nazi party center and was the scene of mammoth rallies. Planned by the Nazi Organization Section for Party Rallies, these events included columns of marching soldiers and party officials, thousands of flags, and even antiaircraft searchlights requisitioned from Germany's strategic reserve to lend drama to evening spectacles. European Picture Service.

headquarters on May 2, 1933; thousands of labor leaders were put in concentration camps. And a Nazi Labor Front was formed. Political parties were next: first the Social Democrats, then the Nationalists were disbanded. In Italy Mussolini had allowed Corradini's people to join the government. Hitler was more exclusive; by the end of July the other parties had "voluntarily" dissolved. A complete control over cultural life was established by means of a National Chamber of Culture. This body not only exercised censorship; it purged books and all other media that might circulate ideas of Jewish and left-wing decadence. As early as April Jews were purged from the civil service, the professions, the arts, teaching, and even denied the right to keep certain kinds of businesses. A boycott of Jewish merchants was organized.

What opposition there remained was from three sources: Communists and the outlawed Social Democrats, some Protestant clergy, and, curiously, Röhm's SA. All paid heavily, not least of all Röhm. The *Reichswehr* had no intention of surrendering power to the party "militia." Röhm, for his part, disliked civilian control over the SA. The SS commander Heinrich Himmler convinced Hitler that Röhm was a threat, the planner of a *Putsch*. In mid-1934, therefore, in an atmosphere charged with hostility between SA, SS, and the army, Hitler instructed Himmler to put down the "revolt" in Bavaria (Röhm's old center of power), with Göring's help. The result was a massacre of SA men, including Röhm, and "suspect" generals like Schleicher, who had been chancellor after Papen. Old friends were swept to death—von Kahr and Strasser from the old days of 1923—in the infamous "night of the long knives."

The purge of June 30, 1934, may be said to mark the end of the Nazi Revolution, for it swept aside the last "enemies," real or imagined. A combination of dynamism and depression, mass unemployment and the psychological needs of the young, nationalism and daring, anti-Semitism

Lenin, shown here, was born to a middle-class family in 1870; his father was a school inspector whom the czar raised to the nobility. Lenin's brother was hanged in 1887 for his membership in a group plotting the assassination of Czar Alexander III, turning Lenin forever against the czarist regime. Studying German so that he could read the works of Marx and Engels (he could read in six other languages as well), Lenin devoted himself to revolutionary politics, leading the Bolshevik Revolution of 1917 and founding the Soviet Russian state. Radio Times Hulton Picture Library.

and the pledge to "revise the peace" of 1919 had put in complete control of a civilized society a one-party state led by a dictator pledged to mass murder and a new era of warfare. The German army was itself guilty of misjudgment in 1934; the SS emerged from the night of the long knives a more potent rival than the SA had been. And to the east and west politicians wondered what the Nazi regime portended for Europe.

TOTALITARIANISM ON SOCIALIST PRINCIPLES

In 1944 the Yugoslav Partisan[65] leader Milovan Djilas[66] visited Moscow to settle some political and military issues arising out of the entry into northern Yugoslavia of Russian troops from the Red Army. In the struggle to aid the revolution in that country, Red Army soldiers had committed 121 rapes, 111 of them with murder. This was a moral as well as a political problem, because the Partisans had expected better of the fraternal soldiers sent by Stalin, not only in the case of their women, but also in the 1,204 cases of looting with assault. "Could this be that ideal . . . Red Army?"[67]

There were more shocks waiting for Djilas in Moscow, however. Not only was he abused for supposing that the Red Army behaved like the troops of fascist and capitalist states. Djilas was a Communist of old vintage; he had joined the party in 1933, had gone to prison for its ideals,

65. The Yugoslav Communist opposition to German occupation of Yugoslavia.
66. Born in 1911 in Montenegro; Djilas was dismissed from the Communist party's central committee in 1954.
67. Djilas, *Conversations with Stalin* (New York: Harcourt, Brace & World, 1962), p. 89.

because the fascist king Alexander systematically purged Marxist enemies. Now, with all the emotion of a pilgrim visiting a holy shrine, he was about to enter Russia's citadel, where Slavs had for centuries sought salvation. Before Djilas met him, Stalin was in the Yugoslav's eyes Lenin's heir, the guardian of the sacred flame of Marxist revolution. Djilas also regarded the Russian state as a "revolutionary" one, the Communist avant-garde.

Slowly, he began to understand that Stalin was a dictator, however Soviet officials explained his role as the result of Stalin's genius, which was that of the statesman, soldier, and philosopher combined in one leader. Djilas saw men struggle to dress up naked hero worship in Marxist formulas. The great Yugoslav leader Tito[68] could not be praised in Moscow, because this seemed somehow to derogate from Stalin's majesty and Russia's unchallenged leadership of the "world revolution." Also, Djilas soon grasped that Stalin had absolute control of the army, which was pledged to him personally, not merely to the party and the state, as theory prescribed. Fed in a luxurious way, regaled with tales of Stalin's universal gifts, Djilas was surprised to find that the dictator allowed such antisocialist excesses. Was it a Marxist hero who presided over this "court" of Oriental splendor? Stalin was short, plain, even austere, crippled in one arm, with discolored teeth, speaking in accented Russian, and knowledgeable about no political history outside of Marxism and the limits of what had been czarist Russia. Moreover, Stalin never spoke of the Soviet Union, but always of "Russia," in a nationalist way; above his desk, on a wall, Stalin kept a photo of Lenin, but it was surrounded by small images of Suvorov and Kutuzov, heroes of the czarist struggles against Napoleon.

The Soviet Revolution had obviously come a long way from the 1917 days, when Molotov[69] remembered the party as weak, disorganized, scattered, and without means to hide him, except in the house of Lenin's sister in Moscow. By 1939, Soviet Russia was in the grip of the "man of steel." Stalin was a fanatical dogmatist who could justly say that he, not Lenin, had transformed Russia into a modern industrial state, and that state into a totalitarian dictatorship! How this happened is no longer obscure.

We will recall[70] that Lenin took Russia out of the war in 1917 and had then to fight a strong Allied intervention in 1918–1919. The National Constituent Assembly elections of November 25, 1917, had returned 410 Social Revolutionaries (members of the peasant party) and only 175 Bolsheviks, in a total of 708 seats. This accurately reflected Lenin's strength at large with the electorate, which numbered 30,000,000, of whom only 9,000,000 supported his party. He therefore dissolved the legislature and with it the mixed support for the provisional government of Kerensky. Having relegated that "liberal" regime to oblivion in 1917, the Bolsheviks did not intend to reconstitute it. They tried to rule through a council of people's commissars, headed by Lenin, but including also Trotsky (1877–1940) to take charge of foreign affairs and Stalin (1879–1953) to supervise the many "nationalities." This turn against majority rule and toward "class rule," a dictatorship of the proletariat executed by the Bolsheviks, served to introduce Communist party rule in Russia; for so Lenin renamed his movement in March 1918.

For the next four years, the new regime was as insecure as the defeated Western states, or more so. A civil war raged against a variety of "enemies"

---

68. His real name was Josip Broz. Born in 1892, he became president of Yugoslavia in 1953.
69. V. M. Molotov, a Bolshevik from 1906; born in 1890, he was a loyal Stalinist, a party organizer.
70. See Chapter 13.

who had Allied supplies and even troops: liberals, Mensheviks, democrats, Social Revolutionaries, and others eager to turn out the regime of councils (soviets) and commissars. To do combat with all opposed forces, Lenin gave Trotsky command of the Red Army. His accomplishment against great odds was striking; by 1920 Russia had reestablished control over some areas taken by Germany at Brest Litovsk[71] and over others confirmed as independent states by the Versailles peace. This was true in the Ukraine, the Caucasus, Siberia, and eastern Russia. Trotsky then turned his forces against Poland, regaining some territory. But the Baltic states, Poland, and Finland remained independent.

The Soviet Union thus started life with a quadruple legacy from the First World War: lost territory produced a strong motive for Russian "revision" of the 1919 settlement; Russia under the Communists had conceived a bitter distrust of the West as a result of their intervention; the Soviet state was ideologically isolated from Europe and physically isolated from groups of "Russian" people; and the great civil war, coming as it did on top of the collapse of the society and the economy in the world war, made it seem doubtful that a viable new state and society could be reconstructed. What resources had the Communists?

The answer was simply that they had themselves. Lenin came to power as a Marxist who drew from theory a course of action. Having made "the Revolution," he knew what he wished to do to establish a regime. Together with other theorists and with the help of men of action, Lenin knew that the conquest of power was only the entry into its use. As a Marxist, he was committed to using power to transform Russian life completely, in every social and political aspect, culturally and economically. Unlike Stalin, however, Lenin, while demanding absolute obedience to policy or the "line" of party action once it was decided, gladly encouraged real debate over alternatives. Lenin also had great personal qualities: he was scholarly but not condescending to the people he wished to convert to Communism; he was powerful in logic and expounded policy clearly; he was unselfish, even humble in contact with ordinary people; he lived simply; and in public he always seemed to obey the rules he prescribed for others.

Lenin was also dictatorial in politics. He had little regard for Western ideas of legality. This was made clear even during the civil war. In a country besieged, Lenin began to convert the government into a party state, giving offices to Communists, even legal offices to men without training in the law. By removing the old bureaucrats, Lenin shocked Western opinion; but the party needed to remove obstacles to "Soviet justice." The West was more shocked by other measures. In line with socialist doctrine, Lenin attacked private property. All bank accounts were seized and banks nationalized. The czarist foreign debt was repudiated. All private commerce was abolished, even at the retail level. Land was entirely nationalized, factories put in the hands of worker soviets. Even under the strain of civil war, therefore, Lenin and his party began to practice Communism as Lenin interpreted it. The bourgeoisie were to have no place in the new society ruled by the party for the people. All *rentiers* and middle-class profiteers were to be eliminated from the economic chain leading from production to distribution.

The peasants were at last to enjoy the fruits of their labor, each according to need, with no surplus "extracted" or stolen from them, except for the portions given to the state for distribution to city workers. The peasants were not Marxists, however, and this "war communism" alienated them

71. The armistice of November 11, 1918, forced Germany to renounce the Treaty of Brest Litovsk and thus to lose the territories acquired by it.

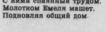

profoundly, because the new state seemed as reluctant to fully redistribute land as the old one had been. Peasants and large farmers joined opposition groups, as did expropriated middle-class people, professionals, industrialists, and noblemen.

Politically, the importance of the phase of "war communism" (1917–1921) was that the internal dissent and Allied intervention encouraged in Lenin an authoritarian response. But this direction had already appeared in December 1917. The party had organized the Cheka,[72] or secret police, for combatting "counterrevolution." This force was an instrument of terror and a part of government policy. It was the forerunner of successive embodiments of the political police: OGPU, NKVD, and MVD. The terror was partly against obvious "class enemies," but also was used against revolutionaries who deviated from the Communist "line." Among the victims were the Kronstadt sailors who rose against party rule in 1921; originally instrumental in bringing Lenin to power, they had become "petit bourgeois" four years later. What this in effect meant was that they had failed the test of absolute obedience. Others fell merely because they belonged to the wrong parents, had the wrong education, or said the wrong thing.

Slaughter was a price Lenin, then Stalin willingly paid to establish a regime which European socialists branded a perversion of Marxism. Like the czars, Lenin rejected "bourgeois" liberties such as press freedom, freedom of speech, and freedom of worship. It was under such repressive conditions, in which "enemies of the state" were killed without their having committed a particular crime, that the new order was consolidated.

72. From the Russian for "All-Russian Extraordinary Commission." The Cheka was also to hunt down "capitalist" speculators and saboteurs.

The purpose of this order was twofold: to establish in Russia a sound state, and to make this Bolshevik state the base for a world revolution.

The goal of spreading Soviet socialism to the rest of the world was the motive behind the creation in 1919 of the Communist International. But this "Comintern" drew scant support in its first congress. In 1920, however, Marxists from many countries attended the second congress. It was at these congresses that the Soviet Marxists served notice on the Marxists elsewhere, or at least those Moscow-oriented Marxists who accepted Lenin's authority. Unlike the old socialist International, in which all parties were sovereign, Lenin's Communist International demanded adherence of the "world parties" to the "line" decided upon by the Soviet-inspired congresses.[73]

The first congress demanded a pledge from all foreign parties to support the Soviet Union and maintain its regime. Tactically, the demand meant erecting in every country Communist parties, youth movements, trade unions, and other agencies subject to Soviet discipline. The explicit purpose of the parties in Europe was to work for the overthrow of all capitalist regimes. Also, because the movement was to a worldwide revolutionary stroke, the Comintern in 1919 made explicit its intention to free the "colonial slaves" of Asia and Africa. All of these points were repeated in 1920. To the West the doctrine of "fraternal liberation" was simply one more incentive to work to isolate the Soviets, or even to expunge the state founded by Lenin.

That the European powers had failed to do so was clear by 1921. In that year Lenin launched the New Economic Policy, or NEP.[74] War and "war communism" had ruined production. The sailors' revolt of 1921 convinced Lenin that "socialism" had come too quickly. Always a supreme tactician as well as a Marxist, Lenin initiated the NEP to give the state ownership and control over basic industry.[75] Commerce for profit was reintroduced, along with peasant rights to sell produce in markets. The effect was to reintroduce middlemen and the profit motive in order to encourage reliable rural-urban exchanges and calm the furor of domestic opposition.

This program saved the Revolution; by fixing the share of surplus extracted from the peasants, NEP encouraged them to be loyal. By permitting a neobourgeois class to arise in town and country, NEP made the shock of Soviet reality less profound. Lenin called NEP a compromise between the proletariat and the peasants. The result was that by 1923 over 75 percent of retail trade was in the hands of "Nepmen"; 88 percent of all facilities of industry was similarly controlled by "Nepmen" in 1923. It is, however, possible to exaggerate the impact of the compromise with capitalism and the peasantry. The state controlled 88.4 percent of all workers in heavy industry, the so-called commanding heights of production. Private enterprise accounted for only 5 percent of gross production. Moreover, the situation resembled that of earlier industrializing systems. The large units set the tempo within a framework where the impetus was supplied by banking and finance; and the state controlled all credit and foreign trade.

This state capitalism (as Lenin called it) restored production to the 1914 levels by 1927. It also split the ruling party. When Lenin died in 1924,[76] the

73. With headquarters in Moscow, under Zinoviev.
74. NEP lasted until 1927.
75. An illustration of the "commanding heights" theory of Communism, in which heavy industry alone is socialized.
76. He had suffered the first of a series of strokes in May of 1922.

cult of his leadership began officially, as his successors deified him and raised him to the level of equality with Marx as a founder of Communism. But this unity did not carry over into political life. Stalin, the powerful party secretary, and Trotsky, the war commissar, contested openly for the succession. Trotsky condemned NEP as inconsistent with socialism; he had the support of some theorists who argued that NEP was meant by Lenin to be temporary only. Trotsky also argued for "permanent revolution" at home and active revolutionary agitation abroad. He denounced bureaucratism, the rise of rich peasants, and the failure to collectivize agriculture. He also urged total social planning. Stalin took a more "Leninist" line and also was nationalistic, urging that Communism in Russia must be built strongly before foreign adventures were launched. The differences came to a head in 1927, at a party congress. Stalin used his control over the party to procure the exile of Trotsky to Siberia and then to banish him from the Soviet Union.[77]

Stalin quickly moved the party to accept many of Trotsky's ideas, after having won the succession struggle. In 1928 the party worked out the first Five-Year Plan. The central purpose was to industrialize and collectivize agriculture and to plan all economic activities and thus to make society *socialist in its direction*.[78] The plan rested on Stalin's interpretation of Marxism, which he held to predict the elimination of the bourgeoisie and the generation of a classless society. But Marx himself had given no blueprint for achieving modernization through industrialization. Engels, however, had seen that the most successful industries were ones in which rationalization took place through the elimination of competition and the total integration within a factory system of all productive functions. Stalin also recognized that in World War I planned economies had arisen from the challenges of defense needs. Because the Soviet state was besieged by encircling enemies and beset with counterrevolution within, it was Stalin's view that planning was justified by theory and fact.

In 1929 Stalin predicted that the Five-Year Plan would be succeeded by others, which came to pass. In the year 1932 the goal of the first plan was said to have been achieved: the building of heavy industry without foreign capital. To do so, it had been necessary to appropriate peasant capital to make up the deficiencies of capital ordinarily available from abroad to industrializing states. Russia had to repeat the agricultural revolution Britain had made as the prelude to industrialization; and Russia had to do so by transferring surpluses from farms to towns, without losing anything to middlemen. This meant the establishment of collective farms on a large scale and the declaration of war against the *kulaks*, or rich peasants, who resisted. While exact statistics are lacking, we can estimate that hundreds of thousands of peasants were murdered or exiled; and it is likely that even more starved to death between 1929 and 1937, when the second Five-Year Plan ended.

In reality, the regime of large industrialized farms (Machine Tractor Stations) and scientific agriculture did not increase total production greatly; but it did increase production per worker, as capital was applied to large-scale farming. And this freed over twenty-million farm workers for industrial jobs by 1939. This enabled Soviet industrial production to more than double by 1937, before falling off as a result of bad harvests after 1937 and the devastation of the Second World War from 1940 to 1945. The rise in production did little to benefit consumers, however. Analysis of the Soviet

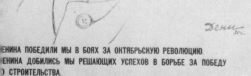

77. Trotsky was murdered in Mexico in 1940 by Stalinist assassins.
78. That is, to achieve the state of society leading toward absolute Communism.

economy in the 1930s shows that the chief sectors of advance were in mining, metalworking, heavy industries for plant construction, and military preparedness. Housing remained at the level achieved under Nicholas II. There were severe lags in all food production, clothing, writing paper; and in the area of food production there were real increases only in canned foods and the fish catch.

Iron and steel production quadrupled from 1928 to 1938, however; and in 1938 the Soviet Union led the world in producing farm machinery and locomotives. Amazingly, this production was achieved in plants built since 1928; at least 80 percent of the industrial system was new. The distribution of industry was changing the face of Russia also. In Siberia and the Urals new cities grew up around new plants set near natural resources. Mining was developed in the Urals, eastern Siberia, and Turkestan. New granaries were developed in several republics, served by a new railroad network. In 1939 total production in the Soviet Union lagged that in only two other countries, Germany and the United States. Therefore, Stalin could rightly claim successes, even if production had not yet raised levels of consumption to Western standards in either food, books, newspapers, electricity, or soap. The Soviet Union needed to concentrate on heavy machinery, like rails for the great system linking eastern Siberia and the Ukraine, in a world which contained two industrial giants opposed to Communism in principle: fascist Germany and democratic America.

How else could the Revolution be held in place, but by decisions as to what goods should be exchanged at what price, how and when schools should be built, whether this or that child should be educated for medicine or left on a collective in the bliss of socialist labor and illiteracy? Building a new society was under any circumstances an intricate task requiring total obedience and discipline. Under the conditions obtaining in Soviet Russia and its larger "Union," only totalitarian control would suffice.

Politically, the Soviet Union was a union of soviet[79] socialist republics (hence USSR), with a federal constitution adopted in 1924 as its basic political document. Even in 1922 the USSR controlled one-sixth of the earth's land and at least sixteen large "national" groups speaking over one hundred languages. Originally the federal system was a bulwark against nationalism, but Stalin accepted the necessity for cultural autonomy—that is, the tolerance of local dress, languages, schools, and mores. In the conditions of the 1920s every means toward unity was exploited, and the constitution conceded even the right of secession to member republics.[80] By 1940 no republic formally taken into the Soviet Union had ever done so, but in 1936 the original four had been reorganized into eleven federated republics; in 1940, with the addition of five more, there were sixteen in all.[81] These republics contained various regions and districts for the minorities; and in extreme cases autonomous "national republics" were allowed within soviet republics. The whole structure of autonomy was emphasized in a Soviet of Nationalities. But in fact the Russian Soviet Federated Socialist Republic dominated all life in the USSR.

Russia was the centralizing element, and within it the Communist party under Stalin ruled everything. The essence of the totalitarian state lay in the complete parallelism of state and party, not in the formal trappings of

79. A soviet was a worker's council.
80. In the early 1920s Georgia, Armenia, and the Caucasus tried to secede but were kept within the Soviet Union by the Red Army.
81. The total of sixteen endured until 1956, when the Karelo-Finnish Republic ceased to be an autonomous republic.

liberty, people's democracy, and constitutions. Actual government in each republic and in the Union was *constitutionally* entrusted to the party in 1924 and 1936. Both constitutions distinguished the state and the party. But the 1924 document excluded from the franchise "parasites" who did not labor.[82] It also provided that all elections to local soviets were indirect, and so up the line to the Congress of Soviets, the legislature for the whole USSR. The various soviets also picked the appropriate executive, culminating in the Union Council of People's Commissars.

These practices were modified in 1936, when franchise restrictions were removed and direct elections allowed. There was also a two-house legislature elected with one member for every 300,000 people. This Supreme Soviet still elected the Presidium, or combined executive-legislative organ which governed when the Supreme Soviet was not sitting. The chairman of the Presidium was "president" of the USSR, empowered to supervise all other council officials and bodies.

What vitiated the democratic "form" of Soviet totalitarianism was the role of the party. Communism was the only party lawful. It was a hierarchic party at the top of which was a Central Committee with several dozen members. The general secretary (Stalin) supervised the work of the executive secretariat with the help of two crucial bureaus, one for organization of the party and another for politics.[83] At all lower levels rigid chains of command existed, through which the policies of the party reached into every republic. The principles of Soviet politics were corporate and not checked from the outside. Stalin was president, party secretary, head of the Politburo, directly in control of the men who ran the secret police. His party had only 3,000,000 members in 1940, when total USSR population was about 195,000,000.

And it was from these 3,000,000 that all state officials and elected officers were named. Thought was controlled throughout the USSR by the rigorous indoctrination of future party members in Marxism-Leninism and by the placement of loyal party people in every shop, on every farm, at every school, and in every army unit. These political officers guarded the state's purity by enforcing adherence to party doctrine. Only in this way, Stalin said, could the Marxist dictatorship of the proletariat really work and bring the people to socialism. The party as a whole, especially the "inner party" close to Stalin, was the guardian of the Revolution.

Elitism was therefore built into the structure of Soviet life as the principle of government in a one-party state. Non–party members must follow where they were led; and, in the event that anyone strayed from the "line," party and nonparty people might be "purged." The new ruling class used totalitarian means, not only on the peasants after 1929, when millions were killed in purges. Grumblers against low wages were "purged"—either exiled in prison camps or killed. In exchange for full employment and a steadily rising rate of literacy and the emancipation of women, the Soviet government exacted as its price obedience. The USSR had no paupers. But Stalin conducted political purge trials in 1936 and 1937, against alleged Trotskyists and right-wing "deviationist dogs." Even top Bolsheviks like Zinoviev were sacrificed in 1936, as earlier (1934) Kirov[84] had been. That old Politburo man was murdered in his office, and his alleged "murderers" were executed later for plotting to murder Stalin! Show trials were staged before the Western press in 1937, at which loyal party members publicly confessed

82. E.g., priests, retail traders.
83. Hence Orgburo and Politburo.
84. One of Stalin's oldest associates.

unspeakable crimes. The purges were extended to all military units and any organized group or individual member of the party thought to pose a threat to the "Leader."

The "new society" therefore led to the inequalities of status of other Western societies. And it exhibited the bench marks of the one-party states of the West. In it error was often seen as sabotage. And there was practically total control over all human expression. Yet it would be wrong to suppose that the totalitarian regime in Russia was any more alien to the people than the regimes of Mussolini and Hitler were. The new societies inspired pride as well as fear in their citizens. And in them there was none of the limping reality of the capitalist depression. State control over economies seemed to work, even if all thought tended to become propaganda for the regime. Democracy in the West seemed weaker than either fascism or Communism and on a collision course with both, as the totalitarian states were with each other.

BIBLIOGRAPHY

ARENDT, HANNAH. *The Origins of Totalitarianism.** New York: Meridian, 1965. Traces the impact of nineteenth-century racism and imperialism on political ideology.

BRACHER, K. D. *The Nazi Dictatorship.* New York: Praeger Publishers, 1970. The greatest work on the Hitler period of German history.

BUCHHEIM, HANS. *Totalitarian Rule.* Translated by Ruth Hein. Middleton, Conn.: Wesleyan University Press, 1968. Treats the character of political and social life and thought in fascist and communist societies in the 1920s and 1930s.

CARR, E. H. *The October Revolution.** New York: Random House, Vintage Books, 1969. Carr's massive history of the Soviet regime, now in seven volumes, stands behind these essays on early Soviet hopes, industrialization, and conflict within the Communist party.

CARSTEN, F. L. *The Rise of Fascism.** Berkeley: University of California Press, 1969. A systematic survey of the various national fascist movements; very good on Eastern Europe.

DEUTSCHER, ISAAC. *The Unfinished Revolution.* London: Oxford University Press, 1967. Sympathetic account by a hopeful Marxist.

FERMI, LAURA. *Mussolini.** Chicago: University of Chicago Press, 1961. The best study of Mussolini and Italian Fascism.

FRIEDRICH, C. J. *Totalitarianism.** New York: Grosset & Dunlap, 1964. A published symposium of forty essays on these facets of totalitarian systems: freedom, expression, ideology, psychology, social and economic life, and organization.

HOFSTADTER, RICHARD. *Social Darwinism in American Thought.** Boston: Beacon Press, 1955. Very good on the "conservative" politics of the Social Darwinists in America and Europe.

KOCHAN, LIONEL. *The Making of Modern Russia.** London: Penguin Books, 1962. The best short history, very good on the period 1890–1930.

MOORE, BARRINGTON. *Social Origins of Dictatorship and Democracy.** London: Penguin Books, 1967. An analytic scheme to show how political systems derive from the mode of agrarian transformation in each state.

NOLTE, ERNEST. *Three Faces of Fascism.** New York: Holt, Rinehart & Winston, 1966. Especially good on the social and psychological aspects of the movement.

PULZER, PETER J. *The Rise of Political Anti-Semitism in Germany and Austria.** New York: John Wiley & Sons, 1964. Focuses on the sources of racism and racist politics.

ROBINSON, G. T. *Rural Russia under the Old Regime.** New York: The Macmillan Company, 1957. A basic work on peasant society before the Revolution.

WILSON, LAWRENCE. *The Road to Dictatorship, Germany 1918–1933.* London: Wolff, 1964. Ten essays on aspects of politics and the enemies of democracy in the Weimar Republic by leading post-Nazi German historians.

Asterisk indicates a paperbound edition.

Our basic demand is: Off with the Peace Treaty! To this end we must use everything we can, especially the difference between France and Italy.
HITLER, *Speech* (July 6, 1920)

Is it right that there is eighteen times more land per head for every Russian than there is for a German?
HITLER, *Speech* (December 10, 1919)[1]

17

A SPECIAL PROVIDENCE: WAR WITHOUT PEACE

HITLER AGAINST THE WORLD: THE BLUEPRINT

German statesmen before World War I had argued for the civilizing role Germany had played and defended the function of the German Empire as providential in the sense that it was imperially and divinely sanctioned. In the 1920s those who were against reinstituting democracy in Germany and still had dreams of the great nationalism of the German people used the concept of a special providence as a rallying point to resist the consequences of defeat. We have already dealt with the slow process by which Germany's republican politicians put their state back into Europe. Germany was not the only state with revisionist aims; and Hitler was not the only politician looking for revenge against the French or for some means of cutting into the area under Soviet control. But Germany was the center of Europe, and it seemed more crucial to Western statesmen in the 1920s to solve the problem of Germany than to seek a real peace with the Marxist revisionists in Moscow or to ease the slights the Italians had suffered at Versailles.

And few indeed were the Western statesmen who noticed the building resentment of colonial rule in Africa or of economic imperialism in Asia. The movements of Indians against the British, led by Mohandas K. Gandhi,[2] and the great civil war in China seemed distant distractions to the peacemakers. The Turkish Republic under Kemal Atatürk after 1923 was more noteworthy, because in ten years it underwent a rapid process of Westernization and was in 1933 no longer dependent on European capital for industrial development. Europe was disturbed by Kemal's acceptance of Russian aid. The British were very worried when in 1935 neighboring Persia showed Westernizing tendencies.[3]

Asia did get some attention, however. At the Washington Conference of 1921–1922 to regulate

---

1. From Eberhard Jäckel, *Hitler's Weltanschauung: A Blueprint for Power* (Middletown, Conn.: Wesleyan University Press, 1972), pp. 29, 33.
2. The Mahatma, or holy one.
3. Changing its name to Iran in the process.

navies and police the Pacific, the "Open Door Policy" was reaffirmed. This undermined the pro-Western regime of Sun Yat-sen (1866–1925), the organizer of the Nationalist party and hero of the 1911 revolution against the Manchus. Dr. Sun was democratically inclined but accepted Marxist aid and practiced a liberal dictatorship. He was also pledged to rid China of imperialist domination, which Versailles had winked at. Moreover, he had been frustrated in his hope that the League of Nations would strip Japan of the German concessions it had acquired. China turned to Russia in 1924, and the Kuomintang[4] merged with the Chinese Communist party.[5] Lenin's successors gave up the Russian concessions in China, inducing Britain to follow suit by way of a bid for the favor of Chiang Kai-shek, the new Kuomintang head. China lapsed back into civil war in 1927, when Chiang purged Russian and Chinese Communist influences.

This rupture led to the formation of a Red Army under the leadership of Mao Tse-tung,[6] a scholarly Marxist, and Chu Teh,[7] a former general in the Kuomintang forces. Chiang drove the Red Army into the mountains and turned his increasingly reactionary forces against the Japanese. In 1931, therefore, "revisionist" China seemed no threat, divided as it was and under pressure from Japan, which in that year began a seizure of Manchuria. A year later the Japanese attacked Shanghai to the south, before withdrawing to focus on the conquest of the Chinese north. A League of Nations commission did condemn Japanese aggression, but no effective sanctions were applied. The West was too busy fighting the Depression.

It was also true that the West in 1932 was in diplomatic disarray. Stresemann had died in 1929, and he was the architect of the German policy of "satisfaction." In return for the Dawes Plan, Locarno, and the Young Plan,[8] as well as admission to the League of Nations, Stresemann had pledged Germany to forsake any efforts to revise the Versailles peace treaty. What Stresemann had not been able to do was prevent former members of the general staff from undertaking secret rearmament operations. The future chancellor Kurt von Schleicher himself collaborated with the *Reichswehr* in establishing commando forces of division strength in eastern Germany. In 1924 a secret Armaments Office planned to mobilize support for sixty-three divisions, about six times the 100,000-man strength allowed by the Versailles Treaty. Toward this end, the clandestine leaders enlisted industrial support at home.

Abroad, Stresemann had once hoped to secure French terms of a more relaxed nature. But as early as 1918 he had talked with representatives of Europe's other outlaw state, Soviet Russia. Stresemann sought economic aid agreements and a military understanding, on the premise that both states were the victims of hostile Western capitalism. In 1921 Lenin had asked German help in reorganizing the Red Army. Because both powers feared Polish aggression with Western support, a special secret military mission of cooperation had been established. A commercial agreement followed. Thus, when Stresemann came to power he had helped Germany to reduce its isolation. Although the generals and Hitler labeled him defeatist, he knew of the secret agreements; and he never renounced the

4. The Chinese name for Sun's party.
5. Organized in 1921.
6. Born in 1893.
7. A Westernized Chinese born in 1886.
8. The Dawes Plan (1924), which had been superceded by the Young Plan (1929), reduced Germany's reparations to a level it could pay. The Locarno Pact (1925) had, by declaring inviolable Germany's western frontier as established by the Treaty of Versailles, brought to Western Europe the first tranquillity its people had known in a generation.

open entente between Germany and Russia signed in 1922 at Rapallo. Indeed, Stresemann extended this in 1926, in the Treaty of Berlin. It was, he said, a "bridge between East and West . . . in the development of Europe."[9] Others said that Stresemann had openly provoked the West; but in fact what he aimed at was a breach in the encirclement of Germany and the evacuation of the Rhineland. That was the meaning of Locarno (1925) and the award of a seat on the council of the League of Nations in 1926, an achievement crowned in 1929 by the Young Plan.

Within the framework of Hitler's world outlook, Stresemann's achievement meant only that he had mortgaged Germany's future. In Hitler's thoughts on international affairs, which were already well developed in 1919–1920, there were a few fixed points, absolute and incompatible with any interpretation of him as a mere pragmatist or opportunist, or even merely a madman. Hitler was filled with a demonic need for power and with hatred of a psychotic sort. His personality was compounded of the urge to hate and the urge to destroy—impulses directed especially against the Jews. But the development of Nazi foreign policy, which in 1939 produced a global, total, war, was consistent with Hitler's ideas about Europe. And these ideas had a certain logical consistency in the area of foreign policy, in *Mein Kampf* and in the long-secret *Second Book*.[10]

Hitler was a *revisionist*, but instead of requiring alterations in the 1919 treaty, he demanded its abolition. As early as 1919 he said in speeches this could come only by war. This war would be directed primarily against France. But war against all the allies of France at the same time was unthinkable. Thus a German revisionist war must be prepared for by campaigns to divide the Allies. Given the postwar estrangement of Italy from France, even before Mussolini's coup Hitler insisted in speeches that Italy was Germany's natural ally. Hitler grasped that no alliance was possible unless Germany ceased to contest Italy's control of the southern Tyrol. This he did when in power, despite the famous 1920 pledge to bring all ethnic Germans into one German state.

With the "enemy on the other side of the Rhine,"[11] Germany might seek alliance with Italy. But Italy was not as useful as either Britain or Russia. In England's favor was Hitler's racist enthusiasm for the Anglo-Saxons; and against Russia was the Revolution itself, which had "brought the Jews to power." Other things were more decisive, however. Britain was an island with vast imperial resources; Russia was a land-based power from which Germany might seize "living space" (*Lebensraum*) for the people of the Aryan race who were "prisoners" in the Slav states.[12] Moreover, England in 1923 opposed France's occupation of the Ruhr. Hitler therefore hoped that England, which had battled France's "hegemony" for 140 years (going back to the Paris peace treaty of 1783), might be detached from alliance with the French. In 1923 Hitler actually advocated taking back the Ruhr by force, in order to force Britain toward the reestablishment of a balance of power.

These ideas were not the insane wanderings of a madman, but rather an old approach to some traditional German objectives. In 1924, however, Hitler added a new element, or rather extended the logic of old elements in his thought. He began to see the necessity of a war of conquest against Russia, beyond mere opportunism. In 1924 Hitler wrote an article in which he played off two foreign policies: either win farmland or opt for sea power

9. Hans W. Gatzke, *Stresemann and the Rearmament of Germany* (Baltimore: The Johns Hopkins Press, 1954), p. 270.
10. Also known as the *Secret Book* (New York: Grove Press, 1962).
11. That is, France.
12. If the Soviet state broke apart.

and a trade empire. The latter meant conflict with England, the former war with Russia. War for "living space" was something beyond *revisionism*, as was the vision of Germany as either a continental power or a colonial one. William II had tried to make Germany both, succeeding only in reducing Germany to the status of an outlaw. The land-based empire was clearly chosen on July 18, 1925, when *Mein Kampf* appeared.

Arguing that the moral right to make war sprang from the fact of hunger, Hitler said that to get farmland, the sword is in reality the plow! From "the tears of war there will grow the daily bread of generations to come."[13] As early as the publication of *Mein Kampf*, therefore, Hitler looked to the future of German youth; there was an annual increase of 900,000, he said. And this demographic surplus could end only in hunger and pauperization without either the acquisition of new land, a program for controlling population growth, production for export to gain credit for foodstuffs, or internal German colonization. Of the four alternatives, Hitler found only a war to seize land in Europe meaningful. He did not shrink from the conclusion: this must be done at Russia's expense.

Thus Hitler in 1924[14] had created a problem of choice: either Germany should seek Italian and British aid in a war against France, or England must join Germany against Russia. In the event that Germany chose the second plan, what would France do? Hitler gave no answer in *Mein Kampf*, but in 1925 he wrote its second volume. In it, the thirteenth chapter dealt with the "policy of alliance." And this chapter Hitler *published as an article in 1926*. It retreated from anti-Russian war, while renewing the French-oriented revisionist line. But Hitler specifically called this the short-run goal. In the next chapters, kept secret for another year, Hitler wrote of his "eastern policy." Here, he combined also all of the elements in a program to eliminate discrepancies between population and territory. The pre-1914 frontiers now no longer sufficed. Long-range policies tending toward the destruction of France were prescribed, but only because the victory in France would insure a free hand for Germany against Russia and its border states, from the Baltic to the Balkans. Italian and English acquiescence were to be assured by spheres of influence for Italy in Africa and for Britain everywhere else overseas.

Hitler also prescribed the tactics for what was a three-phase program to solve the problems of diplomacy, Jews, Bolsheviks, and German needs. In the first phase, rearmament and alliances must be achieved; in the next phase, war with France would be provoked; then, in the third phase, Germany would absorb Eastern Europe, after a war of conquest against Russia. Hitler confirmed this analysis in the long-secret *Second Book*, which he wrote in 1928. There, Hitler dwelled on the rivalries between France, Italy, and Britain, which he correctly predicted would grow greater, because of Mussolini's plans to expand in Africa and because of Anglo-French rivalries elsewhere. The dilemma was that Britain had historically resisted not only France's hegemony, but any European hegemony. Hitler recited the evidence but disregarded it, apparently on the theory that Britain would not fight if Germany respected the British Empire overseas.

In this he was mistaken. He had exposed a contradiction in his global strategy, but he had not resolved it. And he had not satisfied legitimate doubts as to what America would do, as Hitler rolled up the map of Europe and put it in his pocket.

---

13. Quoted in *Mein Kampf*, trans. Ralph Manheim (Boston: Houghton, Mifflin Co., 1939), Chapter 1.
14. The time of the composition of *Mein Kampf*.

Hitler did not forget his early blueprint for hegemony in Europe—we will show in fact that he followed it methodically. Before 1914 war had been for soldiers, and diplomacy for statesmen. After 1918 the masses were convinced that neither could be trusted with one or the other. Hitler understood this popular mood and by reflecting on it, altered it. It was as if the principles of modern science were coming into play in international diplomacy: Hitler, like the physicist Heisenberg, was altering facts simply because he analyzed them.[15] In politics, as Hitler practiced the art, this was true. His purposes were father to his actions; and these purposes were warlike. He was encouraged in his belief that a belligerent posture taken by Germany would not provoke effective sanctions against it because the League of Nations had *never since 1919 applied effective sanctions to any belligerent.* From this he calculated that a strong action would induce the response he wanted—acquiescence.

His guess proved right up until September 1939, when the Nazi invasion of Poland brought about a world war. Hitler understood the general drift of European diplomacy, despite that miscalculation. When he came to power in 1933, the record of the League was a sorry one. The League was based on aspirations for an international order, and these aspirations in turn rested on the illusion that all statesmen wanted peace. Yet the 1919 League of Nations Covenant itself did not prohibit war. Instead it proclaimed a limit to the "causes" for which wars might be lawfully made. Moreover, the sanctions embodied in the Covenant against "aggressors"[16] and later made "automatic" in application[17] had no real support among the powerful members.

The Geneva Protocol and the Kellogg-Briand Pact[18] had a dangerous effect, because these hopes for peace encouraged pacifists to suppose that paper protocols could indeed keep peace. The triumph of this illusion helped to kill realism, as Churchill noted in 1932, saying he could not recall a time when so large a gap existed between the speeches of statesmen and what was happening in the world. The belief that "public opinion" would compel France to disarm because Germany had been forced to do so was obviously disproved by the Ruhr seizure of 1923. Yet delegates to the League said public opinion was their most powerful weapon against aggressors. Public opinion did not curb Japan in 1932, however, when yet another former ally and League power violated a neighbor. Churchill concluded that the League was hopeless. Hitler thought it was weak-willed. Mussolini tested its resolve by invading Ethiopia in 1935. Before this Fascist conquest was completed in May 1936, Hitler had ordered his own troops to remilitarize the Rhineland, on March 7, 1936.

This violation of the Locarno Pact and the Versailles Treaty was directly based on his guess that Europe would do nothing to stop him. Against the Italians only mild economic sanctions had been imposed. Despite this guess, he prudently ordered a pullback if the French opposed the German forces. His gamble paid off, however, much to the amazement of the German military, who had predicted a French assault. Thus in one daring

15. Werner Heisenberg, a physicist born in 1901, formulated the principle of indeterminancy in 1927. He observed that in seeking to measure the position or mass of electrons with powerful electron microscopes, the field necessary for doing so altered both. Hence every "analysis" altered the "facts" of nature.
16. Defined by resolutions in 1921.
17. In the 1924 Geneva Protocol.
18. 1928: to define aggressors and outlaw war.

step Hitler had regained the full might of the Ruhr under militarily secure conditions. Germany had overnight become the strongest continental power. Darwinism applied to politics was resurrected, by Japan, Italy, and Germany: the strong survived at the expense of the weak. These results in 1932, 1935, and 1936[19] ought to have confirmed statesmen in two views: that it was utopian to regard Hitler as peaceful, and that no equilibrium could be had by sacrificing weak states or accepting the bullying of strong ones. Instead, there were rewards given to governments who justified their aggression by giving the opposition a bad name.[20]

The League was thus proved guilty of moral hypocrisy by those who stood to gain from its fall in reputation. But such hypocrisy was nothing new to the major European powers. France had opposed any justice for Germany in the 1920s, because the 1919 peace favored it. The various conferences to limit arms in the 1920s inevitably produced double standards. England wished to abolish submarines on the ground that they were wholly "offensive" weapons. But the weaker naval powers (Italy, Japan, France) favored their "legal" use, protesting that it was duplicitous for Britain to say battleships were purely defensive weapons. The same debate raged over tariff walls, until Britain converted to protection in 1932. Thus Hitler could indict all of the former Allies for chauvinist nonsense, pointing out that the claim that national policy was in the interest of the world was no National Socialist invention. President Wilson had said so, in taking America to war in 1917.

The point of the matter is not that Japan, Italy, Britain, and France were responsible for the coming of the Second World War, either because their aggressions inspired Hitler or because their weakness when challenged encouraged him. It would be just as pointless to blame Mussolini's diplomacy for the war, because in 1936 he allied Italy with Nazi Germany in the Rome-Berlin Axis; or to suppose that Stalin brought about the war, because in 1939 he made a pact with the Nazis;[21] or yet again to claim that the Polish government caused the war, by mistakenly believing it could actually fight Germany and Russia at the same time. The point is, however, that the Rhineland gamble was the decisive turning point on the road to war. In Germany the Nazi *Führer* gained enormously because of it. But the events which came so quickly after March 7, 1936, cannot be understood without a consideration first of Hitler's domestic situation.

Hitler in 1933 had shown he would not be a chancellor in chains. What was not clear even in July, when he decreed the one-party state, was whether he could transcend the divisions of class, religion, political creeds, and general culture among Germans. Hitler's propaganda sought to replace intellect with emotion on such issues, with the aid of anti-Semitism and what in *Mein Kampf* he had openly called "the Great Lie," the lie useful to people inside themselves. This force could penetrate small chinks in all personal armor better than blackmail, terror, or bribery. Thus from the beginning Hitler had concentrated on the peace, which he called the *Diktat*, and the manliness of war as a force of national self-realization. The *Kampf* he predicted would be total, total in its involvement of the whole *Volk* in a chain of authority and responsibility. Hitler also stimulated national pride with the myth that was the reverse image of anti-Semitism: the Germans as a *Herrenrasse*, or master race. From this were drawn the 1935 decrees of the

19. At the expense of China, Ethiopia, and France.
20. Japan complained of atrocities by Manchurians in 1931; Italy issued a "Green Book" about Ethiopian horrors in 1935; Hitler had for years inveighed against the wrongdoings of the French.
21. The infamous Ribbentrop-Molotov Pact, also known as the Nazi-Soviet Pact.

Nuremberg Reichstag depriving Jews of citizenship and the right to marry "Aryans."

Using Göring's Gestapo (or secret state police)[22] to enforce the policy of "coordination," Hitler, as we have shown, had transformed Germany's political, social, and economic structure by 1934. By 1935 the whole life of the people had passed under Nazi control, especially that exercised by cultural leaders who took their cue from Goebbels' National Chamber of Culture. Goebbels also controlled the propaganda ministry. Dr. Hjalmar Schacht managed the economy, in order to avoid inflation. Unemployment had been reduced by many means: the firing of non-Aryans; labor conscription; military levies; the rearmament program of 1935, against which Britain protested but did little; and various public works for land drainage, slum clearance, and road building. Toward the end of 1935 Hitler's policies had put four million people back to work. The slogan *Arbeit und Brot* (Work and Bread) expressed an achievement unrivaled in democratic states.

Hitler had consolidated his control over industrialists by his policy of allowing cartels and forbidding strikes. His expansionist policies had their support also, especially when these forced Hitler to crank up the armaments industry. Even the Prussian landed nobility were won over, because Hitler's Food Organization[23] fixed prices over costs. The nobles also were aided by the revitalization of hereditary estates, while a similar system benefited prosperous peasants. But the supreme reconciling force between the Austrian corporal and the Prussians was the *Reichswehr*. Hitler's massacre of the SA in 1934 and the foreign policy of adventure promised traditional employment for Prussia's youth. A few days after the "night of the long knives" the *Reichswehr* swore personal oaths to Hitler, and in August 38 million citizens voted him the office of president. Every element of importance accepted Hitler.

The only practical question was whether the foreign policy of Hitler's "minimum program" would work. This embraced *Lebensraum*, the expulsion of the Jews, the overthrow of the Bolshevik-Jewish regime, the absorption into the Reich of all Germans living abroad,[24] and the reoccupation of the Rhineland.

This policy was actually set in motion in 1934 when Hitler concluded a pact with Poland to secure the eastern border while moving to build his power militarily. He annexed the Saar in a plebiscite in 1935 and openly defied the League by reintroducing conscription and creating an air force.[25] Britain was Hitler's accomplice in this, *as he had predicted*: it restrained France in the hope that giving Hitler "fair play" would satisfy his legitimate needs. The year before (1934), Russia had been admitted to the League; and Germany "feared" the Bolsheviks. Moreover, the conservative and often pro-Nazi British politicians were not above thinking they could "use" Hitler to check the Communists. The British went further in 1935; they concluded an Anglo-German arms agreement governing navies, in clear violation of the League's demand for collective security. This, as much as Mussolini's success in Ethiopia, encouraged the next step, the march into the Rhineland.

Six months after the remilitarization, on September 2, 1936, Hitler had Göring read to a ministerial council his order for war preparations to be completed within four years. Three years later (less one day) Hitler invaded Poland.

22. *Geheime Staatspolizei.*
23. *Reichsnährstand.*
24. The *Auslanddeutschtum*; abroad included Austria.
25. The *Luftwaffe.*

The Spanish Civil War became a contest of international character, ranging fascists (Franco's troops aided by Hitler and Mussolini) against antifascists (Communists, socialists, anarchists, and those from all over the world opposed to Franco and fascism). One of the antifascist international brigades produced this poster of the bombing of Madrid. Its purpose was to rouse world opinion against the atrocities being committed by Franco's fascists and their German allies: Hitler's bombers were bringing German Kultur to Spain. By the end of the war, 15,000 had been killed in air raids and the Spanish Republic had fallen, at a total cost of a million lives. Victoria and Albert Museum; John R. Freeman.

Before that time, he had several other major chances to test the democracies. Britain and France urged the lifting of sanctions against Mussolini, apparently in the hope of reattaching Italy to its old alliances. But Mussolini was supporting General Franco's fascist onslaught against the Spanish Republic. Hitler saw this was an opportunity to do two things: test his weapons and consolidate the fascist movement. He therefore supported Mussolini and Franco with guns, tanks, and dive-bombers, perfecting in Spain the air raid against towns as a tactic of terror. Shortly after the April 1937 bombing of a small, defenseless Basque town called Guernica, Picasso painted his famous mural of that name,[26] portraying the surrealist horrors of the war. The Soviets aided the Republicans at first, but drew back because the Moscow "line" was violently against the anarchists and non-Communist left. Thus, again, daring had its rewards. Mussolini signed the Rome-Berlin Axis pact in 1936. A year later Mussolini visited Berlin.

In 1937 Hitler also revealed to a few confidants what is now called the Hossbach Protocol.[27] This was a plan of aggression to gain *Lebensraum* and achieve reunion with Germans in Austria or Czechoslovakia, whichever

26. 1937; in the Museum of Modern Art, New York.
27. Because it was in the keeping of a military aide named Hossbach.

was more inviting at the time. The military were frightened again, and in 1937 they won over Schacht, who was in despair because armament demands were dislocating his economic miracle. Hitler made a deep purge of the general staff in February 1938 and reorganized the military and the economics ministry under Nazi loyalists. This he followed in March with open threats against Austria's Chancellor Schuschnigg.[28] When the demand for a Nazi take-over of Austria backfired—Schuschnigg had proposed a plebiscite—Hitler invaded that country, delaying the election until the Nazis could guarantee the result desired. Then elections were held simultaneously in Germany and Austria on April 12, with 99 percent voting for unification.

28. Kurt von Schuschnigg, 1897–1966.

The Thousand Years' Reich, 1935–1942

Allied Powers
Axis Powers
Axis Allies
Neutral Nations

Under Axis Control, End of 1939
Annexed by Russia, 1940
Occupied by Germany
Held by Vichy France

Mussolini was amazed at this sudden union (*Anschluss*). Germany was now Italy's neighbor on the Brenner Pass.[29] Britain's Chamberlain said the League powers had no commitment, because the "unification" was an internal German matter. The British diplomat Anthony Eden was more clearheaded, however. He warned that more would come, but the French and British sent protests only.

On March 28 it did. Hitler demanded that the Czech government allow the secession of several million Sudeten Germans[30] and a German takeover of the region, including its industry. The Czechs refused. Hitler gave orders to the army. Eden again sounded a warning, in April, while events were still unfolding:

> It is futile to imagine that we are involved in a European crisis which may pass as it has come. We are involved in a crisis of humanity . . . in one of those great periods of history which are awe-inspiring in their responsibilities and in their consequences. Stupendous forces are loose, hurricane forces.[31]

While Churchill and Eden tried to stem the tide of appeasement in England, Hitler's orders to the army were leaked to the Czechs, who gave their own forces partial mobilization orders on May 20. With British, Russian, and French support, the Czechs requested guarantees, to which Hitler responded favorably. But on May 28 he directed all-out preparations for *Fall Grün*, or Operation Green. Within Germany Hitler brushed aside the fears of industrialists and army men, saying that the Western powers would do nothing to stop a seizure of Czechoslovakia. For the time being, however, he turned to diplomacy. At Munich a conference with the French, English, and Italians resulted in an agreement to give Hitler three million "Germans" in the Sudetenland. Russia had been excluded, perhaps because Stalin alone urged a firm stand; so, too, were the Czechs, who learned their fate only afterward. This "peace in our time," as Chamberlain called it, was a warrant of death for Czechoslovakia, a warrant for Hitler to invade that country, and, as it turned out, a warrant for the most destructive war in history. In March 1939 Hitler marched into Moravia-Bohemia, the Czech part of Beneš's state.

Earlier, he had gained a French pledge of "disinterest" in central Europe. Perhaps Paris regarded Prague as doomed when Hitler occupied Vienna, a city *east* of Prague and thus part of a pincer movement against the Czechs. There was no warning, however, when Hitler turned to Lithuania, which was forced to cede the port of Memel little more than a week after the invasion of Czechoslovakia. Hitler's move in the Baltic was the prelude to war against Poland. Britain feared this might come as early as May 1938, *before Munich*. London made pacts guaranteeing the independence of Poland, Rumania, and Greece. Hitler, encouraged by victory, and totally held in awe by the German generals who had been proved consistently wrong, gave orders for *Fall Weiss*, Operation White.

This was the plan to invade Poland; and it was given on April 3, allowing five months for preparations. Hitler had prepared the way with a treaty with Japan[32] and another with Italy.[33] The Japanese pact worried Stalin into

29. An alpine pass which became the border between Austria and Italy after World War I.
30. The German-speaking population in the regions of Czechoslovakia bordering on Germany.
31. Quoted in E. H. Carr, *The Twenty Years' Crisis, 1919–1939* (New York: Harper & Row, Publishers, Torchbooks, 1964), p. 40.
32. The "Pact of Steel" of 1938.
33. The Anti-Comintern Pact.

signing the Nazi-Soviet Pact. Earlier Britain had guaranteed Poland's independence, offering an alliance on March 31, 1939. Stalin had tried to widen the agreement into a triple alliance with France on the condition that Russia's *right* to guarantee the independence of the Baltic republics be recognized. Poland joined Estonia, Latvia, and Lithuania in rejecting Stalin's offer, apparently out of fear of the role Russian troops might play once let in as "guarantors."

Hitler seized on the opportunity thus provided, looking back to Bismarck's policy of publicizing the Polish threat to Russia in order to neutralize Stalin in case of an attack on Poland by Germany. The Nazi-Soviet Pact had in it a secret protocol, however, which was not meant to intimidate the democracies, as the pact itself was. The protocol concluded in secret gave to Russia the states of Finland, Estonia, and Latvia, with Poland east of the rivers San and Vistula. Germany was to have western Poland and Lithuania. Britain thus made public its alliance with Poland on August 25; on August 26, three days after the Nazi-Soviet Pact was signed, Hitler considered the new alignment of states. On September 1 the German blitz began in Poland, turning loose the "hurricane forces" Eden had recognized.

If we ask, then, why the war to create the "New Order of Europe" began, we may find our clues in the events of 1938–1939: the chief former outlaw nations were now going to revise the Versailles peace totally, not in parts, with the complicity of former members of the Allies, Italy and Japan. War might be said to have come because the "Peace" needed in 1918 had never been made; instead, Europe had had its map redrawn, and that was a game more than four[34] could play. Marshal Foch had said as much in 1919, when he noted that Versailles was not a peace, but an armistice for *twenty years*. But to say that this alone explained the new war would be to discount Hitler's *blueprint*! And it would be to ignore altogether Japan's aims. That Eastern industrial power went to war also in 1939, not to make some minor adjustment of borders, but to achieve hegemony in the Far East. Japanese propaganda regarded East Asia as Japan's "Coprosperity Sphere." Unless China surrendered and Russia did too, Japan's aggression in Asia meant a huge war there. The reaction of America was also important, given the Pacific interests of that power, still at that time sometimes mistakenly described by Europeans as only an "Atlantic" power.

IN THE EYE OF THE STORM

That Hitler had decided on a great war as early as November 10, 1938, is now clear. To several hundred newspaper people on that day in Berlin, he spoke frankly, spicing his outline of the events ahead with references to the need to exterminate skeptics. What Hitler said was this: circumstances since 1929 had forced him to talk peace in order to buy time to prepare for war. The time was soon to come for giving freedom to the German people. Just as he, Hitler, had overcome odds within Germany, he would do so in war. The reason was that "racial improvement"—Hitler's euphemism for the terrible persecutions of the Jews—had given to Germany a stronger people than any other country had. Germany had 80 million Germans.[35] Some pointed to the great forces likely to be arrayed against Germany. The United States, for example, might enter a German war, and it had 127 million people. What was left though, Hitler asked, if you subtracted the Irish, Negroes, Jews, and Slavs? Barely 60 million Anglo-Saxons! Germany

---

34. The Big Four.
35. Including the 6 million Austrian Germans (as a result of the *Anschluss*) and 3 million Sudeten Germans (as a result of Munich).

was stronger also than the British, with their 46 million Anglo-Saxons at home; the British Empire was black and yellow, and of no account. So ran the logic of aggression, from Prague to the strike at Poland.

Schematically, the war had three great phases: the vast German offensive in Europe, Russia, and Africa, from 1939 to 1942; the entry of the United States against Japan, which produced a global war in 1942–1943; and the great Allied offensives of 1943 and 1944, which produced a German collapse, after first knocking Italy out, and then the total defeat of Germany and Japan in 1945.

The first German sweep into Poland confirmed the tactics of the Spanish intervention. Poland fell to the tank (panzer) and air force (*Luftwaffe*) assault in twenty-seven days. This result was produced by the combined use of mechanized infantry and artillery on the ground, after air assaults had caught the Polish air force on the ground, destroying it. This allowed the Germans to bomb at will roads and railroads and also cities, to disrupt communications and terrorize the people. Hitler wanted to break his enemies' *will to resist by any means*. After the preliminaries, his officers concentrated an enormously superior tank force at crucial points in the Polish line. Once a breakthrough was secured, the tanks and mechanized infantry ranged the open country, encircling the split Polish forces, which they then *annihilated*. The *blitzkrieg* left no resistance in the countryside, but in cities like Warsaw the defense was courageous. Hitler therefore *destroyed* the city by aerial bombardment: the first example in warfare of the destruction of a city in this manner. Two days after Poland's surrender, Russia and Germany divided the country, on the basis of the 1939 pact.

There then ensued what historians call the "phony war." Britain and France gave no effective support to Poland, concentrating instead on a power buildup in the West in an effort to prevent further *blitzkrieg* tactics from succeeding. A period of inactivity followed, except in Finland, which Russia crushed in a short campaign late in 1939 and early in 1940. Since the Allies had tried to protect the North, Hitler preempted this by an occupation of Denmark, which did not resist, and a short war against tiny Norway. The Norwegian campaign was important, however, because it unveiled another tactical novelty: a combined naval and air attack with the "dropping" of *paratroops*. Also important was the effect of the campaign in Britain: Winston Churchill replaced Chamberlain as prime minister, and he set up a war cabinet of all parties on May 10, 1940.

That was the day the Germans launched their western offensive. Seventeen days later, after the central districts of cities had been obliterated by air strikes, the Belgian king[36] capitulated. The Dutch queen[37] had surrendered thirteen days before, with part of Rotterdam in ruins. But over 330,000 British and French troops were rescued from the beaches at Dunkerque, despite relentless air assaults; the British navy provided cover for a fleet of small boats piloted by civilians. Southward, the Germans drove into France with tanks, having split the Allies along a line from Amiens to Abbeville. Breakthroughs on the line of the Somme opened the way to Paris, which the *Wehrmacht* entered on June 14, 1940. German planes relentlessly strafed the roads clogged with civilian refugees.

Churchill desperately tried to keep France in the war, but Prime Minister Reynaud[38] was overruled by the military, who thought resistance useless. Marshal Pétain, the hero of Verdun, then organized a profascist govern-

36. Leopold III (1934–1951).
37. Wilhelmina (1890–1948).
38. Paul Reynaud (1878–1966).

ment, after the surrender of three-fifths of France on June 22. Under the terms, France was left in charge of the southeast and North Africa, which obeyed the government at Vichy. This government rallied the pro-Nazi forces under Pierre Laval (1883–1945). Even unoccupied France therefore fell to fascism, with those unconvinced that this was France's future following General Charles de Gaulle (1890–1970) into exile.[39] In London and North Africa de Gaulle constituted the Free French Government.

The imminent fall of France brought Mussolini into the war on Hitler's side. This gave Hitler security in the Mediterranean, while Germany turned to consider Britain, which was now alone in the Western resistance. The dilemma Hitler faced was how to defeat the island fortress. Despite plans for an amphibious assault, it was decided to force a surrender, or at least weaken resistance, from the air. The Battle of Britain thus produced another novelty: the massive use of bombardment against all military and civilian centers. From July to September the attacks focused on troops and military sites, but then the air blitz went to London. The RAF (Royal Air Force) lost strength but resisted heroically. On September 16, Churchill committed the reserve, and on that day 185 German planes were destroyed. Until November, night raids continued, with hundreds of bombers involved, for the sole purpose of breaking the spirit of the British people. While hundreds were killed in single raids and treasured buildings were destroyed, the British stood firm. Hitler was checked for the first time, and Churchill was correct in his judgment; in the Battle of Britain the West gave hope that Germany could be withstood.

Hitler absorbed the lesson of his failure to bring Britain to terms. He abandoned the plan to invade, and the war machine turned eastward. Hitler now believed he could defeat Russia, since he had won in the West and thought Britain no longer any threat. Moreover, Stalin had moved rapidly into the Baltic; and Molotov had refused to accord Hitler a free hand in the Balkans. This rebuff in 1940 provoked the *Führer* to activate his "blueprint," but not before he had corrected the Italian failures. Molotov's hostility in 1940 was due to the fact that Mussolini had used the western campaigns to invade Greece. But instead of defeating the Greek forces in an Italian version of *blitzkrieg*, the Italians had been pushed out of Greece into Italian-occupied Albania. Moreover, the British had severely beaten the Italians in North Africa. Thus Hitler had to secure the two other fronts (the Balkans and North Africa) before invading Russia.

This he did by sending the armored forces of General Rommel[40] to North Africa, where a prolonged desert war began. Hitler also moved resolutely in the Balkans, combining diplomacy and war. Germany used threats to force

39. A tank commander, de Gaulle escaped in a British plane.
40. Erwin Rommel, 1891–1944; a great tank commander.

The German blitz in London, a harrowing and incessant series of Luftwaffe attacks, began on September 7, 1940. German bombs struck everywhere, even near Buckingham Palace; one unexploded bomb lodged in the outer foundations of St. Paul's Cathedral (shown in the background of this view of London during the blitz). After almost three days of work, the bomb was removed and detonated safely; miraculously St. Paul's survived the blitz, which lasted into June 1941. More than 12,000 tons of German bombs were dropped on London, taking almost 30,000 lives and wounding more than 120,000 people. The attacks, however, failed in their objective; the British people and the RAF fought on, stubbornly withstanding Hitler's onslaught until, at last, he sent his Luftwaffe elsewhere. Radio Times Hulton Picture Library.

the native Balkan fascist states into the Axis system: Hungary, Rumania, and Bulgaria. When Yugoslavia later declined the alliance, Hitler invaded, crushing resistance, and rolled into Greece as well. Within a few weeks the Balkans were in German hands and paratroops had seized Crete. Meanwhile, by mid-1941 Rommel had driven the British in Africa all the way east to Egypt's borders. The whole Near East lay open to conquest.

Such a diversion was never in Hitler's mind, however, and on June 22, 1941, the real "eastern front" was opened. The invasion of Russia began, despite Stalin's efforts to avoid it. Stalin had been optimistic about combat, though, because he believed *blitzkrieg* worked only against decadent capitalist forces. But tank breakthroughs and air superiority worked as well in Russia as elsewhere, even though the Red Army fought stubbornly for every position, thus assuring their own encirclement. When Kiev fell, over 175,000 prisoners of war were taken. In October Leningrad[41] and Moscow were under siege. While a mass evacuation of Moscow took place, the battle for the former imperial capital in the northwest endured the onslaught with nearly the full civilian population. Stalin remained in Moscow, directing the defense of Russia and broadcasting radio speeches of great passion to the Soviet peoples, urging resistance to the death against the Nazi barbarians.

November had come, and with it a second Nazi thrust against Moscow and Leningrad. The new offensive was hampered by an early winter; logistics became difficult. Stalin found great commanders in the field who were more effective than the party men promoted in 1937–1938, in the army

41. Czarist Saint Petersburg had been renamed.

The siege of Leningrad lasted twenty-eight months, from the fall of 1941 until January of 1944. The Germans cut off virtually all means of supply, leaving only one route—a road across the ice of Leningrad's Lake Ladoga. During the first two months of 1942, as many as 3,500 to 4,000 people died each day, primarily from starvation and disease but also as a result of German artillery fire and aerial bombardment. In the spring of 1942, the Nazis, renewing their attack, began a round-the-clock artillery barrage, blasting Leningrad block by block; at left, Leningraders killed by a German shell lie in the city's most famous avenue, the Nevsky Prospect. When the German encirclement began, Leningrad had a population of 3,000,000 people; according to Russian figures, the siege took the lives of 632,000. Sovfoto.

purges. The Soviets also performed the heroic feat of transporting part of their industrial capacity into the vast Urals and the Siberian interior. There, a steady rise in production of all military goods took shape, as the siege of Leningrad stretched into 1942. Also, the entry into the war of the United States late in 1941 brought about a "convoy" system of supplying Soviet needs, despite the natural dangers of the ice-locked and submarine-infested northern route to Murmansk and Archangel.

Hitler had thrown three million Axis troops[42] into Russia, on a line from the Baltic to the oil fields of the Caucasus, with sieges against Leningrad, Moscow, and Stalingrad—the gateway to the Caspian Sea. Yet the Russians held, retreating, burning standing crops in 1942, trading space for time, even the food and oil of the whole Ukraine, in order to fight. The war, which had by then become truly global, was revealing yet another aspect in Russia. Stalin formed guerrilla units, both to harass the Germans and to destroy factories and farms not gutted in advance of their occupation. Hitler had taken personal command on December 19, 1941, and his fanatic determination to hold the whole Russian line alienated military men. This stubborn indifference to advice also produced a delay in launching the Battle of Stalingrad, which began in the summer of 1942. When that siege began, Nazi power had reached its territorial limits. Victory in a quick campaign in Russia had proved beyond Hitler's grasp. The war in Europe had reached an impasse; and from the moment Hitler failed to take Russia out of the war, his defeat began.

We have said that in 1942 the war became truly global in character. Earlier, the Asian theater had witnessed a long row of Japanese triumphs: Indochina, Burma, Singapore, and the East Indies were lost to France, Britain, and Holland. The American President Roosevelt had already followed a course of belligerent neutrality, sending aid to Britain by trades of war supplies as early as 1940. Opinion in the United States was against an entry into the "European" quarrel, a stance that was part of the long heritage of isolationism dating from the refusal of America to enter the League in 1919–1920. But Japanese domination of the Pacific threatened American interests in that area—in Alaska, the Hawaiian Islands, the Philippines, and elsewhere. Thus Roosevelt in 1941 put increasing diplomatic and economic pressure on Japan, but negotiations collapsed late in the fall. On December 7, 1941, the Japanese naval forces made a daring air raid with carrier-based forces, wrecking a good part of the Hawaii-based United States fleet in Pearl Harbor. Congress declared war against only Japan on December 8, in response to Roosevelt's speech and request after the "day of infamy."

Germany and Italy were bound by treaty to aid Japan in any war resulting from the actions of a state *not at war in Europe*. On December 11 the Axis Powers made declarations of war against the United States, a decision urged by Hitler in the face of the tough resistance of the Red Army in Russia. Now Roosevelt could go beyond the mere modification of neutrality acts,[43] which allowed the sale of arms but not their transport in American ships. A year before Pearl Harbor, Roosevelt had spoken of America as "the arsenal of Democracy."[44] In March 1941 Congress had passed the Lend-Lease Act, allowing the United States to aid states to survive, where their endurance was vital to American security. In August Roosevelt and Churchill had met and pledged the Atlantic Charter, the basic statement of

42. Finns, Rumanians, Hungarians, Italians, and Germans.
43. Passed in 1939 and "bent" in 1940, by the deal to give destroyers to Britain.
44. Radio speech, December 29, 1940.

war aims, which held the Western democracies to the faith of freedom and social welfare. The ground had thus been prepared for the visit of Churchill to Washington, where from December 22 to January 14 he and Roosevelt agreed on the overall plan for victory. This plan had two features: it gave priority to the European war and to Hitler's defeat; and it created a single command structure in each "theater" of war, under the staff direction of General George C. Marshall (1880–1959) and Sir John Dill (1881–1944). Russia was not included because of Stalin's suspicious nature and the basic strategy.

This strategy unfolded in the war's second phase. Briefly, it was to open a "second front" to take pressure off Russia. Stalin wished this done at once, in 1942, because his forces were being ravaged by their heroic withstanding of the great sieges. Roosevelt had sympathy for this idea, but Churchill was not above wanting to see the Bolsheviks weakened at the war's end. He had from 1917 on suffered from the "dreadful malady of Bolshevism on the Brain," as Lloyd George said in 1919. But there were also good military reasons not to invade France in 1942; Germany was awfully strong in 1942, while the United States had not yet geared up to war. Moreover, the Pacific war at first went badly for the United States. Japan was threatening to control the whole Far East and by July 1942 had taken the Philippines and Malaya, the Dutch East Indies, and a string of South Pacific islands. In early naval engagements, the American Pacific fleet had suffered further heavy losses.

Hence Churchill resolutely argued that the correct strategy was to defeat the Axis in North Africa, thus breaking the pincer Hitler held on Europe in the Mediterranean. Then, Italy might be taken out of the war, by amphibious assault through Sicily and southern Italy. Only in that way, it seemed, could the second front in the West finally be decisive. Meanwhile, "Uncle Joe" Stalin would have to hold on, until the tide had been turned elsewhere. It was decided that Hitler was simply too strong in Europe for direct assault in 1942. And there was much to be said for this view. For over a year (since July 1941), Hitler had held all of continental Europe except Britain, Sweden, Switzerland, and Iberia, which was a neutral fascist region.

Elsewhere, regimes like the Vichy French government were established in states allied with Germany. And in the conquered regions direct German control was in effect. These arrangements had allowed Hitler to put in his service virtually all European resources, from manpower to raw materials, in a tribute labor system. Local Nazi party and Gestapo groups terrorized the people, especially in states where strong resistance movements grew up, carrying on a variety of guerrilla warfare. The resistance forces were usually either Communist-dominated or Social Democrat–oriented, but there were also large networks of Christian resisters, both Catholic and Protestant, as well as Jewish groups such as the one in command of the Warsaw ghetto in Poland.

While the importance of the Resistance in Nazi Europe is sometimes overestimated, the activities of the various undergrounds should not, in any case, be overlooked. The French *Marquis* carried out wide intelligence and sabotage operations. So, too, did the Norwegian forces opposed to the fascist regime there, the Quisling government.[45] In Yugoslavia Tito led the Partisans into a regular civil war against the fascist-oriented royalists[46] under Draza Mihajlovic. Everywhere, the cost was high. In retaliation for

45. Headed by Vidkun Quisling, 1887–1945; his name was given to other collaborators; they were commonly called Quislings.
46. The "chetniks."

This is Nazi brutality

RADIO BERLIN.--IT IS OFFICIALLY ANNOUNCED:-
ALL MEN OF LIDICE - CZECHOSLOVAKIA - HAVE BEEN SHOT:
THE WOMEN DEPORTED TO A CONCENTRATION CAMP:
THE CHILDREN SENT TO APPROPRIATE CENTERS-- THE
NAME OF THE VILLAGE WAS IMMEDIATELY ABOLISHED.
6/11/42/115P

The Germans retaliated for the assassination of Reinhard Heydrich, Nazi Reich Protector of Bohemia and Moravia, by marching into the Czech village of Lidice on the morning of June 10, 1942, and obliterating it. Acting under Hitler's direct command, Gestapo agents killed or deported all the inhabitants, looted and destroyed every building because they suspected (falsely, as it later turned out) that the town was harboring Heydrich's killers. The Nazis admitted their brutality, claiming they had destroyed a population of 438; according to Czech figures, the population had been 1,200. Within less than three months, a town in Illinois and one in Mexico had changed their names to Lidice; the American artist Ben Shahn commemorated the atrocity in this 1943 lithograph. Lidice was rebuilt in 1948. Collection, the Museum of Modern Art, New York, gift of the Office of War Information.

the assassination of a Gestapo leader by Czechs, the entire village of Lidice was destroyed, the men executed and the women and children dispersed in concentration camps.

Thus it was at the height of Hitler's fortune that the Allies took the offensive. The Battle of Stalingrad in mid-1942 was terrible, raging until January 31, 1943. In November it had seemed that Stalingrad would fall; Hitler even announced that it had. But a Russian counterattack broke the lines of General Paulus, encircling his army of 300,000; Paulus surrendered on the last day of January, together with the 123,000 men that were left alive.[47] This forced a German retreat northward beyond the hole in the vast line within Russia. Meanwhile, in North Africa the British under General Montgomery pushed Rommel's overextended tank forces westward, after a decisive victory at El Alamein, aided by superior naval and air forces. As Rommel moved westward in Libya and Tunisia, General Eisenhower

47. A pocket of Germans held a tractor works in the northern suburbs of Stalingrad and didn't surrender until February 2.

achieved an American landing late in 1942, in French North Africa. The Vichy French surrendered quickly, and by mid-May 1943 Rommel's forces had been beaten in detail.

At the same time, in the Pacific, the war against Japan was turning in America's favor. Three great naval battles, with powerful carrier-based air forces proving decisive, were fought. And in 1942 the Japanese fleet had been crippled in the engagements of the Coral Sea (May), Midway (June), and the Solomon Islands (November). Elsewhere, the British revived the war in Burma, the Chinese fought with the aid of American forces, and India was kept out of the Japanese net.

It is probably correct to say that by mid-1943 the Allied offensives made the defeat of the Axis inescapable. But Hitler was now bent on saving "fortress Europe" by any means. He urged his research scientists to devise superweapons, and they did produce unmanned rockets which were used in a new bombardment of London in 1944. German scientists were also working on harnessing atomic energy for bombs, but this race was eventually won by America, with the help of refugees from fascist ideology—the Italian Fermi, the Hungarian Szilard, and Einstein himself. The real determinant of victory, however, was industrial power, in which Hitler now no longer enjoyed superiority.

Hitler had some hope of causing defections from the Allied side, notably because of the bad will between Churchill and Stalin. This was widely known to exist, even after the Casablanca Conference in early 1943, where Roosevelt and Churchill met to reassure Stalin that a "western front" was to be opened soon, and where the demand of "unconditional" German surrender was set forth. This was also to reassure Russia that no separate

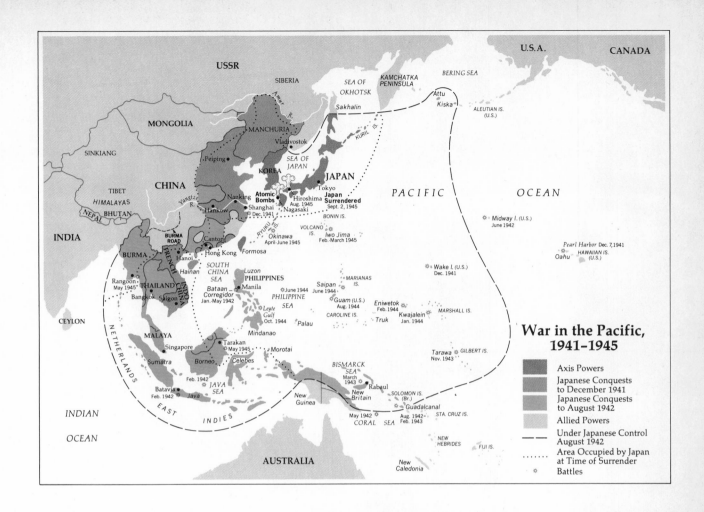

War in the Pacific, 1941–1945

- Axis Powers
- Japanese Conquests to December 1941
- Japanese Conquests to August 1942
- Allied Powers
- – – – Under Japanese Control August 1942
- ·········· Area Occupied by Japan at Time of Surrender
- ✿ Battles

(Map labels: USSR, SIBERIA, MONGOLIA, MANCHURIA, SINKIANG, TIBET, HIMALAYAS, NEPAL, BHUTAN, INDIA, CHINA, CEYLON, BURMA, BURMA ROAD, FRENCH INDO-CHINA, THAILAND, MALAYA, Peiping, Nanking, Hankow, Shanghai, Canton, Hong Kong, Hanoi, Hainan, Rangoon May 1945, Bangkok, Saigon, Singapore, Sumatra, Batavia Feb. 1942, Java Feb. 1942, Borneo, Celebes, Tarakan May 1945, Morotai, Mindanao, Luzon, PHILIPPINES, Manila, Bataan Corregidor Jan.-May 1942, Leyte Gulf Oct. 1944, Palau, SOUTH CHINA SEA, PHILIPPINE SEA, JAVA SEA, NETHERLANDS EAST INDIES, INDIAN OCEAN, AUSTRALIA, New Guinea, New Britain, Rabaul, BISMARCK SEA March 1943, SOLOMON IS. (Br.), Guadalcanal Aug. 1942-Feb. 1943, CORAL SEA May 1942, STA. CRUZ IS., NEW HEBRIDES, FIJI IS., New Caledonia, KOREA, Vladivostok, Amur R., Sakhalin, KURIL IS., SEA OF JAPAN, SEA OF OKHOTSK, KAMCHATKA PENINSULA, BERING SEA, Attu, Kiska, ALEUTIAN IS. (U.S.), JAPAN, Tokyo, Atomic Bombs Aug. 1945, Hiroshima, Nagasaki, Japan Surrendered Sept. 2, 1945, Okinawa April-June 1945, Formosa, RYUKYU IS., BONIN IS., VOLCANO IS., Iwo Jima Feb.-March 1945, Yangtze R., PACIFIC OCEAN, Midway I. (U.S.) June 1942, Wake I. (U.S.) Dec. 1941, MARIANAS IS., Saipan June 1944, Guam (U.S.) Aug. 1944, Eniwetok Feb. 1944, Kwajalein Jan. 1944, Truk, CAROLINE IS., MARSHALL IS., Tarawa Nov. 1943, GILBERT IS., Pearl Harbor Dec. 7, 1941, Oahu, HAWAIIAN IS. (U.S.), U.S.A., CANADA)

The great battle of El Alamein, "the gateway to Egypt," began with a British offensive on October 23, 1942. The German General Rommel, earlier replaced by a new commander, was called back within hours, but lack of fuel and supplies had already spelled defeat. German tanks had run out of gas and were under attack by R.A.F. planes; some of the outdated Italian tanks had fallen apart when their guns were fired. At left, Allies capture a German tank at El Alamein in October 1942; in November, British newspapers announced the capture or destruction of 260 Axis tanks. A decisive Allied victory, the battle forced the westward retreat of the Afrika Korps and marked the beginning of the end for German forces in North Africa. Imperial War Museum, London.

peace with Hitler would be made. Before the "Big Three" met for the first time, in the historic Teheran Conference of December 1943, however, it was the Italian front that had been opened. Sicily had been invaded on July 10, 1943, and this led anti-Fascist leaders to overthrow Mussolini. He was subsequently rescued from prison by German paratroops, but in the interim the new government[48] negotiated secretly to pull Italy out of the war. The Allies were now on the mainland and driving toward Rome from the south, while German tanks were coming toward Rome from the Alps. The armistice of September 8, 1943, brought no real peace, but instead a war between German and Allied forces between Naples and Rome. Mussolini had headquarters in northern Italy,[49] where he was now a German puppet.

The net effect of the Italian collapse is hard to estimate, but two things must be attributed to it. Antifascists everywhere enlarged the resistance struggle; and German forces now had to take the place of Italians in the Balkans. This weakened Hitler's armies everywhere, especially on the Russian front. Units in the "Battle for Italy" were withdrawn from tank divisions needed in what was in retrospect the last German offensive there.

In early 1944, therefore, it was the case that the Russians were moving westward on a front extending from the region of Kiev to that of the Baltic, racing into Poland early in the spring and threatening the whole Danube line of approach to Germany from the southeast. The Italian front was also

48. Under General Pietro Badoglio (1871–1956).
49. His "republic" was established in the small town of Salò.

in disarray, and in the summer Florence was in Allied hands. These offensives, while equally as important as what was to come, were less startling than the vast invasion of France launched by Eisenhower's command in June. "D-Day" was June 6, 1944, when a cross-channel amphibious force of huge size effected a landing on the beaches of Normandy under conditions of total sea and air superiority.

While troops beached in artificial harbors made in Britain, the Allies continued a heavy air attack on Germany's cities. This was aimed not only at wrecking German production—which it never did—but also at destroying whole cities, whether these had any strategic value or not. The point was to defeat Hitler by destroying the support he had at home. That there was some hope of doing this is shown by a plot against Hitler's life on July 20, 1944. A group of generals and civilian officials joined "liberal" and socialist plotters in the hope that, with Hitler dead, the Allies would make a separate peace and keep Germany itself from conquest, especially by Russians, who counted 25 million dead as a cost of Hitler's invasion. This plot backfired, however; the bomb exploded just after Hitler had moved from his position at the conference table. The "treason" was exploited in the media to justify a now fanatically destructive determination either to gain a miraculous victory or to destroy a German people now found unworthy of their Leader.

During the European conflict in World War II the American social realist Ben Shahn painted Italian Landscape, 1943–44. Only dejected figures are left to wander among the desolate rubble of a battered continent. Physically the war was the most appalling in history. With the advent of air power it was possible to destroy vast urban areas in a few days' time, and such historic cities as Dresden, Berlin, Cologne, and large sections of London were obliterated. The industrial base, too, was largely gone, and even many agricultural areas were a shambles. In the first dark postwar years Europe was highly dependent on America for aid which was given through the Marshall Plan. Gradually the old societies found the strength to revive and achieve a still growing sense of cooperation. Collection Walker Art Center, Minneapolis. From the Gilbert M. Walker Fund.

This suicidal twilight of the gods was not long delayed. Allied commanders had achieved the liberation of France and Belgium by the end of September 1944, and had penetrated to the Rhine as well in the southern sector under General George Patton. A determined German counteroffensive in the Ardennes Forest region on the northern front failed late in 1944. This set the stage for the push into Germany in 1945, from the east by Russia in February and across the Rhine by American forces in March. The two forces met on the Elbe River on April 25; on the twenty-ninth the troops in Italy surrendered. On April 30 Hitler committed suicide in his command bunker in Berlin. The Russians seized the capital, and on May 7, 1945, at Reims in France the German High Command surrendered to Eisenhower, with a similar surrender made to the Russian Zhukov two days later. Hitler's tactical daring and strategic genius had proved *he could defeat Europe*, but the combination of Russia and America could not be overcome. His suicide came only two days after the execution of Mussolini.[50]

Fascism was defeated in Europe, but the war had been global in scope. Thus "V-E Day" saw the struggle against Japan still in full swing. General MacArthur[51] had since 1942 conducted a brilliant "island-hopping" campaign across the South Pacific, while in southern Asia Lord Louis Mountbatten liberated Burma, after a three-year struggle. Late in 1944 the position

50. See Walter Langer, *The Mind of Adolf Hitler* (New York: Basic Books, 1972), in which the pathology of the suicide actually committed in Berlin is discussed and Hitler's end predicted in a convincing study made *during* the war.
51. Douglas MacArthur, 1880–1964.

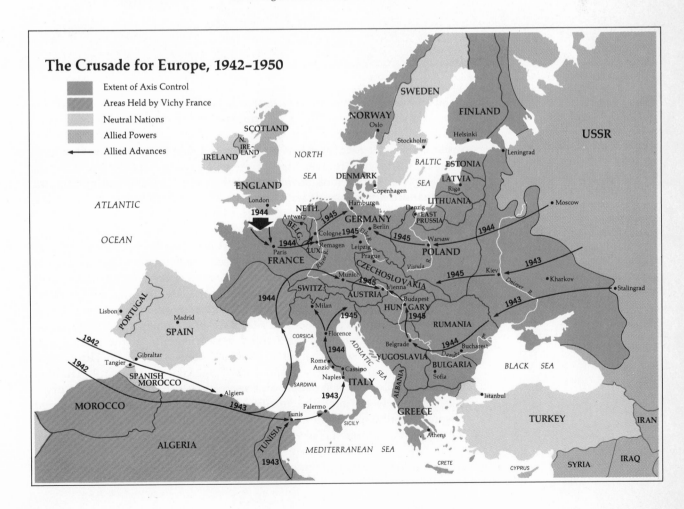

The Crusade for Europe, 1942–1950

Extent of Axis Control
Areas Held by Vichy France
Neutral Nations
Allied Powers
Allied Advances

It was about 11:00 A.M. Tokyo time on August 9, 1945, when the second atomic bomb struck Japan. Its target was the supply port of Nagasaki, a city renowned for the beauty of its harbor. When the bomb hit, a giant fireball rose from Nagasaki; some 75,000 Japanese were killed or injured, and the municipal area, three miles by two miles was reduced to debris. More than a third of Nagasaki had been destroyed. The photo above, from September 13, 1945, shows a Japanese civilian pushing his bicycle along a cleared path in the center of the devastated area. UPI.

of Japan was precarious, therefore, as some of the Philippines were retaken, in an operation at Leyte Gulf that crippled the Japanese air force and fleet. That battle marked the last occasion in which a great fight between warships was waged, for it was air power and submarine warfare that won the day, destroying forever the old premise that in battle sea power was decisive. MacArthur took advantage of the superiority he had to hammer the Japanese home islands with combined heavy explosive and incendiary air raids, from Iwo Jima and Okinawa, which Marines had taken after costly assaults.

But the Japanese resisted even after the outer defense had been collapsed in May 1945. President Truman[52] thus faced a difficult campaign to take the home islands, in which his staff estimated over a million lives would be lost. We now know that Japan was ready to surrender late in the summer; supplies of oil, coal, and food were exhausted and could not be replenished, because MacArthur controlled the sea. But America didn't know this at the time; hence on August 6, the United States ushered in the atomic age, dropping a bomb with the force of 20,000 tons of TNT on Hiroshima; another of equal force was dropped on Nagasaki on August 9. The two explosions killed 130,000 people and seriously wounded an equal number. Less than a week later the terrified and exhausted Japan surrendered unconditionally; on September 2 came the formal surrender, aboard a battleship[53] anchored in Tokyo Bay, with MacArthur as the Allied acceptor.

52. He succeeded Roosevelt in 1945, when FDR died of a cerebral stroke in April.
53. The *Missouri*.

A comprehension of this global war cannot rest solely on the fact that Hitler crushed countries like so many soft-boiled eggs, or on the mistaken belief that these results were obtained because of mere military superiority. On the western front in 1939 Hitler had 134 divisions; the combined Allied force, however, had exactly as many.[54] But the Nazi forces were better equipped and better organized for modern war. Tank strength was imbalanced in favor of the Allies, 3,200 to 2,500. But the German tactics were superior. It was only in the air that Germany had a marked numerical edge, about 3,500 planes to 1,200.

Still less can we understand the war in any other military terms, however sophisticated our analysis. For example, was Hitler right or wrong to seek to hold the whole Russian line in 1942? Was the war prolonged into 1945 in Europe because Eisenhower and Bradley[55] refused to allow Patton to make an armored dash to Berlin? The war was total—economic, psychological, scientific, and above all else political. When the Big Three met at the Teheran Conference (1943) and at Yalta (1945), they did so to discuss strategy. But every strategic decision shaped a political one. How the West was divided after 1945, into the Soviet and American "blocs," was a consequence of how the war was fought—and for what aims. Even more important to us, however, was the evidence provided about the nature of war between 1939 and 1945.

Indeed, as Hitler said in 1925, modern war was economic war, war against the total capacity of industry and the labor resources of a people. This meant economic planning, rationing, inter-Allied planning: even economic conservatives like Churchill achieved essentially dictatorial power during the war. Moreover, in every state the old idea that financial solvency meant everything was overthrown. Deficit financing for production of war goods converted people en masse to the twin ideas of controlled economies and resource manipulation *without regard for debt*. In 1944 Britain's work force was one-third "wartime" (civilian war employment). Manpower control was established everywhere; and people accustomed to debt in the national interest until 1945 were to ask why debt for social reconstruction after 1945 was any less in the national interest!

Therefore, the Western economies were at last "catching up" to the Soviet system of five-year plans. Moreover, within the USSR the war induced a transfer of production eastward and so transformed Asian Russia. In 1942 the eastern regions of the USSR produced 39 percent of Soviet steel and 50 percent of Soviet tractor equipment. A decree in the same year mobilized all men aged sixteen to fifty-five not in uniform, and all women sixteen to forty-five, for the eastern migration. In the same year a four-year plan reorganized German production on the basis of the labor and resources of the captive peoples, a program headed by Albert Speer. This system enabled Hitler's index of production to climb from a base of 100 to 322 late in 1943, despite air raids of enormous intensity. Even as late as September 1944 Germany produced 3,538 planes in one month, a number equal to the whole Luftwaffe of 1939!

Psychologically, the war brought to prominence what Hitler always understood to be a dominant weapon in mass societies—propaganda. Goebbels' "Ministry of People's Enlightenment and Propaganda" later inspired George Orwell's savage parody in *Nineteen Eighty-Four*: the

54. France, 94; Britain, 10; Belgium, 22; Holland, 8.
55. General Omar Bradley, European theater commander of the American field forces.

Ministry of Truth, in business to tell lies. But propaganda for the people at home existed everywhere. More significant was the technique of broadcasts into enemy territories, often by foreign nationals. Hitler used William Joyce, a British Nazi, to speak to the British. Japan used "Tokyo Rose" to undermine American troop morale. Goebbels also exploited films in unoccupied Europe, showing the effect of *blitzkrieg* in France and Poland to convince governments not to resist and to coerce whole peoples.

Psychological warfare as practiced by democratic and by totalitarian countries became more and more the same as the war continued. This is not to say that the techniques merged. For there were differences between Nazi styles and Allied ones. But the end in view was the same: to add persuasion by psychological means to the anxiety produced by physical destruction. The fire-bombing of Dresden toward the end of the war killed more people than the atomic-bombing of Hiroshima and Nagasaki combined. But the purpose was only partly to kill; what made mass death *more evil than "banal,"* as some critics have, rather perversely, called it, was the light which such carnage threw on all governments. There were literally no means off limits in a war in which the stake was really the survival of civilization as each belligerent knew it or wished it to be. So, in 1944, BBC broadcast 160,000 words daily in twenty-three languages, employing Britons and Axis war prisoners, to reach the twenty-three countries within Hitler's Europe. Mass slaughter was another form of language, and it spoke directly to the point.

If the science of psychology made a major contribution to the war effort,[56] so did every other science. Churchill appointed "Tizard the Wizard" (Henry Tizard) to direct scientific war research. Of course, "scientific methods" in war were nothing new. Rulers had wanted military inventions from biblical times to our own; and in the First World War we recognize poison gas, the airplane, the tank, and the bomb dropped from aircraft as historic "advances" in military technique.

We live, however, in a world transformed by the scientific applications of the Second World War. For the war was significant in at least three respects of a novel nature: the power scientists achieved within governments, the array of devices they produced, and the potential for good and evil inherent in these devices.

In Britain, for example, Lord Cherwell[57] was judged to have more influence with Churchill than any other adviser, and more power than any other scientist in history. There was no parallel in either Russia or Germany, where totalitarian party ideologies were antithetical to the exercise of *political* influence by scientists. On the contrary, Stalin's hostility to genetic theories of mutation caused Soviet biology, and hence agriculture, to follow a disastrous course. And Hitler's anti-Semitism gave to America the great physicists Einstein, Meitner, and Szilard. With their aid it is entirely possible that atomic bombs might have been in Hitler's hands, not Truman's, in 1945!

Devices worth special mention, because of their civilian uses after the war was over, are too numerous even to catalogue. But a few must be mentioned. Radar[58] was in use in 1935 in Britain, as an application of the "directional" finding qualities of radio waves. This was vital in the Battle of Britain in

56. In broadcasting, films, journalism, and drops of leaflets encouraging resistance; it was also at the heart of Dr. Langer's study of Hitler's mind. See footnote 50 of this chapter.
57. The Oxford teacher F. A. Lindemann.
58. Developed by Robert Watson-Watt in 1935.

detecting Nazi bombers. Later, bombs dropped from planes guided to targets by navigational radar[59] were also guided electronically. Similarly, electronics detected subs ("sonar") and optical science perfected various camouflages for every habitat. Degaussing machines—minesweepers—cleared minefields; but there was no good defense against the rocket-propelled machines used to terror-bomb London until the RAF perfected the Gloster Meteors to shoot down the V-1 guided missiles. Rocket and jet-fuel crafts were to remake the future of civilian aviation.

In the medical sciences, research councils were at work even before the war. They were responsible for developing concentrated diet substitutes or "rations" to guard troops against malnutrition and for finding substitute remedies against malaria, once the Japanese cut off supplies of quinine from Java. The Germans had synthesized quinacrine in 1917. American research-ers perfected DDT to protect troops against jungle pests. Dozens of sulfa and penicillin compounds revolutionized the treatment of battle casualties, thus bringing the world across the threshold of the antibiotic age. Whether this compensates for the crossing of the missile threshold is difficult to say. As early as 1934 Russian and German researchers had experimented with long-range rockets. The German V-2s of World War II, however, 4,500 strong, created the atmosphere of invisible death in which we all live, the early weapons of destruction having given way to nuclear intercontinental ballistic missiles.

What made the prospect of missile warfare so terrifying was the prospect that Rutherford's "smashing of the atom" principle[60] might be linked to that of the rocket. Mass slaughter delivered without warning and over thousands of miles was not achieved before 1945. But in our own time it is an ever-present part of reality, because a former German rocket scientist who came to America[61] linked the results of the Manhattan Project to his own research.

The Manhattan Project was the code name for the experiments carried on in America to build and detonate an atomic bomb. The actual plutonium chain reaction fired in July 1945 in New Mexico was an international achievement, however. As early as 1928 George Gamow, a Russian, had formulated the theory of bombarding atomic nuclei with accelerated pro-tons. In 1932 this idea was applied by British and American teams[62] to the disintegration of atoms. Two years later Fermi in Rome used neutrons to disintegrate nonradioactive elements and produce radioactive ones. The Dane Niels Bohr explained the event in 1936. In 1938 Otto Hahn in Berlin tested the Bohr theories with elements lighter than uranium, and the refugee Otto Frisch also split nuclei into nearly equal fragments, liberating great amounts of energy in even small "atomic reactions."

Before the war broke out, therefore, it was widely understood that a self-sustaining chain reaction, or continuous nuclear fission and energy release, was possible. The British physicist C. P. Snow published specula-tion on *atomic weapons* in 1939. French scientists advanced the effort in 1939, but failed to sustain a chain reaction. In Germany the preparation for a short war short-circuited similar research. Therefore two refugees now in Britain[63] established in theory the *critical mass* for such a reaction; and they

59. The forecaster of weather today.
60. In 1919, Rutherford bombarded nitrogen and hydrogen atoms with alpha particles liberated by radioactive uranium.
61. Wernher Von Braun.
62. Headed by J. D. Cockcroft and E. O. Lawrence, respectively.
63. Frisch and Rudolf Peierls.

showed that less than a pound of U-235[64] was required. In 1941 five million pounds was assigned to build such a "mass" and thus a bomb. America was in the race too, however, and with its greater resources won the battle for production. But a crucial element in the success was the courage of the Norwegian underground, which in 1943 destroyed the Norsk-Hydro plant producing heavy water for a German bomb.[65] The Russians were far behind, because G. N. Flerov, the "father" of the Russian bomb, was not successful in his campaign for it until 1942. The first Russian atom smasher (cyclotron) was completed in 1945, but no success came until 1949, four years after America began its period of world domination under the cloud of its nuclear umbrella.

Yet even the atomic bomb, however significant it proved for the future of the West and of the world, was not the most startling aspect of the total nature of war *within Europe*, where democracy and totalitarianism were locked in a struggle for the soul of the West. The Nazi liquidation of the Jews was.

The extermination of Europe's Jews arose out of the confluence of ideological motives, wartime opportunities, and the scientific application of technology to the task of murdering men, women, and children who were neither combatants nor bystanders in the path of shells or bombs. The Nazi dictatorship brought the full force of war to bear on the people Hitler had pledged to abolish as early as 1924[66] but the way was prepared by events inside Germany and in Eastern Europe between 1938 and 1941. The inhumanity of the Nazis emerged clearly in what was called the *Kristallnacht*. On November 9, 1938, Hitler loosed a pogrom against the Jews in Germany who had not fled since 1933[67] or been put in concentration camps.[68] Jews were baited, beaten, killed, or confined; and their synagogues were burned and shops broken apart. The glass[69] had scarcely been swept from the streets when, almost a year later, the invasion of Poland confronted Hitler with the three million Polish Jews.

The turn toward the eastern lands posed also the larger problem of "inferior races" in general. Hitler was adamant that the "New Order" must not contain such elements. From 1933 the SS had charge of concentration camps. By 1936 the special SS Death's-Head units (*Totenkopfverbände*) had 3,500 men trained in torture and willing to commit any act under orders. The population in the camps swelled steadily in 1938–1939, after the Austria and Czech conquests. The Polish Jews could not be accommodated in the rapidly expanding camp system, even after Auschwitz[70] was opened. Hitler decided in 1939 to murder the whole Polish intelligentsia, Christian and Jewish, together with every Communist party member. Proclaiming that wars were not won with "Salvation Army methods,"[71] he debated with other officials the relative merit of deporting 20,000,000 Poles or exterminating them. By 1940, SS units were murdering thousands systematically. One commander boasted that the forests in Poland would not grow enough trees to provide paper for the final toll of death notices.

64. A highly fissionable isotope of uranium.
65. Under the direction of Werner Heisenberg.
66. Hitler made a definitive statement in a radio speech on January 30, 1939; it is incorrect to claim, as some do, that the "final solution" was produced by war hysteria.
67. About 280,000 Jewish refugees reached America, Britain, and South America from 1933 to 1939.
68. There were 250,000 Jews in German camps by 1941.
69. *Kristall*, hence "Crystal Night."
70. (Oswiecim), Polish death center.
71. As quoted in Gordon Wright, *The Ordeal of Total War, 1939–1945* (New York: Harper & Row, Publishers, Torchbooks, 1968), p. 125.

Within the Reich meanwhile, as early as 1939 Hitler had ordered the death[72] of "misfits" and persons with incurable diseases. This "eugenics" program used rifles at first but soon graduated to gas for speed. Relatives in Germany were told of death by disease. Despite postwar protests by the civilians in Germany that this program was top secret, churchmen knew about it and preached publicly against it.[73] In behalf of the Jews, however, or the Slavs, no stand was made. Again, within Germany, a new invasion provoked no problems. The Russian campaign, Hitler reckoned, meant another 30,000,000 "irredeemables," the existence of whom was at odds with planning in eastern regions. For the German Jews, this meant a decree that all Jews in Germany had to wear yellow stars, if age six or older. A month later, their deportation eastward, to new camps, was ordered. New camps were opened at Lodz, Sibibor, and Treblinka.

Thus, on the surface, the fate of the Jews seemed linked to the general question of "inferior elements" in the total subject population, as the Reich expanded. Yet the surface is deceiving. Of the 11,000,000 people deliberately murdered by the Nazis, excluding "ordinary" casualties of war, 5,138,000 are known to have been Jews. Or, put another way, of the 8,650,000 European Jews known to be alive in 1941, over 5,000,000 were exterminated by 1945. The real slaughter amounting to genocide was a conscious, racially motivated one, carried out after 1942 by "Action Squads" (*Einsatzgruppen*) in camps or in areas marked by mass execution by gunfire, such as Babi Yar near Kiev.

The first hint of the "final solution" of the Jewish question came in an order of May 20, 1941, which blocked Jewish emigration from France and Belgium "in view of the imminent final solution of the Jewish question."[74] In July Göring had ordered a plan for extermination; and it was prepared by Heydrich[75] of the SS. Even before this plan was approved specifically in January 1942, I. G. Farben's[76] chemists had designed mobile-van gas chambers equipped with Zyklon B gas, a much quicker agent than carbon monoxide. At its peak Auschwitz was able to take in a "convoy" of 12,000 a day, from the trains to the burial pits, in one mass production line of death, as the "historical task to be gotten over with bravely."[77] Urging secrecy, Himmler, who was charged to carry out the "solution," nevertheless glorified it as the road to new values, in a speech at Poznan in 1943. There were prizes for the best action groups, and *Einsatzgruppen A* under Heydrich could personally account for 229,052 executions. Everything was precisely organized, from rail convoys to the squads of camp inmates who stole the rings from fingers and picked the gold out of teeth in skulls.

72. Under the guise of euthanasia.
73. The Catholic bishop of Münster, for instance, on August 3, 1941.
74. Quoted in Karl Dietrich Bracher, *The German Dictatorship,* trans. Jean Steinberg (New York: Praeger Publishers, 1970), p. 425.
75. Reinhard Heydrich, assassinated in Lidice.
76. The great German chemical trust.
77. Bracher, *German Dictatorship*, p. 420.

The Nazis, who had so quickly overrun Poland, despised the Poles. "The Polish collapse . . .," declared a German official, "has proven anew the inferiority of the Poles." Millions were forced from their homes or sent to Germany as slave laborers, while extermination, by firing squad or gas chamber, awaited many of the rest. This photo shows one German technique of mass murder in action: a Pole, clutching what appears to be a quilt, is about to be executed as he kneels before a pit filled with bodies of those already killed. Library of Congress.

Rentabilitätsberechnung der SS über Ausnützung der Häftlinge in den Konzentrationslagern	Table of profits (or yield) per prisoner in concentration camps (established by SS)
Rentabilitätsberechnung	**Rental accounting**
Täglicher Verleihlohn durchschnittlich RM 6,–	Average income from rental of prisoner, per day RM [Reichsmark] 6.00
abzüglich Ernährung RM –,60	Deduction for nourishment, per day RM 0.60
durchschnittl. Lebensdauer 9 Mt. = 270 x RM 5,30 = RM 1431,–	**Average life expectancy:** 9 months: 270 [days] by RM 5.30 = RM 1431.00
abzüglich Bekl. Amort. RM –,10	Minus amortization on clothing RM 0.10
Erlös aus rationeller Verwertung der Leiche:	Profits from rational utilization of corpse:
1. Zahngold 3. Wertsachen	1. Gold teeth 3. Articles of value
2. Kleidung 4. Geld	2. Clothing 4. Money
abzüglich Verbrennungskosten RM 2,–	Minus costs of cremation RM 2.00
durchschnittlicher Nettogewinn RM 200,–	Average net profit RM 200.00
Gesamtgewinn nach 9 Monaten RM 1631,–	Total profit after 9 months RM 1631.00
zuzüglich Erlös aus Knochen und Aschenverwertung.	This estimate does not include profits from [sale of] bones and ashes.

SOURCE: *Macht ohne Moral,* Roderberg-Verlag, Frankfurt am Main.

The horror of German extermination camps was well documented by the prisoners. Shown here are two drawings from Terezín, a camp in Czechoslavakia. At left, Karel Fleischmann shows in Registration *the prisoners filling out forms. After this they would be hastily lined up for inspection by the SS doctors—the gas chambers and crematoria awaited those who remained unselected for work. Those prisoners who were temporarily spared were packed together in shockingly squalid quarters, shown at right by Bedrich Fritta in* In Terezín. *By courtesy of the State Jewish Museum, Prague.*

And so there were 5,138,000 Jews killed, a number equal to Stalin's estimate of Red Army dead from combat! In the piles of corpses made by the war some other numbers need notice: military dead, at least 15,000,000; civilian dead, at least 23,000,000; and these figures exclude Russian losses, which must have been about 20,000,000.[78]

Perhaps, though, the horror of this slaughter can better be appreciated not through statistics, but through Himmler's own words about the Jews:

Most of you know what it means to see 100 corpses piled up, or 500, or 1,000. To have gone through this and—except for instances of human weakness—to have remained decent, that has made us tough. This is an unwritten, never to be written, glorious page in our history.[79]

78. 1939 totals for USSR estimate population at ca. 170,000,000; 1959 totals run about 209,000,000, including all peoples not formerly within the USSR. There was thus no real gain in twenty years from natural increase, or else the birthrates we know would have pushed Soviet levels closer to 250,000,000 in 1959.
79. Address to the SS, Poznan, October 4, 1943; quoted in Bracher, *German Dictatorship*, p. 423.

Eighteen years later in Jerusalem Adolf Eichmann, the transport genius who made the convoys run on time to Treblinka and Auschwitz, said that his main problem was not to refine the "possible methods of killing," but to *camouflage* from others what exactly was happening inside the Third Reich, where mass murder was, for example, officially disguised as "Operation Harvest Festival" in one of its parts.[80] About 2,600,000 of Poland's 3,000,000 Jews died in the slaughter; 750,000 of 1,000,000 Rumanian Jews; 40,000 of 48,000 in Bulgaria; 58,000 of 70,000 in Yugoslavia; 60,000 of 67,000 in Greece; only 100 of 6,000 in Denmark, where the king himself wore the yellow star in protest. Perhaps the statistics do not drive home the horror as effectively as a single poetic line by Dylan Thomas, mourning the death of a child killed in the London blitz: "After the first death, there is no other."[81]

A WORLD WITHOUT PEACE

After such a war there could be no peace, at least not in the way men ordinarily used the term. Before the war values and institutions had been in a constant process of reevaluation and reform. Now, in the wake of genocide and the atomic-bombing of Hiroshima, when Russia alone had lost perhaps 20,000,000 people, and Europe over its whole central and eastern sectors was devastated beyond belief, the world was in a revolutionary state. None could see a brave new world beyond the terrible real one in which societies, economies, and polities had collapsed utterly among victor and vanquished alike.

What would happen to the familiar political structures? Could democracy be put back together in Italy, in France, in the states occupied by Soviet forces—all of Europe between Moscow and Berlin, except for the Scandinavian countries? How could people be made to believe again in parliaments and societies with class structures? What would be the attitudes of the victors toward the ruined states and societies of Japan and Germany? What would happen in the colonial world of Asia and Africa, where the oppressed "natives" had shared the burden of throwing off totalitarian efforts at world domination?

It was, after all, hard to believe that either the Chinese or the Vietnamese would welcome back French or British overlords, or that the peoples of Africa would patiently lie down again under the same pains as those inflicted on them before the global war by "democratic" imperialism. It was just as hard to think that the British, who loved Churchill in war, could rally to him in peace. The war had produced such things as the Beveridge Report,[82] which exposed the "social deficiencies" of the British system as it touched millions of people who were now known to be ill fed, ill clothed, and ill housed. Scores of Britons "queued up" to get copies, despite the danger of air attack. And who could believe that the countries of Eastern Europe would ever return to "normal"? The war there had swept away the traditional systems with the improvised democracies set on top of them in 1919. The Germans had liquidated the political and intellectual elites wherever they could. Hence even if the Soviet forces were to go home—and it was doubtful that Stalin would retreat from the lands buffering Russia from the west as the Soviets counted their dead—it was unlikely that the old order would ever return.

80. This was the name given to the machine-gunning of tens of thousands of Jews near Lublin in Poland.
81. Quoted from "A Refusal to Mourn the Death, by Fire, of a Child in London."
82. In 1943, by the Liberal economist Sir William Beveridge. The actual title was *Social Insurance and Allied Services.*

Those with a monopoly of power and status before 1939 were displaced everywhere, even among the victors. Consider for a moment the social upheaval produced by the war in the United States. Millions of black workers found in the wartime demand for industrial labor the chance to break the bonds of peonage and the sharecropping system in the South. Millions of whites never before closely associated with blacks in daily life, or with Mexican-Americans, Indians, and American Jews, now had been thrown together with them in factories and in trenches, in the common struggle for survival. Would these underdogs of life in "democratic" America go quietly back to the farm or the reservation, or fail to break the barriers of quotas in colleges and "white only" signs in railroad rest rooms?

And in addition to the psychological losses, what of the physical losses of the war? We mean here not the dead, because they were beyond reconstitution. We mean Berlin, in which 75 percent of the houses were destroyed, and Düsseldorf, the flower of the modern city movement, in which 95 percent of all houses were uninhabitable. Almost everywhere in the West *outside* the United States[83] food production and industrial output were more than halved. Britain was so poor that rationing remained in effect into the early 1950s. Everywhere, the basic necessities of life were in short supply: food, clothing, medical care, housing. The Allies owed the United States over $30 billion for Lend-Lease, while American industry had expanded to a gross product level of $166 billion a year in 1945, from $91 billion in 1940. The American merchant marine was in 1939 only 17 percent of the world total, while Europe's share had been 63 percent. In 1945 the United States ships were larger in total tonnage than those of the rest of Europe combined.

To make peace in the West in 1945 thus meant to make new structures, not to repair old ones or improvise brilliantly, as the peacemakers in 1919 had tried to do. Even before the new war had ended, one of the keenest students of the interwar years pointed to the problems the future peacemakers might face:

If and when peace returns to the world, the lessons of the breakdown which has involved Europe in a second major war within twenty years and two months of the Versailles Treaty will need to be earnestly pondered. A settlement which, having destroyed the National Socialist rulers of Germany, leaves untouched the conditions which made the phenomenon of National Socialism possible, will run the risk of being as short lived and as tragic as the settlement of 1919. . . . The next Peace Conference, if it is not to repeat the fiasco of the last, will have to concern itself with issues more fundamental than the drawing of frontiers.[84]

After the war was over and before the era of decolonization set in, rolling back the Western conquest of the world, which had taken four centuries, in as many years, de Gaulle described the war as "the greatest revolution the world has ever known."[85] Immediately after the suicide of Hitler, some commentators dared to hope that a new order might indeed be made, not the one envisioned in Nazi ideology, but one in which the struggle to make the world safe "from the pestilence of tyranny"[86] would be justified by dedication to peace and the values of Western civilization. Roosevelt was in

---

83. And Portugal, neutral Sweden and Switzerland (Spain had been devastated in the 1930s).
84. Carr, *Twenty Years' Crisis*, p. ix.
85. Quoted in Wright, *Ordeal of Total War*, p. 234.
86. Churchill in the House of Commons, September 3, 1939, in the debate on the British declaration of war.

his grave and so could not speak to the point. But he had earlier expressed such hopes, and his successor Truman often spoke in that vein. Stalin's opinions were not so well known in the West, but as early as 1943 at Teheran American advisers predicted that the Russians would seek to control Europe east of the Elbe and be the only important force in all Europe. Churchill concurred, advising Eisenhower to "shake hands with the Russians as far east as possible."[87]

Churchill's reasons for saying this stemmed from the conversations he had with Stalin at the various conferences during the war. Stalin disliked Churchill and distrusted the English. He spoke of Churchill as a petty thief who would "slip a kopeck out of your pocket."[88] Roosevelt at least wanted big money! More to the point, however, was Stalin's view of the war, which he set forth candidly to other Marxists, Tito for instance:

This war is not as in the past; whoever occupies a territory also imposes on it his own social system. Everyone imposes his own system as far as his army can reach. It cannot be otherwise.[89]

A little while after Stalin had expressed in a nutshell the fundamental issue of the postwar years—the East-West split—Churchill contemplated the world that must come of this attitude. The coalition against Hitler had always been one of self-interest only: democrats and socialists against fascists. But the surrenders in May and August ended the reason for that coalition; and what the world was left with was not peace but the stark reality of a confrontation as global as the war had been: between what remained of liberal democracy and what emerged as the socialist world. Churchill told Stalin of his unease as he viewed what lay ahead.

There is not much comfort in looking into a future where you and the countries you dominate, plus the Communist Parties in many other States, are all drawn up on one side, and those who rally to the English-speaking nations . . . are on the other. It is quite obvious that their quarrel would tear the world to pieces and that all of us leading men who had anything to do with that would be shamed before history.[90]

BIBLIOGRAPHY

ARENDT, HANNAH. *Eichmann in Jerusalem.** New York: The Viking Press, 1963. A provocative, controversial account of the last great war-crimes trial.
BULLOCK, ALAN. *Hitler: A Study in Tyranny.** New York: Harper & Row, Publishers, Torchbooks, 1963. The best biography to date, although weak on psychology; compare Walter Langer's *The Mind of Adolf Hitler* (New York: Basic Books, 1972).
CARR, E. H. *The Twenty Years' Crisis, 1919–1939.** New York: Harper & Row, Publishers, Torchbooks, 1964. A brilliant analysis of the crisis, written at its zenith, in 1939.

Asterisk indicates a paperbound edition.

87. Wright, *Ordeal of Total War*, p. 202.
88. Milovan Djilas, *Conversations with Stalin*, trans. Michael B. Petrovich (New York: Harcourt Brace Jovanovich, 1962), p. 73.
89. *Ibid.*, p. 114; the words were spoken in Djilas's hearing, April 1945.
90. Churchill to Stalin, April 29, 1945, in Winston S. Churchill, *The Second World War*, 6 vols. (Boston: Houghton Mifflin Co., 1948–1953), 6:497. This volume is aptly called *Triumph and Tragedy*.

GATZKE, HANS W. *European Diplomacy between the Two Wars, 1919–1939.** Chicago: Quadrangle, 1972. A major collection of essays on the diplomacy of the 1920s and 1930s.

GILBERT, M., and GOTT, R. *The Appeasers.** Boston: Houghton Mifflin Co., 1962. A good survey of British reactions to fascist aggressors.

GRUNBERGER, RICHARD. *Germany, 1918–1945.* London: Batsford, 1964. A very good account; very valuable on the war and the barbarism of the Reich. See also the chapters in Karl Dietrich Bracher's *The German Dictatorship*, trans. Jean Steinberg (New York: Praeger Publishers, 1970), on the extermination of Europe's Jews.

HILBERG, RAUL. *The Destruction of the European Jews.** Chicago: Quadrangle, 1961. The most detailed general history of the "final solution."

JÄCKEL, EBERHARD. *Hitler's Weltanschauung: A Blueprint for Power.* Middletown, Conn.: Wesleyan University Press, 1972. A detailed demonstration of the "blueprint" for power derived from Hitler's often discounted writings.

LANGER, WILLIAM L., and GLEASON, S. E. *The Challenge to Isolation.* New York: Harper & Row, Publishers, 1952. This book and the authors' *The Undeclared War* (New York: Harper & Row, Publishers, 1953) are the standard works on American policy before 1941.

LIDDELL-HART, B. H. *History of the Second World War.* New York: G. P. Putnam's Sons, 1970. The posthumously published massive study by the foremost military scholar of our age.

THOMAS, HUGH. *The Spanish Civil War.** New York: Harper & Row, Publishers, Torchbooks, 1961. Judicious and complete, although passionately antifascist.

WERTH, ALEXANDER. *Russia at War.** New York: E. P. Dutton & Co., 1964. Valuable for the eastern front.

WHEELER-BENNET, SIR J. *Munich: Prologue to Tragedy.** New York: Duell, Sloan & Pearce, 1948. The best account of Hitler's successful rape of Czechoslovakia.

WISKEMANN, ELIZABETH. *Europe of the Dictators, 1919–1945.** New York: Harper & Row, Publishers, Torchbooks, 1966. A passionate democrat's lucid examination of the grip of "democratic forces" on Europe; superbly done.

WRIGHT, GORDON. *The Ordeal of Total War, 1939–1945.** New York: Harper & Row, Publishers, Torchbooks, 1968. By far the best account of the war in all its phases, military, political, economic, psychological.

18

WHO GUARDS THE GUARDIANS?

There are crimes of passion and crimes of logic. The boundary between them is not clearly defined. But the Penal Code makes the convenient distinction of premeditation. We are living in the era of premeditation and the perfect crime. Our criminals are no longer helpless children who could plead love as the excuse. On the contrary, they are adults and they have a perfect alibi: philosophy, which can be used for any purpose—even for transforming murderers into judges.

ALBERT CAMUS, *The Rebel* (1951)[1]

THE BEGINNING OF AN END

It is hard to assess the record of the first half of the twentieth century, to know whether its two global wars betoken a coming doom or the beginnings of a new world community sobered by its recent lessons.

Camus viewed the nature of mid-twentieth-century reality close at hand when in 1951 the war-time Allies gave independence to the former Italian colony of Libya, as if to give a sign that from the 70,000,000 dead in the two world wars some good issue might come. Although himself the son of a French family of *colons*, or settlers, in Algeria, his sympathies were more with the 8,000,000 Algerian Algerians than with the 1,000,000 French Algerians who controlled the state and the society there. Camus understood that the liberty of Libya was galvanizing all of North Africa, as in the Asian subcontinent of India the British withdrawal in 1947 set in motion the events which forced the Dutch out of Indonesia in 1949 and the French out of Vietnam in 1954.

Camus did not live to see the victory over France of the Algerian rebels of the FLN (the National Liberation Front) in 1962, ending a century and a quarter of foreign rule, by plebiscite. But he was alive in 1954, when the French soldiers routed in Indochina by General Giap and the great leader Ho Chi Minh[2] fell on Algeria like some biblical plague. Fresh from the defeat at Dien Bien Phu, the army came 400,000 strong to crush the Liberation Front, which had support from Egypt and other Arab states. Urged on by the *colons* and a combination of military men and right-wing politicians in Paris, the government of France acted as if the prestige lost in Vietnam could be recouped in Africa. Seven years later, and with the dead counted by the tens of

1. Born in 1913, Camus died in 1960, in a sports car crash; the quote is from Anthony Bower's translation (New York: Alfred A. Knopf, 1956), p. 3.
2. 1890–1969; Ho was a Communist who rose to the top after 1946, in the thrust against French restoration efforts in Southeast Asia.

thousands on each side, General de Gaulle led France out of the moral sink of that war, but not before it had brought down the Fourth French Republic in 1958.

The war against the FLN provided Camus and other horrified observers everywhere with an object lesson in the politics of irrationality. Camus's *The Rebel (L'Homme révolté)* began with an analysis of the kind of crime that took refuge in doctrine. It was his view that "crime" had become universal, since states now applied "reason" to criminal acts. The mid-century world was one of "slave camps under the flag of freedom" and of "massacres justified by philanthropy." Without naming the specific atrocities he had in mind, he leaves no doubt that he is speaking of the totalitarian ideological systems in existence *after the Nazi defeat.* In an earlier "age of negation" (the 1920s) the problem was suicide; now, in the "age of ideologies," the problem is murder, which has been elevated to the rank of a political principle. In the one age the denial of our own life was the problem; now it is the denial of the lives of others on a mass scale.

Hence the transition from negation to assertion as a dominant mode of expression has raised the question: In a world where old faiths are exhausted and nihilism itself has been discarded and defeated, what approach to ideology can thinking people make? Objectively, Camus argued, the politicians had already given several answers. The world was amoral, beyond good and evil, according to Nazi nihilism, which thus licensed Nazis to stoke the crematory fires. In the world after 1945, however, the superpowers—the United States and the USSR—were giving answers just as murderous. There was either a tragic dilettantism, in which the world was viewed as a game board of global politics with lives as the counters, or there was pragmatism, a world in which good and bad were judged wholly by results: the strongest and most efficient divide the world; the "just" are the "masters," the "slaves" are the "unjust"; and murder maintains its privileged position.

Indifference to life triumphs, in suicide and murder. For this view, the Hitler apocalypse of 1945 was the best evidence: to destroy oneself and drag the world to death are aspects of the same system. The question was thus simply whether the errors and horrors of a whole period of history based on despair would continue in the 1950s and 1960s. Perhaps no answer is yet possible, but there is some evidence to consider.

THE WORLD DIVIDED

Perhaps the most fundamental problem facing the Western Allies in 1945 was whether the world's economy could be reconstructed. But the most immediately pressing one was what sort of peace could be made *with Russia*. Britain and France went to war in 1939 to guarantee the freedom of Poland against Hitler. Six years and 70,000,000 lives later, Poland was in Russian hands. The United States had recognized the Polish government in exile in 1940. And, on the plane of self-interest, none of the Western powers wanted Stalin to control Poland's resources or the strategic Polish situation in central Europe. Thus, while in terms of technology and motivation, the war had drawn together East and West in one world, it now seemed likely that peace would leave intact the technological unification only.

This prospect was already clear at Yalta in February 1945, where the Big Three met for the second time. Stalin, Churchill, and Roosevelt agreed in principle, but vaguely as to details, concerning the postwar world. Austria and Germany would be separated and also entirely occupied, with the Big

Three having "zones" of occupation even in the capital cities.[3] Berlin and Vienna, under tripartite control, were to be commonly administered by the Big Three while democratic national governments were built and stabilized. Another agreement was that the liberated countries were also to be reestablished as democracies. Finally, at the insistence of Roosevelt, Stalin agreed on joint participation to create a new international body to maintain peace in the world.[4]

These major agreements were, however, put somewhat in the shadows by the fact that Stalin had established a Communist government for Poland at Lublin in 1945, after having broken relations in 1943 with the government in exile in London which the other Allies supported. Churchill was not above trading Polish interests for British spheres of influence elsewhere. But Roosevelt thought Stalin's ambitions were not "imperialist." He therefore sided with one group of his advisers[5] against Churchill, who was suspected of caring less about peace than about establishing a British dominance again. Roosevelt was naïve about Eastern Europe; and his intimate friends Joseph Davies and Harry Hopkins seemed to regard Stalin as a benign force for peace and brotherhood.

They had no grasp of the truly totalitarian nature of Soviet politics and no understanding of the ideological gap between Stalin's version of "Communism in one country" and fraternal socialism. Churchill, who had little understanding of Marx or Lenin, viewed the whole conference at Yalta in terms of traditional conflicts among powers. Hence his needs were met on the surface when Stalin gave a promise to "enlarge" the Lublin government and conduct "free" elections, in exchange for an East-West boundary compromise. This seemed a good bargain, because Russia also pledged to enter the war against Japan.

Five months later Roosevelt was dead of a stroke, and Churchill had been voted out of office in the middle of the third Big Three meeting, at Potsdam. Of the world leaders at the peak of their powers only Stalin remained. Truman and Attlee[6] lacked experience and prestige in 1945. Moreover, the positions had changed. America wanted to "pastoralize" Germany; but Russian policy was to extract heavy reparations, which could be done only from an industrial system. Further differences existed on Germany's eastern frontier.[7] There were also differences about the Baltic and Balkan states, colonial regimes, and German prisoners of war. The Russians refused to repatriate some three million prisoners, because they considered their labor part of reparations. Substantial agreement was reached, however, on some German problems. War-crimes trials must be held to bring home to the defeated peoples the enormities of their actions. This goal would also be achieved by the fact that neither Japan nor Germany would be allowed a central government until democratic "education" was completed.

At Potsdam the Russians also expressed interests in North African and Turkish territory, the latter in order to control the Black Sea and its straits.

3. France was eventually made a party to this arrangement; the French zone was carved out of those governed by Britain and America.
4. Stalin agreed to the formation of a United Nations only after he was promised veto power in the body's Security Council.
5. Stettinius (secretary of state), Stimson (secretary of war), and General Marshall; the "hard-liners" against Stalin were diplomats with experience in Moscow: Averell Harriman, George F. Kennan, and General John R. Deane.
6. Clement Attlee (1883–1967), prime minister of the United Kingdom from 1945–1951.
7. All parties agreed on the line of the rivers Oder and Neisse, but the Neisse had two branches about sixty-five miles apart; the Russians wanted the western Neisse for the boundary, the Allies the eastern Neisse.

Stalin also said that the Red Army had won for the USSR the right to organize the political life of Rumania and Czechoslovakia as well as that of the Baltic states and other regions of southeast Europe. Hence the only unmitigated success of these conferences had been the formal creation of the United Nations, at a meeting in San Francisco,[8] and the subsequent ratification of its charter[9] by all countries who had been at war with Germany and Japan.

Unlike the old League, the United Nations was global from its inception. Also, the United Nations was on an egalitarian footing: each nation had one vote in the General Assembly. This advantage was offset, however, in the Security Council, where politically critical issues were settled. Each of the permanent members[10] had a veto, at Russia's insistence. Yet the United Nations was a great hope in the immediate postwar years. Its Economic and Social Council, together with special agencies concerned with health care and famine, contributed to the development of policies to aid in the relief of disease and overpopulation. Such agencies as the International Bank for Reconstruction and Development tried to play a positive role in the modernization of Africa and Asia, in competition with direct American aid.

In addition to the Security Council veto power, the United Nations has been burdened by external factors. As the nuclear age developed, a new elite of nations has grown up. The membership in this elite has gradually come to correspond to the membership of the Security Council, but the entry price is wholly technological: the possession of nuclear weapons. The American monopoly was broken first by Russia in 1949, then by Britain in 1952, France in 1960, and China in 1964.[11] Within this exclusive club, the United States and the USSR have resources not at the disposal of even the other nuclear powers, whether we consider economies, technology, or military strength.

Hence the United Nations took shape as a forum for peace maintenance under American hegemony, but it has become the place where small nations are effective only in combination with the superpowers. When Russia and America combine, other powers must obey; and when they clash, other powers tremble. In the years since 1945, war and peace exist anywhere because the giants of politics have global interests which are often in confrontation, especially in Asia and Africa, where the dominant powers have been locked in a struggle for the loyalties of the states created by the decolonization movement.

8. Beginning April 25, 1945.
9. By October 24, 1945.
10. The United States, Britain, France, the USSR, and China; six other members are elected for two-year terms by the Assembly.
11. The bomb was a development with Communist China; in 1971 Red China was made a member of the United Nations, occupying the Security Council seat held by Chiang Kai-shek since 1945.

The guiding personality behind the United Nations during its formative years was that of Dag Hammerskjold, the Swedish secretary-general. An aloof, shy man who wrote tortured, mystical poetry, Hammerskjold relied on his inner strength to deal with the complex problems of the Cold War era. Despite weaknesses inherent in the structure of the organization he managed to arrange peaceable solutions to many crises. Hammerskjold was killed in a 1961 plane crash, and the American artist Ben Shahn painted this portrait as a memorial. Inscribed at the bottom is Hammerskjold's working ethic: to protect the weak countries of the world from the greed and excesses of the powerful. Nationalmuseum, Stockholm.

This pattern, which was unsuccessfully challenged by various "Third World" powers seeking to break the bipolarity of power through the formation of "neutral" blocs of unaligned nations, took shape in 1945. Thus it is to the origins of this Cold War that we look in order to understand modern politics and relations between states as well as the reconstruction of Europe.

COLD WAR AND COEXISTENCE

The most important fact of the Cold War is not ideology, although the ideological origins of the split were profound. It was a simple fact that in 1945 the victors could not merely put troops in the countryside of the vanquished or the states overturned by Hitler. The Russians and the "Atlantic" powers recognized that economic, social, and political reconstruction was necessary in order to revive Europe. But here agreement ended. For each "bloc"—essentially America and Russia at first—intended to reconstruct Europe along lines already traditional for the superpowers at home. Thus the "Atlantic" allies agreed to impose their own pattern wherever their armies had been the "liberators"; and Stalin clearly meant to maintain the lands beyond the eastern frontier from the Baltic to the Balkans as a Russian zone of control.

In fact, what this meant was that only the old established Western democracies were put back on their feet as liberal democracies: Britain, France, Belgium, Holland, Sweden, Norway, Denmark, Italy, and Greece. Minor frontier adjustments only were made. France gained a right to the Saar coalfields, although the region was to be officially German. The Low

Countries made very small gains at Germany's expense. The Italians lost Istria to Yugoslavia and also ceded a bit of their northwestern borderland to France and the Dodecanese Islands to Greece. And Italy also lost its entire colonial empire. None of these changes were a result of the sort of formal comprehensive peace conference held at Versailles in 1919. Instead, separate agreements were concluded between the states concerned and the Allied Control Council, which acted for the dependent Germans.

In Eastern Europe the formal changes were a little more extensive but also slight. The Soviet Union made some direct incorporations of territories once parts of Rumania and Finland. Hungary gave up small regions to Rumania and Czechoslovakia. Russia also gained a large piece of eastern Poland. Where Stalin made great additions to the USSR was on the Baltic, where all of the once independent states were absorbed as well as the northern edge of East Prussia. The real problems, however, concerned the East-West frontier zone on a line from the Baltic through Germany which reached the Italian-Yugoslav region after curving along the Czech-Austrian borders.

The map of Europe was redrawn on principles other than those obtaining in 1919, when the great issues were territorial, ethnic, and linguistic, within the framework of self-determination. In 1945 these were dead issues; what counted was the balance of power between Russia and the West. Once Stalin made good his claim to control Eastern Europe as a series of Communist satellite regimes, it made little difference in the West where the borders were made. The question mattered only to the millions of central and eastern Europeans who did not want to live under the Stalinist regime. Millions escaped to the western side of the dividing line. More millions were shifted around within the Soviet bloc, by treaties for the resettlement of minorities. Together with returning soldiers and the surviving Jews, about 45,000,000 displaced persons were in motion within Europe, undoubtedly the greatest *Völkerwanderung* since the Germanic tribes invaded the Roman Empire. Perhaps 10,000,000 Germans fled to the West from the Russian zone before the Berlin Wall was built to stop the flow in 1961.

Thus a new balance of power was being struck immediately.

On the Western side, "denazification" and the prosecution of war criminals and collaborators went on until 1948 as a major concern in the American and British control areas. The French and the Russians hunted down only major offenders, while in Italy and France collaborators were often given vigilante justice only. In Belgium, a tiny state with only 8,000,000 people, charges were brought against 634,000![12] Holland filed charges against nearly 200,000, because of offenses ranging from luncheon dates with Nazi officers to actual killings. But the big purge was in the trials of major Nazi "criminals" at Nuremberg in 1945–1946, where twenty-two top party officers and generals were tried for the murder of millions of innocent people. These trials aroused much public outrage everywhere, sometimes because of the enormities revealed, sometimes because the law used was not equipped to prosecute individuals.[13] The real question for the future, however, even if every offender had been detected and punished, was not asked at the trials.

It was put at the polls in the Western states. Postwar politics in the West turned toward the left nearly everywhere. In Britain Labour won a landslide victory; elsewhere Communist party people were part of the government in the German states, Belgium, and Denmark. The Communists in France,

12. Of whom 77,000 were actually sentenced.
13. International law is a "law of nations," not of individual offenders.

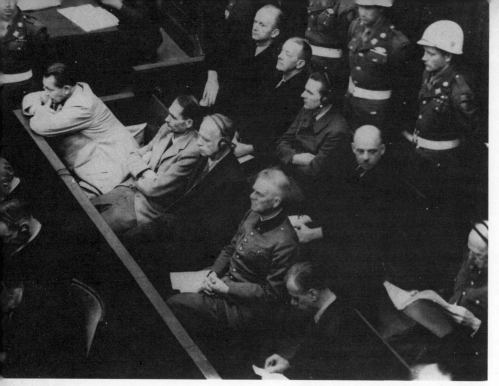

Norway, Greece, and Belgium won many legislative seats, which were used to attack the few vestiges of liberalism left over from the 1930s. This turn to the left was exhausted nearly everywhere by the late 1940s; it ended in Britain, for example, in 1951, when Churchill returned to power on a wave of enthusiasm for more centrist politics.

This revolt against the left was abetted by two powerful forces, one internal and the other external. Western intellectuals like George Orwell wrote books exposing the essence of Soviet totalitarianism, the best known in English being Orwell's *Animal Farm* and *Nineteen Eighty-Four*. Also, Western Europeans were frightened by the Soviet effort to take over Greece in 1947 and the attempt to cut Berlin off from the West by the Russian blockade of rail and auto traffic to the city. In each instance President Truman had acted decisively to thwart the Soviet bid, with arms and aid to the Greeks and Turks[14] and the great Berlin airlift to supply that city. This growing military dependence of Europe on America ran parallel to the economic dependence of the Western states. Britain borrowed over £1.1 billion in 1945 in order to fashion welfare policies in a state bankrupted by the war. But American aid had strings; it was anti-Communist.

In this respect it is vital to consider the postwar reconstruction as a necessary American investment in its own security. The war had discredited liberalism and any semblance of free enterprise in countries like Britain. Labour politicians in Britain and those on the Continent campaigned to eliminate gross want, to curtail unemployment and the hazards of sickness and old age, to assist children, to rebuild the basic stock of housing, and to maintain sufficient security forces so as to discourage aggression by any European power. This seemed essential to curtail Communism at home, in France for example, where de Gaulle faced a threat from the 900,000-strong Communist party. In the 1945 elections the Communist party polled 26 percent of the vote, while Léon Blum's Socialists

When the Russians blockaded the western sector of Berlin, the United States responded almost immediately with a directive to the air force to begin transport of food and medicine to West Berlin. In what came to be known as the Berlin airlift, planes such as the one shown here daily flew in coal and food, flying round the clock and landing as often as every three minutes. Every day American and British planes delivered an average of 4,000 tons of food and supplies; at the height of the airlift, in April 1949, almost 13,000 tons reached West Berlin on a single day. The blockade was lifted the following month, but the airlift continued until September 1949, so as to build up West Berlin's reserve stocks. In all, more than 2,000,000 tons of supplies were flown in to West Berlin, at a cost of over $181,000,000. Fenno Jacobs from Black Star.

14. Under the "Truman Doctrine" of *containing* Communism, that is, allowing no extension of it.

took 24 percent. In Italy the Communist party had 2,000,000 members and was the strongest such unit in Europe west of the Oder-Neisse Line. The monarchy had been dissolved in 1946 by referendum, but the republican Christian Democrats were unable to exclude the Communists from a share in government until 1947. Elsewhere, the Communist party was weak in its appeal because the traditional Social Democrats were united and quite radical, as in Norway for instance.

The need for American capital and political management was most obvious in Germany. Divided into four zones plus Berlin, which was itself divided similarly, Germany had become two states: the western Federal Republic of Germany (*Bundesrepublik*) and the Soviet-dominated eastern German Democratic Republic. America had reason to build a showcase for Western democracy in West Germany, if only to continue to drain, perhaps through the appearance of a better life in the West, skilled people from the Russian sector.[15] This was done at first without any normal German

15. East Germany was the only European state to decline in population from 1945 to 1960.

political life, just as in East Germany Walter Ulbricht, the Communist party boss, ruled because he had Russian support. By 1947–1948, however, a real political revival struck the *Bundesrepublik*. The Allies backed the Christian Democratic Union led by the Catholic mayor of Cologne, Dr. Konrad Adenauer, a staunch anti-Nazi. They considered the Liberals weak, and entirely disliked the Social Democrat leader Dr. Kurt Schumacher, a man committed to radical socialism with an anti-Communist framework. Adenauer was paternalistic and even authoritarian; he thus distrusted real parliamentary politics. And the style of *Der Alte*[16] was thus suited to Allied needs for democracy without conflict.

In Germany, therefore, the aims and means of East and West blended together to clarify the outlines of the early postwar struggle for Europe. Ulbricht's Communist party crushed opposition parties, beginning with the Social Democrats, in favor of a genuine "Bolshevik democracy," or one-party state. This dictatorship was already in being early in 1946. In order to combat it, the Allies had by 1947 decided to accelerate Germany's rehabilitation. Toward that end they coordinated economic policies in the zones, ended denazification, revived German industry, and installed a central government under Adenauer. The new Bonn regime lacked control over defense and foreign affairs but was increasingly able to follow the market in other developments. By late 1948, the German economy was strong enough to eliminate rationing for most commodities, after a short period of instability. A year later there was a good basis for the "economic miracle" of the 1950s.

Before this new Allied policy had progressed very far, however, the Russian members of the Control Council had protested it and left the council, adjourning it *sine die*.[17] And on June 23, 1948, the breakdown of cooperation was total, for on that night all land traffic from the West to Berlin was stopped. The Russians were determined to starve into submission the focal point of resistance to Communist rule in central Europe, just as earlier in the year Stalin had engineered a coup d'état in Czechoslovakia to consolidate the Russian control of the East-West frontier. For more than a year the airlift[18] answered the blockade in an atmosphere which might have produced a new war. Then, on May 12, 1949, Stalin ordered the blockade lifted, convinced that America's full strength was committed to maintaining Berlin's freedom.

The West had won a skirmish in the Cold War between former Allies, but the war was still on, in central Europe and elsewhere. Indeed, it had been on as early as March 1946, when Churchill coined a famous phrase in describing the struggle in Europe:

From Stettin on the Baltic to Trieste on the Adriatic, an *iron curtain* [italics ours] has descended across the Continent. Behind that line lie all the capitals of the ancient states of central and eastern Europe . . . from what I have seen of our Russian friends and allies . . . there is nothing they admire so much as strength and nothing for which they have less respect than military weakness.[19]

On the other side of the Iron Curtain, Russia under Stalin was on the verge of achieving every one of the traditional aims of its foreign policy. The defeat at Japan's hands in 1904–1905 was avenged; Poland was again a

---

16. "The old man"—Adenauer's nickname.
17. That is, with no day appointed to meet again.
18. Over 200,000 supply flights. The airlift actually continued until September 30, 1949.
19. Quoted in Walter Laqueur, *Europe since Hitler* (Baltimore: Penguin Books, 1970), p. 48.

satellite; the border regions were secure; it seemed certain that the Black Sea straits were soon to pass under Russian control, and with them would come new strategic strength in the Middle East; finally, the Soviet goal of exporting Communism was rapidly progressing. There were, of course, setbacks: steel production was off by more than half from the 1939 high, while food supplies were down by 60 percent. Currency inflation was severe by 1947, as the demand for scarce commodities grew. Stalin threw all Russia's resources into economic reorganization, and by 1947 the prewar levels had been reached, only to be exceeded by 40 percent in 1950, a consequence of the new Five-Year Plan adopted in 1946. The West had put it down to Stalin's boastfulness in 1946 when he predicted that the USSR would produce 500 million tons of coal in 1951 and over 60 million tons of steel and barrels of oil; but these targets were reached by 1950.

Partly this was the result of the forced labor of German prisoners; partly it was due to Western loans and German reparations, and to the confiscation of Manchurian resources after the defeat of Japan. But the chief credit was due to the people of the USSR, who triumphed over bad planning in the agricultural sector. This was closely related to the rebirth of older traditions of patriotism and personal freedom in wartime and the doubling of the Communist party to over 6,000,000 members in 1947. In fact in 1946 Russians confidently expected no return of the spirit of oppression familiar in the 1930s. They were wrong, however. Stalin insisted that the Cold War of political ideas and cultural values was as real a threat to the Revolution as fascism had been. He therefore reimposed the oppressively bureaucratic regime of party officials and secret police, enforcing strict discipline and total indoctrination. Stalin often alleged as a reason the difficulties presented by incorporating directly into the USSR nearly 24,000,000 "acquired" citizens, and an area larger than the whole Iberian peninsula.

"Stalinism" also extended throughout the eastern satellite state system, from which only Albania and Greece were exempt. On paper the regimes were "popular democracies." But the peoples of some states were officially Slav brothers[20] while others were not.[21] This made a difference even in 1945, when the Red Army treated the Hungarian "fascist" peoples more harshly than they did the Slavs; but this point cannot be stressed heavily, because Stalin was as repressive toward the Czechs after 1948 as he had been toward Poland and Yugoslavia right after the war. It was Stalin's goal to establish Communist dictatorships in all satellite regimes and use the puppet governments to tap the national resources of every country in behalf of Soviet rebuilding needs. This often necessitated tremendous purges within the local parties as well as abolitions of monarchy—in Yugoslavia, Rumania, and Bulgaria.

The Communist technique was to stage "revolutions" against the majority parties. In Hungary, for example, the Communist party was only one-quarter as strong at the polls as the Smallholders' party. This made it necessary to seize the press, radio, army, police, and domestic agencies of government before reconstituting the society from above. The lack of real support in Hungary—to use this example again—meant that it was only in 1948 that the state was secure enough to take over retail trades or force collectivization of agriculture. Then, as these programs showed appeal for the masses, the inner party bosses followed the "salami technique" of cutting off opposition one slice at a time, especially the various peasant parties. Where too much independence remained, as in Czechoslovakia,

20. Poles, Czechs, Serbs, Bulgarians.
21. Rumanians, Hungarians, East Germans.

open force was used, in 1948 and again in 1968, when the Soviet invasion
ended the "Prague Spring" liberal experiments of Alexander Dubcek.

The net effect was that the policy of all Eastern European countries was in
reality that of Moscow. Stalin would not annex the satellites, but he would
not allow them to form any independent associations within the Soviet
bloc, as Tito wished to do in 1946, when he discussed a Balkan union with
the Bulgarian leader Dimitrov. The proposed customs union would have
undercut Stalin's scheme, which was simply to make the satellites sell their
goods into Soviet markets below the levels set on world markets. The
satellites also had to buy Soviet goods at artificially high prices, in order to
support the hated Red Army occupation forces. The overall purpose of the
scheme was to achieve a rapid restoration of total production to pre-1939
levels. This eventually made Communism acceptable in Yugoslavia, Czechoslovakia,[22] and Bulgaria, but less so elsewhere.

The Stalinist regimes were always based on terror, however, and the
subordination of even national party leaders to the Soviet ambassador. By
1948 the situation was roughly that obtained by the United States after 1965
in South Vietnam, where the puppet regimes "made" policy only within the
limits determined in a foreign capital, in this case Washington.

22. The increasing "popularity" of the regime is not contradicted by the repression of the
Dubcek "liberals" in 1968, when the Soviets invaded. The invasion of 1968 expressed
Russian hostility to the *popular regime!*

If we were to characterize the Soviet system under Stalin until his death on March 5, 1953, we could do worse than begin with a description given by Soviet scholars in 1965, when the campaign by Khrushchev to free Russia from the tyranny of Stalinism was at its peak:

The Stalin personality cult took deep roots after the war. It tainted all aspects of Party work, and the work of its central bodies. The Leninist principles of collective leadership went by the board. Only one plenary meeting of the Central Committee was held in post-war years, and no party Congress was convened, although none had been held for 14 years. Many fundamental questions . . . were not given deep enough study, and the solutions took no account of what the party membership thought. . . . Stalin created a rift between theory and practice. . . . The works of Marx, Engels, and Lenin were in effect relegated to obscurity. No written works of any worth appeared in the fields of political economy, philosophy, and history.[23]

Even this criticism gives no impression of Stalinism, for which we need to turn to the novels of the anti-Stalinist writers who have again been repressed in the 1970s: Alexander Solzhenitsyn,[24] for example, who won the Nobel Prize for literature in 1970 but was forbidden to accept it in person. There we find the living color of a totalitarian dictator's handiwork; we see Russia not as the freest and happiest country in the world, but as a jail, the "first circle" of hell, a place were all economic activity was geared for war and in which the ruler was pathologically fond of murderous purges to crush even the whisper of opposition.

The "Boss," as Stalin was rightly called, had the help of some younger stars of the Politburo: Malenkov, one contender for power after 1953, a specialist in party organization and industrial management; Beria, a police terrorist; Zhdanov, the great ideologist; Bulganin, head of the state bank and also active in Moscow government; Khrushchev, a Moscow party builder and also the organizer of the party in the Ukraine. Slowly but surely these men were even in Stalin's lifetime transforming the party from the style of intellectual revolutionism into a party of "white-collar Communists," managers of the economy, agrarian experts, and builders of schools in which the Marxist classics would again play a part. It was this party regime that the West faced after 1953, in the struggle for coexistence in circumstances of Cold War.

THE WESTERN STANCE

The Cold War was actually almost over before Stalin died (1953), and it certainly was over in 1955, when Khrushchev began to consolidate power. Even while it raged, it would be naïve to suppose it was really an ideological struggle between Stalinism and Western democracy, whatever the slogans used in America to justify actions taken in what successive presidents saw as the national interest. The Cold War was waged over the balance of power among two superpowers. Its most important battles derived from two facts: the Russian inability to directly challenge America, which remained the only nuclear power until 1949; and the American willingness to use its "balance of terror" to prevent Soviet aggrandizement by subversion. And the theaters of this war, inasmuch as they were not European, took shape because of the movement for decolonization, which the Russians played on to show America as the heir to Western colonialism.

23. *A Short History of the U.S.S.R.* (Moscow: Soviet Academy of Sciences, 1965), 2: 270.
24. In his *First Circle, Cancer Ward, August 1914, The Gulag Archipelago: 1918–1956,* and *One Day in the Life of Ivan Denisovich.*

The inability of the Russians to make a direct challenge and the consequences of subversion as a tactic show clearly in the case of Greece. There,
a British occupation army had aided the Greek liberal monarchists until
1947, in an effort to suppress the Communists. Russian aid to the Greek
Communists and threats against the Turkish flank of the Balkans converted
President Truman to an active stance when the commitment to Greece's
defense became too much for Great Britain. Not only did he announce the
policy of containment in 1947 (which became known as the Truman
Doctrine) and provide the aid which defeated the Communists in Greece in
1949. In 1947 his secretary of state, George C. Marshall, made a speech at
Harvard committing the United States to the struggle over the distance.
Marshall said the only bulwark against subversion was prosperity, and this
required economic reconstruction beyond the means of the battered European states. He pledged American aid toward such ends, inaugurating the
Marshall Plan, or the European Recovery Program.[25] Before this program
ended in 1951, when it was replaced by a variety of "foreign aid" programs
focused on military aid, the United States had given $12.4 billion to sixteen
states.[26] Russia intervened to prevent Czechoslovakia and Poland from
accepting aid under the ERP. In 1949, Stalin intervened effectively on behalf
of Mao Tse-tung against the Chinese Nationalist regime of Chiang Kai-
shek. And also in the same year the USSR vetoed an American plan to
control the spread of atomic bombs.

In the Free World, as it was called, it was easy to represent these steps as
wholly aggressive on the part of Russia. And it suited American policy to do
so. But the Russians looked on the arms control scheme as a plan to
perpetuate America's monopoly of decisive weapons and thus the "imperialist" threat to the world's anticapitalist revolutions. Also, Lend-Lease was
cut off in 1945; American credits were delayed; America opposed land
reforms in socialist countries and expropriations elsewhere; even more
basic was the fact that America was intent on reconstructing Europe to
block Soviet-oriented socialism in the democratic states.[27] Russians could
therefore argue plausibly that America was trying to force a showdown in
which the United States would hold the highest card; Zhdanov certainly
pushed that hard line at Stalin. In Washington, on the other hand, the
secretary of defense James Forrestal (1892–1949) and diplomats like Dean
Acheson and John Foster Dulles were partisans of the hard line of anti-
Communism.

In these explosive circumstances, events such as the Greek civil war and
the Berlin blockade merely served to confirm the "Cold Warriors" in
Moscow and Washington in their views. The guerrilla wars in Indonesia
and Indochina, against the Dutch and the French, were also fuel for the
fire. Stalin revived the policy of the First Comintern, which had aligned
Russia with the "nationalist" revolutionaries against colonialism. Ho Chi
Minh, who had been educated in Paris and London, was a Marxist, but
most of all anticolonial. The United States, meanwhile, was seen to support
colonial powers like France in its determination to hold on to Indochina.
More to the point, President Truman had openly intervened on behalf of
Chiang, when negotiations between the Nationalists and Red Chinese
broke down in 1946; the Russians backed Mao. This new focus of the Cold

25. Russia was invited to participate in discussions of this plan, held in Paris, but withdrew
early in the proceedings.
26. Austria, Belgium, Denmark, France, Great Britain, Greece, Iceland, the Republic of
Ireland, Italy, Luxemburg, the Netherlands, Norway, Portugal, Sweden, Switzerland,
Turkey, and western Germany.
27. Aid did go to socialist governments in Britain and France, however.

War produced a tremendous defeat for the United States in 1949, when the Nationalists fled to Taiwan.[28] A Red revolution had succeeded in Asia's most important state, where it balanced the American-controlled regime in occupied Japan.

Indeed, the next three great confrontations of East and West were not European. In 1950 Asia became what it has remained ever since: the chief campaign ground for America's efforts to "contain" Communism. The most important American intervention was in Korea, a country divided at the thirty-eighth parallel of north latitude after the defeat of Japan. The Russians occupied the North, while the United States held the South. Each power established puppet regimes, a Red dictatorship in the North and a so-called democracy, in fact a military dictatorship, in South Korea. On

28. The Europeans called it Formosa.

Taking their cue from Russian "socialist realism" art the Chinese Communists erected this enormous banner of Mao Tse-tung to commemorate their 1949 victory over Chiang Kai-shek. The military and a well-armed, committed people pledge their support of the new regime. The Communist success ended nearly two years of general civil war during which Chiang's nationalists had steadily lost ground to Mao's forces. These events were a blow to American foreign policy which had been openly used to support Chiang, and further aggravated Russian-American tensions. The outbreak of the Korean War in 1950 brought China and the United States to the brink of open conflict, and their positions vis-à-vis one another were not to soften for over two decades. William Sewell; Weidenfeld and Nicolson, London.

June 25, 1950, the North invaded the South. Truman ordered American troops to fight, getting congressional support and a United Nations mandate for his action afterward.[29] The United Nations forces included "peace-keeping" troops from many nations, and the invaders had supply support from China and Russia.

The Allied forces under General MacArthur were generally successful until late in the year, when MacArthur failed to heed repeated Chinese warnings that bombardment of the Yalu River frontier[30] or hot pursuit across it would bring Red China's armies into the war. About 800,000 Red troops entered the struggle, supported by Russian-built jet planes (MIGs). As the Red Army rolled the Allies back to the thirty-eighth parallel, MacArthur grew insubordinate, and President Truman relieved from command the hero of World War II and the Japanese occupation.[31] Some two years later a truce[32] ended this war in which fifteen nations had participated together with the United States in the United Nations combat forces.

In the next year America faced another difficult choice. As Ho Chi Minh's forces besieged the French colonial regime's paratroops at Dien Bien Phu in Vietnam, the French sought United States aid. President Eisenhower resisted Dulles's advice to use American air power openly, and the United States acquiesced in the victory of Ho's Communist guerrillas. Vietnam was divided at the seventeenth parallel, and in the South the United States began the support of the various antidemocratic regimes which by 1965 had involved America in its second major land war in Asia.[33] Another country had been divided into pro-Soviet and pro-Western halves, as earlier Korea in Asia and Germany in Europe had been.

Ironically, the accelerated tempo of conflict came at a time when it is fair to say that the Cold War was beginning to thaw. This thaw was in part due to Stalin's death in 1953 and the internal struggle for power in Russia, which reduced the unity required for adventurism. More fundamental was the Russian advance as a nuclear power. When Americans learned that Russia had the bomb in 1949, the hysterically anti-Soviet right wing created great tension in an already worried country. Blaming the "loss of China"— as if it were an American trinket—on "Red sympathizers" in public life, reactionaries also blamed loyal public servants like Dean Acheson and General Marshall for the loss of America's monopoly of ultimate weapons. Voices had been raised in favor of a "preventive" nuclear war against Russia. Within Russia such talk accelerated the arms race. Truman responded to the pressure by authorizing the development of the hydrogen bomb, which was made and tested late in 1952.

Within a year, the Russians had caught up again. By 1954, therefore, each great power had reason to seek some other forms of confrontation than proxy wars and the nuclear arms race. Despite "provocations" from both sides too numerous even to list exhaustively, let alone discuss critically, the superpowers avoided direct engagement, recognizing that in a nuclear war fought with bombs rated in *megatons*,[34] neither side could win. The passage

29. Russia was boycotting the United Nations at the time, or would certainly have vetoed the "police" action.
30. The boundary of Chinese Manchuria.
31. MacArthur ceaselessly advocated bombing the North Korean-Chinese border regions and criticized Truman's "no-win" strategy.
32. Restoring the 1950 frontiers.
33. America refused to sign the 1954 Geneva Accords on Vietnam and encouraged their violation in 1956, when elections to unify the country were not allowed.
34. One megaton is the measure equivalent to the force of one million tons of TNT, if it were detonated.

of time encouraged Russians and Americans to see the earlier confrontations in more realistic, less apocalyptic terms, rather than as the evidence of America's encirclement of the USSR or part of some Soviet grand design for world conquest.

The Cold War gave way to a more traditional system of relations between states which, while dominated by the superpowers, took on the appearance of a balance of power based on alliances. The balance of terror based on total destruction still existed; and the arms race went beyond ballistic missiles armed with 100-megaton bombs into the realms of nerve gas and bacteriological warfare. But both blocs began to look more and more to the establishment and maintenance of detailed and limited alliance systems.

On the Soviet side the Cominform[35] took shape in 1947 as the successor to the Comintern. This propaganda network was supplemented in 1948, when Stalin concluded a series of mutual-assistance treaties with its European clients. China entered this framework in 1950, bringing with it North Korea and later North Vietnam. The Soviet scheme matured in 1955, early in the "thaw," when the Warsaw Pact tied together in one Soviet-dominated bloc all satellites, including East Germany. The practical effect of the pact was twofold: it forbade entry by members into any other system, and it insured security by providing for military aid against all aggressors. Beyond these mutual advantages, the pact gave legitimacy to the heavy Soviet occupation forces still in the eastern bloc countries ten years after Germany's defeat.

The era of "fraternal" maneuvers had begun, and it was under the pact aegis that Moscow moved to crush dissent in the "people's democracies" after 1955. Earlier, repression had less protection from the glare of publicity: in the Polish purges of 1945, those of 1953 in East Germany and Czechoslovakia,[36] or the several waves of purges in Hungary from 1953 to 1955, culminating in the 1956 uprising against Soviet "pact" troops. The pact came at a time of unprecedented troubles in the eastern bloc, as the satellites were restive under the direct controls over political, economic, and military affairs derived from the 1949 COMECON[37] agreements. Soviet leaders saw in the pact a way to diminish the servility and cynicism prevailing in the satellites, but even more it was an answer to NATO.[38]

COMECON itself was a response to NATO, the comprehensive alliance system embodied in the Brussels Treaty of 1948, by which the former European Allies guaranteed one another against attack. In 1949 this "attack"-conscious network was expanded by the North Atlantic Treaty, in which the United States joined all the Western powers except Spain, Sweden, and Switzerland. Greece and Turkey came into NATO in 1952, and Turkey subsequently became the link to CENTO, the Central Treaty Organization, embracing also Britain, Pakistan, and Iran. The American system then leapfrogged India, which was stubbornly neutral, to embrace SEATO,[39] formed in 1954. The member states were Britain, the United States, France, Pakistan, Australia, New Zealand, the Philippines, and Thailand.

These mutual defense networks also stood in a clear relationship to patterns of events within the Soviet Union and the Western states.

On the Communist side Stalin's death brought to power first Malenkov

---

35. Communist Information Bureau.
36. Some 350,000 were purged in Czechoslovakia, about 250,000 in Poland and East Germany.
37. The Council for Mutual Economic Assistance.
38. North Atlantic Treaty Organization.
39. Southeast Asia Treaty Organization.

and then Bulganin and Khrushchev. Malenkov had two main policies at odds with Stalinism: he saw the need to meet Soviet citizens' demands for consumer goods, which required a diversion of investment away from war-related industries; and he realized that a more conciliatory foreign policy was necessary, as he said in March 1954, in a world where war would destroy civilization itself. Bulganin, soon to be Malenkov's successor, followed this line in 1954, going to Geneva to meet Eisenhower, Eden,[40] and Mollet.[41] One fruit of the initiative for reconciliation was the signing of an Austrian peace treaty in 1955. But Khrushchev quickly gave evidence in that year to warn against optimism. The relaxation of tension in Europe did not extend to the rest of the world. Khrushchev concluded an arms deal with Egypt's Nasser and began a new era of Russian penetration of the Middle East; he visited New Delhi in November, paving the way toward amity with India's pro-Soviet leader Nehru; and he patched up relations with Tito and Yugoslavia.

Yet the thaw was real at home and abroad. Symbolically, the Russian author Ilya Ehrenburg showed this in the title of his 1954 novel *The Thaw*, from which we name the period as a whole. And in 1956 Khrushchev told the twentieth party congress some frank things about Stalinism, beginning the de-Stalinization campaign which ended only when Stalin's body was moved from Red Square to an obscure grave inside the Kremlin walls.

On the Western side, political and military steps had been supplemented with the economic aid of the Marshall Plan. Some European planners wanted to work toward a Western economic union. In 1948 the Ruhr statute allowed collaboration in distributing Ruhr coal and iron.[42] This was a step toward a European free trade area for basic industrial resources, which was the design of Robert Schuman[43] called the European Coal and Steel Community. Britain remained aloof from this plan in 1951, even though Churchill supported its main immediate goal, which was to guard against German power growing too great. The price paid was exclusion from the European Common Market, when this was formed in 1955–1957.

This, then, was the face the West showed the Soviet bloc in 1956, a year of convulsions in both camps. The Hungarian Revolution revealed the fragility of the Soviet hold on popular support in the satellites. A workers' strike at Poznan threatened to produce a Polish rising and was settled by a compromise allowing a measure of autonomy. Among the Western powers just as much consternation was produced by the Suez Crisis, which broke on October 29, three days before Hungary began its attempt to secede from the Warsaw Pact. Britain and France occupied the Suez Canal in ostensive support of Israel, which was involved in a second round of war with its Arab neighbors.[44] Actually, the main reason for the Western action, to which the United States was bitterly opposed, was Colonel Nasser's[45] move to nationalize the canal. Khrushchev backed Nasser, and this made Washington force on Britain and France a retreat, in the hope of staving off a total alignment of the Asian and African "Third World" countries with Soviet policy against "imperialism." Nasser then agreed to impartial operation of the canal, but not for Israel.[46]

40. Sir Anthony Eden.
41. Guy Mollet, the French premier from January 1956 to June 1957.
42. Germany was allowed to join in 1949.
   French foreign minister; his dates are 1886–1963.
44. The first Arab-Israeli war was in 1948, when Israel emerged as a state under United Nations pressures.
45. Gamal Abdel Nasser, the hero of the 1952 revolution that deposed King Farouk.
46. This was part of Israel's "education" about reliance on the great powers.

Sites of Wars, Rebellions, and Revolutions

1. Greece: 1944–1949, civil war; 1967, monarchy overthrown, 1973, government overthrown
2. East Germany: 1948–1949, Berlin airlift; 1953, uprising and Soviet intervention; 1962, Berlin wall
3. Poland: 1956, uprising and Soviet intervention
4. Hungary: 1956, revolution and Soviet intervention
5. Czechoslovakia: 1968, revolution and Soviet intervention
6. Yemen: 1962–1967, civil war
7. Israel: 1967, Six-Day War; 1973, October war
8. Kenya: 1952–1959, Mau Mau uprising
9. Congo: 1960–1965, secession and civil war
10. Nigeria: 1967–present, secession and civil war
11. Guatemala: 1954, U.S. assists in overthrow of pro-Communist government
12. Cuba: 1959, revolution; 1961, Bay of Pigs invasion
13. China: 1945–1949, civil war and Communist victory
14. Philippines: 1949–1955, Huk rebellion
15. Malaysia: 1948–1957, Communist rebellion
16. Korea: 1950–1953, Korean War
17. Vietnam: 1946–1954, French-Indochinese war; 1961–1973, Vietnam war
18. India: 1962, Sino-Indian border war; 1965, Indian-Pakistani war over Kashmir; 1971, Indian-Pakistani war
19. Chile: 1973, Marxist regime overthrown
20. Northern Ireland: 1968–present, civil strife between Protestants and Catholics

Sites of Attempted Coups

21. Dominican Republic: 1965, attempted coup, U.S. intervention
22. Indonesia: 1965, unsuccessful Communist coup

Sites of Crises

23. Cyprus: 1963–1964, Greek-Turkish fighting
24. Egypt: 1956, Suez crisis
25. Lebanon: 1958, U.S. marine landing
26. Cuba: 1962, missile crisis
27. Formosa: 1949–present, Nationalist Chinese government; 1955–1958, Quemoy and Matsu crisis
28. Sino-Soviet border dispute, 1969

States Gaining or Declaring Independence

29. Algeria: 1955–1958, insurrection; 1961, independence gained
30. Rhodesia: 1967, unilateral declaration of independence, 1970 proclaimed republic

Territory Annexed by China

31. Tibet: 1950, annexed by China

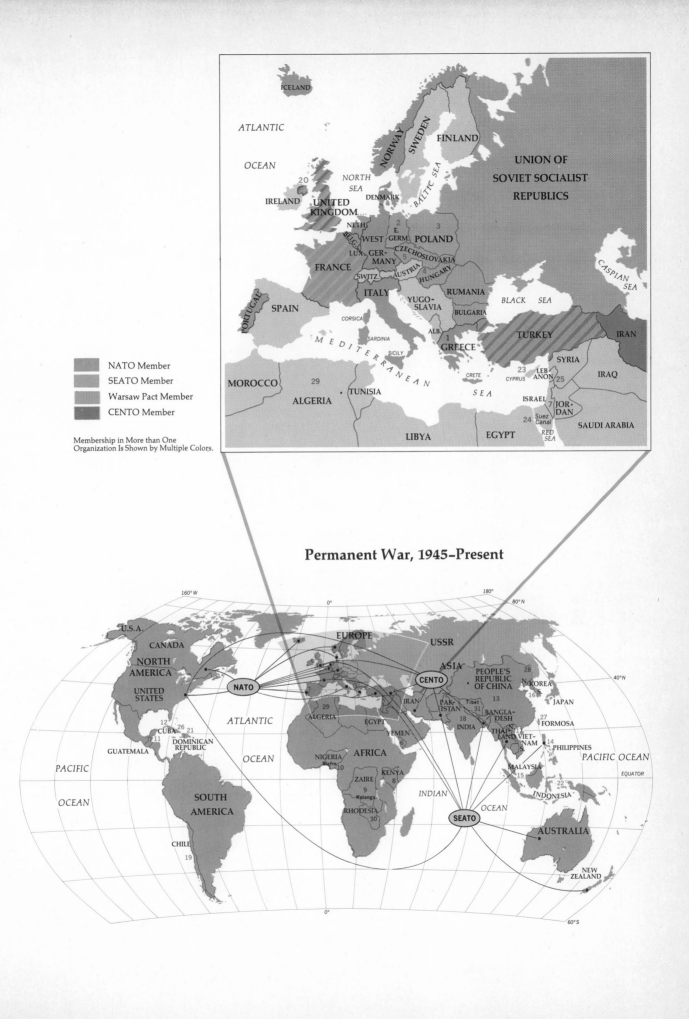

ICELAND

ATLANTIC

OCEAN

NORTH
SEA

IRELAND

UNITED
KINGDOM

DENMARK

NORWAY

SWEDEN

FINLAND

BALTIC SEA

UNION OF
SOVIET SOCIALIST
REPUBLICS

20

NETH.

BELG.

WEST
GER-
MANY

LUX.

FRANCE

SWITZ.

2
E.
GERM.

POLAND

3

CZECHOSLOVAKIA

5

AUSTRIA

HUNGARY

RUMANIA

ITALY

YUGO-
SLAVIA

BULGARIA

BLACK SEA

CASPIAN
SEA

PORTUGAL

SPAIN

CORSICA

SARDINIA

SICILY

M E D I T E R R A N E A N

ALB.

1

GREECE

CRETE

CYPRUS

TURKEY

SYRIA

LEB-
ANON

25

IRAN

IRAQ

23

MOROCCO

29

ALGERIA

TUNISIA

S E A

ISRAEL

7

24

JOR-
DAN

Suez
Canal

RED
SEA

SAUDI ARABIA

LIBYA

EGYPT

NATO Member

SEATO Member

Warsaw Pact Member

CENTO Member

Membership in More than One
Organization Is Shown by Multiple Colors.

Permanent War, 1945–Present

160° W

0°

180°

80° N

U.S.A.

CANADA

NORTH
AMERICA

UNITED
STATES

EUROPE

USSR

ASIA

CENTO

PEOPLE'S
REPUBLIC
OF CHINA

28

KOREA

16

JAPAN

40° N

NATO

IRAN

Tibet

PAK-
ISTAN

31

BANGLA-
DESH

27

FORMOSA

ATLANTIC

12

CUBA

26

21

DOMINICAN
REPUBLIC

GUATEMALA

11

29

ALGERIA

EGYPT

18

INDIA

13

THAI-
LAND

VIET-
NAM

14

PHILIPPINES

PACIFIC OCEAN

OCEAN

YEMEN

6

NIGERIA

Biafra

10

AFRICA

KENYA

8

MALAYSIA

15

PACIFIC

ZAIRE

9

Katanga

INDIAN

INDONESIA

22

OCEAN

SOUTH
AMERICA

RHODESIA

30

OCEAN

SEATO

AUSTRALIA

CHILE

19

NEW
ZEALAND

EQUATOR

0°

60° S

Because of the converging of military units from all parts of the Arab world to front lines around its borders, Israel had no choice but to attack on June 5, 1967. Within six days Israel shattered its enemies on all fronts in one of the most brilliant and decisive campaigns in the annals of war. The Egyptian army and air force were virtually destroyed, and the Jordanian and Syrian armed forces had suffered a crippling blow. Shown here are Israeli parachutists overcome by emotion at the sight of the Western Temple Wall which they reached during the battle for Jerusalem. This liberation of this wall, a site of great spiritual significance to Jews, was perhaps one of the most symbolic acts of the war. Israel Government Press Office.

The principle on which the 1956 interventions took place on all sides was not ideological but programmatic. The Soviets, for example, could not allow secession. America, which was officially pledged to "liberate" the satellites, was unwilling to act in Hungary, or in Egypt for that matter, to risk war. The year 1956 was thus one in which the politics of the Cold War produced the clearest recognition by both superpowers of the limits of saber rattling. Tensions between the United States and the USSR did not reach a boil again until 1961 and 1962, when the Berlin Wall and the Cuban Missile Crisis produced grave possibilities of nuclear war.

By then, however, the politics of coexistence were strong enough to survive even such terrors, and both powers moved closer to the positions they now hold: that by cooperation they can effectively control the regions of their vital interests, guaranteeing one another a tolerance of any course of action *within* their spheres of influence. The United States complains of

Russian tyranny in Czechoslovakia in 1968, when the Soviet tanks crushed the Prague Spring. And the Russians make propaganda gains at the expense of America's past involvement in Vietnam. Both powers play dangerous games in the Arab-Israeli disputes, as they did especially in the 1967 Six-Day War. But each cautiously eyes the emergence of China as a third superpower and seeks security in new combinations. Meanwhile, the rest of the world *within the West* settles down to prosperity.

THE WESTERN MIRACLE

The resurgence of the Western economy from the ruin of total war in the twenty years after 1946 is the dominant achievement of the postwar era. In the prewar period no economists were predicting rapid growth. The Western economy had been mangled by war and depression, between which had come a terrible inflationary period. On the whole the economy was in the middle of an unfinished transformation of industrialization with respect to technique and trade. Much of its productive apparatus was obsolete, restrictive trade and labor practices flourished, industries were stagnating, agricultural outputs were low, there was tremendous unemployment and wide income deficiencies.

Marxist economists saw in these things the symptoms of failure, as predicted in their theory, which were necessary to the proletarian revolution against decaying capitalism. There was a relative pauperization of the working class and a sharpening of class struggle, not the visible economic growth and rising living standards capitalist economics confidently predicted in the 1920s. Fifteen years after V-E Day, however, Western Europe was producing 25 percent of the world's industrial output and controlled 40 percent of the world's trade. This was in any framework a remarkable achievement. Western Europe occupied only 3 percent of the globe's land surface and contained in 1960 only 9 percent of the earth's population. Moreover, in 1946 gross productive levels were on the average about half what they had been in 1939. Observers saw acute hunger, not prosperity; and as late as 1947 poor harvests caused some to fear mass starvation.

From the low point of 1947, therefore, in little more than a decade, a growth took place that was at once unpredictable and perhaps incredible. By 1955 most of European agriculture was mechanized. In 1948, as a matter of fact, except in Germany, major industrial output had passed prewar levels; with the help of the Marshall Plan, Europeans were able to buy what they needed for redevelopment. The tremendous psychological pressure of the pent-up demands, frustrated in wartime, for consumer goods broke loose in an orgy of consumer spending. Average industrial output in 1950 ran 35 percent ahead of levels for 1939, despite the shock given by the Korean War, as the surging defense needs forced raw material prices up sharply. There was no stopping the recovery. Country after country adopted economic planning: France had its Monnet Plan for growth; Europe had the Schuman Plan. Confident forecasts were made in 1951 that industrial production in 1960 would be up at least 40 percent, perhaps as much as 60 percent. In fact those levels were passed in 1955. In 1964 Europe's industrial output was two and a half times as great as it had been in 1939.

This kind of growth was without precedent. Never had there been the consumer prosperity seen everywhere in the decades of the 1950s and 1960s. Never had there been less unemployment or higher rates of growth; nor had there been a period of affluence with less public anxiety about its durability, even when the rate of expansion slowed a bit because of recession in 1957–1958 or again in 1963–1964. The average annual rate of growth[47] from 1948 to 1963 in eleven countries was as follows: Austria, 5.8; Belgium, 3.2; Denmark, 3.6; France, 4.6; Germany, 7.6; Holland, 4.7; Italy, 6.0; Norway, 3.5; Sweden, 3.4; Switzerland, 3.4; and Britain, 2.5. In the subperiod 1960–1965 these rates prevailed: Italy, 5.1; France, 5.1; Germany, 4.8; Britain, 3.3; Japan, 9.6; the United States, 4.5. Thus even sluggish Britain was doing better than it had at any time since 1914. Italy was ceasing to be "backward." And Germany and Japan were becoming industrial giants in the ashes of defeat.

The "capitalist" economies refused to behave as Marxists predicted they must. This was often explained by reference to the essentially "military" character of the boom. Whatever value this had in explaining America's growth, it had none in Europe, which lived under the nuclear shield of the United States, and less in Japan, which remained resolutely antimilitarist in the shadow of the mushroom clouds over Hiroshima and Nagasaki.

Most Western economists deny that any comprehensive explanation is possible, but they point to "factors" obviously influential. The governments, for a start, had learned the lesson of 1919–1939: that consumer purchasing power was essential, as the economist John Maynard Keynes had argued. The governments therefore manipulated taxation, credit, monetary policies, spending and borrowing; they reduced customs barriers[48] to enlarge markets; and they coordinated development.

In retrospect, we can see that the Western economies had followed the "totalitarian" socialist concept of planning for cheaper and more rational production and distribution. Laissez-faire capitalism was a ghost in a civilization operating on the basis of *nationalized* industries,[49] with special stress on what Marxists called the "commanding heights": coal and electricity in Britain, along with airlines, railroads, steel; electricity, air transport, and coal in France, with 37 percent of shipping and 40 percent of banking; in Italy 80 percent of all transport and 60 percent of steel, banking, and mining. The principles were widely accepted that labor supplies should be allowed to move to jobs, that technical innovation was precious, and that unfettered private profit was not the goal of economics in a civilized society.

Industrial production boomed in Eastern Europe as well as in Western Europe and Japan in the period 1938–1967, as the following table shows, where production levels for 1958 are set at an index number of 100.

It is important to notice how false it is to contrast Western "progress" in this regard with Eastern "backwardness." While Western systems continued to show larger gross levels of production than the Soviet satellite systems, the rates of growth and relative indices for some Eastern countries exceeded those for Western nations of comparable size. Thus, while in 1968 Soviet GNP was only half that of America, output by industry in the USSR in 1963 was forty-four times that of 1928, despite the strain of the arms race on what was the weaker economy. The total GNP increase from 1938 to 1964 in Bulgaria, in terms of the same indices used above, was 152, compared with only 147 in Holland, 135 in France, and 132 in Italy. American growth was relatively slow, but its base was larger in any event. The most startling performances were Japan's, Italy's, and Bulgaria's.

Recovery was thus a feature of all industrial economies, even non-

47. Measured as the percent growth in the gross domestic product (GDP). GDP is determined by subtracting foreign income from the gross national product (GNP), or total of goods and services delivered to purchasers.
48. Within the Common Market after 1957 and also in the European Free Trade Association (EFTA) among non-Market members (Britain, Denmark, Norway, etc.)
49. That is, state socialism.

TABLE 1 *Industrial Production Indices, 1938–1967*

	1938	1948	1952/53	1959	1962/63	1965/67
Bulgaria	11	22	55	121	170	238
Czechoslovakia	31	44	64	112	143	159
East Germany	38	27	66	112	137	159
Hungary	28	38	84	111	149	177
Poland	16	28	61	109	145	182
Rumania	25	22	63	110	168	243
Yugoslavia	29	43	53	113	150	217
USSR	23	40	58	111	146	184
United States	33	73	90	113	133	168
West Germany	53	27	61	107	137	158
France	52	55	70	101	129	155
Italy	43	44	64	112	166	212
Holland	47	53	72	110	141	182
Belgium	64	78	88	104	135	153
Britain	67	74	84	105	119	133
Austria	39	36	65	106	131	151
Spain	—	—	—	102	149	215
Sweden	52	74	81	106	140	176
Japan	58	22	50	120	212	347

SOURCE: Walter Laqueur, *The Rebirth of Europe,* p. 142, p. 149. Copyright © 1970 by Walter Laqueur, adapted by permission of Holt, Rinehart and Winston, Inc. The figures for the Eastern states are for 1938, 1948, 1953, 1959, 1962, and 1965; those for the West are 1938, 1948, 1952, 1959, 1963, and 1967.

Western ones, and the achievement had little apparent connection to ideology. The Soviet bloc nations started from a poorer agrarian base and a relatively backward industrial one. Yet they overcame these handicaps as well as the devastation of war, bureaucratic incompetence, the collectivization of farming, and the disadvantageous trade terms forced on the satellites under COMECON treaties. Also, in both East and West other similarities are evident, beyond parallel courses of growth. All of the "backward" countries industrialized; all showed tremendous improvements in living standards, housing conditions, educational opportunity; they shortened work days, achieved lower unemployment levels, and willingly accepted "guest" laborers from neighboring states to solve domestic labor shortages. Yugoslav workers were welcome in Germany and France. Everywhere at least some social security measures were enacted: provisions for medical care, old-age benefits, unemployment pay, or grants or services for working mothers.

It was also the common experience that the social patterns changed rapidly, as unskilled labor gave way to skilled workers on the farms and in the cities. However much Marxists might say there was still poverty and social injustice—and both existed everywhere, especially in America, where blacks, Chicanos, Indians, and other ethnic groups were generally excluded from prosperity—the worker was being unchained by the industrial revolution. Indeed, the proletariat based on factory work was shrinking as economies shifted to automation and moved away from the production of goods toward the provision of services.

In this respect, it is useful to look at another set of figures relevant to growth and its social consequences. The Western European population was 264 million in 1940; in 1970 it was 320 million. The growth from 1940 to 1955 was 12 percent of the prewar total! This was achieved in most instances by a combination of rising birthrates and falling death rates, which also existed in Eastern Europe. Even France experienced a surge of population; in fact the French annual average natural increase from 1960 to 1965 was 1.2 percent, a figure matched in Germany but exceeded only in the USSR, Poland, Switzerland, and the Netherlands.[50] The population of the USSR increased from about 180 million to 227 million between 1950 and 1966. The correlation of the growth of population and output during this new industrial revolution is striking, therefore, and subject to validation by the example of Albania, which remained the least industrialized country in the West and had zero population growth as well!

The social consequences of both sorts of growth are important. Everywhere, things were moving toward what C. G. Jung in 1933 called the "American speed." Chiefly, this meant urbanization, which was more marked in the Soviet Union than anywhere else. The population of the twenty major Soviet cities increased by 13.7 million from 1928 to 1960.[51] Thus growth after 1945 created huge "conurbations" (networks of urban communities) throughout Europe, east and west, with the result that the density of population in some areas of Europe is now four times that of the United States.

The countryside in 1914 had half of the Western European population. In the modern West, agriculture disappeared in the industrial heartlands, and even industry ceased to employ as great a proportion of the work force as the more rapidly growing service sectors did. Even in Spain, where in 1910 some 67 percent of all workers were agricultural, the percentage had fallen to 33 in 1966. Elsewhere the drop was even more startling. In Britain only 3 percent of the people farmed for a living in 1966, and only 17 percent of all workers in the Common Market countries lived on the land. Yet even this number is too great, given the technological revolution that struck agriculture in the 1950s. Western Europe meets over 95 percent of its own food needs with the diminished work force and overproduces milk, butter, and eggs. Should the 50 percent of farms less than 12.5 acres in size be rationally combined to increase production,[52] then the 54 million European farmers would be producing far too much for their region's needs, like the tinier fraction in America, which is only 7 percent of the population.

Thus productivity itself has penalties. As the peasant economies erode everywhere, the young flock to the cities. Europe and America are becoming essentially urban continents in a world where the other 80 percent of the people are living under impoverished systems with scarcely launched industrial bases. The rest of the world watches the West wrestle with the problems of wealth, in stark incomprehension of the economic system that is the greatest fact of modern life. It is as if the whole world outside the West were in the position of black Americans and other minorities within the most powerful Western economy, seeing prosperity but not sharing in it. According to recent projections, the economic prospects for Americans in 1980 are shown in Table 2.[53] Despite great increases in income, the roots of poverty among American minorities are so deeply laid that in 1980 they will not have achieved the white levels of 1967, much less those for 1980 itself.

50. That is, in northern Europe only. In the southern and southeastern countries the birthrates did not rise appreciably, but death rates fell rapidly as industrialization and urbanization went forward.
51. From 7.79 million to 21.49 million.
52. A plan advocated by Common Market managers; the specter of such a program was influential in causing Norway's strong small farmers' party to agitate, successfully, against Norwegian membership in the Common Market in 1972.
53. Andrew Brimmer, "The Black Revolution and the Economic Future of Negroes in the United States," *The American Scholar*, Autumn 1969, pp. 637–638. Copyright © 1969 by the United Chapters of Phi Beta Kappa. By permission of the publishers.

TABLE 2 *White and Nonwhite Income in the United States*

Income Segments	Whites	Nonwhites
Average per capita $ income (1967)	2,590	1,510
Average per capita $ income (1980)*	3,648	2,277

*Assuming GNP grows at the rate of 4 percent; in order to hold the buying power of the dollar constant, 1980 figures are expressed in terms of 1968 prices.

In the world outside the West the general level of agricultural productivity is not high enough to allow adequate levels of food consumption per person, even by the United Nations standard of 2,100 calories per day, which is nearly 1,000 below prevailing Western averages. Even under optimum conditions of population control, domestic capital formation, and external aid, it is unlikely that a per capita income growth rate of 1.5 percent can be achieved in Asia, Latin America, and Africa, where average per capita incomes are lower by half than the lowest European averages and lag United States averages by as much as 90 percent.[54]

Europe has doubled its merchant fleets since 1968, multiplied by a factor of ten its passenger air services, and in 1958 Europe's airlines surpassed its ships in transatlantic passenger volume. Automobiles in private hands in 1948 totaled 5 million; in 1966 there were 44 million cars contributing to the road paralysis long familiar in America, but now also part of the holiday leisure of more than 100 million tourists within Europe. The average European skilled laborer in the West has thirty-three paid holidays a year; in the summer workers participate in mass migrations without parallel, except in the cold winter months, when more than 40 million seek the sun's warmth in Spain, Italy, and North Africa. Tourism is therefore one measure of the general Western prosperity, even allowing for the income disparities between Swedes and Turks, Spaniards and the Swiss.

But a more solid measure of prosperity and a more significant one lies in the social change by which the welfare state eliminated the harshest features of early industrial society. This is not to say there was no poverty in the West in 1970; there was, especially in south Europe and in the United States. But in northwestern Europe material deprivation has become less a problem than the boredom of affluence and the anonymity of city life. Alienation, not hunger, was the watchword of the 1960s, especially among the young, as juvenile crime, drug addiction, and suicide rode the crest of a sharp wave of personal insecurity in the nuclear age.

Despite the alarm over unrest among young people—there is no evidence that it is greater today than in the 1820s or 1920s—Europeans have become conscious of taking part in the greatest social advance in centuries. They enjoy more mobility between classes, and the young especially are less burdened by parental absolutism. The new economy and the welfare state are parts of a permissive society in which church attendance is down and sexual freedom up. The older generations seem to have lost self-confidence in the ravages of war, with the result that the authority of parents and teachers has been shrinking. Moreover, women are actively

54. Rostow, *Politics and the Stages of Growth* (Cambridge: Cambridge University Press, 1970), p. 143. The European nation with the lowest per capita GNP in 1970 is Portugal, with $480; figure for Turkey is about $290; for Sweden, $2,730; United States figure for 1967 was $3,840.

pursuing equal pay for equal work; the availability of a new birth control pill and of sex education is contributing to their sexual freedom. And, if skeptics say this is the road to ruin, because divorce rates were six times as high in 1970 as they had been in 1938, it might be answered that courts once sentencing 1,200 of every 100,000 adults for crimes in 1910 were in 1970 sentencing only 780 per 100,000.

The sharpest contrast exists in the quality of private life, if we compare Soviet youth with their Western counterparts. In the USSR a rigid puritanism and doctrinaire traditionalism frown on sex education, adolescent sexual encounters, abortion, divorce, drugs, women's liberation, and the moral "decadence" obvious in Western art, literature, music, and films. Soviet citizens do enjoy welfare services, however, as well as nominal rents and vastly enlarged educational opportunities. All of the European countries spend more for social services than the United States, in terms of the percent of GNP. And nearly all advanced societies in Europe enjoy lower infant death rates than the Americans, as well as longer life expectancy. The biggest qualitative difference in living standards is the East-West differential in housing. In the most prosperous Western states the index of rooms per person is about 1.5; in the Soviet bloc countries the figure hovers about .6.

Almost everywhere in the West—and as Eastern Europe and Japan approach "Western" levels of affluence we must see the term as less *geographic* and more economic-technological—the Americanization of the life-style is discernible. New mass production techniques are putting into homes the same media for home entertainment—television and the phonograph record. Outside the home there are the common denominators of leisure hours: tourism, hobbies, sports, cars, photography, adult education, the arts, and the film theater—the real temple of mass culture, along with the popular music concert hall. Also, there is the common problem of living with advertisements and artificially induced "wants" and "needs," costly without producing real satisfactions. This is one aspect of the culture of leisure which Soviet citizens have so far been spared.

If the critics of the new culture are correct, however, and the Soviet society meets the Western type, by moving toward a retail-oriented state capitalism as we in the West move toward enlarged welfare statism, perhaps even this distinction will melt away. It seems less likely that the West will join the Soviet society by means of revolution from within, because rapid technological change and economic growth have altered in a fundamental way the class relationships in modern societies. We hear much less of proletarian-capitalist antagonism.

What is a rising concern is the feeling that all classes are equally manipulated by a vaguely defined "establishment" of bureaucrats, opinion makers in the mass media, and the "military-industrial complex" which General Eisenhower warned about in 1962, in his leave-taking from the presidency. As the state expands its control over life, whether in the guise of "bureaucratic collectivism" or "democratic welfare statism," economic equality of status enlarges. Income from earnings increases, while income from property falls. But there does not seem to be the same movement everywhere; and it is not reliably established that the concentration of social and political power in the hands of elites is changing—only that the composition of the elites itself changes. The state is not withering away; it is expanding, and with it the ranks of the educated managers, the meritocracy. Britain stubbornly resists this change, and in 1970 some 5 percent of the population owned 75 percent of the wealth and controlled as well the educational means to dominate top corporation jobs and the government ministries.

The pilgrimage church of Notre-Dame-du-Haut (1950–1955) at Ronchamp, France, is the masterpiece of Le Corbusier's late style. In his early work the architect used reinforced concrete to construct clean, sharply angular, and severely functional buildings which were consciously inspired by machinery design. A political leftist, Le Corbusier was particularly concerned with developing large-scale housing projects for factory workers. Partially because of its religious function, Notre Dame displays a more sculptural, lyric use of concrete which shows the interplay of flat and rounded forms. Despite his belief that twentieth-century architecture ought to conform to the mechanical nature of industrial society, Le Corbusier's concept of the architect's role was humanistic rather than technical. By his arrangement of forms the architect realizes "an order which is a pure creation of his spirit." George Holton, Photo Researchers.

The despair and torment of modern man is captured in Paul Klee's Death and Fire *(1940), painted on the eve of World War II. The German-Swiss artist was a member of the surrealists, who throughout the 1930s looked at a rapidly decaying world with ironic wit. By late in the decade, however, Klee's amusing little post-cubist human figures had taken on the ominous overtones of this work. Klee had a firsthand knowledge of Nazi intolerance; in 1933 the "degenerate" painter was removed from his teaching post in Düsseldorf, and thereafter he lived in Switzerland. Paul Klee Foundation, Museum of Fine Arts, Berne. Permission S.P.A.D.E.M. 1974, by French Reproduction Rights, Inc.*

Socially, therefore, the economic miracle has belied Marxist predictions. The welfare state has eased class antagonisms without eradicating them or the inequities of income distribution. But we must not be blind to the real progress toward greater equality and a more humane attitude toward the weak, the sick, and the aged in Europe, if not yet in America. Nor should we be blind to the equally important fact that the European social revolution came about with America's aid, in dollars and in the resistance to Soviet pressures, especially in the New Germany—and all this without bloody revolutions.

THE SIGHTS AND SOUNDS OF THE SIXTIES

The culture created in the West since the war cannot be encapsulated. It is too diverse for summary, too deserving to be dismissed with easy catch phrases, and too ambiguous in its frenetic energy to allow for neat stylistic pigeonholes.

Some obvious things can be said, of course. The modernist movements in art, architecture, and music have continued trends shown very early in the century. Functionalism in architecture, inspired by the work and philosophy of the designer-craftsman William Morris, began as a revolt against the nineteenth-century love for historical pageantry, for elaborate imitations of classical or medieval styles. Men like Frank Lloyd Wright (United States), Josef Hoffmann (Austria), and Peter Behrens (Germany) found in the needs of bridges, train stations, boat docks, and factories a warrant to make the form fit the function. They shaped glass, concrete, and steel to refrain from deceit and thus show the *reality* of buildings. Likewise functionalism influenced furniture makers and fabric designers, spreading to every aspect of interior decoration.

After the First World War functionalism established itself firmly in the work of the architects first coming to notice around 1914, especially Walter

Op Art was founded by the German Josef Albers and the Hungarian Victor Vaserely. Like the Bauhaus movement of the twenties, Op artists of today have tried·to break down the barriers between art and technology. By the use of primary colors and geometric forms, as seen in Vaserely's Supernovae, their art expresses the technology of the twentieth century through its rhythms. The Tate Gallery, London.

Gropius (1883–1969). Together with Mies van der Rohe (1886–1969), Gropius established the Bauhaus in 1919, a school and system of studios dedicated to good design. By the 1920s the "international" style had new prophets, the Frenchman Le Corbusier[55] and the Finn Eero Saarinen. It spread to Japan and almost everywhere that rebuilding took place in the 1950s, except Russia, where all art struggled with the dictates of party bosses who prescribed socialist realism as the only nondecadent art form.

Painting has moved steadily away from photographic realism, but not always along the lines set by the great pre-1914 pioneers like Picasso, Miró,

55. Charles Édouard Jeanneret (1887–1965).

The two leaders of Abstract Expressionism, Jackson Pollack and William de Kooning, gave rise to a new kind of art movement dubbed "action painting." In de Kooning's Woman *series (Woman I is shown here) the female image is presented as a feared and desired object. Through his bold and contrasting strokes the process itself becomes the subject rather than the image. Collection, The Museum of Modern Art, New York.*

Using objects taken from our everyday world, Robert Rauschenberg creates a piece of Pop art entitled Odalisk. *Pop art satirizes art for art's sake and a world surrounded by objects; it nevertheless is concerned with the visual quality of its elements. Wallraf-Richartz Museum, Cologne.*

and Chagall or those indicated by the pioneer expressionists and abstractionists like Klee, Kandinsky, and Piet Mondrian.[56] If there has been a dominant direction it has been away from figurative and objective art, away from likeness, especially of the human form. From that point of view Picasso became a reactionary, where once he had been a prophet, clinging stubbornly to a humanistic content for his drawings and paintings. While artists since 1945 have evolved no common language in the sense that we speak historically of Romanticism or impressionism, geometric forms in two dimensions have found great favor. But there have been competing rages. In 1960 Andy Warhol pushed "pop art" in America and found eager imitators in Europe, where his favorite subjects were just as well known: Coke bottles, Campbell soup cans, and comic-strip renderings of movie queens like Marilyn Monroe. At the opposite extreme are the "action" painters, followers of Jackson Pollock, the American who threw paint at canvas or "walked" it onto the surface, proclaiming that what counted for the artist was not the optical result but the satisfaction obtained by the act itself.

56. Klee, Kandinsky, and Mondrian all died in 1940–1944.

In no realm of art does the revolution of the twentieth century appear more clearly than in sculpture. The great tradition of Western figurative sculpture was in steady decline from the baroque age until the startling revival begun by Rodin. By the time of his death in 1917 he had consolidated anew the style of naturalistic work in the round, focusing on the figure in a humane, sympathetic way. And in such works as *The Three Shades, Eve,* and *The Thinker* he all but exhausted the tradition he revived. While some workers were influenced by Rodin in the direction of a thoroughgoing classicism—Aristide Maillol, for example—others saw in Rodin's roughhewn faces and figures a warrant for abstracting from reality the more formal elements of sculpture and giving prominence to them: mass, space, and volume. And some abandoned altogether the humanistic concerns of Rodin.

Among the leaders whose work continued to emphasize the human form we give increasing honor to Renoir and Degas. But very important work was done by the German masters Wilhelm Lehmbruck (1881–1919), Käthe Kollwitz (1867–1945), and Gerhard Marcks (1889–1972). Their problem was not in the material or the range of themes they treated so expressively. It was rather that the possibility of saying something new seemed exhausted until Constantin Brancusi (1876–1957) made clear the way toward a sculpture based on the figure seen in a new way. A Rumanian peasant by birth, Brancusi pioneered abstract and cubist sculpture in various materials: limestone, marble, wood, brass, and bronze. His *The Kiss* shares only the title with Rodin's work; and a comparison of his two works called the *Sleeping Muse* (1906, 1910–1911) shows Brancusi's rapid movement away from a literal rendering of the human form. By 1930, in such works as *The Fish* geometric forms had entirely usurped the place of realistic representations.

Cubist sculpture in the fully developed sense was perfected by the Russian-American artist Alexander Archipenko (1887–1964) and two Frenchmen—Raymond Duchamp-Villon (1876–1918) and Jacques Lipchitz (1891–1973). Archipenko especially opened up voids within the mass, abandoning solidness entirely in order to present motion in a new way in such works as *A Walking Woman* (1912). Lipchitz's *Reclining Nude with Guitar* (1928) furthered the reduction of the figure to a series of interwoven planes. The American Max Weber quickly mastered the techniques, and in 1915 his *Spiral Rhythm* raised the question of the relevance of the figurative tradition in an age obsessed by the shapes of machinery.

In Britain a great school developed around Henry Moore and Barbara Hepworth. Their works—Moore's *Reclining Mother and Child* and Hepworth's *Figure: Churinga*—clearly show the struggle to maintain some concern with the human figure. But no artist more poignantly illustrated the dilemma of the sculptor after Rodin than the Swiss Alberto Giacometti (1901–1966). His work is alternately primitive and suggestive of a new iron age as in *Spoon Woman*, or brutal and surrealistic as in *Woman with Her Throat Cut* (1932). During the 1930s and 1940s Giacometti responded to the brutality of his time in characteristic fashion. He held on to the idea of the human face and figure; but his heads are severely lacerated, and his repeated "representations" of a woman reduce her to a few spindly swirls with jagged edges, elongated, harsh, and more dominated by the space in which she appears than dominating it.

After looking at Giacometti for a while, it is necessary for us to remember that the humanistic vision has not disappeared completely, although only the Norwegian master Gustav Vigeland has produced in this century a body of work massive in size and dedicated to the phases of life from infancy to

As Picasso and Braque
experimented with cubism and
developed its language in painting,
Jacques Lipchitz explored the cubist
perception—the multiple views,
geometric shapes, intersecting
planes—in sculpture. To Lipchitz,
who became a close friend of
Picasso's and who, like the Spanish
artist, was to continue his creative
work for almost three-quarters of
the twentieth century, cubism
offered the promise of a new
language for art; he called it "a new
view of the universe." Though he
later moved away from the style of
his early more purely cubist
phase—his Standing Woman
(1918–1919), shown here, is a work
from this period—Lipchitz
continued to call himself a cubist,
maintaining that he still shared the
vision, if not the vocabulary, of
cubism. Kunstmuseum, Basle.

old age. His colossal output marks him off from the other great masters in our own age. And the postwar wave of new sculptors move even further away from the figurative tradition, into abstracts, wire mobiles, constructions from scrap parts, and a variety of forms influenced by industrial technology.

These movements are part of a wider revolution against what has been contemptuously called formalism or humanistic realism. The same revolt also seized music in the pre-1914 years, as we know, in the genius of Stravinsky and Schönberg. Their insistence on pulsating rhythms and cacophony drew an eager response even from composers who remained tied to Romantic modes of expression in part: the Finn Sibelius, Paul Hindemith in Germany, and Shostakovich, the great Soviet master. In the second movement of his Seventh Symphony, which he composed during the siege of Leningrad, the cacophonous jar of war is present, in the beat of the drum which heralds the invaders' approach and in the screeching dissonance of the orchestra, as each voice in it cries out against the mangling of form that war itself is.

In music, however, formalistic elements remain as strong as geometric abstraction in art. The Greek expatriate Iannis Xenakis composed music on the principles of higher mathematics. Electronically governed compositions were pioneered by Pierre Schaffer. Time intervals and "stochastic asymptotes" entered the language of music, as this art sought to achieve some unity with the technology of sound manipulation available through electronics. The revolt against tradition even produced such curiosities as "performances" in which violins were publicly burned, while electronic amplifiers blared out the sounds made by twanging rubber bands and breaking glass plates. The American John Cage composed a "silent sonata" called *4.33* in which a pianist sat at the keyboard poised to play for 4 minutes and 33 seconds, without striking the keys.

The general public preferred other forms, however. The old avant-gardists were absorbed in the more traditional repertoire, and nobody is surprised to hear Webern and Stravinsky, or Bartok and Schönberg, on the same programs with Brahms, Mozart, Beethoven, and Chopin. Indeed, in some concert halls in the 1960s Mahler and Shostakovich were heard as frequently as the "masters." A more significant trend in modern music was the export of popular forms from America to the Westernized world. Broadway musicals either were staged abroad or reached foreign audiences in film versions—*My Fair Lady, West Side Story, Hair,* and *Jesus Christ Superstar.* These last-named shows were a development out of jazz, although the parentage is still debated. After the war, black jazz and big-band "swing" caught on in Europe and the Orient, wherever occupation troops and transistor radios appeared. So, too, did American "folk" music, country and western, especially in the sensational "rock" forms developed in America by Elvis Presley and perfected in Liverpool by the Beatles. Rock groups multiplied, with fantastic names often symbolic of the alienation of the young from the "culture" of their parents: "Mothers of Invention," "Three Dog Night," "The Mamas and the Papas," and "Jefferson Airplane." In some sense, however, the rock movement reunited the public to the composer in the wake of the radical breach caused by the esoteric "serious" composers.

If we seek the common denominator of modern culture, however, it is less in architecture and art, perhaps even less in rock groups and shows, than in the world of television and film. The technology of the motion picture at its best absorbs all other art forms, whether in the Russian version of *Hamlet* for which Shostakovich wrote a great score or in the

British *Henry V*, in which Sir Laurence Olivier brought Shakespeare to millions. Great directors can create the sensual world of impressionism, as Bo Widerberg did in *Elvira Madigan*, or evoke the condition of life in medieval Russia as Sergei Eisenstein did in *Ivan the Terrible*. The world of the angry young writers of the late 1940s and 1950s can be revealed to those who do not read many books, because a hit like John Braine's British best seller *Room at the Top* was translated to the screen, where we might all see Joe Lampton's lust for big money.

Stanley Kubrick's *Dr. Strangelove* brought home to audiences—literally home when the film was shown as a TV movie—the plight of life in the nuclear age; and doubtless Kubrick reached a far greater audience than did Max Frisch in *The Chinese Wall*, where one of the characters echoes Camus's concern about mass murder and the absurdity of life:

A slight whim on the part of the man on the throne, a nervous breakdown, a touch of neurosis . . . a moment of impatience on account of indigestion—and the jig is up. Everything! A cloud of yellow or brown ashes boiling up towards the heavens in the shape of a mushroom, no, a dirty cauliflower—and the rest is silence, radioactive silence.[57]

The CinemaScoped play and the film viewed in a movie theater vie with television, however, in translating every aspect of reality into immediate sense experience. What is not clear about the impact of the electronic media is their benignity, malignancy, or utter neutrality. Orwell warned in *Nine-*

57. Quoted in Laqueur, *Europe since Hitler*, pp. 279–280.

Below, a rock group performs before a Boston audience. With its origins in black music, the new sound, known first in the music trade as "race" music, became rhythm-and-blues, rock 'n' roll, and then rock. The Blues Project, a rock group of the sixties, offered this definition of the new music: "The electric band and the Negro changed folk blues into a tremendous external expression of love, protest, and anger. It forced upon the listener, if he really listened, the knowledge that a much broader and wider understanding could be created with its power. . . . For the first time there is an American music reaching all the people, everywhere." Jeff Albertson; Stock, Boston.

teen Eighty-Four that we would ultimately become the victims of police states abetted in their work by electronic Big Brothers in the shape of one-way spy screens. There is enough surveillance of citizens above suspicion to make this nightmare all too real, not only behind the now torn Iron Curtain, but in the so-called freedom-loving countries. In a series of shocking disclosures, the people of America, for example, saw on television the unfolding of a Senate investigation into the "Watergate Affair." Government agents and the political associates of President Richard M. Nixon apparently conducted wide-ranging electronic surveillance under the guise of "national security" operations, while actually committing a variety of common crimes against domestic opponents of the administration.

Furthermore, electronic applications in military situations have produced "smart" bombs guided to targets by laser beams and the planned fleet of Trident submarines, each carrying enough ICBMs to incinerate the 160 largest Russian cities. The stark horror of that fact is one argument for the proposition that the West has indeed built its own Doomsday Machine, by opening an abyss between the heights of our scientific attainments and the general culture capable of using that science for good rather than evil. It is the tension of this possibility, of course, that haunted Camus and which made the great Italian novelist Alberto Moravia speak of the world as an imbroglio of lies.

The unease of our time springs in part from this situation, in which poets and philosophers seem unable to create things in which the riddles of existence are solved. Scientists and engineers at least claim to do so, by economic miracles and technological orchestration (in the successful launching and functioning of a spacecraft, for example). Modern films

dwell often on this painful aspect of modern life, on anxiety, guilt, torture, and the utter collapse of morals. But in doing so they breed rebellion, activism, and in the young a determination not to walk blindly the road to salvation marked Technology.

Spurred by men of letters whose politics were those of protest—Sartre in postwar France, Günter Grass in Germany in the fifties, Norman Mailer in America in the sixties—the new generation seems less inclined to accept as the ultimate mark of civilization the fact that the Russian Major Gagarin flew in space[58] or that American astronauts landed on the moon. They stubbornly insist on a society in which relationships are more symmetrical and no "mandarins" are followed merely because they strike the correct pose.[59] They will not be kept from talking about racial discrimination in America because there are forced labor camps in Russian Siberia, nor could they accept the destruction of tiny Vietnam by American bombs because the Soviets kept Budapest in leading strings and Czechoslovakia in chains. The world is being measured by different yardsticks, and new values are taking shape.

We have seen the politics of confrontation give way to the politics of coexistence; we have seen the old balances of power shift as new powers rise and others clamor to be heard. As man reaches into outer space, the planet itself draws closer together, linked by technology, by at least some degree of political détente, and by crises in population, energy, and environment that affect us all. The civilization of the West has led us to this point; it must now join in global efforts to meet the coming challenges.

BIBLIOGRAPHY

BARRACLOUGH, G. *Introduction to Contemporary History.** London: Watts, 1964. A distinguished historian's effort to state what is essential in the "ethos" of postmodern society.

BLACKETT, P. M. S. *Atomic Weapons and East-West Diplomacy.* Cambridge: Cambridge University Press, 1956. Sympathetic to the USSR in the era of American nuclear hegemony.

BOULDING, K. E. *The Meaning of the Twentieth Century.** New York: Harper & Row, Publishers, Torchbooks, 1964. Good for the "modern" tendency to analyze social questions in economic terms.

DAHRENDORF, RALF. *Society and Democracy in Germany.** New York: Doubleday & Co., 1967. A sociological analysis of the "new" Germany by one of the champions of its role in Europe.

DAICHES, DAVID. *The Novel and the Modern World.** Chicago: University of Chicago Press, 1960. A very useful critical survey.

DJILAS, M. *The New Class.** New York: Praeger Publishers, 1957. The most thorough indictment of the Soviet system ever written by a Communist party member.

EASTON, STEWART. *The Twilight of European Colonialism.* New York: Holt, Rinehart & Winston, 1960. A good survey of postwar decolonization.

EHRMANN, H. W. *Politics in France.** Boston: Little, Brown & Co., 1968. One of the best studies of the problems of democracy and the policies of Charles de Gaulle.

INKELES, ALEX, and BAUER, R. A. *The Soviet Citizen.** Cambridge, Mass.: Harvard University Press, 1959. Deals with the improvements in living conditions after Stalin's death.

KOCH, A., ed. *Philosophy for a Time of Crisis.** New York: E. P. Dutton & Co., 1959. Good for postwar existentialism.

Asterisk indicates a paperbound edition.

58. April 12, 1961, aboard Vostok I.
59. Jean-Paul Sartre, for example.

LAQUEUR, WALTER. *Europe since Hitler.** Baltimore: Penguin Books, 1970. By far the best account, drawn on heavily for economic data in conjunction with W. W. Rostow's books on growth: *Politics and the Stages of Growth, Process of Economic Growth*, and *Stages of Economic Growth*.

LECACKMAN, ROBERT. *The Age of Keynes.** New York: Random House, 1966. A layman's guide to economic planning in the West.

MCLUHAN, MARSHALL. *Understanding Media.** New York: McGraw-Hill Book Co., 1964. The most provocative introduction to the problems of thought and expression in the "electronic age," by the author of *The Gutenberg Galaxy* and *The Medium Is the Message*.

MARCUSE, HERBERT. *One-Dimensional Man.** Boston: Beacon Press, 1964. An attempt to synthesize Marxist and Freudian culture critiques to account for modern "alienation" of men and women from their basic selves.

MOWRY, GEORGE. *The Urban Nation.** New York: Hill and Wang, 1965. The best brief treatment of America in the postwar era.

POSTAN, M. M. *Economic History of Europe, 1945–1965*. Cambridge: Cambridge University Press, 1969. The best book on the "affluent" society of the postwar era.

SETON-WATSON, HUGH. *The East-European Revolution.** New York: Praeger Publishers, 1950. A basic work on the Stalinist system of control.

———. *Neither War nor Peace*. New York: Praeger Publishers, 1960. A balanced approach to the Cold War.

WILLIS, F. ROY. *France, Germany, and the New Europe, 1945–1963.** Stanford: Stanford University Press, 1965. A good survey of the movement toward Western solidarity; also see Hans A. Schmitt, *The Path to European Union* (Baton Rouge: Louisiana State University Press, 1962).

WOODRUFF, WILLIAM. *Impact of Western Man: A Study of Europe's Role in the World Economy, 1950–1960*. New York: St. Martin's Press, 1967. A retrospective view of the effects of colonial and imperial movements.

Asterisk indicates a paperbound edition.

INDEX

Finland, democracy in, 397, 400, 413; invasion of, after World War I, 401; in World War II, 454

First Principles (Spencer), 362–363

First Principles of Government (Priestley), 42

Fisiocritici, 55, 56

Fitzgerald, F. Scott, 409

Fiume, 398

Flaubert, Gustave, 263–264

Flemings, 154

Flerov, G. N., 468

Foch, Marshal Ferdinand, 344, 402, 453

Fonthill Abbey, 247

Formalism, revolt against, 505

Forrestal, James, 488

Forsyte Saga, The (Galsworthy), 407

Fouché, Joseph, 103–104, 107–108

Foundations of the Nineteenth Century (Chamberlain), 418–419

Four Phases of the Day (Runge), 249

Four Stages of Cruelty, The (Hogarth), 14

Fourier, Charles, 181, 190, 320

Fourteen Points, 348–349

Fox, Charles James, 49, 86, 96

Fragment on Government, The (Bentham), 49

Fragonard, Jean Honoré, 6

France, and Algerian war, 476–477; in the American Revolution, 46–47; anti-Semitism in, 304, 417–418; civil war in, 298–301; in Concert of Europe, 148–151; in Crimean War, 220–226; under the Directory, 85, 92–99; economic regulation in, during World War I, 387–388; economy of, after World War I, 390, 392, 402–403; fascism in, 417, 424, 454–455; and the French and Indian War, 38; and German unification, 235, 238, 240–243; and Hitler, 447–452 passim; imperialism of, 290–291, 292, 295; internal politics of, 402–403, 417–418, 454–455, 481, 482–483; and July Revolution, 151–154; labor organizations in, 252–255, 314; literature in, 262–264; under Napoleon I, 100–127; under Napoleon III, 188, 217–218; pre-revolutionary, 2–14, 58–66; pre-World War I diplomacy of, 328–335; Red Revolution in, 186; Republic of Virtue in, 78–84, 91–92; and revolution in Italy, 226–230; Revolution of 1788 in, 32, 67–78, 86–92, 127–133, 138; Revolution of 1848 in, 177–182; and Russian Revolution, 402; social welfare in, 319–320; and Suez Crisis, 492; suffrage in, 311; Third Republic of, 298–301, 303–304; and Vietnam, 476, 488, 490; in World War I, 337–344, 347–350; in World War II, 454–463 passim. *See also Philosophes*

France, Anatole, 406

France libre, La (Desmoulins), 130

Franchise. *See* Suffrage

Francis I, Holy Roman Emperor, 53, 54

Francis II, Holy Roman Emperor, 77, 88

Francis Ferdinand, archduke of Austria, 336–337

Francis Joseph I, emperor of Austria, 186, 218, 224–225, 228–229, 235, 239–240, 306

Franco, Franciso, 400, 450

Frankfurt *Putsch,* 168

Franklin, Benjamin, 18, 20, 22, 31, 43

Frans the Younger, 4

Frederick II (the Great), king of Prussia, 9–11, 14

Frederick III, king of Prussia, 233

Frederick VII, king of Denmark, 177, 219, 236

Frederick Augustus II, king of Saxony, 12

Frederick William II, king of Prussia, 77, 88

Frederick William III, king of Prussia, 118, 164–165

Frederick William IV, king of Prussia, 170, 182, 183–184, 187, 218, 219, 228, 233

Free association, Freudian, 367–368

Free Corps, 427

"Free enterprise system," end of, 385

Freedom, in the Declaration of Rights, 73; *philosophes* on, 18, 30; of press, 41; of speech, 53–55. *See also* Censorship; Slavery

Freie Bühne, 266

French and Indian War, 38

French Labor Congress, 314

French Royal Academy, 2

Freud, Sigmund, 355, 366–369

Freytag, Gustav, 170

Friedland, battle of, 109

Friedrich, Kaspar, 248

Frisch, Max, 506

Frisch, Otto, 467

Fructidor, coup of, 96

Functionalism, in architecture, 501–502

Futurist Manifesto (Marinetti), 407

Gagarin, Yuri, 508

Gainsborough, Thomas, 13

Galsworthy, John, 406, 407

Gambetta, Leon, 241, 242, 303

Gamow, George, 467

Gandhi, Mohandas K., 443

Garden of Love (Rubens), 4

Garibaldi, Giuseppe, 229–230

Gaskell, Elizabeth, 257, 259

Gasoline engine, introduction of, 287

Gastein, Convention of, 237

Gaudin, Martin, 104

Gauguin, Paul, 250

Gaultier, Denis, 9

General Confederation of Labor, 314, 402

General German Students' Union, 166–167

Geneva Protocol (1924), 447

Gentz, Friedrich von, 137, 141–142

George II, king of England, 38

George III, king of England, 38, 40, 42, 43, 92, 96, 157

George IV, king of England, 157–158

Georgofili, 55, 56

Géricault, Jean Louis, 249

Germain, Gabriel, 13

German Democratic Republic. *See* East Germany

Germanic Confederation, 165–167, 175, 182–184, 186–187, 218–219, 232, 236; dissolution of, 237; formation of, 126

Germany, admission of, to League of Nations, 394, 444, 445; anti-Semitism in, 418–419, 426–433 passim; and Baltic states, 400–401; British relations with, after World War I, 404, 405; division of, after World War II, 483; economic regulation in, during World War I, 387; economy of, 388–396 passim, 415, 426–431 passim, 449, 451, 465; fascism in, 400, 413–434 passim; foreign policy of, under Stresemann, 444–445; imperialism of, 292, 293, 297; industrial supremacy of, 288–289; internal politics of, 304–306, 418–434 passim; labor in, 314–316; nationalism in, 143–146; plans for, at Potsdam Conference, 478; popular liberalism in, 167–171; pre-World War I diplomacy of, 324–335; social welfare in, 317, 318; suffrage in, 311–312; and Treaty of Versailles, 388–390, 394, 415; unification of, 232–243; in World War I, 337–344, 347–350; in World War II, 454–467 passim. *See also* East Germany; Hitler, Adolf; Jews; West Germany. *For political developments before 1870 see* Germanic Confederation; Prussia

Germinal (Zola), 289

Germinie Lacerteux (Goncourt), 244

Gerrymandering, 401

Gettysburg, battle of, 346

Ghetto system, for Russian Jews, 417

Giacometti, Alberto, 504

Giap, General, 476

Gide, André, 406

Giolitti, Giovanni, 309

Girl with a Mandolin (Picasso), 381

Girl with Bare Feet, The (Picasso), 375

Girondins, 78–83

Gladstone, William, 302, 328

Glazer, Ernst, 408

Globe, Le, 262

Gneisenau, August Neithardt von, 49, 144

Goebbels, Joseph, 429, 449, 465, 466

Goethe, Johann Wolfgang von, 10, 11, 92, 140, 143, 170, 246

Gogol, Nikolai, 163

Gohier, Jérôme, 99

Gold mining, in the colonies, 284

Gold standard, 386, 394, 396, 405

Goldsmith, Oliver, 34

Gombos, Julius, 400

Goncharov, Ivan, 264

Goncourt brothers, 244

Gordon Riots, 52

Göring, Hermann, 432, 433, 449, 469

Gorky, Maxim, 289

Gotha Program, 315

Government, effect of industrialization on, 310–316; *philosophes* on, 24–33; and phi-

tition with Europe, 386; economic recovery of, after World War II, 496; imperialism of, 291; plans for, at Potsdam Conference, 478; versus Russia, 333; social welfare in, 320; and treaty with Hitler, 452; and World War I, 348; and World War II, 448, 453, 457–466 passim
Jaurès, Jean, 304, 314
Jeanneret, Charles Édouard, 502
Jefferson, Thomas, 20–21, 32, 36, 47, 114
Jellicoe, Admiral, 341
Jena, battle of, 109
Jenkinson, Robert Banks, 158–159
Jesuits, expulsion of, 58, 303
Jewish France in Public Opinion, 417
Jews, 52; extermination of, 416, 468–472; persecution of, in Germany, 433, 448–449, 453, 468, 469. *See also* Anti-Semitism
John of Austria, Archduke, 186
Johnson, Samuel, 32–33
Jones, Inigo, 3
Jonson, Ben, 3
Joseph II, Holy Roman Emperor, 12, 52
Joséphine de Beauharnais, 100, 111
Jourdan, Jean Baptiste, 91
Joyce, James, 355, 374–375, 406
Joyce, William, 466
July Ordinances, 153
July Revolution of 1830, 152–153
Jung, C. G. 384, 385, 498
Junius, 42
Jupiter (Watteau), 5
Jutland, battle of, 341
Juvara, Filippo, 13

Kafka, Franz, 408
Kahr, Gustav von, 428, 433
Kandinsky, Wassily, 373–374, 503
Kant, Immanuel, 11, 16–18, 20, 21, 31, 92, 145
Kautsky, Karl, 316
Kay, John, 204
Kellogg-Briand Pact (1928), 447
Kerensky, Alexander, 435
Keynes, John Maynard, 385–394 passim, 496
Khrushchev, Nikita, 487, 492
Kiel, mutiny of, 348
Kingsley, Charles, 258, 259
Kirov, Sergei, 441
Kiss, The (Brancusi), 504
Klee, Paul, 374, 503
Klopstock, Friedrich, 92
Kneller, Sir Godfrey, 13
Kollwitz, Käthe, 390, 504
Korea, independence of, 332
Korean War, 489–490, 495
Kosciusko, Thaddeus, 49, 115
Kossuth, Louis, 187, 228
Krupp, Friedrich, 278
Kubrick, Stanley, 506
Kuomintang, 444
Kutuzov, Mikhail, 116–118, 435

La Barre, Jean François, 23
Labor, in Britain, 193–194, 206, 209, 210–216, 255–257, 405; in France, 180–181, 182, 252–255, 403; in Germany, 173–174, 185, 186; in Italy, 423. *See also* Labor unions; Social structure; Socialism
Labor unions, 160, 198–200, 288–289, 313–316, 402, 404, 432–433
Labour Representation Committee, 313
Lafayette, Marquis de, 49, 70, 72, 77, 89, 132, 153
Lagarde, Paul de, 364, 418
La Harpe, Frédéric, 161
Laibach, Conference of, 149
Laissez-faire, policy of, 142
Lamartine, Alphonse de, 182
Lamarie, Paul de, 13
Land ownership, by church, 76–77; in pre-revolutionary France, 60
Land reform, in Eastern Europe, 391, 397, 400; in Russia, 437
Lappo movement, 413
Lassalle, Ferdinand, 234, 315
Last Days of Pompeii (Bulwer-Lytton), 258
Lateran Treaty, 424
Latin America, dictatorship in, 400
La Tour, Quentin de, 14
Latvia, 400, 412, 453. *See also* Baltic, republics of
Laval, Pierre, 455
Lavoisier, Antoine Laurent, 83
Law, Bonar, 404
Law, and economic development, 280–281; English, 40, 41; Napoleonic, 104, 106–107; Russian, 307
Lawrence, D. H., 405, 406, 409
League of Nations, 348–349, 391, 394, 449, 452; admission of Germany to, 427, 429, 444, 445; and disarmament, 402; and Japan, 444; powers of, 447, 448
League of Nations Covenant (1919), 447
Leblanc, Nicolas, 204
Leboeuf Edmond, 242
Le Brun, Charles, 4, 8
Le Chapelier Law, 275
Le Corbusier, 502
Lee, Robert E., 346
Le Fascisme, 424
Lefebvre, François, 91
Legislative Assembly, 75–79
Lehmbruck, Wilhelm, 504
Lely, Peter, 3
Lemercier, Jacques, 7–8
Lend-Lease Act (1941), 457, 473, 488
Lenin, V. I., 343, 435–439 passim, 444
Le Nôtre André, 8
Leo XIII, pope, 365
Leopold I (of Saxe-Coburg), king of Belgium, 151
Leopold II, Holy Roman Emperor, 53–57, 77, 88
Leopold III, king of Belgium, 454
Leopold, prince of Hohenzollern-Sigmaringen, 241
Lermontov, Mikhail, 163

Lessing, Gotthold Ephraim, 11, 20, 170
Letters concerning the English Nation (Voltaire), 10, 23
Le Vau, Louis, 8
Lewald, Fanny, 170
Leyte Gulf, battle of, 464
Liberty Leading the People (Delacroix), 249
Lib-Labs, 303
Libya, independence of, 476
Lidice, destruction of, 459
Liebknecht, Karl, 305–306, 427
Ligurian Republic, 97
Lion Hunt (Delacroix), 250
Lipchitz, Jacques, 504
Literature, French, 181; German, 11, 168–169, 170–171; modern, 355, 374–375; realism in, 244–245, 250–252, 257–259, 263–265, 289; romanticism in, 244, 246, 248–249; Russian, 163, 264–265; after World War I, 406–409. *See also* Drama; Philosophy
Lithuania, 400–401, 412, 452, 453. *See also* Baltic, republics of
Lives of the Engineers (Smiles), 251
Livingstone, David, 292
Lloyd George, David, 303, 319, 348, 404, 458
Local Administration Act of 1800, 104
Locarno Pact (1925), 394, 444, 445, 447
Locke, John, 25
Loménie de Brienne, Etienne Charles, 66
London, air raid on, 346
London, Treaty of, 151
London Bridge, 252
London Protocol, 151, 219
London Workingmen's Association, 199
Lord Jim (Conrad), 406
Lorrain, Claude, 7
Lorraine, house of, 11
Louis XIII, king of France, 8
Louis XIV, king of France, 2–3, 8, 9. *See also* Versailles
Louis XV, king of France, 11, 58, 64–65
Louis XVI, king of France, 32, 64, 65–80
Louis XVII, king of France, 119
Louis XVIII, king of France, 93, 119–120, 151–152
Louis Philippe, duke of Orléans, 71
Louis Philippe, king of the French, 153–154, 177–179, 182
Loutherbourg, Philippe de, 251
Louvre, construction of, 8
Love Feast (Pourbus), 4
Love Letters (Fragonard), 6
Ludendorff, Erich, 342, 344, 424, 428
Lueger, Karl, 317, 419, 424
Lully, Jean Baptiste, 9
Luncheon on the Grass (Manet), 356
Lunéville, Peace of, 105
Lusitania, sinking of, 341
Luxemburg, Rosa, 427

MacArthur, General Douglas, 463, 464, 490
MacDonald, Ramsay, 313, 404, 405, 406
Mach, Ernst, 355, 369